Bottom Line's

The Healing Kitchen

Prevent and Reverse Today's Most Common Health Conditions with Delicious Foods and Meals—Medically Proven!

Stephen Sinatra, M.D.
and Jim Healthy
with recipes by Rebecca Bent

Bottom Line Books

www.BottomLinePublications.com

Bottom Line's The Healing Kitchen

Copyright © 2012 by Stephen Sinatra, MD, Jim Punkre and Rebecca Bent

ISBN 0-88723-657–X

10 9 8 7 6 5 4 3 2 1

This book is based on the research and observations of the authors. The information contained in this book should by no means be considered a substitute for the advice of the reader's personal physician or other medical professional, who should always be consulted before beginning any health program.

The information in this book has been carefully researched, and all efforts have been made to ensure accuracy as of the date published. Readers, particularly those with existing health problems and those who take prescription medications, are cautioned to consult with a health professional about specific recommendations for supplements and the appropriate dosages. The authors and the publisher expressly disclaim responsibility for any adverse effects arising from the use or application of the information contained in this book.

Bottom Line Books® is a registered trademark of Boardroom® Inc.
281 Tresser Blvd., Stamford, CT 06901
www.BottomLinePublications.com

Bottom Line Books® publishes the opinions of expert authorities in many fields. The use of this book is not a substitute for health or other professional services. Please consult a competent professional for answers to your specific questions.

Offers, prices, addresses, telephone numbers and Web sites listed in this book are accurate at the time of publication, but they are subject to frequent change.

Bottom Line Books® is an imprint of Boardroom® Inc., publisher of print periodicals, e-letters and books. We are dedicated to bringing you the best information from the most knowledgeable sources in the world. Our goal is to help you gain greater wealth, better health, more wisdom, extra time and increased happiness.

Printed in the United States of America

Contents

Acknowledgments................................... iv

Introduction....................................... v

1. The Two Healthiest Diets on Earth.... 1

2. The Mediterr-Asian Diet: The Best
   of Both Worlds 19

3. Why Organic Matters 28

4. Arthritis 39

5. Cancer....................................... 58

6. Depression.................................. 83

7. Diabetes 98

8. Digestive Disorders......................119

9. Erectile Dysfunction 135

10. Eye Diseases.............................. 148

11. Fatigue 156

12. Heart Disease............................... 168

13. Hypertension 203

14. Insomnia...................................218

15. Memory Loss............................. 228

16. Menopause 246

17. Migraines................................. 260

18. Osteoporosis 269

19. Overweight and Obesity.............. 280

20. Prostate Problems....................... 307

Recipes 323

Select Bibliography 491

Recipe Index 515

Index 519

About the Authors 531

Acknowledgments

To Jim Healthy, who gave me the idea for this book and whose insights and passion for healthy eating made this book possible.

To Rebecca Bent, a phenomenal chef who walks her talk and provides her family and friends with a steady diet of healthful, healing meals.

To Jan Sinatra, my loving wife and number-one nurse, whose hands-on assistance and practical medical perspective is helping to bring healing back home, where it is most effective.

To my son Step Sinatra, for his culinary expertise and commitment to utilizing food and nutrition to heal himself and to reduce human suffering.

To March Sinatra, editor-in-chief of HeartMd Institute.com. Thank you for the outstanding information created on our educational Web site.

To Drew Sinatra, for his special encouragement in educating his patients about the importance of natural ingredients found in foods that support healing. Love those coconut drinks, too!

To JoAnne Piazza, my trusted assistant, long-time friend, and invaluable right hand.

To Brian Kurtz, who believed in the concept behind this book from the beginning and whose ongoing support helped to make it a reality.

To Matthew Hoffman, whose tireless research and accuracy helped make this book the ultimate resource for healing foods.

To Heidi Hough, for her editing skill and devotion to this project.

To Martina Punkre, whose educated palate helped forge the direction of these meals and recipes, and whose continual editorial assistance and emotional support kept this book on track through many ups and downs.

To Terry Warrington, Cinny Green, Rosemary Ademulegun, Fitzhugh Cline and *Debbie Delsignore.*

Stephen Sinatra, M.D.

Introduction

Over twenty-five years ago, a nutritional researcher named Kerin O'Dea conducted a simple experiment that, in my opinion, was one of the most impressive in medical history. Unfortunately, medical historians didn't agree. Had her remarkable findings been heeded by doctors back then, our current generation might be witnessing the near elimination of diabetes, heart disease, cancer, obesity and many other illnesses that now plague Western civilization.

I want to share O'Dea's extraordinary contribution with you because it underlies the premise of this book.

O'Dea's experiment dates back to the summer of 1982, when she conducted an experiment involving a group of sick, overweight indigenous Australian men who were living a "modern" twentieth-century existence in a poor urban settlement outside Derby, Western Australia. In addition to being overweight and afflicted with type 2 diabetes, the Aborigine men were insulin resistant and had severely elevated triglycerides, two conditions that together constitute a major risk factor for heart disease. Although disease free before immigrating to the city, the men had adopted a Western diet of refined carbohydrates that, along with a sedentary lifestyle, soon upset their insulin balance and metabolism.

Kerin O'Dea wasn't alone in noting that the ill health suffered by those urban Aborigine men was (and continues to be) nonexistent among native populations eating an indigenous diet. The journals of medical anthropologists living among tribes in parts of Africa, Hawaii, Polynesia, Alaska and even Native American reservations report the complete absence of heart disease, diabetes, hypertension and cancers before the introduction of commercially refined foods. O'Dea's great contribution is that she was the first to investigate whether a return to a more indigenous diet would, in effect, cure them and restore their health.

To test her hypothesis, she took her group to a remote region of northwest Australia, where they had no access to commercial foods or beverages, and had to rely instead on foods they hunted and gathered. After seven weeks on this diet, O'Dea drew blood samples from the men and was surprised to discover that dramatic changes had occurred in their health. Blood triglycerides, glucose and cholesterol levels had plummeted into the healthy range. In addition, the men had lost an average of nearly 20 pounds and their blood pressure had dropped significantly. In O'Dea's words, "All of the metabolic abnormalities of type 2 diabetes (glucose tolerance and insulin response) were either greatly improved or completely normalized...." Here was clinical proof that food and lifestyle changes (exercise) do indeed have remarkable curative properties.

Today, more than 9,000 scientific studies demonstrate that food and exercise are potent medicine, in many cases more powerful than today's widely used drugs and surgical procedures. This book describes a simple, affordable and highly effective path to reversing the debilitating, chronic and life-threatening conditions that plague developed and developing nations alike. What you are about to read offers you a way to halt your existing symptoms, end the pain and suffering they cause, increase your vitality and enthusiasm and lengthen your

life—through choices you can make in your kitchen and grocery store.

These are significant rewards, yet they will not require you to forgo your love of food and drink or force you to adhere to a slavish exercise regimen. On the contrary, my strategy makes it easy for you to *enjoy* the process of becoming healthier, along with the joy and happiness that are essential components of true wellness.

FOODS, NOT PHARMACEUTICALS

You are about to learn why foods, not pharmaceuticals, and perhaps not even nutritional supplements, represent the ultimate solution to the vast majority of today's serious health problems. *For example, you will see that...*

- **The omega-3 fatty acids** in certain fish actually prevent soft plaque in arteries from erupting and triggering a heart attack or stroke. Medical studies also show that these fish oils can stabilize and reduce plaque existing in your arteries right now, while at the same time reducing blood pressure, lowering LDL cholesterol and normalizing potentially fatal irregular heartbeats. No medication known can even approximate this.

- **Potassium-rich fruits and vegetables,** such as bananas and celery, among others, lower blood pressure by removing excess sodium from the body. Their results are on par with, and often surpass, today's leading hypertension drugs.

- **Homemade soup stock** from animal bones and cartilage contains higher concentrations of *glucosamine, chondroitin, hyaluronic acid*, and other cartilage-rebuilding substances found in expensive arthritis supplements.

Before-and-after X-rays show that these substances actually help restore joint cushioning in arthritic joints.

- **Adding more leafy greens and cruciferous vegetables to your diet** can improve your memory and slow age-related loss of mental function by an astonishing 40%.

- **Consuming more cabbage and Brussels sprouts** not only helps prevent breast cancer, but according to a new study, the cancer-fighting compounds in these foods also *destroy* breast cancer cells now existing in your body.

- *Lutein,* a nutrient present in brightly colored fruits and vegetables, significantly slows the loss of vision caused by age-related macular degeneration.

- **The antidepressant effects of certain foods,** on a par with leading prescription drugs, have been confirmed by a recent medical study.

- **Walnuts** are one of nature's richest natural sources of *serotonin,* a chemical that calms brain activity and induces sleep the same way prescription sleeping pills do but far more safely.

- **A rare nutrient found primarily in blueberries** has been shown to improve memory, while also acting as the most effective protector against Alzheimer's disease known today.

- **Foods high in dietary fiber** have been clinically proven to lower C-reactive protein, a marker for arterial inflammation which produces artery plaque, and is a major risk factor for diabetes, heart disease, stroke, Alzheimer's and kidney failure.

- **A daily half-teaspoon of ordinary cinnamon lowers blood sugar levels** and harmful LDL cholesterol in people with diabetes enough to reduce their need for oral medication, according to a study by the US Department of Agriculture.

I could easily continue to list the plentiful scientific research supporting the extraordinary curative powers of certain foods and the healing nutrients in them, because there is just so much of it. Surprising new studies lie ahead in the chapters of this book, in which I also guide you in using these healing foods to improve your health. You'll discover newly identified micronutrients, such as *carotenoids, polyphenols* and *phytoestrogens*—names that will soon become familiar to you—that tame inflammation, destroy cancer cells, unclog arteries, rebuild bone mass, stimulate natural hormone production and aid the body's detoxification process, all while protecting you from tumors and age-related deterioration. Indeed, the deeper that scientists probe, the more they are awed by nature's astonishing food pharmacy, which contains natural tranquilizers, laxatives, beta-blockers, blood thinners, antidepressants, cholesterol reducers, anti-inflammatory agents, analgesics, cancer fighters, vasodilators, insulin regulators, expectorants, antibiotics, digestive aids and many other healing marvels.

EMBRACE THE WORLD'S HEALTHIEST DIETS

Happily, we don't have to invent this curative gastronomy because several such diets have existed for centuries. In fact, studies show that *all* native diets produce populations that are free of Western diseases, from the Alaskan fishing villages of the Inuit where vegetables are rarely eaten, to the cattle-herding Masai of Africa who subsist on milk and meat, to the nomadic aboriginal Australians who live on roots, wild herbs, berries, insects and wild game. These disparate diets produce populations free of heart attacks, cancers, diabetes, hypertension, constipation and migraines, plus most of the other medical conditions that trouble us in the West.

Of all the world's indigenous diets, two top the list for creating the world's healthiest, longest-living people. These are the cuisines of the Mediterranean and Asian cultures, and this book will introduce you to the dietary secrets that are responsible for superior health and longevity. Coincidently, the Mediterranean and Asian ways of eating are also the world's oldest cuisines. Thousands of years of evolution have perfected food combinations that are not only extraordinarily healthful but also possess superb flavor and exceptional artistic flair. Good health and long life may not have been the prime motives behind these great cuisines, but they are marvelous by-products nonetheless.

THE COST OF FADS AND CONVENIENCE

Old-world cuisine is all but lost in the average twenty-first-century American household, with its preponderance of commercially processed foods. More than 70,000 new so-called food products, some with FDA-approved health claims, appear on supermarket shelves every year. Journalists and nutrition writers turn every new research

viii

wrinkle into a national eating fad, one only to be debunked years later and replaced by the next. In the process, this profit-driven mania is ruining our wellness.

Two-thirds of Americans currently are overweight or obese. More than 50 million Americans have prediabetes, the vast majority without even realizing it. The incidence of type 2 diabetes is increasing at the mind-boggling rate of 5% annually. It now afflicts 7.7% of the US population, or roughly 20 million people, including tens of thousands of children. Due to the increase in this one disease, children born since 2002 will be the first generation in human history to have a *lower* life expectancy than their parents.

There can be no doubt that America is in the midst of a health crisis that threatens to ruin its personal and collective futures, as well as the national economy. In addition to diabetes, and the obesity that leads to it, we are experiencing epidemic rates of hypertension, stroke, arthritis, cancer, Alzheimer's and cardiovascular disease. Even the baby boomer generation, which prides itself on living a healthy, active lifestyle, hasn't been spared. Many boomers are now experiencing the consequences of past bad dietary habits, in addition to the inevitable pains and disability of aging.

MORE DRUGS, NEW MEDICAL PROCEDURES

As a result of all this, the medical industry is booming. Almost half of all Americans now use at least one prescription medicine, while one in six of us take three or more drugs daily. The cost of treating people with chronic diseases in the US currently accounts for more than 75% of its total medical expenditure, which at $2 trillion eclipses the healthcare expense of every nation on earth. Yet, despite this enormous sum, the US trails the world's developed nations in every measured category of wellness. The World Health Organization ranks the US an unbelievable 22nd out of 23 in "healthy life expectancy," just ahead of the Czech Republic. The US ranks 29th in infant mortality.

Clearly, more drugs, new medical procedures and the billions we are spending aren't solving our health problems. Statistics clearly show that the medical establishment is losing its battles against heart disease, cancer, diabetes, osteoporosis and other Western diseases. Medicalizing this crisis has had almost no effect, and much of the responsibility for this defeat can be attributed to the strategy the medical establishment has chosen. Far from using every weapon at its disposal, conventional medicine continues to ignore alternative treatments, nutritional solutions, diet and exercise education and disease-prevention tactics that are proven to be far more effective.

Neither does the medical community fully acknowledge the metabolic and nutritional underpinnings of these ills, despite thousands of research studies implicating this connection. Most recently, the journal *Circulation* reported that people in 52 countries who ate a Western diet including processed meats, refined carbohydrates, sugary junk foods, salty snacks and fried dishes are 30% more likely to have a heart attack, compared with those whose meals were rich in

vegetables and fruit. In fact, the more of a fruit-and-vegetable-rich diet the participants ate, the lower their risk of heart attack turned out to be.

CURING THE CAUSE

I grew frustrated with opening my patients' obstructed arteries, only to see them clog in other locations months later. My primary motivation for becoming a doctor was to help people, but it was apparent that the tools that conventional cardiology offered doctors weren't sufficient to end the suffering we were encountering day after day. That's when my interest turned to identifying the causes of these conditions, instead of reapplying expensive Band-Aids to the problems. This led me to the study of nutrition and psychotherapy, because it was impossible to ignore the role that diet and emotions had on human health.

Years after receiving my degree in internal medicine and cardiology, I realized the powerful effect emotions have on physical health and healing. I earned a degree in psychotherapy and wrote a book, *Heartbreak and Heart Disease*. Later, I educated myself and studied for years to become a certified nutrition specialist, so that I could guide my patients to eat and live in a way that could prevent, and even reverse, their health problems without medical intervention.

At that time, I was sure that the many new discoveries being made in nutrition and the body-mind connection would inspire modern medicine to redirect itself in a more holistic direction. It's a shock to me that it didn't, and still hasn't, especially because of the well-documented success that this multidisciplinary approach has achieved over the past two decades. Although there are a number of wise, courageous doctors who have incorporated these innovative methods into their practices, the medical establishment as a whole hasn't budged from its unquestioning allegiance to the drugs-and-surgery approach, which, despite the billions spent each year by patients and their insurance providers, has failed to reduce the incidence of our nation's leading killer diseases.

I wrote *The Healing Kitchen* to help you escape this dangerous situation and to provide you with a direct escape route. This generation has grown up in an environment in which Western diseases have become so commonplace that many of us believe that they're an inevitable part of the aging process. I assure you that they are not. There are still places in the world, although they are rapidly disappearing, where these ills don't exist, even among the elderly. For example, I focused on the peoples of the Mediterranean and in parts of Asia, who suffer far less degenerative diseases and live much longer, happier lives than we do in the US and other Western cultures. They age at a slower pace, and are able to stay more energetic, active and vibrant well into their eighties and nineties, as well as experiencing less physical and mental deterioration. The reasons for this, which are thoroughly documented, can be found in the foods they eat and the lifestyle they live.

This book shares their age-old dietary traditions, coupled with modern nutritional discoveries, so that you may reap the rewards of both worlds in your own life. You won't have to pack off to a foreign country

or the wilderness to achieve these benefits. As you're about to see, radical health transformation is possible without radical effort, and without leaving your home, except for an occasional trip to your local farmers' market, your natural grocer or a nightly stroll or bike ride around your neighborhood. *Here are some examples...*

MORE SCIENTIFIC PROOF

In his famous Lifestyle Heart Trial, published in the medical journal *The Lancet* in 1990 and presented at the annual meeting of the American Heart Association, internist Dean Ornish, M.D., demonstrated that coronary artery disease, the leading killer disease in the US for more than a half century, could be halted and reversed with a few simple dietary and lifestyle changes. After just one year, the participants in his impressive study showed a significant decrease in deadly plaque in their arteries. By contrast, the arteries of patients in the control group who received standard medical treatment continued to clog and narrow, increasing their risk of heart attack. In those days, no medical treatment, be it bypass surgery, angioplasty, heart transplant or any other, could approximate this success, a fact largely unchanged today, even with the introduction of statin drugs, which have not produced a significant impact on overall heart mortality.

Sadly, although Ornish's research was scientifically impressive and impeccably administered, it was largely ignored by the medical community, as were subsequent studies by other researchers demonstrating the ability of nutrition, exercise and stress reduction to reverse heart disease. One wonders why. Currently, we spend $100 billion annually on medical intervention for heart disease, yet more than 650,000 Americans still die every year of it, and nearly 25 million new cases are diagnosed annually. It is important to note that these rates have remained basically unchanged per capita since the days of Ornish's discovery. This is anything but progress.

Here's another example of how simple it can be to save yourself from the entirely preventable and reversible medical conditions that threaten your health and day-to-day happiness. In one of the largest, most exacting clinical studies ever undertaken, 120,000 women in the famous Nurses' Health Study were asked to follow a health-promoting lifestyle that included not smoking, keeping their weight below the overweight threshold, engaging in 30 minutes of moderate daily exercise and eating a healthy diet similar to the Mediterranean and Asian cuisines presented in this book. Based on the study's results, which include 14 years of careful analysis and follow-up, Dr. Walter C. Willett and his colleagues at Harvard calculated that if all participants had followed these modest guidelines, an astounding 90% of type 2 diabetes, 80% of all heart disease, and more than 70% of the colon cancers diagnosed among the nurses would never have occurred. Those are staggering reductions.

Taken together, the findings presented by Kerin O'Dea, Dr. Dean Ornish and the Nurses' Health Study prove that even the most deleterious diseases can be stopped dead in their tracks, reversed or completely prevented with a few simple, easy dietary adjustments and lifestyle changes. Given the alternative— a life full of doctor visits, prescription drugs, adverse side effects, risky surgery, potential complications and the common slow, painful decline into disability and deterioration—the choice should be easy.

This book describes a simple, affordable and highly effective way out of this dilemma, reversing the debilitating, chronic and life-threatening conditions that will likely be the fate of most people of your generation. *The Healing Kitchen* tells how to halt your existing symptoms, end the pain and suffering that they cause, increase your vitality and enthusiasm and lengthen your life, all through choices you can make on your own. These are significant rewards, and yet they will not require you to forgo your love of food…or life. On the contrary, my strategy helps you *enjoy* the process of becoming healthier, because joy and happiness are essential components of true wellness.

If you currently suffer from any of today's common medical conditions, you'll find solid clinical research in these pages that proves that eating more of the healing foods described in this book can bring about significant improvements in your health and longevity. If you're well and want to stay that way, or feel even better, you'll discover a delightfully easy and delicious new way of eating that eliminates the guesswork and vexing complexity of calories, grams, nutrients, fat, cholesterol, carbs and just plain "What shall I eat?"

If you *love* eating, there's plenty for you here too. By combining the two most delicious and healthful diets on earth into an exciting fusion cuisine called The Mediterr-Asian Diet, you can delight your senses while improving your health. It allows you to eat just like the world's healthiest, longest-living people do, so that you can reap the same benefits. In a surprisingly short time, with a little practice, you'll find yourself instinctively reaching for the foods that build health, while shunning the ones that don't. The meals and nutritional advice that Jim, Rebecca and I have developed for *The Healing Kitchen* include traditional Mediterranean and Asian recipes updated to emphasize specific healing foods, along with creative new dishes that marry these two impressive ways of eating into exciting new combinations. It is our hope that this book helps your family create a healing kitchen of your own—one that becomes the centerpiece of your family's health and happiness, a convivial place where you laugh and love and share intimate life experiences, while savoring the best foods on earth. You can also visit our Web site, *www.myhealingkitchen. com*, for more healing foods and recipes.

Finally, I urge you to remember to have fun while cooking, and to truly relish this aspect of life with Zorba-like gusto, celebrating every day, every moment and every memory of this marvelous *la dolce vita*—the sweet life—given to each of us.

That is, after all, the true essence of health. ■

—*Stephen Sinatra, M.D.*

1

The Two Healthiest Diets on Earth

Somewhere in China, a teenage girl sits down to a meal of rice and stir-fried vegetables. With her food she drinks a cup of green tea. Halfway across the world, her American counterpart digs into a fast-food burger and fries while sipping a supersized soft drink. Fast forward 20 years. As it turns out, the Chinese woman will be 80% less likely to get breast cancer than the American. She'll also have far less risk of developing osteoporosis, heart disease and other chronic diseases.

A similar scenario unfolds in the Mediterranean, where people experience much lower rates of the diseases that have reached epidemic proportions in the US. Why is this? What factors are responsible? What steps can be taken in the US to dramatically increase the chances of a health and longevity profile that more closely resembles that of the world's healthiest people?

A Truly Remarkable Phenomenon

People living in Asian and Mediterranean cultures lead the world in good health. According to United Nations statistics, the average life expectancy for the Japanese is 83 years. In France, it's almost 81 years, and other Mediterranean countries are not far behind. The US, where the average life expectancy is almost 78 years, lags behind 30 other nations, despite its great wealth and lavish medical system.

Those statistics put the US five years behind the Japanese and three years behind the French. This difference may not seem significant (unless, of course, you're a 77½-year-old American male), until you look at the fitness and quality of life that Asian and

1

The Okinawa Secret: Fewer Calories Equal Longer Life

Scientists have known about this little equation for a long time. When animals are given about one-third fewer calories than normal, their life expectancy increases by more than 30%. If the same were true of humans, cutting about 600 calories from your daily diet would increase your life expectancy from the current 83 years (for women) to an average of 100 years. Those extra years wouldn't be characterized by pain, deterioration and helplessness. The centenarians of Okinawa—which has the highest per capita population of 100-year-olds on earth—are a lively, mentally active bunch. That could be your future, too.

The Okinawa Centenarian Study (OCS) investigated more than 900 members of the 100-year-old population to discover the secret to their surprisingly long and healthy lives. One of the keys, in addition to such factors as relatively low emotional stress, high levels of social support and a low-fat diet, was a lower-than-average-calorie diet. Researchers aren't exactly sure why cutting calories increases life span, but it appears to be linked to the resulting reduction in insulin levels.

So far, calorie restriction is the only proven way to extend the human life span, but cutting calories doesn't have to mean eating less. Few of us would want to live that way. The people of Okinawa, like those in the Mediterranean, leave the table feeling full, because the foods they consume are high volume and nutrient dense. These foods satisfy their hunger and provide their cells with optimal nutrition, yet contain the fewest calories. That's the real secret of getting slim and staying that way for life, while keeping peak health at the same time.

Mediterranean senior citizens experience. A majority of American seniors are not able to fully enjoy the final decade of their lives because their health is impaired by one or more chronic diseases. Many are still alive due to recent medical advances that have extended life, but haven't improved the quality of it. This is not the case for 70- and 80-year-olds living in Japan and most Mediterranean countries. Studies show they are much healthier, active and freer of chronic pain and degenerative diseases. They are also more fit, more independent and able to care for themselves, compared with Americans in the same age group.

WHAT'S THEIR SECRET?

Suppose you were living next door to a couple in their eighties or nineties who seemed exceptionally fit and healthy, walking their dog at a good clip every morning, puttering around their garden most afternoons and laughing heartily on their back porch at sundown over a glass of wine. You'd want to discover the secret of their fitness and longevity in the hope that you might enjoy your golden years as enthusiastically as they seem to.

The same curiosity prompted research on the people of the Mediterranean, beginning with the scientist and epidemiologist Dr. Ancel Keys, who, in 1945, began investigating the reasons that the people of Italy, Greece and other Mediterranean countries were so much healthier and longer-lived than other people. His findings revealed that the foods of the Mediterranean region, particularly the high levels of fresh produce and healthy fats in their diet, made the difference. Other researchers (through the 1950s and '60s) began to study the lower rates of heart disease in these countries where individuals consumed olive oil, nuts, butter, pastries and red meat. Keys was the first to refer to this way of eating as the "Mediterranean Diet." However, his efforts to popularize it in the US were unsuccessful until a pivotal article, entitled "Mediterranean Diet Pyramid: A Cultural Model for Healthy Eating," was published in the *American Journal of Clinical Nutrition* in 1995.

Other researchers noticed the impressive health statistics among the Japanese population. In fact, residents of the Japanese island of Okinawa seemed to be even healthier than the Mediterraneans. Okinawans have the longest life expectancy in the world and the largest ratio of centenarians to average-age population. In 1975, scientists launched the Okinawa Centenarian Study (OCS) to discover the how and the why of such extraordinary longevity. Instead of discovering a population of sickly, frail and wheelchair-bound elderly, the scientists found a group of centenarians who appeared to be aging at a much slower rate and were delaying or completely avoiding the typical Western diseases of aging, like dementia, osteoporosis and arthritis. In fact, the three leading killers in the West—coronary heart disease, stroke and breast and colon cancers—had their lowest incidence in Okinawans of anywhere on the planet. Okinawans even displayed remarkably low rates of stomach cancer, a serious problem on mainland Japan.

After 25 years of painstaking research, the OCS scientists determined that the traditional Okinawan diet was the single most important factor contributing to their exceptional longevity. In contrast, when researchers studied younger Okinawans who had adopted a more Westernized diet and lifestyle, they found that they weighed more, had higher rates of heart disease and cancer and that their life expectancy had decreased by a jaw-dropping 17 years.

Decades of other epidemiological and clinical research have confirmed the remarkable health benefits of traditional Asian and Mediterranean diets. Taken together, these two diets are the most rigorously studied ever. Yet, despite the differences in their ethnic and cultural backgrounds, these cultures share distinct similarities in superior health and exemplary longevity. In both cases, the way they eat is the reason. *Let's look at them in depth…*

The Mediterranean Advantage

It's a paradox. Epidemiologists have gazed in wonder at the ultralow disease rates in France, Italy, Greece and other Mediterranean countries. Even though people there smoke more than Americans, eat more fatty foods, such as cheese and pâté, and seem to drink more alcohol, their rates of heart disease, diabetes and cancers trail the US by a mile. They're also leaner people. In France, for instance, the obesity rate is about 11% (unfortunately on the rise as the French consume more Western fast food)—it's four times higher in the US. The French are three

3

times less likely than Americans to get heart disease; the same healthy trend extends across the entire Mediterranean. Studying the eating habits of people in these countries focused scientists on the idea that diet is the single most important factor in good health.

➤ **The HALE Study.** Here's an extremely impressive finding, showing that the foods of the Mediterranean have the extraordinary power to cut the risk of premature death and debilitating disease by more than half. A research study conducted from 1988 to 2000 across 11 European countries had a startling conclusion. The Healthy Ageing: A Longitudinal Study in Europe (HALE) involved a large group of healthy men and women 70 to 90 years old. Researchers found that those who followed a Mediterranean-style diet, including moderate alcohol use, physical activity and not smoking, had a 50% lower incidence of death from all causes, including cardiovascular diseases and cancer, regardless of their age, gender, education or weight.

➤ **Alzheimer's and asthma.** Other studies have found that people who eat a Mediterranean-style diet have lower rates of Alzheimer's disease. The protective effect of the Mediterranean diet on asthma and respiratory allergies was shown in a 2007 study of 700 children living on the Greek island of Crete. Researchers found that the children's diets provided strong, protective effects.

➤ **Heart disease.** Where the Mediterranean diet really shines is in its ability to bash heart disease. Like most heart specialists, I used to advise my patients to follow the American Heart Association's dietary guidelines, convinced this low-fat diet was good for cardiovascular health and weight control. What turned my thinking around was the groundbreaking Lyon (France) Heart Study, the single most dramatic diet-heart trial ever conducted.

In this study, scientists divided patients who had suffered heart attacks into two groups. One group followed the diet recommended by the American Heart Association (AHA) and the second group followed a Mediterranean-style diet, containing far more fat but fewer refined carbohydrates. The results of this study rocked the medical community. After a few years, researchers found that patients in the Mediterranean group had *70% fewer* second heart attacks than those following the official AHA diet. They also were much less likely to suffer from other heart problems, and their death rate from all causes was 50% lower. These reductions were so dramatic that the director canceled the study because he could not in good conscience deprive the AHA diet group, or the general public, of these profound benefits.

There can be no doubt that the Mediterranean diet can reduce the risk of heart attack and sudden death better than any other diet, drug or medical intervention available today. The protection it provides is nothing short of spectacular. People who follow it are also far less likely to get cancer. Furthermore, they have higher blood levels of vitamin C, other antioxidants, plus essential fatty acids, which is a perfect recipe for reducing inflammation in blood vessel linings.

➤ **Cancer.** When researchers examined cancer rates among the Mediterranean group in the Lyons Study, they found them to be 61% lower. A separate study years later found that, in smokers who were not overweight, the Mediterranean diet significantly reduced incidence of cancer as well as mortality from the disease.

➤ **Eat like the Greeks.** More recently, the Italian National Association of Hospital Cardiologists study confirmed the impressive results of Lyons when they found that the more closely people followed a traditional Greek diet, the less likely they were to die from any cause. More specifically, for each component of the Greek diet that participants included in their eating habits, their risk of death dropped an astonishing 17% in 44 months.

…But not like Greek children. Tragically, in 2008, United Nations researchers reported that in Greece the health-giving Mediterranean diet had "decayed into a moribund state," with children turning away in droves from the traditional fish, fresh produce and olive oil–centered diet. What's causing the reversal? Greek children have been eating like US kids—munching fastfood, gulping sodas and packing in ice cream and other sweets. Over the last three years, doctors report seeing children for high blood pressure, elevated cholesterol and diabetes. Their increasingly Americanized diet is producing a generation of obese children at risk for serious conditions that will follow them for a lifetime. Statistics show that the incidence of overweight 12-year-old Greek boys

skyrocketed more than 200% from 1982 to 2002, with up to 34% of them overweight. One researcher at the University of Athens Medical School called the problem "acute" and attributed it to the heavy marketing of convenience foods.

Healing Foods from the Mediterranean Diet

What is it about the Mediterranean diet that produces such superb health and longevity? The answer can be found in the foods that thrive in the subtropical climate of the regions, an ideal environment for a wide selection of fresh vegetables and fruits, all of which possess extraordinary healing compounds. Mineral-rich figs and antioxidant-laden pomegranates thrive there, along with highly nutritious citrus, olives, nuts and a flavorful array of delightful herbs and spices that possess unique medicinal properties. The Mediterranean Sea is also a plentiful source of fish and seafood, which contain high levels of healing omega-3 fatty acids. Even though the cuisines of Mediterranean countries such as Italy, Greece, Spain, Portugal and France vary in flavor and style, they share a common palette of powerfully beneficial foods. *Here are the ingredients of the Mediterranean diet…*

VEGETABLES AND FRUITS

If I could share one secret for immediate healing and long-lasting health, it is this: love thy vegetables and fruits. Some people have never learned to like them and, if you're among this group, you'll want to read closely, because nature's true nutritional wealth is

5

stashed in fresh produce, the cornerstone of the Mediterranean diet. This virtual rainbow of variety features fruits and vegetables that are loaded with fiber, vitamins, antioxidants and cancer-fighting nutrients. Their bright colors signal to us that they contain literally thousands of different *phytochemicals*, plant compounds that fight disease and nourish cells and tissues throughout the human body. From a weight-loss perspective, they're the perfect food because they're low in calories yet bulky with plentiful fiber, so you can eat your fill and shed pounds at the same time.

Fresh produce contains the highest concentration of nutrients of any food group. Each vegetable and fruit is a tiny treasure chest packed with tens of thousands of precious micronutrients with tongue-twisting names like flavonoids, flavanones, proanthocyanidins, anthocyanins, phenolic acids, lignans and stilbenes, including resveratrol. More than 6,000 different flavonoids alone have been identified in plants and separated into a mind-boggling number of subclasses.

However, there's nothing confusing about the vast body of epidemiological and clinical studies that clearly show that eating more fresh vegetables and fruits pumps up the levels of antioxidants in your blood and aggressively neutralizes a range of diseases such as cancer, coronary heart disease (CHD) and diabetes, while reducing symptoms of chronic conditions such as arthritis, hypertension and insulin resistance. In addition, they help to slow down the aging process itself. Veggies and fruits will keep you healthy, young, energetic, mentally alert, physically strong, sexy and deeply attuned

to Mother Nature. The ideal way to enjoy them is exactly the way they're relished in the traditional Mediterranean diet: locally grown, eaten fresh and minimally processed, so that all their delicate healing compounds come to the table at the height of their potency.

LOTS OF HEALTHY FATS

It may seem counterintuitive, but it's common in Mediterranean countries for people to get almost 40% of their total calories from fat. Ponder that for a moment, while I remind you that the American Heart Association and other mainstream Western diets usually cap fat consumption at 20% to 30% of calories. You might believe, given the low-fat propaganda that pervades US medical advice, that a diet containing 40% fat would generate a lot of heart disease and obesity in Mediterranean countries.

Just the opposite is true: These people are among the slimmest and most heart-healthy on earth. That's because the fat in a traditional Mediterranean diet is extremely healthful, coming from fish, olive oil and nuts, rather than the polyunsaturated vegetable oil and trans fats so common in the US.

I advise my patients to shoot for a total fat intake of approximately 30%, as long as the fats are the healthful kind. Keep in mind that all fats are calorie rich, containing more than twice the number of calories as complex carbohydrates. Even though the following Mediterranean-type fats are great protectors of your health, eating too much of them will make you gain weight, and that isn't healthful. Here are the best fat sources from Mediterranean cuisines to incorporate into your diet.

➤ **Olive oil.** When Hippocrates said, "Let food be thy medicine," he may well have been talking about olive oil. We can assume that Hippocrates, a Greek physician, enjoyed his share of this beneficial Mediterranean fat. Don't confuse the flavorful, yellow-green elixir with mere oil. It's more like a healing genie in a bottle. In Mediterranean countries, where it is used liberally, the rates of heart disease, breast cancer, diabetes and even arthritis are far lower than in the US.

One way olive oil fights heart disease is by reducing LDL cholesterol, the form that most easily oxidizes in the blood and promotes artery blockages. Olive oil is also wonderful for blood pressure. A clinical study found that patients with hypertension who consumed more olive oil were able to decrease their medication dosages by half. Studies also show that olive oil lowers blood sugar levels, prevents peptic ulcers and effectively treats peptic ulcers in progress. Still other research shows that it plays a significant role in preventing cancer.

Enjoy one to two tablespoons of olive oil every day. Use in salad dressings, for very low-heat cooking or as a delicious drizzle on fresh fish, pasta or bread. This doesn't mean in addition to butter and other oils and fats, but instead of.

More than 75% of all olive oil comes from three Mediterranean countries—Italy, Spain and Greece. Look for these countries of origin on labels before you buy, and always select extra virgin, which is the only variety that has been cold pressed and not heat treated. Keep it in a cool place, so that its delicate monounsaturated oleic acid doesn't spoil. Your fridge is not the best spot because olive oil turns solid in cold temperatures, which can be a nuisance when you need to use it in a hurry. We keep a small bottle of olive oil at room temperature for everyday use, filling it halfway from the master bottle kept in the refrigerator.

➤ **Nuts and avocados.** Here are two more luscious foods that provide healthy monounsaturated fats in Mediterranean countries. Dieters tend to shun them because they fear their fat and calorie content, but there's no need to avoid avocados and nuts because their fat is extremely healthful and healing. Like olive oil, avocados and nuts contain oleic acid, which can significantly decrease total cholesterol and LDL while kicking up good HDL. These oleic acids also provide significant protection against breast cancer. At least five major epidemiological studies show that eating nuts on a regular basis decreases the risk of CHD and the more often nuts are consumed, the lower the risk. Studies show that about five servings a week provide maximum protection. Even people who ate nuts just once a month had some reduction.

It's worth noting that nuts played an important healing role in the Lyons Study. In addition, some of the largest, most significant clinical trials, such as the Nurses' Health Study, the Iowa Women's Health Study and the Adventist Study, show a consistent 30% to 50% reduced risk of heart

7

attacks and heart disease from eating nuts several times per week. Researchers at Harvard Medical School found that people who ate four servings of nuts weekly reduced their risk of heart disease, even though they ate fewer fruits and vegetables, didn't take a multivitamin, drank more coffee and consumed more saturated fat. That's some pretty impressive healing power.

Another way nuts, particularly walnuts, contribute to heart health is their omega-3 content. Like aspirin, these highly beneficial fats thin the blood so it can flow freely and prevent dangerous clots from forming. Because the omega-3s are anti-inflammatory, they also protect blood vessels from becoming inflamed. This inflammation usually triggers artery disease. Nuts, especially almonds, are high in vitamin E (a powerful antioxidant) and rich in *arginine* (the amino acid that acts as a natural vasodilator, keeping artery walls flexible and relaxed to enhance blood flow). Eating nuts also discourages type 2 diabetes, according to studies from Harvard University.

Don't worry about nuts making you fat. Studies confirm that people who eat nuts as part of a balanced diet tend to be thinner than those who don't. If that sounds like a paradox, it's really not, when you consider how filling a handful of nuts can be. In another Harvard study, people who got 35% of their calories from healthy fats like those in nuts were three times more likely to maintain their weight loss than dieters who restricted total fat intake to 20%.

A TOAST TO GOOD HEALTH

The Mediterranean way of eating is sensual, fun and beautiful to behold. It is filled with fresh, colorful foods, zingy spices, a wide variety of flavors and lots of celebration. Even the most humble meal is usually festive, lasting for hours as friends and family revel in each other's company. And then there's the wine. Not only do these naturally fermented spirits add merriment to mealtime, but overwhelming research shows that wine makes people healthier. Studies consistently confirm that one or two servings of alcohol extend longevity and improve well-being in a variety of ways. Whether one's taste runs to a cup of hot sake or a glass of ruby-red merlot, moderate drinking raises levels of HDL cholesterol, and research shows that high HDL levels are even more protective against heart disease than low LDL. Moderate alcohol consumption also helps you destress, which lowers blood pressure.

The Mediterraneans have a slight edge because the red wine they favor is high in *quercetin* and other *flavonoids*, antioxidants that disarm potentially harmful free radical molecules. Red wine also contains several other uniquely healthful phytonutrients. One of the best-studied polyphenols in red wine, *resveratrol*, has been shown to improve blood flow to the brain and keep heart and artery tissue flexible. *Tannin* and *saponin glycosides* are other substances in red wine that are proven heart protectors because of their ability to boost HDL. The saponins in red wine also help prevent unwanted clumping of red blood cells. If you're not a drinker, no problem. Nonalcoholic red wines and grape juice contain the same beneficial compounds. The darker the grape, the greater the cardiovascular effects.

The Asian Advantage

As impressive as the Mediterranean diet seems to be, its results are eclipsed by those produced by the traditional diets eaten in China, Japan, Thailand and other Asian countries. Currently, they lead the world in producing healthy, long-living people. And, as demonstrated by research done on the Mediterranean diet, this superb health can't be explained by a single nutrient or food. Rather, as Michael Pollan suggests in his book, *In Defense of Food*, the benefits are more likely a combination of nutrients found in a variety of whole, unprocessed foods. In other words, it's the dietary *pattern*, the combination of specific foods, that is responsible. Some of the largest research studies conducted were designed to explore exactly what produces such healthy populations in Asia. Here are a few of the most significant studies and their results.

➤ **The China-Cornell-Oxford Project.** Also known as the China Study, and led by T. Colin Campbell, Ph.D., professor of nutritional biochemistry at Cornell University, this massive project looked closely at the dietary practices and disease rates among 10,200 Chinese men and women from 1983 to 1990. Dr. Campbell and his colleagues found that the rural Chinese diet, which is based on plant foods such as rice and vegetables, is low in animal foods and dairy and contains three times more fiber than the average Western diet, accounted for rates of heart disease, osteoporosis and breast and prostate cancers that were many times lower than those in Western society. Obesity was also rare.

The Chinese, like the Mediterraneans, eat so many fruits, vegetables, whole grains and other plant foods that they achieve levels of antioxidant protection most Americans can only dream of. The numbers tell the story. The death rate among Chinese men from heart disease is 17 times lower than for American men. Chinese cancer rates are dwarfed by those in the US. Obesity is almost unheard of. However, when urban Chinese abandon their traditional diet, Dr. Campbell's research showed that they develop much higher rates of these Western diseases. After years of painstaking research, the China Study had generated the largest database in the world on the multiple causes of disease. The findings of the study were clear. "In the final analysis," reported Dr. Campbell, "we have strong evidence from this and other studies that nutrition becomes the controlling factor in the development of chronic degenerative diseases."

➤ **Asian Diet and Breast Cancer Study.** In the mid-1990s, researchers from the University of California recruited breast cancer survivors to determine the merits of an Asian-style diet in reducing the risk of breast cancer recurrence. Participants were placed on an Asian-style diet rich in vegetables and grains, low in red meat and rich in omega-3 fat from fish. During the three-month study, there was no recurrence of breast cancer in any of the subjects. Researchers also found that the women's breast-fat composition had changed biochemically in response to this diet. The project director was surprised at how quickly the healthy changes occurred in the breast, saying: "I think it shows that not only are you what you eat, you are what you ate very recently."

➤ **The Ni-Hon-San Study.** Initiated in the 1960s to evaluate dietary and lifestyle differences between middle-aged Japanese men living in Japan, Hawaii and San Francisco, this five-year study found that the men living in Japan who generally followed traditional Japanese dietary and lifestyle practices had very low rates of heart disease. By comparison, partly Westernized Japanese men in Hawaii had almost twice the rate of heart disease. Fully Westernized Japanese men in San Francisco had nearly triple the rate of heart disease compared with the Japanese men living in Japan. Because there were no genetic differences among the study's participants, researchers concluded that the adoption of Western dietary and lifestyle practices were responsible for the differences.

➤ **The Okinawa Centenarian Study.** I've already mentioned this landmark study, which looked at the residents of this small Japanese island with the largest per capita population of centenarians on earth. The incidence of the three leading killer diseases in the West—CHD, stroke, and cancers of the breast and colon—are lower in Okinawa than anywhere else on earth. OCS researchers concluded that the Okinawa diet,

consisting of high amounts of rice, grains, vegetables, fruits, soybeans and other legumes, moderate alcohol intake, very little red meat and at least three servings a week of omega-3-rich fish, was the major factor responsible.

Distinctly Asian Healing Foods

The Asian diet features its own food themes, including an emphasis on the following.

➤ **Soy foods.** This plant protein contains copious amounts of minerals, vitamins, omega-3 fatty acids and fiber. The average Japanese adult eats about 20 pounds of soy per year in a variety of forms. Researchers believe this is one reason the rates of heart disease in Japan are so low. Medical studies support soy's role, revealing that soy protein lowers LDL cholesterol, inhibits arterial inflammation, makes blood vessels more flexible, improves circulation and can reduce blood pressure by as much as 25 points.

Soy is an inexpensive legume that contains a mighty arsenal of disease-fighting plant nutrients. It is the richest food source of health-promoting plant estrogens called *isoflavones*, which help prevent and reverse osteoporosis and many cancers, while relieving a range of menstrual and menopausal symptoms. Research indicates that eating soy foods is also responsible for the low rates of breast cancer and endometrial cancer among Japanese women. Asian men who eat traditional diets high in fish, vegetables and soy foods while limiting red meat and dairy products, exhibit prostate cancer rates that are ten times lower than those of US males.

The traditional Japanese *miso* soup uses fermented soy paste to create a broth rich in isoflavones that are heart protective and cancer preventive. A ten-year study of more than 20,000 women by Tokyo's National Cancer Center Research Institute found that those who consumed at least three bowls of miso soup a day cut their breast cancer risk by 40%. Two bowls a day reduced the risk by 26%.

➤ **Sea vegetables.** People in Japan and China have been eating sea vegetables, known in the West as seaweed, for more than 10,000 years. Sea vegetables are rich in minerals, especially natural iodine, needed for healthy thyroid gland function, and also chlorophyll, *alginates*, and magnesium. In addition, sea vegetables contain health-promoting lignans and anti-inflammatory nutrients called *fucans*. If you're a fan of sushi, you know *nori* as the salty dark green wrap that hold a roll's contents together. Seaweed is one of nature's healing miracle foods. Research shows that it contains compounds capable of preventing and treating several types of cancer, lowering cholesterol and blood pressure, thinning the blood, preventing ulcers and even curing constipation. In the rural areas of Japan, where seaweed consumption is high, the rates of breast cancer are lower than in urban areas, where seaweed is falling out of fashion.

➤ **Fermented foods.** Rich in enzymes and beneficial microorganisms that aid digestion, fermented foods promote healthy flora in our digestive tract, and help us absorb vitamins (particularly C and B-12), minerals and omega 3s more effectively from the other foods we eat. Fermented foods regulate the level of acidity in your digestive tract, act as antioxidants, and boost immunity. In addition, fermented foods possess the same *isothiocyanates* found in cruciferous vegetables, which are responsible for their cancer-fighting and prevention powers.

The Chinese have eaten fermented cabbage for 6,000 years and, across Asia, households make their own fermented carrots, eggplant, turnips and cucumbers. Koreans love *kimchi*, a spicy-hot fermented condiment of cabbage and other vegetables. In China, scientists studied 5,000 people who had previously had heart attacks. They divided them into two groups, one taking a purified extract of rice fermented by Chinese red yeast, the other group getting a placebo. After tracking the groups for five years, researchers found that those in the red yeast rice extract group were 30% less likely to die from any cardiovascular-related condition, had 45% fewer second heart attacks than the placebo takers and were 33% less likely to die from all causes.

Cholesterol was also markedly lowered in the red yeast rice group, and participants needed one-third less the number of angioplasties or heart surgeries than those in the placebo group. No drug I know can produce results like these. Subsequent research shows that the red yeast rice extract acts exactly like statin drugs in lowering cholesterol and, in many cases, just as well.

How the Two Healthiest Diets Overlap: Less Is Often More

There's significant overlap between the two healthiest diets on earth. After all, people in both the Mediterranean and Asian cultures de-emphasize red meat while enjoying generous portions of fish and shellfish. Both cultures also eat an astonishing quantity of fresh vegetables, by some estimates a pound daily, and they generously season their meals with fresh herbs and spices that have serendipitous medicinal properties. Additional similarities follow here, including what the two regions *don't* eat for healthful results…

WHOLE GRAINS AND LEGUMES

Here's another food group that's one of the most nutritious components in both the Mediterranean and Asian diets. People in each region get a significant percentage of their daily calories from whole grains and legumes, such as beans, chickpeas, lentils and soybeans. Many experts attribute the low rates of cancer and heart disease in these cultures to the high levels of antioxidants, as well as fiber, found in these foods. Because whole grains, beans and other legumes are low in calories and high in fiber, they are an excellent food for weight loss, which is another reason that the people of the Mediterranean traditionally have a much slimmer profile than our own.

LESS REFINED SUGAR AND CARBS

The people of the Mediterranean love their sweets, but they view this pleasure as a treat, reserving it for dessert after a healthy meal. In Asia, desserts are not a prominent course as they are in Western meals. Both cultures rarely eat candy or drink sodas during the day as we do in the US. There are very few refined, processed carbohydrate foods in the Asian and Mediterranean diets, with the exception of pasta. (Mediterranean breads are made with a hard durum wheat, which digests slowly.) Refined sugar and carbohydrates have been implicated as a major cause of heart disease, cancer, diabetes, Alzheimer's and other inflammation-driven medical conditions. One reason they're so harmful is that they upset the body's metabolism, flooding the bloodstream with glucose and insulin, a deadly duo that is highly inflammatory, generates massive amounts of free radical molecules and accelerates the aging of cells and tissues through the process of glycation.

Eating refined foods also causes cells to become insulin resistant, resulting in the eventual burnout of insulin-producing cells in the pancreas, which is another way of saying "type 2 diabetes." High levels of blood sugar are the main fuel for cancer cells and tumors, so not only are sugary foods and refined carbs toxic, they're also carcinogenic. Replacing these unhealthy foods with vegetables, fruits, nuts, whole grains, and legumes—in short, a Mediterranean or Asian-style diet—exerts an immediate healing effect on the body.

FEWER POLYUNSATURATED FATS, MORE OMEGA-3S

Like sugar, polyunsaturated vegetable oils are pro-inflammatory because their high omega-6 content overwhelms the scant amount of omega-3s in the typical American diet. Studies show that oil made from corn, safflower and soybeans and even highly touted, so-called healthy canola oil are closely linked to cancer. For decades, doctors have believed these polyunsaturated vegetable oils were ideal replacements for saturated fats, lard and butter. However, an overwhelming body of scientific evidence shows that these very vegetable oils and the hydrogenated trans fats made from them are the real culprits behind the surge of heart disease and cancers in America that began in the 1950s, which is the decade during which vegetable oils, margarine and trans fats began to pervade our food supply.

➤ **Saturated fat is not the culprit.** Furthermore, new scientific evidence is confirming what many astute nutritionists and researchers have known all along: Saturated fat is not the culprit we've been told it is, and foods containing it, such as meat, butter and other dairy products, along with stable saturated fats such as coconut and palm oil, are healthful foods that have proven themselves safe through centuries of consumption. In the Mediterranean, lard and butter, both of which are high in saturated fat, are commonly used in cooking. In Asia, coconut, palm and sesame oils are used for stir-frying, because they stand up well to high temperatures without breaking down and oxidizing. These oils are high in saturated fats, but they have been used faithfully for centuries where rates of heart disease and cancers have remained low.

➤ **More omega-3 fats.** Extraordinarily protective omega-3 fats are found in cold-water fish, nuts, flaxseed and a handful of plants, including soybeans. People throughout the Mediterranean and Asia eat far more fish than Americans, and it's one of the main reasons their heart disease rates are so much lower. Studies show that eating just one serving of omega-3 fish a week, as long as it isn't fried, can cut the risk of sudden cardiac death by 50%. Imagine if there were a drug that could reduce the risk of dying as much as this food does! Unfortunately, there isn't one.

Cold-water fish such as salmon, herring, mackerel, sardines and anchovies are loaded with omega-3s, the type of fat that's pure gold for your heart. Research shows that omega-3s prevent the rupture of fatty plaque deposits in your arteries, a common cause of clots and subsequent heart attacks and strokes. Omega-3s also have stunning anti-inflammatory properties that can derail the arterial damage that leads to cardiovascular disease and plaque formation. A remarkable study, known as The Diet and Reinfarction Trial, found that people with the highest intakes of omega-3 fatty acids were almost 30% less likely to die from all causes during a given period than those who received lesser amounts.

In addition to their anti-inflammatory effects, omega-3 foods reduce inflammation throughout the entire body, especially in arthritic joints. Our most up-to-date research indicates that inflammation is the driving force behind many serious degenerative diseases, including diabetes, hypertension, Alzheimer's and heart disease. Scientists believe that one reason the US is plagued by these inflammation-driven diseases is because the American diet contains too many omega-6

Does the Mediterranean Diet Work in the US?

It's obvious that the Mediterranean diet works for people living there, but how does it travel? Can it improve Americans' health on their home soil and elsewhere? The answer is absolutely *yes*. The largest study ever conducted, involving 400,000 adults, evaluated the effect of a Mediterranean-style diet on the mortality of a US population and found that it does indeed reduce deaths from all causes by 20%. Here's more good news about the way they eat in the Mediterranean:

➤ **Just a few good foods can add years to your life.** The study gave points for each major component of the Mediterranean-style diet, including consumption of vegetables, fruits, fish, whole grains, beans and legumes, olive oil and red wine. Participants whose diet reflected the highest component scores had the lowest incidence of disease and death. This study shows that, even if you don't want to adopt a Mediterranean-style way of eating completely, you can improve your health and chances of long life by adding traditional Mediterranean foods a little at a time.

➤ **The secret to longevity.** The Mediterranean diet actually prolongs life. Men and women whose eating patterns were closest to the Mediterranean diet were up to 31% less likely to die over the study's five-year period compared with those whose diets were the least Mediterranean.

➤ **Smokers helped.** Eating a Mediterranean diet was "particularly beneficial" for smokers who adopted it, the study authors found, cutting their death risk by up to 45%.

➤ **Protects against diabetes.** A study conducted in Spain involving 60,000 people showed that those who ate a Mediterranean-style diet were less likely to develop new-onset diabetes. According to a study in a recent issue of the *British Medical Journal*, researchers found that people with the greatest number of risk factors for type 2 diabetes actually received the highest level of protection by adhering to the Mediterranean diet. Those with the highest adherence to Mediterranean eating habits, regardless of their risk factors for the disease, exhibited a stunning 83% reduction in the risk of developing diabetes.

fatty acids, which are pro-inflammatory. The ideal healthy ratio between omega-6s and omega-3s is 2:1, but in the typical American diet, that ratio is closer to 20:1. Where do we get so many omega-6s from? From polyunsaturated vegetable oils and grain products—two foods plentiful in the American diet. A recent UK study reports that omega-3 fatty acids from fish may help prevent the growth of prostate cancer, while the omega-6 fats that

predominate in common vegetable oils seem to accelerate its spread.

LESS RED MEAT

You won't find a 24-ounce porterhouse steak on the menu in Mediterranean and Asian countries. Residents of these countries eat far less red meat than we do in the US. That's not because it is inherently unhealthy—it just isn't nearly as plentiful there. As a result, red meat is a treat, not a staple. Vegetables and whole grains take the dominant position on the plate, which is the reverse of the typical American diet. Also, almost all the meat eaten, whether it's lamb, veal, pork, goat, poultry or beef, is grass-fed, free-range and hormone-free, which means that the servings contain smaller amounts of omega-6 fatty acids and more beneficial omega-3s, the opposite of US beef. In fact, the omega-3 content of grass-fed, free-range beef rivals that of some fish.

LESS DAIRY

Consumption of dairy products in the countries of the Mediterranean and Asia is much lower than in the US, with the exception of cheese and yogurt. I guess that the people of the Mediterranean would much rather drink wine than milk. Yogurt, which is a mainstay in Greece and throughout the region, provides live bacterial cultures called *probiotics*, which strengthen the immune system, regulate intestinal health and discourage constipation. Since the rate of osteoporosis in Mediterranean and Asian countries is considerably lower than that of the US, you have to wonder if milk really "does a body good," as those Dairy Council ads claim. Many vegetables, specifically the leafy greens such as kale, bok choy, mustard greens and collards, provide all the calcium your bones need, even if you're past menopause. A single serving of collard greens, for example, rivals the calcium in a glass of milk, yet in a more absorbable form. The vitamin D necessary to transform calcium into bone tissue can be provided via fish and sunshine, both of which these cultures enjoy in high doses.

LOW SODIUM

Both the Mediterranean and Asian diets are naturally low in sodium because neither culture consumes much processed food. Most of the sodium in the typical American diet is hidden salt, abundant in processed foods from canned vegetables and soups to frozen foods. Sodium is the mineral that causes your body to retain fluids and elevates blood pressure. The Mediterranean diet does just the opposite, by virtue of its bounty of high-potassium foods. Potassium pulls sodium out of the body and helps lower blood pressure. About 50 million Americans currently have hypertension, and studies show that lowering blood pressure can reduce the incidence of stroke by up to 40% and heart attacks by up to 25%. Doctors estimate that every 12-point reduction in systolic pressure (the upper number in the blood pressure reading) that's maintained for 10 years could prevent as many as 10% of all deaths.

The upper daily limit of sodium for optimal health is 1,500 milligrams (about ⅓ teaspoon), but most Americans take in much more than this amount. Research shows that you can decrease your blood pressure five to 10 points by doing nothing more than keeping sodium within the recommended range. By eating a Mediterranean-style diet, or my Mediterr-Asian Diet (see next chapter), you can easily lower pressure 20 points or more, which is often enough to eliminate the need for medication.

HEALING HERBS, BULBS AND SPICES

Ever notice how the neighborhood seems to perk up when a new Italian or Asian restaurant opens, perhaps in anticipation of enticing aromas wafting through the streets? Both of these full-flavored cuisines use a lot of spices, and they do a lot more than just add flavor. *Here are a few of the most popular...*

➤ **Garlic.** Many of the most popular dishes in Mediterranean and Asian countries use this pungent bulb to kick up the flavor, but garlic has a secret: It's also one of the most healing foods in nature. Many of its therapeutic powers come from sulfur-containing compounds including *allicin, diallyl disulfide* and *diallyl trisulfide.* Several studies have shown that garlic decreases total cholesterol levels, while increasing protective HDL. Garlic has been shown to lower blood pressure in numerous clinical trials. One study also found that it lowered triglyceride levels by up to 17%. That's why, for centuries, Asian physicians have relied on it as a remedy for heart disease and diabetes. Modern research shows that it thins the blood like aspirin, reducing the likelihood of harmful clots. Other studies have found that part of garlic's prowess is its ability to destroy unpleasant yeast growths, such as *Candida*, plus many types of infectious bacteria.

Garlic also helps clobber cancer cells. Several laboratory studies have shown it to be highly protective, while epidemiological studies reveal a lower incidence of stomach and colon cancer in areas where garlic consumption is high. Eating garlic regularly also lowered the incidents of ovarian, colorectal and other cancers, according to a meta-analysis published in the *American Journal of Clinical Nutrition.* A clinical trial in Japan

found that after one year of taking aged garlic extract supplements, people with a history of colon polyps experienced a reduction in the size and number of the precancerous growths.

➤ **Fresh is always best.** Powdered garlic and the chopped garlic you find in jars at supermarkets don't pack much healing punch. The convenience isn't worth the price. A superfast way to peel a clove of garlic is to smash it with the flat side of a big knife so the skin just slides off. Chopping, mincing or pressing garlic before cooking enhances its health-promoting properties by boosting the levels of the healing compound allicin. To get the maximum health benefit, let garlic sit for five to 10 minutes before using to permit more allicin to be formed. Gently sauté garlic in olive oil, adding it last to other ingredients to avoid burning it (which makes it bitter and destroys its healing properties). Since it's a blood thinner, talk to your doctor before eating garlic regularly if you are on an anticoagulant drug, such as Coumadin.

I love roasted garlic heads and use them like butter on baked potatoes or as a spread on a warm, crunchy baguette slice. Just pop a head of garlic into a 350°F oven for 45 minutes or until tender. Roasting makes garlic less pungent and sweeter, because the heat turns the starches to sugar. Roasted garlic cloves lower blood pressure and cholesterol, and remove heavy metals from the body, especially mercury and cadmium, which have been linked to Alzheimer's disease.

➤ **Onions.** A close cousin of garlic, onions contain health-protecting allicin as well.

16

Clinical studies reveal that onions and onion extract also decrease levels of unhealthy fats in the blood, prevent clot formation and lower blood pressure. Onions also have demonstrated the ability to lower glucose in the bloodstream at the same rate as the popular diabetes prescription drugs *tolbutamide* (Orinase) and *phenformin*. Research shows that onions accomplish this by increasing the life span of insulin.

In one of the most remarkable research studies of modern times, Dr. N. N. Gupta, a professor of medicine at K. G. Medical College in Lucknow, India, discovered that onions are able to neutralize the health dangers present in an extremely high-fat meal. He fed young and middle-aged men a 1,000-calorie meal that was 90% fat, featuring eggs, butter and cream, both with and without onions. Dr. Gupta knew that such a meal would produce elevated cholesterol and a greater tendency for the blood to thicken and clot. He and his researchers were astonished when they examined the men's blood before and after both meals. The high fat content definitely pushed up blood cholesterol but, to everyone's surprise, the onions brought it back to normal. In addition, the onions restored the blood's natural clot-busting ability. It didn't matter whether the onions were raw, fried, boiled or dried—the results were the same. The bottom line? If you simply must have a greasy hamburger or juicy sirloin, smother it in onions to protect your arteries and heart. And eat onions every chance you get.

By the way, follow-up studies revealed that only a tiny amount of onion was required to counteract these potentially deadly changes in blood chemistry. In another clinical trial involving two groups of healthy adults in New Delhi, patients ate a 3,000-calorie-per-day diet for 15 days. Not surprisingly, their cholesterol shot up from an average 219 to 263. However, when one group was given a mere *tablespoon* of onion per day with this fatty diet, their cholesterol fell to an average of 237. This is a stunning finding, when you consider the large effect such a small amount of onion produced. Subsequent research showed that when more onion was given, it produced even steeper drops in cholesterol.

➤ **Rosemary.** Frying, broiling or grilling meats at high temperatures creates *heterocyclic amines* (HCAs), potent carcinogens implicated in several cancers, especially those of the breast and colon. Kansas State University scientists found that HCA levels are significantly reduced when rosemary is added to meat during cooking. "Rosemary contains *carnosol* and *rosemarinic acid*, two powerful antioxidants that destroy the HCAs," explains lead researcher J. Scott Smith, Ph.D. To reduce HCAs, he recommends marinating foods in a mix that includes rosemary along with any of these other Mediterranean flavors: thyme, oregano, basil, garlic, onion or parsley.

Rosemary also seems to halt tumor development. Researchers found that rosemary extract helps prevent carcinogens in the body from binding with DNA, the first step in tumor formation. When researchers at the University of Illinois at Urbana-Champaign fed rosemary extract to laboratory animals exposed to a carcinogen that causes breast cancer, both DNA damage and tumors decreased. "Rosemary has shown a lot of cancer-protective potential," says study author Keith W. Singletary, Ph.D.

➤ **Curry.** *Curcumin* is an active ingredient in turmeric, the yellow spice best known as the distinctive coloring agent in curry powder. Some researchers believe the predominance of curry in the Indian diet explains why there is so little arthritis or Alzheimer's disease there, compared with the US. Curcumin has a long history as an anti-inflammatory agent in Chinese and Indian medicine, and has proven itself in numerous modern clinical studies. (For more information, see "Arthritis," "Heart Disease" and "Memory Loss" chapters.)

➤ **Ginger, cinnamon and cloves.** It's hard to find an Asian dish without ginger. A natural blood thinner and a common aid to digestion, it is a distinct flavor component in root or powder form. (See "Arthritis," "Heart Disease" and "Digestive Disorders" chapters

for more information.) Cinnamon, a common ingredient in Chinese five-spice powder, is off the charts in antioxidant power (see "Heart Disease" chapter). Cloves, also a frequent ingredient in five-spice powder and in much of Indian cuisine, is a natural anti-inflammatory (see "Arthritis" chapter).

And the Winner Is...

The more closely I examine the Asian diet and the impressive studies done on it, the more I believe it rivals, or even surpasses, the benefits of the Mediterranean diet. But the Mediterranean diet has many components, including specific fresh fruits and vegetables, that are very familiar to those who reside in the US. That's why I decided to combine them both into a new fusion cuisine that can bring you the best healing benefits of both worlds. I'll tell you all about my Mediterr-Asian Diet in the next chapter. ■

2

The Mediterr-Asian Diet:
The Best of Both Worlds

If, as scientists tell us, *diet* is the single most important determinant of good health and recovery from disease, Mediterranean and Asian cuisines are the ones to embrace. The research results are irrefutable: Both produce superlative health and unparalleled longevity. If those are your goals, adopt the best from these two culinary cultures. You don't need to choose one diet over another.

My hope is that a cuisine that combines the two most healthful diets in the world will *multiply* their individual therapeutic effects and healthfulness. By merging the healthiest aspects of Asian and Mediterranean cuisines, I want you to get more healing benefits on the plates compared with either cuisine alone. Thus, there would be *more* meal choices and *more* new flavor experiences. Here is an abundance of nature's most delicious foods,

prepared in combinations that will delight your senses, satisfy your appetite and hunger for adventurous dining, while providing you with a lifetime of eating enjoyment that will never, ever bore you.

A New World of Adventurous Flavors

This fusion cuisine opens up a world of dining possibilities. The Mediterranean part of the diet draws from the delicious cuisines of Greece, France, Italy, Turkey, Spain, Tunisia and Morocco, in itself quite a rich palette. On the Asian side, there's food from Korea, Japan, China, Thailand, India, Indonesia and Vietnam, which makes for a wide variety of interesting flavors and combinations to choose from. Unfortunately, most diets, whether those meant for weight loss, lowering cholesterol or managing blood sugar,

19

don't succeed because people feel deprived of certain foods and eating pleasure. Let me assure you that the Mediterr-Asian Diet includes every food group for just that reason. The only exception is the highly processed junk foods that are proven to be outright harmful to your health. Here's why my Mediterr-Asian Diet is so exceedingly healing and health-promoting.

NATURE'S RICHEST SOURCES OF PHYTOESTROGENS

Both the Mediterranean and Asian diets are based on an extraordinary array of plant foods, including fruits, vegetables, whole grains, nuts, seeds and beans. All are extremely rich in a unique class of cancer-fighting nutrients known as *phytoestrogens*. In Asia, the prominent phytoestrogens are the *isoflavones* found in soy foods such as soybeans, tofu, tempeh, and miso, as well as the *lignans* found in sea vegetables. In the Mediterranean, isoflavone and lignan phytoestrogens are supplied by legumes, seeds, vegetables and fruits. Research clearly shows that these phytoestrogenic foods are one of the main reasons that both styles of eating are linked to reduced risk of disease, especially cancer. Thousands of studies have identified these foods as the most healthful and healing you can eat.

MORE HEALTHFUL ANIMAL PRODUCTS

While neither diet is vegetarian, meat is eaten moderately (unlike the Western meat-centric approach). The principal animal protein is fish, particularly cold-water varieties that are especially rich in omega-3 fatty acids. When meat is eaten, it comes from animals that

have been raised in a free-range environment where the animal feed is chiefly grass and other living plant foods, which results in meat that is hormone-free and high in anti-inflammatory omega-3 fatty acids. Meat and fish that are humanely raised are better for your heath, better for the environment and better for your spirit because it respects the sacredness of all life.

THE BEST OF BOTH CULTURES

Of course, there are differences between these two diets. In Asia, people eat small quantities of soy foods daily, in addition to seaweed and sea vegetables, fermented foods, medicinal mushrooms and healthy spices such as ginger and chilies. In the Mediterranean, olive oil is splashed on just about everything, and wine is relished with meals. Despite their disparities, both cultures have enduring traditions of eating fresh, whole, unprocessed foods that thrive in their respective regions. Virtually none of these foods are refined, chemicalized, hormone-laden, laced with sugar and other additives or possess any other qualities that are detrimental to the healing and health-building processes.

The Mediterr-Asian way of eating is an approach you can live with, and live well on, because it doesn't feel like a diet at all. It includes a generous portion of healthy fat—up to 30% or more. You can eat meats and chocolate; enjoy comfort carbs, such as bread, rice, and pasta; use butter; eat eggs without worry; and savor your favorite cheeses. Irrefutable clinical studies show that you'll be healthier and slimmer as a result, because there's no deprivation involved. Indeed, the

Mediterr-Asian Diet represents a *lifetime* approach to eating enjoyment. It marries the flavors of the most popular Mediterranean and Asian dishes in new, healthier-than-ever combinations that will excite your palate as they heal your body, build your health and trim your figure.

A Real-Life Plan

In recent years, news outlets have featured story after story about the healthful aspects of both the Mediterranean and Asian diets, urging Americans to eat more soy foods, load up on vegetables and enjoy fish more often. If you're like many of us, you may have tried to incorporate these bits and pieces into your diet without turning your life upside down. *How* do I cut back on my consumption of red meat without feeling deprived? *How* do I cook with tofu? *How* can I satisfy my sweet tooth without sabotaging my weight-loss goals? *How* do I keep myself and my family interested, or even excited, about eating the foods that are so good for us without getting stuck in the tedium of eating healthily?

Through years of nutritional study and research, I've learned which foods harbor the greatest healing power for specific medical conditions and have guided my patients to the superhealing foods they should be eating more of. In addition, I was aware of the extraordinary health and longevity that the diets of the Mediterranean and Asia produced among their people. What I wanted was a way to combine these benefits into a broad new cuisine that would align with mainstream American tastes and provide

boundless opportunities for variety, culinary creativity and eating enjoyment.

That's when I had the great good fortune of meeting Rebecca Bent, a rising young Manhattan chef whose cooking style was deeply rooted in the traditions of the Mediterranean cuisine of her Italian heritage—a heritage, by the way, that we proudly share. Rebecca's interest in Mediterranean cuisine takes her back to Italy, France, Greece and other countries every year to continue her study with both renowned big-city chefs and under-the-radar provincial cooks. I am simply amazed by her food knowledge and culinary skills.

Together, Rebecca and I have created more than 150 healing recipes that follow—recipes that feature foods that have been shown by clinical research to possess outstanding healing properties for specific medical conditions. The recipes are organized by condition, so you can focus your healing efforts there first. Rebecca also offers vegetarian and frugal options that suit different preferences and budgets. There are thousands of permutations and combinations possible as you work with the basic recipes. In a short time, you'll know which foods are your greatest allies and healers for the medical conditions you want to overcome. With a little practice, and as you experience the relief and improvement these foods deliver, you'll instinctively begin building healing meals of your own around these foods and dietary guidelines. Rebecca's ingenious preparations are a roadmap to a lifetime of healing and eating pleasure.

How to Start a Mediterr-Asian Diet

You don't have to move to the Mediterranean or to Asia to enjoy the health and longevity benefits of their healing foods and diets. In fact, you won't even need to make one of Rebecca's recipes to get started. You can start healing yourself and family right away by familiarizing yourself with the foods of the Mediterr-Asian Diet. As you age, the greater your chances of developing health problems become, and the best way to protect yourself is to begin eating Mediterr-Asian style at every meal. Here are some broad guidelines that will start you on this path.

➤ **Eat lots of vegetables.** People in Mediterranean and Asian countries eat a pound of vegetables every day and are amazingly healthy and slender as a result. Vegetables are your most trusted healing allies and also a sure way to lose weight without hunger or deprivation. In general, the more colorful a vegetable is, the better it is for you, because those bright hues indicate large quantities of antioxidants and other healing phytonutrients. You'll gain tremendous vitality from eating the widest possible array of vegetables.

➤ **Enjoy fresh fruits.** They are high in fiber and rich in vitamins, minerals, antioxidants and other nutrients. Berries, including cherries, top the list of the most healthful and healing fruits. I love to start my day with a bowl of mixed berries and plain soy yogurt, topped with a couple of tablespoons of ground flaxseed. Other fruits, such as apples, oranges, bananas and grapefruit, make ideal between-meal snacks because they are high in fiber and contain few calories. The more delicate fruit varieties, such as peaches and apricots, make satisfying low-cal desserts.

➤ **Discover beans and other legumes.** Like vegetables, legumes are an ideal healing and weight-loss food. With loads of fiber, protein, and phytonutrients, legumes are ranked right behind vegetables and fruits as the healthiest food group to eat. Canned beans and lentils are fine as long as their sodium levels are low. Soybeans are a mainstay in Asian cuisine and require a little extra cooking to render them fully digestible, but they can be purchased cooked and frozen.

➤ **Consume more fish.** Cold-water fish such as wild salmon, mackerel, halibut, sardines, anchovies and others contain high levels of omega-3 fatty acids, which are extraordinarily good for your heart and brain. Shrimp and other shellfish are good choices, too. Try to eat these healthful varieties of fish two to three times per week. Their omega-3s are natural anti-inflammatories, so they'll also help relieve joint pain. Other studies show they protect your brain from Alzheimer's and dementia. Fish and shellfish are also low in calories, so they're a natural for weight control, and are also an exceptional source of protein. Bake, grill or broil seafood with a light touch, so that you don't destroy the delicate omega-3 oils. Never, ever deep-fry fish (or anything else). Poultry and eggs are also good protein sources.

➤ **Use olive oil.** Olive oil is a healthful monounsaturated fat that's highly stable and keeps your arteries and organs healthy. Always buy extra-virgin olive oil and store it in a cool place, but please don't cook with it other than for gentle, low-heat sautéing. High heat destroys its healthful qualities. For stir-frying or other high-temperature cooking, choose light olive oil, coconut, palm, peanut or sesame oil. Use extra-virgin olive oil to make salad and vegetable dressings and in place of butter or margarine on bread. Go easy, however, because olive oil contains just as many calories as other fats. Limit yourself to about a tablespoon and a half per day.

➤ **Choose whole grains.** Replace white-flour bread and pasta with whole-wheat products. Eat more brown rice, oats, barley and other complex-carbohydrate grains in place of white rice and white potatoes, both of which have higher glycemic index ratings because they transform into blood sugar relatively quickly. In general, eating low GI foods is much better for you, especially if you have blood sugar problems.

➤ **Go light on red meat.** Grass-fed, free-range cattle, lamb, pigs and poultry eat grass and other wild pasture plants, thus their flesh can contain as much omega-3 as some fish. Avoid conventionally raised animal products because they're fed grains like corn, which makes their meat high in omega-6s and pro-inflammatory, not to mention excessively fatty. The challenging part is that most animal products, free-range or not, contain a lot of calories, so move these meats out of the starring role in your meals and let vegetables and beans take the lead, keeping animal foods as co-stars, as they do in Mediterranean and Asian cultures. When choosing poultry, pick free-range turkey breast, because its composition is closest to the wild game our ancestors ate.

➤ **Give soy foods a try.** You don't have to eat large quantities of soy to reap its health benefits. In Japan, for example, people consume a little with each meal, enjoying soy as a condiment. Aggressive marketing and advertising campaigns have portrayed soy as a miracle health food in the US, in an attempt to expand the industry. More than 200 million Americans now eat soy foods in unprecedented quantities, and in highly processed forms, such as soy burgers, soy energy bars, soy ice cream and soy meats. These are not traditional foods and have little (if any) research to support the health claims made for them.

Recommended soy foods are *edamame*, the whole soybean pod steamed and eaten as an appetizer or snack; moderate amounts of soy milk and soy yogurt; soybeans; tofu, often referred to as *the cheese of Asia*; *tempeh,* a fermented form of tofu; *tamari*, a fermented, salty soy sauce; *miso,* a soybean paste most often used for soup and crunchy roasted soy nuts. If you've received a cancer diagnosis, however, consult your doctor before eating soy foods. Their phytoestrogen content can cause problems in treating some cancers.

➤ **Don't be afraid of seaweed.** I encourage you to experiment with sea vegetables, commonly referred to as *seaweed*, because the health and healing payoffs can be huge. Look in the Asian foods section of your grocery or shop in local markets if your town has a Japanese or Chinese neighborhood. The most popular seaweeds include *dulse*, chopped and sprinkled on main dishes or salads; *nori,* used to make sushi rolls; *kombu,* used as a flavoring for soups and beans; and *wakame,* used to make Japanese miso soup. Kelp, *arame* and *hijiki* are other choices.

I've been so impressed with the medicinal properties of seaweed that I sought out a supplement called Seanol, from Korea. I recommend it to my patients and newsletter readers who can't get used to the idea of eating seaweed. This red/brown seaweed combination from the eastern coast of Korea provides the perfect solution. Just two to four capsules per day allows them to reap the benefits of this amazing healing food.

➤ **Try yogurt, cheese and other fermented foods.** The Mediterr-Asian Diet features much less dairy than the average Western diet, with the exception of cheese and yogurt. Both are fermented foods that provide the body with beneficial bacteria. Yogurt, particularly low fat, can be eaten every day and is an excellent source of calcium and probiotics.

Most cheeses tend to be high in calories and should be enjoyed sparingly. Experiment with the strong-flavored artisanal varieties because a little of these cheeses goes a long way toward satisfaction. The exceptions are farmer and cottage cheeses which are naturally lower in calories, as well as organic goat's milk cheeses and skim-milk mozzarella. Women worried about osteoporosis should not cut back on milk, which protects against bone loss. However, yogurt is a far richer source of calcium. Even better are cruciferous leafy greens, which pack almost as much of this valuable mineral as a glass of milk.

Popular live-culture Asian delicacies include fermented black beans, which are soy-beans that have been lacto-fermented; tempeh, a hearty soy product with a chewy, nutty flavor and almost meatlike texture; and *natto,* made from fermented soybean, is a popular Japanese breakfast served with rice. Sticky and strongly flavored, natto's medical benefits are similar to all fermented soy-derived foods. It thins the blood like aspirin and destroys blood clots like expensive anticoagulant drugs.

➤ **Drink wine.** Numerous studies show that moderate consumption of alcohol, particularly red wine, prevents many diseases and extends longevity. In Asia, sake and beer are the preferred alcoholic beverages. Health experts suggest you limit alcohol, staying within their recommendation of two daily servings of alcohol for men, one for women. If you're alcohol sensitive, you can get the same benefits from grape juice.

Physical Activity Is Vital, Too

The traditional diets of the Mediterranean and Asian countries don't exist in a vacuum. Active lifestyles also play an important role in the health and longevity statistics of their populations. I can't emphasize strongly enough the importance of physical activity, whether you're trying to reverse a medical condition or achieve high-level wellness. No matter how perfect your diet is, optimum health and healing simply aren't possible without some degree of movement, even if it's just walking for 20 minutes a couple of times per day. Activity is the spark that sets the body's healing mechanisms in motion. It allows the foods you eat and the glucose they produce to be more fully burned by your metabolism. When you're active, the heart pumps more strongly, blood flows more quickly, less fat is stored, muscle mass is maintained (remember, muscle burns calories even while the body is at rest) and more oxygen and nutrients reach the brain and other organs.

"The data show that regular moderate exercise increases your ability to battle the effects of disease," says Marilyn Moffat, a professor of physical therapy at New York University and coauthor with Carole B. Lewis of *Age-Defying Fitness.*

➤ **Reduces hypertension.** Dr. Moffat is absolutely correct. Research shows that even modest aerobic exercise reduces blood pressure in hypertensive patients.

➤ **Defuses heart disease.** Clinical trials reveal that exercise of any kind reduces the risk of heart disease by more than 50%. Research published in the *Journal of the American Medical Association* reported that men who walk as little as 30 minutes every day reduce their risk of heart attack by nearly 20%. Jogging for an hour per week reduces the risk by 42% and lifting weights for 30 minutes weekly lowers the risk by another 19%. Women reap even greater rewards. One study showed that women who walked a half-hour daily reduced their risk of heart disease by 30%.

Why does exercise work so well? One reason is that exercise lowers levels of the inflammation marker, CRP, in the blood. Getting up and moving quells inflammation in the body. Even moderately fit people can lower their CRP levels to less than 50% of unfit people.

➤ **Disarms diabetes.** Moderate exercise also reduces your risk of developing diabetes. In those who have the disease, exercise improves glucose tolerance, thus lessening the need for medication, and reduces the risk of life-threatening complications.

➤ **Improves arthritis symptoms.** People with joint disorders and arthritis also benefit tremendously from physical activity. Clinical research shows that exercise can reduce pain and depression, while improving joint function, balance and quality of life. Without exercise, osteoarthritis patients become crippled by stiff, deteriorated joints. The same goes for people with rheumatoid arthritis. "The less they do, the worse things get," Dr. Moffat says. Her findings: "The more their joints move, the better."

➤ **Memory sharpened.** If you're looking to boost your brain power, get moving. Exercise increases brain function, which lifts mood, repels depression and pushes back the risks of Alzheimer's disease and dementia. New studies show that exercise actually gives rise to new brain cells and heals old, damaged ones (a phenomenon called *neurogenesis*). Researchers at the University of Illinois at Urbana-Champaign compared the effects of aerobic exercise on two groups of sedentary adults between the ages of 60 and 75. Half followed a walking program, while the control group performed stretching and toning exercises. When scientists measured each group's cognitive function before and after the six-month program, they found significant improvements in the walkers. The conclusion? "Six months of exercise will buy

Dr. Sinatra's 12 Top Healing Foods

1. Broccoli. Broccoli is loaded with antioxidants and compounds that boost immunity, protect you from heart disease and vision loss, build bone and drive down the risk of cataracts. Eating broccoli and its cruciferous cousins, including kale and cabbage, is the single most effective way to keep cancer at bay, according to a review of 85 individual studies.

2. Avocado. Rich in vitamin E and *glutathione,* avocados are also loaded with beneficial monounsaturated fat, which comes from their oleic acid, also found in olive oil and nuts. Eating avocado increases your beneficial HDL cholesterol and drives down cardio-damaging triglycerides. Avocado also enhances the absorption of the *carotenoids* beta-carotene and lycopene.

3. Onions. Eat them as often as you can. Onions support your immune system, improve prostate health and provide magnificent protection against cancer. Researchers found that people who eat the most onions have lower rates of ovarian, colon and throat cancers. And, because they're loaded with antioxidants, onions protect your cellular DNA, helping the body rid itself of cancer-causing substances before they harm cells.

4. Spinach. Eating just a couple of half-cup servings weekly can slash your risk for macular degeneration by 50%. Spinach is also a powerful protector of your lungs and heart; builds strong bones; and cuts your risk of cancers—including lung, colon, breast, prostate and ovarian. In addition, scientists at the Chicago Health and Aging Project found that leafy greens topped the charts for preventing mental decline.

5. Blueberries. Packed with more antioxidants than any other fruit or vegetable, this tiny healer showed incredible anticancer impact when tested by researchers at the University of Illinois. Blueberries also contain *anthocyanins,* the same compounds that make red wine so heart-healthy—except blueberries have 38% more. They're vision protectors too, and also help neurons in your brain talk to each other better. Who couldn't use a little more of that?

6. Pomegranate juice. This is a powerhouse of antioxidants that keeps arteries clear and protects against prostate cancer. It also works against osteoarthritis by limiting inflammation and stopping the enzymes that harm cartilage. Studies show that drinking pomegranate juice also drives down blood pressure in people with hypertension. Pour four ounces over ice and top with club soda for one of nature's healthiest spritzers.

7. Free-range bison. Meat from buffalo that have grazed on open pasture are an outstanding source of protein with minimal saturated fat. This meat comes to you free of added hormones, antibiotics and chemicals. Grass-fed buffalo also contain precious omega-3s, the highly beneficial fats that work body-wide to reduce inflammation, keep your heart healthy and ease arthritis pain.

8. Beans and other legumes. Research shows that regularly eating kidney beans, black beans, pinto beans and other legumes lengthens life span. They also strengthen the immune system while reducing your risk of colon cancer and type 2 diabetes and help control blood sugar in people with either type of diabetes. Legumes also lower total cholesterol and LDL,

continued…

continued from previous page…

cut your risk for heart disease and protect you against cancer with at least five anticancer compounds.

9. Wild Alaskan salmon. This outstanding protein source contains the vital carotenoid *astaxanthin,* which prevents cell damage from free radicals. This carotenoid, which gives salmon flesh its natural orange color, is 17 times more powerful than Pycnogenol and 50 times more powerful than vitamin E. Wild-caught salmon is also loaded with protective omega-3 fatty acids, which fight inflammation, protect your heart and improve circulation.

10. Almonds. A rich source of heart-healthy monounsaturated fat, almonds contain precious *gamma-tocopherol,* a vital nutrient that neutralizes the *peroxynitrite radical,* a dangerous free radical that destroys cell membranes. Almonds are also a high-quality protein and fiber package, a winning combination for con-trolling hunger. The little nut is also bursting with other nutrients such as folic acid, magnesium, copper and zinc.

11. Seaweed. Also known as sea vegetables, seaweed contains all 56 minerals—especially iodine, needed for thyroid function. Seaweed also contains magnesium, chlorophyll and alginates, essential for optimum health. Purchase dried seaweed at Asian markets and drop into soups and stews regularly.

12. Garlic. Whole baked garlic cloves not only assist in control of blood pressure and cholesterol, but also help detoxify the body of heavy metals, especially mercury and cadmium. A natural nutraceutical (food that has both nutrients and pharmaceutical value), it neutralizes dozens of bacteria, viruses and fungi. Mince it and add to meats, fish, salads and slaws. Using garlic—cooked or raw—is a perfect way to help achieve optimum health.

you 20% improvement in memory, decision-making ability and attention," says Arthur F. Kramer, the study's director. "It will also buy you increases in the volume of various brain regions in the prefrontal and temporal cortex, and more efficient neuro-networks that support the kind of cognition we examined."

Fight Frailty—and Love Life!

Yes, what you eat *is* extremely important, but science is also showing that your level of physical activity is one of the most important predictors of whether you'll be old and decrepit by 60, or live to be a vibrant, active, self-reliant 100-year-old. Humans were meant to be physically active. The goal of staying younger is not as much about avoiding disease as it is about avoiding frailty.

The bottom line? If you want to live as long and strong, and remain as healthy as the people of the Mediterranean and Asian cultures do, eat like they do and emulate their lifestyle as much as possible. Cook. Walk. Pray. Dance. Sing. Love. And exult in the everyday joy of being alive. That's how Zorba the Greek lived. To me, this is the very essence of good health.

We hope that you and your family heartily enjoy every morsel of healing food made with these recipes, even as it improves your health and extends your life span. From Rebecca, Jim and me, *bon appétit* and happy healing! ∎

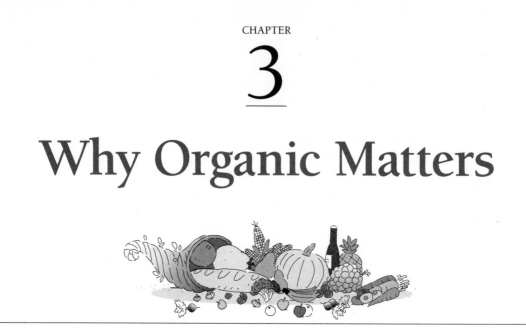

3

Why Organic Matters

You're probably eager to dig into the heart of this book and learn about foods that can relieve or reverse medical conditions you may be struggling with. Isn't that the reason this book appealed to you in the first place?

Of course, you can simply look up your condition right now, but I invite you to wait a while longer, because the information in this chapter will be of enormous help when you're shopping for foods that will improve your health. All foods, even if they are of the same variety, do not have the same micronutrient healing power. Much of this healing power depends upon how they're grown, harvested and processed. These factors affect their flavor, nutritional content and therapeutic value. Foods that are organically grown are superior in each of these categories.

Studies have shown that organic food tastes better, heals better and is better in every way, which explains its explosive growth in recent years. Organic food sales in the US are projected at $32 billion annually. This is small potatoes compared to the $550 billion that the conventional food industry rakes in every year, but, still, the growth of the organic sector is mind-boggling. Nothing is more revealing about the current popularity of organic food than its presence at Wal-Mart, Costco and Safeway stores across the US. In fact, nearly half of all organic food is sold through mass-market outlets. This trend is expected to continue, because the premium prices that organic food generally commands has retailers, growers and food processors scrambling to hop aboard the organic gravy train. This competition is lowering organic prices somewhat and, in some places, prices now rival those of conventionally grown foods. Still, an 18-pound organic turkey can set you back $65. Are these higher prices justified? Let's take a look.

What Is Organic, Anyway?

I don't want to get into a detailed history of the organic movement, only enough to say that it began as a grassroots rebellion against the industrialization farming and our food supply. When giant food companies took over agriculture in the US after World War II, the quality of our food diminished significantly. At the same time, family farmers who took pride in and responsibility for sound stewardship of the soil and environment were forced off their land. The time-honored personal attention to a healthy ecology, as well as conscientious fertilizing of the land with organic waste, were abandoned in favor of the fast bucks made possible by mass-farming vast acreages using chemical fertilizers, pesticides, gargantuan machinery and more recently, genetically modified crops. Quantity, not quality, was the rule.

With the publication of Rachel Carson's *Silent Spring* in 1962, the American public woke up to the true price they were paying for all this so-called cheap food. Carson described how DDT was wreaking havoc on wildlife and poisoning the entire food chain, while causing cancer and genetic damage in humans. Millions were shocked when scientists discovered DDT residue in human breast milk and in the tissue of penguins in Antarctica. The cry for safer food went out, but it's taken nearly 50 years for such food to become widely available.

Technically speaking, *organic* refers to food produced without the use of toxic chemicals, particularly pesticides (which are carcinogenic) and synthetic fertilizers, which destroy the natural fertility of our topsoil. In addition, organic crops are not grown using human waste or sewage sludge, and aren't processed with ionizing radiation, food additives or chemical ripening agents. They are not coated with the wax commonly found on conventionally grown varieties of cucumbers, turnips, eggplant, bell peppers and squash. In most countries, organic crops may not be genetically modified.

As a doctor, I'm especially concerned about the harm done by pesticides and am convinced that their presence in our food supply has been a major factor in the rising rates of cancer and diseases of the nervous system. Chemical pesticides have also been linked to abdominal pain, dizziness, headaches, nausea, vomiting and eye disorders. Peer-reviewed research also ties pesticide exposure to severe medical conditions such as respiratory problems, memory disorders, dermatologic conditions, depression, neurological deficits, miscarriage and birth defects. For instance, the herbicide Atrazine has been shown to cause demasculinization in male frogs exposed to small concentrations, resulting in either malformed genitals or testicles containing infertile sperm. It is not unreasonable to expect similar consequences in humans. Other studies show that nitrate residues from chemical fertilizers bind to hemoglobin, particularly in infants, which significantly reduces the body's ability to carry oxygen.

29

With regard to animal products, *organic* means that the animals were not fed growth hormones, steroids or antibiotics, all of which contribute to an array of health problems, including cancer. However, an animal product being labeled organic doesn't mean it's healthful or humanely raised. Some meat and dairy producers are permitted to use the term if the grain the animals were fed has been organically grown. It doesn't matter if these animals were confined in feedlots under cruel conditions. Meat from grain-fed cattle, for instance, has a much higher ratio of omega-6s to omega-3s, so it will cause more inflammation than grass-fed beef. Unless the label says "free-range," "grass-fed" or "cage free," there will be scant amounts of omega-3s. Pay no attention to any product that claims to be "natural." Legally, it is meaningless.

Until very recently, the term *organic* guaranteed nothing, because there were no universal standards, certification criteria or authority to oversee compliance. Today, organic food is regulated in most countries. Producers are required to obtain organic certification before they can market their products. In the US, certification is regulated by the USDA's National Organic Program (NOP) Standards, established under the Organic Foods Production Act of 1990 and overseen by the National Organic Standards Board (NOSB), an advisory committee of farmers, consumer advocates and scientists. Now that the US has federal standards, you can be confident that when an apple bears an organic label, it's an organic apple.

30

HOW MUCH PESTICIDE IS IN THE FOOD YOU EAT?

Pesticide residue on conventionally grown produce and crops continues to pose a serious problem around the world. The USDA monitors pesticide residue on all food sold in the US and their findings aren't encouraging. Their scientists analyzed more than 94,000 food samples from more than 20 crops and found that 77% of all conventional food contains these toxins. More than 90% of the USDA's samples of conventionally grown apples, peaches, pears, strawberries and celery contained residue. Only 20% of all tested organically raised crops contained residue, and in much lower concentrations. In many cases, pesticide residue on organic produce comes from soil previously polluted by conventional farming and by airborne pesticides drifting over from neighboring farms.

Why does any of this matter? These facts have a direct bearing on your health. What sense does it make to fill your diet with healing foods if they contain toxins that may ultimately harm you? Following the current recommendations to consume five servings per day of conventional fruits and vegetables will mean that you're taking in five or more servings of pesticide residue per day, too.

Organic Food Contains More Healing Power

Perhaps the most compelling reason to buy organic food is that it's far more nutritious than conventionally grown food. Let's start with some actual numbers. The largest study ever done of organic food, completed in 2007 and funded by the European Union, found that organic fruits and vegetables contain up to 40% more disease-fighting antioxidants than their conventional equivalents. (The omega-3 fatty acids are 68% higher in organic milk.) A review of 34 studies undertaken in 1998 revealed that organic foods possess a higher quality of protein, higher levels of vitamin C and more mineral content. In some instances, mineral levels were dramatically higher—the level of iron, for instance, was three times higher than in conventional foods tested. Another review of 41 studies demonstrated that organically grown fruits and vegetables contained 27% more vitamin C, 21% more iron, 29% more magnesium and 14% more phosphorus.

The higher nutrient content of organic foods means more nutrition per calorie, per serving and per dollar. Findings from the University of California at Davis show that organic strawberries, blackberries and corn have significantly more flavonoids than conventionally grown varieties (19%, 50% and 58.5%, respectively), as well as higher levels of vitamin C. A USDA study comparing the lycopene content of 13 brands of ketchup found organic brands contained 57% more than nationally advertised conventional brands and 55% more than store brands. "By buying and consuming organic foods fairly consistently, consumers can easily double their daily intake of vitamins, minerals and antioxidants," explains Dr. Charles Benbrook, chief scientist at the Organic Center for Education and Promotion in Greenfield, Massachusetts.

Why do organic food crops contain higher levels of these healing compounds?

Scientists say they result from a hardiness factor that forces plants and their fruits to develop higher levels of protective *anthocyanins*—one of the most potent of all antioxidants—to repel insect attacks and diseases. (Conventionally raised crops are not pushed to defend themselves as aggressively, because pesticides do this work for them.) In addition, researchers have found this is why levels of *flavonoids,* another powerful antioxidant group, are higher in organic produce.

Eating organically grown unprocessed foods helps protect against chronic inflammation, an underlying factor in cardiovascular disease, colon cancer and arthritis because these foods contain higher levels of *salicylic acid,* the active compound in aspirin that's responsible for its anti-inflammatory effect. Salicylic acid has been shown to reduce levels of C-reactive protein, which helps prevent hardening of the arteries and protects against many cancers. A study published in the *European Journal of Nutrition* found that organic soups sold in the UK contain almost six times as much salicylic acid as nonorganic soups. In fact, the average level of salicylic acid in 11 brands of organic vegetable soup was five times greater than that of the nonorganic variety. Four of the conventional soups had no detectable levels of salicylic acid.

AGRIBUSINESS IS PRODUCING INFERIOR FOOD

Even though it may be cheaper at the checkout, conventionally grown food is no bargain. In the 2004 *Mother Earth News* article, "Is Agribusiness Making Food Less Nutritious?"

authors Cheryl Long and Lynn Keiley report that "American agribusiness is producing more food than ever before, but…the vitamins and minerals in that food are declining. For example, eggs from free-range hens contain up to 30% more vitamin E, 50% more folic acid and 30% more vitamin B-12 than conventional 'factory' eggs." The vast majority of our food now comes from large-scale producers who rely on chemical fertilizers, pesticides, drugs and hormones. The result is less nutritious eggs, meat and dairy products.

The low level of essential minerals in nonorganic produce results from modern agricultural methods that have destroyed the soil bacteria, which makes minerals available to crops. Without these beneficial microbes, essential minerals are rendered unavailable to the plant and, ultimately, to us. Crops grow, but they're deficient in vital trace minerals. Instead, plants take up heavy metals from the soil, including aluminum, mercury and lead. Each of these has been linked to neurological disorders, such as dementia, memory loss and Alzheimer's disease. Between 1950 and 1975, the calcium content of one cup of cooked rice dropped 21% and iron fell by 28.6%. It's no coincidence that we've experienced a parallel increase in the rate of osteoporosis during this period. When trace minerals are scarce in plants, they become scarce in the human body.

As a rule, the quality of the food we eat comes from the quality of the food that our food eats. Unfortunately, because the goals of agribusiness are maximum productivity and profit, our food isn't eating very well

32

these days. Fruits and vegetables are genetically engineered and grown for transport, appearance and size, not nutritional quality. In a study published in *Science Daily Magazine,* researchers at Truman State University in Mississippi found that organically grown oranges contained up to 30% more vitamin C than those grown conventionally, even though the conventional fruits were twice as large. Why the big difference? The conventional oranges had been grown with nitrogen fertilizers that cause the fruit to take up more water, thus diluting the orange's nutritional content.

ORGANIC FOOD IS A BETTER BARGAIN

The nutritional superiority of organic food more than offsets its premium price in some outlets. The math is simple. According to current nutrient analyses, you'd have to eat twice as much conventional food to get the same nutrition as organic provides. That means twice the calories, too. Remember, the trick to staying healthy and lean is to consume the maximum amount of nutrition in the minimum number of calories. A diet based largely on fruits and vegetables satisfies this equation perfectly, and eating organically makes it an even more efficient solution. When you think about organic food in these terms, it really is a bargain, especially when you consider its many other benefits.

➤ **Organic is safer.** Eating organic food means you don't have to worry about potentially harmful additives such as monosodium glutamate (MSG), artificial sweeteners and food coloring agents. Many food additives and dyes have been linked to allergies, hyperactivity, neurological disorders and cancer. You also won't be ingesting added growth hormones or antibiotics in meat or dairy. These hormones, which add muscle bulk to cattle and boost milk production in cows, have been found to trigger premature puberty development in young girls and increase their risk for estrogen-driven breast and uterine cancers.

➤ **Organic food tastes better.** Just as soil minerals add distinction to the world's great wines and cheeses, high-quality soil gives organic foods richer, more complex and unique flavors—which is why the best restaurant chefs demand local, organically raised foods for their kitchens. Nearly every connoisseur agrees that pasture-fed beef tastes better than confined cattle raised on grain. I can still remember my first bite of organic, free-range chicken: It was juicier and more delicious that any poultry I'd ever tasted.

When it comes to eggs, you can see the difference with your own eyes. Compare an egg yolk from a free-range chicken to one that's factory raised and you'll see that the former is a vivid orange due to the high levels of sight-protecting lutein and omega-3s, while the latter is a pale yellow.

Fruits and vegetables grown organically are noticeably sweeter and more flavorful, too. "Organic produce tends to taste better, most likely because of higher antioxidant levels," says nutritional scientist Alyson Mitchell, Ph.D., who led the antioxidant studies at University of California at Davis. A study conducted at Washington State University used a panel of tasters who concluded

---

How to Tell If It's Really Organic

Most supermarkets have large organic and conventionally grown produce departments, with signs indicating which is which. However, the signs can be confusing. The only way to tell for sure is to check the Price Look-Up (PLU) code stickers on individual fruits and vegetables, which will tell you whether produce was organically grown, conventionally grown or genetically modified.

Here's the key to these codes:

➤ **Organic.** The code starts with 9 and contains five digits.

➤ **Conventionally grown.** The code usually starts with 4 and contains four digits.

➤ **Genetically modified.** The code starts with 8 and contains five digits.

---

that organic apples tasted sweeter and were crunchier compared with those grown conventionally. These differences were attributed to the better soil quality produced by organic farming techniques. When fruits and vegetables taste this good, it's easy to follow the recommendations of eating five to 10 daily servings that studies show improve both health and longevity.

➤ **Organic is fresher.** Since many organic farmers are small local producers, their food gets to the market more quickly, often on the day it was picked. For example, Japanese researchers found that spinach contains 200% more vitamin C during the peak of its growing cycle. Locally grown foods are also more environmentally and economically sound because they don't have to be shipped

33

long distances, which requires more fuel and generates air pollution. Michael Pollan, author of *The Omnivore's Dilemma,* points out that just one-fifth of all the energy used by our food system is expended on growing. The rest is used in marketing, packaging and distribution.

Local foods are also good for the local economy. Buying local produce keeps your money home, where it benefits local farmers and merchants. Shopping at the neighborhood farmers' market is one way to achieve this, but a novel, new approach has taken hold in Europe and the US. Called *community-supported agriculture* (CSA) or *subscription farming,* it eliminates the middleman, by matching consumers with local farmers. CSA members purchase shares in a season's harvest and pick up their food dividends weekly from distribution sites, or have them shipped. CSA farmers typically use organic or other sustainable farming methods and pride themselves on providing fresh, high-quality, healthful foods. In some arrangements, CSA members work on the farm in exchange for a portion of their membership cost. To locate a CSA member farm, go to *www.nal.usda.gov/afsic/pubs/csa/csa.shtml.*

IF YOU CAN'T ALWAYS BUY ORGANIC

Some foods are widely available in organically grown and nonorganic versions, while others are primarily offered as conventionally raised. Sometimes, there's no organic choice at all. My advice is to choose organic first, but if you can't find or afford organic produce, you can still reduce your exposure to pesticide residues by 80% by selecting fruits and

vegetables that contain the lowest levels of toxins. Below and on page 35 are two lists of the Dirty Dozen—the most contaminated conventionally grown vegetables and fruits—compiled by the Environmental Working Group (EWG). The third list shows the top 12 least contaminated of conventionally grown produce. The EWG lists are based on test results from the USDA pesticide monitoring program. It's worth taking a look at the complete pesticide analysis of each food and its position on the list: Go to *www. foodnews.org.*

WASHING AND RINSING PRODUCE

It's always a good idea to give produce a thorough washing and rinsing. Here are some tips that can make your fruits and vegetables safer.

➤ **It's the berries.** Strawberries are among the most contaminated of all conventionally grown foods because they contain methyl bromide, a known cancer-causing pesticide. It is impossible to wash off the fruit because farmers apply it to the soil and it's taken up by the plant.

➤ **South of the border.** Conventionally grown fruits and vegetables imported

The Dirty Dozen Vegetables: Highest in Pesticides	
1. Bell peppers	7. Spinach
2. Celery	8. Potatoes
3. Kale	9. Green beans
4. Lettuce	10. Summer squash
5. Carrots	11. Hot peppers
6. Collard greens	12. Cucumber

The Dirty Dozen Fruits: Highest in Pesticides	
1. Peaches	7. Pears
2. Apples	8. Raspberries
3. Nectarines	9. Plums
4. Strawberries	10. Oranges
5. Cherries	11. Grapes (domestic)
6. Grapes (imported)	12. Tangerines

Least Contaminated Conventionally Grown Produce	
1. Onions	7. Asparagus
2. Avocados	8. Kiwis
3. Sweet corn (frozen)	9. Cabbage
4. Pineapples	10. Eggplant
5. Mangoes	11. Papaya
6. Sweet peas (frozen)	12. Watermelon

from Mexico and South America should be avoided because they usually contain high levels of pesticides, including those banned for use in the US.

➤ **Zesty tip.** Dr. Andrew Weil advises that if you use the zest of citrus fruits in recipes, make sure to get organic orange, limes, and lemons, because the peel is the most contaminated part of the fruit.

➤ **Wash or rinse?** Always rinse all produce, even so-called prewashed and organic greens. Pass them under a strong stream of running water, then toss or spin dry. The goal is to remove any potentially harmful substances, such as bacteria, soil and surface pesticide residue. However, with methyl bromide and other systemic pesticides, washing will not remove chemicals that are absorbed during the plant's growing period.

➤ **Removing pesticide residue.** There are quite a few commercial products that claim to remove agricultural chemical residue from conventional fruits and vegetables. However, according to FDA researchers, washing fruits and veggies with or without a commercial wash won't entirely get rid of the pesticide residue. When testing conventionally grown produce for pesticides, the FDA first washes and peels fruits and veggies, yet when they examined apples, for instance, more than 93% of them still contained pesticides. If you use a mild detergent to wash conventionally grown produce, make sure it's well diluted. Detergent residue can dissolve the protective mucous layer of your GI tract and cause gastrointestinal upset or diarrhea.

➤ **Bacterial food poisoning.** Here's where thorough washing really pays off. With recent *E. coli* and *Salmonella* outbreaks involving lettuce, spinach and tomatoes—the very foods we should eat more of—be sure to rinse all your produce with grapefruit seed extract (GSE), a safe, nontoxic and natural antimicrobial disinfectant. Use the homemade vegetable wash on the next page instead of buying a pricey commercial product.

The Power of Your Fork

We can change the world with our forks and chopsticks. This is no fad, but rather a trend,

Grapefruit Extract Vegetable Wash

1 cup water
1 cup distilled white vinegar
1 tablespoon baking soda
20 drops grapefruit seed extract

Combine all ingredients in a bowl. Transfer to a spray bottle with a pump. Spray on produce as needed and leave for 5–10 minutes. Rinse thoroughly. Store mixture in refrigerator.

Caution: May cause irritation in eyes or on skin.

and a vital one that will mean more organic farms…more family farmers working the land…healthier soil across our country …cleaner, purer watersheds and streams… more nutritious food on the world's dinner tables…and inevitably relief from today's burdensome levels of illness and disease. What began as a small group of people who came together for better food and a healthier world has developed into a global movement with far-reaching consequences.

Food has become a rallying point for the change our world needs, whether it is growers demanding more safety regulations so their industry doesn't suffer another E. coli disaster or animal activists calling for more humane treatment of livestock. Nutritionists are demanding new laws banning trans fats and requiring that the nutritional profile of fast foods be posted in restaurants. Concerned parents have demanded that vending machines selling soda and junk be removed from schools. Educators and health officials working on anti-obesity campaigns aspire to the success of anti-smoking campaigns. More consumers are shopping at farmers' markets. More people are discovering that wholesome foods and diets can heal many ills better than any pharmaceutical drug.

"I see this happening everywhere, and it is enormous," says Marion Nestle, professor in the Department of Nutrition, Food Studies, and Public Health at New York University and author of *What to Eat*. "It's the recognition that food ties into extremely important social, economic, environmental and institutional issues. Ordinary people don't have access to these really important issues except through food."

In other words, how you eat may be more powerful than how you vote. Where you shop, what you buy and how it was made or grown should be carefully considered before you plunk down your cash. Your health, your community's health and the health of our planet are intimately tied to the quality of the food you purchase and consume. Every buying decision you make has an impact, even regarding the simple question, "Paper or plastic?" It is encouraging that more and more shoppers are using their own bags instead.

"This is the year everyone discovered that food is about politics and people can do something about it," Ms. Nestle says. "In a world in which people feel more and more distant from global forces that control their lives, they can do something by, as the British put it, 'voting with your trolley.'" ("Trolley" is UK English for shopping cart.)

➤ **What's not for dinner?** Your decision not to serve your family food laced with cancer-causing pesticides is one step closer to the disappearance of those chemicals from the food chain. Giving up farm-raised salmon because it's unhealthy and environmentally destructive can help bring back decimated wild salmon species and revitalize the coastlines that fish farming has destroyed. Demanding more free-range beef will reduce the number of cattle who live dreadful lives standing in their own excrement before meeting horrible deaths, and stop feedlot owners from profiting from this shameful, inhumane suffering. Making some of the dietary changes suggested in the chapters ahead will force the pharmaceutical giants to realize that we know their expensive products aren't the only way to be well. As more people make a deep commitment to personal wellness, environmental and planetary wellness will benefit immensely.

I'm not so naïve as to think this will be a slam dunk. There will be abuses, loopholes and confusion. Right now, you can buy beef and milk from animals that haven't tasted a blade of grass and will have spent all of their lives in absolute confinement, but they get the organic label because they've been fed organically grown grain. The USDA is being petitioned to permit salmon farmers to call their fish "organic" because their fish are raised on organic meal pellets. Giant food corporations like Kraft, Coca-Cola and General Mills are cashing in on the organic movement, with product lines that stretch the letter of the law. Is it fair to call high-fructose corn syrup "organic" because the corn was raised without chemicals?

There is plenty of wiggle room in today's rules and regulations, but the way to avoid most of this confusion is to minimize your consumption of processed foods. These are the leading health disruptors. The more a food is processed, the less nutritious it's likely to be. Choose foods that are as close to their original form as you can get, preferring products with more specific labeling, like "grass-fed," "free-range," "sustainable," "pesticide-free" and "non-GMO." Better yet, get to know the local farmers who raise animals and crops responsibly and purchase directly from them.

The human race did just fine eating food in its natural state for millennia. Start eliminating processed foods from your diet and you will begin to reverse many medical conditions you may be facing. You'll feel an immediate improvement.

SOMETHING ELSE TO CHEW ON

If fresh organic foods already make up the majority of your diet, hats off to you. However, since you may be paying a premium for these incredibly nutritious foods, here's a tip for extracting even more nutrition and healing power from them: *chew*. Giving each mouthful a few extra chews releases more healing nutrients into your bloodstream for your body's repair and regeneration. Eating quickly is like throwing a portion of your food into the garbage, because it won't be as completely digested. Here are some other benefits of slowing down at mealtime.

➤ **Weight loss.** Research shows that chewing your food thoroughly brings you greater satiety from less food. Since it takes about 10 to 15 minutes for your brain to receive the "I'm full" signal from your stomach, speed eating is a major factor in weight gain. A few extra chews with each mouthful means you'll feel satisfied by a smaller portion. You'll lose weight without dieting or feeling deprived, and the extra time will allow you to enjoy yourself and those you're dining with.

➤ **More pleasure.** Better-quality food tastes better, especially when it's artfully prepared. Studies show that diners need less food when meals provide more pleasure. That's the secret behind the best-selling book *French Women Don't Get Fat* by Mireille Guiliano. Even though the French eat bread, cheese and pâté, drink wine, and regularly enjoy three-course meals, they manage to stay slim, live longer and have less incidence of heart disease and other degenerative diseases compared with people in other Western countries. The key to this paradox is that they eat for pleasure, so a little food goes a long way.

➤ **Less kitchen time.** Great chefs insist on the freshest organic ingredients and make these natural flavors and textures the stars of each plate. When you buy top-quality meat, fish and veggies, you don't need to spend hours in preparation. The lightest touch in the kitchen, such as broiling, steaming, sautéing and stir-frying, or even serving some foods raw, allows the delicate sugars, fats and textures to shine through.

➤ **Deeper appreciation.** Obviously, if you've paid a pretty penny for your organic ingredients and fashioned them into a personal work of art, you'll want to get maximum satisfaction from every mouthful. You won't want to eat in front of the TV. Instead, give yourself over completely to your meal and your senses, and share this pleasure with your favorite companion or friends. Chewing slowly allows you to do this, but even before the food reaches your mouth, engage your other senses. Appreciate the colors in the way the food is presented. Enjoy the aromas. Notice the textures as you bite and chew. Pause often and put your fork down occasionally to allow the flavors to linger. This is what enjoyment is all about.

➤ **Consider the connections.** Every spiritual tradition has the central belief that "we are all one" in some way or another. This notion is most obvious when eating. If you think about it, each bite puts you in direct contact with the plant or animal you're consuming…the soil it was raised on…the bacteria and minerals in it…the farmer who cared for it…the worker who harvested it… the rain that nourished it…the atmosphere it breathed (the same that you're breathing right now)…plus the butcher, baker and shipping-container maker. Every mouthful connects you to everything that came in contact with this food, to the very web of life. Why would we want to poison any of this, hurting ourselves, our families and our planet? Though it is not always apparent, what you buy, cook, serve and eat is an important process. Everything matters. And everything depends upon each of us. ∎

4

Arthritis

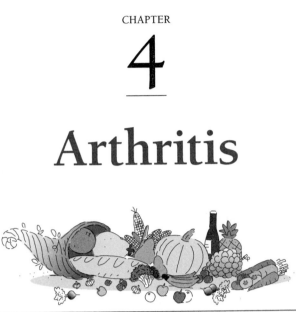

There are more than 100 forms of arthritis. Osteo-arthritis (OA), also called *wear-and-tear* arthritis, is the most common form of the disease, affecting up to 27 million American adults. Rheumatoid arthritis (RA), an inflammatory disease that can literally destroy joints and, in the most severe cases, even damage the heart or lungs, affects close to 1.5 million Americans every year.

OA is usually caused by accumulated stress on, and accompanying inflammation of, the joints, which result in deterioration of *cartilage*, the soft, rubberlike cushion that covers the ends of bones. Joint degeneration also occurs when there is an imbalance in the body of its natural inflammatory and anti-inflammatory substances called *interleukins* and *cytokines*. Without sufficient cartilage, bone rubs against bone, resulting in further

inflammation, pain, deformity, limited range of motion and immobility. Although we tend to associate arthritis with aging, two-thirds of all arthritis sufferers are actually younger than 65.

RA isn't caused by normal wear and tear. Rather, it occurs when the immune system, for reasons that aren't clear, attacks the membrane surrounding the joints, causing intense inflammation. This inflammation triggers the release of proteins that cause the joint membrane to thicken. These proteins can also damage cartilage, tendons and other structures within the joint.

➤ **Here's what creates your pain.** When cartilage is damaged, fatty acids in the cell membranes trigger the release of three key enzymes—COX-l and COX-2, plus 5-lipoxygenase (5-LO), which set in motion the body's inflammatory chemicals called *prostaglandins* and *leukotrienes*. Prostaglandins

39

produced by the COX-2 enzyme increase blood flow and sensitivity in the joint, resulting in inflammation and pain. Anti-inflammatory drugs target pain relief by blocking the COX-2 enzyme. These drugs shut down the COX-2 prostaglandins, but they also inhibit protective COX-1 prostaglandins, causing nausea, vomiting and, in severe cases, stomach ulcers and bleeding. COX-2 drugs don't relieve pain any better than aspirin or other nonsteroidal anti-inflammatory drugs (NSAIDs), but they cause fewer gastrointestinal problems by blocking COX-2 without inhibiting COX-1. These drugs also may increase the risk of heart attack.

SYMPTOMS

While OA and RA share a common name and similar symptoms, they are very different diseases requiring distinct treatments.

➤ **The onset of OA is gradual.** The first symptom is often joint stiffness in the morning, but as the condition progresses, pain is provoked by any movement and is worsened with prolonged activity. Joints become swollen, sore, and tender and may audibly crack or pop. Most commonly affected are the weight-bearing joints of the knees, hips and spine, as well as those of the hands. X-rays may show bony growths called *spurs*, with less space between joints in which healthy cartilage once was. A narrowing of the channels in the spine where nerves pass, called *stenosis*, is a frequent, yet often undiagnosed, cause of chronic backache.

➤ **RA also occurs gradually.** It usually affects smaller joints, such as those in the hands or feet, first. Eventually, as the disease progresses, RA may cause pain and inflammation in the body's larger joints, such as in the hips or shoulders. Most people with RA go through periods of remission, in which the symptoms either stop or are greatly diminished. Eventually, however, remissions are usually followed by extended flare-ups.

CAUSES

RA, like many autoimmune diseases, is largely a mystery. It's three times more common in women, which suggests that hormones may be involved. It's also possible that it's triggered by a viral or bacterial infection in people who already have a genetic tendency toward RA. It tends to run in families, and people who smoke are more likely to get it than those who don't.

OA is more straightforward. Bone-on-bone friction creates inflammation, which hastens damage to cartilage. Certain foods such as refined sugar, trans fats, tomatoes (and other vegetables from the nightshade family) and artificial sweeteners can also cause inflammation, which triggers a cascade of destructive enzymes. The catch-22 of OA is that inflammation is easily switched on by the body, but there's no inherent "off" switch if the body's reserve of anti-inflammatory interleukins is low. In this case, NSAIDs are prescribed to fight inflammation.

Wear and tear also destroys joint cartilage, which the body usually can reconstruct to a certain degree with proper diet and supplementation, but this ability diminishes with age and poor diet. Finally, OA symptoms worsen if the muscles supporting the problem joint are allowed to weaken through inactivity, or if body weight increases. Excess free radical molecules can make the situation worse by further attacking and destroying joint cartilage. That's why people with arthritis must be sure to eat an antioxidant-rich diet that includes plenty of fruits and vegetables to neutralize this onslaught.

TREATMENT

Most patients with RA may eventually need to take disease-modifying antirheumatic drugs (DMARDs). These drugs, which include *hydroxychloroquine* (Plaquenil) and *methotrexate* (Rheumatrex), are most effective in the earlier stages of the disease. They aren't a cure, but can slow the progression of RA and help protect joints from subsequent damage.

Patients with moderate joint deterioration due to either RA or OA experience less discomfort by managing inflammation in both the joints and in the body. To do this, many arthritis sufferers rely on NSAIDS (such as ibuprofen) or COX-2 inhibitors (such as Celebrex), but these drugs carry the risk of high blood pressure, gastrointestinal bleeding, liver damage, kidney dysfunction and cardiac problems, including heart attack and heart failure. To make things worse, frequent use of these drugs further damages the cartilage and actually inhibits the body's mechanism to facilitate its repair. When enough cartilage has been destroyed, the only option is total joint replacement, or if the hip is involved, a technique called *resurfacing.* Unfortunately, few orthopedic surgeons in the US have sufficient experience with it, so most resurfacing candidates have the procedure done in Europe, where surgeons are far more advanced in this area.

One of the most promising developments in the treatment of osteoarthritis has emerged in Germany, where doctors are using a unique technique to boost the body's level of its own natural anti-inflammatory substance, *interleukin-1RA*, plus other natural inflammation-fighting factors, resulting in immediate and long-lasting relief. This often allows patients to delay replacement surgery for years or avoid it altogether. You can read more about this new development at *www.molecularorthopedia.com.*

Fortunately, immediate and highly affordable relief from both forms of arthritis is as close as your grocery store or farmers' market. Hundreds of impressive clinical studies show that what you eat—and, just as important, *what you don't eat*—can substantially reduce trouble-making inflammation, pain and cartilage destruction. These anti-arthritis foods can make a huge difference in your quality of life.

Foods That Make It Better

The key in managing OA is to prevent inflammation. The ideal anti-arthritis diet is built around foods with proven anti-inflammatory effects. Less inflammation means less discomfort, and eating this way can stop pain from getting started. Here are the top foods that have been shown to put a chill on inflammation, decrease your pain and stiffness and encourage natural cartilage repair. You can find additional arthritis-healing foods and recipes at our Web site *www.myhealingkitchen.com.*

THE HEALING POWER OF OMEGA-3

It's well documented that people with RA and/or OA who eat plenty of oily fish experience less inflammation and pain. In fact, studies show that people who load up on fish and other anti-inflammatory foods can see a significant and immediate reduction in joint inflammation.

In one notable clinical trial, Dr. Joel M. Kremer, associate professor of medicine at Albany Medical College in New York, gave RA patients fish oil capsules (the equivalent of a salmon dinner or can of sardines) daily for 14 weeks and found that they reduced joint tenderness and pain by 50% compared with the control group. The benefits lasted for as long as 30 days after the fish oil was discontinued.

"We saw a significant correlation between the drop in leukotriene B-4 and decrease in the number of tender joints," said Dr. Kremer. Leukotriene B-4 triggers inflammation in joints.

Newer studies show that omega-3s relieve joint pain by boosting the body's production of inflammation-fighting fats called *resolvins*, which the body manufactures from *eicosapentaenoic acid* (EPA) and *docosahexaenoic acid* (DHA).

These are major findings, demonstrating that omega-3s definitely protect joint cartilage and may actually reverse arthritic conditions in some cases. The evidence in favor of fish and fish oil is so strong that it would be irresponsible for any doctor not to recommend it to patients suffering from RA and OA. To see which foods are highest in omega-3s, both fish and plants, see page 43.

➤ **Start a fish affair.** If you have arthritis, you'd do well to learn to love fish, if you don't already. Eating three servings of fish every week can keep harmful prostaglandins and leukotrienes under control, so they can't initiate the inflammatory cascade.

➤ **Hook the cold ones.** All fish contain some omega-3s, but the varieties with the highest levels are cold-water fish, such as wild salmon (fresh or canned), tuna, wild trout, herring, mackerel (not king), Pacific oysters, anchovies, scallops and sardines (see page 182 for information about mercury levels in fish).

➤ **Look for the richest colors.** Salmon is one of the best sources of omega-3s, containing a full gram per ounce. The darker the flesh, such as that of wild Pacific salmon, the higher the content of omega-3. Paler Atlantic salmon contains a lesser amount, and may actually contribute to more inflammation.

➤ **Open a can.** Many people enjoy eating fish, but not everyone loves cooking it. If you're one of them, a can of water-packed tuna, sardines or salmon contains the same quality of omega-3s as fresh fish, making them almost as good for you. Canned seafood loses some water and protein, but the amino acid content remains the same.

➤ **Shake on some flax.** Fish are not the only source of omega-3s. Flaxseeds are rich in *alpha-linolenic acid* (ALA), which your body converts to the omega-3 fatty acids EPA and DHA. These small, dark brown seeds are widely available, either whole or ground into flakes. Because the oil in flaxseeds spoils easily, always keep flaxseed, especially ground, in the refrigerator. It's best to buy the whole seeds and use an electric coffee mill to grind a tablespoon or two at a time, then sprinkle them on cereals, salads, casseroles and add to smoothies. Flaxseeds are so nutritious and anti-inflammatory that you should eat some at every opportunity. Other nonfish sources are omega-3-fortified eggs, walnuts, seaweed and walnut oil.

HOW OLIVE OIL COOLS YOUR JOINTS

Olive oil is great for your joints, which helps explain why the rates of RA and OA in Mediterranean countries, where the oil is popular, are much lower than those in the US. Researchers wanted to know if olive oil helps arthritis sufferers, so they fed arthritic laboratory rats a variety of oils and observed the effects. Not surprisingly, the two groups of rats who fared the best were those receiving fish oil and olive oil. Both prevented arthritis-related inflammation. Clinical trials on humans confirmed these animal studies.

Findings published in the journal *Nature* demonstrated that extra-virgin olive oil produces anti-inflammatory effects almost identical to those of ibuprofen, due to a naturally occurring chemical called *oleocanthal*, which blocks the activity of the pro-inflammatory COX-2 enzyme.

➤ **Choose extra-virgin.** Many nutritionists believe that oleocanthal is destroyed when olive oil is heat-processed, so it's always best to use the cold-pressed variety labeled *extra-virgin*. Extra-virgin olive oil is best consumed on salads and in salad dressings, or as a dip for whole-grain bread, a favorite of southern Italians for centuries. Extra-virgin olive oil has a low smoke point and excess heat will damage its nutritional benefits. Low-heat sautéing won't hurt olive oil, but when cooking at higher temperatures it's best to use coconut or other nut oils, which are more stable when exposed to extreme heat.

VEGETABLES AND FRUITS THAT FIGHT INFLAMMATION

Consuming fruits and vegetables provide your joints with a rich supply of antioxidants. These inhibit the damage that free-radical molecules can wreak on cartilage, ultimately relieving arthritis. New research from Japan indicates that these free-radicals actually block cartilage's ability to repair itself. Fruits and vegetables are also rich in *salicylic acid,* a

---

10 Top Omega-3 Fish

1. Mackerel (Atlantic)	**6.** Tuna
2. Sardines	**7.** Anchovies
3. Herring	**8.** Halibut
4. Rainbow trout	**9.** Pacific oysters
5. Wild Pacific salmon (fresh or canned)	**10.** Scallops

10 Top Omega-3 Plant Foods

1. Flaxseeds	**6.** Tofu and soybeans
2. Walnuts	**7.** Kale
3. Cauliflower	**8.** Spinach
4. Cabbage	**9.** Strawberries
5. Broccoli	**10.** Green beans

natural anti-inflammatory substance nearly identical to the active ingredient in aspirin. Dr. David Williams reports on research done in Scotland and published in the British medical journal *The Lancet*, which found that vegetarians have higher levels of salicylic acid in their blood than nonvegetarians—often the equivalent amount of a daily aspirin. "If you get your salicylic acid from food, you get the anti-inflammatory benefits…but none of the bleeding problems caused by aspirin," Dr. Williams writes. This new finding also helps explains why people who consume more fruits and vegetables have lower blood levels of C-reactive protein (CRP), a marker for inflammation in the body.

➤ **Go green**. Leafy greens, such as Swiss chard, spinach and turnip greens, are loaded with vitamin E and *zeaxanthin*, two antioxidants that have been shown to relieve arthritis pain, especially when combined with foods rich in vitamin C, such as oranges and kiwifruit. The research found that adding them to your diet provides relief that is as effective as taking ibuprofen or other pain relievers.

Johns Hopkins researchers recently discovered that broccoli, cabbage and other cruciferous vegetables contain compounds that help protect cartilage and also block joint pain in the same way in which COX-2 arthritis drugs do, but without drugs' dangers and with beneficial effects that last much longer. Their findings, published in *Proceedings of the National Academy of Sciences*, concluded that these veggie compounds possess "the potential for stopping pain and inflammation before they start." These new studies are

helping scientists understand why vegetarians experience arthritis less often than people who follow the standard American diet.

➤ **A hot tip.** For those of you who enjoy a bit of kick in your meals, eating hot peppers, cayenne and chilies can also bring pain relief. These foods contain high concentrations of the compound *capsaicin*, a clinically proven pain reliever. Medical studies from India show that hot peppers may reduce arthritic pain by an astonishing 88%.

➤ **Pile on the garlic and onions.** Both contain sulfur compounds that markedly reduce inflammation by inhibiting two enzymes directly responsible for joint inflammation. This anti-inflammatory effect, coupled with their high content of vitamin C and the bioflavonoid *quercetin* have been shown to reduce arthritis pain and inflammation in medical studies. Sulfur is also important because it is a critical component of healthy cartilage. Researchers analyzing the sulfur content in the fingernails of arthritis sufferers found much less than in healthy people without arthritis.

➤ **Snack on pineapple.** Rich in *bromelain*, a sulfur-based *proteolytic* enzyme that digests proteins, fresh pineapple has been shown in clinical human trials to be a driving force that stamps out inflammation and swelling. Studies show it to be as effective at smothering arthritis pain and inflammation as ibuprofen. To get the maximum benefit, eat fresh pineapple between meals, otherwise its enzymes will be expended in the digestion of your food. Canned pineapple or pineapple juice won't provide this anti-inflammatory benefit.

➤ **Sip pomegranate juice.** The juice of this Biblical fruit is beginning to take the medical community by storm. In addition to its proven ability to reduce artery plaque and reverse prostate cancer, pomegranate juice contains powerful anti-inflammatory and antioxidant compounds that protect joint cartilage. When researchers at Case Western Reserve University of Cleveland dripped pomegranate extract on damaged cartilage tissue in the lab, they found it reduced the levels of an enzyme responsible for inflammation. More studies are ongoing, but there are so many marvelous benefits already linked to this wonder-working nectar that there's no reason to wait. And you don't need to drink very much—a couple of ounces of unsweetened pomegranate juice per day will do the trick.

➤ **Cherries, berries and wine.** How would you like to ease your arthritis pain by eating a delicious bowl of cherries? Research says it works—and here's why. These fruits are the richest sources of *anthocyanins*, a group of antioxidant flavonoids that have impressive anti-inflammatory effects. Anthocyanin pigments are responsible for the bright colors of many fruits, vegetables and flowers, but their most impressive quality is the ability to clobber free-radical molecules that initiate disease and cartilage damage.

Anthocyanins are among the most powerful antioxidants found in nature, which is why you should eat as many brightly colored berries as you possibly can—especially if you have OA. To put this in perspective, a half cup of berries contains more antioxidant activity than five servings of broccoli. In addition, the remarkable *phenol* content of strawberries has been shown to block the COX-2 enzyme just as anti-inflammatory drugs do.

COX stands for *cyclooxygenase*, which is produced in the body as COX-1 and COX-2. COX-2 signals pain and inflammation. Arthritis drugs block the pain and inflammation messages of COX-2 without inhibiting the noninflammatory COX-1. Unfortunately, these drugs can produce unpleasant side effects such as damage to the heart muscle and increased risk of heart attack. Anthocyanins produce the same anti-inflammatory benefit, but without the damages.

Cherries and raspberries have the highest concentrations of pure anthocyanins. In one study, researchers found that the COX-inhibitory activity in cherries rivaled that of ibuprofen and naproxen. Researchers at Michigan State University found that eating 10 tart cherries provides the same pain-relieving effect as aspirin, while providing a healthy measure of antioxidants. Incidentally, red wine contains another anti-inflammatory compound found in many berries and grapes called *resveratrol*. Like anthocyanins, it also blocks the COX-2 enzyme that sets joints on fire. Just another reason to enjoy an occasional glass or two of red wine.

➤ **Eat two oranges.** Scientists at Boston University School of Medicine reported that patients whose blood contained the vitamin C equivalent of two oranges (about 120 milligrams [mg]), were three times less likely to see their OA of the knee get worse, compared with those who had lower blood levels. Another study, this one reported in *American Journal of Clinical Nutrition*, found that high blood levels of vitamin C were linked to a 45% reduction in inflammation.

➤ **Peel a papaya.** Like pineapple, papaya contains protein-digesting enzymes that have been shown to lower inflammation and improve joint healing. In addition, papaya is rich in vitamin C, vitamin E and beta-carotene—antioxidants known for their ability to tackle inflammation. Studies have shown that people with inflammatory diseases such as asthma, RA and OA experience significant improvement when they consume more of these nutrients.

ANTI-INFLAMMATORY SPICES AND HERBS

➤ **Curry brings relief.** *Curcumin* is an active ingredient in turmeric, the yellow spice best known as the distinctive coloring agent in curry powder. Some researchers believe the predominance of curry in the Indian diet explains why there is so little arthritis there, compared with the US. Curcumin has a long history as an anti-inflammatory agent in Chinese and Indian medicine, and has proven itself in numerous modern clinical studies. A recent study of arthritis patients demonstrated that curcumin reduced morning stiffness and joint swelling, while increasing the length of time patients could walk without pain. A daily healing dose is about ½ teaspoon sprinkled on salads, vegetables, or rice.

➤ **Gingerly advice.** Ginger is strong medicine too. It contains potent anti-inflammatory compounds called *gingerols*, which have a chemical structure similar to NSAIDs. A study conducted at Miami Medical School involving 250 patients with arthritis found that

ginger, taken twice daily, reduced pain as effectively as these anti-inflammatory drugs. In two other clinical studies, doctors found that 75% of arthritis patients and 100% of patients with muscle pain experienced significant relief and reduction in swollen joints after consuming ginger. Another 2½-year clinical trial using powdered ginger on patients with RA and OA found that approximately 75% of the patients experienced pain relief and decreased swelling, with no reports of adverse effects.

Similar studies examining the active ingredient in ginger extract showed that it significantly inhibited the activity of COX-2 and *tumor necrosis factor* (TNF), a natural inflammatory agent. Increasing evidence indicates that TNF is a major influence, not only on inflammatory arthritis, usually RA or lupus, but also OA. As little as 2 to 3 teaspoons of fresh ginger or ginger powder daily is enough to provide this benefit. Brew it as a tea or add it to food. Ginger is also well known for soothing an upset stomach, helpful to know if your arthritis medication or pain reliever causes gastrointestinal problems.

➤ **All you need is clove.** Animal studies show that *eugenol*, an anti-inflammatory chemical present in cloves, inhibits the COX-2 enzyme the same way the arthritis drug Celebrex does. Cloves are also rich in antioxidants, which have been shown to slow the deterioration of cartilage and bone caused by arthritis. An effective dose is between ½ to 1 teaspoon, which can be added to hot tea.

➤ **Bank on basil.** This delightful herb gives many Mediterranean and Thai dishes their distinctive flavor. Basil's contribution goes beyond the kitchen. Like clove, it contains COX-2-blocking eugenol, making it a significant anti-inflammatory. Studies show that ½ teaspoon of basil a day is as effective as many NSAIDs, including aspirin, ibuprofen and acetaminophen.

SWITCH TO TEA

➤ **Green tea is 5,000 years old,** but its health and healing benefits are just being discovered by modern science, and what we're finding is quite impressive. For one thing, green tea is plentiful in an antioxidant called *epigallocatechin-3-gallate* (EGCG) that has 20 times the power of vitamin C, making it one of the top defenders against free-radical damage. More important, solid evidence shows that green tea's natural compounds block the inflammatory cytokines that destroy cartilage in arthritic joints.

The usually skeptical Arthritis Foundation was so impressed by this research that it named green tea as one of its Top 10 Supplements Worth Considering for alleviating the symptoms of RA and OA. Dozens of studies have found that drinking green tea reduces inflammation, slows the breakdown of cartilage and may even help prevent arthritis in the first place. And you get all these benefits without any of the adverse side effects that drugs can pose.

Foods That Make It Worse

The incidence of arthritis in the US has increased steadily since the early 1900s, which is about the time Americans began to get less of their food from natural sources and more from boxes and cans. Many processed and

Dr. Sinatra's Anti-Inflammation Tea

Here's a double-duty beverage for relieving painful arthritis symptoms. Brew a combination of green tea and fresh ginger and you'll get a double dose of anti-inflammatory benefits.

Makes 4 servings

Using a pot, bring 4 cups of water to a boil. Add sliced ginger (from about a 2-inch piece). Boil for an additional 30 to 60 seconds. Add 4 green teabags or 4 tablespoons of green tea in an infuser. Remove from heat and steep for 2 to 3 minutes.

Sweeten with no-cal stevia or a little honey. I also like to add a teaspoon of D-ribose as a mild sweetener, because it energizes the body by increasing ATP production in cells, particularly those of the heart. Increasing ATP is also one of the best ways to repair weakened or damaged cells.

Sip the tea hot or let it chill in the fridge for a refreshing summertime drink.

fried foods have profound pro-inflammatory effects, as they trigger the release of inflammatory chemicals in the body that make arthritis worse. In addition, today we are eating far fewer anti-inflammatory foods such as fish, fruit, and vegetables, so it's easy to see why arthritis is such a big problem.

The typical American diet is loaded with pro-inflammatory foods and ingredients that cause pain, or make it worse. Ingesting them triggers the release of cytokines and other chemicals that are directly responsible for joint pain and destruction. That's why it's not enough to just eat more foods that help reduce inflammation. It's equally important to reduce your intake of foods that light these inflammatory fires in the first place.

➤ **Cut back on omega-6 fats.** There are two types of polyunsaturated fats—omega-3s, which are anti-inflammatory, and omega-6s, which are pro-inflammatory when they are dominant in a diet. Omega-6 fats are present in most cheap vegetable-based oils, such as corn, cottonseed, safflower, canola, soybean and sunflower—and of course, the myriad processed and fried foods that contain them. Read food labels carefully if you have arthritis, because too much omega-6 will make your joints stiff and sore by upsetting the balance with omega-3s. And when it comes to inflammation, this balance is all-important.

In the days before their food supply was industrialized, most Americans consumed a ratio of two parts omega-6 fatty acids to one part omega-3 fatty acids, the ideal balance for optimal health. Today, the ratio is closer to 20:1. This imbalance causes the body to churn out hormonelike substances called *eicosanoids*, which throw gasoline on the fires of inflammation. This is one of the main reasons why we're now seeing such a surge in inflammation-driven conditions such as heart disease, diabetes, Alzheimer's and arthritis. Your joints will feel much better if you cut back on these omega-6 oils and foods, while substituting healthy monounsaturates, such as olive oil, and consuming more omega-3 foods.

➤ **Skip the trans fats.** These man-made fats are even worse for you than omega-6 oils and excess saturated fats. Food

scientists created them so that baked goods would last longer on the shelf without spoiling. What was good for the bakers' bottom lines became a nightmare for our joints and arteries. Trans fats are one of the most pro-inflammatory, unnatural substances you can put in your mouth. After more than 20 years of protests from consumer advocates, the food industry is finally taking them off the market—sort of. New laws allow food labels

10 Worst Omega-6 Foods

The typical US diet is top-heavy in omega-6s from three primary sources—corn oil, soybean oil and cottonseed oil—found in the foods listed below. To ease inflammation and joint pain, try to cut back or eliminate them from your diet, while consuming more omega-3 foods, such as flax, walnuts, cold-water fish and omega-3 fortified eggs. Use extra-virgin olive oil for salad dressings. Here are today's leading troublemakers.

1. Refined, polyunsaturated vegetable oils (canola, safflower, sunflower, corn)
2. All fast food, even so-called healthy choices, such as fish and chicken
3. Processed snacks, such as chips and crackers
4. Baked goods, such as coffee cakes and cookies
5. Processsed, store-bought salad dressings and dips
6. Mayonnaise
7. Granola bars
8. Veggie burgers
9. Microwave popcorn
10. Tub margarines

to say "zero trans fats," even though foods may contain a half gram or less. That means you'll still be eating trans fats, which can still accumulate in your body. Despite what the American Heart Association claims, there is no safe, allowable level of trans fat consumption. Avoid trans fats like the plague. Search food labels for the word *hydrogenated* or any of the polyunsaturated fats mentioned here. Stay away from margarine or any vegetable oil that remains solid at room temperature. And be on the lookout for *interesterified fats,* the new Frankenfat replacement that's even worse than trans fats. Better yet, stick with high-quality natural oils such as butter (preferably from grass-fed cows), coconut and macadamia oils, seed oils, fish oils and extra-virgin olive oil.

➤ **Shun refined carbs.** Try to limit your consumption of sugary foods, baked goods containing white flour, bread and crackers, white rice and other refined carbohydrates because they are highly pro-inflammatory and trigger the release of cytokines, which make joints stiff and sore.

➤ **Go easy on meat and eggs.** That includes organ meats (such as liver). Meat and eggs are generally healthful foods, but if you have arthritis you should eat smaller amounts because they contain *arachidonic acid,* which is inflammatory. Cutting back, as opposed to giving up these foods completely, is relatively easy to do. Most people will feel an improvement right away.

➤ **Switch off the nightshades.** Some people with arthritis are susceptible to the alkaloids found in tomatoes, potatoes, eggplant, peppers and tobacco, which belong to the *Solanaceae,* or nightshade, family. If you're nightshade sensitive, these alkaloids can block your body's normal repair of collagen in joints, while also increasing inflammation and cartilage degeneration. Some estimates say that up to 20% of arthritis sufferers have an increase in discomfort when they eat one or more of these foods. One notable advocate of this theory is Dr. Norman E. Childers, Ph.D., a horticulturist and professor at the University of Florida. Dr. Childers claims that by eliminating nightshades, an arthritis patient has a 70% chance of improving his or her condition. You may want to try eliminating these nightshade foods from your diet for 30 days to see if you experience an improvement. For more information, read Dr. Childers' account of how he reversed his own arthritis in his book, *Arthritis: Childers' Diet That Stops It!*

➤ **Be wary of gluten.** It's a protein found in wheat, barley and rye, and is also used as a texture-enhancing or thickening ingredient in thousands of packaged foods. A study conducted in the mid-1990s reported that more than two-thirds of patients with celiac disease (a severe form of gluten sensitivity) showed signs of joint inflammation. I've put patients on a gluten-free diet and their arthritis symptoms have totally disappeared. My son Drew is a good example. After only six weeks of avoiding gluten in his diet, he has had an 80% reduction in his arthritis symptoms. To read more about gluten intolerance, see "Celiac Disease" on page 120.

Do You Have a Secret Food Allergy?

Most scientists believe that food sensitivities—along with the inflammatory characteristics of many foods in the American diet—can make arthritis worse in some patients. Some people with arthritis get better when they stop eating certain foods.

Several studies show that dairy products, corn and wheat worsen arthritis inflammation pain because certain proteins in these foods produce antibodies that exacerbate joint inflammation. Other research shows that these antibodies damage joints directly. The best way to correctly identify food sensitivities is to work with your doctor or a registered dietitian who can put you on an elimination diet. Here's how it works.

➤ **Keep a food diary.** Every day, write down everything that passes your lips. On the same pages, keep notes of your symptoms. Did the pain get better or worse on particular days? Did you have more flare-ups than usual? The more detailed your notes, the easier it will be to make a positive (or negative) identification.

➤ **Start the exclusion phase.** For a week to 10 days, consume a limited number of foods and beverages. Doctors who specialize in food sensitivities have lists of acceptable items to eat during this time, including lamb, rice and some vegetables and fruits. These are neutral foods your body is unlikely to react to—young, grass-fed lamb has few toxins, rice is gluten-free and there are few allergenic fruits and vegetables (except the nightshade family). The goal of the exclusion phase is to clear your body of suspected foods and ingredients.

➤ **Introduce foods slowly.** After the exclusion phase, you'll start reintroducing foods into your diet, one at a time. Be disciplined. If you add more than one food, and have a reaction, you won't know which one was responsible. Continue taking notes in your diary. In general, plan to reintroduce one food per week. This is a time-consuming process, so be patient. It's really the only way to pinpoint the culprit. If you don't notice any improvements within a few months, or the changes are so minor that they hardly seem significant, then you'll know that the foods you are eating are safe.

Supplemental Help

Whole foods are nature's best medicines, but it isn't always possible to get therapeutic doses of certain nutrients from food alone. Take omega-3s, for example. While eating fish three times a week is optimal, this isn't always possible due to availability and expense. In these cases, high-quality fish oil is a good alternative. While nutritional supplements may not be the ideal way to get the nutrients you need, they can provide necessary support. Here are the ones I recommend for arthritis.

➤ **Glucosamine gets the thumbs-up.** *Glucosamine* is a molecule produced by the body to stimulate the creation of *glycosaminoglycans* (GAGs), which are the key components of cartilage. With age, some people lose the ability to produce enough glucosamine or extract it from their food, making cartilage repair difficult or impossible. Some experts believe this is a common cause of OA. Enter the supplement glucosamine and chondroitin sulfate, the over-the-counter joint treatment that has gained tremendous popularity in the past decade. Made from cow cartilage (chondroitin) and shellfish (glucosamine), these supplements promote the repair of damaged cartilage, while also helping new cartilage to form. Both are used regularly by millions of people worldwide and are classified as a drug for the treatment of arthritis in 70 countries. But do they really work?

According to abundant scientific research, yes they do. Glucosamine and chondroitin sulfate have been examined in more than 300 investigations and have produced positive results in over 20 double-blind clinical trials. With arthritis patients, the success has ranged from a rate of 72% to 95%. That's impressive. With OA of the knee, the success rate tops 80%.

In the largest clinical trial ever conducted on glucosamine and chondroitin, a $14 million study funded by the National Institutes of Health in 2006, the Glucosamine Arthritis Intervention Trial (GAIT), researchers examined 1,200 arthritis patients and found that those taking the supplement had "significantly reduced pain." In fact, it relieved pain better than the best-selling COX-2 drug, Celebrex. Patients in the studies experienced improvement in four weeks or less, and the longer the supplement was used, the better the results were. In head-to-head studies, glucosamine has outperformed NSAIDs, such as acetaminophen, ibuprofen and naproxen, in relieving pain and inflammation.

Even though the glucosamine–chondroitin duo relieves pain, it is not a painkiller per se. Instead, it works by helping the body to regenerate lost cartilage, which ultimately results in less bone-on-bone friction, thus reducing inflammation and pain. The supplement not only improves arthritis symptoms, such as pain and stiffness, but it also helps repair damaged joints. This is supported by another study published in the journal *Menopause*, which found that patients taking the supplement were less likely to experience a progression of arthritis than patients on a placebo. In fact, three times as many patients in the nonsupplement group went on to show joint narrowing, a sure sign of progressive cartilage destruction.

One caution, however. Most glucosamine is derived from shellfish, so avoid if you're allergic. However, there are shellfish-free formulations on the market, so read labels carefully. If you have an aversion to meat products, you can also find vegetarian brands. In any case, look for a quality product that provides 1,500 mg glucosamine and 1,200 mg chondroitin per day.

➤ **Fish oil capsules are convenient.** My nutritional preference is always for fresh foods, but fish oil capsules are a convenient way to make sure you're always getting enough omega-3s to suppress inflammation on a daily basis. No need to worry about side effects because fish oil is compatible with prescription medications and other supplements, with the notable exceptions of blood-thinners like *warfarin* (Coumadin).

Soft-gel capsules are the only products to buy because they stay fresh longer. Since omega-3s are extremely sensitive to light, heat and oxygen, keep them refrigerated, if possible. Be sure to select a product that also contains vitamin E, which helps prevent the omega-3s' delicate oils from turning rancid from oxidation. If you experience fish-oil burp after taking your capsules, they may have spoiled and must be discarded immediately. The dose used in clinical studies is about 3,000 mg daily, but I don't believe this is sufficient. If you are experiencing a lot of joint pain and stiffness, I recommend taking three 1,000 mg capsules three times a day (9,000 mg). If you bleed easily, or are on the blood-thinning drug Coumadin, consult your doctor first, and do not take more than 2,000 mg per day.

➤ **Don't be caught D-ficient.** Most health-savvy people know that vitamin D is vital for strong bone strength (more details about this in the "Osteoporosis" chapter, page 269), but it is also essential for joint health. Clinical studies show that upping your intake of vitamin D improves both RA and OA. Research also shows that people with OA who have a vitamin D deficiency develop greater disability faster. Other studies indicate that getting adequate amounts of vitamin D preserves muscle strength, improves physical functioning and retards the deterioration of cartilage. If you want to take a supplement, shoot for at least 1,000 to 2,000 international units (IU) daily. If you're over the age of 70, you should bump that up to 3,000 IU.

Of course, the best source of vitamin D is sunshine. Your skin converts solar rays into the highest-quality vitamin D, which is readily available for immediate use by your bones and joints. While the current wrinkle-

phobia sweeping the US may be making sunscreen manufacturers and dermatologists wealthier, it's also creating a wave of vitamin D deficiency that is pushing up the rates of many cancers, osteoporosis and making osteoarthritis a bigger problem for people who have it. If you can, bathe in the sun for 10 to 20 minutes every day. It's some of the best medicine you can take—and it's absolutely free. For more about the healing properties of vitamin D, read pages 275–76 in the "Osteoporosis" chapter.

Will boosting your levels of vitamin D result in less pain? Swiss researchers recently treated chronic pain patients with vitamin D and reported the pain disappeared within one to three months in most patients. This was confirmed by another study presented to the American College of Rheumatology showing that low vitamin D levels may worsen knee OA. The researchers found that 88% of patients with chronic pain had levels less than 10 nanograms per milliliter (ng/mL) of vitamin D in their body. This lack of vitamin D may explain why many people complain that their arthritis pain is worse during the winter months. Perhaps it isn't the cold in their bones that's causing the problem, as much as the lack of sunshine exposure. If this sounds like you, be sure to take a good-quality vitamin D supplement during the dark winter months.

➤ **The selenium secret.** In a clinical study that included 900 participants, people who had low blood levels of selenium were found to be more susceptible to OA of the knee. And those who consumed the fewest selenium-rich foods were 100% more likely to see their arthritis become severe. Foods with the highest selenium content include Brazil nuts, tuna, crab, oysters, tilapia, whole-wheat pasta, lean beef, cod, shrimp, whole-wheat bread, turkey, wheat germ, brown rice, chicken breast, low-fat cottage cheese, mushrooms and eggs. Selenium supplements are a good insurance policy, but more is not better. Don't exceed a dose of 200 mg per day.

➤ **Pineapple Pacman to the rescue!** Pineapple supplements contain a concentrated source of the proteolytic enzyme bromelain, one of the best-researched natural anti-inflammatory agents around (see page 44). It gobbles up pro-inflammatory protein gunk in your bloodstream like a hungry Pacman. Studies show it works just like an anti-inflammatory drug—*only better!*—because there's no risk of side effects. Bromelain also squashes the production of chemicals that cause joint pain and inflammation. Take 500 to 2,000 mg daily divided into two doses between meals. Swallow them on an empty stomach so that the enzymes aren't diverted into digesting your food. You should feel an improvement in a matter of weeks.

➤ **Ginger, turmeric and cloves.** Their strong anti-inflammatory powers have been lauded as healthful culinary additions (see page 46), but these spices in supplement form allow you to get even larger doses. Just remember that cloves and ginger also thin your blood as aspirin does, so consult your physician if you're on any blood-thinning medications. For ginger, take 500 mg daily. Take 250 to 500 mg of turmeric (which contains curcumin) three times a day with meals. As for cloves, a recent clinical trial study found two to three grams daily is effective in relieving inflammation.

➤ **Help from Uncle SAMe.** SAM-e (*S-adenosylmethionine*) has been shown to be very effective for both RA and OA and has been popular in Europe for decades. It's one of the best supplements you can take for joint pain. A 2002 meta-analysis of 11 clinical trials involving SAM-e showed that the supplement was as effective as NSAIDs, such as ibuprofen, but without the side effects of these drugs. Another study conducted at the University of California, Irvine, tested SAMe head-to-head against the arthritis drug Celebrex, and researchers found that SAMe relieved pain just as well, with joint function improved significantly in just two months. The dose tested was 1,200 mg per day. Remember, SAM-e can be expensive. It can be contraindicated in patients with a family history of manic-depressive illness.

➤ **Stop the pain with MSM.** *Methylsulfonylmethane* (MSM) is a supernutrient when it comes to arthritis pain relief. Rich in sulfur, it is a potent analgesic and anti-inflammatory agent. The body uses sulfur to maintain healthy connective tissue. People with arthritis generally are deficient in it. The result is that cartilage cannot be regenerated efficiently. A double-blind clinical trial conducted at the UCLA School of Medicine found that OA patients who took MSM daily for six weeks reported an 80% reduction in pain. That kind of pain relief is off the charts, even compared with strong prescription painkillers. Yet MSM is absolutely safe and effective for both RA and OA.

My recommendation is to start at 5 grams (g) daily, going up to 10 or 15 g if needed to reduce discomfort.

➤ **Worm your way back to health.** In the process of becoming moths, silkworms produce an enzyme called *serrapeptase* that can have arthritis patients fluttering with increased activity again. Pharmacist and author Suzy Cohen reports that serrapeptase supplements produce the same protein-digesting effect as bromelain, thereby reducing inflammation and arthritic pain. Few people in the US have heard of it, but arthritis sufferers in Europe and Asia have been using it for more than 25 years. Other research shows that serrapeptase also digests blood clots and artery plaque, giving you a two-for-one benefit if you also have heart disease. It's part of the plaque-reversal program described in my book, *Reverse Heart Disease Now*. Use brands that are enteric-coated, so the active ingredient isn't destroyed by your stomach acids. Take 200 to 400 mg daily.

Other Helpers and Healers

➤ **Hot-pepper pain relief.** The capsaicin in cayenne and other hot peppers provides impressive relief for arthritis when applied to the skin as a cream. These creams are so successful in curbing arthritis discomfort that they have FDA approval. They work by blocking the neurotransmitter known as *substance P*, which causes the pain. Repeated applications of capsaicin deplete substance P from nerve fibers, so the more you use it, the greater and more lasting its effect. It's like training your pain receptors to become less

sensitive. Clinical studies demonstrate that capsaicin cream is an effective treatment for arthritis pain that produces impressive results. Apply four times daily during the first for three to four days, reducing your use to twice daily afterward. Be sure to wash your hands with soap and water to avoid burning your eyes or other body parts inadvertently.

➤ **Hands-on therapy.** The pain and stiffness from arthritis can be improved by a variety of physical therapies, including massage, physical manipulation, heat, cold and ultrasound. Ask your physician to refer you to physical therapists, naturopathic physicians, osteopaths and chiropractors who can help improve your joint mobility, while reducing pain and discomfort.

➤ **Keep moving.** Don't let pain and discomfort turn you into a couch potato because it hurts to move. Inactivity can be as harmful to the joints as overuse. Lack of exercise or regular range-of-motion movements can weaken the muscles that support the joints, while decreasing their flexibility. This can increase your pain discomfort in the long run. An underused joint will soon become stiff, painful, dysfunctional and prone to injury and rapidly advancing OA. Staying active is one of the best ways to prevent joint pain and stiffness from worsening.

If you can no longer run or walk without pain, try a recumbent stationary bike. It's easier on your joints and builds the muscles in your knees, legs, butt and back. This will help take some of the stress off of your problem areas. Aqua aerobics are also helpful because the water reduces the gravitational force on your body, making you more able to move

Simmer Up Your Own Glucosamine/Chondroitin

One reason arthritis has become such a widespread problem today is because of a dramatic reduction in our consumption of foods containing collagen, hyaluronic acid, chondroitin sulfate, glycosaminoglycans (GAGs), glycine, proline and sulfur, all of which are necessary in the repair and generation of joint cartilage. The richest sources of these components are animal bones and cartilage, which Depression-era cooks, who wasted nothing, utilized in homemade soups and stocks.

Glucosamine and chondroitin are often taken as a replacement, but this can be expensive. A month's supply can cost as much as $75. And the refinement process used in making these supplements dilutes the potency of the real thing (leftover meat, poultry or fish bones, or scraps obtained from a butcher, simmered slowly into a broth).

Bone Broth Recipe: Here's how you can get an effective joint healer that costs next to nothing: *Homemade glucosamine/chondroitin...*

Place bones (preferably beef with marrow and cartilage), eggshells (the richest source of hyaluronic acid and a good source of calcium) and fatty meat scraps (with plenty of connective tissue) in a pot. Fill with water, enough to cover the bones and scraps. Cover partially and bring to a boil. (You can also make a fish stock version with fish heads and shrimp shells, or a poultry broth with chicken bones and skin.) Feel free to add vegetable peelings for extra nutrients.

Add a couple of tablespoons of apple cider vinegar to release the cartilage compounds and calcium in the bones. Reduce the heat and allow this to simmer on a very low heat for at least an hour. The longer you simmer, the more condensed the flavor. Add more water as necessary. When you're ready to use it, strain the liquid through a colander, then use it for soup stock, gravy or as the liquid in which you cook whole grains or rice. To make soup, simply add your favorite vegetables and seasonings. If you like, the bone broth can be frozen for later use.

If you want high-potency joint supplementation for just pennies, give bone broth a try. I've seen chronic joint and arthritis pain eliminated in a matter of weeks in people who have consumed it on a regular basis.

with less pain. Be creative and look for ways to keep moving without stressing your joints. Exercise can also help you lose pounds and maintain a healthier weight, which reduces the overall stress on joints. Regular exercise, stretching and yoga can increase your flexibility and also help you sleep better.

➤ **Get needled.** Modern clinical studies show that the centuries-old alternative therapy acupuncture can be quite effective in alleviating arthritic pain. A large clinical trial involving more than 3,500 arthritis sufferers, published in the medical journal *Arthritis & Rheumatism,* found that patients with OA of the knee who were treated with acupuncture in addition to routine medical care showed significant improvements in symptoms and quality of life in just three months. In the longest and largest clinical trial of acupuncture ever conducted, patients with OA of the knee who received acupuncture along with standard medical treatment fared significantly better than those receiving medical care alone. Writing in the *Annals of Internal*

Medicine, Dr. Stephen E. Straus, the study director, said, "For the first time, a clinical trial with sufficient rigor, size and duration has shown that acupuncture reduces the pain and functional impairment of osteoarthritis of the knee."

➤ **Drop some pounds.** You don't have to be Isaac Newton to know that a falling watermelon hits the ground with far more force than a falling apple. Excess weight puts extra stress on joints, so one of the most important tips for people with arthritis is to shed as many excess pounds as possible. The National Health and Nutrition Examination Survey found that obese women are four times more likely to get OA in the knee than thinner women. Among men, the risk is nearly five times higher. Why? Because every extra pound you're carting around is equal to four pounds of pressure on your joints. On the flip side, every pound you lose will take four pounds of pressure off your hips and knees.

Losing weight, in addition to reducing the pressure on your joints, will decrease the amount of inflammatory chemicals floating around your bloodstream, which translates into less pain. Body fat cells, particularly in the belly, secrete pro-inflammatory hormones that raise your level of C-reactive protein (CRP) and make your joints stiff and sore. Need a little extra motivation to slim down? Studies show that higher levels of CRP also increase your risk for heart attack, diabetes and certain cancers.

Here's more good news. Research confirms that people who lose as few as 10 pounds and who eat more of the anti-arthritis foods described in this chapter, while limiting their

56

intake of pro-inflammatory foods such as omega-6s, fried foods, fatty meats, full-fat dairy products, vegetable oils, processed foods and baked goods, can reduce their chronic pain by as much as 90%. Just think about having 90% less pain without having to take drugs! Less weight definitely equals less pain—and a follow-up study of 48 obese men and women who underwent gastric bypass (bariatric) surgery proves it. Before surgery, every patient complained of chronic pain in their joints. After surgery, 75% reported significant reduction of pain in their spine, neck, shoulder, hand, leg and foot. Their stiffness and joint function greatly improved, too, as did the quality of their lives.

Bariatric surgery is a risky and radical procedure, and shouldn't be undertaken unless all other attempts at losing weight fail. In most cases, this extreme procedure isn't necessary. Medical studies prove that the vast majority of overweight people can lose enough weight to reduce their arthritis symptoms through simple dietary changes alone. The most effective weight-loss method I've ever experienced involves shifting to a plant-centric (not vegetarian) style of eating such as my Mediterr-Asian Diet (see page 19), reducing your intake of refined and sugary carbohydrates plus fried and processed foods and getting more physical activity. (For more information, see the chapter "Obesity and Overweight," page 280.) Not only will this help you lose a significant amount of weight, but it also provides your body with an abundance of inflammation-fighting foods and nutrients that can alleviate your symptoms.

Jim's Joint Juice

One of the most nutritious drinks is a super-healing fresh vegetable juice developed by my coauthor Jim Healthy. It's like a meal in a glass. I drink a glass every day at lunchtime. It is packed with phytonutrients, vitamins, minerals and inflammation-fighting compounds, such as salicylic acid, which is plentiful in most vegetables. You'll need a good-quality juicer with a wide chute and a motor strong enough to juice hard veggies like carrots and beets. It's one of the best investments you can make in your health. Be sure to choose organic produce only.

Makes one 8- to 10-ounce serving

5–8 carrots
½ red beet, with a few of its greens
½–1 whole sweet apple
piece of fresh ginger (about 2 inches)
small handful of spinach
1 stalk kale
1 stalk Swiss chard
4–5 sprigs parsley
2 stalks celery

Wash, peel and slice up half the carrots and all of the beet. Clean the apple (no need to peel), peel the ginger and slice both into thin wedges. Wash and dry the spinach, kale, chard, beet greens and parsley. Juice sliced carrots and beet. Add all other ingredients and use the remaining carrots to help push them through the chute.

The beet, apple and carrots will sweeten the bitter taste of the greens, so you may want to use more of these until you get used to the flavor. Since we drink this juice often, my wife and I have found a clever way to reduce the prep and cleanup time by making a one-month supply. Every 30 days or so we juice about three gallons and freeze it in 8-ounce plastic bottles. To make a big batch like this, just multiply the ingredients. The whole operation takes the two of us about an hour from start to finish.

➤ **Stay hydrated.** Drinking extra fluids really helps because it increases the amount of synovial fluid in your joints, the lubricating liquid that keeps your joints well oiled and more pain free. However, don't just think "water" because, even though it is calorie-free, water contains none of the nutrients that your joints need for repair or inflammation quashing. Why not choose a drink that adds nutrients to your body, in addition to fluids? People with arthritis would do well to sip on iced green tea or ginger tea throughout the day, or a combination of both, sweetened with a little no-cal stevia or honey. Vegetable juice, such as V-8, is loaded with nutrition as well, though it does contain calories. Water is certainly preferable to sodas and fruit juices, but try to nourish your joints every chance you get.

If you can add a chlorophyll-rich green drink to your diet, as I do, you'll not only stay hydrated, but you'll also get an extra serving of veggies. I enjoy a refreshing drink of green spirulina—an algae powder that stimulates tissue regeneration—mixed with fruit juice every morning. ■

5

Cancer

While there have been many important advances in cancer treatment, the incidence of this dreadful disease remains alarming. Every year, more than 2.5 million Americans are diagnosed with cancer. Overall, some form of cancer is responsible for 20% of all deaths, claiming more than one-half million American lives every year, more than 1,500 a day. Cancer is the second most common cause of death in the US, exceeded only by heart disease.

Cancer is not a single disease. Every cancer, depending on the part of the body in which it originates, behaves somewhat differently, but all cancers have one thing in common: They occur when the body's DNA has been damaged. DNA is the genetic material that tells cells how to grow, when to divide and when to die. Damage to DNA, known

as *mutation*, occurs constantly. Normal cells have built-in mechanisms that recognize mutations and repair them. When repair isn't possible, the cells simply die off.

Some mutations, however, aren't repaired and some damaged cells don't die. These are the ones that cause problems. When a mutated cell survives and divides, the mutations are carried on to future generations. What begins as a few damaged cells can soon become millions, with the potential to turn into cancerous tumors. While not all mutations go on to cause cancer, some multiply at an astonishing rate and, if the body's natural anticancer mechanisms don't recognize and destroy these cells, they can spread to other tissues and organs and coalesce into tumors. Cancer doesn't kill directly but diverts blood and nutrients from the rest of the body so that the patient usually dies of malnutrition.

SYMPTOMS

Very few cancers develop quickly. A cancer diagnosis represents a late link in a very long chain of events that typically extends over years or even decades. Abnormal cells that can lead to cancer are forming all the time, but don't usually develop as cancer because the immune system is surprisingly efficient at recognizing and destroying them with natural killer cells. However, this system isn't perfect. A weakened immune system, poor diet or exposure to carcinogenic substances, combined with a genetic propensity for cancer and DNA damage caused by excessive free radical molecules can create a perfect storm that allows cancer to develop. Unfortunately, this process is generally silent and undetectable by normal diagnostics. By the time cancer symptoms are noticeable, the disease has already begun to invade a certain part of the body—or, in more advanced cases, many parts of the body at once (*metastasis*). Symptoms that patients experience largely depend on the cancer's location.

➤ **What to watch for.** Some of the more common cancer symptoms include chronic fatigue, unexplained weight changes, a lump under the skin, sores that don't heal or unexplained pain. One of the tricky things about cancer is that a patient might experience one, none or all of these symptoms. The best defense is to have regular checkups, particularly if you have any risk factors for cancer, such as a family history of certain cancers, cigarette smoking or exposure to environmental toxins. The earlier a cancer is discovered, the more likely it is that treatment will be successful.

CAUSES

Cancer is known as a *multifactorial* disease, which means that it can be triggered by many different causes, including heredity, environmental factors and personal habits such as smoking or excessive alcohol consumption. Anything that causes genetic changes in the cells may cause cancer. Diet is a major determinant. Experts estimate that 30% to 40% of all cancers are directly linked to obesity, as well as the foods we eat. We now know that certain foods have an immediate neutralizing effect on cancer cells, while other foods can fuel their growth. Obviously, one should consume as many of these anticancer foods as possible, while staying away from those foods and lifestyle factors that act like cancer fertilizer.

Nutrition and cancer expert Dr. Patrick Quillin—vice president of nutrition for Cancer Treatment Centers of America and author of 15 best-selling books on nutrition and health—points out that thousands of oncologists still aren't familiar with the beneficial role that nutrition plays in cancer prevention, even though the research supporting it is overwhelming. More than 200 studies on the benefits of diet in cancer therapy have been published, with approximately 90% confirming a positive relationship between a high intake of fruits and vegetables and the suppression of cancer in general.

Unstable molecules known as *free radicals*—oxidation by-products of breathing and eating—are some of the most common instigators of cancer. Under normal circumstances, free radicals are kept under control by nutrients called *antioxidants*, which are

59

plentiful in fresh fruits and vegetables. However, if the body's supply of antioxidants is generally low—or if excessive free radicals are produced as a result of cigarette smoking, insomnia, stress, pollution, toxic chemicals or poor diet—the defensive perimeter guarding the DNA may be breached and damage to free radicals and genetic material can result. This damage initiates the cancer process.

Our body naturally produces the enzyme *superoxide dismutase* (SOD) to protect healthy cells from free-radical injury. Unfortunately, as we age, we run low on SOD and may not have enough of it to block DNA damage. Diets that include plenty of fruits and vegetables loaded with vitamin C, lycopene, isoflavones and other antioxidants block this free-radical damage and can prevent carcinogenic changes. Does this strategy work? Like a charm. When researchers at the University of California, Berkeley, analyzed studies that looked at the connection between vitamin C and cancer, they found that people who took in the highest levels of this powerful antioxidant had far and away the lowest risk.

TREATMENT

Year after year, pharmaceutical companies develop new types of chemotherapy or other cancer treatments that are considered cutting-edge, but these treatments rarely work as well as hoped. During chemotherapy, for example, patients are given toxic drugs designed to kill cancer cells, but they damage healthy cells and weaken the immune system at the same time. This is one reason why so many patients undergoing chemotherapy experience such miserable side effects. Other approaches, such as surgery and radiation therapy, have similar limitations. Cancer cells, to put it simply, are extremely difficult to kill.

▶ **Prevention is our best cure.** Because cancer is much easier to avoid than to treat, the most effective solution is prevention. None of us can choose our parents or change our genetic makeup, nor can we always avoid air pollution or chemicals in the environment. However, we *can* eat the anticancer foods that have been shown to protect our cells from these and other carcinogenic dangers. Tragically, the majority of Americans aren't eating nearly enough of these protective foods. The standard American diet doesn't give us a chance against cancer, because it is grossly deficient in antioxidants, folate, iron, zinc and other cancer-fighting nutrients. The result? The quarter of the American population that consumes the fewest fruits and vegetables has twice the cancer rate of the quarter that eats the most.

The Mediterr-Asian Diet is designed to provide your body with an abundance of super-healing antioxidants. It is packed with foods that protect the body from free-radical damage. These foods also stimulate the body's self-repair mechanisms, detoxify carcinogens, strengthen immunity, boost natural killer cell activity and may even stop blood vessels from carrying nutrients to nearby tumors. Whether you want to prevent cancer or are trying to treat it, these are the foods you should be eating.

Foods That Make It Better

A most important nutritional study clearly illustrates how powerful a Mediterr-Asian style diet is in defeating cancer. For 27 years, the China-Oxford-Cornell Diet and Health Project tracked the eating habits and disease rates in dozens of rural Chinese provinces. People in these regions consume very little meat. Their diet is primarily grain and vegetable based, naturally low in calories and exceptionally high in fiber and antioxidants. These Chinese provinces were found to have phenomenally low rates of cancer, as well as other chronic health problems, such as heart disease. These rates are barely a fraction of those in the US.

➤ **Breast cancer.** Deaths from breast cancer among women in the study ages 35 to 64 averaged fewer than nine per 100,000 people, compared with 44 per 100,000 among American women.

➤ **Colon cancer.** In the US, colorectal cancer is the second-leading cause of cancer fatalities. In China where people eat far more vegetables, the risk is 47% lower.

➤ **Prostate cancer.** One of the most common cancers in America, prostate cancer affects as many as half of all men 70 years and older. In China, the disease is much rarer.

GOOD HEALTH FROM THE GARDEN

The Mediterr-Asian Diet is a modern fusion of the two most healthful culinary styles on earth: Mediterranean and Asian. It emphasizes whole, unprocessed foods. Unlike the standard Western diet, which is extremely high in calories, refined carbohydrates, polyunsaturated vegetable oils, trans fats and a plethora of food additives, Mediterr-Asian meals are far less likely to initiate the kinds of cell changes that lead to cancer.

Just as important, the vegetables and fruits that make up the bulk of the diet contain chemical compounds that block just about every phase of the cancer cycle.

Recently, Canadian researchers, publishing in the journal *Food Chemistry*, wrote that the most powerful anticancer activity in nature is found in three groups of vegetables: *Crucifers* (including broccoli, cauliflower, kale and cabbage), *alliums* (including onions and garlic) and dark green vegetables. To arrive at this conclusion, scientists used extracts of 34 vegetables and evaluated their impact on tumor cells. Notably, the cruciferous veggies strongly inhibited every type of cancer cell tested, including those of the pancreas, prostate, brain, lung, breast, skin and stomach. As a result, the researchers recommended increased consumption of these three vegetable groups as a possible way to limit tumor development and reduce the incidence of cancer.

I couldn't agree more, but please don't restrict yourself to these vegetables. There's plenty of evidence showing anticancer action in all types of fruits and vegetables, because the vast majority of them contain *pectin*, a component of fiber. Scientists at the UK's Institute of Food Research demonstrated that pectin binds to a protein involved in every stage of cancer development and seems to inhibit its action. This may explain why people who eat more veggies and fruits are better protected against a variety of cancers. To gain the most beneficial effects these foods have to offer, including the pectin/cancer defense, it's best to consume a broad range of veggies, fruits and other high-fiber choices, including whole grains, such as oatmeal and brown rice. Eat fresh produce liberally and be sure to include the other major cancer-fighting foods described in this chapter. Upping your intake can help protect you from cancer, especially if there is a history of it in your family or you currently are under treatment.

➤ **Count on crucifers.** The cruciferous vegetables, such as broccoli, cauliflower and Brussels sprouts, are believed to be the first choice for cancer prevention. Crucifers contain two types of antioxidants that may be responsible for their cancer-protective effects, *isothiocyanates* and *indoles*.

More than 94 studies have identified the cancer-preventive effects of *Brassica* (another name for crucifers) vegetables. In one study, researchers fed volunteers about eight ounces of raw broccoli a day. Then they measured blood levels of *F2-iP*, a marker of cell-damaging oxidation in the body. The volunteers' levels of F2-iP dropped about 22%, indicating broccoli's high level of free radical-clobbering antioxidant activity. Another study showed that one of the isothiocyanates in cruciferous vegetables, *sulforaphane*, reduces the ability of carcinogens to cause dangerous cell changes by deactivating carcinogenic enzymes.

In addition, other compounds in cruciferous vegetables increase the tendency of abnormal cells to self-destruct, a natural process called *apoptosis*. Broccoli sprouts, which are now widely available, are an enormously concentrated source of sulforaphane. Scientists believe that this same protective compound defends human cells against harm, so layer them onto a sandwich and toss them into your salad every chance you get.

62

At Johns Hopkins, researchers directly tested the effects of sulforaphane on living cells. First, animals were given high doses of a cancer-causing agent. Then they were given extracts of sulforaphane. Among the treated animals, only 26% developed tumors, compared with 68% in those that weren't given sulforaphane. From there, the researchers moved on to humans. A study published in *Journal of the National Cancer Institute* found that men who ate cruciferous veggies three or more times weekly were more than 40% less likely to get prostate cancer than those who had less than one serving a week. That's an amazing risk reduction. Another study, this one done in the Netherlands, found that people who ate 14 Brussels sprouts daily for as short a time as one week had significantly higher levels of beneficial enzymes that protect against colon cancer.

The indoles found in crucifers, including *indole-3-carbinol* (I3C), also boost beneficial hormones in your body, while depressing harmful hormones that fuel prostate and breast cancers. I3C is a *phytoestrogen* that fights breast cancer by occupying cancer cell receptor sites that might otherwise house stronger forms of estrogen that fuel the cancer's growth. Another potent broccoli chemical, *diindolylmethane* (DIM), is actually produced in your body from I3C as you chew and digest broccoli. Research on DIM shows that it possesses fantastic promise as an immune booster, an attribute that may be related to its anticancer potency. Currently, the US government is funding clinical trials to study DIM's potential in treating prostate and cervical cancers.

➤ **Combine broccoli and tomatoes.** Eating them together provides more cancer-fighting action than either one alone. According to Dr. John Erdman, a food science and nutrition professor at the University of Illinois, consuming these two foods produces an additive effect, because the chemical compounds in each food attack cancer cells via entirely different pathways. In an interesting study, laboratory animals with prostate cancer were given a diet that included both tomato and broccoli powders. Other animals in the study were given only one of the powders or were given supplements or other treatments with known anticancer effects. After 22 weeks, the prostate tumors in animals given broccoli and tomato powders shrank significantly more than tumors in animals given any other treatment. This prompted one of the study researchers to conclude that men with slow-growing prostate cancers should definitely consider adding more broccoli and tomato to their diets. To get the equivalent effect, a man would only have to eat nearly one-and-a-half cups of raw broccoli and two-and-a-half cups of fresh tomatoes daily or the equivalent of one cup of sauce.

➤ **Ketchup as a cancer fighter.** I generally do not recommend eating processed foods, but ketchup and tomato sauce are exceptions, especially in healthful, natural products. Tomatoes, in all their forms, are among the healthiest foods you can eat. While there are now many varieties and colors of tomatoes, including yellow, green and almost brown, the bright red ones contain the most *lycopene*, a powerful antioxidant

Take Fat with That?

The lycopene in tomatoes is one of the most potent antioxidants in nature.

But there's a catch: It can be only absorbed by the body when it's combined with a little bit of fat. That's not a problem if you're using tomatoes to top a juicy burger, but what should you do when you hanker for the flavor of a simple, summer-fresh tomato? Just slice it up and drizzle about a teaspoon olive oil over it to dissolve the lycopene and make it available to your bloodstream for healing.

that appears to slow the growth of cancer cells. A long-running study of 48,000 men found that those who consumed 10 or more weekly servings of tomatoes or tomato-based foods were 66% less likely to get prostate cancer than men who ate less. Another interesting fact about lycopene is that, unlike many plant-based chemicals, it isn't damaged during high-heat processing. In fact, tomato sauce, tomato paste and ketchup provide *more* lycopene than whole fresh tomatoes because cooking makes it more available.

➤ **Popeye's prostate.** All leafy greens are nutritional gold mines, but spinach is exceptional because it contains at least 13 different *flavonoids*, substances that appear to have strong anticancer effects. Laboratory scientists found that extracts made from spinach slow the development of stomach cancer and reduce the incidence of skin cancers. They also are thought to accelerate the cell death of prostate cancer cells, while encouraging the formation of molecules that help prevent cancer cells from multiplying.

➤ **Cry for onions.** The chemicals that are released when you slice an onion may bring tears to your eyes, but they also cause cancer cells to self-destruct. Studies show that people who eat a lot of onions have a much lower risk for many cancers, particularly those that affect the gastrointestinal tract. Onions contain *allyl sulfides*, healing compounds only found in allium vegetables, a group that also includes garlic and leeks. People who eat onions regularly can reduce their risk for getting breast cancer by 25% and their risk for stomach cancer by up to 30%. In Vidalia, Georgia, home of the delicious Vidalia onions, death rates from stomach cancer are 50% lower than those in other parts of the US.

Researchers have found that people who ate the most onions had the lowest rates of colon, ovarian and throat cancers overall. In fact, those who ate at least seven servings of onions per week slashed their risk for colon cancer by more than 50%, compared with those who didn't eat them. In real life, the benefits might be even higher, because recipes that include onions often include garlic, and the two together are more effective than either one alone.

Onions block cancer cells at different stages, which multiplies the odds that the cells will be stopped before they have a chance to proliferate. Like most fruits and vegetables, onions are high in antioxidants, so they also protect your DNA.

The benefits of onions don't seem to be specific to a particular cancer. That is, their effects aren't limited to a few locations in the body. They appear to produce chemical changes in many different tissues. So even though research has only looked at their effects on a few cancers, it seems likely that they work against *all* forms of cancer.

➤ **Go for garlic.** Since garlic is in the same botanical family as onion, it makes sense that it has equally impressive anticancer effects. Laboratory studies have found that the *S-allylcysteine* in garlic stops healthy cells from turning into cancerous ones. Like onion, it also contains *diallyl disulfide*, which stops any existing cancers from spreading. Furthermore, *diallyl trisulfide,* another compound in garlic, kills lung cancer cells outright. Some years ago, the Iowa Women's Health study reported that people who ate garlic once a week

---

More Tears, Better Onions

The sulfur compounds in onions, known as *phenols*, can literally detoxify carcinogens before they have a chance to damage healthy cells. The stronger the onion is, the greater the anticancer effects are likely to be. A recent study found that the stronger, make-you-cry yellow onions actually have higher levels of phenols than the sweet, white varieties. A good cry is good for you, but all onions, even the mild ones, have generous amounts of fightin' phenols.

Here's a neat trick if your eyes always run like a faucet when slicing onions: Chill the onion in the freezer for about half an hour before slicing in. A cold onion won't release as many eye-burning sulfur compounds. And don't cut through the root end. That's where a lot of the tear-causing chemicals are concentrated.

were 32% less likely to get colon cancer than women who never touched the stuff.

Some scientists speculate that garlic is even strong enough to counteract the carcinogenic effects of the wrong kinds of fat in your diet. Dr. John A. Milner, scientist and former head of the nutrition department at Penn State University, knew that laboratory rats that were fed a high-fat diet, then exposed to carcinogenic agents were likely to develop cancer. He decided to give a similar group of rats garlic along with their fatty foods. As he suspected, the garlic prevented the carcinogenic agent from taking hold. He concluded that when garlic was added to the rats' diet, the ability of fat to trigger cancer was blocked. The optimal dose hasn't been established, but scientists

Unleash the Power of Garlic

Fresh garlic contains high levels of anti-cancer compounds, but Mother Nature doesn't make it easy to get them out. For one thing, *allicin*, the active healing ingredient in garlic, gives it a strong taste and the garlic breath that persists even longer. The most pungent varieties have the most allicin. In addition, the compounds in garlic need to mature to release their full array of healing benefits. Cut or smash a clove of garlic, then wait about 10 minutes before cooking or eating raw. This gives it time to release the anticancer chemicals.

Also helpful: Mince garlic, rather than coarsely chopping it. This increases the surface area and helps facilitate the release of garlic's healing compounds.

speculate that a few cloves of garlic a week may be enough to offer significant protection.

➤ **Swallow a rainbow.** Most produce with bright, vivid colors contain *beta-carotene*, a plant pigment that seems to be the sworn enemy of lung cancer. When Dr. Regina G. Ziegler of the National Cancer Institute (NCI) examined men in New Jersey, she found that those who ate as little as half a cup of carrots, sweet potatoes or winter squash daily were 50% less likely to develop lung cancer as those who didn't eat these vegetables. Intriguingly, this beta-carotene-rich diet appeared to offer the most protection to men who had only stopped smoking in the previous five years. Dr. Ziegler later found, in subsequent research, that the beta-carotene in carrots could even protect people who are frequently exposed to secondhand smoke, such as those who are the spouse of a smoker. It is important to note that beta-carotene supplements did not provide this protection—in fact, they seemed to increase the incidence of lung cancer and mortality in smokers, ex-smokers and asbestos workers.

For some reason, beta-carotene (and perhaps other antioxidants in carrots and foods such as squash) seems to be most effective against the most dangerous cancers, including cancers of the pancreas. An important Swedish study found that people who ate carrots most days of the week significantly reduced their risk for pancreatic cancer. A carrot-rich diet has even been found to reduce colon cancer by up to 24% and breast cancer by up to 44%.

➤ **Crunch more apples.** It's tempting to underestimate the healing power of the common apple. As it turns out, apples are high in flavonoids, substances with super-antioxidant activity. The long-running Nurses' Health Study, one of the most prestigious scientific projects ever conducted, found that women who ate one or more apples daily were 37% less likely to contract lung cancer—even after controlling for risk factors such as smoking. Until recently, flavonoids were primarily thought to provide protection from heart disease. For example, a study in the Netherlands found that men who ate a green apple daily, along with small amounts of onions and tea (both of which contain flavonoids) were about 30% less likely to have a heart attack than men who didn't. It's only in the last few years that the cancer connection is becoming clearer. Finnish researchers have noted that people with the highest intake of flavonoids, particularly from apples, have a 20% lower risk for getting all cancers overall and are 46% less likely to develop lung cancer.

Surveys show that the average consumer wants apple flesh to remain white after cutting, so commercial growers have developed new varieties of old favorites like the Granny Smith that don't brown easily. They've accomplished this by reducing the chemicals involved in the oxidation process. Unfortunately, these are the main protective chemicals in apples, so don't worry about those color changes: An apple that turns brown is actually your healthiest choice.

Apple eaters trying to avoid pesticide residue often get out the paring knife. Others just don't like the taste or texture of the outer peel. However, it's a big nutritional mistake

to throw away the apple skin. Researchers at the French National Institute for Health and Medical Research found that apple peels are exceptionally high in *procyanidins*, substances that inhibit cancer. In laboratory studies, animals fed unskinned apples and then exposed to carcinogens were 50% less likely to develop colon cancer as those who ate the skinless fruit. This is just another reason to make sure you buy organic apples, because their skins won't be tainted with pesticide residues.

If you're one of those people who just don't like the peel, you might include apple cider in your diet because this hearty beverage contains the skin and all. Both apple juice and apple cider are made from apples, but clear apple juice has been filtered many times to remove solids. It's also been heated during pasteurization so that it will stay fresh longer. Cider is a raw apple juice. It is cloudy because it has not undergone a filtration process, so it contains higher amounts of *polyphenols*, the natural antioxidants that protect us from cancer.

➤ **A berry good cancer fighter.** Scientists at Tufts University analyzed the antioxidant effects of more than 40 fruits and vegetables, and found that three of the top five contenders were berries. Leading the list were blueberries, strawberries and blackberries. In one study, researchers recruited volunteers who were asked to drink a beverage that contained the equivalent of one cup of fresh strawberries. This minor addition to their diets increased their bodies' ability to block free radicals by 20%.

➤ **Seek out citrus.** Everyone knows that oranges, grapefruit and other citrus fruits are good for you, if only because they're high in vitamin C and fiber. That's not the whole story by a long shot. Epidemiological studies show that in parts of the world where people eat a lot of citrus fruits (such as the Mediterranean), cancer rates tend to be much lower than here in the US. Scientists have found, for example, that people who eat citrus fruits daily tend to have lower rates of both stomach and pancreatic cancer.

This protection isn't due to vitamin C alone. Although C is a powerful antioxidant, other citrus compounds seem to be involved. For example, Japanese researchers found that injecting grapefruit pulp extract under the skin of mice blocked the growth of tumors and, in some cases, caused a total remission of their cancer. There's something in the rind and pulp of grapefruit that seems to prevent the kinds of cellular changes that can lead to cancer. That something is *limonene*, a phytonutrient also present in varieties of oranges, limes and lemons. Researchers believe this compound stimulates the body's natural ability to counteract the effects of free radicals.

Here in the US, researchers studied residents of sunny Arizona who frequently cooked with citrus peels. They found that their risk for *squamous cell carcinoma*—a precursor to skin cancer—was reduced by a remarkable 50%.

➤ **Life-giving lignans.** There are plenty of good reasons to eat more fruits, vegetables and other plants foods, but here's one

you might not have heard about. Quite a few plant foods, especially beans, flax and sesame seeds, along with fruits and vegetables, contain *lignans*. More accurately, they contain lignan precursors, substances with tongue-twisting names such as *secoisolariciresinol*, which interact with bacteria in the intestine to form lignans.

Why is this important? Lignans are kissing cousins to the hormone estrogen, which is why they're known as *phytoestrogens* (*phyto* refers to their plant-based origin). These weak natural estrogens have captured the attention of cancer researchers worldwide because they are able to occupy space on your body's estrogen-receptor sites that might otherwise be occupied by stronger estrogens, including substances with estrogen-like qualities, such as plastics and petrochemicals, which enter your body through environmental sources. These substances have the potential to flood the receptor cells in your breast, uterus, prostate and other potential cancer target areas with excessive doses of this cancer-fueling hormone. By occupying these sites, lignans and other phytoestrogens protect against estrogen-driven cancers.

Studies have shown, for example, that women with high levels of lignans in their breast tissue are far less likely to develop cancer there. According to Dr. Lillian Thompson, a scientist at the University of Toronto, lignans work in no less than 11 different ways to stop the growth or spread of breast tumors. Because of its estrogen content, a lignan-rich diet also has been found to reduce hot flashes, mood swings, headaches and other symptoms that are associated with the menstrual cycle and menopause.

The Mediterr-Asian Diet is ideal for women's health because it contains an abundance of foods that provide copious amounts of lignans. I recommend that all women, especially those in menopause or who are postmenopausal, consume beans and fiber-rich vegetables. And don't forget the ground flaxseed. It contains 77 times more lignans than any other plant food on earth. Sprinkle it on cereals and salads and add it to your smoothies. It's also the top plant source of omega-3 fatty acids.

BEEF UP ON BEANS

It's a mystery to me why Americans don't eat more beans. Throughout the Mediterranean countries and also in Asia, people eat them with almost every meal, and the cancer-prevention rewards are impressive. Virtually all beans, and particularly the darker varieties like black beans, are extremely high in antioxidants as well as *phytic acid*, a protective substance that makes it difficult for cancer cells to grow and spread. Beans also contain anticancer compounds that help prevent normal cells from undergoing cancerous changes.

➤ **How beans fight cancer.** All beans are your body's best friends because they are extremely rich in *protease inhibitors*, enzymes that help neutralize carcinogens in the gut and other parts of the body. When protease inhibitors are consumed as a normal part of the diet, studies show that they inhibit breast and colon cancers. During one of the largest and longest-running clinical trials ever conducted,

the Nurses' Health Study, researchers found that women who ate four or more servings of beans a week had 33% fewer cases of colorectal precancers than women who ate only one serving or less. Other studies have reported parallel results.

Researchers believe that a bean-rich diet may be the reason that Hispanic women have relatively low rates of breast cancer. However, there's another, less direct way in which beans can help. Beans are very high in protein, which means they can be used as a substitute for meat, thus reducing the calorie and fat content in meals to control weight gain.

SOY VERY GOOD FOR YOU

Soybeans are special. They contain many of the same protective compounds as other beans, plus a few extras. They're excellent sources of *genistein* and *daidzein*, natural compounds that block estrogen receptors in cells and reduce the risk that natural and environmental estrogens and testosterone will fuel cancer growth.

Throughout Asia, people eat soy foods nearly every day, and many researchers believe that may be one reason why women in Asian countries are six times less likely to get breast cancer than their American counterparts. Researchers have found that the humble soybean is like a tiny anticancer chemical factory, filled with compounds that help prevent the disease in a variety of ways.

I've already discussed the cancer-fighting compounds known as protease inhibitors and isoflavones that are found in beans and plant products. Two of the isoflavones in soy, genistein and daidzein, are particularly effective because they help prevent the body's natural estrogen from triggering changes that can promote the growth of estrogen-sensitive tumors. Genistein also inhibits the ability of certain enzymes that fuel tumor growth. A study published in the journal *Nutrition and Cancer* found that people who eat as little as one-and-a-half daily servings of soy are less likely to get cancer than those who don't. You don't have to eat unfamiliar foods such as tofu or tempeh to get the benefits of soy. A glass of soy milk or cup of soy yogurt will provide the same benefits.

Caution: Because soybeans do contain phytoestrogens, cancer patients under treatment should consult their physicians before adding them to their diet.

GO NUTS FOR FISH

Nuts and fish are also fierce cancer fighters. Both are high in omega-3 fatty acids, beneficial fats that help reduce the inflammation that can damage cells and increase cancer risks.

So far, the best evidence for omega-3s is in relation to colon cancer. The Physicians' Health Study, which has looked at more than 22,000 men, found that those who ate fish at least five times a week were 40% less likely to get colorectal cancer than men who ate fish rarely.

A recent meta-analysis published in the *American Journal of Epidemiology* states that you may be able to reduce your risk for colorectal cancer by 12% simply by consuming more fish per week. In addition, researchers from Wageningen University in the Netherlands found that every additional serving of omega-3 fish you eat per week cuts your risk for developing the cancer by 4%.

Which fish are best? Swedish researchers tracked the eating habits of 60,000 people for 15 years and found that those who ate at least one 4-ounce serving of cold-water, fatty fish (such as salmon, mackerel, herring or sardines) each week were 74% less likely to develop kidney cancer. Tuna, which contains significantly less omega-3 fatty acids, didn't lower the risk at all.

➤ **More good news for guys.** The omega-3s in fish have also been linked to a reduction in the risk for prostate cancer. A study of 48,000 men found that eating fish three times a week cut their risk for prostate cancer in half. Conversely, Swedish researchers found that men who never ate seafood were up to three times more likely to develop prostate cancer at some point. And what's good for the prostate also seems to be good for the colon. The prestigious European Prospective Investigation into Cancer and Nutrition study found that people who ate as little as 10 ounces of fish per week lowered their risk for colon cancer by 30%.

➤ **Fish in a bottle.** You don't have to be a fish lover to benefit from the cancer-protective omega-3s in our finny friends. In laboratory studies, fish oil has been shown to slow the rate at which cancer spreads. A study of cancer patients showed that taking 6 grams (g) of fish oil daily caused a major improvement in immune function and increased their survival time. The recommended dose is 1 to 3 g daily.

➤ **Stopping cancer's spread.** Scientists have found that the development and spread of cancer, or metastasis, is regulated by hormonelike substances called *prostaglandins*, which are responsible for the inflammation response in the body. Studies show that cancer patients have higher blood levels of certain prostaglandins and that every tumor overproduces them. Research has found that fish oils discourage the development and metastasis of cancer by squelching prostaglandin overproduction. Scientists believe that the low rate of breast cancer among Japanese and Eskimo women is linked to their high consumption of seafood.

➤ **Or just go nuts.** You can get even more cancer-fighting omega-3s into your bloodstream by snacking on nuts. Walnuts are a great choice because they contain some omega-3s in the form of *alpha-linolenic acid* (ALA). Almonds are also good because they're high in vitamin E, which has been shown to reduce inflammation, along with cancer risks.

DRINKS THAT DROWN CANCER

➤ **Green tea is the beverage of choice.** Throughout Asia, people sip green tea all the time, and it helps explain why cancer rates tend to be lower in that part of the world. According to Dr. Allan Conney, director of the Laboratory for Cancer Research at Rutgers University's College of Pharmacy in New Brunswick, New Jersey, green tea blocks or inhibits a variety of cancers, including those of the colon, lung and skin. In laboratory studies, animals exposed to cancer and then given green tea in the same concentrations that people drink exhibited significantly fewer cancers. By putting additional green tea in

drinking water, "we can actually stop tumor growth," Dr. Conney reports.

Human studies show very similar benefits. When researchers from the University of Minnesota School of Public Health examined more than 35,000 women, they found those who drank as few as two cups of tea a day were able to reduce their risk for stomach, colorectal, esophageal and mouth cancers by one-third, and were 60% less likely to get bladder cancer.

Both green and black teas (though black tea to a lesser degree) contain *polyphenols*, including powerful green tea *catechins* such as EGCG (*epigallocatechin-3-gallate*), which are exceptionally potent enemies of cancer cells. Catechins actually limit development of the blood vessels that nourish tumors. Without a blood supply, tumors can't live. In lab studies, green tea also magnified the impact of radiation on cancer cells, actually promoting their death. It's also a great detoxifier, triggering liver enzymes that usher poisons from your body. I recommend you add green tea to your regular diet if it isn't already part of it. Check Asian shops for genuine Japanese green tea varieties, including such fermented varieties such as *matcha*, *sencha* and *gyokuro*, which carry more EGCG than most Chinese green tea varieties. Polyphenol levels are present in both caffeinated and decaf teas. However, never boil any tea. Instead, steep green tea for 10 minutes for maximum catechin release, then drink the tea within an hour. My prescription is one to three cups daily.

➤ **Sip some pomegranate juice.** It's one of the easiest ways to keep the prostate gland healthy. In the first-ever clinical study involving pomegranate juice and prostate cancer, UCLA researchers reported that men who drank 8 ounces of pomegranate juice a day had significantly lower levels of prostate-specific antigen (PSA), a marker for prostate abnormalities. The juice also possesses strong anti-inflammatory and antioxidant properties, which some researchers believe alters the way that prostate cancer grows. None of the men in the study (all of whom had undergone treatment for prostate cancer) experienced metastasis, the spread of cancer cells throughout the body. That's reason enough to keep a bottle of pomegranate juice in the refrigerator and to enjoy 4 to 8 ounces daily for maximum prostate protection.

➤ **Grab some grapes.** Both nonalcoholic grape juice and red wine contain *resveratrol*, a compound that blocks cancer at just about every stage of its development. Resveratrol detoxifies carcinogens by triggering *phase II enzymes*, the body's natural defense against toxic substances. It also inhibits the growth and spread of cancer cells that happen to escape the notice of these protective enzymes. When scientists at the University of Illinois exposed laboratory animals to known carcinogens, they found that those who had more resveratrol their blood were 50% more protected when the researchers exposed them to cancer. Even among animals that did get cancer, those with higher levels of resveratrol had 66% fewer tumors than animals with lower levels.

➤ **Juice up your day.** Both orange and grapefruit juice are not only high in vitamin C, but also contain impressive amounts of *hesperidin* and *naringin*, chemical compounds that exhibit destructive power against cancer cells. In Canada, studies by the University of Western Ontario's Centre for Human Nutrition show that frequent consumption of orange or grapefruit juices may reduce breast cancer by up to 43%. In one of the studies, mice drank water spiked with hesperidin and naringin. Then, the mice were injected with cancer cells. The results were impressive. The mice that drank the spiked water had only half as many tumors as the animals that drank plain water.

MAGIC MUSHROOMS

People in Asian countries eat a lot of mushrooms. I don't mean the bland, boring and nutritionally inferior button mushrooms found in most American supermarkets. The mushrooms favored in Asia and particularly Japan are loaded with powerful *alkaloids* that stomp all over cancer cells. Here are the most healing varieties.

➤ **The dancing mushroom.** The maitake mushroom is also known as the *dancing mushroom* because Japanese folklore claims that people who ate it danced with joy, both for its good flavor and its health-enhancing properties. Research shows that maitake may be the best anticancer food on the planet. Its chemical structure is similar to that of *beta-glucan*, one of the strongest substances for stimulating the immune system and halting cancer growth. Animal studies indicate that maitake prevents the spread of existing tumors and also blocks environmental toxins from initiating carcinogenic changes. At the same time, maitake can make life easier for

71

Don't Swap a Salad for A Smoothie

An article recently published by the *International Journal of Food Sciences and Nutrition* reported that fruit and vegetable juices prevent cancer just as well as so-called real foods. The article, funded by one of the country's top juice manufacturers, understandably shook up the nutritional community. Is a glass of juice really as healthful as a plate of vegetables or a whole fruit?

Probably not. Fresh juices may contain similar amounts of protective antioxidants and phytonutrients, but they have been separated from the fiber content of the foods.

Remember, fiber binds to potential carcinogens in the intestine and rushes them out of the body. Fiber is also filling, helping eaters to take in fewer calories overall. A glass of juice, on the other hand, concentrates all its calories into just a few swallows. By all means, enjoy a glass of juice. But think of it as refreshment—*not* a replacement for wholesome fruits and vegetables.

people who already have cancer. It relieves many of the side effects of chemotherapy, including nausea, diarrhea and intestinal bleeding.

Furthermore, Japanese research found that substances in maitake mushrooms can reduce the rate of bladder cancer in laboratory animals by an amazing 46%. The healing powers of maitakes are so respected in Japan that doctors often use them to improve chemotherapy treatments. The mushrooms also stimulate immune function and are believed to protect the body's cells from environmental toxins.

➤ **Fight with white.** The white, mild-tasting *enoki* mushroom has only recently come to the attention of Western scientists. It contains *flammulin*, a compound that has been shown to stimulate the immune system and improve the body's ability to detect and destroy cancer cells before they can become established.

➤ **Slice some shiitakes.** They're among the most popular Asian mushrooms in the US because they have a rich, smoky flavor that works well with fish, meat and vegetable dishes. They contain *lentinan*, a substance believed to detoxify carcinogens and also stimulate the activity of immune cells that attack cancer cells.

DETOX WITH PRODUCE

It's impossible to completely eliminate our exposure to cancer-causing agents in the environment. Air pollution, pesticide residues and even some naturally occurring substances can increase our risks for carcinogenic changes. Detoxification can make a difference, especially with cancer patients. Regular detoxing is good for everyone because it removes many potential cancer-causing troublemakers before they have a chance to initiate cell-damaging changes.

It's easy to attain these benefits without complicated fasts. A diet high in fresh, organically grown fruits and vegetables is one of the easiest, most effective ways to remove toxins from the body. Especially beneficial are apples, grapefruit, bean sprouts, as well as many other fruits and vegetables that contain the compound *D-glucarate*. Studies show that it can reduce the risk for a variety of cancers because it has a chemical structure similar to one of the body's natural detoxifying agents, *glucuronic acid.*

One of the ways the body eliminates toxins, including excess hormones, is through compounds that attach themselves to toxic molecules and escort them out of the body, either via urine or stools. D-glucarate inhibits a nasty enzyme that blocks this detox process. Early research indicates that D-glucarate can halt the development of breast tumors and even reduce the size of existing tumors. It also seems to be effective at fighting prostate, lung and colon cancers. If you have a family history of any of these cancers, you'd be well-advised to get more D-glucarate into your diet. Eat more apples, grapefruit, sprouts—especially broccoli sprouts—and cruciferous vegetables such as broccoli, cabbage and Brussels sprouts. You can also take D-glucarate supplements in doses that range from 500 mg to 1,000 mg daily.

GET YOUR FIBER FIX

Official anticancer diet guidelines call for five to nine daily servings of fruits and vegetables, with plenty of whole grains and legumes. The reasons go beyond vitamins, minerals and antioxidants. People who eat more of these foods are far less likely to get cancer than those who load up on sugary refined carbohydrates, fast food, take-out meals and processed commercial groceries. Much of the credit goes to fiber, the roughage portion of plants that passes undigested through the digestive tract. For a long time, scientists were puzzled that a substance that isn't readily absorbed into the bloodstream could be so protective. However, the reasons are now clear.

➤ **Fiber cleans the bowel.** The bulkiness of fiber greatly speeds the transit time of the stool, so digested foods move through the intestine faster. Faster transit means that harmful fats, cholesterol and carcinogens in your diet have less time to cause dangerous changes in intestinal cells. Fiber foods are also a great way to stay regular and avoid constipation, which can result in toxic buildup.

➤ **Fiber manages hormones.** Another wonderful benefit of high-fiber foods is that they bind to estrogen molecules in the intestine and block their reabsorption into the bloodstream. Less circulating estrogen means a lower risk for hormone-driven cancers such as those of the breast and prostate.

➤ **Fiber controls your appetite.** The sugars in high-fiber foods don't convert into glucose as rapidly as refined foods do. This regulates the amount of glucose in your bloodstream and the insulin needed to process it, thus providing a number of healthy benefits. Because these foods are digested slowly, they keep you feeling full and satisfied longer, a big plus if you're trying to manage your weight and control your hunger. Also, if you're concerned about your blood sugar, high-fiber foods are just the ticket because they won't trigger a sudden demand for insulin. Plenty of studies show that excess glucose and insulin damage your arteries and organs through *glycation*, a process that accelerates their aging...and yours.

➤ **Fiber fights cancer.** When researchers reviewed the results of 40 different studies, they concluded that people who ate the most whole grains, which are among the best fiber sources, were 30% less likely to get *any* cancer than those who consumed less.

How much fiber do you need each day? The minimum requirement is 40 g, but more is certainly better. Unfortunately, the average American consumes less than half this amount, which is one big reason why cancer is about to overtake heart disease as our nation's leading killer. Don't fret over the numbers. If you shift your diet to a more Mediterr-Asian style of eating, you'll get plenty of fiber. You can't go wrong if you make vegetables, fruits, whole grains, plus beans and legumes, the central focus of your diet.

➤ **Mix it up.** Fiber actually comes in two main categories. There's soluble fiber, mainly found in beans and quite a few fruits, and the insoluble fiber present in whole grains and vegetables. All whole foods contain a mix of both, which is why eating a varied diet is so important. New research suggests that people who get a mix of both fibers are better able to eliminate bile acids, which are linked to cancer.

CANCER-FIGHTING HERBS AND SPICES

➤ **Season with saffron.** With its intense orange-yellow color and distinctive flavor, saffron is among the most-popular spices in Mediterranean recipes. It's also the most expensive, because it takes 75,000 threads (the *stigmas* of the flowers) to make one pound. Fortunately, a little goes a long way, whether it's for health or flavor. Saffron contains *crocin*, the carotenoid responsible for its vibrant color, which has been found to trigger the death of cancer cells. Studies indicate that it is active against many different cancers, including ovarian cancer, squamous cell carcinoma and leukemia, among others. These new findings confirm the wisdom of using saffron in traditional medicine, which recognizes it as a potent anticancer herb.

➤ **Cook up a curry.** The distinctive color of curry dishes comes from turmeric, a spice that contains the active ingredient curcumin. This powerfully anti-inflammatory substance has been shown in numerous studies to protect cellular DNA from free radicals. Turmeric, in fact, may be the single most potent food-derived anti-inflammatory available. It's particularly effective in the colon, where cells turn over frequently (about every three days) and are especially vulnerable to free-radical damage.

Current medical advice recommends a daily aspirin or other nonsteroidal anti-inflammatory drugs (NSAIDs) to prevent colon cancer, but clinical studies indicate that curcumin is even more effective. Not only does it help stop the initial stages of cancer development, but it is also blocks its growth and progression. In one study, smokers were given small amounts of turmeric daily. The study was designed to measure the effects of turmeric on potential carcinogens generated by cigarette smoke. After one month, the smokers given turmeric showed significant reduction in these toxic compounds. In fact, their levels were nearly the same as those of nonsmokers. Volunteers in a control group, who weren't given the turmeric, showed no changes.

Turmeric has also been found to slow the growth of tumors and boost the death of cancer cells. It even bolsters chemo's effectiveness. Turmeric is easy to buy and use. Purchase ground turmeric and blend a teaspoon—a tablespoon if you're already fighting cancer—per day with a grind of black pepper and a teaspoon of extra-virgin olive oil. Sprinkle it on vegetables, and add to eggs, soups and salads.

Here's another reason that turmeric is such a good ally in the fight against cancer. Research shows that it binds to iron, making the iron unavailable to tissues—including cancer cells, which can't live without iron. This is one reason that the risk for cancer is greatly increased in patients who tend to accumulate excess iron.

➤ **Raise some rosemary.** Sprinkle a teaspoon of rosemary on a leg of lamb for a traditional herbal flavor, or toss rosemary with roasting potatoes. This savory herb is rich in *carnosic acid*, a substance found to inhibit breast cancer in the earliest stages. Other research shows that it stimulates the body's production of enzymes that protect against lung cancer cells.

➤ **Go with ginger.** Knobby fresh gingerroot is a bona fide cancer killer. It not only calms any nausea you may have from cancer treatment, but also works against cancer cells and limits the growth of tumors. If you've been uncertain how to use it, start by steeping slices from a one-inch piece in boiling water for 15 minutes. Sip the ginger tea cool, tepid or hot. You can also grate the root (after peeling), combining with yogurt for a refreshing fish dip, adding raw to salads or cooking up in a stir-fry.

DARK CHOCOLATE, THE CANCER BLOCKER

Nibble a daily square or two of dark chocolate containing a minimum of 70% cocoa. Look for chocolate with an even higher percentage of cocoa, the source of cancer protection. The antioxidant power in a piece of dark chocolate is equal to that of a cup of green tea and twice that of a glass of red wine. Cocoa contains polyphenols and proanthocyanidins, which knock out cancer cells and slow the growth of blood vessels that nourish tumors. Don't eat milk chocolate, which contains polyphenol-inhibiting dairy.

For more cancer-blocking foods and recipes, visit *www.myhealingkitchen.com.*

Foods That Make It Worse

The traditional Western diet—all of those sugary carbs, greasy chips, fast-food lunches and calorie-bloated desserts—are a major reason that cancer is the leading killer disease in America. Time and again, important research studies show that diet *does* make a difference in who gets cancer and who doesn't. It isn't only what we eat that can have a tremendous effect on lowering our chances of cancer—it's also what we *don't* eat. Here are some of the worst cancer-promoting foods that you should avoid at all costs.

SPARE THE SUGAR, PLEASE

You can eat all the healing food in the world, but it won't help if you're also eating refined carbohydrates. In fact, quickie carb foods that rapidly convert to sugar in the bloodstream are highly toxic. Numerous studies have shown them to be a major cause of cancer. Why?

Sugar and high-glycemic (GI) carbs are highly inflammatory, and inflammation is an underlying cause of every major disease. Physicians are beginning to recognize this, but it will be years before mainstream health advice changes. Until then, doctors will continue to blame meat, dairy products and saturated fats, when the unrecognized culprit—excess blood sugar—is right under our noses. The widely respected physician Mark Hyman, M.D., author of the book *UltraMetabolism* and former medical director of the world-famous Canyon Ranch health resort, puts it succinctly: "All the diseases that kill us in our society are related to refined carbohydrates and sugars—cancer, heart disease, obesity, diabetes, stroke and Alzheimer's."

➤ **Breast cancer.** Sugar's role in breast cancer was highlighted by the ongoing, 10-year Nurses' Health Study of 120,000 women, which found that sedentary, overweight women who consumed a diet high in refined carbs and sweets have a greater risk for type 2 diabetes, heart disease, cancer and other potentially life-threatening conditions than those who don't. Indeed, women who ate the most carbohydrates, particularly sugary foods, had 2.2 times greater incidence of breast cancer than women on a more balanced diet. Another study, following nondiabetic women with early-stage breast cancer, found a strong correlation between high levels of blood sugar and the progression of the disease. And sugar's influence isn't limited to breast cancer.

➤ **Colon cancer.** Another study, which examined the eating habits of 38,451 women over a period of eight years, found that a diet of high GI foods increased the risk for colorectal

cancer in women. In fact, women with higher GI diets were nearly 300% more likely to develop colon cancer. Still another study showed that excess sugar in the diet increases the risk for diabetes, and this in turn raises your risk for colon cancer by up to 40%.

➤ **All cancers.** These findings are consistent with other clinical research reporting that people with impaired glucose tolerance are nearly twice as likely to die from any type of cancer as those with normal blood sugar levels. Writing in the *American Journal of Epidemiology*, researchers noted that people with elevated blood sugar levels had more than *quadruple* the chance of developing the cancer as those whose blood sugar levels were normal.

➤ **Cancer cells are sugar addicts.** The German scientist Dr. Otto Warburg won the Nobel Prize Nobel in 1931 for discovering that cancer cells use glucose as fuel. Oncologists from that point on have noticed that tumors are glucose guzzlers, and that very few cancers can survive without a steady supply of the stuff. As one cancer expert put it, "If you strangulated the supply of sugar to a tumor, it actually triggers a form of biological suicide among the malignant cells." This means that when you give up sugar, you are depriving any cancer cells in your body of the food that they need to grow and spread. How's that for motivation for controlling your sweet tooth?

It has taken nearly 80 years since Dr. Warburg's discovery for even a small number of scientists and cancer specialists to recognize the damning role that a high sugar intake plays in the development of cancers of the breast, gallbladder, prostate, colon, uterus and pancreas. Only now are a handful of researchers seeing that high glucose and insulin levels encourage and speed tumor growth. Yet this knowledge is rarely reflected in the dietary advice, or even the hospital food, given to cancer patients. Of the four million cancer patients being treated in America today, very few are provided any scientifically supported nutrition therapy or advised to eat any of the healing foods mentioned in this chapter. This must change… and soon. As another respected cancer authority stated: "I believe many cancer patients would have a major improvement in their outcome if they controlled the supply of cancer's preferred fuel, glucose."

THE RED MEAT RUSE

The average American gets about 40% of his or her calories from protein, in large part from red meat. According to the China Study, which compared the diets, lifestyle and disease characteristics of people in 65 rural counties in China in the 1970s and 1980s, the percentage of protein in their diet was about 20% and it mostly came from plant sources. When they compared the rates of cancer between Americans and rural Chinese, the researchers found that Americans had a much higher incidence. The majority of medical experts cite this as proof that eating red meat causes cancer. However, no direct study has proved this association. The fact that Chinese peasants contracted cancer less often than Americans could easily be attributed to their high intake of plant foods instead of meat.

➤ **Meat is a healthful food.** While it is true that eating as much animal protein as we Americans do can put a strain on your kidneys, liver and other organs, this is not the same as condemning it as a cancer-causing food. Red meat and all animal products—if they have been raised under free-range, grass-fed conditions—are healthful foods that have been consumed for centuries. On average Americans eat about ½ pound of meat a day or 200 pounds a year. This is unhealthy, not because meat is bad, but because it is of poor quality, contains too much excessive protein and fat as well as too many calories. My advice is to enjoy meat as they do in the Mediterranean and Asian cultures—have smaller amounts in relation to vegetables and whole grains.

➤ **Quality versus quantity.** Studies that associate meat-eating with cancer do not make the distinction between the types of meat being consumed. A grass-fed, free-range steak is not the same as a pile of fried bacon or a hunk of salami, both of which are laced with carcinogenic nitrites and hormones. But numerous studies *do* show that processed meats are unhealthy for you. A study of more than 1,500 adults who were treated for precancerous colon polyps found that those who ate a lot of processed meats were 75% more likely to develop an advanced polyp, compared with just 25% of those who ate the least.

➤ **The danger of the grill.** Grilled or fried meat cooked to high temperatures is especially dangerous because it contains high levels of *heterocyclic amines* (HCAs), chemicals that are known carcinogens. Other studies have shown that women who eat a great deal of meat that's been subjected to high-heat cooking may have more than four times the risk of breast cancer than women who eat these same meats rare or medium-done.

➤ **Don't overcook.** Other research reveals that well-done meat is carcinogenic, regardless of the method of cooking. The longer the meat is cooked and the higher the temperature, the more HCA compounds are formed. The studies found no association with total meat consumption or red meat consumption, but uncovered a 100% increase in breast cancer risk in women who consumed well-done meat compared with those who ate it rare or medium.

ALCOHOL AND BREAST CANCER

We've all seen the studies praising the many health benefits of one or two alcoholic beverages per day—unless you're a female. In that case, two daily drinks have been shown conclusively to increase the risk of breast cancer. For women, even moderate alcohol consumption has also been linked to cancers of the colon, rectum, neck and brain.

➤ **One drink per day.** That's what highly credible studies say should be the limit for women. Men are allowed two because their body mass is greater, so alcohol has less effect. Also, the female metabolism processes alcohol differently. Excessive alcohol consumption should be avoided by everyone because alcohol produces a dramatic increase in free radicals, which in turn can produce genetic damage that can lead to cancer. Studies at the University of Mississippi also indicate that alcohol can promote the growth of blood vessels in tumors,

which increases the odds that they'll grow and spread. In one study, animals with cancer who were given alcohol developed tumors twice as large as those in the alcohol-free group, and the alcohol group had an 800% increase in the spread of cancer cells into blood vessels.

Of course, not everyone is going to follow this advice. They certainly don't in the wine-loving Mediterranean countries. Yet these cultures have lower rates of cancers, heart disease and all other degenerative health problems than we do. And they live longer. There have been many explanations for this so-called French paradox, but I feel this seeming contradiction is explained by the generous amounts of antioxidant-rich vegetables and fruits in their diets, their habit of not overeating and their overall enjoyment of life. My advice is to follow their lead and expect similar results.

Supplemental Help for Cancer Prevention

Over the years, dozens (if not hundreds) of supplements have been touted as miracle cures for cancer, and most haven't come close to fulfilling the exaggerated claims. However, a few supplements do seem to make a significant difference.

➤ **Coenzyme Q10 (CoQ10).** Studies show that this vitaminlike nutrient appears to reprogram cancer cells so that they self-destruct, interrupting their ability to multiply at their astonishingly fast—and lethal—rates. In a study of high-risk breast cancer patients, those treated with 90 mg of CoQ10 daily, along with other supplements, had lower-than-expected rates of mortality and also required lower doses of painkillers. Take up to 200 mg of a high-quality soft-gel twice daily for therapeutic benefit. Avoid powdered products because they are not well absorbed.

➤ **Melatonin.** Commonly used as a sleep aid, this supplement is very closely linked with cellular regulation. A number of studies have shown that cancer patients who take melatonin have higher survival rates, as well as a slowing of cancer progression. Research also shows melatonin can induce the death of cancer cells, as well as slow the growth rate of tumors. Start with 1 to 2 mg and work up to 10 mg if the lower dose is found ineffective.

➤ **Vitamin C.** Most people get enough vitamin C from their diets, especially if they eat the produce recommended in the Mediterr-Asian Diet. Smokers, however, need a lot more. Scientists at the University of California, Berkeley, found that smokers who took extra vitamin C reduced free-radical damage caused by smoking by more than 10%. A daily vitamin C supplement also helps vitamin E in the body, prolonging additional lung protection. Smokers—or anyone who's exposed to secondhand smoke—should get an extra 500 to 1,000 mg of vitamin C daily.

➤ **Folic acid.** Researchers at the Mayo Clinic report that women who took a daily supplement that includes folic acid were able to eliminate the risk of breast cancer associated with alcohol consumption. Folic acid is an important supplement even if you don't drink. The Harvard Nurses' Health Study found that women who received extra folic acid from a daily supplement were 75% less likely to get colon cancer. The recommended dose is 400 to 800 micrograms daily.

Nutritional Support for Cancer Patients

As you've just seen, good nutrition is among the most effective strategies for cancer prevention. It's equally important for those with a cancer diagnosis. Even though dietary cancer cures should be viewed with a great deal of caution, nutritional support and supplementation have been shown to help patients fight infections, strengthen their immune systems, maintain a healthy weight and minimize the side effects of treatment—all of which can greatly improve your odds for a successful outcome.

COPING WITH NAUSEA

Nausea and vomiting are among the most dreaded complications of cancer. Sometimes they're caused by the cancer itself. More often, they're a side effect of radiation or chemotherapy. It's not uncommon for cancer patients to feel so ill that they stop eating or, if they do eat, they're unable to absorb the nutrients from foods. This can lead to dramatic weight loss and wasting, a condition known as *cachexia*. As I mentioned previously, most cancer patients die not from the disease itself, but from the malnutrition that accompanies it. That's why it's essential to do everything possible to maintain your strength and eat well when battling cancer. This is particularly true if you're undergoing treatments such as chemotherapy, radiation or surgery, which can greatly increase the body's demand for healing nutrients. The following strategies can make a significant difference.

➤ **Graze.** Whether or not you're undergoing chemotherapy, you'll probably find it's easier on your body to eat small, frequent meals—say, every few hours—rather than a few larger meals per day. People who graze usually experience less stomach upset and are better able to absorb essential nutrients.

➤ **Boost the flavors.** It's common for cancer patients to lose their appetite. This can be due to the illness, the side effects of treatments or even depression. People often find that they're able to eat more—and enjoy it—if they intensify flavor by using a variety of herbs and spices.

➤ **Don't skimp on protein.** Any illness increases the body's need for protein. This is particularly true after surgery, because the body uses protein to repair damaged tissues. Protein also maintains muscle mass, strengthens the lining of the intestine and improves the ability of the immune system to fight cancer. Cancer patients who are undergoing therapy may need 50% more protein than they did before. Just make sure the protein you are consuming is of the highest quality available to you.

➤ **Liquid diets.** If you don't have a big appetite, get in the habit of drinking a high-protein smoothie or green drink once or twice a day. Look for a protein powder that contains whey, or a green drink that is made from blue-green algae, spirulina or dried mixed greens. Whey is a complete dairy-based protein that provides all of the essential amino acids. You can buy whey protein in such flavors as chocolate, strawberry and orange. Mix it with juice, water or soy milk, and add frozen or fresh fruit for flavor and extra antioxidants. It will help provide necessary protein plus extra calories that can help your strength and stamina. Be wary of soy protein powders because of the phytoestrogen in them. Remember to consult your doctor first to make sure your tumor is not estrogen-dependent.

➤ **Blend your vitamins.** Even people who find it's difficult to eat can usually drink without any problems. Get in the habit of blending fruit or making fresh vegetable juice. You can use carrots, celery, apples, grapes or even stronger-tasting veggies, such as broccoli. For an even more nutritious juice, use fruit juice or even a broth for the liquid component.

➤ **Grab some ginger.** Fresh gingerroot is a traditional remedy for nausea, and studies indicate that it works as well as some drugs. Add about a tablespoon of fresh ginger to your fruit-and-vegetable drinks, or brew it as a stomach-settling tea.

SOY: TO EAT OR NOT TO EAT?

With the exception of those who have estrogen-sensitive breast cancer or prostate cancer, soy foods can be very beneficial for cancer patients during treatment. Soy foods are extremely high in protein, yet easier to digest than meat. In addition, the chemical compounds in soy milk, tofu and other soy foods may play a beneficial role in your eventual recovery. As I mentioned earlier, some of the chemicals in soy have been shown to inhibit the development of tumor blood vessels. This can make a critical difference, because these blood vessels are what make it possible for tumors to grow. Studies have also found that soy seems to block some of the enzymes that cancer cells need to divide and grow. Talk to your oncologist or physician to see if soy foods belong in your diet. If so, plan on eating at least one serving of soy food daily. Women with breast cancer receiving radiation should not consume soy as it can interfere with the treatment.

STAY HYDRATED

Drinking plenty of fluids is more important when you're dealing with cancer. Water and other fluids help break down the residues of chemotherapy drugs and other medications, flushing them from your body. Fluids carry away toxins, including those produced by your body in response to the disease, as well as to the treatment. Drinking water regularly, as well as juice and teas, can keep your tissues hydrated, so you're less likely to experience painful sores or irritation. It will also counteract the dehydration that you may experience if you're nauseated from cancer treatments.

➤ **Sip some soups.** Along with stews, smoothies and other moist foods, soup provides your body with extra liquids and nutrition. They're also easy to prepare when your energy is low. People with cancer who have trouble eating often find they're able to enjoy soups without discomfort. Other wet foods to consider include fresh or frozen fruits, ice pops or ice cream and sherbet or sorbet.

➤ **Keep a full glass nearby.** Don't allow yourself get thirsty. Always keep a glass of water, juice or herbal tea close by. Plan on drinking at least one cup of fluid per hour, or even more if you feel like it. Don't guzzle too much liquid at once, however—it can make nausea worse. Small sips will probably be more comfortable than large gulps.

➤ **Give up coffee and alcohol.** Both are diuretics, which means they can cause you to lose more water than you take in. This can deplete precious minerals in your body.

➤ **Elevate your electrolytes.** If you've been losing fluids due to vomiting or diarrhea—or simply because you haven't been drinking enough—your body is probably running low on electrolyte minerals, including calcium, sodium and potassium. Every cell in your body needs electrolytes to function properly. You can purchase electrolyte-replacement solutions at pharmacies, but it's just as easy to make your own. Celtic and Himalayan salts have the full spectrum of minerals and trace elements, making them rich in electrolytes. Mix a teaspoon of either of these salts with a teaspoon of honey and a pinch of baking soda in a quart of water. Stir well and drink some throughout the day. If you've been consuming enough fluids, you probably won't need anything this potent. Drinking a glass or two of organic vegetable or fruit juice once a day will help replace electrolytes that might otherwise have been lost.

Other Helpers and Healers

➤ **Prevent cancer by sunbathing.** Want to lower your cancer risk even more? Then move to a sunnier climate. I'm not kidding. A study conducted by William B. Grant, Ph.D., compared sunlight exposure with cancer mortality rates in the US and found that people who got fewer rays had a higher risk for

13 different types of cancer, including breast, lung and pancreatic cancer. Now he has expanded his study to the entire world using a new data-gathering tool called GLOBOCAN that tracks cancer statistics in 175 countries. When his researchers mapped the global cases of breast cancer, they found that rates were highest at the highest latitudes in both the northern and southern hemispheres, where there is less sunshine.

How can this be? Because solar rays are a major source of vitamin D and plenty of evidence shows this sunshine vitamin offers significant protection against numerous cancers. Studies show that women with the lowest vitamin D levels have a 500% higher risk for breast cancer.

➤ **Vitamin D saves lives.** An estimated 600,000 cases of breast and colorectal cancers could be prevented each year if vitamin D-3 levels among populations worldwide were increased, particularly in countries north of the equator, according to researchers from the Moores Cancer Center at the University of California, San Diego (UCSD). This includes nearly 150,000 cases of cancer that could be prevented in the US alone.

To increase your vitamin D levels, expose as much skin as you're comfortable with to the direct rays of the sun for 10 to 20 minutes daily, taking care not to burn. Contrary to mainstream advice, exposure to sunlight actually helps *prevent* skin cancer. If you are going to be out in the sun longer, be sure to protect your exposed skin with appropriate sunscreen. In colder climates—and on all the days when sunlight is limited—take 1,000 to 2,000 international units (IU) of a high-quality vitamin D-3 supplement.

➤ **A honey of a remedy.** Bee *propolis* is a waxlike substance that honeybees use to seal cracks in their hives. It's been used for centuries as a folk remedy, mainly for fighting infection. More recently, scientists have found that it may have anticancer properties because it contains *caffeic acids,* which appear to prevent the formation of precancerous tissue. Propolis is also high in flavonoids and ethanols, substances that inhibit the cell-damaging action of free radicals, and may reduce inflammation that can damage cells as well as the arteries that carry blood to the heart. Most of the research on bee propolis has been done on laboratory animals, so the optimal dose hasn't been established. A good starting place would be 500 mg, taken one to three times daily. ∎

6

Depression

epression affects the entire body, not just the mind. We're not talking about feeling blue, or transitory grief or sadness. People who are depressed find little or no pleasure in daily activities, including things that they once enjoyed. They may feel suicidal or turn to drugs or alcohol for temporary relief. Many have trouble maintaining relationships, and often experience a host of physical symptoms, including fatigue, stomach upset or back pain. Unlike sadness, depression tends to linger, often for years or decades, unless the sufferer seeks appropriate help.

It's estimated that 15% of all Americans will suffer from depression that's severe enough to require medical attention. Among older adults, the incidence of depression can reach one in four, but the actual figure is probably much higher because many people

with depression don't seek treatment. Many don't even realize they have a treatable condition. Symptoms usually begin in one's twenties, but it's not unusual for depression to first occur later in life. Sometimes, depression is linked to an illness or traumatic event, such as the loss of a spouse. More often, it just happens, and the reasons why aren't always apparent.

SYMPTOMS

Depression can be difficult to diagnose because everyone experiences somewhat different symptoms. Some might have a loss of appetite, while others might use food for comfort and overeat. Some sleep more than usual, while others struggle with insomnia. Depression can be so severe that normal life is impossible, or so mild that the sufferer just feels a little off. Doctors look at eight factors before deciding if a patient is suffering from depression. Those who experience five or more of these symptoms for one month or longer are considered clinically depressed. Having four symptoms still makes some-one a candidate for depression, although in a somewhat milder form. Check yourself against the list that follows.

The 8 Telltale Symptoms of Clinical Depression

1. Appetite changes—either eating more or less than usual.
2. Changes in sleeping habits.
3. Increase or decrease in physical activity.
4. Lack of pleasure in daily activities or hobbies.
5. Low energy and fatigue, noticeable changes in libido.
6. Feelings of low self-worth or persistent guilt.
7. An inability to concentrate or think clearly.
8. Thoughts of death or suicide.

CAUSES

Depression was once believed to be all in one's head, as though someone could choose to switch their feelings on and off. New re-search shows that this is clearly not the case. Neuroscientists now believe that depression is mainly due to alterations in the levels of neurotransmitters, particularly brain chemi-cals such as *norepinephrine*, *dopamine* and *serotonin*, which control mood and emotion-al states. Even slight changes in brain chem-istry can have profound effects on how we feel and behave. Depression has also been linked to hormonal changes. This is why some women feel depressed and irritable at certain points during their menstrual cycles or during menopause, and why men may experience emotional slumps when their testosterone levels decline during middle age and beyond.

Depression tends to run in families, which suggests that specific genes play a role. It's unlikely that genetic factors actually cause depression, but they can make indi-viduals more susceptible. External factors can also have an influence, including death of a loved one, divorce, financial problems and so on. Often, these events can push us into full-blown depression. So can purely physical factors, such as the chronic use of alcohol or drugs, sleep deprivation or un-derlying physical disorders like diabetes or hypothyroidism.

TREATMENT

People who suffer from clinical depression can spend their days in a crushing state of hopelessness. They may have trouble getting up in the morning and lose interest in their hobbies, their friends and their families. Sometimes they give up altogether and take their own lives. Everyone who goes through a prolonged depression needs to see a thera-pist, psychiatrist or at least a family doctor. Today's antidepressant drugs can work won-ders in patients who suffer from severe bio-chemical depression.

Antidepressants are one of the top-selling categories of drugs today and the phar-maceutical industry has pumped billions of dollars into research on them. These drugs are designed to shift the balance among different brain chemicals, particularly those neurotransmitters closely involved with mood, emotions and arousal. About 10% of US adults take one or more antidepressants, up 500% in the past 10 years. Incredibly, a study by the New England Research Institute found that 43% of those who had been prescribed had no psychiatric diagnosis. While today's generations of drugs are far safer than their predecessors, none are free of side effects, nor do they produce permanent alterations in brain chemistry. In other words, they can mask the symptoms of depression for as long as someone keeps taking them, but they are unlikely to eliminate the underlying problems.

The good news and most promising new findings indicate that certain mood-altering foods make it possible to shift brain chemistry in a healthier direction. People who consume more of these antidepressant foods, while avoiding those that disrupt brain chemistry, can achieve dramatic improvements in their moods and emotional states.

Foods That Make It Better

We often refer to food as the fuel that keeps our energy up, but food also powers and influences the brain as well. The various amino acids, vitamins and minerals in certain foods trigger millions of biochemical reactions in our gray matter. While there's still a great deal of controversy among researchers about the precise role that nutrition plays in brain function, no one disagrees that the effects are both real and measurable, or that

they can have a profound influence on how we feel.

We know, for example, that nutritional deficiencies can produce low levels of vitamin B-12 and omega-3 fatty acids, which trigger changes in brain chemistry that lead to anxiety, depression and other mood disorders. People who skip meals will have drops in blood sugar that can cause a temporarily depressed mood. It works the other way, too. People who don't feel well emotionally are probably not taking care of themselves physically. If they quit eating or, just as likely, binge on carbohydrate-loaded refined junk foods, they are likely to receive inadequate amounts of the nutrients that can help prevent or reverse depression.

Some nutrients in foods are directly converted by the brain into neurotransmitters, substances that act as chemical messengers to carry electrical signals from one brain cell, called a *neuron*, to the next. People with imbalances in neurotransmitters aren't likely to feel very well or happy. Certain foods also generate enzymatic activity that stimulates the hormones involved in emotions and moods, as well as in memory and concentration.

Here's an example of how powerful an influence nutrition can be on your mental state. People with clinical depression often have low blood levels of folate, a B-vitamin linked to serotonin, one of the main neurotransmitters involved in mood. When these people receive extra folic acid, the supplemental form of folate, the improvements in their mood were quite striking. Several foods produce this effect.

85

PROZAC IN YOUR BAGEL

Low-carbohydrate diets widely promoted for weight loss are terrible for people struggling with depression. It's no coincidence that we refer to fare like mashed potatoes, mac-and-cheese, pasta and fresh-baked bread as *comfort food*. The connection is clear. Carbohydrates increase brain levels of *tryptophan*, an amino acid that's converted into serotonin, which produces a calming effect. That's why carbohydrate foods are the backbone of the depression-healing diet. We are not talking about refined quickie carbs that can play havoc with your glucose and insulin levels, and also cause rapid weight gain. Stick with carbohydrate foods as close to their natural state as possible, including vegetables, whole grains, whole-wheat pastas and whole-grain breads.

It's estimated that virtually all women, and nearly 70% of men, crave carbohydrates. About 85% of these give in to their cravings at least half the time. This isn't always a good thing, but the neurochemistry behind it is intriguing. When you eat refined carbohydrate foods, the pancreas pumps out insulin, which lowers blood levels of every single amino acid *except* tryptophan. As Elizabeth Somer, M.A., R.D., explains in her book *Food and Mood*, amino acids compete with each other to gain access to the brain. By eliminating other amino acids, insulin makes it easy for tryptophan to hit the target. Once tryptophan is elevated, serotonin rises, which puts the comfort in comfort foods. This is exactly how most popular antidepressant drugs work, especially the *selective*

86

Best Sources of Feel-Better Carbs

People who crave carbohydrates often get them in the form of sugar-rich snacks. But these simple carbohydrates can lower energy and ultimately make depression worse. Feeling better isn't just about eating more carbohydrates. You have to pick the right ones. Complex carbohydrates provide a slow, steady influx of glucose, tryptophan and serotonin. Here are the foods to eat for an emotional pick-me-up.

10 Top Complex Carbohydrates

1. Vegetables, fresh or frozen
2. Fruits, fresh or frozen
3. Legumes, such as beans, peas, and lentils
4. Brown and wild rice
5. Barley
6. Sweet Potatoes
7. Oats
8. Winter squash
9. Raisins
10. Nuts

---

serotonin reuptake inhibitors (SSRIs), of which Prozac is the best known. This class of antidepressants relieves depression by increasing brain levels of serotonin, which is more or less what happens when you eat a bagel or a bowl of whole-grain cereal.

Meals that are rich in protein, on the other hand, lower serotonin, which may explain why people who are feeling down are more likely to order a pasta dish than a sirloin. This was confirmed in a study where people in a weight-loss program who ate more carbohydrates experienced less depression than people in the same program who consumed fewer carbohydrates. Of course, this didn't help much with their weight-loss plan.

KEY VITAMINS AND NUTRIENTS THAT BOOST YOUR SPIRITS

➤ **Get your fill of folate.** Of all the vitamins, folate is the one most closely associated with mood and depression. Harvard scientists have noted that up to 38% of adults diagnosed with depression have low or borderline levels of folate. Doctors have known for a long time that people with a form of anemia caused by low folate often suffer from depression. Folate even affects the action of antidepressant drugs, so much so that patients with low levels of folate don't do as well on medications as those with higher levels.

So far, no one's put his or her finger on the particular mechanism that makes folate so critical to mood. Researchers generally believe that it increases levels of serotonin as well as *melatonin*, another hormone involved in energy and mood. Folate is also used by the body to manufacture a variety of chemicals that keeps nerves healthy and repairs damage to the DNA within nerves. Melatonin is also critical to the sleep process.

Most people generally need only 400 micrograms (mcg) of folate daily. With regard to depression, as little as 200 mcg seems to be enough to make a difference. This is the amount found in a small (¾ cup) serving of spinach. Pumpkin seeds and sunflower seeds are also great sources of folate. In addition, they're high in essential fatty acids, so eat a

small handful instead of those packaged snacks loaded with unhealthy trans fats.

At the same time, try to eat more B-rich foods, and prepare them so that more of the crucial vitamins are preserved. Fresh vegetables have the most folate, particularly when they're consumed within a few days. Don't overcook leafy greens, because this destroys their vitamins. Quickly steam them in just a little water, then use the water in soups or stews to recapture the vitamins. (See page 95 for more information on B vitamins.)

Even though doctors advise patients to eat more vegetables, a lot of people don't. If you're one of them, and you're dealing with depression, here's an appealing option— Drink a glass of orange juice. Many juices are now fortified with folate.

➤ **Don't pass on the protein.** Even though carbs may be the first choice, people suffering from depression need protein, especially meat and dairy products, because these foods are the most plentiful source of vitamin B-12. This is important for brain function because deficiencies in B-12 are a common cause of depression and memory problems. Also called *cobalamin*, vitamin B-12 is used by the body to produce the myelin sheath that insulates nerve fibers. Once this coating starts to break down, people can experience memory loss, confusion and fatigue, accompanied by depression. In addition, since B-12 plays a vital role in the production of red blood cells, a deficiency in it can cause a severe condition known as *pernicious anemia*, which sends your energy levels plunging.

At a minimum, you need 2 mcg of vitamin B-12 daily to prevent depression and its symptoms, but the official recommended daily amount (RDA) is much lower. Once you reach your forties or fifties, however, you should increase that amount because the body's ability to absorb B-12 declines with age.

The best food sources for B-12 are seafood, eggs, lean meats and other animal products, including milk, yogurt and cheese. If you're a vegan, I strongly suggest you take a high-quality B-12 supplement (see page 95).

➤ **Have more turkey days.** Don't wait for Thanksgiving to enjoy the traditional holiday bird. Turkey and other lean meats are superb sources of *tryptophan*, the precursor to mood-calming serotonin. People who don't get enough tryptophan are more susceptible to depression. Until the late 1980s, it was possible to buy tryptophan supplements, which were widely used for insomnia as well as depression. However, the Food and Drug Administration withdrew the supplements from the market because a manufacturing error resulted in a tainted batch. Tryptophan itself is perfectly safe, particularly when you get it from dietary sources such as milk, yogurt, cheese, as well as almonds and pumpkin seeds.

➤ **Eat whole grains and bananas.** A study conducted by researchers at Harvard and Tufts University found that more than 25% of depressed patients were low in either vitamin B-6 or vitamin B-12. Other research indicates that up to 79% are low in B-6. Studies don't come across correlations like this by chance. It's obvious that B-6 is

doing something beneficial to keep mood elevated, although what it does isn't entirely clear to scientists yet. Because so many foods contain vitamin B-6, it's rare to find patients with outright deficiencies in the US, but there are millions of Americans who are borderline. And even slightly low levels can be enough to trigger depression.

How can you make sure you're getting enough of these vital brain nutrients? Bananas and whole-grain cereals are great sources of vitamin B-6, as is nearly every protein-rich food, including beans, fish and chicken, as well as leafy green vegetables such as spinach, kale and Swiss chard. Many processed foods are fortified with essential vitamins, but vitamin B-6 isn't likely to be among them. If you do nothing else, eat several servings of whole grains per day. Forget the white, bleached stuff: Up to 70% of vitamin B-6 is removed during milling and processing.

➤ **Brighten your brain with the sunshine vitamin.** Vitamin D, otherwise known as the sunshine vitamin because it's synthesized in the skin following sun exposure, is another nutrient that appears to increase serotonin. Not surprisingly, exposure to sunlight is one of the most effective approaches for easing *seasonal affective disorder* (SAD), a depression-like mood disorder that mainly occurs in the dark, winter months.

Experts estimate that some 10 million Americans suffer seasonal-related sadness, anxiety and depression. The lucky ones only feel down for a month or two, while others can suffer for up to half the year. SAD is thought to be related to the decline in vitamin D that occurs when people don't get enough sunshine, either because they spend winters indoors, or because they live in northern climates that don't deliver a lot of the sun's rays. Also, *always* using sunblock has been linked to vitamin D deficiency, so try to spend 20 minutes in the morning sun *without* sunblock to activate your vitamin D during every season. Studies show that individuals who typically have normal levels of vitamin D in the summer can suffer reductions of up to 30% or more during the dark winter months, often with SAD results.

Fortunately, vitamin D is one of the easiest nutrients to acquire. In addition to spending 10 to 20 minutes in the sun daily, eating foods that are rich in vitamin D (such as organ meats, dairy products and eggs) can keep you safe. You can also take a high-quality vitamin D supplement during times when you can't bask in the sunshine. Take at least 2,000 to 3,000 international units (IU) of a high-quality vitamin D-3 and double that if you are an African-American or over age 65. To read more about the benefits of vitamin D supplementation, see page 275.

FISH REALLY IS BRAIN FOOD

Doctors have noticed that people with low blood levels of *omega-3s*, the fatty acids found in cold-water fish and flaxseed, are more likely to be depressed than individuals with higher levels. As far back as 1998, an important epidemiological study published in the prestigious medical journal *Lancet* noted that rates of depression are higher in countries where people don't eat a lot of fish.

More recently, researchers put this to a clinical test. They divided patients with a history of depression into two groups, with one group receiving fish-oil supplements and the other a placebo. After four months, 50% of the patients on placebos suffered a relapse into depression, compared with fewer than 20% who were given fish oil.

These findings later were confirmed by scientists at the University of Pittsburgh, who noted that people with the highest levels of omega-3 in their blood are 53% less likely to experience depression. Research has also shown that people suffering from bipolar disorder have better control of their condition when they include fish oil along with their medications.

➤ **Fish on the brain.** In centuries past, humans consumed far more omega-3s than they do today because wild nuts, grains and animals (which have a much greater percentage of omega-3s than our poor feed-lot source of meat) made up the bulk of their diet. In fact, the ideal ratio of omega-3s to omega-6 fatty acids—the oils found in polyunsaturated vegetable oils and refined carbohydrates—is thought to be about 1:2. Today, the average ratio is closer to 1:20, which is way too much omega-6. Fifty percent of the fat in nerve tissue consists of omega-3s, which need to be replenished by our diets. This is one major reason why the rates of depression have increased by nearly 1,000% times in the last century.

Clearly, there's a reason for the high concentration of omega-3s in the brain. We already know that they help maintain healthy brain levels of serotonin, but I'm convinced that brain researchers will discover other benefits in the near future. In the meantime, eating a few servings of fish per week, taking fish oil supplements—or both—clearly have Prozac-like effects on clinical depression, as well as other emotional and mental problems. New research indicates that this boost in serotonin is not only helpful for garden-variety depression but also for postpartum depression and bipolar disorder.

What's the optimal level of omega-3s for depression? No one is quite sure. Studies indicate that a daily dose of about 650 milligrams (mg) of omega-3s, the equivalent of eating a serving of fish every other day, is enough to make a difference. In fact, as little as one weekly serving of omega-3-rich fish, such as salmon, herring, tuna or mackerel, might be enough to keep depression in check. However, since fish oil is beneficial for a number of other medical conditions in which inflammation is the driving force, you can safely double or triple that amount. For best results, take 2,000 to 3,000 mg twice per day. Fish and flaxseed are by far the best food sources of omega-3s. Get mood-boosting levels of these healthy fats by eating a few handfuls of walnuts daily. To see a list of the "10 Top Omega-3 Fish" and the "10 Top Omega-3 Plant Foods," turn to page 43.

➤ If you imbibe, take note. You should definitely eat more fish if you drink alcohol regularly. Alcohol depletes levels of omega-3s, which is undoubtedly one reason that up to 70% of alcoholics suffer from depression. Excessive alcohol consumption also promotes inflammation because it metabolizes to glucose quickly and produces as insulin responds. So, more omega-3s can chill the fires of inflammation in your cranium. (This inflammation has been linked to Alzheimer's,

90

Fatten Up Your Mood

Deficiencies in both vitamins D and E have been linked to depression and both are fat-soluble. This means they're difficult for the body to absorb unless you take them with a little fat. Don't let this frighten you if you're watching your weight. It doesn't take a lot of fat to do the trick. You can add a little half-and-half to your breakfast cereal, for example, or sprinkle a little extra-virgin olive oil on a seed-and-nut salad. There's no need to add the fat directly to the vitamin-rich foods. Just have a little fat with every meal.

memory loss, dementia and other mental dysfunction.)

Find more foods and recipes that fight depression at *www.myhealingkitchen.com*.

Foods That Make It Worse

We've all experienced the sugar blues at one time or another—that crash in energy and mood that often occurs when our sweet tooth has free reign. Actually, it's not just sugar that's doing the talking. Some people can eat sugary snacks without noticing a wrinkle in their moods. But others, for reasons that aren't clear, feel a mood crash after a single cookie or a scoop of ice cream. One study, at the University of South Alabama, examined a group of people with serious depression. They were advised to eliminate all sugar and caffeine from their diets. After just three weeks, their depression was significantly reduced.

It's not necessary, in most cases, for people to completely eliminate certain foods in order to feel better. However, anyone who's suffering from depression should be aware that some foods can potentially make their depression worse. Here are some suggestions.

GIVE UP "SIMPLE" SNACKS

Earlier, I explained how complex carbohydrates can increase brain levels of serotonin and keep them elevated. Quickie carbs, on the other hand, produce the opposite effect. Foods such as white bread, pastries and doughnuts, cookies and chips, snack foods, sodas and anything else that's high in sugar and low in fiber are absorbed almost instantly into the bloodstream, where they trigger an equally sudden surge in blood sugar (glucose), plus rapid rise in tryptophan and serotonin. The result is that you feel good after eating these foods, but the euphoria, known as a *sugar high*, doesn't last very long.

Because refined carbohydrates are absorbed and metabolized so rapidly, the effects wear off quickly, causing a rebound effect. Soon after eating them, many people experience low levels of blood sugar and serotonin, resulting in tiredness, the desire to sleep and a depressed mood, which is often called the *sugar blues*.

Americans like sugar. The average person in the US consumes about 175 pounds of it per year or about one full cup per day. And that doesn't include a tremendous amount of hidden sugars pervading the food supply. In fact, 25% of our total daily calories come from sweeteners, mainly in the form of *high fructose corn syrup* (HFCS). Forget for a moment what all of this sugar can do to your waistline, and focus on what it does to your moods.

When epidemiologists at the University of Texas Southwestern Medical Center investigated the relationship between mood and sugar consumption in six different countries, they discovered a close link. In New Zealand, where people tend to indulge their sweet tooth, the annual rate of depression of the entire population was 6%. Compare that to North Korea (where people eat relatively little sugar)—the incidence of depression was less than 2%.

➤ **Global toxin number one.** Ready for a shock? In the last 200 years, global sugar consumption has risen by more than 1,500%. There's no way that the human body can adapt to such a radical dietary change in a relatively short span of time. The sharp spike in so many modern metabolic diseases is a direct result of our massive consumption of sugar and refined carbohydrates.

Sugar, whether you're spooning it into your coffee or consuming it in the form of sodas or snacks, causes a quick sugar rush, followed by an equally sudden dip in blood sugar, called *hypoglycemia*, as extra insulin is called forth to remove glucose from the bloodstream. We all are familiar with the resulting listless, sleepy feeling sometimes referred to as *midday slump*. Studies show that up to 77% of people who experience hypoglycemia also suffer from depression.

➤ **Your brain on sugar.** Your brain comprises only 2% of your total body weight, but it gobbles 30% of the calories you take in. It needs a steady supply of glucose to function and, because it can't produce its own glucose, it relies on dietary sugar. In other words, your brain craves glucose. But "sugar is good for the brain only if it comes from complex carbohydrates that are released slowly," says Dharma Singh Khalsa, M.D., president and medical director of the Alzheimer's Prevention Foundation International, and author of the best-selling book *Brain Longevity*. This is because when the brain is working properly, it uses sugar very quickly for its fuel. If glucose levels run low, brain function can take a dip, causing you to feel tired and groggy. "Refined carbohydrates and sugars cause your blood glucose levels to swing wildly," Dr. Khalsa says. In other words, these foods create a sugar high followed quickly by a sugar crash.

➤ **Roller-coaster mood swings.** "Sugar sensitivity turns a person into Dr. Jekyll and Mr. Hyde," writes Kathleen DesMaisons, Ph.D., in her bestselling book *Potatoes, Not Prozac*. These intense mood swings are like a roller-coaster ride soaring uncontrollably from high to low. Many researchers believe that sugar is every bit as addictive as alcohol and other intoxicating substances, creating a very real dependence in the brain and leading to feelings of misery, hopelessness and unhappiness when it is removed. To see if this is happening to you, keep a journal of what you eat and how you feel afterward. Kicking the sugar habit isn't always easy, but it's worth the effort because it can save your sanity, your relationships and your health.

➤ **How sugar affects your memory.** Recent studies are providing new insights into how sugar affects the brain. In pioneering research published in the *Proceedings of the National Academy of Sciences*, researchers administered a concentrated sugar drink as

part of a Glucose Tolerance Test to a group of healthy, nondiabetic people, then gave them a memory test. Results showed that those people who did not process blood sugar normally performed worse on the test than those who had normal blood-sugar control. In addition, computed tomography (CT) scans of their brains showed that the people who processed sugar poorly had a significantly smaller hippocampus, the part of the brain responsible for memory and learning. This shows that the longer glucose stays in the bloodstream after a meal, the less it is able to reach the brain, resulting in problems with cognitive function (in this case memory).

These results are confirmed by 25 other medical studies showing that diabetics have more problems with memory and learning function than the general population. However, even in nondiabetics, studies show that elevated blood sugar levels affect memory adversely. As one researcher summarized, "We found that those who didn't metabolize their sugar normally performed worse on the memory tests." (For more information, see "Memory" on page 228.)

➤ **Free radicals love sugar.** Studies conducted at the State University of New York at Buffalo reveal that eating sugary foods and quickie carbs produces a deluge of harmful free radicals, while also lowering levels of vitamin E that might otherwise prevent the oxidation that creates them. Researchers have linked free-radical damage in brain cells as a major cause of Alzheimer's disease. The lead researcher of the study, Paresh Dandona, M.D., Ph.D., a distinguished professor and expert on endocrinology and diabetes, states that for the first time it is now established that sugar consumption increases free-radical production. "Long-term diabetes leads to a decline in cognitive abilities due to the free-radical generation and inflammation," he comments.

➤ **Save your brain now.** There can be no doubt that excessive sugar consumption is harmful to the brain and its functions, as well as every other important organ and metabolic system. I don't think there's any doubt that our collective sweet tooth plays a major role in the dementia that plagues more than four million Americans over age 65. That's a scary statistic, but predictions for the future are even more frightening. According to the National Institute on Aging and Alzheimer's Disease Education estimates, another 14 million Americans will be stricken with dementia by 2050.

To save your brain, start adding more brightly colored, antioxidant-rich vegetables and fruits to your diet, along with foods high in omega-3 fatty acids such as non-farm-raised fish, flaxseed and walnuts, whole grains and legumes and grass-fed, free-range animal protein. Getting sufficient sleep, handling the stress in your life, plus regular physical activity, will also preserve and improve your brain function. And whatever you do, cut back as far as you possibly can on sugary foods and refined carbs. They are, quite literally, brain killers.

CONSIDER THE PICK-ME-UPS YOU DRINK

➤ **Watch your caffeine.** Are you a caffeine junkie? Welcome to the crowd. Americans slurp an astonishing one billion cups of coffee in an average week. That's in addition to the 4.5 billion caffeinated soft drinks we drink every week. A little caffeine isn't a bad thing. In fact, studies show that people who consume moderate amounts of caffeine have improvements in short-term memory. And, believe it or not, coffee is surprisingly high in antioxidants. It's one of the leading sources of antioxidants in the American diet. However, if you're troubled by depression, even low doses of caffeine—as little as 30 mg, or the amount in a cup—of espresso—can produce negative, mood-altering effects. Believe it or not, the average American adult consumes almost 10 times this amount.

Too much caffeine isn't good for sleep, and fatigue and depression are common bedfellows. Curiously enough, animal studies indicate that caffeine *raises* brain levels of tryptophan but lowers levels of serotonin. It's possible that caffeine somehow decreases the body's ability to convert one to the other, which explains why people who consume too much caffeine experience an increase in depression. I'm not suggesting that you give up caffeine altogether, but if you're suffering from fatigue or depression, limiting your intake to one or two cups per day just makes sense.

➤ **Drink lightly.** In moderation, alcohol has been shown by numerous studies to be beneficial for the heart and arteries. People who drink moderately actually score better on several measures of mood than people who never drink. That's the good news. The other side of the coin is that alcohol affects the same parts of the brain that are involved in depressive symptoms. In fact, a large percentage of

93

heavy drinkers regularly experience depression. Even the occasional binge can make depressive symptoms worse. Furthermore, alcohol depletes omega-3s from nerve tissue, which can easily contribute to long-term depression. It only takes a few drinks to sink your body's reserves of omega-3s.

The bottom line is pretty simple. If you're dealing with depression, you should definitely cut back on alcohol consumption. Experimenting with not drinking at all might be a wise choice if you're one of those people who consistently feel emotionally down after raising your glass.

Supplemental Help

A number of natural remedies, including certain vitamins, minerals and herbs, have been shown to play a significant role in fighting depression. In some cases, these remedies can be combined with medications, or for those with minor depression, they can be taken alone. There's an important caveat: Some natural products can change the effects of prescription drugs. So if you're already taking medication for depression, check with your doctor before adding any of these natural remedies to the mix.

➤ **St. John's wort works.** St. John's wort, a traditional herbal remedy for depression, is prescribed by European doctors as frequently as Prozac. Europeans generally look more favorably on herbal treatments than do Americans, and their fondness for St. John's wort is based on solid science. It's clearly as effective against mild to moderate depression as prescription drugs. *Hypericin*,

the active chemical compound in St. John's wort, elevates brain levels of serotonin in the same way most antidepressants do. In a study published in *British Medical Journal*, researchers analyzed the results of 23 published studies that involved more than 1,000 depressed patients. They concluded that St. John's wort does in fact work and is much less likely than pharmaceutical drugs to cause side effects, including reduced libido and poor sleep.

Numerous double-blind clinical trials confirm that St. John's wort is effective for mild-to-moderate depression. In some instances, the herb works even better than drugs, although it isn't strong enough for serious cases. In case you're in the mild-to-moderate category, the recommended dose is 300 mg twice daily. If your mood doesn't start to lift within a week, it's fine to increase the dose to 600 or even 900 mg. Despite its favorable safety profile, St. John's wort does have powerful effects. For example, it can change the ways in which the body metabolizes certain drugs, including oral contraceptives, cyclosporine, theophylline and even other antidepressants. If you're taking any other drugs, talk to your doctor before starting treatment with St. John's wort.

➤ **Sample some SAMe.** In the last few years, there have been a lot of reports about SAMe (*s-adenosyl-methionine*), a substance that occurs naturally in the body that is thought to play an important role in the production of serotonin and other neurotransmitters. We're not yet sure exactly how it works, but people who take it report a significant improvement in their mood.

Start with 200 mg daily, slowly increasing the dose to 400 mg over a period of weeks. Divide the doses to prevent stomach upset.

➤ **Boost your Bs.** The majority of people barely get enough B vitamins in their diets, which can result in real problems with depression. Even marginal deficiencies of B vitamins can produce subtle changes in your mood. If you're suffering from depression, make sure to eat plenty of vitamin B-rich foods and take a B-complex supplement. Look for a supplement that provides 800 mcg of folic acid, 50 to 100 mg of vitamin B-6 and at least 500 mcg of vitamin B-12. For more information on how you can get more B vitamins in your food, see page 254. For a list of the "10 Top Folate-Rich Foods," see page 234.

All the B vitamins are thought to play some role in mood, although folate and vitamin B-12 have been studied the most. One study examined patients who had been hospitalized for severe depression. Subsequent tests showed that about 30% of them were low in vitamin B-12. Other studies indicate that people with low levels of vitamin B-12 were about twice as likely to be depressed as those with normal levels. This deficiency can be significantly higher in vegans.

➤ **Slip in some selenium.** The mineral selenium has gotten a lot of attention in recent years because it is a powerful antioxidant that's been shown to protect the cardiovascular system as well as the prostate gland. More recently, scientists have learned that this trace mineral can also help control depression, in part because it's used by the body to produce *glutathione*, a superantioxidant that fortifies the brain. Studies have found that people who don't get enough selenium in their diets are more likely to experience depressive symptoms. For improving mood, the recommended supplemental dose is 100 to 200 mcg daily. For a list of the "12 Top Selenium-Rich Foods," see page 311.

➤ **Fish in a pill.** The omega-3 fatty acids in cold-water fish are among the most powerful dietary allies for fighting depression. Many Americans, however, don't eat a lot of fish. An alternative is to take fish oil capsules. Look for a product that contains at least 220 mg of DHA (one of the omega-3s) and 200 mg of EPA. In research studies on serious depression, scientists tend to use doses as high as 3,000 mg, although the lower dose has been shown to be effective, especially if you combine supplements with a few delicious fish meals every week. For a list of the "10 Top Omega-3 Fish" and "10 Top Omega-3 Plant Foods," see page 43.

➤ **Try the multitasker 5-hydroxy-tryptophan (5-HTP).** The supplement 5-HTP converts the amino acid tryptophan into other compounds such as serotonin and melatonin. If your depression is caused by serotonin deficiency, it can help balance your mood, as well as help with sleep. It also aids in weight loss by satisfying the serotonin craving in the brain that triggers hunger and oversnacking. Dosages of 5-HTP greater than 100 mg per day should be taken only under the guidance of a physician.

Other Helpers and Healers

➤ **Sniff some cinnamon.** The nasal membranes readily absorb odor molecules, some of which produce druglike effects on the brain, nervous system and body. Cinnamon is particularly good for people coping with depression because the aromatized molecules have been shown to trigger the release of antidepressant neurotransmitters. In fact, a number of studies show that smelling cinnamon can help reduce stress, as well as depression. You can buy an essential oil that can be added to bathwater or mixed in massage oil. A less expensive option is to simmer a few cinnamon sticks in a pan of water and inhale the scent for three minutes or less. Walk away for a while, then come back for another dose, as the therapeutic effects are enhanced by getting the scent in bursts.

➤ **Perk up with dark chocolate.** People crave all sorts of foods when they're feeling down, but chocolate is in a class by itself. For most women, chocolate holds a particular allure, especially during certain days before a menstrual period. One of the chemical compounds in chocolate, *phenylethylamine*, increases levels of endorphins, the same substances that produce the euphoric, so-called runner's high. In addition to its effects on feel-better endorphins, chocolate stimulates the body's production of nitric oxide, a naturally occurring gas that dilates blood vessels and enhances circulation—important for brain health, as well as mood.

Chocolate is also rich in antioxidants, which adds to its mental and physical benefits. A study at Brigham and Women's Hospital in Boston found that women who drank a cup of hot chocolate experienced a 33% increase in blood circulation within the brain. Dark, organic chocolate with a high cocoa content has

almost double the antioxidant load of milk chocolate. Don't bother with white chocolate, as it has no medicinal value.

➤ **Get enough iron.** It used to be called *iron-poor blood*, but now we refer to it as anemia. Whatever you call it, iron deficiency persists as one of the most common nutritional deficiencies in the US. Some people don't get enough iron in their diets, but more often they lose more iron than they take in. This frequently occurs in women who experience heavy menstrual cycles, or in men and women suffering from unidentified internal bleeding, due to an ulcer, for example. Symptoms of iron deficiency include fatigue, poor concentration and sometimes depression. The good news is that depleted iron is easy to replace. In one study, women experiencing postpartum depression recovered quickly when they were given supplemental iron. However, iron supplements should only be taken under a doctor's supervision. Studies show that too much iron can be bad for the heart and is a risk factor for heart disease. Yet supplements are rarely necessary because you usually can get all the iron you need from food sources. Make sure you eat iron-rich foods along with those rich in vitamin C, because it will help your body better absorb the iron. A list of the foods highest in iron is on page 97.

➤ **Get moving.** In addition to a healthy diet, regular exercise is one of the best ways to prevent, relieve and reverse depression. The psychological effects alone are worth it. Studies show that people who exercise tend to feel stronger and more confident. However, that's not the only way exercise helps. People who exercise experience almost immediate increases in *endorphins*, brain chemicals that produce feelings of well-being. Exercise also increases circulation and pumps extra oxygen throughout the body, including to the brain—and more oxygen means more nutrients.

How much exercise is enough? Scientists used to believe that people had to exercise regularly before experiencing the mood-raising benefits. However, new research indicates that it can happen almost immediately. In a study at the University of Texas, patients with depression worked out on treadmills or stationary bikes for 30 minutes, three to five times a week. The results were impressive. Their depression symptoms were reduced by 50%, which compares well to the improvements achieved by psychiatric drugs. And it didn't take tough workouts to get these benefits. Even those who exercised at less intense levels, like doing stretching or yoga, were able to reduce their symptoms by nearly 30%.

➤ **Eat often.** Since low blood sugar is a common cause of fatigue, irritability and mood changes, it's essential to eat regularly so that your brain has a steady supply of glucose. Don't skip meals. People struggling

---

10 Top Food Sources of Iron

1. Red meat
2. Egg yolks
3. Dark, leafy greens
4. Dried prunes, raisins, apricots, dates
5. Iron-enriched cereals and grains (check the labels)
6. Oysters, clams, scallops
7. Turkey or chicken giblets
8. Beans, lentils, chickpeas and soybeans
9. Calf's liver
10. Artichokes

---

with depression need to eat at least once every couple of hours to keep their brain supplied. The idea isn't to pack in a lot of calories between meals, but merely to keep your blood sugar at steady levels. The ideal foods for this are complex carbohydrates, such as fruits and vegetables, a smidge of healthy fat such as a wedge of cheese or cup of yogurt and a bit of high-quality protein. When you're snacking between meals, avoid chips and cookies or quickie carb foods such as candy or energy bars. Instead, have an apple with a small handful of nuts. ■

7

Diabetes

Every time you eat carbohydrates, your body breaks them down into various sugar molecules. The main one is *glucose*. Glucose is the fuel your cells use for energy; when it is in your blood, it is known as *serum glucose*, or blood sugar. During digestion, glucose seeps through the intestinal wall and enters the bloodstream. However, cells can't take in glucose to be converted to fuel without the help of *insulin*. A hormone that basically escorts glucose from the bloodstream into the body's cells, insulin is produced by the pancreas. Insulin is released into the bloodstream whenever the pancreas senses that glucose levels are rising, particularly after meals, so more cells open up to let in the fuel they need.

Type 2 diabetes—by far the most common type of this disease—begins when your cells don't respond to insulin efficiently. This

inefficiency is marked by a fasting blood sugar reading of 126 milligrams per deciliter (mg/DL) and a reading of 200 mg/DL on a glucose tolerance test. Nutritionist Jonny Bowden likens it to being in Times Square, where the noise level is so high that you have to shout more and more loudly to be heard. When glucose levels are consistently elevated, it means that insulin isn't working well enough and it has to knock louder and louder on the doors of your cells. In other words, the pancreas makes more of it. When cells don't open up in the presence of insulin, they have what is called *insulin resistance*. This is the first stage of type 2 diabetes and when this happens, cells don't get enough glucose. As a result, patients will experience various symptoms such as fatigue and dizziness. If glucose is completely locked out, patients can suffer much more drastic complications, such as thirst, severe nutrient loss, infections and even diabetic coma.

Elevated blood glucose levels can also cause excessive urination. Through this loss of water, sugar becomes even more concentrated in the blood, and concentrated glucose is a toxin that can damage the heart, eyes, kidneys, blood vessels and other organs. Excess sugar in the blood also combines with protein and greatly increases oxidation and free-radical production, which speeds up the aging process. This is why people with diabetes often look much older than their biological age. These massive amounts of free radicals wrinkle the skin and damage the body's tissue and organs. Given enough time, elevated glucose in the bloodstream causes permanent damage. Eventually, the pancreas becomes exhausted from pumping out so much insulin and simply halts production, necessitating regular injections of synthetic insulin. At this point, type 2 diabetes has officially set in.

Diabetes is one of the most serious and widespread diseases of the modern, industrialized era. More than 24 million Americans already have type 2 diabetes, and it is three times more common now than it was just a generation ago. Experts predict that one in three children born since the year 2000 will develop full-blown type 2 diabetes in his or her lifetime.

And the statistics get worse. As many as 147 million Americans, or one-half of the US population, already have some form of blood sugar malfunction, either diagnosed or yet to be uncovered. That means the odds might be as high as 50-50 that you or someone you know are included in this figure.

SYMPTOMS

One of the most frightening things about diabetes is that it typically displays no symptoms in its early stages. Nearly one-third of people with diabetes aren't even aware they have it. Before symptoms become apparent, serious harm is being done to nerves, blood vessels and organs. Many patients with type 2 diabetes have the disease for nine to 12 years prior to diagnosis. By the time they are finally diagnosed, most have already suffered damage to the small blood vessels, which impairs circulation and deprives the body of adequate nutrition. That's why diabetes is called a *wasting disease*—when untreated, the body can literally starve even though there is plenty of food.

Telltale signs of impending diabetes are excessive thirst and hunger, along with frequent urination. Diabetics are often chronically hungry because sufficient levels of glucose aren't getting into cells or to their brain, thus creating ravenous cravings—usually for carbohydrates. The excess sugar that is not metabolized is stored as fat, which is why it is extremely easy for those with diabetes to gain weight. Fatigue is another common symptom. Some people also experience blurred vision, frequent infections or slow wound healing due to poor circulation.

The American Diabetes Association (ADA) recommends regular diabetes screenings beginning at age 45, but adults with identified risk factors, such as obesity, hypertension or a family history of the disease,

99

should start testing at age 30. Diabetes can be diagnosed with an oral glucose tolerance test, in which blood sugar is tested after an overnight fast, then again after the patient consumes a glucose solution.

Early testing and diagnosis are critical. Diabetes greatly increases the risk of cardiovascular disease, nerve disease and various infections. People with uncontrolled diabetes will experience significantly shorter life spans, as they are likely to die from its complications.

CAUSES

The most serious type of diabetes, known as type 1 or juvenile-onset, is a less common form of the disease. It occurs when the pancreas makes little or no insulin. People with this form of diabetes require regular insulin injections to survive. Type 1 diabetes is an autoimmune disease. In other words, it is caused by a malfunction in the immune system, in which the body's immune cells attack and destroy its own insulin-producing cells. The vast majority of patients with type 1 diabetes have antibodies to pancreatic beta cells. No one knows what causes the malfunction, but the final onset of type 1 diabetes is often preceded by the presence of a simple respiratory virus.

Far more common is type 2 diabetes. It accounts for up to 95% of all cases and is frequently linked to excess weight. Ninety percent of those with type 2 diabetes are overweight or obese, and carry a large proportion of belly fat. The good news is that type 2 diabetes—unlike type 1—is almost completely preventable through a combination of good nutrition and physical activity. A 16-year Harvard study of 84,000 women found that the
100

vast majority of people can lower their risk of type 2 diabetes by up to 91% with simple lifestyle changes—most notably, losing weight.

More than any other single factor, overconsumption of refined carbohydrates (including sugar and white flour) is responsible for the sudden explosion of type 2 diabetes around the world today. This intake leads directly to weight gain and abdominal obesity. Insulin resistance usually results, followed by impaired glucose tolerance. The end result is diabetes.

TREATMENT

Many diabetics must take supplemental insulin and other medications to help the pancreas release insulin. Some drugs stimulate the pancreas to produce more insulin, while others make the body's cells more sensitive to insulin's effects or reduce the amount of glucose that's released from the liver. However, these drugs come with enormous risks. In fact, the US government suddenly halted a major study of diabetes and heart disease after an unexpected number of participants died. The study had used aggressive drug therapy to push blood sugar down to extremely low levels. Eighteen months before the end of the trial, researchers discovered that the intensive drug strategy was not only ineffective, but increased the risk of death when compared with a more standard, less-intensive drug regimen.

Many people now are being diagnosed as prediabetic (when fasting blood sugar is 100 or higher). Frequently, diabetes drugs are prescribed, even at this early stage. There is much evidence confirming that diet and lifestyle changes provide better protection, whether you're prediabetic, diabetic or simply at risk for diabetes. Such changes address the underlying cause of type 2 diabetes and can also improve other aspects of your overall health.

So what's the first step? If you are overweight, the most important thing you can do is to immediately and dramatically lower your weight. Right now, two out of three Americans are overweight, and half that number is obese. The connection between weight and diabetes is so strong that doctors have coined a new term, *diabesity,* to describe it. According to researchers directing the long-running Nurses' Health Study, being overweight is the single most important factor in the development of diabetes. Losing just 10% of your total weight can reduce your risk for diabetes by up to 60%. A Finnish study of more than 500 overweight men found that those who lost as little as 10 pounds reduced their diabetes risk by 58% on average.

People tend to think of fat as inert body weight, but it is actually quite dangerous. Fat cells secrete hormonelike substances that are highly inflammatory, especially in abdominal fat. Inflammation is the activation of the immune system in response to infection, irritation, or injury. It can have different names when it appears in different parts of the body—for example, when it is the joints, it is called arthritis; when it affects the sinuses, it is known as sinusitis. When inflammation persists and the immune system is always activated, it is known as chronic inflammation and it can lead to chronic disease of the organs involved. In type 2 diabetes, chronic inflammation makes cells more resistant to insulin. What's more, excess weight makes all cells more resistant to insulin. People who are apple shaped, with most of their weight around the middle, have a much higher risk of developing insulin resistance and diabetes.

Diabetes is a metabolic disorder that affects nearly every organ in the body, including the brain. It often goes hand-in-hand with other health problems, such as high cholesterol and blood pressure, and many patients are put on drugs to control these problems. There is no known cure for type 1 diabetes, which occurs when the immune system destroys the cells that make insulin. Type 1 patients must take insulin injections for the rest of their lives.

Type 2 diabetes, however, can be managed and sometimes reversed by strict lifestyle changes alone, including weight loss, a low-fat, low-glycemic diet and exercise, but those changes must be sustained throughout the patient's life to avoid reversal and deterioration. Bariatric surgery (stomach stapling), which produces dramatic weight loss, offers medical assistance, but even then patients must maintain their weight and monitor themselves. Doctors can only try their best to manage a patient's symptoms and delay the deterioration that slowly destroys the body. I know this from personal experience because, as a young man, I watched my mother suffer from this cruel disease. The helplessness I felt as I watched her waste away motivated me to redirect my medical career. Seeing her experience, I began the study and use of therapeutic nutrition to reverse diabetes and other medical conditions, ones for which drugs and surgery fail to provide any significant healing.

Foods That Make It Better

Modern medicine isn't going to bail us out of the current diabetes crisis. There are simply no silver bullets or miracle cures on the horizon—but the tools you need to control your blood sugar, escape diabetes and its complications and possibly even reverse the disease are here right now.

Better diet and weight control are the only ways to reverse the condition. My Mediterr-Asian Diet plan, combined with a simple program of walking, can help you achieve both these goals. Many of the foods in this plan are ideal for people who already have diabetes. The omega-3 fatty acids in fish, for example, help reduce arterial inflammation and reduce the risk of heart disease, one of the main complications of diabetes. The carbohydrates in this diet are the healthy kind, containing plenty of fiber, so they require less insulin from the body. Years of data from some of the largest, most-comprehensive studies indicate that people with diabetes who eat like this can manage both insulin resistance and elevated glucose. Here are some specific foods that directly improve glucose control.

BE CARB SMART

If you're dealing with diabetes, you have to be carb smart. Munch a quickie carb and it will spike your blood sugar in minutes. By quickie carbs, I mean *refined carbohydrates*—foods that have had their beneficial fiber removed during processing. Refined carbs are

everywhere today. They include white-flour products such as breads and pasta, processed foods such as potato chips, crackers, soft drinks, fruit juices, most breakfast cereals, and all foods containing sugar or corn syrup.

Smart carbs, on the other hand, are digested slowly and release their sugars into your bloodstream at a slow, steady pace, because they haven't had their beneficial fiber removed. Smart carbs are found in unrefined, whole foods that remain in their original form or close to it, such as fruits, vegetables, beans, nuts, seeds and whole grains. These foods are powerful disease fighters, as well as being ideal for weight loss and insulin control. Quickie carbs require more insulin; smart carbs minimize your need for it—and keep the damaging effects of excess glucose out of your bloodstream. Foods high in sugars cause the fastest swings in blood sugar. Complex carbohydrates, such as vegetables and whole grains, are much better choices.

➤ **Make small changes.** Being carb smart doesn't mean you have to turn your diet topsy-turvy. Research demonstrates that simply choosing a few smart carbs over a couple of quickie carbs each day can deliver significant health improvements. A Harvard Medical School study tracked more than 40,000 men and found that choosing whole-grain bread, substituting brown rice for white and changing from a sugary breakfast cereal to oatmeal reduced their diabetes risk by more than 40%. Another study discovered that eating brown rice instead of a baked potato just once a week reduced the risk for type 2 diabetes by up to 30%. These are big rewards that resulted from a couple of small changes.

➤ **The carbo-rater.** How can you tell a good carb from a bad one? The Glycemic Index (GI) is a good place to start.* The GI is a numerical rating system that measures the blood sugar response to certain foods—in other words, how quickly the foods convert to glucose. A food with a high number, such as white bread, will cause blood glucose to shoot up quickly and requires extra insulin from the pancreas to process it. In general, white foods (white bread, white pasta and white potatoes) have higher GI scores. A food with a low number, such as oat bran, will cause only a slight rise. These low-GI carbs are ideal for glucose control. With a little practice, you won't need a chart to point you to the good carbs and away from the bad. For instance, you can safely assume that foods that have undergone the least processing— that is, foods in their more natural state—are going to have lower GI scores than foods such as crackers, chips, candy and even energy bars. When in doubt, go for foods with the brightest natural colors and highest fiber content. Avoid the white foods.

➤ **Put yourself on a carb budget.** Since glucose control is critical whether you have diabetes or not, it's a good idea to eat roughly the same amount of carbohydrates every day. If you decide to really pack in the carbs during a Sunday morning breakfast of pancakes, hash browns or bagels, or if you let yourself go hungry because you're

late for work one day, your blood sugar will roller-coaster. If you have diabetes and do this, your medications won't work efficiently. Worse, these swings in blood sugar can damage your nerves, blood vessels and organs. Be consistent—and make the most of your carbohydrate choices by choosing smart carbs.

Portion size counts, too. The good thing about complex carbohydrates is that its pretty difficult for them to send your blood sugar levels out of whack. That's one of the beauties of making vegetables the center of your diet. Bite for bite, vegetables—and to a lesser extent, whole grains—provide more nutrients and fiber with fewer calories than any other food group. This not only makes managing your blood sugar much easier, but it helps you control the amount of food you take in without allowing you to feel hungry.

FABULOUS FIBER

The most important difference between good carbohydrates and bad is how quickly the carbohydrate is broken down into glucose by your body. In other words, the speed with which a carb breaks down depends upon the amount of fiber it contains. There are two types of fiber, and they're both all-stars at helping you manage your blood sugar, regardless of whether you have diabetes. *Insoluble fiber* is the roughage component of vegetables, fruits and grains that fills you up without causing weight gain because it contains no calories. That's extremely important for people with diabetes, because weight loss lowers insulin resistance, permitting the naturally occurring insulin in your body to lower your blood sugar more effectively. For people on diabetes

---

*For an extensive Glycemic Index database, visit *www.glycemicindex.com* and click "GI Database" in the left column.

medication, weight loss drives down blood sugar, which can help them cut back on the amount of diabetes drugs they take, or even halt them altogether.

Soluble fiber, found in oatmeal, oat bran, seeds and beans, turns into a sticky gel when you digest it, trapping cholesterol and other fats so that they can't clog your bloodstream. Eating foods high in soluble fiber delays the rate at which your stomach empties, slowing the digestion of sugars and starches, while controlling blood sugar spikes. Like insoluble fiber, soluble fiber drives down cholesterol levels and the risk for heart disease. Studies have shown that for every 10 grams (g) of soluble fiber that you eat, you lower your LDL cholesterol levels by 5%.

A UCLA study dramatically illustrates how fiber foods can lower coronary heart disease (CHD) risk. CHD is characterized by plaque buildup in the arteries that can result in heart attack. Diabetics have a higher risk of CHD because high blood glucose levels lead to fatty deposits on the insides of the blood vessel walls. Researchers placed a group of obese men on a high-fiber diet for three weeks. They were allowed to eat as much food as they wanted, as long as 75% of it came from fiber-rich fruits, vegetables and whole grains. The participants also walked for 45 to 60 minutes daily. At the study's conclusion, the men displayed remarkable improvements. Total cholesterol fell by almost 20% on average. Of the men who had high blood pressure at the beginning of the study, none had it at the end. Blood sugar and insulin levels dropped by 7% and 46%, respectively. These are exceptional results,

10 Top Fiber Foods

Work these foods into your meals regularly, starting your day with a bowl of oatmeal with ground flaxseed or a fiber-rich fruit smoothie that contains a quarter teaspoon of cinnamon. For lunch or dinner, open and drain a can of beans or chickpeas and dress with extra-virgin olive oil and vinegar. Add raw chopped veggies or apples and a small handful of nuts. You won't believe how filling these fiber foods can be.

1.	Ground psyllium	700 g/cup
2.	Ground flaxseed	30 g/cup
3.	Almonds	28 g/cup
4.	Beans	19 g/cup
5.	Oat bran	15 g/cup
6.	Raspberries	8 g/cup
7.	Sweet potato	8 g/cup
8.	Pumpkin seeds	5 g/cup
9.	Apple	4 g/cup
10.	Grapefruit	4 g/cup

unrivaled by drug therapy. You can achieve the same benefits by consuming a minimum of 40 g of fiber daily and upping your physical activity. That's an easy task with my Mediterr-Asian Diet, because the healing recipes in this book are loaded with health-building fiber. In addition, take a look at "10 Top Fiber Foods" above for selections to include in your diet every day.

GREAT GRAINS

If you already have diabetes, whole-grain foods such as steel-cut oats, brown rice and quinoa can help you avoid dangerous blood sugar swings. Diabetic or not, everyone should eat more whole grains. One study involving 65,000 adults found that those who ate the most whole grains were only about half as likely to get diabetes as those who ate the least.

Whole grains are great because they contain more nutrients than white rice, white bread or other refined grains, plus they have lots more fiber. Since fiber slows the absorption of glucose into the bloodstream, eating fiber-rich foods is the direct route to better glucose control. Whole grains also make cells more sensitive and responsive to insulin's effects. (Remember, you want your cells to be insulin-*sensitive*, not insulin-resistant.)

As terrific as vegetables are, the fiber in whole grains works in a curiously different way from the fiber in fruits and vegetables. James Anderson, M.D., one of the early pioneers in fiber research, found that people who consumed most of their fiber from wheat, oats and other cereal grains reduced their chances of getting diabetes by more than 30%. Other studies, including one that looked at 43,000 health professionals, found that those who ate the most whole grains reduced their risk by up to 41%. Here are some practical ways to benefit from the unique whole-grain advantage.

➤ **Golden oats.** Both oatmeal and oat bran are high in fiber, including a type called *beta-glucan*, which slows the passage of sugars into the bloodstream and puts less strain on insulin-producing cells. Studies show that people who eat oats tend to have slower and steadier releases of blood sugar, compared with those who eat refined carbohydrates such as white bread and pasta.

➤ **Try rye.** Like oats, rye triggers a less sudden insulin response than refined carbs. In addition to its fiber load, rye is unusually high in protein. Its unique mix of protein and carbohydrates seems to be ideal for diabetes control.

➤ **Whip up some buckwheat pancakes.** Despite its name, buckwheat is not a type of wheat, but rather a seed related to sorrel and rhubarb. People with wheat sensitivities often eat buckwheat as a grain substitute because it has many of the beneficial effects of whole grains but without the gluten found in wheat. Oklahoma scientists found that people who regularly ate buckwheat pancakes tended to have lower blood sugar surges after meals. Their pancreas didn't have to churn out as much insulin, which is important for diabetes control as well as prevention.

THE CHROMIUM SOLUTION

Antioxidant vitamins like C and E get all the glory, but unglamorous and under-the-radar minerals are vital to good health, too, especially for people with blood sugar problems. One of these minerals, chromium, is essential for helping the insulin you have to process sugar more efficiently. It does this by making your cells less insulin resistant. Unfortunately, 90% of Americans are estimated to be deficient in chromium. People with diabetes, who need chromium the most, lead the pack.

Certain foods are chromium rich, such as romaine lettuce and other leafy greens. If you have diabetes, prediabetes or any blood sugar concerns, I recommend that you eat

10 Top Food Sources of Chromium	
1. Brewer's yeast	112 mcg/¾ cup
2. Beef	57 mcg/¾ cup
3. Calf's liver	55 mcg/¾ cup
4. Egg yolk	183 mcg/¾ cup
5. Sweet potato	35 mcg/each
6. Onions	24 mcg/cup
7. Oysters	14 mcg/¾ cup
8. Basil, fresh	16 mcg/cup
9. Tomato	9 mcg/cup
10. Romaine lettuce	8 mcg/cup

one or more servings of the high-chromium foods listed above and perhaps take a supplement. The same foods are equally effective for the prevention of diabetes. This means that those who already have diabetes and a diminished supply of insulin can still keep blood glucose where it should be by getting more chromium through foods, supplements or both. There's even some evidence that whole grains can protect the insulin-producing (islet) cells in the pancreas.

➤ **Opt for extra onions.** You can make a fresh green salad even better by adding plenty of onions. Like leafy greens, onions are high in chromium. Studies have shown that people with diabetes who eat more onions tend to have lower fasting blood glucose levels. They also have lower LDL cholesterol and triglycerides, the blood fats that increase the risk of heart disease. In addition to their high chromium content, onions contain a chemical compound, *allyl propyl disulfide*, which in-

106

creases the amount of available insulin in your body to lower blood sugar after meals.

DISCOVER DIABETES-FIGHTING VEGETABLES AND FORMERLY FORBIDDEN FOODS

➤ **Add some artichoke hearts.** Artichokes contain a type of carbohydrate known as *inulin*, which has been shown to improve blood sugar in patients with diabetes. Artichokes also contain liver-supporting *phytonutrients* (nutrients from plants), which all of us need, particularly diabetics.

➤ **This spud's for you.** Americans have a love affair with potatoes, particularly when they're mashed, baked or deep fried. Unfortunately, none of these choices will help your blood sugar, because white potatoes have a relatively high GI rating, meaning they convert into glucose rapidly.

Nutritionists have a love-hate relationship with the average spud. On the one hand, white potatoes are loaded with magnesium, potassium and vitamin C. On the other hand, their high ranking on the GI scale should put them off-limits for people with diabetes, according to some experts. My advice is to enjoy them occasionally and healthfully—baked or boiled instead of served as French fries. And hold the sour cream and butter, or at least be moderate. Try healthful accompaniments such as steamed broccoli or roasted red peppers. Or you can slather a small baked potato with pesto. Eating the fiber-rich skin lowers the GI rating considerably. Just make sure you scrub it well before baking.

The sweet potato is another story. It contains twice as much fiber as white spuds, which significantly slows their transformation into glucose. Studies show that sweet potatoes also make insulin work more efficiently. Much has been made of the sweet potato's antidiabetic personality, which stems from its higher fiber content. The more sweet potatoes you eat, the more stable your blood sugar levels will be.

➤ **Get your fruit fix.** People with diabetes are sometimes reluctant to eat fruit. The natural sweetness, they assume, can't be good for blood sugar control. However, that's a mistake, because whole fruit is great for glucose control. Even though fructose, the main sugar in fruits, can be 150% sweeter than white sugar, the body processes it differently. Specifically, it isn't utilized by the body until it's first been converted by the liver into glucose. This lag time means that blood sugar levels rise relatively slowly after eating fruit. This is not the case with fruit juice, which will spike your blood sugar levels immediately. Eating fresh fruit regularly also helps control your weight because of its fiber content. Eating fruit also helps control your appetite because it satisfies your sweet tooth better than sugary snacks or fattening desserts.

➤ **Citrus is sensational.** Diabetes isn't just about blood-sugar levels, but also about the many complications that occur when blood sugar and insulin levels run high. Complications can be fairly common, even in people who do their best to keep their glucose stable. Here again, diet is crucial. Statistically speaking, people with diabetes have a shorter life expectancy, usually 12 years fewer than the general population,

even if their blood sugar is well-controlled. That's why another important goal is to minimize the many diabetic complications that can develop, such as heart disease and circulatory problems, that result in vision loss and limb amputations. Citrus fruits can make a big difference. They're one of the best sources of vitamin C, a nutrient that's needed by people with diabetes because it competes with glucose to get into their cells. Suppose there is the usual amount of vitamin C floating around in the blood, plus an abundance of blood sugar. These two molecules will fight to get into the cells, and the result is that some of the vitamin C will lose. Adding more vitamin C to your diet will give it a better chance to succeed. Also, many of the complications of diabetes are caused by free-radical oxidation, a biochemical process that is blocked by vitamin C and other antioxidants.

If you eat a lot of oranges, grapefruit and other citrus fruits, it's hard to fall short on vitamin C. One orange provides close to 60 milligrams (mg), the recommended daily amount. But citrus fruits don't have the lock on vitamin C. One kiwi packs more than 100 mg. Red peppers have about 140 mg each, and broccoli delivers about 116 mg per cup. In fact, virtually all fruits and vegetables contain good amounts of vitamin C.

➤ **Dig into beans.** Nothing is better for controlling blood sugar than beans. Three-bean salad, baked beans, pinto, navy beans and soybeans have all been found to contain compounds that help control blood sugar, improve the body's insulin response and reduce the risk of diabetes. Like whole grains, beans generally have low GI scores because of their high fiber content. People who eat a lot of beans have a much lower *glycemic load*, the rush of blood sugar that can occur after meals. And because they're loaded with fiber, beans also help you feel full longer, which is also important for weight control.

Here's how great beans are: Groundbreaking research by Dr. James Anderson showed that people with type 1 diabetes who ate a lot of beans were able to reduce their need for insulin by an amazing 38%. In those with type 2 diabetes, a high-bean diet all but *eliminated* their need for insulin. Eating beans got people off their insulin injections and glucose-controlling medications. In other words, beans helped reverse their diabetes.

Beans produced this miraculous effect because they are high in pectin and other fibrous substances that encourage cells to produce additional insulin-receptor sites. The extra receptors on cell surfaces make it easier for insulin to bind to them and remove glucose from the blood. That's like installing more doors on cell walls to get glucose out of the bloodstream faster. And, like other high-fiber foods, beans greatly reduce the blood sugar spikes that occur after meals.

Research shows that people who add just three cups of beans to their diet weekly are less likely to get diabetes than those who eat fewer beans. People who substitute beans for quickie carb foods do even better. One study found that people who ate a serving of beans instead of refined carbohydrate foods had glucose levels that were approximately 50% less than those of the refined-carb eaters.

➤ **Have a peanut butter sandwich.** Peanuts control blood sugar, too. If you're not a peanut butter fan, just eat more nuts of any type. They're all high in fiber and magnesium, both of which help control blood glucose and the body's insulin response. Plus, nuts are among the best sources of healthy fats that promote better cardiovascular health. When Harvard scientists looked at the diets and health of 83,000 women, they found that those who ate at least two tablespoons of peanut butter—or a handful of nuts—five or more times a week were about 20% less likely to get diabetes than those who rarely ate those foods.

➤ **Break out the olive oil.** Scientists are discovering that olive oil is one of nature's greatest healing foods. Not only is it good for the heart and arteries, but it also appears to make a significant difference in diabetes. When researchers in Spain examined a group of patients with a high risk of heart disease, they found that those who consumed a lot of olive oil showed big improvements in blood sugar. They also had lower blood pressure and cholesterol. Olive oil has just as many calories as other fats, so moderation counts. The recommended amount is about one tablespoon per day, used in place of—not in addition to—other healthy fats in your diet.

➤ **Coffee clobbers diabetes.** If coffee doesn't give you the jitters, you might want to enjoy a few extra cups. A new study reports that drinking coffee can significantly reduce the risk for developing diabetes. Scientists already know that coffee contains chemical compounds that aid in the body's ability to process glucose. Now, it seems that coffee can prevent people from getting diabetes in the first place. The study, which followed 126,000 people for 12 to 18 years, found that men who drank six cups of coffee daily reduced their diabetes risk by a whopping 50%. Women who drank the same amount cut their risk by nearly 35%.

Paradoxically, earlier studies found that coffee—or at least caffeine—increases the risk for diabetes. This suggests that decaf, which contains the beneficial chemicals minus the caffeine, might be the best choice. One theory is that the antioxidants in coffee protect the insulin-producing cells in the pancreas. Coffee also contains a substance, *chlorogenic acid*, which seems to slow the passage of glucose into the bloodstream.

ANTIDIABETIC HERBS AND SPICES

➤ **More cinnamon, lower blood sugar.** Studies show that ordinary cinnamon can significantly reduce glucose levels in people with diabetes. Better yet, it doesn't take a lot to do it—good news if you happen to love cinnamon-laced applesauce. The secret is a chemical compound in cinnamon known as *MHCP*. Scientists have found that it mimics the effects of insulin in the body, while helping to make cells more sensitive to insulin's effects. A study of people with diabetes found that those given cinnamon—in doses ranging from 1 to 6 g—had blood sugar readings that were, on average, 20% lower than people in a control group. When the volunteers quit taking cinnamon, their blood sugar readings crept back up.

Another interesting finding about cinnamon is that people had the same reductions in blood sugar whether they were taking a little cinnamon, or a lot, although the higher doses worked more quickly. Researchers estimate that about one-quarter teaspoon of cinnamon, taken two to three times daily, produces dramatic glucose-lowering effects. You can use it in baking or add it to coffee, tea and breakfast cereal. The study used powdered cinnamon, but stick cinnamon steeped in a cup of hot tea should deliver the same results. The most potent effects are found with true cinnamon, which is not the same as what's found in most spice racks. The rarer, more expensive spice can be found in health food stores or from sources online.

➤ **Go along with tarragon.** Traditional healers often recommend tarragon for people with diabetes. It clearly works, although the reasons aren't entirely clear. In laboratory studies on animals with diabetes, tarragon reduced appetite, leading to weight loss. It also helped control excessive thirst, another common symptom of the disease. The curious thing is that tarragon doesn't have an appreciable effect on either glucose levels or the amount of insulin in the body. This suggests that tarragon must work by a different mechanism altogether, and could give people with diabetes yet another treatment option.

➤ **Fight diabetes with fenugreek.** Often used in curries, the spice fenugreek has been shown in both animal and human studies to improve blood sugar. For example, Indian researchers divided diabetes patients into two groups. Those in one group were given 1,000 mg of fenugreek seed extract daily. Those in the second group were only given traditional care, such as exercise advice and dietary management. At the end of the study, patients in the fenugreek group had significant improvements in blood sugar control and a decrease in insulin resistance.

➤ **More cilantro, more insulin.** Cilantro and coriander are different names for the same plant, although coriander is often attributed to the seed. Whatever you call the parts of this herb, they are both good for diabetes. When researchers added cilantro to the food of laboratory animals with diabetes, they saw a natural increase in the release of insulin and a reduction in blood sugar. Currently, there are no human studies to confirm this effect, but cilantro has many other healing attributes, such as helping to detoxify mercury in the body.

➤ **Not so sweet.** No one has to give up sugar completely. Can you imagine life without the occasional scoop of ice cream or chocolate mousse? Sweets do raise blood sugar, but so does just about everything else. The trick is to manage your sugar intake so you that can have your cake and enjoy it, too. Whether or not you have diabetes, it makes sense to limit the amount of sugar you consume. Remember, refined carbohydrates like bread, chips and crackers count as sweets. You must learn how to make smart substitutions. Want that serving of ice cream after dinner? Have it. Make room for dessert by giving up something else during the day, like a baked potato or a slice of bread.

A lot of people ask me if honey is a healthier choice than sugar. It's always a good idea to eat natural, minimally processed foods and honey fits the bill. However, honey is chemically very similar to sugar. It does have minerals, but not enough to make a difference. It actually has more calories per teaspoon than sugar. If you like the taste of honey, go ahead and use it, but just a little bit.

➤ **Capillary tea.** One of the main dangers of diabetes is long-term damage to the capillaries, the tiny blood vessels that branch off and carry blood throughout the body. Damaged capillaries, referred to as *microvascular complications*, can lead to stroke, blindness, numbness and nerve pain, known as *neuropathy*. An herbal tea known as *rooibos*, also called African Red Bush tea, is high in antioxidants as well as quercetin, a substance that strengthens capillaries. Ask for it at your local health food store.

➤ **Raise your glass.** A Harvard study found that small amounts of alcohol can reduce the risk of developing diabetes by nearly 35%. As a bonus, mild alcohol consumption has been shown to reduce the risk of a heart disease, one of the most serious complications of diabetes. The recommended level of consumption is one drink per day for women and two for men. I suggest that you keep two days a week alcohol free.

There are more foods and recipes that fight off diabetes at *www.myhealingkitchen.com*.

Foods That Make It Worse

I've already been up on the soapbox about the evils of sugar and quickie carb foods. No other food group is more harmful and dangerous to your health, whether you have diabetes or not. Other foods can cause problems too, so they should be eaten in moderation or not at all.

➤ **Cut back on fatty foods.** Some fats are superbly healthful and I advise people to eat more of them. Extra-virgin olive oil is among the healthiest fats you can consume, as are the beneficial fats in fish and nuts. However, polyunsaturated vegetable oils that are rich in omega-6s, such as those made from corn, soybeans, safflower and canola, should be avoided. You should also avoid trans fats and fried foods in general. Not only are they highly inflammatory, but there's some evidence that they can contribute to diabetes by interfering with the secretion of insulin. If you already have diabetes, too much of the wrong kinds of fat also can increase the risk of diabetic complications. About 65% of people with diabetes will die of a heart attack or stroke because their risk for developing CHD is 400% higher than it is for those without diabetes.

➤ **Red meat.** The usual advice for otherwise healthy people is to limit foods containing saturated fats, such as red meat, butter and dairy products. Researchers at Harvard's School of Public Health conducted a study and found that as little as one daily serving of meat increases the risk of developing type 2 diabetes by 26%. The risk rose to 40% for two daily servings. As I've said before, you have to be careful as to how you interpret these studies. Two servings of fast-food burgers, highly processed cold cuts or nitrite-laced bacon is not the same as eating grass-fed, free-range beef or organic chicken. Also, people who consume more meat tend to eat fewer vegetables and fruits, which can skew study conclusions. My position is that humanely raised and organically fed animal products are healthful foods. That goes for dairy products and butter, too, as long as you don't overdo it, because they are calorie-rich. Personally, I'd rather have a smaller portion of an artisanal cheese than a bigger chunk of a reduced-fat cheese. There's simply no comparison in flavor or quality.

The bottom line to remember about all fats is that they contain more calories gram-for-gram than carbohydrates, and that too many calories make you fat no matter where they come from. If you have type 2 diabetes, the single most important way to improve your condition is to lose weight. This means centering your diet around bulky, high-fiber plant foods that contain the fewest calories, such as vegetables and whole grains. You don't have to give up meat, just trim back the portions you're used to and make up the difference with more veggies and grains. This way, you'll lose weight, control your blood sugar *and* enjoy eating.

➤ **Can the sodas.** Have you noticed the size of the soda cups at convenience stores and fast-food restaurants lately? Either Americans are a lot thirstier than they used to be or they've developed a powerful craving for jumbo, supersweet drinks. Whatever the reason, people have come to expect these huge sizes in spite of the fact that soft drinks are the single largest source of calories in the American diet, adding up to about 7% of our total caloric intake. Scientists have argued for years about the effects of all of this liquid sugar on diabetes. Anyone who sucks down soda after soda is obviously going to have problems with blood sugar because soft drinks are even worse than quickie carb foods.

Findings from the long-running Nurses' Health Study reveal that women who consumed the most sugary drinks, such as fruit punch and sodas, *doubled* their risk of developing diabetes compared with those who drank them less frequently. One explanation is that the high-fructose corn syrup (HFCS), which sweetens soft drinks and many juice products, overstimulates the secretion of insulin and impairs the hormone's ability to remove glucose from the blood. On top of that, HFCS does not satisfy hunger. People who drink a 150-calorie soft drink won't be any less hungry than they were before, so it's very easy to drink too many of them. These beverages also contain a lot of calories and make gaining weight easy.

Supplemental Help

Researchers have looked hard to find supplements that can make an appreciable difference to the many people who struggle to control blood sugar in order to manage their diabetes. Here are some of the best, based on the most recent findings.

➤ **Better control with ginseng.** Many people with diabetes use medication to improve the ability of their insulin to remove glucose from the blood. Diet and lifestyle changes can be a big help, too. Now, there might be a third approach to make the usual treatments even better—ginseng. Studies show that ginseng lowers both fasting and

after-meal glucose levels all by itself. It also improves scores on the A1C test, a measure of average glucose levels over three months. A study published in *Diabetes Care* reports that patients given a 3 g dose of ginseng had blood sugar levels that were nearly 60% lower than those given a placebo. Scientists aren't entirely clear how ginseng helps, but believe it increases cellular sensitivity to insulin. It also may increase the output of insulin by the pancreas.

Ginseng is among the safer herbal treatments, but might cause blood sugar to fall too low in patients who are also taking prescription drugs. I think ginseng is worth a try—but take it under your physician's supervision.

➤ **CoQ10 works wonders.** Studies show that coenzyme Q10 (CoQ10) increases the body's sensitivity to insulin's effects, which both lowers and stabilizes blood sugar. This marvelous supplement is particularly helpful for those with long-standing diabetes. The oxidative stress that occurs with diabetes can quickly deplete natural levels of CoQ10, so it is imperative that you replace it. My recommended dose is 100 to 200 mg daily.

➤ **Crank up the chromium.** Sometimes, good things come in small packages. Chromium is a trace mineral that improves the ability of insulin to remove glucose from the blood. The body uses chromium to manufacture *glucose tolerance factor* (GTF), a substance that aids in the metabolism of sugar. Studies show that people with diabetes who receive additional chromium have lower blood sugar, as well as lower cholesterol and triglycerides, two serious risk factors for heart disease. When researchers test the effects of chromium, they often find that 50% or more of their patients achieve better glucose control. In one study, people given chromium supplements had drops in blood sugar of as much as 50% in as little as five weeks.

Even though the recommended daily amount of chromium is only 120 micrograms (mcg), deficiencies are common, especially in people with diabetes, because foods that have high GI ratings accelerate the loss of chromium from the body. Also, refined carbohydrates have been stripped of chromium and other trace minerals due to the refining process.

For more than a decade, scientists with the U.S. Department of Agriculture (USDA) have suspected that chromium can help fight diabetes. When researchers finally studied a group of type 2 diabetics in China, one scientist documented "spectacular" results when patients were given 1,000 mcg of *chromium picolinate* daily. "Nearly all of them no longer had the classic signs of diabetes," reported chief researcher Dr. Richard Anderson. Their blood sugar and insulin levels became normal. Even more impressive, blood levels of hemoglobin A1C, which is considered the gold standard diagnostic measure of long-term blood sugar control, fell within the normal range.

Millions of Americans are prediabetic (also known as *insulin resistant*), a condition that causes chronically high blood sugar and makes insulin less effective. Dr. Anderson believes that taking at least 200 mcg of chromium supplements daily could help prevent 50% of these high-risk people from slipping into full-blown diabetes. Despite dozens of positive clinical studies, the American Diabetes Association (ADA) still does not endorse chromium therapy, maintaining that more studies are needed. It steadfastly claims that the majority of people with diabetes are getting enough chromium. Dr. Anderson's research clearly contradicts this. His studies show that up to 90% of the general US population are chromium deficient.

I side with Dr. Anderson's research. Do yourself a favor and make sure you include more chromium-rich foods in your diet. For added insurance, take 50 to 200 mcg of chromium daily. If you are diabetic, take up to 400 mcg twice daily, 30 minutes to an hour before meals. Check with your doctor first.

➤ **Maximize your magnesium.** Just about every biological function in your body depends on magnesium. Like chromium, it's often in short supply in people with diabetes. In fact, it's estimated that up to 25% of people with diabetes aren't getting enough, even when they eat a balanced diet. Research confirms that a deficiency of magnesium reduces insulin production and makes cells less sensitive to its effects.

When researchers at the Harvard School of Public Health looked at the nutritional status of about 125,000 men and women, they found that those with the highest intakes of magnesium were least likely to develop diabetes. A second study found that women who got large amounts of magnesium were 22% better protected against the disease, even if they were overweight. Since low magnesium combined with diabetes can increase the risk for retinopathy, a serious eye disease that is a common complication of diabetes, people with the disease really need to get more of this important mineral. Good food sources include halibut, whole grains, beans, almonds and other nuts.

It's also a good idea to get additional magnesium insurance in the form of supplements. A recent, double-blind, placebo-controlled study of people with diabetes—all of whom were found to have low magnesium at the start of the study—found that those who took the supplement showed significant improvements in insulin sensitivity as well as blood glucose control. The recommended dose is 400 to 800 mg daily. If you have kidney problems, don't take more than 400 mg —after discussing it with your doctor. Chelated magnesium or *magnesium glycinate* or *citrate* supplements are the forms most readily absorbed by the body.

➤ **Excellent E.** A long-running study that looked at more than 4,300 volunteers found that those who ate the most vitamin E-rich foods, such as leafy greens and nuts, were over 30% less likely to develop diabetes. Everyone should try to get 200 to 400 international units (IU) of vitamin E daily. To make sure you get enough, I encourage you to take a daily multi that includes vitamin E with mixed *tocopherols.*

➤ **The dynamic duo.** Vitamin C, one of the most powerful antioxidants, gives vitamin E a boost so that it can work more effectively. Studies also show that vitamin C helps curtail damage to the nerves and blood vessels in patients with diabetes. How much do you need? One study found that people given

1,000 mg of vitamin C daily had a significant improvement in the body's ability to use glucose. Other studies have found that a dose as small as 500 mg daily might be enough to prevent some diabetes complications.

➤ **Team calcium with vitamin D.** Speaking of dynamic duos, a long-running Boston study found that women who got plenty of daily calcium (1,200 mg daily) and vitamin D (800 IU) were 33% less likely to develop diabetes than those who got lower amounts.

➤ **The alpha dog of blood-sugar healers.** Alpha-lipoic acid (ALA), a substance that helps many of the body's metabolic processes work more efficiently, has been found to lower levels of blood sugar and can also reduce nerve-related complications of diabetes. The recommended dose is 100 to 300 mg daily.

➤ **Eye bark.** *Diabetic retinopathy* is one of the main complications of diabetes. It is the result of damage to the tiny blood vessels that nourish the retina. The longer a person has diabetes, the more likely he or she will develop this blinding condition. In France, doctors routinely prescribe *Pycnogenol*, a potent antioxidant derived from pine tree bark. Studies show it can repair damaged capillaries in the eye and help reduce retinopathy and that it's 190 times more effective than the leading medication prescribed to slow the body's uptake of glucose after meals. The recommended dose is 30 to 60 mg daily.

➤ **Blood sugar and vitamin D.** True or false? Your blood sugar is closely associated with your vitamin D level. The correct

114

answer is "absolutely true!" Researchers in Australia recently reported that a deficiency in vitamin D (also known as the sunshine vitamin)—caused in part by current health advice to shun the sun and such vitamin D-rich foods as organ meats, animal fats, dairy foods and eggs—may be contributing to the epidemic of type 2 diabetes in the US and other Western countries. The Australian research findings were straightforward and powerful. "The higher your vitamin D level, the lower your blood glucose."

Whether or not you have diabetes, getting more vitamin D will improve your health and protect you from a number of serious diseases, including cancer and osteoporosis. *Here's my advice…*

➤ **Get tested.** Ask your doctor for the 25(OH) D blood test, which measures your blood level of vitamin D. If your results aren't in the 45 to 52 nanograms per milliliter range, you need to take corrective measures—more sun exposure, more vitamin D-rich foods in your diet and supplementation.

➤ **Get more sun.** Without question, the ideal way to increase your levels of vitamin D is through UV ray exposure. Get 10 to 20 minutes of sun exposure on as much skin surface as you feel comfortable baring. Take care not to burn, because sunburn generates free radicals and is linked to skin cancer. Do not wear sunscreen unless you are going to be in the sun for longer periods. If you live north of the 42-degrees latitude (imagine a line from the northern border of California to Boston), you will have a difficult time getting enough vitamin D from the sun during the winter. You will probably need to eat

more vitamin D-rich foods or take 2,000–3,000 IU of vitamin D-3.

➤ **Moderation is important.** Studies show that lily-whites have higher rates of skin cancer than people who are moderately tanned. The key is not to sunburn. The extra vitamin D makes the difference, and it won't cost you a cent.

Other Helpers and Healers

➤ **Exercise is vital.** While a healthy diet and weight management are the cornerstones of diabetes control, exercise is also essential. That's because it's difficult to lose weight just by watching what you eat. With dieting alone, you'd have to give up about 500 calories a day to lose a pound per week. But with exercise, you can burn off about half those calories and take care of the other half by cutting back on calories slightly. Usually, this can be accomplished by giving up a soft drink or holding the mayo when you make a sandwich. Exercise doesn't only help with weight loss. It also pulls glucose out of the blood and escorts it to muscles where it gets burned up. People who exercise 30 minutes a day can expect to lower their blood sugar by as much as 20%.

Losing weight and exercising provides a double boost in diabetes protection. An important study, the Diabetes Prevention Program, looked at more than 3,000 overweight people who had a high risk of diabetes. After three years, only 14% of those in an exercise–weight loss program went on to develop diabetes, compared with more than twice as many in a nonexercising and nondieting group. Exercise doesn't have to be hard or intense to produce significant health benefits and weight loss. Something as simple as a regular walking program can do the trick.

➤ **Diabetes and depression.** Diabetes and depression often go hand in hand. New research shows that each can cause the other. A recent study published in *The Journal of the American Medical Association* shows that depressed people have an increased risk of type 2 diabetes and those with diabetes may be at increased risk for depression. "The complications and burdens of managing diabetes can increase the risk for depression," said Dr. Sherita Hill Golden, the study's director and an associate professor of medicine at Johns Hopkins. On the other hand, the study also showed that "people who had depression ate more, smoked more and were more obese—all of which can increase the risk for diabetes." People with diabetes who also have depression don't take very good care of themselves. According to data published in the journal *Diabetes Care*, depression disrupts a patient's self-care, causing him or her to be less diligent about glucose monitoring, medications, dietary changes and exercise.

The bottom line is that you need to be proactive in either instance. If you suffer from depression, you should be especially on guard for diabetes or prediabetes. Consult your physician right away. If you have diabetes, be aware that you are vulnerable to depression. If you have any symptoms, such as insomnia, sadness, listlessness or loss of energy, see your doctor or specialist immediately.

"It's No Big Thing"

Too many people with diabetes don't take their condition seriously enough. Others, who may be on the brink, don't seem to think that developing diabetes is a big deal. Both groups are dead wrong.

Health writer Tara Parker-Pope of the *New York Times* described a large-scale 2008 survey conducted by the American Diabetes Association (ADA) in which they asked people to rank the seriousness of various health problems, including cancer, heart disease and diabetes, on a scale from one to ten. Cancer and heart disease consistently ranked in the nines and tens, but diabetes scored only fours and fives. It's obvious from this response that people don't seem to be aware of how dangerous and deadly diabetes is.

"The general consensus seems to be, 'There's medication,' and 'Look how good people look with diabetes' or 'I've never heard of anybody dying of diabetes,'" said Larry Hausner, chief executive of the ADA.

"There was so little understanding about everything that dealt with diabetes," Parker-Pope said.

Diabetes is not something to take lightly. It takes a devastating toll on the entire body, destroying important bodily functions, including hearing, eyesight, sexuality, sleep and mental health. Most people don't realize that diabetes is a leading cause of blindness, amputations, kidney failure and raises the risk for heart attack and stroke by 400%. A diagnosis of diabetes subtracts an average of 12 years off the person's life and costs an additional $13,000 in extra medical costs a year.

116

It is absolutely true that the disease is treatable and that by following a careful program of glucose monitoring, medication and lifestyle adjustments, a patient stands a very good chance of enjoying a normal life and life span without ever encountering diabetes-related complications. Unfortunately, too many diabetes patients aren't doing this. Some are too busy. Others are ill-informed. Many low-income patients simply can't afford proper care. As diabetes spreads around the globe, helped by the proliferation of junk food that's replaced traditional and indigenous diets, the World Health Organization (WHO) has declared the disease an international health crisis.

➤ **Avoiding complications.** Diabetes and its complications take a terrible toll from head to toe. In the brain, it can increase the risk for depression, create sleep problems and make a patient more vulnerable to stroke. Because it impairs circulation, diabetes can lead to vision problems and poor dental health. *The Annals of Internal Medicine* reports that the disease doubles the risk for hearing loss. It also leads to liver and kidney disease, as well as severe gastrointestinal complications, such as paralysis of the stomach and loss of bowel control. A study published in the journal *Diabetes Care* reports that 70% of diabetes patients also have fatty liver disease. Poor circulation also results in *neuropathy*, degeneration of peripheral nerves, which causes loss of feeling in the extremities and severe skin ulcers and infections. Each year in the US alone, there are 86,000 diabetes-related amputations.

Relationships and sexuality also suffer. Up to 80% of men with diabetes have some form of erectile dysfunction. Women often lose their sexual desire and are plagued by vaginal dryness.

➤ **Lack of official action.** Although the specter of diabetes has been rearing its ugly head for many years, the ADA has been a little late in raising the alarm. This disease is now so common that it strikes every 20 seconds, yet the public earned a mere 51% when asked a series of questions on basic facts about diabetes and its serious complications. As a result, in 2009 the ADA finally launched a public awareness campaign and sent new directives to US physicians about the seriousness of the disease.

This effort strikes me as a bit hypocritical. The ADA has recently revised its guidelines for product approvals after getting soundly criticized for receiving support from—and implicitly endorsing—products such as SnackWell's Sugar-Free Lemon Creme cookies, Eskimo Pie's No Sugar Added ice cream bars and Post Frosted Shredded Wheat cereal, which have nearly as many calories as some sugar-rich foods. Last year, it also had to back out of the "Smart Choices" seal of approval program when the FDA determined that the health standards for "smart" were deceptively weak and included notoriously unhealthy products such as sweets and cereals. Isn't it the obligation of the foundation whose mission is "to stop diabetes" to denounce the products that contribute to the disease instead of support them for financial gain?

The ADA does provide good advice to individuals about what to eat. Yet treating diabetes isn't just about sugar control. Equally important is curbing and reversing obesity, yet the ADA may not be able to focus on these goals adequately when so much of their funding comes from the very corporations they would have to criticize. For instance, the organization has a three-year, $1.5 million sponsorship deal with Cadbury-Schweppes, the world's largest confectioner. Under the deal, Cadbury is promoted as an ADA sponsor in several settings, and has permission to use the ADA logo on its Diet-Rite sodas, Snapple unsweetened tea and Mott's Apple Sauce, among other products. The affiliation helps position Cadbury as a concerned corporate citizen despite its production of sugary, fattening, diabetes-causing foods like Dr Pepper and the Cadbury Creme Egg. "Maybe the American Diabetes Association should rename itself the American Junk Food Association," said Gary Ruskin, director of Commercial Alert, a consumer advocacy group.

This echoes the mixed record of the American Heart Association (AHA), which had its heart-healthy Seal of Approval affixed to boxes of Lucky Charms, Cocoa Puffs and Trix cereals; Yoo-Hoo chocolate drink; and Healthy Choice's Premium Caramel Swirl Ice Cream Sandwich. Meanwhile, as Michael Pollan points out in his illuminating book, *In Defense of Food*, "the genuinely heart-healthy whole foods in the produce section, lacking the financial and political clout of the packaged goods a few aisles over, are mute."

➤ **A modern-day plague.** Forgive me for sounding cynical, but I think there's an-other reason this crisis has been overlooked until now. And that's the huge income potential of medicalizing the problem. Michael Pollan agrees: "Apparently it is easier or at least a lot more profitable to change a disease of civilization into a lifestyle than it is to change the way that civilization eats."

Despite estimates that 80% of type 2 diabetes cases could be prevented by simple changes in diet and exercise, medical establishments are busy creating a massive new diabetes industry, complete with a wide array of new gadgets and drugs. (The latest is a new glucose monitor, ergonomically designed to fit in the palm of your hand, which gives an audio readout of your blood sugar.) Since 80% of all diabetics will also develop heart disease and kidney disease, the medical industry must be licking its chops at all the new heart bypass surgeries, kidney dialysis and transplants coming its way. With so much new income to be earned, it's hard to believe that the ADA, AHA or any other disease-oriented medical organization that collects royalties for use of its official logo would earnestly want to prevent this surge in new business.

Instead, diabetes—just like heart disease—is becoming normalized in our society as another unavoidable consequence of growing older that can be dealt with by taking a pill. I urge you not to fall for this dangerous misconception. Diabetes is not only usually entirely preventable, it is often reversible with a few simple dietary and lifestyle changes. You can do it. Too much is at stake for you not to give it your all in trying. ■

8

Digestive Disorders

 With the exception of infectious diseases, many of the digestive problems that plague us today were barely a blip on the radar screen a century ago. Our intestinal health began going downhill in the late 1800s, when manufacturers developed the technology to make refined white flour accessible to more than the wealthiest few and to kill off disease-causing bacteria in a food supply that was being stretched to feed an ever-increasing population. These processes stripped away valuable food fiber and gave us sterile dairy products. People were taking in a lot less fiber and beneficial bacteria. Today, the average American consumes a small fraction of the amount recommended for both in order to keep the digestive system healthy.

The story of fiber is a good example of how certain foods can be an important part of the healing process or the very trigger that can make us ill. Digestive conditions such as celiac disease, constipation, heartburn, irritable bowel syndrome and chronic flatulence are all food-related in some way.

The National Institutes of Health (NIH) estimates that more than 20 million Americans have some type of chronic digestive disease. Much of this misery is preventable. Like many of the other conditions discussed in this book, most digestive disorders can be managed without expensive medical care or drugs, and some can be cured altogether with appropriate nutrition. Even when the underlying problem can't be resolved, it's often possible to achieve complete control—no symptoms and no internal damage—with nutritional changes alone. For more ways to take control of your digestive challenges, visit the Web site *www. myhealingkitchen.com.*

119

Celiac Disease

Barley and other whole grains are among the healthiest foods you can eat. I wish everyone would enjoy them more often. For people with celiac disease (CD), however, there's no choice at all. Also known as *celiac sprue* or *gluten-sensitive enteropathy*, CD is an often inherited autoimmune disorder in which the nutrient-absorbing projectiles of the small intestine (called *villi)* are damaged, interfering with their ability to absorb nutrients from food. The villain in CD is *gluten*, a protein found in wheat, barley, rye and the vast number of products made with these grains, from pizza crust and soy sauce to condiments, even some envelope glues. When a person with CD ingests even a tiny amount of gluten, his or her immune system goes on a rampage, damaging the small intestine's plush carpet of villi and limiting his or her ability to absorb nutrition.

If you're gluten sensitive and continue to eat gluten, repeated assaults by your immune system will flatten the villi, eliminating their ability to absorb nutrients altogether, leading to malnutrition and brittle bones. Even when people with CD eat a perfect diet, they can't get enough of the nutrients they need to be healthy. There's good news about the recuperative power of villi, however. Since the intestine renews itself every 72 hours, villi are able to regenerate themselves and begin absorbing vital nutrients again if gluten foods are avoided.

One in every 133 Americans has full-blown CD and, by some estimates, up to one in three men, women and children have some degree of gluten sensitivity. CD is one of the most common genetic conditions in the world, which means that it tends to run in families. No one knows exactly what causes it, though a provocative theory is that it first occurred when humans made the transition from hunting and gathering to growing grains. It's possible some humans never developed the internal biochemistry to process the gluten in cultivated grains. Put another way, gluten may be a completely unnatural part of the human diet. Some research seems to back this up. People who are sensitive to gluten apparently don't produce the enzymes needed to break it down, which irritates the immune system. Sensing foreign gluten molecules, the immune system unleashes cytokines and other inflammatory substances to combat the perceived threat.

Symptoms of CD are wide-ranging and can include intermittent diarrhea, cramps, foul-smelling stools, missed periods, tooth discoloration, bloating or gas, headaches, an itchy rash, fatigue, constipation, irritability, depression, joint pain, or some combination thereof. Because calcium is among the nutrients not absorbed by people with CD, severe osteoporosis is a common outcome. Some people with CD have no digestive discomfort and others rarely experience any symptoms. If you do have symptoms, ask your doctor for a blood test that looks for the *anti-tTg antibody*, which is elevated in people with CD. Your physician may also test for *anti-endomysium*, an antibody that's more specific to the mucosal tissue lining the small intestine. If your blood tests are positive for CD, the diagnosis can be confirmed

Diverticulosis: Intestinal Blowouts

If you regularly fill up on processed foods or fast foods, there's a good chance that your insides aren't as solid as you may think. Ever see a car tire with a bubble on the side? You might have dozens of similar bubbles inside your large intestine if you've been eating poorly for some time. There's a lot of pressure in there that rises dramatically when you strain to have a bowel movement.

Diverticulosis is a condition in which a weakened intestinal wall produces marble-sized pouches that bulge outward, usually growing larger with time. The condition isn't dangerous in and of itself, and most people with pouches have no symptoms. However, the risk is that one or more of the pouches will become inflamed and infected, a condition called *diverticulitis*. This condition can produce severe abdominal pain, along with symptoms such as fever or changes in bowel habits. In fact, without treatment it can be life threatening.

Most people can prevent or correct diverticulosis simply by eating more high-fiber foods. An impressively large Harvard study found that people who ate the most fiber-rich foods were 40% less likely to get diverticulosis compared with those eating few fiber-rich foods. The reason is simple: A high-fiber diet makes stools softer and easier to pass.

by using an endoscope to take a biopsy sample of the villi in your small intestine.

Despite numerous public awareness campaigns drawing attention to CD, many doctors still consider it a rare condition, and often don't test for it in response to symptoms, which can be mistaken for those of a broad range of other conditions. CD may be misdiagnosed as irritable bowel syndrome. Celiac disease could be passed over as a possible cause of infertility or lack of proper weight gain in children. Less-severe cases of gluten sensitivity are more difficult to spot. Even if your blood test results are negative, you might want to eliminate gluten from your diet to see if your symptoms (however minor) improve. Most adults with CD aren't diagnosed for 10 or more years after developing symptoms. That's a long time to suffer, and needlessly, because CD has a straightforward treatment.

Once gluten is removed from your diet, your small intestine will start to heal itself immediately. Your symptoms may quiet within days, but it can take a few months for the villi in your small intestine to begin absorbing nutrients again. In severe cases, it can take two to three years before intestinal healing is complete. Remember that any amount of gluten will set off an autoimmune response, trigger intestinal inflammation and worsen tissue damage. The goal isn't to reduce gluten but to eliminate it completely.

There's an abundance of information and support available for people who need to live a gluten-free life. Take advantage of celiac support groups on and off the Internet.

FOODS THAT MAKE IT BETTER

You can't reverse gluten sensitivity by eating specific foods, but you can replace missing nutrients and minimize your body's inflammatory response by eating from the gluten-free foods in my Mediterr-Asian Diet (see page 19). Attitude is one of the most important factors in living with CD. You'll have to say goodbye to some of your favorite foods and begin to focus on a delectable new array of problem-free ones. The good news is that the vast majority of foods I recommend for peak health are gluten free. You can use this book to eat well from the naturally gluten-free range of whole foods I recommend for everyone, including the following.

➤ **Fancy fish.** The omega-3 fatty acids in fish act like natural aspirin, reducing inflammation and helping to quell your body's immune response if you accidentally eat a little gluten. Plus, cold-water fish such as wild-caught salmon and mackerel are loaded with healing omega-3 fatty acids. Even in small amounts, omega-3s reduce your body's production of inflammatory substances. That's good for everyone's heart, blood pressure and brain health, and is especially beneficial for people with CD.

➤ **Learn the good grains.** There's a long list of grains and flours you can eat—brown rice, corn, soy, potato, tapioca, sorghum, arrowroot, teff, oat groats, amaranth, millet, buckwheat groats, nuts, wild rice and quinoa. None of these contain gluten, but they can easily become cross-contaminated with wheat during harvesting or processing. If you're eating good grains and notice CD symptoms returning, pay attention. Your gluten-free grain might not be as pure as you think it is. Look for gluten-free labels and stick with brands you know and trust.

➤ **Love those legumes.** Beans and other legumes are one of the most potent sources of disease-fighting, health-promoting antioxidants. They're also packed with B vitamins and help satisfy your hunger because they fill you up quickly on a minimum of calories. Some companies are even milling beans and legumes into flour for use in gluten-free products. Enjoy protein-rich, high-fiber legumes such as kidney beans, black beans, pinto beans and chickpeas as often as possible.

➤ **Choose real food.** Gluten is so often present as a texturing or thickening agent in canned and boxed foods that I'd run out of space listing all the processed foods to avoid. Whether or not you have CD, it's best to avoid processed foods. Choose instead from the enormous array of unprocessed fruits and vegetables that make up the Mediterr-Asian style of eating. Your body will thrive as a result. Emphasize leafy greens. They're loaded with calcium, which people with CD can run frighteningly low on, especially those who are also lactose intolerant.

➤ **Become fond of flax.** Flaxseeds are the best plant source of health-protecting omega-3 fats and are loaded with cholesterol-lowering fiber. They also contain cancer-protective lignans, antioxidants and lots of B vitamins. Purchase flax whole and mill small portions in a coffee grinder, and store it in a tightly covered container in the freezer to keep the delicate oils from going rancid. Flaxseed oil contains alpha-linolenic acid, which is an omega-3 precursor, meaning that the body breaks it down into DHA and EPA. It's also highly perishable, though, so never cook with it, keep it refrigerated, and drizzle a tablespoon daily onto your salad or veggies.

➤ **Go a little nutty.** People with active CD have trouble absorbing fats, which limits their intake of the fat-soluble nutrients, including vitamin E. Nuts and seeds are high in vitamin E and healthy fats, making them an exceptional choice for replacing lost nutrients. In addition, the type of vitamin E in sesame seeds, pecans, walnuts and sesame oil, called *gamma-tocopherol*, has been shown in lab studies to limit the multiplication of cancer cells, particularly in the prostate and lungs.

➤ **Be pro probiotic.** Populate your GI tract with beneficial bacteria by eating plain yogurt with live cultures and drinking acidophilus milk. Both are digestible, even by those who are lactose intolerant, because helpful bacteria in these products produce the enzyme *lactase*, which digests milk sugars. Yogurt and acidophilus milk are also top calcium sources, important for everyone, especially those with CD who can't tolerate cow's milk.

➤ **RSVP yes, but BYOF.** The safest way to attend a party, if you have CD, is to bring a gluten-free dish you've made yourself. Because gluten-containing foods can cross-contaminate gluten-free foods easily, even the most well-intentioned host may serve you some gluten in error. Make smart choices at the bar too. A glass of wine is fine, since wine is made from grapes, which are gluten free, while beer is usually derived from grain. Assume beer contains gluten unless it's labeled gluten free. Spirits such as vodka and Scotch that are made from grain may also make you sick. Some patients consume liquors labeled "triple-distilled," while others drink only spirits made from grapes, corn or other gluten-free ingredients.

FOODS THAT MAKE IT WORSE

The treatment for CD is simple. Avoid gluten in all its forms. This becomes a lot easier once you're armed with information. To start learning about gluten's presence in food, visit the Celiac Disease Foundation at *www.celiac. org*. Foods containing gluten are abundant on supermarket shelves. Sometimes its presence is obvious, as in products like croutons and flour, but more often gluten is hidden away in marinades, condiments, processed lunch meats, soy sauce and even nutritional supplements. Many groceries have gluten-free sections, but it's still smart to learn how to read labels and spot hidden gluten.

Challenges go beyond just picking the right food product for a family member with CD. Gluten-free foods must never come in contact with foods containing gluten, which can easily occur if meals are prepared on the same surface or using the same utensils. Even a toaster used for a slice of wheat bread can transmit gluten to a gluten-free slice inserted afterward. Here are the main CD food culprits.

➤ **Banish the big three.** Wheat, barley, rye and everything made from them are the primary sources of gluten in the diet. If you have CD, avoid them completely. There are still some unanswered questions about the ability of people with CD to tolerate oats. Some folks are able to eat about a half cup daily. Oats themselves don't contain gluten, but it's not unusual for them to be contaminated by wheat at some point in the manufacturing process. Look for gluten-free oats, and work with your doctor or nutritionist when

123

adding them to your diet. Also, be aware that processed foods often list ingredients that contain wheat, even though the word *wheat* does not appear, including semolina, spelt, matzo meal, triticale, graham flour and quite a few others. Don't eat anything without being certain that the big three, in any form, aren't part of the product. Remember that a food product labeled wheat free may not be gluten free and still may contain rye or barley-based ingredients.

➤ **Keep good grains pure.** If you're eating gluten-free grains and notice your symptoms returning, pay attention. Your grain may have been cross-contaminated with wheat, rye or barley during processing. Companies in North America producing uncontaminated oats include Bob's Red Mill Natural Foods. CD groups and online resources can help you locate uncontaminated gluten-free grains.

➤ **Monitor milk.** Because of the damage gluten has done to their small intestines, some people with CD aren't able to digest the lactose in dairy products, a condition known as *lactose intolerance*. However, once you get gluten out of your diet, your healed intestine may once again be able to accept milk and other dairy products. If you're having difficulties with dairy, ask your doctor or nutritionist for the best way to reintroduce these products.

OTHER HELPERS AND HEALERS

➤ **Work with an expert.** Ask your doctor for a referral to a nutritionist or dietician who specializes in gluten-free eating. Meeting with a specialist will give you a broad overview of foods to avoid and those to emphasize to meet your individual CD requirements.

➤ **Hook up with a group.** The Internet site *www.meetup.com* brings together communities of people with shared interests, from model trains to CD. A recent search of the site turned up 111,000 listings for CD meetups in North America. Your local hospital may also offer a CD support group.

➤ **Eat out gluten free.** Everyone enjoys dining out from time to time. Some restaurants advertise gluten-free selections. Talk to chefs at organic restaurants and other establishments. Most will happily accommodate your gluten-free requests. Also, check the Internet for gluten-free restaurants in your area.

➤ **Prep your food.** Google "gluten free" and you'll find recipes galore, as well as Web sites run by people who love to cook gluten-free. Or go to *www.celiac.com* for a recipe listing to get you started. Celiac Chicks (*www.celiacchicks.com*) bills itself as the guide to a hip and healthy gluten-free lifestyle. The site will convince you that having CD is not the end of the world.

➤ **Learn the terms.** Understand the language of gluten, which appears on packaging in many different word combinations, including amino peptide complex, filler flour, triticum and vegetable starch. Most health food stores and some large supermarkets have areas devoted to gluten-free products. You can also shop online at places like Arico Natural Foods Company or Gluten Smart. There's also help from the FDA, which has required food manufacturers to clearly identify gluten-free products on their labels since 2008.

Constipation

A lot of people worry when they occasionally miss a bowel movement, but it's no cause for alarm. Doctors define constipation as hard, dry stools passed fewer than three times weekly—a condition that is uncomfortable, sometimes painful and definitely unpleasant. It's normal for some people not to have a bowel movement every day and equally normal for others to have them several times a day. The alarming situation is when there's an ongoing disruption in your usual habits. Some medications, including iron pills, antidepressants and narcotic pain medication, can cause constipation, but more often it's how you're living. *If you have occasional constipation, these food fixes are just what the doctor ordered...*

FOODS THAT MAKE IT BETTER

Here's an amusing medical secret. Doctors like talking about constipation. There are plenty of problems that we're not great at treating, but constipation isn't one of them. It makes us feel good when we can give patients advice that really works. You can almost always reverse constipation by cleaning up your nutritional profile and a few other habits.

➤ **Say spinach.** It's an excellent source of magnesium, a mineral that increases the strength of intestinal contractions and improves bowel regularity. It also contains compounds that encourage *peristalsis*, the wavelike contractions that move waste products through the intestines. Spinach juice is an excellent remedy for constipation. Toss a handful of spinach in your juicer along with some carrots to cut the

Turn on the Water Works

As you can see, a high-fiber diet is the ideal solution to many digestive problems, but take note: Adding fiber to your diet without upping your water intake is like dumping cement into your gut. Fiber absorbs a lot of liquid in the intestines, so if you don't drink plenty of water, there won't be enough moisture to lubricate stools. Try to drink eight glasses of water a day; more if you exercise or live in a hot climate. Never depend on thirst to tell you when to drink. Your thirst mechanism becomes less sensitive with age and can't be relied on to alert you when you're dehydrated. Drink eight ounces when you wake up and keep bottles of water or other low-calorie fluid close at hand, sipping throughout the day. One of my patients has a neat trick. She fills up a 64-ounce pitcher in the morning and makes sure it's empty by dinner time.

green's bitter taste. Eat something from the magnesium-rich food roster daily—Swiss chard, turnip greens, molasses, broccoli and summer squash.

➤ **Be fiber-optic.** Look for chances to eat more fiber by building the foundation of your diet on vegetables, fruits, whole grains, nuts and seeds and legumes and beans. The insoluble fiber in veggies, fruits and grains contains no calories—it's pure roughage. In your intestines, it pulls toxins out of your body while softening stools. It even scrubs the walls of your intestines like a broom as it moves through. On the other hand, soluble fiber from oatmeal, seeds and beans transforms into a gel-like substance during digestion and soaks fats and cholesterol in the intestine so they can't reenter your bloodstream. Aim for 40 grams (g) of fiber every day, along with plenty of water, which should put an end to your constipation.

➤ **Stop to sip.** Dehydration is one of the main causes of constipation, and with all the extra fiber you'll be adding to your diet, drinking more is essential. Water adds bulk to your stools and increases the fluid in your large intestine, softening bowel movements and helping them on their way. Drink plenty of fluids every day to avoid dehydration. You'll need even more if you're losing fluids through perspiration. Start your day with a glass of pure water, even before enjoying your coffee or tea. It's a good way to rehydrate after eight hours of sleep.

➤ **Grow fond of fermentation.** All fermented foods contain active bacteria cultures that are beneficial not only to your GI tract but also your entire immune system. Called probiotics and produced through a process known as *lacto-fermentation*, fermented foods contain healthful bacteria that inhabit the intestine and are critical for digestive health. Try to eat a little fermented food—such as soy sauce, miso, yogurt, sauerkraut and sourdough bread—every day.

➤ **Pop a prune.** Prunes, or dried plums, really do promote bowel movements because they contain a chemical, *dihydroxyphenyl isatin*, that stimulates intestinal contractions. Prunes also soak up impressive amounts of water, which adds bulk to your stool. Their high fiber content makes them universally loved for preventing constipation by speeding up the transit time of waste

126

Herbs That Attack Gas

Flatulence is harmless and normal, but it sure can be embarrassing, especially when you consider that the average adult passes gas up to 15 times a day. You can get relief with *carminative* (gas-fighting) herbs. Here are the best choices.

➤ **Ginger.** It has antispasmodic action to reduce the pressure and subsequent gas generated by intestinal contractions. Slice about an inch of fresh gingerroot, peel and brew it in a few cups of water for 20 minutes. Sip hot or cool up to three times daily.

➤ **Fennel seed.** There's a reason most Indian restaurants keep a bowl of fresh fennel seed near the cash register. They've been used for centuries as a digestive aid and to reduce flatulence. Nibble a few after meals.

➤ **Chamomile tea.** Like ginger, it reduces the frequency of intestinal contractions and also limits gas production. Steep in hot water for about 10 minutes and sip after supper.

matter in the bowel, which also drives down your risk of colon cancer. A quarter cup every morning—about three or four prunes—will do it. So will a small glass of prune juice. Prunes are also high in antioxidants.

➤ **Just the flax.** Flax is a great source of fiber, as well as brimming with inflammation-fighting omega-3 fatty acids. Sprinkle 2 tablespoons of ground flaxseed on your breakfast oatmeal or add it to a morning smoothie. Purchase whole flaxseed and grind a few days' worth in a coffee grinder.

Keep the flax meal in the fridge or freezer because it is highly perishable. The whole seed is too tough for your digestive system to break down.

FOODS THAT MAKE IT WORSE

The typical American diet is a virtual prescription for constipation, with its emphasis on meat, processed foods and refined carbohydrates that have been stripped of their fiber. It's no surprise, then, that Americans have nearly twice the rate of constipation as their Mediterranean and Asian counterparts, where the emphasis is on vegetables, fruits, whole grains and beans. For regularity, make sure you cut back on these constipating foods.

➤ **Downplay dairy.** A study in the *New England Journal of Medicine* of children with frequent constipation found that milk was the culprit about 65% of the time. Too much dairy isn't good for constipated adults, either. Milk contains a protein called casein, which is known to cause constipation.

➤ **Limit saturated fat.** Doctors in Asia and throughout the Mediterranean don't see many patients with constipation, partly because people in these cultures consume lots of plant foods that have their natural fiber intact. In addition, their meals are lower in saturated fats, which are difficult for the body to digest. Rather than speeding up *motility*, the rate at which stools move out of the body, saturated fats slow it down, resulting in fewer bowel movements.

OTHER HELPERS AND HEALERS

➤ **Walk it off.** Get moving to improve the muscle tone in your digestive tract and encourage bowel movements. Even brisk walking kicks up your breath rate and heart rate, which stimulates your intestinal muscles to contract and move stools toward the exit. Being active also speeds up the transit time of stools, which limits the amount of fluid your body absorbs from them, keeping them well hydrated and easy to pass.

➤ **Start your day warm.** Warm liquids wake up the intestine and help promote morning bowel movements. It's not just the temperature of tea or coffee that makes it work. Caffeine has been shown to jump-start intestinal contractions. If you're not a java or tea lover, try a cup of hot herbal tea and you'll still benefit from the first part of this equation. In all cases, have a glass of water first.

➤ **Lose the laxatives.** It may seem counterintuitive, but using laxatives and/or stool softeners can weaken the muscles of your large intestine, limiting their ability to move stools on their own. Supernutritious, high-fiber meals are the only medicine you need to beat constipation for life.

Heartburn

It's a law of physics that what goes up must come down. However, where your digestion is concerned, what goes down should definitely not come back up. Nonetheless, close to 50% of all adults in the US get heartburn at least once a month, and millions have it all the time. This pain can be intense, and so can the long-term damage. Chronic heartburn can permanently scar the esophagus and throat, increasing the risk of asthma, pneumonia and cancer.

Heartburn has nothing to do with your heart and everything to do with your esophagus, the channel connecting your mouth to your stomach. Heartburn happens when a tight, ringlike muscle at the base of the esophagus, called the lower esophageal sphincter (LES), is weaker than it should be or when it relaxes at the wrong time. The LES is designed to keep stomach acid from moving upward into your esophagus, but when the sphincter doesn't work as it should, corrosive stomach acid splashes upward. Your stomach is designed to withstand the acid, but the delicate lining of the esophagus is not.

Heartburn is a chemical burn. Occasional heartburn is one thing, but if you have it all the time, it is called *gastroesophageal reflux disease* (GERD), or acid reflux disease. Why might your esophageal sphincter not be closing as it should? Obesity or pregnancy can be to blame, since both place extra pressure on the stomach. A big factor is simply eating too much. Smoking also causes the sphincter to relax, as can some medications. Aspirin, alcohol and caffeine also enhance reflux.

FOODS THAT MAKE IT BETTER

Millions of people manage heartburn by taking fistfuls of antacids or drugs that suppress acid production or neutralize it. Drugs are expensive, never free of side effects and usually unnecessary, because most people with heartburn can control it with dietary changes. Add some of these heartburn healers to your diet and slow down during mealtime, setting down your fork between bites and chewing each mouthful thoroughly.

➤ **Focus on fiber.** People who eat a diet high in fiber are 20% less likely to have heartburn, according to one study. My Mediterr-Asian Diet doubles as a heartburn-healing diet because it contains plenty of high-fiber foods, such as beans, nuts, seeds, vegetables, lean meats, fruits and whole grains.

➤ **Sip away.** Have a glass of water after eating to wash down any stomach acid making its way north. Also, when you feel heartburn coming on, drinking water will dilute the acid and help flush away acid splashes, causing the pain to subside temporarily.

➤ **Take ginger tea.** Ginger increases the holding power of the esophageal muscle, making it more difficult for acid to surge upward. A slice of fresh ginger might be too spicy for some people. I recommend drinking a cup of ginger tea once or twice a day, made from a teaspoon of freshly grated ginger added to a cup of hot water. Let it steep for 5 to 10 minutes before sipping.

➤ **Go "grazey."** Another solution is to stop eating large meals and start grazing. Sending a lot of food down to your stomach at one time increases the chances of reflux and heartburn. Instead, eat the same amount of food (or less!), but spread it out into five or six small meals eaten throughout the day. Your stomach is only a litter bigger than your fist and can only hold so much before it backs up into your esophagus.

FOODS THAT MAKE IT WORSE

It's not only what you eat but *when* you eat it. Lying down after a big meal puts gravity to work against you, encouraging stomach acid to travel sideways into your esophagus. Stay upright for at least a few hours after eating, allowing digestion to occur and food to leave your stomach before you lie down. Better yet, go for a stroll. You'll also definitely want to avoid foods that trigger heartburn. Believe it or not, spicy foods are rarely the problem.

➤ **Forgo the fryer.** Fried foods can weaken the muscle at the base of your esophagus that keeps acid where it belongs. These foods also spend more time in the stomach before moving along because they are digested slowly.

➤ **Ease off chocolate.** It's among the most common causes of heartburn, partly because it contains chemical compounds that reduce the strength of the esophageal muscle. One study found that, for some people, acid splashed upward into the esophagus for up to an hour after eating chocolate.

➤ **Minus the mints.** It's ironic. Restaurants often have a bowl of mints by the cash register, presumably because they freshen the breath and have a reputation as digestive aids. Mints have been used for centuries to aid digestion, but they're one of the worst choices if you suffer from heartburn. Mints relax the esophageal muscle, often within just a few minutes.

➤ **Take down high fat.** Studies have shown that people who eat high-fat meals experience far worse acid onslaughts than those eating leaner foods. Much of the fat in the American diet comes from large servings of meat, particularly fatty cuts of poorer quality. With the Mediterr-Asian Diet (see page 19), you'll still enjoy the flavor of meat but in heartburn-controlling portions.

➤ **Note the sore spots.** It seems everyone has a different heartburn trigger. For some it's chocolate, while others feel the flames when they eat onions and garlic or drink alcohol. Next time you have heartburn, make a few notes, jotting down what (and how much) you ate before it occurred. Once you've identified the culprits, make a mental note to go easy on these problem foods or drinks.

➤ **Cut back the caffeine and alcohol.** The caffeine in coffee, cola and tea relaxes the esophageal muscle, making stomach acid more likely to kick upward and cause you pain. Alcohol and aspirin do the same thing. These liquids also increase the acidity of your stomach. If you want to enjoy an occasional coffee, tea or glass of wine, make sure you're well hydrated with water first and drink another large glass of water afterward.

OTHER HELPERS AND HEALERS

➤ **Elevate at bedtime.** According to a study published in the journal *Chest*, up to 25% of Americans have heartburn at night. To calm nighttime heartburn, sleep on your left side or use a wedge pillow to slightly raise your head while you sleep. Some people have success raising the incline level of their bed by placing a block of wood under the legs of the headboard.

➤ **Whittle your waist.** Having a large midsection puts extra pressure where you need it least—against your stomach and the sphincter muscle that keeps acid below, not above.

➤ **Tight's not right.** Wear looser clothes to keep the pressure off your midsection. Better yet, see the item just above.

Irritable Bowel Syndrome

It's one of the great mysteries of digestive medicine. Irritable bowel syndrome (IBS) affects up to one in five adults and its symptoms account for more than 10% of all doctor visits. However, when doctors run tests and view a patient's intestines, they find nothing to blame for this persistent and dreadfully uncomfortable condition.

Here's what we do know. The intestine is lined with layers of thick, strong muscles that normally contract and relax in a rhythmic pattern called *peristalsis*. These contractions are what propel food through the small intestine and solid waste through the large intestine, but in people with IBS, contractions seem to be somewhat erratic, with the intestines contracting more intensely and for longer periods. This can cause extreme pain. Since food is moved through the system more erratically than it would normally, many people with IBS experience a constellation of digestive symptoms, including gas, constipation, bloating, pain, cramps and diarrhea.

What causes the erratic contractions in the first place? Doctors aren't sure, but stress is suspect, since it's involved in many cases of IBS. Women, who tend to experience IBS at a rate twice to three times of men, may be feeling the effect of a hormonal abnormality, with flare-ups often occurring near their periods. If you think you have IBS, work with your doctor to rule out other causes of digestive symptoms, including celiac disease and lactose intolerance. You might also have a comprehensive stool analysis to see if you're lacking any digestive enzymes or whether

you're infected with parasites. A food sensitivity panel uses a small blood sample to see if your immune system is reacting to any of about 100 common problem foods. Ruling out other causes of IBS-like distress is essential. Most people can successfully treat themselves with nutritional changes and stress reduction.

FOODS THAT MAKE IT BETTER

IBS symptoms are like a hall of mirrors. For one person, certain foods can cause flare-ups, while, for another, these same foods are benign. A nutritious diet can help everyone.

In addition, eat only small amounts of food at a sitting and see if that calms your symptoms. At the same time, eliminate all refined white-flour foods from your diet, including pastries, cookies, white bread and pasta. Make it a habit to check food packaging labels to make sure there aren't any unwanted ingredients.

Don't eat any meals that you haven't prepared yourself, so you'll know exactly what went into them. It takes a little preparation, a convenient lunch bag and a thermos, but your digestive system will thank you.

Conventional IBS recommendations include adding over-the-counter fiber supplements in the form of psyllium or miller's bran. This is unnecessary once you start eating the Mediterr-Asian way, because you'll be getting an ample supply of fiber. Here are a few food approaches that can make a difference.

➤ **Keep your catch.** Many people who increase the amount of fish they eat see an immediate reduction in IBS symptoms, according to one study. We know that the

From the Cabbage Patch: Get Ahead of Ulcers

For years people with ulcers were told to drink milk, avoid spicy foods and reduce the stress in their lives. Now we know that most ulcers are caused by screw-shaped bacteria called *Helicobacter pylori*, which bore into the stomach or intestinal lining. Not a pretty picture but, fortunately, it can be eradicated with antibiotics. If you have recurring ulcer pain, ask your doctor to test you.

In the meantime, eat more cabbage. As far back as Roman times, cabbage was part of the treatment for ulcers and, like many time-honored home remedies, this isn't just folklore. Cabbage is high in vitamin C, thought to inhibit *H. pylori,* and also contains glutamine, an amino acid that boosts stomach circulation and accelerates the ulcer-healing process. One study found that people with ulcers who drank cabbage juice healed more quickly. It takes about half a cabbage to get enough juice to make a difference, but eating raw cabbage likely has the same effect. For even better results, douse the cabbage with a couple of capfuls of extra-virgin olive oil. Preliminary studies indicate the polyphenols in olive oil are extremely powerful inhibitors of *H. pylori*. Now, there's a recipe for a pain-free belly.

omega-3s in cold-water fish, such as mackerel and wild-caught salmon, are natural anti-inflammatory agents. Put them to work on your inflamed bowel by eating fish several times weekly and taking two fish oil capsules daily.

➤ **Lean up.** Choose lean meats such as turkey or chicken breast, minus the skin, and enjoy a smallish portion, about the size of half a deck of cards, with a little cooked brown rice, barley, oats or other whole grains. Steam some veggies for an accompanying side dish and splash with a little extra-virgin olive oil for its healing polyphenols.

➤ **Go pro(biotic).** Eating probiotic foods, such as plain yogurt with live cultures, restores the balance of helpful bacteria in your intestines, which is especially vital for those with IBS. Enjoy one cup of plain yogurt daily, ensuring that it has no added real sugar or artificial sweeteners of any kind and that the label promises "live cultures" inside.

➤ **Bring on the beans.** It sounds like eating more beans would be the opposite of good IBS advice. After all, don't they cause gas and digestive discomfort? For some people, yes, but they're also one of the best sources of soluble fiber, which can reduce diarrhea without bulking up the stools the way insoluble fiber does. Less-bulky stools can reduce painful cramping. Enjoy a small amount of well-cooked beans each day, starting with a quarter cup of drained, cooked chickpeas that have been tossed gently with a teaspoon of olive oil.

➤ **Stay hydrated.** Water and other uncaffeinated fluids help your digestive tract operate efficiently and are essential for moving the fiber foods you're beginning to eat through your system.

➤ **Get fond of fiber.** The foods of Asia and the Mediterranean contain different types of fiber, and a lot of it. There's plenty of soluble fiber in beans and insoluble fiber in whole grains and vegetables. In fact, all plant foods have a blend of different fiber types. For most people with IBS, increasing fiber intake is the best way to control symptoms. If your IBS is constipation dominant, you'll want to consume more fiber because it soaks up water in the intestine and makes bowel movements softer and more regular. Fiber is good for diarrhea too, since it bulks up stools.

FOODS THAT MAKE IT WORSE

IBS trigger foods vary enormously from person to person, but good nutrition is crucial for everyone. I can guarantee that eliminating any junk you currently eat and replacing it with the foods of the Mediterr-Asian Diet (page 19) is a big first step toward getting IBS under control. Cut back on or eliminate all refined and white-flour foods, as well as all prepared foods. Make your own meals, reducing portion sizes and eating more frequently. Food you don't prepare yourself often contains ingredients that people with IBS need to watch out for, such as the following.

➤ **Lower the saturated fat.** A high-fat diet is a problem for nearly everyone with IBS because the body has to work overtime to digest fats, particularly the saturated variety. Not only does your gallbladder contract like crazy after a high-fat meal, squeezing out the bile that's needed to break down fat, but your large intestine is stimulated as well, causing intensely painful contractions for some people with IBS. Cut way back on saturated fats and eliminate all foods containing trans fats.

➤ **Forget the high-fructose corn syrup and fake sugars.** Sugar is hard for your body to digest and a common cause of gas, cramping and diarrhea. Your glucose levels zoom skyward after eating sugary foods and refined carbs, which your body treats just like sugar. If you're following the Mediterr-Asian Diet, your main sugars are coming from healthful sources such as fruit. This will help you cut back on the fake sugars, found in everything from so-called healthy breakfast cereals to sodas and candy. One of the fake sugars, *sorbitol*, is notorious for triggering IBS flare-ups.

➤ **Identify your problem foods.** Some people with IBS find that caffeine triggers their symptoms. If that's true for you, avoid it. The same applies to any food or drink that seems to cause your IBS to flare up. Take note of the food and eating habits that cause problems. One of my patients with IBS finally figured out that eating nuts before noon triggered her intense abdominal pain.

OTHER HELPERS AND HEALERS

➤ **Jot in a journal.** Make a note of everything you eat, tracking your intake for a month or so. In the same journal, record any symptoms you may have. Track the links between diet, stress and symptoms. Some people with IBS have a good sense of what triggers their symptoms, while others don't have a clue. If your IBS is well controlled and you have a flare-up, stop and ask yourself if there's a stress component or food factor that could be responsible.

➤ **Learn to destress.** Since there's a link between IBS and stress, start engaging in a daily stress-lowering activity like yoga, *tai chi* or aerobics. Learn to meditate, and discover

132

Powerful Probiotics

Probiotic foods and supplements contain many of the same beneficial living microorganisms that populate your digestive tract and keep disease-causing bacteria and viruses in check. They also keep your GI tract regular and in peak health.

The power of these good-guy bacteria to generate health and healing bodywide is enormous.

Consider this: A staggering 70% of the human immune system is located in the mucous membrane of the digestive tract. Your immune system relies on beneficial bacteria for its very strength and vitality.

Until recently, most probiotic products were a lot less effective than their labels and marketing campaigns indicated. In some formulations, the live bacteria died in the harsh, acidic environment of the stomach before they could ever reach the intestine. Certain products couldn't be absorbed from the small intestine and still others were unable to attach to intestinal cells.

A selection of new products are far more effective. Bio-K Plus, part of a line of fermented milk and soy-based drinks, inoculate the GI tract with 50 billion live organisms in one glass. Starting your day with this healthy drink will boost your digestive system…and more.

New research on the benefits of probiotics shows that they do a lot more than improve digestion. Some probiotic organisms support the production of B vitamins, lower your cholesterol levels, deactivate toxins and enhance immunity. What's good for your gut is also good for your heart. An important study published in *The American Journal of Clinical Nutrition* found that one organism, *Lactobacillus plantarum 299v*, caused significant drops in inflammatory mediators such as fibrinogen and interleukin 6. Probiotics also lower blood pressure in hypertensive patients and reduce harmful LDL cholesterol.

Supplements are the easiest way to get adequate amounts of probiotics, but you can also eat probiotic-rich foods, such as live-culture yogurt, tamari, sauerkraut, Korean *kimchi* and Japanese miso. Look for foods that have been lacto-fermented and *not* pasteurized. They're usually found at health food stores, farmers' markets, local farms and the refrigerated section of your grocery store. Some delis still make their own lacto-fermented pickles and sauerkraut, keeping it in crocks right on the floor of the store. Anything sitting on a unrefrigerated shelf has been pasteurized, which means all its live organisms were killed when the product was heated.

how this ancient practice can still your mind and calm your body's symptoms.

➤ **Get good at grazing.** Eating big meals can cause intestinal contractions. My advice is to switch to a Mediterr-Asian menu (page 19), enjoying five or six small meals daily.

➤ **Move and improve.** Studies show that people with IBS who exercise regular-

ly have a significant decline in symptoms. Choose an activity you can do every day.

Lactose Intolerance

Nearly three-quarters of adults worldwide have some degree of *lactose intolerance*, which is the inability to completely digest one of the natural sugars in milk, *lactose*. People who are lactose intolerant lack the enzyme *lactase*, which is produced by the cells lining the small intestine to digest lactose. When people with lactose intolerance drink milk, the milk sugar pours into their intestines virtually undigested, where the bacteria living in their gut break down its lactose. The by-products of their digestion are what cause the gas, diarrhea, cramping, nausea, bloating and other distressing symptoms.

There's good news if you're lactose intolerant: You may not have to give up dairy products altogether—and that's a good thing since they're loaded with much-needed calcium for strong teeth and bones. *Here are a few simple strategies that can help...*

➤ **Sip milk.** Many people with lactose intolerance do fine with a cup of milk once or twice a day, sipped slowly. Smaller servings are also less likely to cause digestive problems.

➤ **Substitute yogurt.** You'll get all the calcium your bones need from yogurt, which contains very little lactose. The live bacteria in yogurt also help break down milk sugar and reduce discomfort. Look for yogurt labeled "live cultures."

➤ **Drink milk with foods.** Sipping milk while eating slows the rate at which lactose enters the intestine, giving the body more time to process it.

➤ **Say cheese.** Swiss and hard cheddar have relatively little lactose and don't usually cause symptoms, while softer cheeses, which have a higher milk content, generally do.

➤ **Monitor mystery milk sugars.** Prepared foods such as cake mixes, instant soups and salad dressings often have milk sugar added. These can cause problematic symptoms. You won't be consuming any of these if you're eating from the Mediterr-Asian menu, which is real food, not manufactured foodlike products. Other sources of hidden lactose include medications, both prescription and OTC. Be sure to read labels carefully to protect yourself.

➤ **Take supplemental lactase.** Put a few drops of lactase into a glass of milk and let this supplemental enzyme digest the milk sugars for you. This form doesn't completely break down lactose, but it minimizes the amount your body has to process. Milk that's been especially formulated for people with lactose intolerance is also available.

➤ **Go pro.** Read "Powerful Probiotics" on page 133 to learn about the extraordinary benefits of getting appropriate beneficial bacteria into your GI tract. Evidence shows that live bacteria cultures can help you digest lactose more effectively. There are several over-the-counter probiotic/digestive enzyme supplements available.

➤ **Concentrate on calcium.** If you're past menopause, you need up to 1,500 milligrams (mg) of calcium every day to keep your bones strong. However, if your tummy isn't happy with milk, it can be more challenging to get this much from dairy foods. See "Osteoporosis" beginning on page 269 and take special notice of the advice about nondairy sources of calcium. ■

9

Erectile Dysfunction

If you have problems with erections, you're definitely not alone. It's common for a man to experience this from time to time, so it's nothing to panic over. However, if it is a frequent occurrence, chances are it's a sign of an underlying health condition. What doctors call *erectile dysfunction* (ED) affects nearly one in five men, according to a Johns Hopkins study, with more than half of men 40 and older having some kind of erection problem. These problems can include the challenge of getting an erection or maintaining it long enough to have sex.

A few decades ago, this condition was called *impotence*, and men were often referred to a psychologist because it was thought that underlying emotional issues were at play. We now know that most men with erection problems have a physical disorder that prevents an adequate supply of blood from reaching the penis. For you and your partner, this can be good news. New medical and research advances now allow the vast majority of men to regain all or most of their normal sexual function with lifestyle changes, improvements in diet, help from the doctor or a combination of all three.

SYMPTOMS

Failing to maintain an erection or not feeling aroused occasionally is normal. Erectile dysfunction is officially defined as the inability to get an erection about 25% of the time. It's important to reiterate that virtually every man has had occasional difficulties due to excess alcohol, fatigue, underlying cardiovascular problems, medication side effects or a decline in his available testosterone.

CAUSES

Erections have everything to do with blood flow, and unsatisfactory erections are usually caused by circulation problems. Coronary artery disease and diabetes are primary culprits. Atherosclerosis, which is the buildup of fatty deposits in the arteries, also can restrict normal blood flow to the penis. Arteries carrying blood to the heart are relatively large, so a significant blockage must occur before a man notices symptoms. The main artery supplying the penis is only about half a millimeter in diameter, about the size of a small spaghetti strand. Any degree of atherosclerosis here will significantly restrict blood flow. That's bad news for erections, but it can be good news for your health, because it may alert you in time to prevent a heart attack.

The penis is a built-in barometer of a man's cardiovascular health. When you have erection problems, the first thing your physician should do is investigate the health of your arteries, not give you an ED drug. Fortunately, doctors are beginning to get the message. A study of nearly 1,000 men with erection problems found that 18% had undiagnosed high blood pressure and 5% had heart disease. An additional 16% had diabetes, which damages blood vessels and the nerves that make erections possible. Nerve damage can also contribute to erection problems in men who've had prostate surgery or who have a neurological condition such as stroke, Parkinson's, multiple sclerosis or spinal cord injury.

Occasionally, a hormone imbalance can be the cause of ED. Men begin losing the male sex hormone *testosterone* in their thirties, while beginning to accumulate *estrogen*, particularly if they're overweight. (That's because estrogen, the so-called female hormone, is produced and secreted by fat cells.) A man

with an unfavorable testosterone–estrogen ratio may notice a decline in his libido, in addition to erection problems.

In many cases, male arteries are just fine and the real problem is being caused by the medications they're taking for other conditions. Quite a few prescription drugs, especially antihypertensive beta-blockers, can put a damper on libido (sex drive or desire) and erections. It may help to switch medicines. For many men, a calcium channel blocker works just as well as a beta-blocker to bring down blood pressure, and these drugs are less likely to affect sexual function. Antidepressants often cause low libido and contribute to erection problems, too, as do certain sedatives, diuretics and antipsychotic medications.

Other causes of sexual problems include excessive alcohol consumption, illness, fatigue, depression, stress and worry or relationship trouble. Men are understandably embarrassed when they can't perform sexually and often become defensive, angry or both. This is the time when talking to your physician or a knowledgeable friend can really help. Bottling up your emotions in this case will only make things worse. A more healthful, positive reaction would be to look deeper into the causes.

➤ **Are you drinking more than you used to?** Too much alcohol can compromise your nervous system, a key component of your sex life. It's in charge of sending signals to the blood vessels in your penis that tell them to open and fill with blood to produce an erection.

➤ **Are you smoking?** Cigarette smoke damages the lining of blood vessels in the penis, limiting blood flow and your ability to achieve and/or maintain a full erection.

➤ **Are you overweight?** Lugging around extra pounds and being a couch potato can hurt sexual performance. Studies show that men who are overweight or who don't exercise are far more likely to have sexual problems than men who stay fit.

➤ **Are you eating poorly?** Too much fat, sugar, refined carbohydrates and polyunsaturated vegetable oils increase inflammation in your body, which ups your risk of atherosclerosis, diabetes and sexual difficulties.

TREATMENT

Most cases of impotence can be prevented or reversed with better nutrition and minor lifestyle changes. Before I discuss diet and lifestyle changes, let's take a quick look at the medical treatment of ED.

Drugs such as Viagra, Cialis and others have revolutionized the treatment of sexual problems. These drugs, known as *phosphodiesterase inhibitors*, magnify the effect of nitric oxide (NO), which relaxes blood vessels in the penis, allowing more blood to enter its spongy tissues when you're aroused. The drugs don't cause an erection, but they open the pipes if you have an underlying circulatory problem that may be impairing circulation. Another medical option is to inject *alprostadil* (Caverject, Edex) into the base of the penis, which triggers an instantaneous erection that can last for up to four hours. An alternate method is to drop a tiny pellet of alprostadil into the tip of the penis, which

produces the same effect. In either case, the drug is absorbed by tissue in the penis and rapidly increases blood flow. Sometimes supplemental testosterone in the form of a prescription gel or cream or even an over-the-counter testosterone precursor is all that's needed.

The downside of ED drugs is that they are expensive and carry risks, including adverse side effects. The most popular pharmaceuticals for improving erections—Viagra, Levitra and Cialis—should be used in small doses only. Men taking certain medications, including nitrates for angina, blood thinners and some types of alpha blockers for prostate enlargement or hypertension are not good candidates for Viagra, Levitra or Cialis. You also might not be a good candidate for these drugs if you have diabetes, hypertension, heart disease, congenital heart failure or if you've had a stroke. If you want to try one of them, it's essential that you discuss it with your doctor first.

A small percentage of men go the surgical route, in which underlying vascular problems are repaired or a penile implant is inserted. The most common implants are inflatable tubes that can be pumped up when an erection is wanted and deflated thereafter. Implant surgery is expensive and usually not recommended until after other potential solutions have been tried and any underlying causes resolved. This is an important point, because virtually every man who has difficulty getting an erection usually has an existing health problem or one that is developing. If blood isn't getting to the penis properly, there's a reason. Again, discuss this with your physician so that the underlying problem can be resolved.

Some individuals or couples find that psychological counseling helps resolve the stress and emotional factors that can be involved in erection problems. Sexual difficulties can strain relationships. Discussing these problems with a counselor, alone or with your partner, can point you toward a solution. Finally, take to heart the fact that most erection problems can be resolved through good nutrition and by making healthy lifestyle changes, such as limiting alcohol, quitting smoking, losing some weight and getting more exercise. Here are some of the most effective nonmedical solutions to try.

Foods That Make It Better

Many of the same steps you can take to reduce heart disease and hypertension also help resolve sexual problems. The most important of these is to eat in a heart-healthy manner, such as by following the Mediterr-Asian Diet (see page 19). It is chock-full of foods and meals that limit inflammation, which is the stealth cause of most circulatory problems. Be sure to consume plenty of fresh vegetables and fruits, whole grains and legumes, along with lots of fish and small amounts of red meat. You'll also want to take advantage of these specific sexy foods.

➤ **Sex on the beach.** Oysters have long enjoyed a reputation as an aphrodisiac. Now we know that there's real science behind their fabled ability to make a difference in the bedroom. A team of American and Italian scientists analyzed bivalve mollusks, a group of shellfish that includes clams, mussels and oysters, and found that these foods are surprisingly high in two unusual amino acids, *d-aspartic acid* and *N-methyl-D-aspartate,* both of which trigger the body's release of testosterone. Extra testosterone works for both men and women, helping them to become aroused and enjoy better sexual performance.

There's also the zinc factor. Oysters and other shellfish are very high in zinc, a mineral that's essential for testosterone production as well as male fertility and prostate health. Most men don't get anywhere near enough zinc, especially those who are sexually active. A man can lose more zinc every time he ejaculates than he takes in during the course of a day's diet. Oysters have about 100 milligrams (mg) of zinc per gram of oyster. They're the very best food source of zinc, with half a dozen containing about 27 mg, far more than the recommended 15 mg daily. Also at the top of the zinc list are gingerroot, with about 7 mg per gram, and lamb and beef, with about 6 mg per gram.

➤ **The arginine advantage.** For men who want to improve sexual health, eating oats, walnuts and seafood regularly is a great way to naturally increase levels of L-arginine, an amino acid that promotes stronger, more reliable erections. L-arginine passes through the intestines and into the bloodstream, where it quickly penetrates the endothelial cells that line arteries. There, it's converted to nitric oxide, a chemical that causes blood vessels to dilate. In other words, it makes the blood vessel openings larger, which helps more blood circulate with less force. That's good for blood pressure as well as for erections. By the way, this is exactly the way in which those expensive ED drugs work. Other good sources of L-arginine include milk, chickpeas, soybeans and coconut.

➤ **Red, red wine.** Shakespeare got it right about alcohol—"It provokes the desire, but it takes away the performance." In small amounts, a drink or two can loosen inhibitions and fire up sexual interest. In larger quantities, it can wipe out male sexual performance. With self-control on your side, a nightly glass or two of wine can be great for your sex life. Alcohol dilates arteries so that blood can flow more freely, which is why men who drink lightly tend to have lower blood pressure than those who don't. Dilated arteries and good blood pressure can translate into reliable erections.

Although any alcoholic beverage can improve circulation, red wine is a better choice than a mixed drink for sexual health and cardiovascular fitness because it's high in the flavonoids *resveratrol* and *quercetin,* antioxidant compounds that limit artery narrowing by making LDL cholesterol less likely to oxidize and stick to artery walls. Red wine contains more flavonoids than white because the entire grape is squeezed to make red wine, so the antioxidants in the skins enter the mix. When choosing a wine, select a full-bodied red, such as cabernet sauvignon, red zinfandel, or pinot noir.

➤ **Salmon is sexy.** Men who eat a few servings of cold-water fatty fish every week, such as wild salmon, mackerel, sardines or and anchovies are far less likely to have sexual problems than meat-and-potato guys

who load up on turf and skip the surf. The omega-3 fatty acids in these fish can dramatically lower triglycerides, the high-risk blood fats which increase the chances of arterial blockage. (For a list of the "Top 10 Omega-3 Fish" and other foods, see page 43.) Omega-3s also reduce inflammation, one of the main causes of heart disease and the irritation to the blood vessels that initiates artery disease. One study found that men who ate as little as one serving of fish a week reduced their risk of a fatal heart attack by 52%. Remember, anything that helps keep your coronary arteries clear above your navel also opens the your blood vessels down below.

➤ **Avocado and lime: A potent combo.** Here's a flavorful way to load your system with nutrients that have long-term effects for erections, as well as for your heart. Avocados are high in the beneficial monounsaturated fat *oleic acid,* which lowers total cholesterol and artery-clogging triglycerides. Research shows that regular avocado eaters often experience a drop in dangerous LDL cholesterol and an increase in the good HDL. Avocados are also very high in potassium, with nearly 500 mg in half an avocado. Potassium relaxes blood vessels and promotes better circulation. This star ingredient in guacamole also contains vitamin E, a powerful antioxidant that reduces arterial inflammation and inhibits fatty deposits. Limes and avocados are a perfect mix for sexual health because limes are high in vitamin C, which reduces oxidation and inflammation in blood vessel linings. Studies show that people who get a lot of vitamin C are far more likely to have clear arteries than those who don't. Vitamin C also makes blood vessels more flexible, so they can expand more readily and permit more blood to circulate. That's good medicine in the bedroom.

➤ **Well-watered and ready.** Millions of Americans go through life in a mild state of dehydration, or not so mild if they drink a lot of coffee, which is a mild diuretic that pulls water out of the body. That's bad news if your erections aren't as reliable as you'd like. There's nothing mysterious about the role of water and other liquids in male sexuality. When you don't drink enough, your blood volume drops, resulting in less blood flow to the pelvis and genitals. Research shows that men who remain well-hydrated have better blood flow where it counts. Underhydrated guys also have thicker blood, which doesn't flow as freely.

While drinking 64 ounces a day may sound like a lot, it is easily managed if you sip throughout the day. Keep a bottle of liquid on your desk and take a drink now and then.

You needn't depend solely on water—this is a good opportunity to get more healing, health-promoting nutrients into your body. One of my favorite hydrating drinks is a mixture of sun-brewed green tea and hibiscus leaves (great for cardiovascular health and blood pressure), plus a small amount of pomegranate juice (which is good for your heart and prostate), all sweetened with a bit of no-cal stevia (a powder derived from a South American herb that can be 30 times sweeter than sugar). Whatever you choose, be sure to drink a large glass of liquid before you leave the house in the morning and choose low-calorie fluids or water whenever you're thirsty, replacing soft drinks and

juices, which add unnecessary calories and increase your weight. Remember to drink a glass of water between each cup of coffee. How can you tell if you're drinking enough? A well-hydrated person has urine the color of weak lemonade.

➤ **Magical melon.** The juicy seductive crunch of watermelon can heat things up in the bedroom. Watermelon contains *citrulline*, a compound that acts like a low dose of Viagra to stimulate production of arginine, which increases levels of NO in your blood and relaxes blood vessels so that they can accommodate more blood flow. As a bonus, boosting NO also eases high blood pressure and angina. Be sure to eat your melon all the way down to the rind, where 60% of citrulline is located. Also, choose yellow watermelon whenever possible, because it contains a higher concentration of citrulline than red.

➤ **Feel your oats.** Cereals are particularly good medicine if your arteries aren't carrying as much blood as they should. I wish more doctors would prescribe a daily bowl of oatmeal before jotting "Viagra" on a prescription pad. I have nothing against drugs in general, and I recognize that medications have made life better for millions of people. However, when it comes to cardiovascular health and sexual fitness, eating a bowl of whole oats for breakfast can't be beat. It's one of the best ways to get a head start on your daily fiber while protecting your heart and arteries. Studies show that increasing your fiber intake by as little as 3 or 4 grams (g) a day can produce drops in total cholesterol of up to 15%. That's pretty significant. Whole grains, such as oatmeal and barley, are especially good because they're high in soluble fiber, which forms a gel in the intestine to trap cholesterol molecules and prevent them from moving into your bloodstream. Less cholesterol means less atherosclerosis, easier blood flow and better erections.

➤ **The love food.** Chocolate has been called the food of love, and it's wildly popular with women. Many women say that chocolate makes them feel sexy, and they're right. Italian research showed that women who ate chocolate regularly had sex more often and enjoyed it more than those who didn't eat chocolate. Chocolate doesn't seem to make men feel sexy in the same way, but it clearly has some effect. It is a complex substance for sure, containing more than 300 different chemical compounds, including stimulants such as caffeine and *theobromine*, both of which can ignite sexual flames. Other chemicals in chocolate trigger the activity of neurotransmitters that affect mood and emotions in a sexy way. It is also unusually rich in *flavonoids*, the same antioxidants found in red wine. Chocolate's flavonoids relax tiny blood vessels, including those that make up the spongy tissue of the penis, and men who regularly eat a little chocolate suffer less from high blood pressure, one of the conditions linked to erection problems. Get in the habit of eating a small square of dark chocolate every now and then—the darker the better, since dark chocolate contains the most flavonoids. Why not pick up a chocolate treat for you and your special sweetie today?

➤ **Pump up with pumpkin.** Pumpkin is loaded with protective antioxidants,

which are beneficial for overall health. Pumpkin also has the curious ability to fire up a man's sexual interest and performance. Studies at the Smell & Taste Treatment and Research Foundation in Chicago show that men who merely smell pumpkin pie get a 40% increase in blood flow to the penis. Men who smell a woman's perfume, by contrast, have an increase of just 3%. How does it work? Odor molecules in foods act like drugs, stimulating the release of neurotransmitters that produce chemical signals in the brain. For men, pumpkin pie (along with the scent of vanilla and doughnuts) is exceedingly stimulating. Before asking your partner to dab a little pie behind her ears, you might want to crack open a can of organic pumpkin and stir it into your morning oatmeal along with the spices that make pumpkin pie so alluring: cinnamon, ginger, nutmeg and cloves. Breakfast takes on a whole new dimension!

➤ **Splash on the olive oil.** Consuming olive oil instead of polyunsaturated vegetable oils, such as corn, sunflower and canola, can produce a significant drop in total cholesterol, without lowering your protective HDL levels. Extra-virgin olive oil, which is one of the very best fats found in nature, is high in chemical compounds that inhibit artery blockages. That means a man's blood flows more freely *everywhere* it's needed.

➤ **Select sterols.** You don't need to buy the expensive healthy spreads and other margarine surrogates to get adequate cholesterol-lowering plant *sterols*. Naturally occurring in certain plants, sterols block the absorption of cholesterol from the foods you eat and the cholesterol that's manufactured by your liver, which is why food manufacturers are beginning to add sterols to certain foods, such as margarines and butter substitutes. This way they can advertise these synthetic products as being "heart healthy." Don't be fooled. Some research shows that eating foods with added sterols, such as the sterol-enriched spreads, can actually lower the concentration of antioxidants in your blood. You're much better off getting your sterols in their natural form. Best sources of natural sterols include sesame seeds, wheat germ oil, sunflower seeds, peanuts, olive oil, soybeans, almonds, walnuts and avocado.

➤ **Pack in the plant foods.** Overall, the easiest way to reduce your consumption of fat and refined carbs is to focus on eating more fruit, vegetables, beans, nuts and whole grains. All of these healthful, healing foods contain copious amounts of heart-healthy fiber. They're also naturally high in antioxidants, which help maintain good levels of erection-promoting nitric oxide.

Visit *www.myhealingkitchen.com* for more healing foods and recipes.

Foods That Make It Worse

Eating more vegetables, fruits, and whole grains and less of the stuff that plugs up the arteries will definitely improve your erection quotient. However, most men usually want a faster fix, so they reach for an ED drug. It may seem easier to take Viagra, but these types of meds have serious limitations and risks, while ignoring the underlying issues causing the problem. Men who are constantly exhausted aren't likely to have good sex,

142

even if their arteries are healthy. And men who drink too much, overeat and who are overweight have a diminished blood supply where and when it's needed. The only sure-fire way to count on getting erections is to keep your arteries clear. This means eating better and getting more exercise, while cutting way back on the ones that inhibit blood flow. Here are some tips that will help.

➤ **Go easy on the fat and sugar.** The American diet is awash in fat and sugar, and today's high rate of erection problems will never decline until men get serious about eating less of both. There's no mystery about this. Guys who eat a lot of fat and sugar in the form of red meat, fast food, doughnuts, bread, cakes, chips and processed snacks usually suffer the consequences in the sack, because these foods increase the body's production of inflammatory chemicals, which causes thick blood and clogging plaque deposits. Inflammation in your arteries can persist for decades, and is the primary cause of atherosclerosis, in which fatty deposits narrow arteries and let less blood reach the heart and other organs essential for satisfying sex.

There's also the cholesterol connection, because fat and sugar raise the levels of total cholesterol and bad LDL. Some research has identified a link between high cholesterol and erection problems. Studies show that men with cholesterol readings of 200 or higher are more likely to suffer from impotence than those with lower levels. These guys also may be more likely to have a heart attack or stroke.

Lower cholesterol may be good for your heart and arteries, but cholesterol that's too low can cause a decrease in testosterone, particularly when lower levels result from taking cholesterol-lowering drugs. Your body actually needs a certain level of cholesterol to manufacture testosterone. Although a desirable level is below 200 milligrams per deciliter (mg/dL), a reasonable compromise seems to be a cholesterol reading in the neighborhood of 200 to 220 mg/dL, which can usually be achieved by eating small amounts of fat, sugary foods and refined carbs, as well as more veggies and fish. The following are the specifics of a potency-enhancing diet.

➤ **Limit the red.** To keep your arteries clear and your erections strong, eat red meat no more than a couple of times per week. When you do, keep portion sizes sensible. In 2006, according to the US Department of Agriculture, Americans ate a robust average of 36 ounces of red meat every week. A sexier choice is to enjoy a three- or four-ounce serving, which is about the size of a deck of cards, twice weekly (8 ounces). Meat does contain valuable nutrients, including zinc, protein, iron and vitamin B-12, but moderation is essential. Men who consumed less meat, including pork and chicken, and who eat more fish, almost always see a significant drop in cholesterol, by as much as 50 points in some cases! When you do eat red meat, make sure it is organic, grass fed and pasture raised. Meat raised in this manner contains far less proinflammatory omega-6 fatty acids and no additional growth hormones (meat contains some natural growth hormones) or chemical pesticides.

➤ **Avoid the trans fats.** Fast food is crammed with saturated fat and refined carbohydrates. That's bad for your arteries and your erections. Even worse are the deadly trans fats these foods contain. Trans fats are one of the main causes of heart disease, and are even worse than saturated fats because they clog arteries, decrease levels of protective HDL cholesterol and increase harmful LDL. Studies show that eating foods containing trans fats doubles your risk of a heart attack. Trans fats abound in deep-fried foods like French fries, doughnuts and fried chicken. While laws are being enacted to ban them from our food supply, they still remain in most crackers, cookies and chips.

➤ **Eat lean for love.** Want some extra motivation for eating lean? Researchers studied a group of overweight men who were having erection problems. Nearly one-third of them were assigned to a weight-loss program, which included exercise and smart eating. Guess what happened? The boys who lost weight completely regained their ability to have erections! Sexual health means eating well.

SHAKE THE SALT

Hypertension is a major risk factor for erection problems, partly because high blood pressure can damage the arteries that carry blood to the penis. Also, some hypertension drugs routinely cause sexual side effects. Salt consumption doesn't boost blood pressure in every person, but you'd lower your risk substantially if you keep your sodium intake to about 1,500 mg a day, or less than one teaspoon. Your body closely regulates its salt content, and men who eat a lot of sodium retain more fluids, which is nature's way of diluting it. More fluid means greater blood volume, which raises blood pressure. Men who reduce their salt intake to 1,500 mg typically have a drop in blood pressure of five to 10 points. Here are a few tips on kicking the salt habit. (See also "Hypertension," page 203, for more information.)

➤ **Cook without it.** Next time you're making a pot of chili or soup, leave the salt shaker in the cabinet. If you do want a little salt, choose unrefined sea salt. It tastes more "salty" (so you'll use less) and it's also full of beneficial trace minerals. In fact, most foods can easily be prepared without added salt, because most people usually add their own before eating.

➤ **Say no to processed foods.** The biggest source of stealth sodium is commercial foods. For example, one packet of ramen noodles contains 1,350 mg of sodium. A leading brand of frozen meatloaf dinner contains 1,300. Canned chili comes close at 1,250. Many canned soups have higher levels. By contrast, whole unprocessed foods contain virtually no sodium. Fruits, veggies, seafood and beans all begin with no added salt, so you can shake on a little if needed.

➤ **Substitute herbs for salt.** Sure, unsalted foods can taste bland, but many herbs and spices can take up the slack and reduce your salt tooth. I've found that one's craving for salt is a learned habit that is easily unlearned within two to three weeks of cutting back. Substituting zesty herbs, spices and peppers can help you feel less deprived. You can grow your own herbs on your kitchen countertop or windowsill, or purchase them fresh at the market. Make coleslaw with generous amounts of chopped oregano, mint

and basil. Cook fish with rosemary and other fresh herbs. This herbal zing will take the sting out of using less salt.

Supplemental Help

A man's ability to have an erection has as much to do with his lifestyle as his penis. Impaired circulation is obviously key, but so are factors like stress and fatigue. A guy who's exhausted or stressed all the time isn't likely to think much about sex, even if he's able to have it. Certain supplements can raise your energy level and help support the fundamentals of eating well, sleeping enough, working out and limiting stress.

➤ **Get going with ginkgo.** This leaf of the oldest living tree species is a potent antioxidant and *vasodilator*, which means that it opens up your arteries, and that can translate into stronger, more reliable erections. It's been used in traditional medicine for curing circulation disorders for centuries, and modern research is confirming its healing powers. One study found that more than three-quarters of men with ED who took ginkgo regained their ability to have normal erections. Because it improves circulation to the brain as well as the penis, many people also use it to boost their memory. Ginkgo also seems to reduce the erection difficulties that can occur as a side effect of some antidepressant drugs. The recommended dose is 40 mg, three times daily.

➤ **Go with yohimbe.** This is the only supplement approved by the FDA for treating sexual problems in men, and yohimbe (pronounced yo-HIM-bee) tea has been taken

Mediterranean Diet Reverses Erection Problems

Reversing erection difficulties can be accomplished simply by eating a Mediterranean-style diet, according to a new study conducted in Naples, Italy. Scientists studied men with ED and metabolic syndrome, a cluster of dangerous health conditions including obesity, high blood pressure, high blood sugar and high LDL cholesterol with low HDL. Researchers put half of the men on a Mediterranean diet, and noted 24 months later that nearly 50% of them scored higher than 22 out of 30 on a widely used erectile function scale. The lucky guys ate whole grains, fish, vegetables and fruits, along with walnuts, olive oil and avocados. The last three are all rich sources of healthy-heart monounsaturated fats. At the same time, they cut back on processed foods, high-fat dairy, red meat and refined carbohydrates, such as white bread and chips. The guys eating the Mediterranean way had better and stronger erections. They also reported more sexual desire and satisfaction.

for centuries in West Africa, where the tree it comes from grows. Yohimbe stimulates the release of *norepinephrine*, a hormone that improves circulation to the penis and increases sexual desire. Most sex supplements can take weeks or months to work, but yohimbe can improve erections within a few hours. Take 15 mg to 25 mg once a day, but talk to your doctor before trying it because yohimbe can cause spikes in blood pressure and dizziness. It can also interact with several prescription drugs and a variety of medical conditions. Never take Yohimbe without your MD's supervision!

➤ **The amorous amino.** In a recent study of men with ED, those who took supplemental *L-arginine* experienced significantly improved erections. L-arginine is an amino acid that occurs naturally in your body and increases nitric oxide, a chemical that opens blood vessels and gets blood moving. Taking the supplement produces the same effect. Women also seem to benefit. In one study, nearly three-quarters of women who took L-arginine had increased sexual desire. Recommended dose is 3,000 mg daily.

➤ **Ginseng for endurance.** Used for centuries in traditional Chinese medicine, Siberian ginseng can increase energy and libido, while improving overall health. Also called *Eleuthero*, Siberian ginseng stimulates the adrenal glands, offsetting the effects of stress, a common cause of low sex drive. Recommended dose is 500 mg to 3,000 mg daily of dried root capsules or tea. Or you can take 100 mg to 200 mg twice daily of a standardized liquid extract containing 0.8% to 1% *eleutherosides*.

➤ **C your performance improve.** Just about every man can benefit from extra vitamin C, which improves the activity of nitric oxide. By now you know that more nitric oxide means healthier erections. Unfortunately, millions of American men don't get enough vitamin C, and this is especially true among smokers. Smoking depletes vitamin C from the body, and according to the most recent estimates, more than one in four smokers is dangerously deficient. If you're eating the Mediterr-Asian way, you shouldn't need a supplement, but if you're smoking or experiencing stress, take a 500 mg to 1,000 mg supplement daily. You can also get a tasty vitamin C blast by popping an acerola berry. Popular in the Caribbean, it's a pure vitamin C powerhouse, with 80 mg in a single berry.

Other Helpers and Healers

➤ **Work it out.** Quite a few of my male patients were once vigilant exercisers but, in their later years, started to let physical activity slide. This is easy to do, but it's not good for your sex life. Exercise improves the tone of many different muscles, among them the ones that are vital to orgasm. Exercise triggers the production of the sex hormone testosterone and keeps it stable as we age, and encourages the release of brain neurotransmitters that scientists believe are involved in releasing the hormones that fuel our sex drive. Exercise improves your overall cardiovascular health, boosts blood circulation and enhances your stamina and endurance when you need it most. I've also found that guys who exercise regularly look younger, sexier, more fit and have more self-confidence. You don't need to be a marathoner or gym rat to achieve this. Hitting the weights a few days a week is usually all you need. Simply walking, along with a healthy diet, can keep you lean and fit. Using a pedometer and a pair of walking shoes can bring you more stamina within weeks. You can put the brakes on weight gain and accelerate your sex life.

➤ **Get your z-z-zs.** Human growth hormone (HGH), critical for muscle strength

146

as well as libido and erections, is mainly produced when you sleep. Men who are in the habit of staying up late and getting up early are shorting themselves of this sexy hormone. Six hours a night is not enough to replenish low HGH levels. To make sure you're getting enough sleep, go to bed at about the same time every night and get up after eight good hours of quality sleep. About an hour before you go to bed, start dimming the lights to help prepare your body's internal clock for sleep. Minimize bedroom distractions, such as watching television, using your phone or working on your laptop. Use the bedroom solely for sleep and—you guessed it—sex.

➤ **Check your thyroid.** Nearly 10% of men 60 years and over produce low levels of thyroid hormone. This essential gland, situated just below the Adam's apple, produces hormones that regulate energy. Men with insufficient levels of thyroid hormone (called *hypothyroidism*) frequently have problems with erections as well as very low energy. In fact, a study published in the *International Journal of Impotence Research* found that a majority of men with thyroid disorders experience erectile difficulties. Thyroid imbalance is easily diagnosed with a simple blood test to check levels of thyroid stimulating hormone (TSH) or to measure levels of T3 and T4, the key thyroid hormones. It's easily treated, too, with supplemental thyroid hormone.

➤ **Stress less.** Sex and stress don't mix. Men who are stressed out don't perform particularly well at any task, those in the bedroom included. Chronic stress interferes with body chemistry to diminish levels of testosterone and generates excess cortisol. You can reset both levels by exercising regularly and by starting a daily stress-reducing activity. Your body craves a little quiet. Plus, when you shift your focus from whatever's stressing you to your loved one, you're making room for romance. Many activities can help you release stress, from *tai chi* in the park to 15 minutes of quiet prayer or meditation in your favorite chair.

➤ **Manage your blood sugar.** Diabetes is responsible for as many as 40% of cases of ED. Many blood sugar problems are usually the result of how we live, be it gaining too much weight, not exercising enough or eating a lousy diet. Diabetes and other blood sugar problems damage nerves and blood vessels, accelerate the rate at which fat is deposited in arteries and reduce the body's production of nitric oxide, which helps blood vessels in the penis relax and fill with blood. Men with diabetes are about 400% more likely to have erection problems than those without it.

If you really want to protect your sex life, get in the habit of eating carbohydrate foods that are low on the glycemic index, including beans, produce and whole grains. Cut back on the take-out and baby back ribs. Eliminate processed foods like chips, frozen meals and cookies. I promise you won't go hungry. At the same

time, become more physically active. Men with prediabetes, a condition that often progresses to the real deal, can cut their risk 58% by exercising aerobically five days a week. Isn't your sex life worth it? I wish there was a shortcut or magic bullet, but there just isn't. Remember: Real men cook. Rebecca's recipes are the perfect excuse to immerse yourself in a new pastime (see pages 325–486), and I bet that cooking for your partner will add a new dimension to your love life.

➤ **Eat fiber for breakfast.** A high-fiber diet is among the best ways to lower your cholesterol and keep blood flowing where it counts. Research shows that men who eat a minimum of 25 to 40 g of fiber a day are far less likely to contract atherosclerosis or suffer from erection problems. For optimal circulation, make high-fiber plant foods—fruits, vegetables, nuts, seeds and whole-grain cereals—the center of your diet. (See "10 Top Fiber Foods" on page 104.) The time of day that you eat fiber helps. Men who load up on fiber early in the day are less likely to experience spikes in blood sugar that can damage delicate arteries in the penis. Plus, fiber is a dieter's best friend because it fills you up while slowing the rate at which your stomach empties, which means you'll stay full longer and be less likely to load up on surplus calories later on. ■

10

Eye Diseases

Cataracts and macular degeneration are among the leading causes of vision loss in the United States. Even though we have five senses, we use vision to understand about 80% of incoming data. Losing eyesight is a big loss indeed. While macular degeneration and cataracts damage the eyes in different ways, the underlying causes, and the power of certain foods to make a sight-changing difference, have a lot in common.

Cataracts occur when proteins in the lenses of the eyes gradually begin to disintegrate. Once the proteins lose their structural integrity, individual protein fibers form little clumps. Over the years, these clumps become thicker and spread over a larger area of the eye, causing vision to become cloudy. You can see but not distinctly. Eventually, you might lose some or all of your vision.

Macular degeneration is less likely than cataracts to cause total blindness, but it greatly impairs the quality of your sight. The most common type occurs when a layer of tissue that covers the *macula*, which is the part of the retina that permits central focus, but not peripheral vision, breaks down and accumulates metabolic waste products. This process damages the light-sensitive cells in the macula. Vision becomes blurry, and some people develop a blind spot right in the center of their vision.

SYMPTOMS

Both cataracts and macular degeneration usually progress slowly, so most people don't know what's happening until their vision is significantly impaired. However, a less common type of macular degeneration, known as the wet form, occurs much more quickly. One of the first warning signs is the inability to see things up close, such as a newspaper, without needing brighter lights. As the damage progresses, people notice they can't see well at night or recognize people at a distance. Colors appear washed out and everything starts to appear blurred.

Cataracts are more likely to affect the entire field of vision. People may find that both their distance and near vision are impaired. They may see halos around streetlights or traffic signals and almost certainly have difficulty seeing at night.

CAUSES

Both cataracts and macular degeneration are thought of as age-related conditions, and many doctors believe it's normal for the eyes to break down over time. However, this isn't entirely true. Even though older adults have a higher risk for cataracts and macular degeneration, the underlying changes that occur in the eyes have little to do with age alone. Some researchers now believe that the underlying issue is nutritional, because virtually every serious eye disease is either caused or made worse by free radicals, tissue-damaging oxidizing molecules that the body produces in reaction to excessive glucose and insulin in the bloodstream, too much sunshine, smoking, air pollution and polyunsaturated vegetable oils. Free radicals can destroy vision by ripping apart the molecules that make up individual cells in the eye.

Cataracts, for example, occur when free radicals damage proteins in the lenses of the eyes. Macular degeneration, on the other hand, is caused in part by free-radical damage to the center of the eye. It's estimated that about 80% of eye diseases, including most cases of cataracts and macular degeneration,

could be prevented with a free radical–fighting diet high in antioxidant-rich foods.

TREATMENT

The sun's ultraviolet rays are toxic to the eyes, so the first precaution is to wear sunglasses and a brimmed hat or cap to protect your eyes. This alone could make a huge difference, experts say.

There are no simple fixes for these conditions. Some try to get by with lifestyle changes, like using brighter lights or reading with a magnifying glass. Most people with cataracts will probably need surgery if they hope to regain normal vision. Macular degeneration is a more devastating condition. Once it has advanced, most people are unlikely to experience marked improvement in vision.

Luckily, people who eat an antioxidant-rich diet can neutralize the harmful effects of disease-causing free radicals before they cause lasting damage.

Foods That Make It Better

The incidence of cataracts and macular degeneration would plummet if everyone ate several weekly servings of brightly colored vegetables and fruits, which are the best source of antioxidant nutrients. Such a diet is equally important for patients who already have existing eye damage and those who wish to prevent it. The National Eye Institute's Age-Related Eye Disease Study reported that people who got the most beta-carotene, vitamin C and other antioxidants from the foods in their diet and supplements were almost 30% less likely to experience the progression of these conditions compared with those who consumed lower amounts.

FRUITS AND VEGETABLES TO THE RESCUE

Over the last decade, scientists have looked extensively at the antioxidant nutrients found in fresh produce. What started as an interesting hypothesis is now an established fact: People who eat generous amounts of fruits and vegetables—between five and six half-cup servings of vegetables and three to four half-cup servings of fruits daily—are far more likely to maintain healthy eyes. An important Harvard study that followed participants for a decade found that those who ate an abundance of fruits and vegetables were able to reduce their cataract risk by up to 15%.

➤ **Make a C change.** Vitamin C is among the most important nutrients for eye health. It's not only a powerful antioxidant but is also concentrated in the cornea and retina, where 60 times more vitamin C can be found than in the blood. Vitamin C also boosts protective action of vitamin E, another potent antioxidant. Can eating more vitamin C-rich foods help your eyesight? Yes, indeed.

In a study published in the prestigious *British Medical Journal*, researchers looked at diet and diseases in 50,000 women. They found, over a 10-year period, that participants who got the most vitamin C were 45% less likely to contract cataracts. Another study, this one conducted by scientists at Tufts University USDA Human Nutrition Research Center on Aging, found that people with very low levels of vitamin C were 11

150

times more likely to get cataracts than those with the highest levels.

We all know that citrus fruits are loaded with vitamin C. However, just about every vegetable, including bell peppers, broccoli and even onions, provides healthy amounts of this important nutrient. For a list of 10 top vitamin C foods, see page 161.

➤ **Quercetin pie, anyone?** Apples are a traditional symbol of health, but it's only recently that scientists have learned why. It's not so much the flesh, but the skin that's so impressively healthful. Apple peel contains high concentrations of an antioxidant known as *quercetin*. Also found in onions and tea, quercetin greatly reduces free radical damage in the lenses of the eyes. There's even some evidence that getting more quercetin may promote greater lens transparency in already-damaged eyes. So crunch an apple every day and you'll be doing your vision a big favor.

➤ **Eat like Popeye.** A lot of people don't like spinach. Here's a fact that might make you see spinach and its close cousins, Swiss chard and kale, in a new light. These greens are high in *lutein*, a member of the carotenoid family that includes beta-carotene. Lutein is a yellowish plant pigment that is concentrated in the retina. Its job is to reflect the harmful rays in sunshine, protecting it from cellular damage and reducing the risk of macular degeneration and cataracts.

A study at Harvard found that people who consume 6 milligrams (mg) of lutein daily had a 43% lower risk for macular degeneration compared with those who ate less. Studies show that those who get this much lutein, along with its sister carotenoid chemical, *zeaxanthin*, are significantly less likely to need cataract surgery than people who get smaller amounts. Leafy greens are the best food sources of both lutein and zeaxanthin. Since lutein is one of the few carotenoids that are absorbed directly by the eyes, you should consume as many lutein-rich foods as you can. One serving of spinach has anywhere from 1.7 mg to 13.3 mg of lutein. You'll get good amounts from just about any green vegetable. Zeaxanthin is equally important to better vision. One study found that when eye tissues were treated with these pigments, then exposed to sunlike radiation, they had up to 60% less damage than cells that didn't get a similar treatment. Vegetables such as kale, spinach, turnip greens, collard greens, romaine lettuce, broccoli, zucchini, garden peas and Brussels sprouts are among the best sources of lutein and zeaxanthin.

Because lutein concentrates in fatty tissue, people who are obese have less of it in their eyes. Researchers at Tufts University found that women who were obese were more than twice as likely to develop cataracts as those who kept their weight in check. The Mediterr-Asian Diet (see page 19) is ideal for weight control and it also helps maintain healthy blood sugar, critical for healthy eyes.

➤ **Bunnies do see better.** The brilliant color of carrots says that they're extremely high in beta-carotene and other carotenoids. Your body converts beta-carotene to vitamin A, which forms a pigment in the eye that helps you to see in dim light. Researchers have noted that people who are deficient in vitamin A may have trouble seeing at night.

Studies show that people who consume more beta-carotene foods and have higher blood levels of vitamin A are less likely to have problems with night vision.

➤ **Spread some bilberry jam.** Bilberries are a tart cousin of blueberries and cranberries and are amazingly high in flavonoids and *anthocyanosides*, the antioxidants that improve eye circulation. Here's an interesting bit of history. In the Battle of Britain, a certain unit of the Royal Air Force had significantly higher kill rates than other squadrons. A flight surgeon identified the reason why. The sharp-shooting pilots were eating wild bilberry jam.

➤ **Stalk better vision.** Asparagus is among the best sources of *cysteine*, an amino acid used by the body to manufacture *glutathione*, a powerful antioxidant that also blocks free-radical damage in the eyes. Studies have shown that virtually all eye lenses with cataracts are so deficient in glutathione that they contain only about one-fifteenth the amount they should. People with macular degeneration also have reduced levels of glutathione. Obviously, you should do everything possible to increase levels of glutathione in the eyes—it also improves the circulation of amino acids and minerals in and out of the eye, keeping the tissues nourished. You can achieve this by eating cysteine-rich foods, including eggs, onions, avocado and asparagus. Or, you simply can eat more foods that naturally contain glutathione. This means *any* vegetable or fruit. Eat produce raw because cooking reduces levels of glutathione.

12 Top Beta-Carotene Foods

1. Peppers, hot chilies
2. Lettuce, green leaf or red
3. Kale, cooked
4. Spinach, cooked
5. Carrots, cooked
6. Mustard greens, cooked
7. Swiss chard, cooked
8. Watercress, raw
9. Beet greens, cooked
10. Cilantro leaves, raw
11. Squash, winter and butternut, cooked
12. Pumpkin, cooked

OIL YOUR EYES

Like glutathione, vitamin E is one of the most powerful antioxidants known. It's important for eye health because it works in the fatty parts of the eyes, where vitamin C is ineffective. One study found that those with the highest blood levels of vitamin E were 50% less likely to get cataracts than individuals with lower amounts. Other studies indicate that people who have a high intake of vitamin E and other antioxidants can reduce their risk for macular degeneration by about 25%.

The best food sources of vitamin E include fish, olive oil, wheat germ, nuts and sunflower seeds. The recommended daily amount for vitamin E is 30 international units (IU), which is about what you'd get from a half cup of almonds or a handful of sunflower seeds.

FISH FOR BETTER VISION

➤ **Put salmon on the grill.** A Harvard study found that people who eat one or more weekly servings of salmon (or other fatty fish such mackerel, sardines and anchovies) reduced their cataract risk by up to 12%. This is because salmon and other cold-water fish are high in omega-3 fatty acids. These beneficial fats concentrate in the eye membrane and play a critical role in vision. Omega-3s also reduce the tendency of blood to clot and help improve blood circulation in the arteries of the eyes. The famous Nurses' Health Study found that women who ate four or more servings of fish per week had significantly lower instances of macular degeneration than those who ate fish three times or less each month.

➤ **Buy it wild.** Wild salmon, available at most higher-end supermarkets, is better for the eyes than its farm-raised cousins. Wild salmon eat algae as part of their regular diets, which increases their production of DHA, a type of fatty acid that's used by the body to repair cell damage caused by free radicals. Farm-raised salmon contains less DHA.

➤ **Eye those oysters.** It's more than a myth that raw oysters can fire up your sexual appetite. The mineral responsible for this, zinc, also perks up your eyesight. Oysters are loaded with zinc, which is also found in high concentrations in the retina of the eye. Studies indicate that people who are deficient in zinc may have a higher than normal risk of macular degeneration. In a study at Louisiana State University, patients with early signs of macular degeneration were either given zinc supplements or a placebo for up to two years. Later eye and vision tests showed that people in the zinc group had better vision than those given the placebo.

To learn more about foods and recipes that can improve your vision, visit *www.my healingkitchen.com.*

Foods That Make It Worse

➤ **Unhook yourself from sugar.** The same foods that you'd avoid in order to protect your heart and arteries, namely sugary foods and quickie carbs, such as fatty burgers and fries, trans fats, polyunsaturated vegetable oils and processed foods in general, are also the ones that can destroy your eyesight. Sugar and high glycemic index (GI) foods trigger the release of extra insulin into the bloodstream, which can gunk up blood flow in the tiny capillaries of the eyes and cause obstructions known as *plaques*. To make things worse, excess blood sugar creates a crusting called *glycation* on tissue and in organs, which generates huge amounts of free radicals and inflammation. Glycation accelerates the wrinkling of the skin, the aging of organs and tissue in the body and diminishes blood circulation to all parts of the body, especially the eyes. This is why people with diabetes frequently look 10 to 15 years older than their biological age and commonly suffer blindness as a complication of their disease. You'd be wise to cut back on, or eliminate, these foods from your diet.

➤ **Ease up on meat.** Studies show that people who have more than one weekly serving of beef, pork or lamb are 35% more likely to develop macular degeneration than those who eat these meats less often. While there's

nothing wrong with enjoying a juicy steak, people with macular degeneration would do better to consume more fish or chicken, along with generous portions of leafy greens and other vegetables.

➤ **Ditch the doughnuts.** Prepared pastries, particularly fried treats such as doughnuts, are invariably high in fat and sugar. It's been estimated that just one daily doughnut or a single serving of other processed baked goods can increase your risk for macular degeneration by 150%.

➤ **Consider your condiments.** It's easy to sabotage the most healing foods and meals with health-ruining condiments. For instance, you could wisely open a can of omega 3-rich tuna for lunch, but then smother it in mayo. Or order a fresh green salad, but then douse it with creamy ranch dressing. Most creamy dressings are high in polyunsaturated vegetable oil—usually corn, safflower, soybean or canola. Each of these oils is very high in omega-6 fatty acids. A long-running Harvard study found that a diet high in omega-6s increases the risk of cataracts. Stick with extra-virgin olive oil and balsamic vinegar. If you enjoy a creamy dressing, blend your own, using yogurt or buttermilk as a base.

➤ **Drink lightly.** The evidence linking alcohol with cataracts is mixed. In one study, researchers found that even women who drank lightly—two drinks per week—increased their risk of one form of cataracts by 13%. Other studies, however, have found that alcohol isn't a significant risk factor, or may even provide a benefit in some cases. Until the evidence is sorted out, I advise patients to use common sense and follow the recommended guidelines of no more than one daily drink for women or two for men. Just to be on the safe side, abstain for one to two days per week.

➤ **Skip the salt.** When Australian scientists studied nearly 3,000 subjects, they found that people who use more than a teaspoon of salt—daily—have double the risk for cataracts compared with those who consume only a half teaspoon. It's possible that excess salt in the diet interferes with the normal balance of sodium in the eye. In general, salt from the shaker isn't the main problem. Most of the salt in our diets is hidden in processed foods, such as canned soups, sliced meats and even foods that don't seem salty, such as baked goods. Dill pickles and fast-food chicken (broiled or grilled) contain more than 1,000 mg of sodium per serving. This is half the recommended daily allowance. Protect yourself by reading nutritional labels carefully.

Supplemental Help

Most of the nutrients and antioxidants that play a pivotal role in eye health are readily available from food sources. If you need extra help, you can use nutritional supplements to provide higher levels of the nutrients that help both of these conditions. Here are the ones I recommend.

➤ **Above C level.** Since so many foods contain vitamin C, it's easy to get the official recommended daily allowance (RDA) of 85 to 90 mg just by eating several daily servings of fresh fruits and vegetables. Unfortunately, this amount is the bare minimum, and nowhere near enough to provide optimal eye protection.

154

To prevent cataracts and macular degeneration, try to get between 500 mg and 1,000 mg of vitamin C daily. There's good evidence that people who consistently get this amount can reduce their risk for cataracts by up to 70%. Supplements are particularly important

More Beta per Bite

Beta-carotene and other carotenoids are among the most important antioxidants for vision and eye health. That's the good news. However, until Americans change their eating habits and start consuming more fruits and vegetables, their levels of these important substances will always be on the low side, and that means poor vision is on the horizon for many of us, if it's not already here. Don't let it happen to you.

➤ **Add a little fat.** Like other fat-soluble nutrients, beta-carotene can't get into your system unless it's combined with a little fat. It doesn't take much, perhaps a little avocado or a drizzle of extra-virgin olive oil. Research indicates that avocado is the best food to enhance absorption of carotenoids, especially beta-carotene, which turns into vitamin A in the body.

➤ **Cook your carrots.** The fiber in raw carrots traps some of the beta-carotene, making it unavailable to your body's cells. Cooking carrots helps break down the fiber and allows the beta-carotene to be released.

Also helpful: After steaming, save the cooking water and add it to a soup or sauce to preserve nutrients that might otherwise have been lost.

➤ **Crank up the juicer.** Another way to extract more beta-carotene from carrots is to juice them.

if you smoke, or used to. Why? Smoking increases the risk for cataracts and macular degeneration. In fact, every cigarette you smoke depletes about 25 mg of vitamin C from the body. The best thing, of course, is to quit smoking. However, until you're ready, take a daily vitamin C supplement to keep your eyes healthier.

➤ **Better flow with ginkgo biloba.** Studies show that ginkgo biloba, taken in supplement form, can increase circulation to the optic nerve by more than 20%. It also appears to improve vision in patients who already have glaucoma. Take 120 mg, twice daily. You can also drink gingko biloba tea. Never take ginkgo biloba with aspirin or any anticoagulant, such as *warfarin*, because of its blood-thinning effects.

➤ **Give yourself a digestive boost.** It's common for older adults, even those who eat a healthy diet, to experience nutritional deficiencies because of impaired digestion. That's because the body's production of stomach acid declines with age, so food isn't digested completely. The result is that the nutrient-hungry cells in your eyes don't get all of the nourishment they need. I advise patients 65 years and older to take daily supplements that contain *betaine hydrochloride*. It's similar to the hydrochloric acid produced by the stomach. Better digestion can increase the levels of nutrients to the eye cells, as well as everywhere else in your body. The usual dose

is one to three capsules daily—about 1,000 micrograms—taken with meals.

➤ **New breakthrough supplement combo.** About 90% of patients with age-related macular degeneration have the dry form. Until recently, no treatment was shown to have a real impact on this disease. But researchers participating in the Age-Related Eye Disease Research Study recently announced a groundbreaking finding: Certain supplements *do* make a significant difference.

In the study, 3,640 men and women were divided into one of four groups: those taking a placebo, antioxidants, zinc or antioxidants plus zinc. The researchers followed the patients for five years and discovered that those in the zinc-antioxidant group experienced a 25% reduction in the progression of the disease. The same nutrient combo reduced the risk for vision loss by 19% in high-risk patients. This is a truly remarkable finding, one that you should put to use right away if you have an intermediate or advanced macular degeneration. Based on these results, I recommend the following daily supplements to be taken together.

• **Vitamin E.** 200 to 400 IU, preferably mixed tocopherols, along with tocotrienols.

• **Beta-carotene.** Up to 7,500 IU.

• **Zinc.** Up to 50 mg balanced with 1 mg of copper for every 20 to 30 mg of zinc. (Zinc without copper can have a negative effect on cholesterol.) ■

CHAPTER

11

Fatigue

Are you one of the millions of people who feel so drained or rundown that you can't summon the energy to enjoy life? Half of adult Americans complain about fatigue when they consult their doctors, indicating a level of chronic exhaustion that isn't the same as being a little tired now and then. Constant fatigue dulls memory and concentration, kills clarity of thought and simply makes it difficult for some people to stay awake.

Americans work the longest hours of all industrialized nations. It's no surprise, then, that nearly 40% of us are sleep deprived. Research shows that sleepy drivers are just as dangerous as drunk drivers, and nearly two-thirds of US drivers say they've driven while drowsy! In fact, about 100,000 annual car crashes are attributed to fatigue. At the same time, we're gulping down copious amounts

of caffeine, about 4.5 billion speedy drinks per week, just to get an energizing lift or to feel what we think is normal.

SYMPTOMS

However, chronic fatigue is *not* normal. People who feel exhausted are often borderline sick and far more likely to make serious errors of judgment. Fatigued workers don't function well either, because they lack focus and concentration. Marriages and relationships also suffer, and studies show that the fatigued are more likely to die prematurely than those who sleep well and face the world well rested.

CAUSES

It may sound obvious, but not sleeping long enough, or well enough, is one of the primary causes of fatigue. Most of us require at least six to nine hours of good sleep per day and, if you're not getting that much, fatigue will result. However, millions of Americans *do* get enough sleep and still experience a constant sense of tiredness. Too much caffeine or stress can cause fatigue, as can poor nutrition, vitamin B-12 deficiency and a condition called *adrenal fatigue*. It can also be a symptom of many underlying health problems, including anemia, depression, diabetes and even cancer. It can also result from low thyroid function, with symptoms making you feel cold and sluggish, as well as causing dry skin and hair.

TREATMENT

If you have fatigue without a clear cause, see your doctor. Some conditions, such as low thyroid, which affects women far more often than men, can be diagnosed easily with a series of tests, then treated with thyroid replacement hormone. This usually restores energy levels quickly.

If you get a clean bill of health from your physician and your sleep patterns are more or less normal, the next step should be to examine your diet. Certain foods make us sleepy, while others provide an energizing boost. Refined carbohydrates cause blood sugar to surge, then crash. The best energy foods—high-quality proteins, monounsaturated oils such as extra-virgin olive oil, and complex carbohydrates such as whole grains, vegetables and nuts—provide steady and lasting energy. It's only during the last few decades that science has truly begun to understand how foods work in our bodies, and we can use this knowledge to acquire and maintain significant energy.

Foods That Make It Better

Every mood you experience is affected to some degree by *neurotransmitters*, brain chemicals that relay messages from one brain cell to the next, carrying messages. Two important neurotransmitters, known as *dopamine* and *norepinephrine*, have such profound effects on our energy levels that they're sometimes called the *wake-up chemicals*. The foods you eat can significantly affect your brain's neurotransmitter balance. At the same time, what you eat largely controls not only the amount of fuel that's available to your body's cells but also how long that fuel lasts. Glucose from carbohydrates is the body's primary fuel, but vitamins, minerals and amino acids also determine whether your energy ebbs or flows. Let's start with the most important meal of the day.

BREAKFAST COMES FIRST

Your mother was right. You need to eat breakfast. The word itself indicates that you are "breaking the fast" of the previous eight to 10 hours since your last meal. Imagine not eating for that long during the day! When you wake up, your blood sugar is low and a cup or two of strong coffee can trick your body into believing it's energized, but only for so long. You simply can't operate at your best without fuel in the morning, because your body and brain are waiting for glucose to get their engines started.

If you're dealing with fatigue, missing breakfast usually makes it worse. About one-quarter of adults skip breakfast and fully half eat it only sometimes. People give all sorts of reasons: They don't want to gain weight, don't have time, aren't hungry in the morning. These end up being weak excuses when you need to power your morning.

Without fuel, your metabolic rate drops, making you feel sluggish. Even if you pack in those missing calories at lunch, you'll never fully recover from these metabolic doldrums. Starting your day with a good breakfast, on the other hand, causes your metabolic rate to jump by about 25%, which is why most people say they feel better when they eat something in the morning. Researchers found that eating breakfast regularly was the most common trait among people who lived to be centenarians.

Skipping breakfast to lose weight is a counterproductive strategy. Research shows that those who miss their first meal of the day often consume more calories later. Eating when you wake up puts your energy levels at the starting line for the morning's performance, but you also need to eat a smart breakfast. Here are some pointers.

➤ **Hold the juice and white toast.** The carbohydrates in these foods are almost instantly transformed into blood sugar, with virtually the same effect on glucose levels as eating a doughnut. Your blood sugar and energy levels will crash before the morning is half over.

➤ **Toss the cold cereal.** Most boxed cold cereals are made of refined carbohydrates dressed up with vitamins and minerals, but with little fiber and other complex carbs to provide a steady supply of energy.

➤ **Plan ahead.** Stock up on all kinds of fruit, washing enough for several days and placing it in bowls in the fridge or on the counter so it's always ready to eat. If you absolutely can't sit down for breakfast, bag a few pieces of fruit to eat during your commute.

If you walk part of the way to work—and I hope you do—eat some fruit before setting off and enjoy the rest when you arrive. Add a handful of walnuts or a small chunk of your favorite cheese to slow glucose conversion, which will keep your energy levels stable and longer lasting.

➤ **Stay smooth.** Yogurt is a breakfast all-star. Choose plain yogurt with a label indicating that it has live cultures. Spoon out a cup and top with a few prunes or a sliced banana or, my favorite, fresh berries. Add some chopped walnuts or ground flaxseed. Or, you might choose to blend frozen berries, yogurt, protein powder, ground flaxseed and a splash of pomegranate juice to create a super smoothie that will keep you going all morning.

➤ **Milk is good protein.** Milk in the morning is a good idea. All types of milk—cow's, soy or nutty almond—are good sources of protein, which enhance the steady release of energy. Pour it on your oatmeal or into a smoothie or enjoy a cold glass with one of the breakfast sandwiches described on the next page.

➤ **Make it complex.** Complex carbohydrates deliver sustained energy, and oatmeal is queen of the morning complex carbs. Buy a box of steel-cut or Irish oatmeal and make a big batch on Sunday, cooling and storing it in your fridge for the week ahead. Then, each morning, scoop out a cup, toss in some raisins, cinnamon and a little milk and heat. Summer or winter, this breakfast will keep your energy levels stable. For even more nutrition, sprinkle on some berries or other fruit, crushed walnuts and ground flaxseed.

➤ **Make a breakfast sandwich.** Keep a loaf of sliced whole-grain bread in your freezer and take two slices out before bedtime. When you wake up, slather one slice with a tablespoon or two of natural peanut butter and some all-fruit preserves, or sprinkle with raisins or banana slices. Top with the other slice, cutting your sandwich into quarters and eating the first quarter with a big glass of milk before you leave the house. Pack the rest to finish during your commute. Or make a morning sandwich of turkey and cheese or a hard-boiled egg. Find true whole-grain bread (whole grain is the first ingredient on the list) with at least 3 grams (g) of fiber per serving and make your own magnificent morning sandwiches. For a list of my favorite "In a Hurry" Breakfasts, see page 290.

COMBINE CARBS WITH PROTEIN

Many people find that their energy fades midmorning or after lunch. You can minimize this slump by combining complex carbohydrates and a protein source at every meal. Protein contains amino acids, which help fight fatigue and elevate serotonin levels in the brain. Combining protein with complex carbs controls your hunger and sustains your blood sugar for steady energy.

The ratio of fats to carbohydrates also comes into play. In one study, volunteers were given a variety of lunches. Some lunches were high in carbs and low in fat, others had medium levels of both and still others were high in fat and low in carbs. People who consumed too many carbs and too much fat tended to get sleepy in the afternoon. The optimal mix, the researchers concluded, was a lunch that consisted primarily of complex carbohydrates, but that also included adequate amounts of fat and protein. Think of raw veggies with a hummus dip. Or a whole-wheat pita with chicken salad.

If your usual lunch is a plate of pasta, you're probably spending a good chunk of the afternoon in snoozeland. However, a serving of lean chicken breast on whole-wheat pasta, or a green salad topped with hard-boiled eggs, delivers balanced fat, protein and carbohydrates. A lunch like that should definitely improve your afternoon energy levels. Beans are another great complex carb that can be added to the lunch mix. Try a bean burrito with chicken. Or black bean soup with chopped egg.

WHOLE-FOOD ENERGY

The typical American diet has been processed to within an inch of its nutritional life, which is why millions of people don't get anywhere near enough B vitamins and why fatigue is such a widespread problem in the United States today. You've probably heard of *beriberi*, a disease caused by an extreme deficiency of thiamine or vitamin B-1. It literally means "I cannot, I cannot," which is an apt name for a disease that causes extreme exhaustion. A deficiency of any B vitamin can have similar effects, because your body uses these nutrients at virtually every point in the energy cycle.

Shockingly, many people are borderline deficient in B vitamins. Even if you eat a mainly whole-foods diet, emotional stress can deplete a lot of B, and stress, as most of us know, goes hand in hand with fatigue.

People who take diuretics or birth control pills also may run low on B vitamins. There are eight different B vitamins, and low levels of any can cause fatigue, difficulty in concentrating and a general sense of weakness. Don't let this happen to you. B vitamins are found in virtually every unadulterated plant food: beans, grains, fruits and vegetables.

The one exception is vitamin B-12, which occurs only in animal foods. It's an essential antifatigue vitamin because its function is essential to energy production, from cell formation to helping produce adrenal hormones. B-12 works with folic acid to control the production of oxygen-carrying red blood cells, and keeps your nervous system healthy by helping your body use iron. If you don't eat many animal products, you need a vitamin B-12 supplement. Taking a B-complex 100 tablet every day will cover your B requirements not met by foods.

In addition, start eating more salads, whole grains, fresh fruits and vegetables and you'll quickly notice an increase in energy and, in many cases, a decrease in emotional stress. Here's another instance in which beans are the ideal food. Add them to salads along with chopped raw veggies, drizzled with an extra-virgin olive oil and balsamic vinaigrette. Beans are loaded with *folate*, one of the B-vitamins vital for the development of red blood cells that carry oxygen and thus, energy, throughout your body. You can't get too much of the Bs because they're water soluble, so any extra is flushed out of your body in urine.

➤ **Raw veggies rule.** Keep a stash of cut-up raw vegetables in the fridge, washed and ready to snack on. You'll be amazed at how good they taste at 3:30 PM when the urge for sugar strikes. Or pile them onto a plate to enjoy an hour before dinner. You'll eat less at mealtime, which is an easy way to control, or lose, weight.

➤ **Bean salad bonanza.** If you're hungry at 10:30 in the morning after your oatmeal or yogurt-and-fruit breakfast has been metabolized, have a cup of kidney bean salad with chopped onion and green pepper, dressed in extra-virgin olive oil and balsamic vinaigrette. You may think bean salad is a bizarre morning snack, but the results will change your mind. Becoming more productive while everyone else in the office is struggling with midmorning slump might be valuable to you in the form of a raise or promotion.

MINE FOR IRON

Your body uses iron to create hemoglobin, which carries oxygen in red blood cells. If you don't get enough iron in your diet, tissues throughout your body and brain may not get enough oxygen, which is a recipe for persistent fatigue. Iron deficiency is the most common nutritional deficiency in the world, including the food-rich United States. Up to one-third of American women are iron deficient. Even a minor deficiency of iron can make you feel tired and weak, an occurrence so common that doctors often assume people experiencing fatigue are deficient in iron. Here's how to get more iron safely and easily.

➤ **Lean on meats and seafood.** There are two forms of iron: the readily absorbed *heme* iron in meats and seafood and the less-absorbable *non-heme* iron in plant foods. Beef, pork and poultry are good sources of iron, but some seafood choices actually contain more. A three-ounce serving of clams or oysters has about 7.4 milligrams (mg) of iron. That's more iron than in three ounces of beef, which contains 7.0 mg.

➤ **Pair meats and vegetables.** Pairing meats and vegetables in the same meal can increase the absorption of non-heme iron from 10% to 15%.

➤ **Cook in cast iron.** Some of the iron in that trusty black skillet is released during cooking. This can increase your iron intake by about 5% more than the iron in the foods alone.

➤ **Space out calcium and iron.** High-calcium foods, such as milk, block the absorption of iron by your body. This isn't a big issue with dietary iron, but it can significantly reduce the effects of iron supplements. If you're taking iron, don't load up on calcium at the same time.

➤ **Citrus and salad.** You can get some iron from plant foods, even though it's not as easy for the body to absorb as iron from meat. Here's a trick to significantly increase your iron absorption from iron-rich plant foods, such as spinach and whole grains: Eat them with a vitamin C-rich food. Vitamin C increases the body's ability to take in iron. Try orange slices on a spinach salad or a whole-grain sandwich with high-C sweet red peppers. Read on for more ways vitamin C can boost your energy levels.

REV UP WITH C

Over the years, I've occasionally diagnosed patients with vitamin C deficiency anemia. This occurs when individuals don't get the

vitamin C they need to produce healthy red blood cells. Low vitamin C also impairs the body's ability to absorb iron, so it can contribute to iron-deficiency anemia as well. While low C anemia is rare, there's some evidence that those getting enough vitamin C in their diets can boost energy by getting a little more. One study that looked at health professionals and their spouses found that those who got at least 400 mg of vitamin C daily had significantly more energy than those who consumed lower amounts. It's possible that the energy boost is linked to vitamin C's effects on neurotransmitters. The body uses C to synthesize *norepinephrine*, one of the energizing brain chemicals. It also plays a role in powering up *mitochondria*, the energy plants inside our cells. There's nothing wrong with taking vitamin C supplements,

10 Top Vitamin C Foods	
1. Guava	188 mg/½ cup
2. Red bell pepper, raw	142 mg/½ cup
3. Orange juice	76 mg/¾ cup
4. Kiwi	70 mg/1 medium
5. Grapefruit juice	60 mg/¾ cup
6. Strawberries	49 mg/½ cup
7. Brussels sprouts, cooked	48 mg/½ cup
8. Broccoli, cooked	37 mg/½ cup
9. Cauliflower, cooked	28 mg/½ cup
10. Kale, cooked	27 mg/½ cup

but if you're eating a fruit and vegetable-based diet, you'll get your fill of C.

PERK UP WITH POULTRY

There are many reasons to eat more poultry and less red meat. Better energy is one of them. Turkey and chicken are high in *tyrosine*, an amino acid that's one of the building blocks of the brain chemicals dopamine and norepinephrine. People who get their protein from poultry, as well as fish and low-fat dairy, get additional tyrosine with relatively little saturated fat and fewer calories. That's good for your heart, your weight and your overall energy.

AN ALMOND SNACK

A study published in the *European Journal of Applied Physiology and Occupational Physiology* looked at the effect of carbohydrates and fats on how people experience fatigue after exercise. Researchers found that people who ate almonds reported a significant delay in exhaustion, whereas 50% of those in the control group, and a group that ate sugar cubes, complained of exhaustion. This isn't surprising. Almonds are high in carbohydrates, as well as protein and healthy fats. They provide a slow burn that keeps energy levels flowing steady.

PASS THE POTASSIUM AND MAGNESIUM, PLEASE

Fatigue is one of the main symptoms of potassium deficiency, and potassium levels are one of the first things doctors check when patients tell them that their energy is in the dumps. You can avoid this deficiency by loading up on fruits and vegetables for maximum potassium, a mineral essential for cellular energy. Excellent sources include Swiss chard,

162

romaine lettuce, cremini mushrooms, cooked spinach and raw celery. For a list of "10 Top Potassium-Rich Foods," see page 207.

Potassium doesn't work alone, however. It must be balanced with magnesium. In some studies, up to 90% of participants had significant boosts in energy when they received extra potassium and magnesium in tandem. It's fine to take a multiple or combo supplement to ensure you're getting enough of both these minerals, but they're widely available in foods. Thanks to Mother Nature's perfect packaging, these two often occur together. So, eat your magnesium-rich and potassium-rich spinach and Swiss chard. Add some extra magnesium by enjoying pumpkin seeds, Chinook salmon, black beans and halibut.

WATER, WATER EVERYWHERE

With water bottles everywhere, you'd think most Americans would be adequately hydrated. Not true. Millions spend their days in a state of mild dehydration, without enough fluid in their circulatory system. This can deplete blood flow to vital organs, including the brain. And depletion of blood flow means more fatigue.

The Institute of Medicine recommends that women get about 11 eight-ounce cups of water daily. Men need more, about 16 cups a day. This may sound like a directive to swig water by the quart, but about 20% of our fluid intake comes from food. Get your share, which is about nine cups daily for women, 12 for men, from pure water and herbal noncaffeinated teas, plus natural soups and broths. Scratch sodas and sugary fruit drinks off your shopping list.

For other ways to fight fatigue with food, visit *www.myhealingkitchen.com.*

Foods That Make It Worse

If you love big meals, you may also love frequent naps.

Here's why: When you consume a lot of calories at once, blood rushes to your stomach to aid digestion. That blood has to come from somewhere, and quite a lot drains from your brain. Even a slight drop in brain circulation, with the accompanying drop in oxygen, can cause fatigue. Heavy meals also cause extreme fluctuations in your body's insulin response, which is why nearly everyone gets sleepy after holiday feasts. Here are some recommendations to prevent postmeal fatigue.

BEWARE OF BIG MEALS

Eating three square meals a day doesn't lend itself to good insulin control or steady glucose supplies. It's much better to eat five or six smaller meals scattered throughout the day to keep your energy up and fatigue at bay. What you eat matters, too. Focus on whole foods. Eating a bag of chips, full of highly refined carbohydrates, as your midmorning snack will push up your glucose briefly before it crashes, leaving you feeling sluggish and hungry for carbs again.

EASE OFF THE SWEETS

One of the ironies of corporate life is that the same companies that try to wring the last drop of performance from exhausted employees are the same ones stocking doughnuts in meeting rooms or near the coffee pot. The problem with sugar, whether it comes from the sugar bowl or in the form of highly refined carbohydrates like pastries, is that it surges into the bloodstream immediately, delivering a quick hit of energy that doesn't last. Worse, the energy jolt is invariably followed by a crash as reserves are depleted. In no time, those employees will be sleepy or hungry again.

There's no mystery as to *why.* When your blood sugar spikes, your body releases a wave of *insulin,* the hormone that ushers sugars from the blood into individual cells. This gives cells immediate energy, but at the same time removes glucose from your bloodstream and brain. Low blood sugar, as everyone knows, makes you weak, tired and drowsy. A sugary snack produces another negative effect. When you eat sweets or refined carbs, the excess sugar stimulates brain chemicals that make you even sleepier.

To avoid this energy crash, kick the refined snack habit. Try replacing most of the sugar in your diet with the natural sugars found in fresh fruit or dried fruit, such as apricots or prunes. Sprinkle a bit of cinnamon on a sliced pear and see if it satisfies your sweet tooth. If you simply must have a cookie, minimize the energy-draining effects by first eating other foods that provide a slower, longer-lasting energy source. Munch a cookie after you've eaten a turkey sandwich on whole grain with vegetables, for example. Look for other healthful combos that will satisfy your sweet tooth, such as a small piece of dark chocolate with a half dozen walnuts or an apple with a piece of cheese.

CUT BACK THE COFFEE

A cup of coffee, depending on its size and preparation, can contain between 30 and

150 mg of caffeine. At these doses, caffeine is a drug, and one with powerful physiological effects. This isn't necessarily bad. New research indicates that coffee drinkers are better protected from diabetes and may have a lower risk for heart disease than people who don't drink it. Caffeine gets your heart beating, raises blood pressure and generally cranks up your nervous system. Studies show that people do better on tests and feel more alert when they have their morning java.

But there's a limit. Even in small amounts, caffeine signals the pituitary gland to secrete a hormone that increases levels of adrenaline, one of our fight-or-flight hormones that revs up just about every system in the body. The caffeine rush feels good for a while. However, what goes up must come down, and the caffeine high is usually followed by a caffeine crash. If you slug coffee by the mugful, your energy is likely to suffer.

The human body isn't designed to stay in a perpetual state of high alert. People who drink a lot of caffeinated drinks every day are pushing their adrenal glands to exhaustion. At some point, the body can no longer keep up. This is especially true when you drink coffee late in the day. Caffeine stays in your body for hours and, while you might sleep through the night, caffeine can disturb the architecture of sleep, so you aren't as rested the next day.

In one study, people with fatigue were put on a caffeine-free (and sugar-free) diet for a few weeks. Many reported significant improvements in their symptoms. Then, when they resumed their regular caffeine- and sugar-laced routine, nearly 50% of them experienced

a return of their fatigue. Those who drink moderate amounts of coffee, between one and three cups daily, can usually enjoy the stimulating effects without dropping into the doldrums. This response is highly variable. If you're sensitive to caffeine, a single cup might be too much. If it doesn't seem to bother you, two or three cups are probably okay, but try some new drinks, too. *Here are some examples…*

➤ **Go herbal.** Sometimes, we just want something to sip. A cup of hot or iced green tea, loaded with health-giving antioxidants called *polyphenols*, can satisfy that urge without a huge caffeine jolt.

➤ **Sparkling fruit.** Sparkling water takes on a satisfying new dimension when you mix in a little 100% fruit juice. Start with ice in a tall glass, pour in some healthful 100% juice, including pomegranate, cranberry or grape, before filling your glass to the brim with fizzy water like seltzer or sparkling mineral water. It refreshes your thirst and sweet tooth, but with only a tiny fraction of the calories that a soda delivers.

➤ **C water.** For a vitamin C boost, squeeze a whole lemon or lime into a glass of iced or un-iced water. The citrus will perk up your taste buds and the C will energize your cells.

Supplemental Help

The same supplements that can help relieve chronic fatigue can also help with general fatigue. In addition, you might experiment with some of these and see if they perk up your energy levels.

Chronic Fatigue: Running on Empty

Chronic fatigue syndrome (CFS) is a debilitating medical condition that affects more than 14 million Americans, leaving them not just tired, but bone tired. In many cases, they are so exhausted that their lives grind to a halt.

Most people with CFS have symptoms for about six months before seeking help, but some suffer for years before being diagnosed. Doctors still don't know what causes CFS, though some believe it might be linked to a prior viral (or retroviral) infection. New research indicates that CFS is accompanied by degeneration of the *mitochondria*, energy-producing parts inside cells. The Centers for Disease Control and Prevention (CDC) defines CFS as unexplained lack of energy for at least six months, accompanied by four or more of the following: muscle aches, sore throat, headaches, postexertion fatigue, joint pain, memory dysfunction, insomnia or swelling or tenderness of the lymph nodes.

Since we don't know what causes CFS, physicians focus on relieving individual symptoms, usually with medications. My approach is different. I've had considerable success with supplements that help individual cells work harder.

➤ **NADH.** *Nicotinamide adenine dinucleotide* (NADH) is a cofactor that facilitates the energy-transfer reactions in mitochondria. In studies performed at Georgetown Medical Center, patients given NADH supplements for four weeks reported a 31% reduction in fatigue symptoms, increasing to 81% after a year. Start with 5 mg a day.

➤ **Coenzyme Q10.** Like NADH, coenzyme Q10 (CoQ10) affects the electron-transport system in mitochondria, and allows cells to generate energy more efficiently. The recommended dose is 100 to 200 mg a day of a water-soluble form.

➤ **L-carnitine.** This amino acid is involved in moving fatty acids to the mitochondria, where the fats are burned for fuel. After combustion, L-carnitine removes the waste products, which allows cells to work at peak efficiency. I recommend a broad-spectrum carnitine that combines 500 to 1000 mg per day of L-carnitine, acetyl-L-carnitine and propionyl L-carnitine.

➤ **Magnesium.** This mineral is involved in more than 300 enzymatic reactions in the body, and is the main player in cellular energy dynamics. Take 400 to 600 mg of magnesium citrate, *glycinate orotate* or *taurinate*.

➤ **Folic acid.** A study of 60 CFS patients found that 50% had low levels of folic acid. A daily supplement or multivitamin that includes folic acid is fine, but you should also eat generously from folate-rich foods including beans and other legumes, spinach and collards. Make sure your multivitamin contains 800 micrograms of folic acid or purchase an individual supplement.

➤ **D-ribose.** This metabolic sugar is critical for cellular production of *adenosine-5'-triphosphate* (ATP). Research shows that 80% of people with CFS who take D-ribose will experience improvement in symptoms. One teaspoon three times a day in juice or water will increase your energy significantly.

In addition to supplements, many people with CFS undergo a detoxification program to restore their immunity to an optimal level. This means temporarily abstaining from makeup, hair spray, perfume and all other products containing chemicals that accumulate in our bodies to see if this causes an improvement. Avoid excessive use of cell phones, computers and microwaves. Eating fresh, whole foods helps you avoid chemicals that can weaken your immune system.

ZING FROM GINSENG

Ginseng is commonly used in traditional Chinese medicine as an energy-boosting tonic. Western doctors have been slower to embrace it, but that's starting to change. Ginseng contains chemical compounds, called *ginsenosides*, that help the adrenal glands to improve your energy and alertness.

Ginseng is classified as an *adaptogen*, an herb that reduces the effects of stress. Russian athletes have utilized it for decades to improve physical performance. It was even given to Russian cosmonauts to improve their energy and alertness in space. When researchers analyzed data from more than 20 years of scientific studies, they concluded that ginseng is consistently beneficial and unlikely to cause side effects. Unlike caffeine, ginseng does not produce a rapid burst of energy. Most people need to take it daily for about a month before feeling the effects. If you'd like to try it, take up to 200 mg per day.

RESTORE ADRENAL HEALTH

Your adrenal glands produce hormones, among them those that manage stress, including cortisol and adrenaline. People who suffer from chronic stress can experience adrenal fatigue, which occurs when the hormone-producing cells of the adrenal glands are unable to keep up with relentless demand. The result is profound tiredness (especially in the afternoon), difficulty waking up in the morning and even low-grade depression.

Each of the B vitamins affects the ability of your adrenals to function at peak by helping to manufacture cortisol. Strengthening your adrenal health will usually result in improved energy. To do this, take a B-complex 100 tablet every day, or shop for an adrenal health supplement that includes 50 to 100 mg of vitamin B-6, 75 to 125 mg of vitamin B-3 or niacin and 200 to 400 mcg of vitamin B-12. In addition, start to reduce the stress in your life that's causing the adrenal fatigue in the first place. Your adrenal glands will actually heal themselves if you lighten up their stress load. See below for a few ideas.

Other Helpers and Healers

➤ **Say yes to exercise.** In a recent review, scientists have analyzed dozens of studies examining the effect of exercise on fatigue. More than 90% of this research found that people who were previously sedentary received a significant energy boost when they started moving. In fact, exercise generally worked better than stimulant drugs.

When you're feeling tired, there's nothing wrong with the occasional nap, but exercise is a better choice for revving up your energy. According to Dr. Patrick O'Connor of the Exercise Psychology Laboratory at the University of Georgia, being just a bit more active helps people suffering from fatigue. This can be as easy as walking for 20 minutes a couple of times per day or choosing the stairs instead of the elevator. Make a habit of taking a brisk walk whenever possible. Exercise will also help you sleep better.

➤ **Offset stress.** Stress floods your body with stress hormones such as adrenaline and cortisol, which can leave you feeling drained. This is the fight-or-flight response in action. You need those stress hormones

Fatigue and Heart Failure

Fatigue is also a major symptom of heart disease, especially in any patient who is suffering with congestive heart failure (CHF). I've found that when patients whose cardiac function is impaired receive certain supplements that increase cardiac output, their energy not only improves but soars. In patients with heart disease and congestive heart failure, the production of ATP—the molecule that transports chemical energy within cells for metabolism—is reduced in heart cells because of faulty metabolism. I coined the term *metabolic cardiology* to describe the interventions that we employ to directly improve energy metabolism in heart cells. Increasing ATP energy production with cellular nutrients such as coenzyme Q10, magnesium, carnitine and d-ribose has given my patients a better quality of life, while increasing longevity. The same supplements and doses recommended to remedy CFS (see page 165) will improve CHF.

to fend off an attacker, but you don't need it repeated every day. Even mild, background stress produces similar effects. Start taking chronic stress seriously as a cause of fatigue, and get help in coping with it. Anything that helps you relax, including exercise, an engaging hobby or meditative practices such as deep breathing, will lower your level of stress hormones and will leave you more energized and alert.

It's easy to work brief stress reducers into your life. Walk briskly for 20 minutes in the morning and again during the day. The fresh air, sunshine and movement will increase your level of feel-good *serotonin*, a brain chemical closely tied to relaxation. Work out vigorously any way you can: Take a yoga class, learn *tai chi,* bike to work or swim laps. Start meditating for ten minutes daily to relax your mind. Clearing your mind of its busyness is the first step in gaining the upper hand on stress.

➤ **Breathe through your nose.** Many of us are in the habit of breathing through our mouths rather than our noses. The problem with mouth breathing is that it causes us to breathe too rapidly and shallowly, which reduces the amount of oxygen available to tissues, according to Dr. Robert Fried, author of *The Psychology and Physiology of Breathing in Behavioral Medicine*. Breathing deeply through your nose and into your belly, slowly and deeply enough to expand your abdomen, is the best way to increase whole-body oxygenation.

➤ **Snuff the cigs.** Smoking not only decreases the amount of oxygen that's available to the body, but it also increases levels of carbon monoxide, a toxic gas. Nicotine can also disrupt sleep. People who quit smoking often report a rapid increase in overall energy.

➤ **Take a break from alcohol.** Alcohol can cause sleep disruption that leads to daytime drowsiness and fatigue, according to the National Institute on Alcohol Abuse and Alcoholism. Drinking can disrupt your sleep cycle, causing you to wake up in the middle of the night and have difficulty getting back to sleep. Take a break from alcohol and see if your fatigue eases. At the very least, enjoy your glass of wine with a meal and not on an empty stomach. ■

12

Heart Disease

Heart disease, also called *cardiovascular disease* or *coronary heart disease* (CHD), kills 650,000 people in the United States each year, making it the country's leading cause of death. Most heart disease is caused by *atherosclerosis*, in which fatty deposits called *plaques* accumulate in the arteries that carry blood to the heart. Heart disease is really artery disease, and it is inflammation of the arteries that triggers atherosclerosis in the first place.

When inflammation damages the delicate inner lining of blood vessels, your body lays down plaques in an attempt to repair the damage. The mortar it uses to seal these microscopic cracks is composed of cholesterol and other oxidized fats in the bloodstream. Unfortunately, bacteria may also become sealed under the plaque cap. It is as if your

arteries contain festering pimples with the potential to rupture. When one of these artery pimples pops, a blood clot (*thrombosis*) is formed just as it would on the surface of your skin. Usually, the body's anticlotting factors dissolve these clots and no harm is done. Occasionally, however, a clot doesn't dissolve and either blocks arterial blood flow, or a piece of it drifts downstream and jams a tiny capillary that feeds the heart. As a result, a portion of the heart muscle can die from lack of oxygen, impairing proper function. This is a heart attack.

More than one million Americans have a heart attack each year, and just under half die as a result. In middle-aged adults, the incidence of CHD is roughly 181 per 100,000. In the mid-seventies age group, that figure rises to well over 1,200 per 100,000. It's estimated that more than 70 million Americans, about one in five adults, has some form of heart disease. The medical industry likes to boast about the amazing progress it has made in treating heart fatalities by cutting the death rate in half over the last 40 years. This figure can be misleading, because the incidence of heart disease has barely budged in the past 20 years.

The progress made is due largely to better emergency treatments. We are saving more heart attack victims from death, but not reducing the rate of CHD. The truth is, conventional medicine is losing the battle against heart disease.

SYMPTOMS

People with severe, artery-narrowing blockages often experience chest pain during physical activity called *angina*. What happens is that the heart needs more oxygen-rich blood than the arteries can supply. For the same reason, people with atherosclerosis may find themselves short of breath or fatigued with even minor exertion. If the blockages aren't severe enough to cause chest pain, most people have no symptoms, which is why atherosclerosis is sometimes called a "silent killer."

Half of all deaths from cardiovascular disease occur in people with no diagnosed symptoms. The most common symptom of heart attack in both women and men is chest pressure, pain or discomfort. However, women experience more subtle symptoms, including nausea or vomiting; sweating; discomfort in the upper back, neck, jaw, shoulder or abdominal region; dizziness or lightheadedness and unexplained fatigue. The only way to know if you have heart disease, assuming you don't have chest pain, is to be tested.

However, today's standard tests are inadequate for identifying who's really at risk. The majority of cardiologists depend primarily on cholesterol evaluation, yet the cholesterol theory of heart disease is highly controversial. The fact that one-half to two-thirds of all heart attacks occur in people with normal cholesterol levels indicates that this is not a reliable predictor. More people with cholesterol under 200 milligrams per deciliter of blood (mg/dL) (the benchmark for good heart health) die of CHD than those whose levels are over 300. More accurate diagnostic tests are available, but most cardiologists do not use them, nor will most insurance companies pay for all of them.

CAUSES

Artery-narrowing plaque deposits are extremely common, with some degree of accumulation occurring even in those in their twenties. Over time, these deposits tend to get thicker, more extensive and harder, which prevents arteries from normal contracting and relaxing. This often can cause high blood pressure (*hypertension*). Various factors related to inflammation play a role in the formation of plaque and hardening of the arteries. The inner lining of arteries, called the *endothelium*, is quite delicate (just one cell thick) and is easily damaged by high blood pressure, excess glucose or insulin and any type of inflammation. Smoking also irritates it, as do free-radical molecules, which initiate tissue deterioration and disease. Free radicals are produced by natural oxidation in the body, but also are generated by cigarette smoke, air pollution and poor dietary choices, especially the consumption of foods containing trans fats.

► **Inflammation.** More and more cardiologists are becoming aware that inflammation is the primary cause of atherosclerosis. Heart disease can no longer be viewed simply as a clogged-plumbing problem. Controlling inflammation is becoming the number-one strategy for preventing CHD and heart attack. As many as 35 million Americans with normal cholesterol are believed to have above-normal inflammation and, with it, an elevated risk of heart disease. The effectiveness of cholesterol-lowering drugs known as *statins* is now believed to be linked to their anti-inflammatory effects, and not the lowering of cholesterol.

Are there ways to tell if you have inflammation? Absolutely. The Harvard Physicians' Health Study, which tracked healthy male doctors for 10 years, found that those who had high levels of certain inflammatory chemicals were significantly more likely to have a heart attack or stroke than those with lower levels. What this means, in practical terms, is that traditional approaches to preventing and treating heart disease aren't sufficient. Evaluation and treatment must pay attention to chemical markers that indicate blood vessel inflammation and plaque buildup, along with changes in the viscosity of blood that can make it sticky, thick, slow-moving and clot inclined. Although research published in the *New England Journal of Medicine* nearly ten years ago described these blood chemicals as reliable predictors of heart disease risk, most doctors have been

170

slow to recognize the importance of testing for them. Fortunately, this is beginning to change. Let's review the other important risk factors for CHD.

► **C-reactive protein (CRP).** When silent inflammation is present, the body's inflammatory response sends a message to the liver to produce CRP; thus, elevated levels of it signal inflammation's presence. Ask your doctor to check your CRP using the newer, high-sensitivity blood test called *hs-CRP*. It's an inexpensive test, easy to perform and the results can be a very good predictor of future cardiovascular risks. By some estimates, it is 100% more effective than standard cholesterol tests.

A study of postmenopausal women discovered that those who had the highest CRP levels were more than four times as likely to have a heart attack as women with the lowest levels. Taking a daily aspirin reduces CRP, but following the Mediterr-Asian Diet, with foods rich in fiber, antioxidants and anti-inflammatory omega 3s, will help drive down CRP naturally. If you do have inflammation, you won't necessarily need to take drugs, but you'll definitely want to make some important changes in your diet. Most people can significantly lower inflammation and cholesterol with a better diet, weight loss and moderate exercise.

► **Fibrinogen.** Elevated levels of this blood-clotting component encourage heart attack by causing the blood to thicken and coagulate excessively. People with high levels are referred to as having "thick blood" and are twice as likely to have a fatal heart attack. Ideally, fibrinogen should be under

300 mg/dl, with levels over 360 considered risky. Smoking is the greatest single cause of high fibrinogen. Natural blood thinners include a diet rich in fish oil, garlic, ginger and turmeric. Aspirin also thins the blood.

➤ **Homocysteine.** This amino acid occurs naturally in your body, as a result of metabolizing meat and other dietary protein. High levels of homocysteine cause oxidation of LDL cholesterol and can irritate the inner lining of your arteries. In fact, homocysteine is often the initiator of the blood vessel damage that encourages LDL to oxidize and fibrinogen to build up. Even people who have normal triglyceride and cholesterol levels but display elevated homocysteine are at greater risk for arterial blood clots and atherosclerosis. Women who have high blood pressure and high homocysteine have up to a 25 times greater risk for stroke. Vitamins B-12, B-6 and folic acid, all of which are found in Mediterr-Asian foods, can neutralize homocysteine naturally.

➤ **Lipoprotein(a).** Lp(a) is a cholesterol particle, or *subfraction*, that is sticky and therefore can cause cholesterol molecules to bind into plaques. It's a significant early predictor of genetic predisposition to heart disease. In fact, people with high levels of Lp(a) are 70% more likely to have a heart attack than those with low concentrations. Statin drugs do not lower Lp(a); in fact, research shows they raise levels. (More than 30% of people who take statins have an increase in Lp[a].) If you're already taking a statin drug, or are considering it, ask your doctor to order one of the new cholesterol tests that also checks levels of Lp(a).

TREATMENT

A majority of people with coronary artery disease don't need surgical treatment. Even though atherosclerosis is extremely common, the heart is surprisingly resilient. About 65% of men and 55% of women in their mid-sixties and older have arterial deposits that are extensive enough to be considered moderate to severe blockages, although most people don't experience symptoms until the deposits block 70% or more of an artery.

It's also important to know that the clots that cause most heart attacks rarely form in the calcified blockages that are readily seen on imaging tests. Still, these blockages get doctors' attention, even if the patient isn't having symptoms. Every year, millions of people are encouraged to have angioplasty, bypass surgery or other invasive procedures that they don't actually need. When physicians see something in an artery, their impulse is to remove it, even though 60% of heart attacks originate in blood vessels that appear normal. This obsession with calcified blockages has also led the medical profession to overfocus on cholesterol as a risk factor for heart disease.

I'm not saying atherosclerosis and high cholesterol should be ignored. Some people do need surgery and those with high inflammatory cholesterol need to lower it. Surgery is one solution, but should only be done if there is an impending emergency. However, up to two-thirds of people who have these procedures don't need them and do just as well on drug therapy, as well as dietary and lifestyle changes.

171

Is Cholesterol Really the Culprit?

Many people believe that cholesterol is bad, but it's actually essential to human life and good health. Cholesterol is a helpful fat made by your body and is present in every cell, where it's used to reinforce cell membranes, make hormones and convert vitamin D into a form your body can use. It's also essential for healthy brain function.

Cholesterol becomes a risk factor for heart disease when it is oxidized by free radicals. In addition, it isn't involved in plaque formation unless there's already damage to the lining of the arteries, which is caused by inflammation.

We've been taught that there are several forms of cholesterol, with low-density lipoprotein (LDL) getting the most attention because it can become oxidized most easily.

However, LDL and HDL aren't cholesterol at all, but rather vehicles called *lipoproteins*, which carry cholesterol around the body. LDL transports cholesterol from your liver to wherever it's needed. The job of HDL, or high-density lipoprotein, is to attach to any unused LDL, escorting it back to the liver for elimination or recycling before it can become oxidized. You can see how HDL earns its title as the "good cholesterol." If there isn't enough HDL to move excess LDL back to your liver, that LDL stays in your bloodstream, where it can be oxidized and cause trouble.

Furthermore, lipoproteins come in three basic sizes: Small, medium and large. Small LDL particles are the most dangerous because they fit neatly into tiny cracks and arteries. Medium and large LDL particles are basically harmless. Large HDL particles are the most beneficial because they can scoop up more excess LDL, and even remove some of it from existing artery plaques.

The standard cholesterol test doesn't measure lipoprotein size, so you can have a normal cholesterol reading, but if most of your LDL particles are small, you could be in danger without you or your doctor realizing it. Likewise, you may have a high HDL reading (normally a good thing) but if most of your HDL particles are small, your protection is actually minimal. On the other hand, your LDL level could be high based on National Institutes of Health guidelines (see page 173), but if your particles are not small you're probably not in danger. You may not need a cholesterol-lowering drug, even if your doctor has prescribed one. The only way to know for sure is to test for cholesterol size.

Many cardiologists are beginning to order the advanced lipid profile test that measures lipoprotein size. If your doctor isn't, you should request one at your next visit. You should also ask to be tested for high-sensitivity CRP, Lp(a), homocysteine and fibrinogen.

Old-school cardiologists continue to focus on cholesterol as the primary cause of heart disease, while newer studies are more likely to implicate inflammation and other risk factors. These distinctions greatly influence how heart disease can be prevented and treated, especially when it comes to choosing whether to take drugs. The best research indicates that the incidence of heart attacks could be reduced by up to 70% by combining good medical care with anti-inflammatory lifestyle habits, especially diet.

THE PUSH FOR EVEN LOWER CHOLESTEROL

The current cholesterol-control guidelines from the National Institutes of Health (NIH) call for people with risk factors for heart disease to maintain LDL at 100 or below, down from 130. For patients already diagnosed with heart disease, the guidelines recommend dropping it to 70. A multi-author review by internists and researchers in cardiovascular disease concluded that the panel's evidence to set such levels and the treatment goals to obtain them were limited. The reviewers felt that more research is needed. Indeed, there's mounting evidence that the aggressive anti-cholesterol push of the past decades has been a red herring, because there's no solid proof that only lowering cholesterol prevents heart disease.

Consider the prestigious Multiple Risk Factor Intervention Trial (MRFIT), which examined cholesterol levels in 362,000 men. Researchers found that the annual death rate from coronary artery disease in men with very low cholesterol, below 140 mg/dL was less than one fatality per 1,000. In men with very high cholesterol, above 300 mg/dL, the annual death rate from heart disease was about two per 1,000. This difference is statistically insignificant, and even less impressive when you consider that the vast majority of people don't have cholesterol numbers at either of these extremes.

THE SATURATED FAT CONTROVERSY

The hypothesis that dietary fat, especially saturated fat, is the main cause of high cholesterol and heart disease has been accepted for 50 years. The theory is that people who consume a lot of fat, particularly saturated fat found in meat and dairy, tend to have higher blood levels of cholesterol. These fats, it was thought, would tend to accumulate in the coronary arteries as plaque, causing atherosclerosis.

However, the evidence against saturated fat is thin to nonexistent. For one thing, consumption of fat in the US has decreased in the past 40 years, while heart disease has continued to rise. In 1970, the average American fat intake was about 40% of total calories. Today, it's closer to 34%. Although the average US cholesterol level has dropped over the same time period, heart disease continues to be the nation's number-one killer. If cholesterol were the main cause of atherosclerosis and heart disease, you would expect Americans to be having fewer heart attacks. This isn't the case, which suggests that there's something fishy about the cholesterol theory, and perhaps even more so about the dietary fat connection.

According to Dr. Walter Willett, chair of the Department of Nutrition at the Harvard School of Public Health, the intense focus on lowering dietary fat has actually made our nation less healthy, by driving Americans toward highly processed carbohydrates. Data from the long-running Nurses' Health Study show that saturated fat, long considered the main risk factor for elevated cholesterol and heart attack, is far less culpable than experts once thought.

Consider the French paradox. Despite the rich, high-fat diets that are typical in much of France and the fact that the average French citizen has a cholesterol level well above 200, France and other Mediterranean countries have among the lowest incidence of heart disease in the world. Also keep in mind the famous Lyon Heart Disease Study of 1988, which showed that heart attack survivors who followed a Mediterranean diet with a fat content of 30% were 70% less likely to experience a second heart attack or other cardiac problems than patients who followed the typical low-fat diet recommended by the American Heart Association. The heart-healing effects of the Mediterranean diet could be observed in patients within the first two months.

CHOLESTEROL IS INNOCENT

Neither dietary fat nor cholesterol is the real cause of heart disease. Instead, the initiating factor is inflammation, most of which is caused by inflammatory foods such as sugar, refined carbohydrates, processed foods, polyunsaturated vegetable oils, margarine and trans fats, as well as consuming too many omega-6 fatty acids and not enough anti-inflammatory omega-3s. Other factors that cause inflammation are cigarette smoking, auto exhaust, air pollution and environmental toxins. Of these inflammatory factors, we have the greatest control over smoking and diet.

The current NIH cholesterol guidelines take none of this evidence into account. What's more, the guidelines establish such low cholesterol numbers that it's virtually impossible for most people to achieve them without drugs.

Statins, the main pharmaceuticals prescribed for lowering cholesterol, are a good choice for certain patients, particularly men ages 45 to 75 who've had a heart attack or already have heart trouble. However, too many doctors hand these drugs out unnecessarily. Statins can cause serious side effects, such as muscle weakness, flu-like symptoms and liver damage, plus memory and vision problems. The cost of treating tens of millions of people with statins just to drive down cholesterol to these unreasonably low numbers is enormous, and the risks aren't worth it. The cardiology community likes to call statins "lifesavers," but that's hardly true. In every major study done on these drugs, even the ones in which heart fatalities have been slightly decreased, mortality rates from all other causes among statin takers are higher.

Yes, there is substantial evidence that people who already have heart disease and take these drugs may reduce their cardiovascular risk. What isn't clear is why. Is it because cholesterol is being lowered? Or is it because of the anti-inflammatory effects of statin drugs? If it's the latter, then doctors should first investigate other inflammation-fighting agents, beginning with foods and diet.

WHY DON'T MORE DOCTORS CONSIDER DIET FIRST?

As you're about to see, there's a preponderance of solid scientific evidence showing that diet, exercise and simple lifestyle changes may be the most effective strategy for avoiding a heart attack, even in people who have already suffered one. Dietary strategies are effective for the vast majority of people who might otherwise be prone to CHD. Indeed, there are foods that thin the blood so it is less likely to clot. Others can neutralize inflammation. Still others reduce the amount of glucose and insulin, which damage arteries when their presence is excessive. There are even foods that reduce blood cholesterol.

One study, published in the *Journal of the American Medical Association*, reported that people who ate a diet consisting of nuts, soy foods, fiber and plant sterols experienced drops in harmful cholesterol that rivaled those produced by *lovastatin*, one of the primary statin drugs. This illustrates just how powerful dietary changes can be, and it's one of the reasons I advise the majority of my heart patients to switch to a Mediterr-Asian–style diet (see page 19). You'd be surprised at how often these simple changes work. Clinical studies too numerous to mention prove it.

Foods That Make It Better

Back in the 1950s and '60s, when the rate of heart disease in the United States was just beginning to skyrocket, epidemiologists noticed an unusual phenomenon in Greece, France and other countries bordering the Mediterranean Sea. People living there regularly consumed quantities of fat-rich foods that would make a Western cardiologist cringe—cheese, olive oil, nuts, butter, pastries and red meats—and they washed it down with red and white wine. They also smoked more cigarettes than Americans did. However, in Greece, the rate of heart disease in middle-aged men was a stunning 90% lower than in comparable groups of Americans. This certainly contradicted medical theories that consumption of fats was at the root of heart disease. Then, the researchers looked east and examined eating habits in China. Back in the 1970s, before the Chinese population had begun to adopt a more Western way of eating, heart attacks were considered a medical curiosity. Even today among Chinese who eat traditional foods, the rates of heart disease are much lower than in the United States, even though the Chinese smoke much more.

Researchers concluded that the diets of these two cultures made the difference. The people of the Mediterranean and Asia in general live longer and experience better health than populations in the West, especially the United States. Studies confirm that their way of eating is the primary reason.

My diet plan combines the best features of the Mediterranean countries and those of Asia. It is high in fruits, vegetables, whole grains, beans and small servings of animal products. In my opinion, it is the most healing diet known. Virtually anyone who switches to it will achieve significant reductions in heart attack risk, as well as lower levels of inflammation, which has been linked to nearly every degenerative and chronic disease that plague Americans. Clearly, what we eat can save our lives. Let's take a look at the specific healing foods that can make the greatest difference. There are additional heart-healing foods and recipe ideas at *www.myhealingkitchen.com*.

HEART-PROTECTING PRODUCE

You can't ignore the scientific proof. Chemical compounds in fruits and vegetables douse the artery inflammation that initiates heart disease. Fresh local vegetables and fruits are loaded with *flavonoids*, those powerful antioxidant compounds that neutralize free radicals and protect arteries from damage. An antioxidant-rich diet is the best way to keep your arteries clear. In a fascinating study, Swedish researchers examined why Lithuanian men had a four times greater mortality from heart disease than Swedish men. Curiously, the high-risk Lithuanians had lower cholesterol (including LDL) than the Swedes. Scientists discovered that what really put them at higher risk were significantly lower levels of antioxidants in their blood, particularly lycopene and beta-carotene. Even though the more vulnerable men had better cholesterol profiles, they clearly weren't eating enough antioxidant-rich foods to prevent inflammation and plaque accumulation in their arteries.

Here's some incentive to up your intake of fruit and vegetables. When you eat as little as one and a half extra servings of fruit or vegetables daily, your risk of hypertension drops significantly. Since hypertension is another serious risk factor for heart disease, this is a huge benefit. For each additional serving of fruits and vegetables you eat daily, your risk of heart disease drops by about 5%. The power of produce is astonishing. Harvard scientists monitored more than 800 men for 20 years and discovered that those eating the most vegetables and fruit had a staggering 59% fewer strokes that those who ate the least.

This protection is universal. In 2008, the journal *Circulation* published an impressive study showing that people around the world whose diets were low in vegetables and fruits but high in meats, fried foods and salty snacks, or what researchers refer to as the typical Western diet, experienced a 30% greater heart attack risk compared with those whose meals were rich in produce. The study revealed that the more fruit and vegetables the participants ate, the more their risk of heart attack dropped. Consider, too, the massive amounts of vitamin C in produce. One study found that people who got as little as 300 mg per day (one orange has about 60 mg) were up to 42% less likely to die of heart disease than those who got lower amounts. This protection isn't limited to vitamin C. All vegetables and fruits possess different antioxidant effects, which is why I recommend eating the widest possible variety.

I can't think of an easier or better way to dodge a heart attack or to repair arteries already damaged than eating a few extra servings of produce daily. For maximum healing, try to eat at least 10 servings of fruits and vegetables every day, especially vegetables. Doing so will provide your body with potent ammunition to neutralize unhealthful oxidation and inflammatory free radicals. For a list of the top food sources of antioxidants, see the chart on page 191.

Fruits and veggies have more than just antioxidants to offer. They come packaged with *salicylates,* natural blood thinners that work like aspirin to prevent blood clots and keep your circulation flowing smoothly. Studies bear this out. Harvard scientists found that of 50,000 men, those who ate the most vegetables and fruit had 41% fewer heart attacks than men who ate less. These foods produce a significant cholesterol benefit too. Scientists in Toronto put two groups of adults on a low-fat diet, with one group fed more vegetables and fruit. Interestingly, the produce eaters experienced an impressive reduction in cholesterol, which was 34% to 49% lower than that of the nonproduce group. Can any drug make this claim? Apparently the cholesterol-lowering drug Crestor makes this claim, but there has been much controversy about its side effects, which include potential kidney and muscle damage.

Eating more fresh fruits and vegetables produces another positive benefit. You can actually watch your blood pressure numbers drop by eating more produce, according to the famous DASH (Dietary Approaches to Stop Hypertension) study. People with high blood pressure who cut back on total fats and ate diets rich in vegetables, fruits and low-fat dairy products brought down their upper-number systolic pressure by 11 points, while the lower-number diastolic pressure dropped by nearly seven.

All produce protects your heart, each in a slightly different way. *Here are some of the best choices...*

➤ **Crank up the crucifers.** Broccoli and other cruciferous vegetables, such as cabbage, kale, cauliflower, Brussels sprouts and radishes, appear to be among the most powerful foods for reducing inflammation. They curtail your body's output of inflammatory substances called *prostaglandins*. Plus, a compound in broccoli called *sulforaphane* may actually be able to repair damaged heart blood vessels. Studies show that sulforaphane seems to activate antioxidant enzymes, which are detoxifying. Eating broccoli is strongly linked to a reduced risk of heart attack in postmenopausal women. Flavonoids in broccoli limit the oxidation of LDL cholesterol and prevent it from attaching to artery walls, where it can clog arteries and boost your risk of heart attack.

➤ **Top off with tomatoes.** They're loaded with lycopene, a chemical compound that lowers the risk of cancer as well as heart disease. Lycopene prevents LDL cholesterol from *oxidizing*, which is the process that initiates atherosclerosis. In one study, researchers found that men with the lowest levels of lycopene in their blood were three times more likely to have a heart attack than those who had more. Cooked tomatoes are a concentrated source of lycopene, so enjoy tomato sauce and low-sodium juice as often as you'd like.

➤ **Start the day with organic strawberries.** Strawberries are powerful heart protectors, as they are one of the best sources of *ellagic acid*, an unusually powerful antioxidant that reduces the inflammatory effects of free radicals. They also contain flavonoids, which drive down the activity of the enzyme *cyclooxygenase*, linked to atherosclerosis and other inflammatory diseases. Be sure to choose the organic varieties because conventionally grown strawberries are among the most pesticide-laden fruits on the market.

➤ **Get the blues.** Scientists use a laboratory test called ORAC (for oxygen radical absorbance capacity) to measure the antioxidant activity of fruits and vegetables. The greater the antioxidant capacity in food, the lower the risk of heart disease for those who consume them. Blueberries rate high on the ORAC chart (see page 191), as do strawberries, plums, apples and cherries. Blueberries are also high in *resveratrol*, a plant compound that's been linked to reductions in heart disease and cancer, as well as increased longevity. Raw blueberries are best, as cooking breaks down resveratrol.

➤ **Eat like Bugs Bunny.** Carrots are among the most cardioprotective foods you can eat. A Scottish study found that people who ate seven ounces of carrots daily (about two average carrots) reduced their cholesterol by more than 10%. Other studies show that people who eat a lot of carrots are also about a third less likely to have a heart attack than those who don't eat any.

➤ **Onions on everything.** Research shows that people who eat the most onions tend to enjoy longer and healthier lives. A Finnish study that tracked more than 5,000 men and women for 20 years found that women who consumed the most onions were about half as likely to develop heart disease compared with women who ate the least.

➤ **Declot with garlic.** Reducing your risk of blood clots is another smart way to prevent a heart attack, and garlic can help. One of its active compounds, *diallyl disulfide*, helps keep platelets from clumping together and forming clots. This antiplatelet effect is so pronounced that doctors advise people taking blood-thinning drugs, such as *warfarin*, to beware of eating too much garlic. In an exciting study at Brown University, volunteers were given the equivalent of six cloves of garlic a day, which reduced their tendency to form clots by up to 58%. Garlic is also often recommended as a cholesterol-lowering agent, and studies show it can lower LDL from 4% to 12%.

➤ **Power in the peel.** All apples, and especially the peel, are high in the flavonoid *quercetin*, an inflammation-fighting antioxidant that lowers the risk of heart attack by preventing free radicals from oxidizing LDL cholesterol. Even if you already have atherosclerosis, flavonoids can help by inhibiting the blood clot formation that causes heart attacks and strokes. Apples also contain generous amounts of soluble and insoluble fiber, a healing duo that can help lower cholesterol and overall risk of heart disease and stroke.

➤ **Load up on kiwi.** Dr. Paul LaChance of Rutgers University ran a nutritional analysis of kiwis and other fruits and found that kiwis supply twice the vitamin C of oranges, along with other antioxidants that neutralize free radicals before they have a chance to oxidize LDL. Kiwis also contain the amino acid *arginine*, which dilates blood vessels and promotes easier circulation.

➤ **Grab a grapefruit.** All citrus fruit are good for your heart, but grapefruit is especially rich in *pectin*, a type of fiber that appears to be as powerful as some drugs at lowering cholesterol. Dr. James Cerda, a cholesterol researcher at the University of Florida, found that people who ate about a half ounce of grapefruit pectin daily had drops in cholesterol between 10% and 19%. Even more notably, many of his volunteers saw improvement in beneficial HDL, one of the best predictors of cardiovascular risk. The study used a supplemental form of pectin, but the whole fruit is undoubtedly an even better source, both because it offers additional antioxidants and because the vitamin C in grapefruit apparently intensifies the action of pectin.

➤ **Don't skimp on spinach.** It's extremely high in antioxidants and other nutrients, particularly folate, that protect your heart. Folate is a B vitamin that drives down levels of *homocysteine*, an amino acid that produces inflammation in artery linings. Too much homocysteine damages the endothelium, encouraging the development of scarring and fatty deposits of plaque. One study found that people with low blood levels of folate were 2.64 times more likely to die from CHD than those with higher levels. The Harvard Nurses' Health Study, which followed 80,000 women for more than a decade, found that those with elevated homocysteine had three times the rate of heart disease compared with those with lower levels. It's thought that as little as 400 micrograms (mcg) of folate daily is enough to lower homocysteine levels. That's the amount in about a cup of spinach or any green leafy vegetable, such as kale, Swiss chard or mustard greens.

➤ **Spear more asparagus.** These harbingers of spring are another great source of folate, as well as vitamin B-6. Both nutrients control homocysteine and help reduce your risk of heart disease. It's been estimated that the annual number of heart attacks would decline by 10% if everyone got at least 400 mcg of folate daily.

➤ **The colors of health.** The deep orange and yellow hues of winter squash indicate their exceptionally high levels of antioxidants, including lutein, zeaxanthin and beta-carotene. Squash is also high in *alpha-linolenic acid*, an omega-3 fatty acid that lowers harmful blood fats and keeps the heart beating in a regular rhythm.

➤ **Dip into guacamole.** Enjoy a little avocado, which is rich in heart-healthy monounsaturated fat, as often as you want. In an interesting study, researchers put two groups of people on a relatively low-fat diet, with one group eating avocado. When they were evaluated, both groups had reductions in LDL, but only the avocado group had reductions in cardio-risky triglycerides and an increase in protective HDL. Avocado also enhances the absorption of other carotenoids, especially beta-carotene and lycopene, both of which are found in many fruits and vegetables.

➤ **The mighty bean.** Beans are tiny heart healers to the extreme. They're loaded with heart-protecting nutrients, fiber and an abundance of antioxidants. One 20-year study looked at more than 9,500 participants, none of whom had cardiovascular disease at the start of the project. As you'd expect, some did develop heart disease in the ensuing years, but when scientists examined the groups' diets, they found that those who ate beans four or more times a week were 22% less likely to get heart disease. The bean eaters also had lower cholesterol and hypertension, plus a lower incidence of diabetes.

Beans contain eight different phenol compounds with antioxidant properties in their outer covering. Pinto, kidney and tiny red beans have more disease-fighting antioxidants than virtually any other food.

Researchers are discovering new phytonutrients in beans all the time. Black beans, for example, are extremely rich in *anthocyanins*, the compounds that make grapes and wine so heart healthy. One study found that black beans and grapes have equal antioxidant power.

Beans are also loaded with folate, one of the B vitamins that most of us are deficient in, even if we eat folate-fortified processed foods. Folate, also called folic acid, has real power to lower your heart disease risk because it repairs cells damaged by oxidation. Folate deficiency can cause high levels of *homocysteine*, an amino acid that ups your risk of stroke, peripheral vascular disease and heart attack. Research shows that up to 40% of people with heart disease show elevated levels of homocysteine in their blood.

➤ **Pumpkin keeps it pumpin'.** Pumpkin seeds are among the richest sources of magnesium, a mineral that improves the metabolic efficiency of heart cells and relieves chest pain and other symptoms of angina. More important, magnesium can greatly reduce your risk of heart disease. Magnesium relaxes the muscle walls of arteries in much the same way as prescription calcium channel blockers do. It also restores normal heart rhythm in those who have *ectopic* (skipped) heartbeats. Magnesium is so powerful that it's even used in emergency situations for people with sky-high blood pressure or irregular heartbeat. Several studies have evaluated the relationship between magnesium and atherosclerosis. Researchers involved in the Honolulu Heart Program looked at the magnesium intake of more than 7,000 men and, in 30

years of followup, found that men who consumed the least magnesium were almost twice as likely to develop heart disease compared with men who got the most.

You can also get plenty of magnesium from nuts, beans and figs, as well as leafy green vegetables such as spinach and Swiss chard.

➤ **Pack in the C.** Virtually all fruits and vegetables in the Mediterr-Asian way of eating have generous amounts of vitamin C. Research conducted at Harvard and Boston University found that people who get high levels of vitamin C are able to repair arterial damage caused by atherosclerosis, while also improving circulation and reducing the odds of a vessel-blocking clot.

➤ **Load up on watermelon.** Don't save it for the Fourth of July. This succulent melon is among the best sources of *lycopene*, the protective antioxidant also found in tomatoes, cooked tomato foods like pasta sauce and in other red or pink foods such as papaya and pink grapefruit. One study found that people who had the highest blood levels of lycopene were more than 30% less likely to develop atherosclerosis.

THE FIBER FIX

Fiber-rich foods contain antioxidants, some of which seem to inhibit cell damage that can lead to a depletion of nitric oxide (NO), which is a natural gas your body produces to dilate blood vessels, thus lowering blood pressure. It also reduces arterial clots and, according to some research, the fatty accumulations that cause atherosclerosis in the first place. In recent years, scientists have come to recognize the importance of NO in cardiovascular health. It's so essential, in fact, that some experts suspect that increasing NO levels could be the secret to eliminating heart disease altogether.

People who get at least 25 grams (g) of fiber daily see a significant increase in NO, and those eating high-fiber foods in place of polyunsaturated fat do even better, because these fats (found in vegetable oil such as corn, soy, sunflower, and canola) inhibit NO production. This might explain why a study of nearly 22,000 Finnish men found that those who ate slightly more than a third of an ounce of whole-grain fiber daily were 17% less likely to die of cardiovascular disease. That's about the amount in a scant tablespoon of ground flaxseed, an exceptional food for adding protective fiber to your diet, since it also contains heart-healthful omega-3s. Men who ate more fiber had an even greater reduction in risk.

California scientists found that people who regularly eat 100% whole-grain bread are far less likely to have a heart attack than those who eat the refined white bread. Oats and other whole grains contain folate, a B vitamin that lowers inflammation-promoting homocysteine, cholesterol buildups, and clots. The message? Pack your diet with fiber from whole grains, beans and produce.

THE CARDIO-PROTECTIVE CATCH

The omega-3 fatty acids in fish are critical for heart health. Americans eat a lot less fish than Asians and the Mediterraneans, which may have a lot to do with our soaring rates of cardiovascular disease. William Castelli, former director of the Framingham Heart Study, said that people with heart or high cholesterol problems are crazy not to eat fish at least twice a week. Cold-water fish, such as salmon, mackerel and tuna are high in omega-3s. These species are the best source of *eicosapentaenoic acid* (EPA) and *docosahexaenoic acid* (DHA), the most healing of the omega-3 compounds.

Research shows that omega-3s thin the blood, heal damaged arteries and stabilize soft plaque in arteries so that plaque is less likely to erupt and trigger a heart attack or stroke. Omega-3s in fish also keep arteries soft and flexible, thereby lowering blood pressure and decreasing the likelihood of atherosclerosis. A study published in the *Journal of the American Medical Association* found that as little as one serving per week of omega-3 fish could reduce the risk of cardiac arrest by 50%. Recent Japanese research found that people who ate fish every day showed a 56% lower risk of heart attack and 37% lower risk of heart disease than the occasional eaters. People who never eat fish do much worse. When researchers examined the diets of nearly 1,100 middle-aged men over a 20-year period, they found that those who ate no fish had a 100% higher risk of heart attack as those who enjoyed two weekly servings.

Omega-3s are like powerful drugs without the side effects. Even in small amounts, they reduce the body's production of inflammatory prostaglandins, as well as *leukotrienes* and *thromboxanes*, substances that cause blood vessels to tighten, elevate blood pressure and increase the risk of clots. The healing effect of omega-3s on blood pressure was a centerpiece of the INTERMAP study of nearly 5,000 people (published in the *Journal of Human Hypertension*). Researchers found a direct link between omega-3 consumption and lower blood pressure.

Researchers aren't certain how much omega-3 fat is optimal for cardio-protection, but the Japanese average 1.3 g per day (the amount in about six ounces of salmon), compared with 0.2 g in the United States. Also in Japan, middle-aged men have twice the level of omega-3 fats in their blood and, perhaps not so coincidentally, fewer clogged arteries than Americans. Two weekly servings of fish is the usual recommendation, while three or four will provide additional benefits to those with a diagnosed heart condition.

However, there's a catch. Many fish are now contaminated with mercury. The Finnish Heart Study found that men with high levels of mercury in their blood were twice as likely to have a heart attack compared with those with lower levels. How can you reap the benefits of the omega-3 fatty acids in fish without the risk? The best advice is to buy fish species that accumulate the least mercury. Fish with the highest mercury loads are those at the top of the fish food chain. *Here are some recommendations for safely increasing your intake of omega-3s with fish…*

➤ **Choose safe high-omega-3 species.** These include Atlantic herring, wild Pacific salmon, domestic shrimp, cod, scallops, anchovies, Atlantic mackerel, Atlantic halibut, canned light tuna, oysters, mussels, sardines and freshwater trout.

➤ **Leave the big feeders.** Don't eat shark, swordfish, king mackerel, tilefish, grouper or large tuna, as all are high-mercury species.

➤ **Avoid farmed salmon.** They may resemble their wild-caught cousins, but they're as different as night and day. Farmed salmon are fed mostly grain and as a result are low in omega-3s and high in proinflammatory omega-6s. They contain antibiotics and carcinogenic chemicals, such as PCBs and pesticides. Atlantic salmon is almost always farmed raised. Choose salmon specifically labeled wild, Alaskan or Chinook.

➤ **Check your tuna can.** Select chunk light tuna when shopping. It has about one-third the mercury of albacore. Also limit consumption of light canned tuna to 6 ounces per week (3 ounces for a child).

➤ **Say *sí* to sardines.** This little fish is one of the most concentrated sources of the omega-3 fatty acids EPA and DHA. Sardines are also an excellent source of vitamin B-12, essential for keeping homocysteine in check. They're high in calcium and coenzyme Q10. They're also low in mercury.

➤ **Eat fish this often.** If you have any inflammation-driven medical condition, such as heart disease or arthritis, eat a minimum of two to three servings of high-quality fish per week, more if possible, especially wild-caught, cold-water fish, such as salmon. One serving equals four ounces of cooked fish or six ounces raw.

➤ **Not fond of fish?** Fish oil supplements are an adequate substitute, as long as they come from uncontaminated fish. Tainted fish oil isn't usually a problem because mercury occurs in the fish's flesh rather than the oil. Purchase supplements with labels that

182

indicate they've undergone molecular distillation, a process that eliminates toxins. Take one to three capsules daily.

JUST THE FLAX, MA'AM

Flaxseed is one of the best sources of alpha-linolenic acid (ALA), one of the heart-healthy omega-3s. According to Harvard researchers, people who get the most ALA in their diets may reduce their risk of heart disease by about 50%. Ground flaxseed has also been shown to lower cholesterol. A clinical trial involving postmenopausal women showed that one tablespoon eaten daily for 90 days reduced their total cholesterol by 6% and triglycerides by 12.8%. More significantly, the flaxseed group showed significant reduction in the small-size cholesterol carriers apolipoprotein A-1 and apolipoprotein B by 6% and 7.5%, respectively. Researchers now think that these tiny lipoproteins are more dangerous than elevated LDL cholesterol levels.

➤ **Your daily flax.** Enjoy two tablespoons of ground flax meal daily (whole flaxseeds can't be digested), sprinkled into cereal, smoothies, fruit, yogurt, salad or vegetables. This amount provides more than the Institute of Medicine's total daily recommendations for ALA.

You can purchase flaxseed whole or ground. If you buy whole flaxseed, keep it tightly covered in a cool, dry spot and use an electric coffee grinder to make enough for a week. Keep all ground flax (stored in a tightly closed container) in your refrigerator or freezer. It spoils quickly when exposed to air.

Seven Ways It Works: Why Your Heart Loves Fish Oil

Here are seven reasons to eat more omega-3 fish or start taking fish oil capsules. *Both…*
1. Counteract inflammation.
2. Drive down levels of cardio-risky triglycerides.
3. Contribute to healthy blood vessels, especially the *endothelium* (the vessel lining).
4. Reduce blood pressure.
5. Help prevent irregular heartbeats and improve heart rate variability, the beat-to-beat alterations in heart rate that signal a healthy nervous system.
6. Keep the inside of your coronary arteries free of deposits that can block blood flow.
7. Thin the blood and help prevent clots.

OIL YOUR ARTERIES

Olive oil is a celebrated staple in Mediterranean countries, and is generously splashed on salads, fish, pasta and bread. Extra-virgin olive oil is the product of the first pressing of olives and contains the most antioxidant compounds, called *polyphenols*, which account for the oil's magnificent cardiovascular benefits. Polyphenols are anticoagulating and anti-inflammatory, making it the most heart-healthy oil there is. While you're enjoying the flavor, your heart will be humming happily.

Using olive oil can cut your risk of heart disease by a full 50%. Researchers in Greece looked at more than 800 men and women with heart disease, reviewing their diets and use of olive oil, while considering their smoking habits, alcohol consumption, physical activity levels, blood pressure, weight and history of diabetes and heart disease. Regardless of other risk factors, the use of olive oil was connected to a 47% reduction in heart disease. Another study found that men who had as little as one-and-a-half tablespoons of olive oil a day had improvements in cholesterol in just one week.

What makes olive oil such a potent elixir? Research is ongoing, but we do know that it's one of the best sources of *oleuropein* and *hydroxytyrosol*, two antioxidants that reduce inflammatory chemicals in the body. It also makes cholesterol less likely to stick to artery walls. Scientists at the University of Athens in Greece wondered whether it was olive oil specifically or the Mediterranean diet in general that was so effective at reducing blood pressure. They studied the eating habits of more than 20,000 Greeks and discovered that while the Mediterranean diet in total lowered diastolic and systolic blood pressure, it was olive oil that was mostly responsible for the reductions.

Remember to enjoy olive oil as a replacement for other fats, not in addition to them. Olive oil has just as many calories as any other fat. Keep in mind that more isn't better at one sitting. Research recommends consuming no more than two tablespoons at a time. Moderation is key. *Here are a few suggestions for enjoying olive oil...*

➤ **Purchase with care.** Keep extra-virgin olive oil in dark bottles that protect it from exposure to light, which can reduce the power of its heart-helping polyphenols. The words "cold pressed" on the label tell you that destructive heat was not used in pressing the olives into oil. Virgin, pure and light grades should be used for cooking, but they don't have anywhere near the healing power of extra virgin.

➤ **Use in dressings.** Start all your salad dressings with a couple of tablespoons of extra-virgin olive oil. You can add sherry vinegar, rice wine vinegar, lemon or lime juice and a little Dijon mustard to create a vinaigrette.

➤ **Don't use for high-heat cooking.** It's fine to gently sauté foods with light olive oil (not extra virgin), but avoid using it in higher-heat cooking. Heat destroys the oil's healing polyphenols.

➤ **Dip some bread.** Whole-grain bread dipped lightly in extra-virgin olive oil is a real treat. For outstanding flavor, crush a clove of garlic into the oil and let stand for a few minutes before dipping.

➤ **Toss with veggies.** While you're steaming any vegetable, place a tablespoon of extra-virgin olive oil into a large bowl with a shake of vinegar or a squeeze of citrus. When your veggies are ready, pour directly into the bowl and toss for a heavenly blend.

➤ **Store it carefully.** The benefits of this delicate oil can be compromised by exposing it to heat or light, which also may cause the oil to turn rancid. Store it in a cool, dark spot. Your refrigerator is a fine place to keep the main supply, after pouring a cup or so into a smaller bottle you can keep handy for frequent use.

MUNCH SOME NUTS

A landmark study found that people who ate nuts at least four times a week were nearly half as likely to die of a heart attack as those who ate few or none. This is partly due to nuts' heart-protecting monounsaturated fat. Nuts are also an excellent source of plant sterols such as beta-sitosterol, along with both kinds of unsaturated fat—monounsaturated and healthful polyunsaturated.

Nuts also contain the amino acid *arginine*, which dilates blood vessels, allowing more blood to reach the heart under lower pressure. In one study, researchers interviewed members of the Seventh-day Adventist Church to find out what foods they ate most often. Those who ate nuts five or more times weekly were half as likely to die from heart disease compared with those who ate the least nuts, though members who ate nuts one to four times a week still had a 25% lower risk.

Nuts also contain appreciable amounts of vitamin E, which reduces inflammation in your arteries and inhibits the oxidation of cholesterol. A Harvard study found that people with the highest intake of vitamin E were about a third less likely to contract heart disease than those who got less. There's a huge market for vitamin E supplements, but if you're eating the Mediterr-Asian Diet (page 19), which includes nuts and other vitamin E foods, you won't need capsules. Foods are certainly safer and a lot more delicious than capsules. Eating three servings of almonds, peanuts, pecans or walnuts per week as part of an overall heart-healthy diet can decrease total cholesterol by up to 16% and lower LDL cholesterol by up to 19%, according to a study published in the *Journal of Nutrition*.

➤ **Mix 'em up.** Each nut has its own specific health benefits, so enjoy a variety, including macadamia nuts, which help drive down LDL. Peanuts are another good choice, because they are high in monounsaturated fats, which are ideal for cholesterol control. One study found that people who ate a lot of peanuts, peanut butter and other foods rich in monounsaturated fat were able to reduce their risk of heart disease by more than 20%.

Here's another peanut bonus. They contain resveratrol, the antioxidant that's also found in red wine and is linked to longer life span.

CHOCOLATE LOVERS, REJOICE!

Finally, some good news for your sweet tooth! The cocoa beans that are used to make dark chocolate are exceptionally high in anti-inflammatory *flavonoids*, the antioxidants that neutralize artery-damaging free radicals. Dark chocolate, the darker the better, lowers high blood pressure, according to two studies published in the journal *Nature* and in the *Journal of the American Medical Association*.

In addition, dark chocolate is powerfully effective against inflammation. Italian researchers reporting in the *Journal of Nutrition* found that eating about 6.5 g (0.23 ounces) of dark chocolate daily, which is an average Hershey's bar (43 g) a week, drives down CRP, an inflammatory marker. Lower CRP means less inflammation and a reduced risk of heart disease. People in the study who ate dark chocolate regularly showed CRP reductions of 17%, which is enough to lower women's risk of heart disease by one-third and men's by one-quarter. This benefit doesn't apply to milk chocolate or the combination of dark chocolate and milk because milk interferes with the body's ability to absorb chocolate's antioxidants.

The science behind chocolate is getting a lot of attention these days. Harvard scientists who studied the Puna Indians, who live on an island near Panama and drink about five cups of unadulterated cocoa per day, found that hypertension was rare, which means less risk of heart disease.

Even though chocolate contains a saturated fat, called *stearic acid*, it doesn't raise cholesterol. More chocolate won't make you healthier, of course. It will make you fat. However, a small piece of dark chocolate eaten two or three times weekly appears to be enough to protect your heart. Look for chocolate labeled with its percentage of cocoa. Bittersweet chocolate has less sugar than other choices, and some contain as much as 85% (or more) cocoa.

ENJOY EGGS...PLEASE

Since the early days of cholesterol research, many doctors viewed eggs as dangerous since the yolk of a single egg can contain upward of 200 milligrams (mg) of cholesterol. Eggs got a bum rap. Thank goodness, all that has changed. A recent study showed that people who eat three or more eggs a day experience a beneficial rise in protective HDL. They also experience a spike in LDL, but eggs produced larger particles of LDL, which are less damaging than smaller, inflammatory LDL particles. The egg eaters in the study also benefited from larger HDL particles, which remove LDL cholesterol from the blood more effectively.

186

The best advice for now is to enjoy eggs, but don't eat more than six a week if your cholesterol is close to or over 200 mg/dL. Eat all the egg whites you'd like, because only the yolks contain cholesterol.

There's one caution: Some people, known as *hyperresponders*, show a disproportionate spike in blood cholesterol when they eat eggs or other cholesterol-rich foods. If your cholesterol runs high even when you make every effort to eat a healthful diet, you might fall into this group. If so, avoiding egg yolks altogether might be the best choice for you. Ask your doctor to check if you're a hyperresponder.

SIP A GLASS OF RED WINE (OR GRAPE JUICE)

I mentioned the French paradox earlier, the phenomenon that allows the French to consume butter, cheese, pastries and fatty pâtés while experiencing far less heart disease than Americans. Part of their cardiovascular good fortune is thought to be red wine. Researchers believe the flavonoids in red wine, whose antioxidant powers lower the risk of heart disease, elevates levels of protective HDL cholesterol. Any alcoholic beverage consumed in moderation can raise HDL.

Red wine also contains resveratrol and other antioxidants that limit atherosclerosis. White wine isn't as protective as red wine nor does it contain as many antioxidants. Wine makers produce red wine using the entire grape, including the skin and seeds, where the heart-healthy flavonoids reside. White wine is fermented without the grape skin. Scientists at the University of California at Davis performed tests on a variety of red wines to find out which were most potent in flavonoids. They discovered the biggest antioxidant bang is found in zinfandel, with cabernet sauvignon, pinot noir and petit syrah close behind. Choose a dry red because the sweet varieties have far fewer flavonoids.

Studies also show that people who drink moderately, with an upper limit of two drinks daily for men and one for women, are about 25% less likely to get coronary artery disease than nondrinkers. Obviously, the word *moderately* is significant. Those who overindulge actually have a higher risk of heart attack or stroke. If you're alcohol sensitive in any way, substitute 100% grape juice. Evidence shows it offers benefits similar to those of red wine.

"SOY" GOOD FOR YOU

Soy foods, even after all these years, still reside on the fringes of American cuisine. Not so in Asia, of course, where people eat soybeans and soy foods, such as tofu, nearly every day. This alone might explain, at least in part, why the rate of heart disease in Asian countries is so much lower than it is in the United States. When scientists study people with elevated cholesterol (total levels over 240), they find that soy protein consistently causes a significant drop in LDL, as well as an increase in beneficial HDL. An analysis of clinical studies found that soy protein lowers LDL by 13% and increases HDL by 2.4%.

The known benefits of soy, such as being a rich source of *isoflavones* and other heart-healthy plant chemicals, are reason enough to strongly recommend it.

➤ **Enjoy soy all week long.** Try to eat a total of at least 25 g of soy protein throughout the week. One serving of tofu or a glass of soy milk supplies roughly one quarter of this amount. It's worth noting that while most Asians eat some soy every day, they don't eat large portions of it at any one time. A couple of ounces per serving are usually sufficient. They don't eat processed soy foods, such as soy dogs or "tofurkey."

ENJOY YOUR COFFEE BREAK

Good news about coffee. One cup has more antioxidants than a serving of blueberries! In fact, coffee is the main source of antioxidants in the US diet. (This says a lot about what we're not eating—the vegetables, fruits, whole grains and beans that are packed with antioxidants.) As part of the Iowa Women's Health Study, the coffee-drinking habits of 27,000 women were tracked for 15 years. Those drinking one to three cups daily had a lower risk of heart disease by 24%.

Decaf, incidentally, has the same amount of beneficial antioxidants as regular coffee, so you can still get the cardiovascular benefits without the caffeine jitters. Many people with heart conditions, and especially those with hypertension, are told to stay away from caffeine. However, a meta-analysis of ten different research studies tracking more than 400,000 people could find no increase in heart problems of any kind in people who drink coffee every day. This was regardless of whether people drank caffeinated or decaffeinated. It's true that caffeine kicks up your blood pressure a tiny bit, but the effect is temporary.

➤ **And tea time, too.** Tea lovers can count on adding extra years to their lives while protecting their arteries and hearts. About 30% of tea's dry weight consists of potent antioxidants called *polyphenols*, one of which is up to five times more effective than vitamin C at blocking the oxidation of cholesterol in artery walls. A study conducted by Brigham and Women's Hospital in Boston found that people who drank one or more cups of black tea daily had a lower incidence of heart attack—a remarkable 44%. Even in people who already have heart disease, tea can make a difference. One of the characteristics of atherosclerosis is that the blood vessels grow rigid and lose their ability to contract and relax normally. Tea has been shown to restore this ability of blood vessels to dilate, which can increase circulation and lower blood pressure.

➤ **Drink a wide variety of tea.** Like vegetables and fruits, different types of tea contain various polyphenols and have a range of antioxidant effects. Green tea has a wide range of remarkable health benefits, from immune boosting to cancer fighting. You might want to try gingko tea too. It contains a chemical compound called *ginkgolide*, which lowers levels of platelet-activating factor, a substance that increases the risk of artery-blocking clots.

➤ **Use the real thing.** The amount of caffeine in tea depends on the variety and method of brewing. (A pound of tea actually has more caffeine than an equal amount of coffee, but tea is usually brewed weaker, so coffee emits the bigger jolt.) To get the

188

cardio-protective benefits without the caffeine blast, make your tea with full-leaf tea rather than tea bag dust. The full-leaf variety will release just about half as much caffeine. In addition, brew your own tea instead of purchasing it in a can or bottle. The green tea sold in containers has a miniscule 5% of the flavonoids present in loose-leaf tea that is freshly brewed.

DIP INTO HONEY

Honey, particularly the darker varieties, is high in antioxidant compounds that protect the heart and arteries. People who eat honey regularly have been shown to experience a reduction in *lipid peroxidation*, the free-radical damage that makes LDL more likely to stick to artery walls. Some honeys have antioxidant levels that rival fresh fruits. Plus, people who eat honey regularly, such as a teaspoon or so per day in place of other forms of sugar, can significantly increase their blood levels of antioxidants.

HEART-LOVING SPICES

➤ **Protection from clots with curry.** Turmeric, the bright yellow spice that's a component of curries, is loaded with healthful antioxidants and has been widely studied as a cancer-preventing spice. It's so effective, in fact, that India's National Institute of Nutrition has launched campaigns to encourage people to eat more of it. Now, Western researchers are discovering that many of the same antioxidants in turmeric that protect against cancer may also be good for your heart. Turmeric is believed to inhibit the harmful oxidation of LDL cholesterol and also seems to lower triglycerides, the blood fats that are closely linked to heart disease. It also contains chemical compounds that inhibit clots, the cause of most heart attacks and strokes.

➤ **Hottest heart-healer.** *Capsaicin*, the chemical that puts the heat in chili peppers, is very good for the heart. Doctors noticed that people in Thailand rarely suffer from *thromboembolism*, the clots that can cause heart attacks, and believe that frequent use of chilies in Thai cuisine may be the reason. In a research study, Dr. Sukon Visudhiohan of Bangkok served spicy noodles containing two teaspoons of ground jalapeños to a group of volunteers. Others were given plain noodles. Researchers then analyzed the blood of both groups, and found that volunteers who had eaten the fiery fare had an almost immediate reduction in their ability to form dangerous clots. No such change was seen in the plain-noodle group. Additional studies suggest that capsaicin, and perhaps other chemicals in chili peppers, also lower cholesterol and triglycerides.

➤ **Ginger makes blood thinner.** Many herbs and spices inhibit the body's ability to form clots, and ginger is more effective than most. This zingy spice actually inhibits the ability of blood cells to manufacture *thromboxane*, a signaling agent that tells platelets to stick together. People who eat ginger regularly retain the ability to form necessary blood clots, which are needed after getting cut, for example, but seem less likely to form dangerous clots in their arteries.

➤ **Less inflammation with cinnamon.** This aromatic spice is a superpower of antioxidants. The more antioxidant power in a food, the greater its ability to squash the free-radical molecules that trigger inflammatory conditions. Cinnamon contains five antioxidants, the most powerful being *cinnamaldehyde*, which reduces arterial inflammation as well as blood clots (see ORAC chart, page 191). At the University of South Florida, scientist Dr. David Fitzpatrick found that cinnamon stimulates the release of nitric oxide, which causes blood vessels to dilate, an essential for healthier blood flow and circulation. Sprinkle cinnamon on your oatmeal, fruit salad and even on chicken and vegetables. Use it daily along with your other antioxidant foods. For a bigger dose, take one of the many available cinnamon supplements.

CHOOSE YOUR FATS WISELY

The standard advice regarding fats dates back to the 1950s when we were told to avoid saturated fats, such as butter, animal products and coconut oil, because they raise cholesterol and cause heart disease. We were also told to substitute the so-called "heart healthy" polyunsaturated fats, such as corn and soybean oils, to reduce our cholesterol. But little was said about monounsaturated fats such as olive oil, because they were thought to have a neutral effect.

Saturated fat is actually a healthy food source that provides valuable fat-soluble vitamins and nutrients and is essential to the body. And monounsaturated fats, which play a beneficial role in insulin management, are anything but neutral. Polyunsaturated fats, the ones that were supposed to save us from heart disease and cancer, actually have been a major influence in today's epidemic rates of both conditions (see page 194).

➤ **Saturated fat.** Your body needs and manufactures saturated fats from carbohydrates, and they are also present in animal fats and tropical oils, such as coconut and palm. A three-year study of 235 postmenopausal women, published in the *American Journal of Clinical Nutrition,* showed that saturated fats (butter, lard, coconut oil) actually protected their arteries and slowed the accumulation of plaque. At the start of the study, researchers took X-rays of the women's heart arteries. The women kept comprehensive records of the foods they ate and how much, including what kinds of oils they used for frying and baking. At the end of the three-year period, researchers took a second set of images and found that women who had regularly eaten the highest amounts of saturated fats had the least additional plaque buildup in their arteries. The saturated-fat group also had a healthier balance of good and bad cholesterols.

Not only do foods such as butter and cheese excite and satisfy our senses (unlike laboratory-engineered processed carbohydrate foods) but they also serve important biological functions. Both saturated fats and cholesterol provide cell membranes with stiffness and stability.

Saturated fat and cholesterol also contain vital nutrients necessary for growth, reproduction, hormones and energy production, while providing protection from many degenerative diseases. The body needs saturated fats to properly utilize essential fatty acids and for proper calcium utilization in the bones.

190

➤ **Monounsaturated fat.** The fats in this category tend to be liquid at room temperature, though they solidify when refrigerated. Like saturated fats, they are relatively stable and tend not to oxidize easily. The most common food source of monounsaturated fatty acid is *oleic acid,* found in the oils of olives, almonds, avocados, pecans, cashews, peanuts and other nuts. Monounsaturated fat is the main fat in the Mediterranean diet, which has been shown in virtually every research study conducted to be associated with lower levels of heart disease and cancer, not to mention longer life spans. The health benefits of monounsaturated fats were unrecognized until the late 1970s, when researchers discovered that monounsaturated fats were highly heart-protective because they raise HDL, lower LDL and reduce inflammation.

THE MOST HEART-HEALTHY OILS

There are safe modern techniques that extract monounsaturated oil and its delicate antioxidants under low temperatures. Look for labels that say "expeller-expressed" or "unrefined." These oils will remain fresh for many years in the refrigerator or if packaged in opaque containers or dark bottles.

➤ **Olive oil.** The high percentage of oleic acid in olive oil makes it perfect for salads and cooked veggies, but only if the olive oil is labeled extra virgin. Use only olive oil labeled cold-pressed. It is the most healthful vegetable oil you can use. Remember, olive oil is high in calories. Use no more than a tablespoon or so at a time, and always *in place*

Cinnamon: Queen of the ORAC and Other Foods High in Antioxidants

Scientists at the National Institutes of Health (NIH) developed the ORAC (oxygen radical absorbance capacity) score to measure antioxidant activity. The higher the score, the more effectively a food neutralizes damaging free radicals.

Studies show that foods with a high ORAC score can increase antioxidant levels in the blood by up to 25%. Nutritionists recommend shooting for a total daily ORAC score of 5,000 or more. Here's a partial list of the highest ORAC-ranking foods.

Food	Serving size	Antioxidant capacity per serving size
Cinnamon, ground	1 tablespoon	38,220
Small red bean	½ cup dried beans	13,727
Wild blueberry	1 cup	13,427
Red kidney bean	½ cup dried beans	13,259
Pinto bean	½ cup	11,864
Blueberry	1 cup cultivated berries	9,019
Cranberry	1 cup whole berries	8,983
Artichoke hearts	1 cup, cooked	7,904
Blackberry	1 cup cultivated berries	7,701
Prune	½ cup	7,291
Raspberry	1 cup	6,058
Strawberry	1 cup	5,938
Red Delicious apple	1 apple	5,900
Granny Smith apple	1 apple	5,381
Pecan	1 ounce	5,095
Sweet cherry	1 cup	4,873
Black plum	1 plum	4,844
Russet potato	1 potato	4,649
Black bean	½ cup dried beans	4,181
Plum	1 plum	4,118
Gala apple	1 apple	3,903

of other fats, not in addition to them. For low-heat sautéing, use light olive oil because it remains more stable when heated.

Olive oil has been shown to protect against heart disease by reducing blood pressure and artery inflammation. I recommend replacing any polyunsaturated oils you may be using with monounsaturated oils in salad dressings and for cooking. Use saturated fats such as virgin coconut oil or butter for baking. Use nut (such as peanut) and certain seed (such as grape and sesame) oils for high-heat frying.

Ten Easy Ways to Boost HDL

Studies show that increasing beneficial HDL cholesterol maximizes your protection against heart disease. Women should shoot for HDL levels over 40 mg/dL and men for levels over 50 mg/dL.

1. **Quit the cigs.** Your HDL should rise significantly in just two months.

2. **Focus on fruits and veggies.** Researchers at the University of Western Ontario showed that eating oranges and other fresh produce boosted HDL by 21%.

3. **Munch macadamias.** A study from the University of Newcastle in Australia, looking at the effects of the humble macadamia nut on cholesterol, found that daily consumption increased HDL by 8%. Participants ate about one-third of a cup daily. Be sure to eat macadamias in place of, not in addition to, other fats.

4. **Reach for the extra virgin**—the olive oil with the most polyphenols. A study in the *Annals of Internal Medicine* found that the higher the content of polyphenols, the higher the HDL level is raised.

5. **Nibble some niacin.** Take 500 mg of nicotinic acid (niacin) daily, upping the dose by 500 mg every week until you're taking 2,000 to 3,000 mg daily, in three doses with food. Niacin can cause flushing and itchiness. If these bother you, choose *inositol hexanicotinate,* a flush-free form, or take your niacin at bedtime. Another study in the *American Journal of Cardiology* found that time-release niacin, available by prescription, can boost HDL by nearly 8% in just 12 weeks.

6. **Crave curry.** Eating more curcumin, a component of turmeric, one of the spices used in curry, can kick up your HDL by an astonishing 29%.

7. **Move around.** As little as 10 minutes of exercise three times daily increases HDL and lowers cardio-risky triglyceride fats.

8. **Eat an onion a day.** Tufts University scientists found that eating a raw onion every day kicked up HDL by an average of 30%. Choose yellow or white onions, not the sweet variety, and eat them raw (on salads or sandwiches) for maximum HDL benefit.

9. **Fish for higher HDL.** Fish and taking fish oil supplements can boost HDL.

10. **Count on cranberries.** Cranberries, rich in antioxidant flavonoids, are showing promise as a significant HDL booster. The dose researchers cited as most effective was about one cup. Choose 100% cranberry juice with no added sugar.

➤ **Flaxseed oil.** One of nature's richest sources of omega-3s, flaxseed oil provides a remedy for today's widespread omega-6/omega-3 imbalance. Because it is so rich in omega-3s it can spoil easily, although new techniques for extraction and bottling have minimized the problem. Use it sparingly in salad dressings, never cook with it and always keep refrigerated and protected from light.

➤ **Peanut oil.** Peanut and other nut oils haver a high level of monounsaturated fat. It is relatively stable and, therefore, appropriate for higher-heat stir-frying. One caution, however. Due to its high percentage of omega-6s, use of peanut oil should be strictly limited.

➤ **Sesame oil.** Similar in composition to peanut oil, it can be used for frying because its unique antioxidants are not destroyed by heat. As is the case with peanut oil, it shouldn't be used frequently because of its high omega-6 content.

➤ **Grapeseed oil.** This healthful monounsaturated fat is pressed from grapeseeds that have been extracted after winemaking. It is also very stable, and is a neutral-flavored oil that can be heated at high temperatures. Again, its omega-6 content is on the high side, so use sparingly.

➤ **Coconut oil.** Tropical oils have fallen victim to the hysteria surrounding saturated fat in the health community. This is unfortunate, because their molecular structure allows them to withstand high heat, making them ideal for cooking and baking. Their bad reputation is the result of intense lobbying by the vegetable oil industry, which sought to replace coconut oil once in refined foods.

Standard medical advice claims that consumption of saturated fats can increase the risk of CHD, but a 2004 study published in the journal *Clinical Biochemistry* found that virgin coconut oil actually reduces LDL cholesterol, while raising beneficial HDL levels. Convincing research shows that saturated tropical oils do not contribute to heart disease.

Nutritionist Jonny Bowden has described a long-term, multidisciplinary study that examined people living on the coconut-eating islands of Tokelau and Pukapuka. Although up to 60% of the population's calories came from the saturated fat of coconuts, the islanders were lean, healthy and virtually free of atherosclerosis, heart disease, colon cancer and digestive problems. Coconut oil is extremely rich in *lauric acid*, a natural antiviral and antibacterial compound that also makes mother's milk protective.

Coconut oil is also rich in *myristic acid,* an important fatty acid used by the immune system to fight tumors. Most Westerners are deficient in myristic acid because we are told to avoid coconut oil and its other main dietary source, dairy fats.

➤ **Palm oil.** Both palm kernel oil and palm oil are saturated vegetable fats that contain high levels of lauric acid. Like coconut oil, both are extremely stable and can be kept at room temperature for many months without becoming rancid. Palm oil for cooking is difficult to find in US supermarkets, but you can purchase online.

➤ **Shopping tips.** In summary, your choice of fats and oils is one of the most important factors influencing your health. Don't be afraid of saturated fats. The research is very clear—avoid the PUFAs made from safflower, corn, sunflower, soybean (which is often labeled as "pure vegetable oil"), cottonseed and canola (see page 194). These oils oxidize rapidly in the body, creating free-radical molecules that deplete the body of its antioxidants and damage organs. Shun any processed foods containing them or *hydrogenated* fat, which is another term for trans fat. See "Get Off the Trans-Fat Train," pages 195–96.

➤ **What to use.** Use extra-virgin olive oil, small amounts of unrefined flaxseed oil or walnut oil for salad dressings. I prefer small amounts of coconut, grapeseed or refined sesame oils for stir-frying, because these all have a high smoking point and stay molecularly stable at high heat. When baking, stick with coconut oil or animal fats, such as butter. Contrary to what you've heard, they are much safer and healthier than polyunsaturated oils. You could also use extra-light olive oil in baking, depending on the flavor component you're looking for.

Never heat any oil to its smoking point, and never inhale that smoke because it is toxic and carcinogenic. Any oil that has gone rancid is toxic. Ingesting it is like pouring free-radical molecules into your body. Rancid oil has an unpleasant odor similar to varnish or oil paint. Discard it immediately. To prevent oxidation, buy high-quality oils in small containers and protect them from heat and light. Refrigerate delicate omega-3 oils.

Foods That Make It Worse

There are many powerful inflammation-fighting foods that can heal your arteries, lower your blood pressure and save you from a heart attack, but that's just half the equation. Cutting back on, or completely eliminating, foods that contribute to inflammation is also essential. You can greatly reduce your risk of CHD by controlling both factors, eating more of the foods and spices that reduce inflammation and less of those that are proinflammatory.

PASS ON POLYUNSATURATED FAT

This is the most unstable form of fatty acid, making it highly susceptible to oxidation and spoilage. The most common food sources of polyunsaturated fatty acids (PUFAs) are omega-6 linolenic acid and omega-3 linolenic acid. Since your body cannot manufacture them, they are referred to as *essential fatty acids* (EFAs) and must be obtained from diet. The greater the degree of unsaturation in a fatty acid, the more vulnerable it is to lipid *peroxidation*, commonly known as rancidity.

The ease with which these oils become rancid is the main reason that they cause so many health problems, especially CHD. Their oxidation creates a barrage of free radical molecules that attack cell membranes, artery linings and DNA/RNA strands, causing artery disease, cancers, Alzheimer's, cataracts and arthritis, as well as wrinkles and premature aging. They rob the body of its protective antioxidant supplies, exacerbating these health problems and weakening the immune system.

Standard health advice recommends that you substitute polyunsaturated vegetable oils for the saturated fats in your diet, and that they comprise approximately 30% of your calories. However, highly reliable scientific research indicates that this is bad advice. Avoid polyunsaturated oils, including those made from soy, corn, safflower, cottonseed and canola, entirely, especially in cooking. Studies confirm that PUFAs should comprise no greater than 4% of your total calories and should come directly from food sources such as grains, nuts, green vegetables and fish—not from commercially refined vegetable oils.

CUT BACK ON OMEGA-6

Processed PUFA oils are troublesome because they contain too much omega-6 linoleic acid and too little omega-3. Excess omega-6 in the diet has been found to interfere with the production of *prostaglandins*, hormonelike substances that help control blood pressure and modulate inflammation. Research shows that this disruption can result in blood clots, increased inflammation, high blood pressure, cancer, weight gain and immune system dysfunction.

We are learning that omega-3 fatty acids have powerful anti-inflammatory effects in the body, and that their absence from our diet may be a significant reason for the current epidemic proportions of inflammatory-based diseases such as CHD, diabetes, arthritis, asthma, Alzheimer's and many cancers.

When you eat a food that contains more omega-6s and fewer omega-3s, the omega-6s use up the available enzymes to produce pro-inflammatory compounds, which prevent the manufacture of anti-inflammatory prostaglandin. The result is a tendency toward inflammation throughout the body.

Unfortunately, the American diet is awash in inflammation-causing omega-6s, mainly in the form of vegetable oils made from corn, canola, soybean, safflower and peanut oil. In addition, these refined vegetable oils are widely used in processed foods such as crackers, cookies and other snack foods, as well as fast foods. Americans eat so many so-called "foods" that experts estimate a staggering 20% of their calories come from soybean oil alone.

The fastest and easiest way to improve your ratio of 6s to 3s is to avoid all fast foods and processed foods, and to stop using PUFA vegetable oils when you prepare food. Increase your intake of omega-3s by eating fish a few times a week, taking fish oil supplements and incorporating other omega-3–rich foods into your diet, such as flaxseed, walnuts and omega-3–fortified eggs. (For a list of the 10 Top Omega-3 Fish and Plant Foods, see page 43.) Another way is to upgrade the quality of the meat you are eating, either by preparing more wild game or choosing grass-fed beef. According to a study done at Iowa State University, truly free-range cattle have an omega-3 content on a level with some fish.

Safflower, corn, sunflower, soybean and cottonseed oils each contain more than 50% omega-6 and, except for soybean oil, only minimal amounts of omega-3. Use of these oils should be strictly limited. They should never be consumed after they have been heated, as in cooking, frying or baking. High-oleic safflower and sunflower oils, which are produced from hybrid plants, have a composition similar to olive oil and are more stable than traditional varieties. However, it is nearly impossible to find truly cold-pressed versions of these oils.

GET OFF THE TRANS-FAT TRAIN

Trans fats are completely artificial and appear on food labels as "hydrogenated" or "partially hydrogenated" oils. The introduction of these

The Canola Oil Hoax

Canola oil, marketed as the so-called heart-healthy alternative, is no better than other PUFA vegetables, and may actually be worse. Processed from a hybrid strain of rapeseed, shortening made from it can contain as much as 50% trans fat. It goes rancid easily, and baked goods that contain it quickly become moldy.

Researchers have found that during the deodorizing process, the omega-3 fatty acids of processed canola oil are transformed into trans fats, similar to those in margarine and possibly more dangerous.

A recent study revealed that canola oil creates a vitamin E deficiency in the body, which can lead to heart disease. Other studies indicate that canola oil causes heart lesions, particularly in a diet that's low in saturated fat.

Modern methods of oil processing destroy much of oil's inherent nutritional quality. Antioxidants originally present in the seeds, such as vitamin E, are also destroyed and replaced by the preservatives BHT and BH, both of which have been implicated in causing cancer and brain damage. Don't fall for the hype that canola oil is the heart-healthy alternative. It isn't by a long shot.

oils into the US diet parallels the surge in heart disease. This phenomenon was blamed at one time on the saturated fats in butter and meats. Trans fats more likely are to blame. These oils push up harmful LDL cholesterol while lowering beneficial HDL. Trans fats also increase inflammation in the arteries, inflammation that makes cholesterol far more likely to form plaques and cause a heart

attack. The Harvard Nurses' Health Study tracked 80,000 women and discovered that those who ate the most trans-fat-containing foods experienced a whopping 53% more heart attacks than those who ate less.

Consuming foods containing trans fats doubles your risk of heart attack. *The New England Journal of Medicine* published a report stating that trans fats, more than any other food, increase the risk of heart disease.

Also beware: Despite new laws requiring the labeling of trans fats content, the listings can be deceiving. Food labels can claim that the package's contents contain "zero trans fats" if they comprise .5% of total calories. Since trans fats accumulate in your body, eating one or two of these foods daily can accumulate trans-fat buildup in your arteries. I strongly urge you to avoid them completely. Many restaurants also continue to use trans fats, mostly in fried foods. As a general rule, avoid all deep-fried foods and most chips, crackers, cakes, candies, cookies, doughnuts and processed cheese.

HOLD THE REFINED CARBS AND PROCESSED FOODS

Most consumers and many doctors aren't aware that sugar is one of the leading causes of heart disease. Since the advent of refined grains and processed foods a century ago, Americans have eaten more and more processed white carbohydrates, the high-glycemic (GI) refined carbs that push up your blood sugar to damaging levels.

Many Americans eat a diet high in refined carbohydrates, including white bread, white pasta, cookies and crackers, plus other

Good Fats, Bad Fats

Use sparingly, no heat:
   Flaxseed oil
   Extra-virgin olive oil
   Walnut oil
Use sparingly, high heat and baking:
   Virgin coconut oil
   Palm oil
   Peanut oil
   Sesame oil (refined)
   Grapeseed oil
   Butter (for baking only)
   Lard
   Light olive oil
Avoid completely:
   Safflower oil
   Corn oil
   Sunflower oil
   Soybean oil (often labeled "pure
      vegetable oil")
   Cottonseed oil
   Canola oil

We know that a diet high in refined carbohydrates is a major factor in weight gain, and more recent studies show that these foods are among the worst substances for your heart. Refined carbohydrates elevate blood sugar almost as rapidly as eating refined sugar, which triggers inflammation. Sugar and other refined carbohydrates also put more insulin into the bloodstream, which in turn boosts cholesterol and triglycerides, while raising blood pressure. When glucose and insulin are chronically present in the bloodstream, they inflame and damage artery linings, a process known as *glycation*. People who eat refined foods regularly are far more likely to develop cardiovascular disease than those who eat whole foods, such as vegetables, fruits, whole grains like oatmeal and lean meats and dairy.

My advice is to eat virtually no refined or processed foods. Of course, if you go to your granddaughter's birthday party, it's okay to enjoy a small piece of cake. Exceptions should be just that—exceptions. Better yet, make your granddaughter a carrot-nut cake. You'll be amazed at how much energy you have from whole foods, since they keep your blood sugar steady and prevent the roller-coaster highs and lows of glucose-insulin spikes.

Supplemental Help

➤ **Nature's miracle heart-attack buster.** There's some exciting research being done on a particular fermented food. Red yeast rice, a staple in some Asian countries, is helping hearts and arteries. Chinese scientists tracked 5,000 people who had previous

starchy foods that have been processed to within an inch of their lives and stripped of their fiber. Without fiber, these refined carbs become a highly concentrated form of sugar (glucose) in your bloodstream. Most processed foods are highly refined, including most packaged breakfast cereals, such as corn flakes, puffed wheat, frosted anything and any cereal with added sugar, including allegedly healthful granolas. Drinks with added sugar, such as many fruit juices, are also processed foods. In general, this is the junk food category, and there's a lot of crossover between this group of manufactured foods and those in the trans-fat group.

heart attacks, giving half a placebo and the other half a purified extract of Chinese red yeast rice. After following the two groups for five years, researchers discovered that the red yeast rice group had 45% fewer second heart attacks than the placebo takers, were 30% less likely to die from any cardiovascular condition and 33% less likely to die from any cause. Cholesterol was also significantly lowered in the red yeast rice group, and their need for angioplasty or heart surgery was reduced by one-third. No drug currently produces results like these. Note that red yeast rice acts like a statin drug in depleting coenzyme Q10, so you should chase it down with a minimum of 200 mg of CoQ10 daily. And, if you are already taking a statin drug, yeast rice extract may not be appropriate for you. Consult your doctor.

➤ **Feeling fine with L-arginine.** The Nobel Prize for Medicine in 1998 was awarded for important research into the role that nitric oxide (NO) plays in heart health. Scientists at the time discovered that NO molecules lower blood pressure by relaxing blood vessels and also reduce dangerous clotting in arteries. Sounds like something we could all benefit from, right? Yes, indeed. However, because NO is a gas that breaks down almost instantly when exposed to air, you can't take it as a supplement. You can, however, get more nitric oxide into your bloodstream by eating high-fiber foods and taking an amino acid called L-arginine. Naturally present in grains, fish and other foods, L-arginine moves into the cells that line blood vessels, where it's converted to NO. Studies indicate that people who take about

198

2,000 mg of L-arginine daily have healthier blood vessels and improvement in circulation. It also reduces symptoms of coronary artery spasms, improves immunity and offsets the risks associated with having high cholesterol. Since L-arginine doesn't readily penetrate cells, it should be combined with another amino acid, *L-citrulline*, to help it enter cells more readily. As little as 200 mg daily of L-citrulline is enough to allow L-arginine to make the NO conversion.

➤ **D right vitamin.** Vitamin D is a heart-healing necessity. German scientists found a strong link between low levels of D and incidence of heart failure. They measured the blood levels of vitamin D in a group of heart-failure patients and also in a group of healthy people. What they found was startling—those patients with heart failure had 50% lower blood levels of vitamin D. In addition, the severity of D deficiency correlated to the severity of their heart failure. Scientists believe the connection may have to do with D's role in regulating the body's calcium, which helps the heart pump and contract effectively.

Vitamin D can also protect against peripheral artery disease (PAD), in which restricted blood flow to the arms and legs causes numbness and pain, even interfering with walking. A US government survey of 5,000 people with PAD examined their vitamin D levels and found that those who were lowest in D were 80% more likely to have PAD than those with the highest blood levels of D. More recently, a study tracking 13,000 people for an average of eight years found that low vitamin D levels increase the risk of death from all causes by 26%.

Your skin manufactures vitamin D when it's exposed to sunshine, and many people, especially in northern states where winter's overcast skies can make getting enough sun impossible, have dangerously low levels. I recommend getting 10 to 20 minutes of direct sun exposure without sunscreen several times a week and take a minimum of 1,000 to 2,000 international units (IU) of vitamin D-3 every day, doubling the dose in winter. If your skin is dark, you may need twice those amounts.

➤ **Niacin is a busy B.** Don't underestimate the power of over-the-counter niacin, a B vitamin that can increase heart-protective HDL by as much as 50%. Niacin also is very effective in reducing levels of lipoprotein (a) [Lp(a)] and other risk factors for heart disease. (No drug decreases this dangerous plaque-forming factor, and statin drugs can actually increase it.) Therapeutic levels of niacin may cause flushing and headaches. I suggest you gradually increase your dose over several weeks or use the flush-free form of niacin, *inositol hexaniacinate*. Start with 100 mg twice daily, increasing to 1,000 mg daily. Or, ask your doctor about Niaspan, a time-release formula that requires a prescription.

➤ **Deoxidize with coenzyme Q10.** In addition to helping the heart muscle beat more strongly, CoQ10 supports healthy HDL cholesterol levels and prevents excess oxidation of LDL. It also lowers high blood pressure, a serious risk factor for heart disease. Take 60 to 120 mg of liquid, water-soluble CoQ10 daily in soft gel capsules.

➤ **Slip in some psyllium.** Consuming sufficient levels of heart-protecting fiber is easy if you're following the Mediterr-Asian Diet. Food sources are the best way to get fiber, because they also include antioxidants and healing nutrients. Rebecca's heart recipes (see page 413) contain plenty of fiber in its most delicious whole-food form. A fiber supplement can help when you aren't eating well, but it won't provide nutrition. Choose a psyllium supplement, such as Metamucil or Fiberall, taking 5 to 10 g daily. Or try supplements made from seaweed fibers, such as alginate, carrageenan or glucomannan, derived from an Asian plant, *konjac*.

➤ **Fish oil in a pill.** The omega-3 fatty acids are among the best nutrients for your heart, but that doesn't help if you're one of the millions of Americans who don't eat much fish. If you are, I suggest you take a high-quality fish oil supplement, which provides many of the same benefits. Most fish oil capsules contain 1,000 mg of fish oil. Use a product that contains 220 mg (or more) of EPA and 240 mg of DHA. If you're using fish oil to lower triglycerides, take 2,000 to 4,000 mg daily, the amount in two to four capsules, but check with your doctor before starting these higher doses.

➤ **Help from hibiscus.** An extract from the hibiscus flower appears to have the same beneficial effects on cholesterol as red wine and green tea. A study published in the *Journal of the Science of Food and Agriculture* found that laboratory animals given hibiscus extract showed a significant drop in cholesterol and were less likely to experience artery-clogging deposits. Previous research has shown that people who drink red wine or green tea are less likely to experience atherosclerosis. This is the first study to show that hibiscus produces similar effects and probably for the same reasons. Hibiscus, a traditional remedy for hypertension, contains powerful antioxidants that prevent LDL cholesterol from oxidizing, the process that makes it more likely to stick to artery walls and trigger blood clots that can cause a heart attack or stroke.

➤ **Check out artichoke leaf.** Scientists at the University of Reading, England, discovered that artichoke leaf extract (ALE) from globe artichokes lowers cholesterol in people with moderately elevated levels. Volunteers took four capsules equaling 1,280 mg of ALE daily for 12 weeks and experienced a statistically significant lowering of their total cholesterol. ALEs are a good source of flavonoid antioxidants that characterize all the vegetables and fruits of the Mediterr-Asian Diet.

➤ **Consider an aspirin.** This old standby reduces inflammation and the risk of blood clots. Taken daily (or every other day), aspirin can reduce the risk of heart attack by up to 30%. Doctors routinely recommend a daily 81-mg aspirin for those who already have heart disease or who are at high risk. In fact, the Nurses' Health Study, which tracked nearly 80,000 women for 27 years, found that women taking aspirin, ranging from daily 81-mg low-dose to 325-mg regular-dose aspirin, had a significantly lower risk of death from all causes. Older women and those at risk for heart disease gained

200

particular benefit. You shouldn't need this, however, if you're eating the inflammation-fighting foods in the Mediterr-Asian Diet.

Other Helpers and Healers

➤ **Regular physical activity lowers CRP.** One of the primary markers of chronic inflammation is a substance called C-reactive protein (CRP), and Harvard researchers report that men with the highest levels have a 300% higher chance of having a heart attack than those whose levels are lower. The anti-inflammatory foods featured in the Mediterr-Asian Diet combined with regular physical activity can produce even greater reductions—as much as 50%.

➤ **Low intensity or high?** Doctors used to believe that only hard-core aerobic workouts produced positive effects on HDL, but new research indicates that even low-intensity exercise, such as walking, can elevate HDL by at least 8%. Walking briskly for 30 minutes a day can reduce your risk of heart disease by as much as 30% to 40%. Don't be afraid of working up to more vigorous exercise, no matter how old you are, just as long as your doctor approves. Research on largely inactive people aged 60 to 75 showed that an hour of endurance exercise such as walking, cycling or slow jogging three to five times per week produced significant improvement in heart health, with participants' hearts acting metabolically like younger hearts. Participants even told researchers they felt as though they were in their best shape in years.

➤ **Drop some weight.** Being overweight is hard on the heart, but many people don't understand exactly why. It's not just the extra strain that those excess pounds place on your heart, but the extra inflammation it generates. Fat is a metabolically active tissue that secretes inflammatory chemicals. Studies show that obese people produce higher levels of C-reactive protein, and also tend to have higher blood pressure and poor cholesterol profiles. Being overweight increases your risk of dying from heart disease by about 40%. (See chapter 19 to define "obesity" and "overweight.")

Here's the good news, though—people who lose as little as 10 pounds through calorie control, regular physical activity and other strategies can quickly lower their risk and make significant improvements in blood pressure and glucose control.

➤ **Release the stress.** Here's another reason to get your body moving—it's a great stress reducer. Studies show that dispelling negative emotions and stress can save your life. Did you know that you're twice as likely to have a heart attack on a Monday, typically the most stressful day of the week? Research also reveals that the risk of a heart attack can double in the hours after an anger-provoking encounter. Take a positive step toward lowering the stress in your life by signing up for a yoga class, learning to meditate or trying biofeedback, in which you slow your breathing and heart rate using a monitor that guides you toward your calming goals.

➤ **Kick the habit.** Smoking isn't only bad for your lungs. It triggers inflammation throughout your arteries, and increases the risk of atherosclerosis, blood clots and heart attack. The risk is even higher if you smoke and have hypertension, high cholesterol or other CVD risk factors. If you haven't been able to quit on your own, talk to your doctor. People who use stop-smoking strategies such as nicotine patches and smoking-cessation counseling (often done in groups) have about twice the success rate as those who try to quit through willpower alone.

➤ **Take a nap.** Here's a happy prescription for a healthy heart—take a daily nap. Napping is very beneficial for your heart, according to researchers in Greece who tracked 23,000 women and men in good health. For the study, published in the *Archives of Internal Medicine*, researchers followed the group's napping habits along with whether they developed heart disease. Those who took regular naps had 37% less heart disease than participants who never napped, results that should make you eager to put up your feet for a little siesta.

➤ **Brush and floss.** Poor dental hygiene raises your risk of stroke and heart attack, according to two studies reported by the Society for General Microbiology. Inadequate brushing and flossing permits the nastiest bacteria in your mouth to flourish and spread. When they get into your bloodstream—via bleeding gums, for example—they start a wave of biological action that can lead to artery disease, heart attack and stroke. One study noted, "…it doesn't matter how fit, slim or healthy you are, you're adding to your chances of getting heart disease by having bad teeth."

Women and Heart Disease

Heart disease is the top cause of death in women, but men are the primary subjects of heart-disease research. This has allowed male data to set the standards for detection and treatment in women. Worse, women with heart disease are sometimes treated less aggressively than men because their heart attack symptoms differ from the man's typical crushing chest pain. Women's heart attack symptoms are more likely to include difficulty breathing, abdominal pain and indigestion, unexplained fatigue, and pain just under the breastbone or in the jaw area. As a result, women are often misdiagnosed with anxiety attacks, indigestion or gallbladder problems.

Women's heart disease tends to develop ten years later than men's, a lag attributed to the reduction in estrogen and increased risk after menopause. When heart disease does develop in women, it also seems to occur in the smaller blood vessels, a condition called *microvascular disease*. Hormone replacement therapy (HRT), once thought to lower a woman's heart disease risk by replacing lost estrogen, now appears to raise it.

The same overall risk factors that apply to men apply to women: Inflammation, obesity, hypertension and chronically elevated blood sugar. However, for women, some factors carry even greater risk, including depression and stress, smoking and metabolic syndrome (the combination of high blood sugar, high triglycerides, belly fat and hypertension). What can you do? Get a handle on those risks right away. *Here's how…*

➤ **If you smoke, quit.** Ask your physician for help with nicotine replacement and in locating a smoking-cessation group in which members work together to stay cigarette free.

➤ **Check your iron level.** Women in menopause or past it should have their iron levels checked. Elevated iron can lead to significant damage of blood vessels by oxidation. That's why you should never take an iron supplement, or a multivitamin containing it, without consulting your doctor first.

➤ **Eat well for heart health.** Follow the Mediterr-Asian Diet to maximize antioxidants and other inflammation-fighters. Eating this way will also help to bring down your weight, cholesterol, blood pressure and blood sugar.

➤ **Move to save your life.** Cardiovascular health relies on regular exercise. Shoot for 30 minutes of moderate to intense activity daily. Brisk walking is fine, or get your heart rate up with an aerobics or spin class.

➤ **Relax for better heart health.** It's enormously important for women to let go of stress. Make room for some me time every day and destress in your favorite way: taking a yoga class, napping, walking, meditating, having a massage, or soaking in a hot bath.

Other research shows that mouth germs can trigger atherosclerosis, and older studies clearly support these newer findings. Scientists also know that people with advanced gum disease, or periodontal disease, have a higher risk of heart problems. When data was analyzed from 11 studies on heart disease and gum disease, it was found that people who had the highest levels of bacteria in their gums also had the highest levels of whole-body bacterial exposure and the most arterial blockage. ■

CHAPTER

13

Hypertension

The heart's job is to move blood. Every time it beats it pushes blood through a complex network of the arteries and smaller blood vessels with great force, or pressure. Doctors use two numbers to measure this blood pressure. The top number of the reading is called the *systolic* pressure, which measures the pressure in the arteries when the heart contracts. The number below it is the *diastolic* pressure, or how much pressure there is in the arteries between beats.

Under normal circumstances, blood moves smoothly through the blood vessels, somewhat like water running through a garden hose. However, when blood pressure is high, it exerts extra force on your arteries, especially where they bend and turn. This turbulence can wear away portions of the *endothelial* cells, which line the arteries, creating weak, thin spots that are later patched by cholesterol-filled plaques. When these soft plaques are hardened by calcium deposits, they make arteries narrower and less flexible, a condition known as *atherosclerosis* (hardening of the arteries), which can increase blood pressure even further. High blood pressure, also known as *hypertension*, can also damage blood vessels in the kidneys, eyes, brain and other organs, leading to dementia and other forms of cognitive impairment. A study published in the *Archives of Neurology* shows that hypertension increases the danger of mild cognitive impairment (MCI), which often leads to dementia and Alzheimer's disease.

About 50 million Americans have hypertension, and an additional 45 million have *prehypertension*, a newly identified condition that puts one at high risk for full-fledged high blood pressure. Until a few years ago, a normal blood pressure reading

203

was thought to be 120/80, but recent studies show that those with blood pressure in that range have a higher likelihood of developing full-blown hypertension and related health problems. The new normal for all age groups is 115/75 or lower, and experts advise anyone with higher numbers to take steps to bring it down. Doctors use terms such as "mild" or "moderate" hypertension to describe slightly elevated blood pressure, but there's nothing mild about the risks this condition poses. About 80% of those with hypertension fall into this mild range, and the majority of heart attacks and strokes occur there.

A new report from the American Heart Association (AHA) finds that untreated hypertension is particularly serious for females. Moreover, midsection obesity (another way of saying belly fat) is a major risk factor for high blood pressure, and occurs in 79% of hypertensive women. One more caution: Women with a history of taking oral contraceptives have up to a 300% higher risk of hypertension. If that's you, be sure to have your blood pressure monitored regularly.

SYMPTOMS

One of the most frightening facts about hypertension is that it usually presents no symptoms, even in patients whose pressure is extremely high. This means that it may persist for decades, causing severe damage to blood vessels, before you become aware of it. While some hypertensive people may experience headaches, dizziness or frequent nosebleeds, these symptoms are rare. Most often, people don't know they have hypertension until it's detected during a routine doctor's

visit, or after they've suffered a heart attack or stroke. Once you reach your mid-fifties, your chances of developing hypertension are greatly increased. Maintaining healthy blood pressure is vital, because it can reduce the risk of a heart attack by up to 25%, stroke by up to 40% and heart failure by 50%.

CAUSES

Only about 5% to 10% of hypertension cases are linked to an underlying medical problem, such as kidney disease or an adrenal tumor. The vast majority of cases, known as *primary hypertension*, don't have an identifiable medical cause. This doesn't mean that we don't know how to prevent it. Lifestyle changes, such as exercising and not smoking, can have profound positive effects on hypertension. So, too, can a healthier diet.

TREATMENT

Hypertension can be one of the easiest medical conditions to control without drugs or medical treatment. Studies reveal that drugs usually don't solve the problem. A 2002 survey revealed that only 41.5% of patients taking drugs for hypertension achieve adequate blood pressure control. In addition, antihypertensive drugs carry a worrisome array of side effects, including fatigue, erectile difficulties and chronic coughing. Many of the newer drugs are also expensive, putting them out of reach for people with no health insurance. The bottom line is that drugs are usually unnecessary, particularly for patients with mild-to-moderate hypertension. Simple dietary and lifestyle changes can be just as effective as drug therapy, and even more so.

The landmark 1997 study called Dietary Approaches to Stop Hypertension (DASH) clearly demonstrated that patients who eat more fruit, vegetables, whole grains and switch to low-fat dairy foods are able to lower their systolic blood pressure by 11.4 points and their diastolic pressure by 5.5 points. Moreover, DASH participants achieved these gains *without* deliberately losing weight or cutting back on sodium, two of the most effective nonmedical tools for lowering blood pressure. For more foods and recipes that control blood pressure naturally, visit the Web site *www.myhealingkitchen.com.*

Foods That Make It Better

Dietary changes produce rapid results. The DASH Diet, developed by the National Heart, Lung and Blood Institute (NHLBI), was shown to lower blood pressure in as little as two weeks. It is very similar to the Mediterr-Asian Diet, and includes an abundance of fruits, vegetables, beans and whole grains, with less red meat and full-fat dairy products than the typical American diet. Both DASH and the Mediterr-Asian Diet are rich in dietary fiber and provide plenty of potassium, magnesium and calcium, which are minerals proven to lower hypertension. These diets also include many of the foods shown to exert significant pressure-lowering effects, while improving the kidneys' ability to regulate fluids in the body. Some of these foods, which I'll discuss in a moment, also help maintain the elasticity of blood vessels and inhibit the buildup of plaque deposits, which narrow arteries and can increase blood pressure.

Another important benefit of DASH and the Mediterr-Asian Diet is that they make losing weight easier. This is critical, because excess body weight is a major contributor to hypertension. Studies show that those who lose as little as 10 pounds can reduce their blood pressure by 10 points or more. If you're in the borderline category, that could be enough to get your blood pressure back into a healthy zone and get you off drugs. Even if your hypertension is severe, losing weight could allow you to take a lower dose of medication.

One of the most important clinical trials of all time, the Harvard Nurses' Health Study (NHS), has been tracking the health and eating habits of more than 120,000 nurses since 1976. So far, researchers have found that women whose diets most closely follow the DASH guidelines have suffered

The DASH Diet

The landmark 1997 Dietary Approaches to Stop Hypertension (DASH) studied the healing power of certain foods and diet over hypertension. Patients were able to lower their blood pressure significantly by eating more of these foods...

Whole grains	Seven to eight daily servings
Fruits and vegetables	Four to five daily servings per day
Low-fat milk or cheese	Two to three daily servings
Lean meat, poultry or other animal proteins	Two or fewer daily servings
Nuts and legumes	Up to five servings per week

25% *fewer* heart attacks than those who eat the standard American diet. In broad terms, DASH is the same type of diet that many nutrition experts recommend for overall good health. More specifically, the DASH and the traditional Mediterranean and Asian diets all feature many of the foods that directly target blood pressure and act remarkably like today's drugs. *Let's take a look at the most prominent and well-researched...*

➤ **Oil your arteries.** People of the Mediterranean consume a lot of olive oil. It's no coincidence that hypertension isn't much of a problem in these countries. A number of studies show that consuming more olive oil can significantly reduce both systolic and diastolic blood pressure, even if they don't make other dietary changes. In one clinical trial, researchers at the University of Barcelona recruited men from Germany, Denmark and Finland, where olive oil isn't used as often, and had them add about one-and-a-half tablespoons of olive oil to their regular daily diets. By the end of the study, the men saw reductions in their systolic blood pressure of about 3%. While it's still not clear exactly how olive oil lowers blood pressure, researchers think it may be due to the large amount of *polyphenols* it contains. These high-powered antioxidant compounds help protect arterial linings and promote better circulation by keeping them free of plaque buildup.

➤ **Garlic lowers blood pressure.** Garlic is one of the most extensively studied healing foods and has been found to reduce both systolic and diastolic pressure consistently. In one study, scientists at the Centre for Cardiovascular Pharmacology in Wies-

baden, Germany, wanted to measure the effects of garlic on hardening of the arteries by selecting 200 middle-aged men and dividing them into two groups. One group was given 300 milligrams (mg) of garlic extract daily for two years (the equivalent of one to two fresh cloves) while the second group received none. At the end of the two-year period, those in the garlic group had significantly more flexible blood vessels.

➤ **Eat onions, drink wine.** The people of the Mediterranean consume onions and wine regularly, and their cardiovascular health really benefits. Both are rich in *quercetin*, a type of flavonoid with potent artery-opening effects. In recent research, published in the *Journal of Nutrition*, doctors at the University of Utah studied a group of adults with hypertension, giving them either a placebo or quercetin supplements every day. The patients receiving the quercetin experienced reductions in blood pressure of 7 systolic points and 5 diastolic points, compared with the placebo group. Researchers speculated that the quercetin may reduce the body's production of a compound called *angiotensin II*, a protein that constricts blood vessels.

➤ **Dig a spud.** Eating a large potato—baked, steamed or boiled—every once in a while can help knock out hypertension, because it is rich in potassium, a superhero mineral when it comes to blood pressure. In one study, people with hypertension who ate more potassium-rich foods, including potatoes, saw their blood pressure levels decline so much that they were able to reduce their doses of blood-pressure medicine. Sweet potatoes also contain a wallop of potassium. In a review of 33 studies examining the effect of potassium on blood pressure, researchers found that people who get at least 2,340 mg of potassium daily, from foods, supplements (under a physician's supervision) or both, lowered their risk for hypertension by an average of 25%. Those who had the highest blood pressure benefited the most.

Potassium is vital for normal blood pressure because it counteracts sodium in your diet, which can cause fluid retention and high blood volume. The higher the fluid volume in your bloodstream, the greater the pressure will be. Sodium retains fluid, but potassium moves sodium out of the body to control fluid buildup. In preindustrial cultures, the ratio of potassium to sodium in the diet is 7:1, which is ideal. In Western diets, sodium consumption is three times *higher* than potassium.

Potassium also causes arteries to relax and dilate, allowing more blood to circulate with less force. When researchers analyzed the most significant causative factors for hypertension across five countries, they found that potassium deficiency accounted for up to 17% of all cases. Other epidemiological studies confirm that, in communities where potassium consumption is high, blood pressure levels are generally in the normal range.

The advice here is obvious. Eat more potassium-rich foods. Many of the foods featured in the Mediterr-Asian Diet, such as dried and fresh fruits, nuts, beans, seeds and lentils, are high in potassium. Here are some other examples.

➤ **Unzip a banana.** This tropical fruit is a great source of potassium. A study track-ing more than 40,000 men for four years found that those who ate more bananas or other potassium-rich foods had significantly fewer strokes than those who consume smaller amounts. Another study, from the University of California, San Diego, found that men and women who ate just one daily serving of bananas or other high-potassium foods were able to reduce their stroke risk by 40%. The great thing about bananas is that they're like Mother Nature's version of fast food. Just unzip and eat. Or you can put a banana in the blender, with a tablespoon of whey or soy protein powder, add a cup or two of low-fat milk, yogurt or soy milk and you'll have a high-potassium smoothie in seconds.

➤ **Give a fig.** Six fresh figs have 891 mg of potassium, nearly 20% of the recommended daily intake and twice the content of a large banana. In a recent five-year study from the Netherlands, high-potassium diets were linked with lower rates of death from all causes in healthy adults age 55 and older.

➤ **More magnesium, please.** Plentiful in green vegetables, beans, whole grains and

10 Top Potassium-Rich Foods	
1. Tomato sauce	909 mg/cup
2. Winter squash	896 mg/cup
3. Figs, fresh	891 mg/six
4. Spinach, fresh	839 mg/cup
5. Papaya, medium	781 mg/each
6. Cantaloupe	494 mg/cup
7. Banana	460 mg/each
8. Avocado, medium	450 mg/each
9. Potato	422 mg/cup
10. Green beans	374 mg/cup

many other plant foods, magnesium relaxes the tiny muscles and blood vessels to promote better blood flow. Studies show that people who increase their consumption of magnesium-rich foods tend to see a decrease in blood pressure. On the other hand, a deficiency in magnesium, which most Americans have, is strongly linked to hypertension and heart disease.

To pack more magnesium into your diet, eat more of the foods listed here. If you're taking drugs to lower your blood pressure, ask your doctor if you should also take a daily supplement to replace the magnesium that many blood pressure drugs deplete. Ironically, some of the diuretic medications that are used to lower blood pressure also leach away magnesium, which can be counterproductive.

➤ **Have a guava.** Doctors at the Centre of Nutrition and Heart Research Laboratory in Moradabad, India, fed hypertensive patients about 16 ounces of guava daily for three months and found that they experienced a decrease in blood pressure by 11 to 13 points. Not only that, their cholesterol fell 27 points and triglycerides dropped by nearly 9%. This represents a major reduction in their overall risk for heart disease on a level that surpasses most drug therapy.

➤ **"C" your pressure go down.** The vitamin C from oranges provides significant benefit to people with hypertension and heart disease. Researchers have found that foods rich in vitamin C can actually lower blood pressure, while increasing levels of HDL (good cholesterol) and relaxing hardened arteries. (For a list of "10 Top Vitamin C Foods," see page 161).

10 Top Magnesium-Rich Foods

1. Pumpkin seeds — 151 mg/oz
2. Brazil nuts — 107 mg/oz
3. Haddock, cooked — 81 mg/3 oz
4. Spinach, cooked — 78 mg/½ cup
5. Buckwheat flour — 75 mg/¼ cup
6. Pine nuts — 71 mg/oz
7. White beans, canned — 67 mg/½ cup
8. Swiss chard, raw — 65 mg/½ cup
9. Artichoke hearts, cooked — 50 mg/½ cup
10. Brown rice, cooked — 42 mg/½ cup

➤ **Fill up on fiber.** Wise cardiologists advise their patients to consume more fiber, because studies show that it helps lower cholesterol and reduces other cardiovascular risk factors, such as diabetes and obesity. Fiber-rich foods, particularly fruit, also have a significant positive effect on blood pressure. A Harvard medical study of 30,000 men found that those who got relatively little fiber in their diets were 60% more likely to have hypertension compared to those who ate more. All fruits and plant foods contain fiber, but some of the best picks are apples, pears, berries and oranges.

➤ **Tomatoes are tops.** The brilliant red color of fresh tomatoes is due to *lycopene*, a nutrient proven to reduce the risk of prostate cancer. Now, scientists have learned it tames hypertension, too. Tomatoes are one of the food best sources of *gamma-aminobutyric acid*, a chemical compound that lowers blood pressure. In fact, tomatoes contain a number of compounds that help protect the arteries and improve circulation.

208

➤ **Holy mackerel!** In a study at Berlin's Central Institute for Cardiovascular Research, researchers divided hypertensive men into two groups. Both groups ate a standard Western diet, but one also consumed two daily servings (about 14 ounces) of canned mackerel, an especially rich source of omega-3 fatty acids. They followed this diet for two weeks, then cut back to three cans of mackerel a week for eight months. While they ate the mackerel, their blood pressure dropped by 7%, which is enough of a reduction to take most people with mildly elevated blood pressure out of danger.

More good news about fish: A meta-analysis of several studies examining fish oil's effect on blood pressure found that eating omega 3–rich fish three times per week is as effective at reducing high blood pressure as taking megadoses of fish oil supplements. Omega-3s reduce blood pressure by softening and improving the flexibility of artery walls.

Mackerel isn't the only fish that lowers blood pressure. *Peptides*, which naturally occur in skipjack tuna and sardines, also reduce hypertension by inhibiting the *angiotensin-converting enzyme* (ACE) that constricts blood vessels. By the way, this is exactly the way ACE-inhibitor drugs work, and these fish peptides were shown to block ACE better than any naturally occurring substance thus far known. Five separate clinical studies have demonstrated that the peptides in skipjack tuna and sardines perform just as well as many antihypertensive prescription drugs. Blood pressure reduction in these studies was significant, usually dropping

people with borderline hypertension into the normal range.

➤ **Stalk some celery.** In traditional Chinese medicine, celery is a time-honored treatment for high blood pressure. Several modern studies show that people who eat more celery experience significant drops in blood pressure. Celery contains a chemical compound called *apigenin*, which dilates blood vessels and reduces the circulatory force of the bloodstream. Another chemical in celery, *3-n-butylphthalide*, not only relaxes arteries but also reduces levels of adrenaline and other hormones that cause blood pressure to rise. University of Chicago researchers found that animals given 3-n-butylphthalide had a 12-point drop in blood pressure. Extrapolated to humans, these results would be enough to shift a patient with mild hypertension into the safety zone.

Some doctors hesitate to recommend celery because it's high in sodium. They forget that a three-ounce serving of celery has more than 340 mg of potassium, which can neutralize the sodium's pressure-raising effects. I advise patients to have no more than four or five stalks of celery a day, and to check their blood pressure regularly, just to be safe. In most cases, they notice that their pressure goes down.

➤ **Beet hypertension now.** A study by the London School of Medicine and Dentistry found that volunteers who drank 16 ounces of beet juice daily experienced reductions in blood pressure of more than 10 points, and that their pressure remained lower for 24 hours. The researchers explained that beets and other green leafy vegetables are converted

209

into *nitric oxide* (NO), a gas that opens arteries wider, so that blood is able to flow with less pressure. "There have been some very large studies showing that when people were put on a fruit-and-vegetable diet—particularly green leafy vegetables—their cardiovascular function and cardiovascular health improved," says Dr. Amrita Ahluwalia, senior author of the study. In the past, doctors have credited the antioxidants in beets and other vegetables for their cardio-protective effects. Now it seems that NO is the real hero.

One of the easiest ways to get plenty of these antihypertensive vegetables into your diet is by drinking vegetable juice. According to a study published in the *Journal of the American Medical Association* in 2004, Low-Sodium V8 juice lowers blood pressure significantly. Dr. Julian Whitaker of the Whitaker Wellness Institute in Newport Beach, California, regularly prescribes it to his hypertensive patients because of its effectiveness.

➤ **How Popeye keeps his cool.** Spinach, along with other leafy greens, such as dandelion, mustard and beet greens, are high in folate, an important B vitamin that appears to be very effective against hypertension In an eight-year study, researchers at Brigham and Women's Hospital in Boston tracked folate consumption among nurses. They found that women who got more than 1,000 micrograms (mcg) of folate daily had 50% fewer cases of hypertension.

Another recent study discovered that an enzyme in spinach acts exactly like ACE-inhibitor drugs to lower blood pressure by blocking the enzyme that constricts and tightens blood vessels. When laboratory animals with hypertension were fed spinach, it significantly dropped their blood pressure within two to four hours.

➤ **Ask for asparagus.** When researchers examined the health and dietary habits of people over age 60, they found that those who ate the most *glutathione*-rich vegetables, such as asparagus, had lower blood pressure and cholesterol, in addition to fewer instances of arthritis, diabetes or heart disease.

➤ **Milk does your pressure good.** A two-year study of 6,000 people published in the *American Journal of Clinical Nutrition* found that people who drank skim milk experienced 50% less hypertension than those who drank whole milk. Scientists explain that the calcium in milk counteracts the pressure-raising effects of sodium-rich foods. For blood-pressure control, any milk seems to help. Dr. John Laragh, who studied hypertension at Weill Cornell Medical College, found that patients with mild hypertension, defined as a diastolic reading between 90 and 104 (the bottom number of your reading), showed significant improvement just by drinking more milk.

Another study, this one conducted at the National Heart, Lung and Blood Institute, looked at the dietary habits and blood pressure of 8,000 adult males. Researchers discovered that men who drink about two cups of milk a day are half as likely to develop hypertension as men who don't drink as much. It confirms other reports, including research from the famous Framingham Heart Study, which found that people who consume more calcium-rich foods are the least likely to

210

develop high blood pressure. Another study done in Spain demonstrated that both men and women who consume more low-fat and fat-free dairy products have half the risk for hypertension.

The recommended daily intake of calcium depends upon age and sex: Women need more calcium than men. Everyone should get at least 550 mg of calcium (up to 1,500 mg may be ideal for postmenopausal women, but only women should consume this much). Studies show that adult males who consume more than 2,000 mg of calcium per day may increase their risk of prostate cancer.

➤ **Lactose intolerance.** Millions of Americans are deficient in calcium because they are lactose intolerant and can't digest cow's milk. For them, soy milk is a good alternative, because most brands today are fortified with calcium. Soy also contains *genistein*, a chemical compound that increases levels of NO, the gas that dilates blood vessels to help lower blood pressure. Research shows that animals on a soy-based diet tend to have lower blood pressure than those on a regular diet. Soy seems to have similar effects in humans. A recent study of men and women with mild-to-moderate hypertension found that those who drank soy milk had a decrease in systolic blood pressure of about 18 points and a drop in diastolic pressure of about 15 points.

➤ **Move over, Wheaties.** Oatmeal, it seems, is the real breakfast of champions, according to a study involving hypertensive men and women taking at least one prescription drug, reported in the *Journal of Family*

Practice. After just eight weeks of eating oatmeal every morning, more than 70% of the patients were able to have their doses of antihypertensive medication reduced by at least half. More than a third were able to eliminate it completely. Researchers estimated that the oatmeal breakfast would save almost $200 per individual a year in drug costs.

➤ **Chicken soup for the heart.** Scientists in Japan found that *collagen* in chicken soup act just like the blood pressure-lowering medicines called *ACE inhibitors*. These drugs work by enlarging blood vessels so blood flows more readily through them with less resistance, making easier work for the heart. Earlier research discovered that breast meat from chicken had small amounts of collagen, but the Japanese scientists say chicken bones and cartilage (often used in soup) have much more. They discovered four proteins in the legs and feet that behaved like ACE inhibitors. I encourage you to enjoy this type of chicken soup for its wide range of healing properties, including arthritis relief. Make your own broth for best results and keep the salt to a minimum. Salt can limit or completely neutralize the positive benefits collagen has on your blood pressure.

➤ **The 911 emergency diet.** If your blood pressure is high and you need to bring it down quickly, but don't want to use medications, let rice come to your rescue. In the 1940s, Dr. Walter Kempner of Duke University demonstrated that a diet of steamed rice, fruit and vegetables, known as the Kempner Rice Diet, reduced blood pressure by at least 20 points in a matter of days. This is an old trick used by commercial airline pilots, who routinely are checked for hypertension, but aren't allowed to use medications to bring it down. The doctor's rice diet really produces fast results. While the diet is restrictive, as no other foods are allowed, including oils, sweeteners, spices, alcohol, caffeinated beverages, meat and dairy products, the rapid results are worth it. (Be sure to use brown rice to get maximum fiber.) Eating such a bland diet won't hold anyone's interest for more than a few weeks, but once you get your hypertension under control you can shift over to the Mediterr-Asian Diet.

Foods That Make It Worse

Whole foods are always the best choice for fighting hypertension because processed foods are typically high in polyunsaturated vegetable oil, trans fat, sodium, sugar and chemical preservatives, all of which are bad for blood pressure. Adopting the Mediterr-Asian Diet is an easy, delicious way to achieve significant improvement in your blood pressure and cardiovascular function in a relatively short time, usually within a few months. However, there are some foods you'll definitely want to limit, or avoid entirely, if you have hypertension.

➤ **Shake the salt habit.** The average American consumes between 3,000 and 6,000 mg of sodium daily, which is far too much. Just about every canned and packaged food is high in sodium, as are most restaurant and take-out foods. Even those healthy-looking whole-grain bread loaves in supermarkets and bakeries often contain too much

212

salt. Your body does need sodium to generate nerve signals and muscular contractions, but it only needs a tiny amount. In excess, sodium stresses the kidneys and causes fluid retention, which results in hypertension.

For reasons that are still a mystery, some people can eat large amounts of salt without experiencing a significant rise in blood pressure. Others, known as *salt sensitive*, experience sharp spikes in blood pressure when they consume sodium. It's estimated that between 15% and 25% of Americans are sensitive to salt and you may be one of them. Among people with hypertension, the rate of salt sensitivity is as high as 50%. Since there's no easy way to tell if you're sensitive to salt, doctors advise everyone to keep their salt intake on the low side.

Aim to keep your daily sodium intake at 1,500 mg. That's not very much, considering that one teaspoon contains more than 2,300 mg. Most people who shave their salt consumption will see a drop in blood pressure of as much as 10 points. Those who cut back on salt in combination with eating a healthier diet can achieve a drop of 20 points or more. A recent study published in the *British Medical Journal* found that lowering your sodium level also reduces heart disease risk.

People with hypertension should also increase their consumption of potassium. Remember, potassium pulls sodium out of the blood to neutralize its fluid-retaining effect. To improve your blood pressure, it's important to cut back on sodium, while eating more fruits, whole grains and other potassium-rich foods. A clinical study demonstrated that when people ate a diet low in sodium and high in potassium, it produced a significant decrease in blood pressure.

Only about 11% of our salt consumption is added from the salt shaker and salty condiments. The vast majority of sodium in our diet comes from processed foods such as canned soups and vegetables, commercial baked goods and frozen dinners. Your best defense is to read food labels carefully, so you know how much salt you're getting.

If you must have salt, be aware that sea salt is much better for you. Toss out your iodized table salt—or save it for ice storms—because it is treated with aluminum to prevent caking. Some salt is even bleached to make it whiter. Sea salt, which tastes much better, is made by evaporating seawater in the sun, making it higher in the essential minerals your body needs.

➤ **Don't trust your taste buds.** Foods with a lot of sodium don't always taste salty. Baking soda in baked goods is a secret source of it. An innocent-looking bagel can pack more than 400 mg of sodium. The sodium in most restaurant meals is through the roof. Be sure to check what's in a food product or restaurant meals even if you have to ask for clarification. If you dine out a lot, get in the habit of requesting low-salt appetizers and entrees, or ask the chef to prepare your meals with a minimum of salt. Bring your own sea salt with you and season to taste.

➤ **Spice up your recipes.** Dishes with less sodium than those to which you're accustomed can taste a little flat, although most people who cut back on sodium lose their "salt tooth" in a few weeks. Get acquainted with spices and herbs that can add more flavor to your food so you won't miss the salt.

➤ **Drink defensively.** Many people enjoy a glass of wine with dinner, which is fine, because studies show that mild alcohol consumption does good things for the heart, such as raising beneficial HDL cholesterol and making blood less likely to form clots. However, more than two glasses of alcohol a day for men and one for women can elevate blood pressure, which is why most heavy drinkers are also hypertensive and have a 69% higher risk for stroke. Cutting back can result in a significant drop in blood pressure. Alcohol also contains a lot of calories, which can contribute to weight gain, another major risk factor for hypertension and stroke. If you're currently taking drugs to lower blood pressure, ask your doctor if it's okay to have a drink or two. Alcohol may reduce the effectiveness of some of these drugs and increase their side effects.

➤ **Rein in the caffeine.** Coffee is both good and bad for your heart. On the plus side, it is rich in the antioxidants that reduce arterial inflammation and inhibit plaque deposits on artery walls. On the other hand, caffeine is a stimulant that can raise blood pressure for about an hour after drinking it. So, where do you draw the line?

Researchers at Duke University found that people who drink four to five cups of coffee per day can experience increases in adrenaline of nearly 30%. Adrenaline is one of the stress hormones that may significantly elevate blood pressure. If you drink coffee or other caffeinated beverages throughout the day, your blood pressure could easily stay

213

high. Researchers from Duke University and the University of Vermont discovered that the first cup of coffee of the day increases both heart rate and blood pressure. They also found that the cardiovascular system has very little tolerance for caffeine from one cup to the next. That means each extra cup of coffee you drink continues to increase heart rate and blood pressure. If you absolutely must have a caffeine kick, switch to green tea, which contains one-third the amount of caffeine and is much better for you nutritionally.

Supplemental Help

Only about two-thirds of Americans diagnosed with high blood pressure manage to keep it under adequate control. Diet is the most important hypertension healing factor, but it's not always enough by itself. Drugs obviously can help, but many patients struggle with both the side effects and the expense. Fortunately, there are a few supplements that make a difference.

➤ **Depressurize with CoQ10.** Co-enzyme Q10 (CoQ10), also called *ubiquinone*, is a substance that powers the mitochondria, the energy-producing machinery inside cells. It's also a top antioxidant that's good for your heart and can significantly lower blood pressure. In one study, people with hypertension who were given 100 mg of CoQ10 daily for 10 weeks had reductions of about 10%. Doctors also saw drops in cholesterol of about 20 points. The body produces its own supply of CoQ10, but this output begins to decrease with age. By the

214

time you've reached your seventies, you're only producing half as much CoQ10 as you did earlier. Studies of heart patients, including those with congestive heart failure, indicate that supplemental CoQ10 can help reverse this debilitating condition.

Many foods contain CoQ10, but not enough to make a difference. If you decide to try supplementing with CoQ10, start at the lower dose of 60 mg. Take it daily for about three weeks. If you don't notice much difference, bump it up to 240 mg. For better absorption, take CoQ10 in divided doses after breakfast and dinner.

➤ **Hawthorn and garlic.** Taken together, these two herbs interrupt the conversion of the hormone angiotensin I to angiotensin II—the same effect created by some antihypertensive medications. The recommended dose is 1,000 to 1,500 mg of hawthorn daily, along with 500 to 1,000 milligrams of garlic. Split your consumption into two daily doses for maximum benefit.

➤ **Vitamin C.** Vitamin C is an all-purpose nutrient that's best known to reduce the duration of colds. Now, there's evidence that it can also lower blood pressure. In a study at Boston University School of Medicine, people with hypertension were given a starting dose of 2,000 mg of vitamin C, followed by 500 mg daily for the next month. Other volunteers in the study received placebos. At the end of the study, people in the vitamin C group saw their systolic pressure (the top number) drop from 155 to 142. There were no blood pressure changes in the placebo group.

➤ **L-carnitine.** This very useful amino acid enhances fat metabolism in cells, including the removal of waste products, which has been shown to improve blood pressure. Take 1 to 3 grams (g) daily.

➤ **L-arginine.** Another common amino acid, L-arginine acid promotes the release of nitric oxide, the gas that opens and dilates blood vessels, allowing them to carry more blood with less pressure. Take 2 to 4 g daily.

➤ **Doctor-induced hypertension.** You should get your blood pressure checked every time you see a doctor—even if you're in the office for nothing more than a wart on your pinkie. Don't be surprised if your numbers are a little high now and then. Just about everyone becomes anxious when they see a doctor, which can nudge blood pressure readings upward, a phenomenon known as *white-coat hypertension*. This happens often enough that doctors routinely take multiple readings before making a diagnosis of hypertension.

A single high reading usually doesn't mean much, but as we've recently learned, white-coat hypertension isn't necessarily harmless. A study published in *Journal of Human Hypertension* followed patients for 10 years and found that those with white-coat hypertension actually did have an elevated cardiovascular risk. Another study reported that white-coat hypertension may contribute to a serious condition called *carotid arteriosclerosis*. These findings have led some experts to suspect that doctor-induced hypertension could be a precursor to the real deal. If you experience white-coat hypertension, you might want to start some kind of stress-reduction program. Activities such as yoga, *tai chi*, biofeedback and meditation can help keep your numbers down.

➤ **Blood-pressure flower power.** Hibiscus tea (*Hibiscus sabdariffa*) has been a respected remedy for high blood pressure in many countries for centuries, so researchers decided to clinically measure its validity on hypertensive patients. The participants stopped taking their high blood pressure medication for one week prior to the study and drank a cup of hibiscus tea one hour before having their blood pressure taken, which was done three times throughout the 15-day study.

After 12 days, the subjects who drank the hibiscus tea experienced an average 11.7% drop in systolic blood pressure and a 10.7% drop in diastolic blood pressure from their initial readings. For someone with a blood pressure of around 160/115, this would be a reduction to roughly 145/95, which is so impressive that the results of the study were reported in the *Journal of Ethnopharmacology*. While the hibiscus tea produces reductions rather quickly, they may not be long-lasting, so it would be wise to drink the tea on a regular basis. Hibiscus is brewed made from the flowers and fruit of the plant, using a teaspoon or less per cup. Sweeten to taste.

A word of caution: Never discontinue any medication without speaking to your doctor first.

Other Helpers and Healers

➤ **Monitor yourself.** If you have hypertension, it's a good idea to purchase a high-quality digital blood pressure monitor and check yourself a few times every day. For the most accurate results, take three readings each time and average them. Monitoring your own blood pressure will show you which foods and supplements are causing improvements in your condition.

➤ **Shed some weight.** A 15-year study reported in the *American Journal of Hypertension* found that weight gain increases your risk of hypertension. A body mass index (BMI) of 18.5 to 24.9 is considered normal, 25 to 29.9 is overweight and a BMI of 30 or greater is obese. Compared with men who had a BMI below 22.4, those at 22.4 to 23.6 were 20% more likely to develop high blood pressure, while men at 26.4 or higher were 85% more likely to have hypertension. Being overweight makes your heart work harder, which increases blood pressure. Research shows that returning to your normal weight can lower your blood pressure by as much as 25 points. That's a better outcome than most drugs produce.

➤ **Stop smoking.** Most people know that cigarette smoke is not good for them but may not realize how harmful it is to the cardiovascular system. Nicotine constricts blood vessels, which raises blood pressure and also increases the oxidation of fats and LDL cholesterol in your bloodstream. In addition, the carbon monoxide in cigarette smoke decreases the blood's ability to carry oxygen, thus forcing your heart to work harder. Finally, smoking depletes every protective vitamin and mineral your body needs. Secondhand smoke is just as bad. Kicking the habit can lower your blood pressure by 10 points or more. Giving up both cigarettes and coffee can produce reductions of up to 20 points.

➤ **Become more active.** Getting at least 30 minutes a day of exercise is so beneficial

Punch Out Hypertension Punch

This is one of my favorite beverages, which I recommend to my patients with high blood pressure and heart problems. I often drink it when hiking or working in the yard. It keeps me hydrated and packs a triple health benefit. The pomegranate juice keeps my arteries clear and protects my prostate from cancer. The green tea is a superb source of antioxidants that are especially good for arthritis. And the hibiscus is good for my cardiovascular system and blood pressure. Plus, I love the way it tastes. *Here's my recipe…*

> *Makes 1 gallon*
> 3¾ quarts of water
> 4–8 decaffeinated green tea bags or ½ cup leaves
> 2–3 cups of unsweetened pomegranate juice
> 6–8 tablespoons of hibiscus leaves (wrapped in cheesecloth)

Bring the water to a boil, then stir in the remaining ingredients and steep for six minutes before discarding. Or make a sun-tea version: Place all ingredients in a one-gallon glass jar with a screw-on lid. Set out in the sun to brew for two to three hours. Sweeten either version with no-cal stevia or raw honey and store in the refrigerator. Drink throughout the day.

to your cardiovascular system and blood pressure that it should be included in every medical prescription for treating hypertension. Exercise not only helps prevent heart problems, but several studies show beyond a doubt that exercise lowers blood pressure in individuals with hypertension and those taking hypertensive medications. According to the National Institutes of Health (NIH), 70% of all people who exercise experience a reduction in blood pressure of 10 points, on average. The American College of Sports Medicine (ACSM) has found that these reductions last for approximately one to three hours.

You won't even need to break a sweat to reap these benefits. "Moderate intensity exercise has been scientifically documented to effectively lower blood pressure in people, perhaps more so than vigorous exercise," says Linda Pescatello, PhD, who chaired the ACSM study. These reductions in blood pressure can be achieved by walking, biking or other activities that moderately raise the heart rate.

➤ **Chill out.** Chronic stress, whether caused by relationship troubles, financial worries or a troublesome boss, generates chronically high levels of the adrenal hormone cortisol, which can affect your health adversely. Cortisol elevates blood pressure and blood sugar and weakens the immune system. High levels of stress can also lead to chronic low-grade inflammation, which contributes to numerous diseases.

Reducing your stress level can have a major impact on lowering your blood pressure. One insight that will be immediately helpful is to realize that it isn't the stress that's causing the problem, but rather how you're reacting to it. Relaxation techniques that utilize yoga or biofeedback have been shown to lower blood pressure dramatically when employed on a regular basis. An easy and inexpensive way to begin is by purchasing a pulse monitor. This small, inexpensive device slips over the tip of your index finger and displays a continuous readout of your pulse as you watch the monitor. Concentrate on lowering your pulse rate through relaxed breathing and you'll soon discover how to bring yourself to a calm state. Then, use this new information whenever stress starts getting the better of you. Pets are another stress reliever. Studies show that people who have animal companions suffer less from hypertension and live longer. ■

14

Insomnia

Every night, 70 million Americans toss and turn, thoughts racing, desperately hoping to fall asleep. Others start out snoozing, but awaken in the middle of the night and can't get back to sleep. Bleary eyed and depleted, anyone with a sleep problem knows the scrambled thinking and unfocused blur that plagues us the morning after. *Insomnia* is difficulty falling or staying asleep, and one in 10 of us encounter it regularly. The National Sleep Foundation says up to 60% of adults have sleep problems several nights per week or more. Most of us need about eight hours for health and physiological reasons alone, but how much sleep we require varies from person to person.

Sleep is essential for restoring your levels of the rejuvenating *human growth hormone* (HGH), which isn't released in most people until after the sixth hour of sleep. Long-term

memory improves with eight hours of sleep, but not with fewer than six. Virtually everyone who regularly suffers through sleepless nights would swear that they have a medical condition, but insomnia is actually a symptom. A symptom of *what*? That's when this bedtime story becomes more like a nightmare.

SYMPTOMS

Insomnia comes in three forms: Difficulty falling asleep, problems staying asleep and nonrestorative sleep, meaning you do sleep, but it's not rejuvenating. Most of us have had an occasional night of poor slumber, but those with chronic insomnia go through this horrible experience almost every night. Millions of Americans are walking around sleep-deprived, creating an enormous pool of lost productivity and accidents waiting to happen. On the road, sleepy drivers cause more than 100,000 collisions annually.

Not sleeping well at night means you're not concentrating well during the day, which can adversely affect your ability to listen, problem solve and make sound decisions. You feel exhausted and run the risk of falling asleep when you shouldn't. Insomnia may cause relationship problems, too, from interrupting your partner's sleep to your predictable irritability the day after a sleepless night. Debilitated by fatigue, you're also vulnerable to depression and a variety of physical and mental health problems. If all this weren't bad enough, the Nurses' Health Study found a direct link between inadequate sleep and weight gain, with those getting five or fewer hours of sleep per night gaining substantially more weight than women who regularly got seven hours.

Sleep is essential for a healthy immune system, because your body does much of its healing during the deepest period of sleep cycle, called *REM* (rapid eye movement). Research confirms that people who sleep well feel better and actually live longer.

Little wonder why. Sleep is the third angle, along with good nutrition and exercise, of the health triangle. It restores us by slowing down every physiological process in the body, including heart rate, breathing and blood pressure. Insufficient sleep radically disrupts your body's delicate hormone balance. Research published in *The Lancet* reports that chronic sleep loss can cripple hormone production and metabolism in a way that mimics diabetes and the aging process. In other words, not sleeping well makes you old before your time. Its effect on blood sugar is freakish. Scientists have discovered that just one week of sleep deprivation dramatically increases the amount of time it takes blood sugar levels to fall after a high-carb meal, meaning sugar stays in your bloodstream longer and browns artery walls, organs and tissue (the process called *glycation*). It also inhibits the release of insulin by 30%. The sleep-deprived participants in the study also had more of the stress hormone *cortisol* in their systems at night, similar to the levels doctors see in older people.

Without enough sleep, your body and mind are constantly stressed, which weakens your immune system and leaves you more vulnerable to infections and degenerative disease. Insufficient sleep also leads to falls, according to a study published in the *Archives of Internal Medicine*. Researchers found that women over 70 who slept five hours or fewer each night were 47% more likely to suffer at least two falls during the year-long study than those who slept seven to eight hours nightly. A report from the Centers for Disease Control (CDC) implicates insomnia as a cause of high blood pressure, diabetes, stroke, obesity and depression, as well as seriously complicating these conditions. Statistics show that personal health costs for insomniacs are triple those of normal sleepers.

CAUSES

A constellation of factors can disrupt sleep. Researchers at Washington State University discovered that many people seeing their doctors for insomnia also suffered from depression or other underlying mental health conditions. Anxiety, stress and tension top the list of insomnia inducers for many. In fact, scientists who have studied sleep disorders found that chronic insomniacs have higher levels of stress hormones circulating in their blood day and night. These are the very same hormones linked to an increased risk of osteoporosis, obesity, high blood pressure and depression. In the study, those who had the most trouble sleeping displayed the highest levels of cortisol in their blood, especially in the evening hours and through the night. Researchers think that this *hyperarousal* could actually be the underlying cause of chronic insomnia.

Your job schedule can also affect sleeplessness, especially if you work early-morning or late-night shifts, frequently change shifts or travel across time zones. Men with enlarged prostates often have disturbed sleep because of their need to urinate throughout the night. Women going through menopause have their sleep buffeted by hot flashes and night sweats.

Other causes of sleep disorders include sharing a bedroom with a snorer, having restless leg syndrome and sleep apnea (in which you stop breathing briefly and wake up breathless). Any condition that causes physical pain, including fibromyalgia, backaches and arthritis, can make sound sleep difficult. Curiously, some people with sleep problems find that they sleep well when they're away from their usual environment.

Several medications are notorious for disturbing sleep, including over-the-counter decongestants, headache drugs and weight-loss products containing caffeine and other stimulants. There are hundreds of prescription drugs that make sleep difficult or block

220

normal sleep patterns, most notably, blood pressure drugs and antidepressants.

What we eat and drink also interferes with sleep. Caffeine, sugar and/or excessive alcohol can cause real problems in falling and staying asleep. Overeating or eating anything more than a snack close to bedtime can cause digestive distress and may push acidic digestive juices into your esophagus while you are lying down.

TREATMENT

Sleeping pills may help occasionally, but because they mask the underlying cause of insomnia you should use them judiciously as you explore the source of your problem. Also, with regular use, sleep medications lose their effectiveness, can lead to dependency, and often cause rebound insomnia (a recurrence of stronger insomnia after you stop taking them).

In fact, a compelling study on sleeping pills from researchers at the University of California recommends against their regular use. Scientists reviewed data on more than a million sleeping-pill users and discovered that those taking more than 30 per month had a 300% greater risk of death. People taking between one and 29 pills monthly had a 50% to 80% higher risk of death. And, like all prescription drugs, sleeping medications come with side effects, such as facial puffiness, allergic responses and bizarre behavior, such as driving or eating while asleep. Many over-the-counter sleep aids, such as Tylenol PM and Sominex, are sleep inducing because they contain antihistamines, which make you drowsy the same way allergy drugs do. Just like prescription meds, they may lose effectiveness over time and produce unpleasant hangover effects the next day. If you think that depression or a similar condition may be causing your insomnia, talk to your doctor.

Very often, insomnia can be overcome without doctors or drugs. Plain old exercise is extremely effective because it reduces anxiety, eases depression and boosts your body temperature, which plays a significant part in helping you fall asleep and stay asleep. Exercise also helps your body regulate its wake-sleep cycle, synchronizing it with natural darkness and daylight rhythms. Research supports the sleep benefits of moving your body, and a little workout goes a long way.

Scientists at the University of Arizona Sleep Disorder Center monitored more than 700 people with sleep problems and discovered that just a half-mile walk daily remedied many sleep problems. Participants who exercised were the ones who slept the longest and deepest. Scientists at Stanford found that adults over 50 especially benefited from exercise. The *Journal of the American Medical Association* published a study in which insomniacs age 50 to 76 did low-impact aerobics or walked briskly for a half hour daily, four days a week. Within four months, they were sleeping better for longer periods and with fewer awakenings. They also fell asleep more quickly.

Other studies show that regular exercise can help shed the extra pounds that are linked to sleep apnea. Also important to note is that vigorous aerobic exercise most days of the week calms the adrenal glands' production of stress hormones, which results in sweet slumber at night.

Foods That Make It Better

What you eat has a powerful impact on how you sleep. The ideal bedtime snack should include one or two foods rich in *tryptophan* (see pages 224–225), an amino acid your brain uses to make *serotonin*, the neurochemical that governs mood. When your brain is happily loaded with serotonin, you become calm and drowsy. Turn out the lights and your brain transforms serotonin into *melatonin*, the sleep-regulating hormone.

Shift Your Perspective

If you're a shift worker, you're probably well acquainted with sleep challenges. Shift workers often have more problems than daytime workers, including sleep quality, falling asleep and staying asleep. Research shows that shift workers have lower levels of the feel-good, sleep-regulating brain chemical serotonin in their blood.

The way your shifts rotate could offer some relief, according to Dutch scientists, who discovered that workers with forward-moving shifts had far fewer health problems than those with backward-moving shifts. If you have to rotate, request shifts that move forward: 7 AM to 3 PM, 3 PM to 11 PM, and so forth. Those with backward-moving shifts had triple the rate of health problems. As challenging as it may be, try to keep the same bedtime schedule on your days off to regulate your sleep cycle.

10 Tips for Better Sleep

1. **Pull the plug.** Get your television, computer, phone and all other electronic entertainment and communications devices out of the bedroom. Electronics stimulate the brain, disrupting your pineal gland's production of sleepy-time melatonin. Keep a good book near your bed, but otherwise: The bedroom is for sleep and sex only.

2. **Leave the sheets.** If you can't fall asleep, or go back to sleep, get up after 30 minutes. Lying in bed will only increase your stress. Head for another room and read something calming until you're sleepy, or listen to a guided imagery tape.

3. **Dark, calm and chilly.** Keep the bedroom dark, quiet and cool. Darkness is essential for your brain's pineal gland to produce sleep-including melatonin, so remove all night-lights. Don't turn on the light in the bathroom if you need to use it during after hours. Use earplugs or turn on a fan to mask any noise.

4. **Limit pain.** If you have chronic pain, it's hard to sleep well. Talk to your doctor if you aren't getting enough pain relief to afford a good night's sleep, which you need to bolster your body's innate healing.

5. **Go to sleep camp.** Start your own sleep-training camp to prepare your body and mind for zzz's. Start by going to bed at the same time every night, weekends included, and getting up at the same time each day. Establish a sleep routine that you'll follow every night before sleep. Have a tryptophan snack, take a warm bath with calming lavender oil, sip a cup of chamomile or passionflower tea and read five pages of a meditative book. Then go to bed. Count your breaths backward starting from 100, and give your full attention to the sensation of your breathing. If you lose count, go back to 100 and start again.

6. **Jot in a journal.** If stressors such as work priorities and to-do lists revisit your consciousness every night, start a journal during the day. Record your concerns, as well as how and when you'll deal with them later.

7. **Closet the clock.** Stash your bedroom clock where you'll still hear your wake-up alarm, but in a location you can't see from bed, such as under it. Watching the digital progress of your sleeplessness is stressful.

8. **Quit disturbing me.** Talk shows, news programs and "nighttime dramas" are filled with disturbing images and stories. If you find that real or fictional violence is upsetting your slumber, go on a media fast for a week to see if it improves your sleep.

9. **Let the daylight shine.** Improve your sleep by exposing yourself to daylight. If your problem is getting sleepy in the afternoon, brief exposure to outdoor light, such as taking a 30-minute walk, can help decrease afternoon drowsiness, according to scientists in the journal *Sleep*. In the winter, use a full-spectrum light box. At night, make sure it's absolutely dark in your bedroom.

10. **Get the worm.** If you love to stay up late, your insomnia is probably worse than that of the early bird. Stanford School of Medicine researchers surveyed more than 300 people with sleep problems and discovered that those with the most fatigue during the day and the poorest sleep at night were night owls. Shift your sleep cycle so that you're heading to bed earlier and rising with the sun.

In addition, eating a nutritious diet can restore your tired adrenal glands and help reduce their production of stress hormones, a common underlying cause of chronic insomnia. The diet recommended to reverse adrenal fatigue emphasizes whole grains, vegetables and fruit, beans, nuts and seeds. Smaller, regularly spaced meals also support adrenal health. It may seem obvious, but if you have insomnia, it's best to eat lightly at your last meal of the day, so that your digestive system has several hours to process food before you lie down. Read on for specific food ideas that can clear your path to dreamland.

➤ **Have a little honey.** It's true that honey is pure sugar, but according to research at MIT, it increases serotonin in the brain and settles down brain activity to encourage relaxation and sleep. Having just a little glucose also signals the brain to quit its production of *orexin*, a chemical that helps keep it bright and alert.

➤ **Open wide for oats.** A cup of oatmeal can trigger sleep by virtue of its melatonin content, which gets your brain ready for slumberland. Pump up oatmeal's sleep-inducing properties by enjoying it with a little honey and milk.

➤ **Reach for high-GI carbohydrates.** The glycemic index (GI) measures how quickly carbohydrate foods are converted into blood sugar (glucose). I generally advise people to stay away from high-GI carbs, such as refined wheat products and sugary foods because they're full of empty calories that can lead to weight gain and blood sugar problems, notably type 2 diabetes. However, if you are otherwise healthy and have

trouble falling asleep, you may want to include one more high-GI foods with dinner or as a bedtime snack. One study found that when people with sleep problems ate white rice, which has a GI rating of over 100, they fell asleep 50% faster, according to research published in the *American Journal of Clinical Nutrition*. Other high-GI foods that produce a similar effect include white potatoes, rice cakes, a bagel or toast, and many commercial breakfast cereals.

➤ **Nosh on nuts.** Nuts, seeds and leafy greens are rich in magnesium which, like calcium, relaxes muscles and also helps to produce sleepy-time serotonin. Studies show that low levels of magnesium can be a contributing cause of restless leg syndrome.

Potassium is also essential for proper adrenal function and is found in kelp, sunflower seeds, wheat germ, almonds, raisins, parsley, peanuts, avocado, pecans, Swiss chard, garlic and yams. Loading up on these foods is also beneficial to your blood pressure, because potassium pulls sodium from your cells and lessens fluid retention. Pantothenic acid is another nutrient needed for peak adrenal health. Foods such as salmon, sweet potatoes, tomatoes, broccoli, cauliflower, whole grains and legumes—especially kidney beans—are rich in it.

➤ **Go with grains.** Eating whole grains throughout the day generates lots of feel-good serotonin. Your brain will use that supply later to help produce the melatonin that triggers sleep. Two easy ways to accomplish this are enjoying oatmeal for breakfast and brown rice with dinner. Whole grains are also rich in an array of B vitamins, essential for a calm nervous system.

➤ **Have an herbal fix and zzz.** A cup of herbal tea taken about an hour before retiring can soothe the anxiety and stress that keeps you awake at night. Choose chamomile or passionflower for best results. Chamomile contains an antioxidant-rich flavonoid called *apigenin*, which finds its way into your nervous system to ease anxiety and mellow your response to stress. Passionflower calms the central nervous system and acts as an antispasmodic on the smooth muscles, relaxing your arteries and veins, GI tract and breathing. Limit yourself to one small cup so that your bladder doesn't become overloaded in the middle of the night.

➤ **Sip away stress.** Stress is often a hidden factor in insomnia. Decaffeinated green tea can help. New studies show that green tea contains an unusual amino acid called *L-theanine* that has the ability to disarm stress that builds up in the body and nervous system. The *Alternative Medicine Review* reports that L-theanine calms the nervous system and increases alpha wave levels in the brain to create a state of relaxed alertness. L-theanine is also available in supplement form.

➤ **Finding Nemo.** Eating a diet rich in omega-3 fatty acids raises your brain's serotonin levels so that it can work with melatonin to induce sleep. Eat other cold-water fatty fish such as mackerel, wild-caught salmon and sardines, as well as walnuts and flaxseed, to get more omega-3s and thus more serotonin. This feel-good neurotransmitter is clinically proven to produce positive effects on mood. If

224

you suffer from depression, a factor for many with sleep problems, serotonin can help.

➤ **Bet on the Bs.** If sleep eludes you, you may have a deficiency of B-vitamins, essential for nervous system function and to keep stress under control. I regularly recommend my patients take a B-complex 100 supplement every day. Vitamin B-6 and niacin are intimately involved in your body's production of serotonin, the precursor to sleep-inducing melatonin. Your brain also needs other B-vitamins to help regulate sleep. If restless legs are keeping you up, the folic acid in your B-complex will ease this condition. Eating a Mediterr-Asian style diet provides B-vitamins galore in whole grains, seeds, nuts and eggs, as well as legumes like pinto beans and chickpeas.

SLEEPY-TIME TRYPTOPHAN

Have one of these tryptophan snacks an hour or so before bed for a wave of serotonin, which brings on sleep. For more sleepy-time snacks, visit *www.myhealingkitchen.com*.

➤ **Indulge in good leftovers.** The last banana on the counter. A slice of turkey or chicken on whole-grain bread. A few teaspoons of cottage cheese. A piece of cheese. Even a scoop of leftover bean salad will do the trick. These are all sedative foods, high in tryptophan.

➤ **Warm up some milk.** Add a tablespoon of honey to trigger your body to release insulin, which helps more tryptophan to reach your brain. Heat helps magnify the effect of tryptophan. All dairy products contain calcium, which helps your brain use the tryptophan effectively and also helps relax your muscles.

➤ **Munch these.** Almonds contain tryptophan and magnesium, both of which act like a muscle relaxant. Peanuts, although they are legumes, will do the trick too.

➤ **Create a classic combo for easy sleep.** Have a slice of whole-wheat bread spread with a little peanut butter and drizzled with honey, plus a small mug of warm milk. Nighty-night!

Foods That Make It Worse

Using caffeine dates to the Stone Age, when Paleolithic man stumbled on this stimulating compound, which is present in 63 plant species. Caffeine is just one in a group of compounds called *xanthines*, including *theophylline* and *theobromine*. Xanthines are all stimulants, which means that they buzz up your central nervous system and keep you alert. Theophylline accounts for your racing heartbeat after drinking too much coffee. Caffeine isn't the only thing keeping us awake at night, however. If you're getting up to use the bathroom, cut the liquids a couple of hours before bedtime. In addition, follow these guidelines for sounder sleep.

➤ **Forego the fat.** Eating a high-fat meal late in the day (or any time) can bring on heartburn and indigestion, both of which can interrupt a good night's sleep. Keep meals light throughout the day, especially at dinner. Eat dinner at least several hours before you head to bed. Feeling full is not conducive to sound sleep.

➤ **Cross off caffeine.** Even if you don't drink coffee, you might be getting doses of caffeine or other stimulants from hidden sources like soft drinks, chocolate, or even medications. Cut back where you can.

➤ **Cut back on alcohol.** Alcohol in moderation is a sedative and can make you sleepy. However, as your body metabolizes the alcohol after you go to sleep, its sedative effect wears off, and you can easily awaken. Alcohol also prevents you from slipping into the deeper REM sleep states, which are necessary for repair and regeneration. Furthermore, alcohol is a diuretic that pulls fluids into your bladder, making you hit the bathroom during the night. Finally, alcohol relaxes the muscles you use to breathe, which can exacerbate sleep apnea and snoring, two other culprits in nighttime awakening.

➤ **Say so long to sugar.** Table sugar and refined carbohydrates can trigger erratic blood glucose levels and stimulate your nervous system. Low blood sugar can actually awaken you in the night when your glucose levels crash, as your body cries out for more of it. Eating beans and whole grains, plus vegetables and fruits during the day, will help stabilize your blood sugar at night, so that you sleep better.

Supplemental Help

➤ **Valerian.** Used for thousands of years as a mild sedative, valerian root helps you fall asleep more quickly and improve the quality of your sleep. Plus, it won't leave you with a hungover feeling the next day. In some people, valerian takes a while to work. One study showed that a single dose provided minimal help but that sleep improved after two to four weeks of use. Valerian works by preventing the breakdown of a brain chemical called GABA (*gamma-aminobutyric acid*), which has a tranquilizing effect. More than 200 studies support its effectiveness in sleep disorders. Take 800 to 900 milligrams (mg) with a little food about an hour before heading to bed.

➤ **Melatonin.** Melatonin supplements can be a boon to good sleep, especially for older people. Your body makes the sleep hormone *melatonin* in the pineal gland of your brain, but production starts dropping off when you're in your twenties and continues to fall with age. Extended-release melatonin is a good product choice. Research published in the *Journal of Sleep Research* shows that it increases the restorative value of sleep. One caveat: It's important to take extended-release melatonin before your pineal gland starts up its own production for the night. If you don't, melatonin supplements may not be as effective. Take a 300-microgram (mcg) time-release product a full four hours before bedtime.

➤ **Fish oil.** To boost your serotonin, which works with melatonin to induce sleep, take two fish oil capsules daily. I recommend 1,000 to 3,000 international units (IU) of fish oil for cardiovascular protection, too, as well as for its mood-enhancing properties.

➤ **5-HTP.** The supplement *5-hydroxytryptophan* (5-HTP) transforms into serotonin in your brain and can provide genuine support for sleeping. If you're taking an SSRI antidepressant, though, skip the 5-HTP. These antidepressants themselves boost the serotonin in your brain, just like 5-HTP. Too much serotonin will keep you awake. Take 100 to 150 mg about an hour before you head to bed.

Other Helpers and Healers

➤ **Loving lavender.** Scatter a few drops of lavender oil on your pillow before bedtime. Research published in the *Journal of Alternative and Complementary Medicine* found that people with insomnia who slept in a room with lavender-scented air reported that their insomnia improved by 50%.

➤ **Nix the naps.** If an afternoon snooze makes nighttime sleep elusive, get some exercise during naptime instead. Try brisk walking, stair climbing, a light jog or whatever revs up your system.

➤ **Early to bed.** Your adrenal glands have their own sleep schedule, recovering from the day's stresses and charging up for tomorrow's challenges between 11 PM and 1 AM. If you're awake and alert, they can't recharge. Your gallbladder also releases toxins during this same time frame. If you're not sleeping, the toxins accumulate in your liver. Try to adjust your schedule to nature's light and dark schedule, with some natural variations with clock changes in winter and summer.

➤ **Switch off stress.** Fully 75% of Americans say they're stressed, with 33% admitting to extreme stress and half reporting that their stress has shot up in the past five years. Begin a stress-reducing technique such as yoga, meditation or deep breathing, and practice it every day to help minimize stressful thoughts at bedtime.

226

Sleep Cycles

Your body's internal clock knows when it's time to sleep because of the light and dark of day and night. In addition, during daylight hours when you're busy moving and using energy, the chemical *adenosine* accumulates in your brain. The more of it you have, the sleepier you'll be. When you do get to sleep, you move through four stages.

Stage 1. **Transitional sleep.** This is when you're drowsy and drifting off. The transitional period lasts five to ten minutes.

Stage 2. **Light sleep.** Your heart rate slows, eye movement stops and body temperature decreases.

Stage 3. **Deep, restful sleep.** Blood flow to your brain slows down, and your brain takes a little nap. Blood instead moves to your muscles to replenish physical energy and repair tissue. This is when your immune system does important repair work.

Stage 4. **REM (rapid eye movement) sleep.** This is when you dream, release the pressure valve on stress, process emotional information and store memories. Your first REM cycle usually occurs about 90 minutes after Stage 1, and you can have three to five REM cycles in a night's sleep. Research shows that good REM sleep bolsters daytime mood. As you work on improving your ability to sleep, let yourself sleep a bit more on the back end of your sleep cycle, which is in the morning hours for most people. REM sleep is so important that if it's interrupted one night, the body will move into extra REM the following night to catch up. Sleep patterns can change with age, meaning you might go to sleep earlier and awaken earlier. Older adults spend more time in the first two stages of sleep and less in Stages 3 and 4. As a result, their sleep may feel less restful.

➤ **Guided to sleep.** Picture a blue sky padded with fluffy clouds moving slowly across your field of vision. Imagine tall trees sheltering you as you inhale the scent of pine forest. It's very relaxing to fill your mind with calming images and thoughts. Take a guided imagery recording to bed with you and relax your way into slumber. Look for Belleruth Naparstek's "Healthful Sleep" guided imagery recording (available as CD or MP3 download) at bookstores or online (*www.healthjourneys.com*).

➤ **Kick the smokes.** Nicotine keeps you awake and alert, one of the reasons smokers find the addiction so hard to break. If you're a smoker, stop smoking a few hours before bedtime. Better yet, quit altogether.

➤ **When to work out.** Exercise energizes your body, which is just what you don't want if you're having trouble with sleep. Work out at least five hours before going to bed, and shoot for at least 30 minutes of vigorous exercise daily to help your body relax into sleep.

➤ **Hydrate early.** If nighttime bathroom visits are a problem, drink most of your water early in the day, stopping all fluids at least two hours before bedtime. ■

15

Memory Loss

It's happened to you. You've misplaced your keys, forgotten your cell phone, or found yourself absolutely unable to recall the name of a friend you bump into at the market. You may call this *synapse lapse, brain fade* or something else altogether, but the result is the same: you feel as though your brain is betraying you. Scientists call this disheartening occurrence *age-related-cognitive decline.*

We've heard for so long that it's normal to become forgetful as we age that we've come to believe it, and even expect it. Don't buy into this misconception. Many memory problems have nothing to do with age, driven instead by stress, poor nutrition or doing too much at once. While brain cells do shrink with age, scientists aren't sure this actually affects brain function. In fact, your brain continues to generate new brain

cells as you age, relying on good nutrition to function optimally.

The brain itself is composed of fats that play a major role in relaying the chemical messages between neurons or nerve cells, in your brain. These fats are extremely delicate, however, and free radicals can literally punch holes into cell membranes, causing damage that shows up in your memory function.

Memory decline can be subtle. For many of us, the first and most frightening thought is—*Could it be Alzheimer's?* But there's a big difference between occasional forgetfulness and chronic dementia such as Alzheimer's, which affects 13% of Americans 65 and over. Severe lapses in memory require a doctor's attention. For the rest of us, new studies are showing that aging brains take in more information and sift through it all to decide what should be kept, making older adults better problem solvers than younger people, but often less able to retrieve a fact, name or date. As one research professor put it, "Wisdom is what results when the mind is able to assimilate data and put it in its proper place."

SYMPTOMS

Problems with memory run the gamut from simple forgetfulness to mild cognitive impairment. Early signs of Alzheimer's, on the other hand, include sudden changes in behavior or mood without any obvious cause, such as not understanding directions for a new game, becoming lost while walking or driving in an area you've always known, having problems finding easy words in conversation, putting common objects in odd places (such as the phone in the oven) and confusing words that may be loosely related, such as car and bike.

Mental deterioration progresses steadily in Alzheimer's, leaving the sufferer unable to carry out daily tasks we usually take for granted, such as how to use the toilet or squeeze a slice of lemon or even understand what a lemon slice is. Personality changes, aggression and increased anxiety also occur in Alzheimer's and the disease progresses to banish treasured memories, including the familiar faces of dearest loved ones.

CAUSES

If you're having a memory problem, consider the constellation of factors that can cause it. Chronic medical disorders such as kidney, heart, lung and liver disease all affect mental function. Your kidneys and liver transport toxins out of your body. When they're not performing properly, these toxins can accumulate and damage your brain. Like all cells,

in order to function well, those in your brain require a free-flowing blood supply to deliver oxygen and nourishment. Lung disease and heart disease limit blood flow and thus the amount of oxygen reaching your brain, which can cause cognitive problems.

High blood pressure, diabetes and high levels of small, dense cholesterol particles all damage your arteries, which further compromise blood flow to your brain. Research on thousands of civil servants in England shows that low levels of beneficial high-density lipoprotein (HDL) cholesterol might be a risk factor for dementia, as we know it already is for stroke and heart disease. Studies have shown that people with low HDL are 53% more likely to have impaired memory than those with highest HDL levels. *Let's look at some other common causes of impaired memory…*

➤ *Hypothyroidism,* or underactive thyroid, means you're not producing enough thyroid hormones, which are essential for proper brain function. People with this disorder who take thyroid replacement hormone often report significantly improved concentration, memory and mental focus.

➤ **Stress** is another significant factor in muddied mental performance. Research shows that the stress hormone, *cortisol,* released by your adrenal gland when you're chronically stressed, actually blocks your brain's ability to think clearly and recall details.

➤ **Chronic anxiety and depression** both involve falling levels of important neurotransmitters. Your mind needs these "brain chemicals," neurotransmitters such as *dopamine, acetylcholine* and *serotonin,* for clear

229

thought and memory. That's why some Alzheimer's drugs work to increase neurotransmitter levels, just as antidepressants do.

➤ **Poor nutrition** has an enormous impact on how you think. Some studies show that consuming a lot of sugar, refined carbohydrates or excess alcohol can interfere with cognition, as does any nutritional deficiency. Without proper nourishment, your brain puts the brakes on generating new neurotransmitters that carry thoughts and memories. Dehydration and medications can also cause problems with clear thought.

➤ **How Alzheimer's changes the brain.** It's not exactly clear what causes Alzheimer's, a chronic and progressive dementia that causes personality changes, severe memory problems and, ultimately, death. Connections between brain cells are blocked by the accumulation of *beta-amyloid plaque*, a usually harmless protein. Also, many of the neurons that generate acetylcholine die off. Without the neurotransmitter, brain signals can't jump from one neuron to the next, resulting in compromised thinking and memory loss.

Brain autopsies of people with Alzheimer's also show tangled clumps of nerve fibers. Inflammation, caused by oxidative damage in the brain by cell-damaging molecules called *free radicals*, is also involved in Alzheimer's. It may even be one of the primary causes. One study found that high levels of *homocysteine*, a marker for inflammation, were linked to an increased risk for the disease.

Genetic factors are definitely involved and certain medical conditions increase your chances of developing it. For example, people with diabetes have up to a 65% higher risk

230

of developing Alzheimer's, according to research published in the *Archives of Neurology*. In fact, scientists at Northwestern University in Chicago suggest that Alzheimer's may actually be a form of diabetes occurring in the brain. For a well-functioning memory and a continuing ability to learn, your brain cells must have working insulin receptors and it's known that people with Alzheimer's have fewer of them. These researchers discovered that a toxic protein in the brains of those with Alzheimer's effectively makes neurons resistant to insulin by knocking out insulin receptors. The result is blocked memory. Scientists believe the process may be reversible and suggest that Alzheimer's patients be treated with the same diet, lifestyle changes and drugs used to treat type 2 diabetes.

TREATMENT

Research shows that a full 65% of the effects of age on our bodies, including our cognitive ability, are caused by lifestyle factors. In short, it's the day-to-day choices we make. That's good news for anyone experiencing brain fade; it means that making a few changes in daily habits can get your cognition back on track. Research demonstrates that people can boost their thinking and memory abilities with regular physical exercise, stress reduction, challenging brain exercises and a more healthful diet.

At the University of California in Los Angeles, scientists studied the effects cardiovascular exercise, stress-relief practices, brain-friendly nutrition and mental games had on brainpower and memory. After just two weeks, brain scans confirmed that the brains of participants in this program were working more efficiently.

Don't forget the role that stress plays in compromised memory function. Stress, anxiety and depression directly block the ease with which your brain tags memories for storage and retrieval, thus causing a negative impact on cognitive function. Maintaining elevated levels of the feel-good brain chemical serotonin will ensure that your brain is awash in mood-elevating neurotransmitters. Conversely, people who endure lengthy periods of untreated depression have reduced levels of serotonin, which can increase their risk of Alzheimer's.

Especially important is taking steps to limit your risk of diabetes, since having it quadruples your risk of Alzheimer's (see "Causes"). See the guidelines for preventing and controlling diabetes on pages 98–118.

People who have heart disease, especially those with elevated *homocysteine*, an important marker for inflammation, have twice the risk of Alzheimer's. While research into Alzheimer's continues, minding your heart and the risk factors that can hurt it, including type 2 diabetes and high blood pressure, can reduce your chances of contracting Alzheimer's.

For people with Alzheimer's, drugs can help slow the disease's progression, but they don't cure it. Still, there are steps you can take to distance yourself from the worst manifestations of Alzheimer's. The same recommendations for people who are having garden-variety memory problems apply to those with early Alzheimer's and those who fear it. At the top of this list is eating a Mediterr-Asian diet (see pages 19–27) rich in antioxidant foods with an emphasis on folic acid and omega-3s fish, which has been linked to the reduced risk of Alzheimer's. You'll also find more "memory foods" and recipes at the Web site, *www.myhealingkitchen.com*.

Foods That Make It Better

Overwhelming research shows that a healthy diet improves cognitive ability, including memory. Harvard researchers tracking 13,000 women for over 25 years found that those who ate the most vegetables were less susceptible to age-related memory problems. Veggies that confer the most protection are leafy greens, such as spinach, and the cruciferous veggies, such as broccoli, cabbage and kale.

Another study funded by the National Institutes of Health National Institute on Aging discovered that people whose eating habits most closely paralleled those of the Mediterranean diet, which is rich in vegetables, fish, fruits, nuts, legumes and olive oil, were 40% less likely to suffer from dementia or Alzheimer's. Participants were tested on cognitive ability throughout the four-year study, receiving neurological exams that included tests of memory, reasoning and language. While eating a Mediterranean diet has already been shown to reduce risk for heart disease, cancer and premature death, this was the first research to show that it also lowers the risk for Alzheimer's. Later studies confirm these findings. Researchers explain that the Mediterranean diet guards against narrowing of the arteries, which contributes to dementia by reducing blood flow to the brain.

They also think it helps prevent Alzheimer's by decreasing inflammation and keeping the brain well nourished with antioxidants.

Foods that are good for your brain are loaded with antioxidants and B vitamins, both of which limit inflammation and support brain cells, called *neurons*. These nerve cells help you retrieve memories, names and places. Neurons are especially vulnerable to attack by free radicals, the molecules that damage cells and their DNA. If you eat a regular diet of vegetables, fruits, fish, nuts and legumes, the antioxidants in these foods will work throughout your body to neutralize free radicals. Antioxidants also shield your neurons from free-radical damage. Talk about brain food!

Research tells us that, for the elderly especially, mental ability is tied closely to nutritional intake. Put plainly, older people who eat well are better at thinking, learning and recalling information. Nutrition and the thinking process are inextricably linked. It's been shown, for example, that older adults with dementia often are deficient in vitamin B-12 and folic acid, two vitamins that are essential for clear thought.

For years, we've known that eating a variety of rainbow-colored foods is essential for good health. These vibrant colors indicate their *phytochemical* content, many of which are antioxidants. Phytochemicals put the purple in grapes and eggplant, the green in spinach and broccoli and the red in tomato and pink grapefruit. Just one tomato can contain more than 100 of these compounds, which are highly protective of memory and thinking.

232

My recommendation for better cognition and memory at any age is to eat from the range of whole foods that make up the Mediterr-Asian Diet, including fish and extra-virgin olive oil for their brain-strengthening qualities. Here are some more brain foods that will have you thinking more clearly and remembering better.

HIKE YOUR HDL

We know that having a high level of the heart-healthy HDL cholesterol protects against heart disease and stroke. Research indicates that it can protect you against dementia too. According to research in the United Kingdom, people with lower HDL were 50% more likely to have memory problems than those with higher HDL, and the higher HDL also seemed to decrease the incidence of Alzheimer's. HDL-elevating foods include extra-virgin olive oil, instead of polyunsaturated vegetable oils. Make vegetables and fruits the largest part of your daily diet. Eat fish regularly. And enjoy snacking on nuts, particularly macadamias. In one study, eating a handful of macadamias daily boosted HDL by 8%. The goal is 50 milligrams per deciliter of blood (mg/dL) or higher for men, and a minimum of 40 mg/dL for women.

➤ **Flavonoid-rich cranberries also raise HDL,** making 100% cranberry your juice of choice. Just make sure there's no added sugar.

There are two other powerful nonfood ways to get your HDL number to shoot up: Quit cigarettes and get 30 minutes of daily exercise, such as brisk walking.

NIBBLE SOME NIACIN

Getting enough niacin, or vitamin B-3, can protect you from age-related cognitive decline and Alzheimer's, according to a study published in the *Journal of Neurology, Neurosurgery and Psychiatry*. Scientists studied niacin's effects on 4,000 people aged 65 and older. None had dementia at the start of the study. The study discovered that those with the highest intake of niacin-rich foods experienced half the rate of cognitive decline as those who got the least. Those who took in less niacin were also 80% more likely to be diagnosed with Alzheimer's than people who had the highest intake. Niacin is vital for nerve cell signaling and well-functioning DNA and is a powerful antioxidant for brain cells. Doctors sometimes prescribe it to elderly patients to prevent mental confusion, though researchers state that its role in Alzheimer's prevention hasn't been sufficiently explored. I would agree. The RDA for niacin is 14 mg for women and 16 mg for men.

Niacin is mostly found in meat and fish, which is why I don't recommend strict vegetarianism. If you sometimes skip eating meat, you can see from the list here how easy it can be not to reach your optimum level of niacin. I urge you to take a B-complex 100 supplement daily to cover your niacin requirements, and to continue to get as much as possible from your diet.

FOLATE AND OTHER BOUNTIFUL Bs

You'll triple your risk of dementia if you don't get enough folate from your diet. Also called *folic acid* when it's in supplemental form, folate is found in leafy green vegetables, such as turnip greens and spinach. It also occurs naturally in legumes like kidney beans and chickpeas. Scientists aren't exactly sure why folic acid is essential for good memory, but they think it may affect neurotransmitters, which carry messages from one brain cell to the next. Research published in the *Lancet* found that taking 800 micrograms (mcg) of folic acid daily, which is twice the recommended amount, boosted the mental abilities, including short-term memory, of participants in the study, all of whom were over 50.

Folic acid is just one of eight B vitamins that, along with B-12, B-6 and B-3 (also known as niacin), are essential for proper cognitive function. Folic acid helps control homocysteine, a marker of inflammation and itself a known risk factor for Alzheimer's. This important B vitamin is linked to clear thinking, and there's a wealth of research on the effects of folic acid and homocysteine on memory.

10 Top Niacin-Rich Foods

1. Yellowfin tuna, 4 ounces baked — 14 mg
2. Chicken breast, 4 ounces baked — 14 mg
3. Salmon, chinook, 4 ounces baked — 11 mg
4. Calf's liver, 4 ounces braised — 10 mg
5. Halibut, 4 ounces baked — 8 mg
6. Lamb, 4 ounces baked — 8 mg
7. Cremini mushrooms, 5 ounces raw — 5 mg
8. Peanuts, ¼ cup raw — 4 mg
9. Shrimp, 4 ounces boiled — 3 mg
10. Green peas, 1 cup boiled — 3 mg

233

10 Top Folate-Rich Foods

A slew of studies show that folate acts to protect memory. Daily recommended intake is 400 mcg. Folate is so important to brainpower that you should also take it in supplement form, preferably from a daily B-complex 100 tablet.

1.	Calf's liver, 4 ounces cooked	861 mcg
2.	Lentils, 1 cup cooked	358 mcg
3.	Pinto beans, 1 cup cooked	294 mcg
4.	Garbanzo beans, 1 cup cooked	282 mcg
5.	Asparagus, 1 cup cooked	263 mcg
6.	Spinach, 1 cup cooked	262 mcg
7.	Kidney beans, 1 cup cooked	229 mcg
8.	Turnip greens, 1 cup cooked	171 mcg
9.	Lima beans, 1 cup cooked	156 mcg
10.	Romaine lettuce, 2 cups fresh	152 mcg

Tufts University scientists tracked more than 300 men for three years and discovered that those who ate folate-rich foods had better memories, while those with high homocysteine levels had more problems with recall.

Low levels of B-12 and B-6 were also linked to poor memory in this same group. In addition, British researchers discovered that lower levels of B-12 in older adults may actually shrink the brain. Their study measured brain volume using brain scans and blood tests to gauge levels of B-12. After five years, people in the study who had the least amount of B-12 in their blood had twice the loss in brain size as those with the highest amounts.

Finally, a study published in the *Archives of Neurology* tracked 1,000 people over six years and found that those who took in the most folate experienced a significant reduction in Alzheimer's risk. It didn't matter if they got their folate from food or supplements—I recommend you get it from both. Take a B-complex 100 supplement daily and check the box to the left for a list of folate-rich foods.

BE FRUITFUL

Flavonoid-rich foods deliver massive amounts of antioxidants that neutralize free radicals and drive down inflammation. This healing power in these fruits and vegetables develops as protective agents for the plants themselves as they mature, shielding them from ultraviolet radiation and warding off predators and diseases. Flavonoids live up to their reputation as healing compounds, with solid evidence that you can lower your risk of dementia with every bite of flavonoid-rich foods you take. Scientists have identified more than 4,000 flavonoids to date and there are countless more to be discovered, which is why I recommend that you eat widely from nature's fruit basket. Apples and berries are richly endowed with antioxidants, specifically *quercetin* and *anthocyanins*. Each helps reduce memory loss by boosting the flow of blood to your brain.

➤ **Apple a day.** With the second highest antioxidant activity level of all fruits, apples offer a diverse array of healing components, including the flavonoid quercetin, which pops up repeatedly in studies as vital to cognitive health. One trial showed that this flavonoid was a more powerful protector of oxidative damage to delicate brain cells than vitamin C. Quercetin is found in apple skin, so eat the peel along with your daily apple, as long as it has been organically grown.

➤ **Brain berries.** The blueberry is packed with more antioxidants than just about any other food known, and studies show that the little berry can actually change the way your brain works by improving memory and learning capacity. Rich in anthocyanins, which are responsible for the blueberry's color, these healing antioxidants are able to cross the blood-brain barrier, your body's mechanism for keeping toxins out of your gray matter. Once in your brain, the blueberry strengthens brain cell connections and enhances your brain cells' ability to communicate with each other. Two British research teams added blueberries to the normal diets of volunteers over a three-month period and discovered that memory improved within several weeks. Lead researcher Dr. Jeremy Spencer was quoted as saying "This study not only adds science to the claim that eating blueberries is good for you, it also provides support to a diet-based approach that could potentially be used to increase memory capacity and performance in the future."

SIP SOME WINE

Don't drink alcohol excessively if you want to preserve your brain cells, because studies show it can cause premature aging of your gray matter. However, consuming small amounts, such as five ounces of wine with meals, seems to deliver a brain benefit. Scientists at the University of Bari in Italy tracked a group of people ages 65 to 84 who had mild cognitive impairment. After three and half years, they found that Alzheimer's developed at an 85% slower rate in those who enjoyed a drink a day, usually wine, compared with those who didn't drink. (Drinking more didn't confer added protection, in case you're wondering.) One glass, five or six times a week, seems to improve the health of the brain's blood vessels, and red wine is recommended.

Researchers at Litwin-Zucker Research Center for the Study of Alzheimer's Disease and Memory Disorders in New York found that *resveratrol*, the antioxidant in red grapes and red wine, neutralizes the *amyloid-beta* protein that destroy the brains of those who have Alzheimer's. Separate research suggests that people who have a daily drink also reduce their risk for memory problems. This may occur because alcohol stops blood from clotting, which impairs oxygen from reaching your brain.

SPINACH IS BRAIN FOOD

We know that our brain cells are especially vulnerable to free radicals, those rogue oxygen molecules produced as a part of eating and breathing. We also know that antioxidant-rich vegetables can protect delicate brain cells from the oxidative damage free radicals cause. With most scientists agreeing that oxidative damage plays a central role in age-related disorders, including declining memory, researchers publishing in the *Journal of Neuroscience* propose that eating vegetables frequently can help prevent the mental decline brought on by oxidization-damaged brain cells. Their research shows that eating vegetables, especially spinach, can help protect against age-related problems of the central nervous system and brain.

Green leafy vegetables, again particularly spinach, also came out on top for preventing mental decline, according to the Chicago Health and Aging Project (CHAP) at Rush University Medical Center. Researchers there found that those who ate about three servings of vegetables a day, compared with people who ate just one daily serving, decreased cognitive decline by 40%. Leafy green vegetables provided the greatest protective effect, though cruciferous and yellow vegetables were significant too.

➤ **It's in the bag.** Prewashed baby spinach is one of my favorite fast foods for its ease of preparation and extraordinary nutrient profile. Pile raw baby leaves into your salad and on sandwiches. Or shake the contents of the entire bag into a pot and steam for a minute or two. Don't overcook it; spinach is best when it is slightly wilted and bright green. Top with a capful of extra-virgin olive oil for a brain-booster extraordinaire.

➤ **Egg it on.** Many of spinach's beneficial nutrients need a little fat to be fully absorbed by your body, and a hard-boiled egg gives your brain a double memory-boosting hit. Egg yolks are rich in B-12, which reduces inflammatory, memory-compromising homocysteine levels. Plus, eggs contain choline, another supporter of brain health and memory. Translation: A spinach omelet is a great brain-boosting meal!

➤ **Choose organic.** Spinach is one of those super-healing foods that should always be purchased in the organic form. Conventionally grown spinach is among the foods containing the highest levels of pesticides.

236

NOSH ON NUTS AND SEEDS

You won't find a better brain snack than nuts and seeds. Each nut variety has particular value, but they're all rich sources of vitamin E. One trial showed a 32% reduction in cognitive decline in people who got the most E from their diets, compared with people who got the least. Enjoy a variety of nuts every day. A small handful is sufficient.

Sunflower seeds, sesame seeds, pumpkin seeds and flaxseeds contain healthful polyunsaturated fats along with vitamins, protein and minerals such as magnesium, which are vital for healthy brain function. Walnuts contain vitamins B-6 and E, an all-around treasure trove for a healthy nervous system, clear memory and focused thinking. Almonds are a great source of riboflavin and *phenylalanine*, which perk up your brain and your attitude. Pecans and peanuts contain *choline*, a must nutrient for a good memory. Cashews are rich in compounds that dilate blood vessels so that oxygen-rich blood can flow to the brain, where it's needed for optimum performance.

OPT FOR OMEGA-3s

Omega-3 fatty acids are surely nature's best brain food. Found in cold-water fish such as sardines and wild-caught salmon, they're a rich source of *docosahexaenoic acid* (DHA), which is necessary for strong and healthy outer membranes of nerve cells in the brain. Research shows that omega-3s improve memory, concentration and mood. Eating omega 3–rich foods also maintains high levels of the feel-good neurotransmitter serotonin. Making fish a regular part of your diet can reduce your chances of dementia, according to scientists at Rush-Presbyterian St. Luke's Medical Center in Chicago. Their research showed that Alzheimer's risk was lowered by 60% in people who ate fish once per week.

Omega-3s are so important to overall health that I recommend you put fish on the table several times a week and also take a fish oil supplement. Evidence shows that not getting enough omega-3s, especially DHA, increases the risk for developing Alzheimer's. This protective effect likely occurs because omega-3 fats reduce brain inflammation. Our brains are, after all, composed of about 60% fat, much of it DHA. Another study showed that people who ate small servings of fish every day did better on verbal, visual, attention and memory tests.

For people who don't enjoy fish that much, fish oil capsules can be invaluable. All omega-3s are active against inflammation in your brain. Eating fish and taking fish oil, however, aren't your only alternative. *Here are some other options…*

➤ **Take some tyrosine.** In addition to omega-3s, fish contains *tyrosine*, an amino acid that feeds the chemical messengers dopamine and *norepinephrine* in your brain, perking up alertness and giving your brain more energy. You need only about three to four ounces of fish to get this mental lift, so open a can of tuna, top it with a little extra-virgin olive oil and chopped olives.

➤ **Pick omega-3 fortified eggs.** These have been laid by hens whose feed is enriched with omega-3 feed, or who are allowed to range free to do their own foraging.

➤ **Use olive oil.** Stay away from salad dressings made with polyunsaturated vegetable oils such as corn, soybean or canola. These so-called healthful oils contain more than 50% omega-6s and can upset your ratio of omega-3s to 6s. Use extra-virgin olive oil as the base for homemade dressings by adding lemon juice, herbs and balsamic vinegar. Drizzle steamed veggies with extra-virgin olive oil and add a few capers.

➤ **Go nuts.** A quarter cup of walnuts provides about the same amount of omega-3s as a three-ounce piece of salmon.

➤ **Take flaxseed or walnut oil.** One teaspoonful of either daily keeps your omega-3 levels high. Store it in the fridge because it's highly perishable. Or sprinkle ground flaxseed onto your oatmeal and salads for a fiber-rich omega-3 blast.

➤ **Choose grass-fed animals or wild game.** An Iowa State University study showed that the omega-3 content of these animals is higher than that of fish. Meats from conventionally raised animals have low amounts of omega-3s and are loaded with inflammatory omega-6s.

"I LOVE JAVA, I LOVE TEA"

Caffeinated coffee boosts memory and actually increases the activity in your brain, according to researchers from the University of Innsbruck, who studied people before and after drinking two cups of java. The scientists used brain imaging to monitor the neuron activity of volunteers while they were involved in memory tests. The noncaffeinated group revealed no boost in brain activity, but the caffeinated volunteers had better memory and more activity in brain areas involved with concentration and memory. Scientists in France found that caffeine appears to reduce cognitive decline in women. They spent four years tracking the mental sharpness and coffee intake in 4,000 women. Those who consumed caffeine equal to about three or more cups of coffee daily were 30% less likely to show a decline in memory. Plus, women 80 and older getting their daily dose of caffeine were 70% less likely to have memory problems.

Tea drinkers get a cognitive boost too. Researchers tracked the habits of more than 2,500 Chinese adults. After just two years later, 35% of those who didn't drink tea showed a decline in cognition, but a whopping two-thirds of those who drank tea maintained their recall ability. Researchers believe that one of the compounds in tea, *catechins*, helps hold on to the brain's mental abilities by protecting them from destructive protein accumulation. Black tea and green tea have different antioxidants than fruits and vegetables but they both slow the action of the enzyme *acetylcholinesterase*, which is linked to Alzheimer's, according to researchers at Newcastle University. This effect in tea actually mimics the one in Alzheimer's pharmaceutical drugs Aricept and Exelon.

Green tea was the subject of a 2005 study that discovered that one of its antioxidants, *epigallocatechin-3-gallate* (EGCG), reduced the body's production of the protein beta-amyloid, which forms tangled plaques in the brains of people with Alzheimer's. A separate study found that drinking just two cups of green tea daily reduced the risk of cognitive dysfunction.

Ginkgo tea is also protective because it increases oxygen-rich blood flow to the brain. Its active ingredient, *ginkgolide*, also limits production of the substance that triggers blood clots. With these twin effects, ginkgo reduces the chance of clots in both your heart and brain.

BRAIN-BOOSTING HERBS AND SPICES

The fragrance and healing properties of certain herbs and spices can enhance your brainpower and liven up your meals.

➤ **Cinnamon** is a potent antioxidant with anti-inflammatory effects. It also can help keep your brain young and active. In one study, participants chewing cinnamon gum did better on a variety of mental tasks compared with those who chewed a different flavor or chewed no gum at all. Cinnamon is a versatile spice that also slows the rate at which sugars are absorbed into your bloodstream, helping to keep blood sugar stable and your brain well nourished. So sprinkle cinnamon on oatmeal and fruit, and into stews and smoothies.

➤ **Bright yellow turmeric,** one of the spices in curry, contains an antioxidant substance called *curcumin*. In one study, it appeared to trigger the destruction of beta-amyloid protein plaques that clog the memory circuits in the brains of Alzheimer's patients. In some regions of the world, including India, where turmeric is consumed regularly, the rates of Alzheimer's disease are lower than in Western cultures. Look for turmeric on the spice shelf and start using it daily, sprinkling it into tomato juice and scrambled eggs and onto fish or chicken. One-tenth of a teaspoon daily is all you need to boost your HDL by an incredible 29%, too.

➤ **Rosemary** is a memory herb with a rich history, and studies are finding that its magical scent can improve alertness and recall. Sprinkle rosemary on chicken or place a fresh branch of the herb in the cavity of your bird before roasting.

➤ **Garlic** has a distinctive scent and equally unusual antioxidant powers. Its sulfur components are responsible for reducing the inflammation that can lead to cognitive problems. While you're enjoying its unique flavor, you'll also be calming your blood pressure and lowering your cholesterol too. Chop a couple of garlic cloves and add to soups and stews, salads and meat dishes every day. Let them rest for a few minutes after chopping to maximize their healing power.

Foods That Make It Worse

If you're experiencing memory problems, or have mental illness in your family, it's wise to avoid certain foods that are proven to make things worse. Eating the Mediterr-Asian way limits two important factors that contribute to problems with mental function and dementia: insulin resistance and inflammatory fats.

SUGAR AND FOODS THAT MIMIC IT

One of the common symptoms of insulin resistance is brain fog. You may know the feeling: lack of concentration, inability to focus and a craving for carbohydrates. Foods containing either a lot of sugar or a lot of refined carbohydrates act the same way in your body. Blood sugar elevates rapidly, but then it quickly plummets as glucose is

To Prevent Dementia, Whittle Your Waistline

Carrying extra weight around your midsection is risky business, raising your chances for heart disease, diabetes, stroke and dementia. We already knew that simply being obese ups your risk for dementia, but a recent study finds it's a greater risk in people in their forties who have abdominal fat, even if they aren't obese.

Researchers tracked 6,500 people for an average of 36 years each, comparing those with normal weight and modest waistlines to people with normal weight and large waistlines. People with large midsections were 89% more likely to develop dementia, and that risk spiked even higher in people who had big waistlines and were overweight or obese. Research published in the journal *Neurology* suggests that abdominal fat produces substances that harm the brain.

Inflammation is likely to be the critical link between belly fat and dementia. Fat in the midsection seems to work with immune cells to depress the immune system itself and, in the process, creates substances that can set off inflammation. Nearly half of all adults in the United States have central obesity.

rushed out of the bloodstream, which leaves you hungry again and disoriented. Refined carbohydrate foods increase the amount of insulin in your bloodstream, speed up the rate at which your blood vessels and organs age, trigger inflammation, and encourage diabetes, which dramatically increases the risk of Alzheimer's and other forms of dementia.

Take an inventory of all the refined carbohydrates in your pantry, from white bread to white pasta, rice and flour and then consider getting rid of them. You should also limit your consumption of sugar and sugar-rich foods, including soft drinks, refined breakfast cereals and commercial snacks. Eating them not only increases the amount of fat stored in your body, but also leads to a poor insulin response, which a long-term study identifies as a factor in the development of Alzheimer's. Scientists tracked data from more than 2,000 men who were given a glucose tolerance test at the start of the study and then again during a follow-up. A low insulin response in the first test was linked to a 30% increased risk of Alzheimer's. Those with impaired secretion of insulin, glucose intolerance and a high fasting blood level of insulin were at higher risk for cognitive problems and dementia.

Just like type 2 diabetes, insulin resistance leads to brain-cell death when cells can't get the fuel they need to function effectively. Problems with insulin may also clog the communicative areas of the brain. The simple solution is to cut back or eliminate your consumption of soft drinks, sugar and most fruit juices and emphasize the brain-healing foods in the Mediterr-Asian Diet (see page 19). They'll keep your blood sugar stable and your brain clear of fog.

AVOID INFLAMMATORY FATS

I encourage daily consumption of extra-virgin olive oil, omega-3 fatty fish, nuts and avocados. The good fats in these foods bolster mental performance and protect against Alzheimer's. Inflammatory fats, on the other hand, are the "antibrain" fats. Avoid polyunsaturated veg-

etable oils such as canola, corn, soybean and safflower, because they are high in proinflammatory omega-6s. Having too high a proportion of omega-6s cancels out the beneficial effects of omega-3s. You should definitely eliminate foods that contain vegetable shortening and those made with hydrogenated oils, also called trans fats. Stay away from all fried foods in restaurants, especially fast-food restaurants. Eating these fats, along with a lot of corn-fed beef, increases inflammation, which has been shown to block the blood flow that your brain relies on for optimal performance.

Scientists studying cognitive problems at Chicago's Rush-Presbyterian-St. Luke's Medical Center found that diets high in trans fats increased the risk of dementia. Good thinking and memory skills will become a distant memory if your diet is heavy in polyunsaturated oils and trans fats from chips, baked goods and doughnuts, fried chicken and French fries. To improve your memory, follow the Mediterr-Asian Diet, which features moderate amounts of grass-fed beef and other healthful protein sources. Remember, you don't have to give up every food containing saturated fat, just the low-quality types, such as cheap burgers, cold cuts and processed meals.

Supplemental Help

Nutritional supplements can change the way your medications work and the way your body functions. If you're taking any drugs, ask your doctor for an okay to rule out potential interactions with medications. Pregnant women and those who are breastfeeding

240

should also check with their physicians. That said, these top brain-boosting supplements have solid research behind them.

➤ **High-potency multiple vitamin.** Ask your doctor if you need one with iron, especially if you are a woman who is still menstruating. Memory problems often occur with iron-deficiency anemia, since red blood cells need iron to move oxygen to your brain. Take one daily.

➤ **B-complex 100.** A 10-year study of more than 1,600 men and women 65 and over, published in the *American Journal of Clinical Nutrition*, found that cognitive function could drop with too little B-12. In fact, scientists suggested that by doubling the amount of B-12 taken in supplement form, the decline could be slowed by a third. Older adults can have trouble absorbing B-12 from eggs, milk, meat and fish, so look for dissolvable sublingual supplements, which you place under your tongue. Liquid forms work well too.

Two other studies attest to the importance of B vitamins. Dutch researchers discovered that older adults had the memories of people five years younger after taking 800 mcg of folic acid for three years. You'll get 400 to 800 mcg in a typical B-complex 100 tablet. All of the B vitamins are water soluble, with any extra leaving your body in urine, so don't worry about getting too much.

➤ **Acetyl-L-carnitine (ALC).** This amazing substance occurs naturally in your body. In supplement form, it's one of the few that can cross the blood-brain barrier and help regenerate neurons damaged by free radicals. Once in your brain, ALC boosts the production of acetylcholine, which is vital for short-term memory and learning capacity. It also works directly on the nerve cells in your brain to increase energy production. People with Alzheimer's are deficient in acetylcholine and ALC has been found effective in slowing the rate of decline in those with Alzheimer's, especially younger patients. For better memory, take 250 to 500 mg daily. Alzheimer's patients should take at least 1 to 2 grams (g) daily.

➤ **Alpha-lipoic acid.** This helps protect against free radicals in your body, before they can even reach your brain. Take 50 to 150 mg daily.

➤ **Ashwagandha.** The root of this shrub prevents breakdown of acetylcholine, increases the body's resistance to stress and balances a variety of your body's important functions. It may also reduce your level of stress hormones, which can impede memory. Take 100 mg daily.

➤ **Coenzyme Q-10.** CoQ10, for short, works on the energy-producing mitochondria in your brain cells and throughout the body. It's extremely important for energizing the brain. Take 50 to 300 mg once daily.

➤ **Ginkgo.** Ginkgo biloba provides antioxidant support, plus boosts and maintains blood circulation to the brain, a major factor in preserving brain function and increasing memory. Take 120 mg daily. Do not take it if you're on aspirin or Coumadin, as excessive blood thinning may occur.

➤ **Huperzine A.** Derived from a Chinese herb, huperzine boosts brain levels of acetylcholine, which is essential for learning and short-term memory. It's also an antioxidant that keeps brain cells healthy. Take 50 mcg per day, increasing to twice per day if you choose. Check with your doctor before taking this supplement, since it can lower your heart rate.

➤ **Vinpocetine.** Used by European doctors for many years, it supports brain circulation and cognitive function and is helpful for mild memory problems associated with aging. Take 5 to 10 mg twice daily.

➤ **Fish oil or krill oil.** These supplements provide the higher levels of omega-3 fatty acids that your brain needs to manufacture the feel-good brain neurotransmitter serotonin, which supports mental function and mood. Take two capsules daily.

➤ **Galantamine.** FDA-approved for Alzheimer's, *galantamine* is derived from daffodil bulbs and is sold over the counter as GalantaMind and as the prescription drug Razadyne. Finnish researchers discovered that people who had Alzheimer's or a type of dementia called *vascular dementia* scored higher on both behavioral and cognitive tests after taking galantamine for six months. The study was published in the medical journal *The Lancet*. Start with 8 mg per day, increasing to 24 mg if needed. GalantaMind can cause upset stomach in some people, so it's wise to start slowly.

➤ **Dimethylaminoethanol (DMAE).** Sold as Deanol in Europe, DMAE has been shown to increase levels of acetylcholine. It may also reinforce the delicate membranes that encase brain cells. DMAE is especially helpful because it's able to cross the barrier between circulating blood and cerebrospinal fluid, and it is quickly utilized to improve

concentration, memory and focus. Take 150 mg on an empty stomach twice daily.

➤ **Phosphatidylserine (PS).** Popular in Europe, PS keeps brain cell membranes fluid, flexible and ready for nutrient absorption. It acts on acetylcholine, which is required for memory and focus, and also helps with the conduction of nerve impulses, keeping memory-related pathways healthy and intact. Take 200 to 400 mg daily, but check with your doctor if you're taking a blood-thinner, since PS thins the blood.

➤ **Vitamins E and C.** A study of more than 4,700 older adults in Utah found that vitamins E and C offered significant protection against Alzheimer's and other dementia when they were taken together, possibly because the water-soluble C may help break down fat-soluble E for better use by the body. Researchers cautioned that while supplements were linked to a 72% lower risk for these dementias, people could reduce their risk by eating a Mediterranean-style diet along with exercise, plus moderate alcohol consumption. Take 500 mg of vitamin C and 200 to 400 international units (IU) of vitamin E (mixed tocopherols) daily.

➤ **Vitamin D.** Researchers in Ireland discovered that vitamin D-3 works on aging brains as an anti-inflammatory agent, preventing and possibly even ameliorating age-related memory problems. Our bodies make vitamin D when skin is exposed to sun. We get small amounts from fortified foods, but the sunshine vitamin is showing great promise for a range of healing. I recommend you take a minimum of 1,000 IU daily.

➤ **Sage.** Used for hundreds of years to increase memory, sage protects acetylcholine, which people with Alzheimer's often lack. Research on sage continues, but evidence shows that it can boost cognitive function in people with Alzheimer's, possibly by also decreasing inflammation. Iranian researchers discovered that sage extract worked better for this group than a placebo. You can perform your own at-home trial by sipping sage tea, made by steeping a couple teaspoons of dried sage in hot water for a few minutes. Or take 300 to 600 mg of dried sage supplement daily.

Other Helpers and Healers

➤ **Start the day with brain food.** Eat breakfast every day to power up your brain. Without food, your brain lacks the nutrition it needs to get a quick start and operate effectively throughout the day. Research repeatedly shows that schoolchildren who eat breakfast learn better and remember more. If you starve your brain, there's little wonder that your mind doesn't work well. If you're pressed for time in the mornings, check page 290 for 10 in-a-hurry breakfasts that provide top nutrition.

➤ **Check your meds.** Prescription drugs for anxiety, depression, allergies, high blood pressure and pain can cause muddled thinking. Make a list of every drug you're using and take it to your physician. Ask if you can cut back or quit using any of them that might be causing brain fuzz.

➤ **Silence stress.** Chronic stress is like a tourniquet wrapped around your brain.

Result? You can't think straight, much less remember important things. Scientists at the University of California in San Diego found that the higher the stress level, the worse memory was in people they studied, who were an average age of 79. You don't have to be close to that age to understand how chronic stress boggles your mind. Being chronically stressed for just a week exposes your brain to the stress hormone *cortisol*, which damages thinking, memory and other cognitive functions. On-and-off spurts of stress are no better. Best solution? Learn and practice a stress-relief technique such as yoga or meditation daily. Research studies support the health benefits of meditation and relaxation exercises. Participants who meditated in a training course over a two-month period had elevated activity in the areas of their brains that control positive emotions. Their bodies also produced more antibodies to a flu vaccine, revealing the powerful impact of stress relief on your immune system.

➤ **Get moving.** Regular physical activity moves oxygen to your brain via better blood flow, and that's one of the best things you can do for your memory. Exercise also plays a role in triggering your body's production of nerve growth factors and hormones responsible for *neurogenesis*, the creation of new brain cells.

In fact, research shows that regular exercise cuts your chances of Alzheimer's and other dementia by half. Scientists at the University of Washington spent six years studying 1,700 people 65 and older, none of whom had any serious memory problems. All were asked how frequently they exercised. At the end of the six years, dementia had developed in 158 people and Alzheimer's in 107. What's significant is that those who exercised for at least 15 minutes three or more times weekly were 38% less likely to have dementia. Merely walking 10 minutes a few times per week drove down the risk of Alzheimer's by 32%.

Exercise also helps offset type 2 diabetes, which dramatically increases your risk of dementia. Just 30 minutes a day will boost your brainpower and protect your precious brain cells from disease and decline.

➤ **Alzheimer's and exercise.** Moving your body is so important that even people who already have Alzheimer's can benefit. Researchers in France studied Alzheimer's patients living in nursing homes over the course of a year, putting them through a twice-weekly exercise program for an hour each session. The exercisers showed a slower decline in their ability to dress, bathe, use the toilet and eat. Most researchers believe the improvement occurs because exercise increases the flow of oxygen-carrying blood to the brain. It also offsets stress and jump-starts the release of brain-cell strengthening compounds.

➤ **Choose your routine.** There's evidence that breaking out of your normal routine helps create new brain connections. Easy ways to accomplish this is to use your non-dominant hand to eat oatmeal, brush your teeth or operate a computer mouse. It's like a jungle gym for your neurotransmitters.

➤ **Get organized.** If you're a person who's often confused and misses appointments due to an overstressed life, get a calendar and log in all birthdays, social activities and appointments. Note important dates and

244

anniversaries for the next 30 days in one spot, and organize yourself at the start of the month by purchasing gifts and cards for everyone in a single outing. Keep your keys in a bowl near the door and find a spot for anything else you misplace frequently. Update your to-do list every day, crossing off and adding to it. I have patients in their thirties who are rigorous list makers. Most people can't remember very well without them.

➤ **Clear the smoke.** Smoking limits the flow of blood to your brain and can seriously impede memory. Search for a smoke-cessation group to provide support as you quit. Many hospitals sponsor them.

GIVE YOURSELF MORE BRAIN CELLS

For years, scientists thought that once brain cells died they couldn't be replaced. We now know that everyone, regardless of age, is able to generate new brain cells, a process called neurogenesis—literally, the "birth of neurons." Researchers haven't yet determined whether older adults who are mentally sharp have kept their smarts *because* of certain behaviors or whether those behaviors have caused them to retain their mental acuity. "It's probably a two-way street," according to Bruce S. McEwen, chief of the neuroendocrinology lab at Rockefeller University in New York. Whichever way it works, the list of ways to trigger neurogenesis is more than enough to get you started. In studies, older people with sharp minds generally do the following.

➤ **Stay connected socially.** Maintaining friendships and having strong social ties with community and relatives is linked to healthy brains. Staying socially connected may involve regular bridge games, performing volunteer activities or frequent lunch dates. If television is filling your time at the expense of interaction with other people, find the off switch. Scientists at the University of Washington discovered that young children develop memory and thinking problems years after TV exposure. Television does the opposite of connecting you to other people. Limit your viewing to a couple hours daily.

➤ **Stay physically active.** Your brain functions better with physical activity. Even older adults who haven't exercised much can benefit tremendously. Scientists at the University of Illinois organized a study with adults ages 60 to 75 who had been sedentary. They assigned half of the participants to meet three times weekly for nonaerobic exercise, such as stretching. The others met with the same frequency to walk together. After six months, the cognitive improvement in the walkers was stunning. According to Arthur F. Kramer, professor of psychology at the University of Illinois, "Six months of exercise will buy you a 15% to 20% improvement in memory, decision-making ability and attention span... plus increases in the volume of various brain regions in the prefrontal and temporal cortex and more efficient neuro networks that support the kind of cognition we examined."

➤ **Engage intellectually.** Researchers have discovered that giving your brain an intellectual workout is the best way to generate new brain cells, which become part of the very structure that keeps memories and thought clear. Older adults with sharp minds tend to be involved in activities that stimulate brain activity, such as volunteering, traveling, continuing education and playing music. Also helpful is engaging in mind-challenging games, such as crossword puzzles, Scrabble or chess. The old adage "use it or lose it" applies to the brain as well as your muscles. Here are some suggestions for keeping your brain fit: Memorize a poem. Use your hands to build, sculpt, paint or otherwise create. Learn a new computer program.

➤ **Manage stress effectively.** Chronic stress can reduce brain function to devastating levels. It also can cause your brain to deteriorate in areas that are responsible for memory, emotion and decision making. Nonstop stress also resets your brain's recall ability, so that your gray matter is less capable of storing information and more prone to depression, anxiety and a less flexible approach to decision making.

➤ **Adapt to change readily.** Older adults who are open to change and who stay flexible in their approach to life are well served, according to gerontologist and psychologist K. Warner Schaie, PhD. He began following the psychological profiles of a group of people in 1956 with the Seattle Longitudinal Study. In a nutshell, here's what he learned: "You have to expect things will shift over time and won't be the same as when you were young. Those who manage to roll with the punches and enjoy change rather than fighting it tend to do well." ■

16

Menopause

Menopause, often referred to as *the change of life,* is the biological shift that marks the end of a woman's menstrual periods. About 1.5 million women hit menopause every year, and 42 million more American baby boomers are moving in that direction. More a transition than a single event, the process includes *perimenopause,* the time leading up to menopause (beginning around age 45) when a woman's periods become increasingly irregular and hormone levels shift. Technically, a woman doesn't reach menopause until a year after her final period, about age 50 for American and other Western women, though it can occur as early as 40, or as late as the mid-fifties.

SYMPTOMS

The symptoms and signs of menopause are apparent to most women long before their final period. Usually, sometime in one's forties, the nature of periods change, becoming more or less frequent, plus lighter or heavier and lasting longer or shorter than normal. As menopause approaches, about 85% of women begin showing some symptoms, including hot flashes, persistent fatigue, vaginal dryness leading to painful intercourse, mood changes, memory problems, disturbed sleep, low libido, depression and increased belly fat. Most women have only some of these symptoms and to varying degrees.

The classic symptom of menopause is the *hot flash,* which occurs when a decrease in estrogen levels causes blood vessels to rapidly expand, triggering an intense burst of heat in the face, neck or chest. This can be a brief flash or an agonizing, embarrassing event several minutes long. Just as women's symptoms differ in menopause, their outlook toward it varies as well. Some are elated by the imminent end of troublesome periods and PMS, while others view menopause as a loss of what makes them womanly. Two serious health conditions that pose increased risks for women around menopause include weaker bones and an elevated risk for heart disease.

CAUSES

It's important to remember that menopause is not a disease or disorder, although the pharmaceutical industry has portrayed it as such as a marketing ploy by which to sell hormone replacement drugs. Menopause is a natural biological process that starts when the ovaries gradually curtail their production of estrogen and progesterone, the hormones that control menstruation. A woman still has periods during perimenopause, but hormone production can be erratic. However, she may still be fertile and become pregnant. About one year after her final period, a woman's ovaries produce very little estrogen and no progesterone at all. As a result, eggs are no longer released. At the same time, the pituitary gland boosts its production of other hormones. In both perimenopause and menopause, fluctuating hormone levels are responsible for uncomfortable symptoms.

Certain medical conditions and procedures can trigger immediate menopause, such as having a total hysterectomy, in which the ovaries and uterus are removed. Some cancer treatments that include radiation or chemotherapy can also interrupt hormone production. A minority of women have a condition called *premature ovarian failure*, in which the ovaries stop functioning before

age 40 due to autoimmune disease, inherited genetic factors or other causes.

TREATMENT

Hormone replacement therapy (HRT) was once the primary treatment for menopausal women who were experiencing uncomfortable symptoms such as hot flashes, vaginal dryness, mood changes and insomnia. Doctors at one time believed that HRT offered increased protection from heart disease. It also had the added bonus of boosting bone density. Then, in 2002, the Women's Health Initiative (WHI), the largest study ever to examine the effects of HRT, was halted early when it was discovered that HRT (in the form of equine estrogen plus progestin, a synthetic progesterone), actually *increased* the risks of certain cancers and other serious medical conditions, while offering no protection against heart disease. Data from the study showed that women using HRT were 29% more likely to experience a heart attack, 26% more likely to develop breast cancer and 41% more likely suffer a stroke. In addition, scientists found that the elevated risk for both lung and breast cancers endured for two years after women stopped taking HRT.

The conclusion derived from this large study was that women with disabling menopause symptoms should weigh the risks of short-term HRT against its benefits. As a result, many women went off HRT altogether. It should be noted that many women make an easy transition into menopause without much problem at all, especially those who eat properly and exercise regularly.

If you are experiencing specific symptoms, you'll find nondrug solutions in this chapter. There's a wide range of choices for treating menopausal symptoms and it's generally best to start with the most natural methods, since these support your body's innate capacity to heal and regulate itself. Feel free to experiment until you find the natural remedies that work for you. In all cases, proper nutrition and regular physical activity are essential cornerstones of a healthy menopause.

Foods That Make It Better

Hormones are perhaps the most powerful substances in the human body, controlling practically every function. So, it should come as no surprise that a woman's body experiences dramatic changes in the years leading up to and after menopause, just as it did during the years of puberty. Most women gain weight during the process and the distribution of those pounds shifts from hips and thighs to abdomen, a location that increases risk for heart disease. Women's arteries tend to thicken during this time, also increasing risk for cardiovascular disease. Optimal nutrition, along with regular exercise, is critical at this time, not just for weight control, but also to minimize inflammation and other risk factors for heart attack and stroke.

If you've been busy taking care of everyone else for most of your life, now is the time to shift your attention to your own health and well-being by eating more vegetables, fruits, fish, legumes and whole grains. Coax your partner and family in this direction, too; it's

the healing foundation for optimal health throughout all stages of life.

➤ **Eat estrogenic.** In Mediterranean and Asian countries, where a plant-based diet takes center stage, women display dramatically lower rates of menopause-related ills and discomforts compared with women in the United States. When they do have hot flashes or vaginal dryness, it tends to be less severe. Mediterranean and Asian women also have lower rates of breast and other cancers, as well as osteoporosis.

What exactly is it about the diets of these two regions that seem to ease women's transition into menopause? Researchers credit the *phytoestrogens* (literally, "plant-based estrogens") in the foods they eat. These chemical compounds in certain plants possess estrogenlike qualities, and the compounds replace some of the estrogen lost at menopause. Studies show that a phytoestrogen-rich diet can significantly reduce hot flashes and other symptoms while protecting the bones and heart.

It's a win-win proposition with some cautions: If you're being treated for an estrogen-sensitive breast cancer, talk to your doctor before loading up on soy-rich foods. Also, don't take soy supplements, which can interfere with the antitumor action of drugs like tamoxifen. In fact, the jury's still out on the safety of soy supplements in general, so stick with foods that have mild estrogenic effects: alfalfa sprouts, nuts, whole grains and ground flaxseed. Some of the best-known estrogenic foods follow.

➤ **Cool off with soy.** About 80% of American women experiencing menopause will have a hot flash at some point in their lives, compared with 16% of women in Asian countries, where soy is eaten nearly every day. Tofu, tempeh, soy nuts, miso soup and soy milk all contain *isoflavones*, a type of phytoestrogen. Soy has many different isoflavones but the two we know most about, *daidzein* and *genistein*, produce powerful beneficial effects. They match the shape of estrogen receptors in your body's cell membranes, making it possible for the isoflavones to lock in to those receptor sites and produce safe, mild estrogenlike effects.

Women who eat soy regularly are getting a gentle form of estrogen replacement. At Harvard, scientists asked 250 menopausal women to take either a daidzein-rich soy extract or a placebo. Over three months, the soy group experienced a 52% reduction in hot flashes.

Overall, when scientists analyzed the results of 19 clinical studies, they found that approximately 33% of menopausal women who ate soy foods had a significant reduction in hot flashes, with the benefits most pronounced in women who had eight or more hot flashes daily. If you're in this group, eating soy could cut your hot flashes by nearly 40%. That's cool news you can use.

Soy has other health benefits, too. Isoflavones enhance the ability of your blood vessels to flex and contract, helping to control blood pressure and improving circulation once you start moving into menopause, when a woman's risk of heart disease rises sharply. Other studies show that soy protein also can lower low-density lipoprotein (LDL) cholesterol by up to 5%. Soy is also a good source of heart-healthy polyunsaturated fats, which can reduce arterial inflammation, the underlying cause of atherosclerosis, blood clots and heart attacks.

To get maximum soy-related benefits, shoot for at least 50 milligrams (mg) of isoflavones daily from foods. Three ounces of tofu provides about 20 mg. You'll get 30 mg from a cup of soy milk, but be sure to choose a type with no added sugar. Tempeh, a fermented form of soy with a smoky flavor, is loaded with protein. A three-ounce serving has nearly 37 grams (g) of protein and 37 mg of isoflavones. One ounce of roasted soy nuts has about the same amount.

➤ **Try tofu.** To increase your calcium and get a protein blast too, eat more tofu. A half cup has about the same amount of protein as tempeh, along with 258 mg of calcium and 13 mg of iron. If you've never tried tofu, start at an Asian restaurant by ordering a noodle or rice dish with tofu instead of meat or fish. If you like it, you can purchase tofu at your grocery store and start adding it to stir-fry meals, green salads and bean salads. The firm style is best for cooking.

➤ **Make some miso.** Miso soup is made by dissolving miso paste, a type of fermented soy, in hot (not boiling) water. For a delicious broth, add a little *kombu* seaweed, sliced spring onion or scallion greens and cubed tofu. The soup will contain varying amounts of isoflavones, depending on how much miso paste is used.

➤ **Protein power from soy powder.** Add powdered soy protein to your morning smoothie for an isoflavone punch. You can also sprinkle it on soups and morning breakfast cereals.

➤ **Say yes to yams.** Like the sweet potato, yet in a class of its own, the humble yam contains a chemical compound called *diosgenin*, which has estrogenic properties. Studies suggest that yams help relieve menopausal discomfort. They are also rich in vitamin B-6, which is thought to modulate the effects of estrogen in the body.

➤ **Sprouts and more.** Alfalfa seeds and sprouts are a great source of phytoestrogens and have powerful antioxidant effects, important for protecting your heart and arteries against menopausal changes. Purchase alfalfa sprouts regularly or start a grow-your-own sprout farm in a jar on your kitchen counter.

➤ **Pump up the produce.** Research shows that fresh organic vegetables and fruits are a woman's best pals in life, especially during menopause. Studies at the University of Helsinki tested eight berries for their phytoestrogen levels and found blackberries highest, followed by strawberries.

The mineral *boron* occurs in most produce. Derived from the soil, it seems to increase the female body's ability to retain and use the estrogen that remains after menopause. That's good news, because more estrogen means fewer hot flashes and other uncomfortable symptoms. Boron also boosts bone strength by limiting the amount of calcium lost at this stage of life.

My prescription for a comfortable, problem-free menopause is to eat richly every day from the healing vegetables and fruits featured in this book, especially boron-rich selections,

which also contain phytoestrogens: cabbage, broccoli stems, beets, bell peppers, asparagus, cauliflower, carrots, cucumbers, onion, lettuce, sweet potatoes, soybeans, turnips, dates, raisins, nuts, oranges, grapes, grapefruit, red raspberries, blackberries, prunes and plums, strawberries, apples, bananas, tomatoes and pears.

➤ **Get a daily dose of grains.** Current medical thinking has it that many menopause symptoms are caused not only by declining estrogen, but also by a buildup of hormonal *metabolites*, produced when hormones break down. These metabolites are largely made up of fat-based molecules.

An overlooked approach to menopause is to eat more whole grains, which absorb these metabolites so they don't cause symptoms. Some of the best whole grains for menopause relief include brown rice and cereals such as oatmeal. However, just about every whole grain contains large amounts of insoluble fiber, often described as *lipophilic*, because this fiber is attracted to fats, including those in hormonal metabolites that are present in your intestines waiting to cause trouble. (The same is true of excess cholesterol and other fats.) The insoluble fiber in grains binds to them and whooshes them away via stools. Presto—fewer menopause symptoms!

Studies show that women who eat high-fiber diets have lower levels of these hormonal waste products in their blood. Three to five daily servings of whole grains will protect you, as long as you're also eating other high-fiber foods including fruits, vegetables and beans. Aim for 40 g of fiber daily to gain maximum menopause symptom control.

I strongly urge you to learn more about whole grains. Visit the organic dry bins at your local health food store or food co-op. Try each of several grains you've never tasted before. One such grain is *groats*, buckwheat grains whose inedible hulls have been removed, but which retain their highly nutritious bran, germ and endosperm.

These grains take a little longer to cook, so when you do prepare them, make a big batch and freeze individual portions. Familiarize yourself with grain terminology, so that you will know that pearled barley, for example, means that the grain has had much of its highly nutritious germ and bran polished away. Start using brown rice instead of white. It has a rich, nutty flavor and protects your health by increasing your fiber consumption. You'll never miss the white, denatured variety. Buy some wheat berries and cook them with raisins for breakfast or to serve with fish for dinner. You won't believe how much more energy you'll have when you eat whole grains instead of white rice, white bread and white potatoes, all of which are rapidly transformed to blood sugar and blood fats (triglycerides.)

➤ **Nibble on nuts.** Research confirms that women who snack on nuts every day are likely to have fewer hot flashes, one of the first signs of menopause. A Mayo Clinic study found that women who received extra vitamin E had a decrease in hot flashes, and nuts are one of the few whole food sources of the mighty E. All nuts contain some vitamin E, but walnuts and almonds are especially rich in it. A third of a cup of either provides about 40% of your daily E needs. Many nuts,

like walnuts, are also high in monounsaturated fat and omega-3 fatty acids, so they're good for your heart and arteries too.

➤ **Go fishing.** The seafood-rich dishes of Asia and the Mediterranean can dramatically lower your risk of heart disease. Although the myth persists that heart disease is somehow a man's disease, statistics prove that's not true. More women die from cardiovascular disease than men. They get it later in life and menopause is the reason. Estrogen helps protect a woman from heart disease in her younger years, but when menopause brings reduced estrogen levels, this protection melts away.

Eating fish helps compensate for this loss. Studies show that women who eat fish at least twice a week, especially omega 3–rich cold-water fatty fish like mackerel, sardines or wild-caught salmon, have a significant drop in triglycerides and welcome improvements in LDL and high-density lipoprotein (HDL) cholesterols. The protection is cumulative the more fish is eaten. One study found that people who ate fish every day might have a 23% drop in triglycerides in just 12 weeks. It would be great if we all could eat a little high-quality fish every day, but that's not realistic for most of us. Try for twice a week and take a daily fish-oil supplement.

➤ **Crank up the calcium.** Another serious downside of menopause is the rapid loss of bone density that leads to *osteoporosis*. Women begin to lose some bone mass in their mid-to-late thirties, but the rate accelerates steeply when estrogen levels go into decline around menopause. Estrogen is vital for helping bones absorb and retain calcium, which is why I emphasize phytoestrogen foods in this section. Osteoporosis, which means "porous bones," can be a life-threatening condition. For a large percentage of older women, a broken bone is a direct path to nursing-home care or death. Health declines rapidly with the loss of mobility.

Once a woman reaches menopause, she needs 1,500 mg of calcium daily. You can protect the bone mass you have by eating more calcium-rich foods. One study found that women who got as little as 1,000 mg of calcium a day, about the amount in two cups of plain low-fat yogurt, reduced their total bone loss by nearly 50%. Since a cup of skim milk has about 300 mg, you can cook your morning oatmeal with milk instead of water and pour on a little more when you eat it. Don't forget leafy greens, including collards and turnip greens, each with about 200 mg of calcium per cup. Tofu delivers calcium as well as phytoestrogens, which help block bone loss. Consider buttermilk, too, which contains just about 2 g of fat per cup and delivers 285 mg of calcium. Use it to make salad dressings and sauces. If you can't reliably eat your 1,500 mg daily, take a calcium supplement.

➤ **Add some D.** The so-called sunshine vitamin is just as important as calcium for strong bones because it escorts calcium into your bones. I recommend that you get between 1,000 and 2,000 International Units (IU) of vitamin D-3 daily; double this dose if your skin is darker or if you are over age 65. Your body will naturally produce vitamin D when you spend time in the sun with your skin exposed, but virtually all women need to supplement.

➤ **Count on K-2.** This recently discovered subtype of vitamin K is a boon to strong bones. Here's how it works: Your body uses a protein called *osteocalcin* to carry calcium from the blood into bones, but osteocalcin can't work efficiently without vitamin K-2. Even if you have a lot of calcium in your blood, it will remain locked out of your bones without sufficient levels of K-2. That's bad news for bones. (Arteries, too, since excess blood calcium tends to end up in artery walls.) You can kick up your K-2 intake by eating nonprocessed cheese and *natto*, a fermented soy food that contains more K-2 than any other food source. In one study, Japanese researchers compared 1,000 menopausal women from Tokyo and Hiroshima to their counterparts in Britain. The Japanese women consumed a lot of natto, while the women in Britain ate none. The more natto they ate, the stronger their bones were.

➤ **Lube your arteries with olive oil.** Increased risk for heart disease as a result of menopause is something that deserves your keenest attention. One delicious way to reduce this risk is extra-virgin olive oil. It is high in heart-healing antioxidants, drives down inflammation and helps thin the blood. Olive oil can actually reduce the ability of cholesterol to cling to the inner walls of your arteries, while boosting beneficial HDL. As little as two tablespoons daily is enough to provide significant cardiovascular protection. Switching to extra-virgin olive oil can also calm hot flashes, due to its high vitamin E content. Use it to dress your vegetables and salads and as a substitute for butter and polyunsaturated vegetable oils.

➤ **Flax to the max.** I advise women of all ages to eat a couple tablespoons of ground flaxseed daily. Flaxseed is high in omega-3 fatty acids, which protect the heart. It's also an important source of phytoestrogenic *lignans*, containing from 75 to 800 times more of these compounds than any other plant source. Lignans are powerful hot-flash reducers that quell other menopausal symptoms, too. In one study, a group of menopausal women ate about four tablespoons of ground flaxseed daily, blending it into yogurt, sprinkling it on fruit or mixing it into their cereal in two doses. Within six weeks, the intensity of their hot flashes was reduced by 57% and the frequency was cut by 50%. Women in the study also reported improvement in mood and in the muscle and joint pain that afflicts some women in menopause. Ground flaxseed is highly perishable, so purchase whole seeds and grind them in your coffee grinder as needed. You can also buy ground seeds in resealable bags. Either way, store flax tightly covered in your freezer to maintain its extraordinary healing benefits. Don't try to eat the whole, unground seeds. Your GI tract can't break them down.

➤ **Go for good carbs.** Food really does influence your mood, and for the mood swings that often accompany menopause, complex carbohydrates are the best comfort foods to eat. Choose fruits, vegetables and whole grains. These are the good carbs that your body requires to support *tryptophan*, an amino acid that boosts brain levels of *serotonin*, the same brain chemical that's

---

How to Host a Bone-Building Party

➤ **Serve bone-building snacks.** Make smoothies with calcium-rich yogurt and powdered soy protein, plus blueberries for brain health.

➤ **Dance together.** Ask each woman to bring her favorite music and throw a dance party. Dancing, like all weight-bearing physical activity, builds bone mass.

➤ **Take the party outside.** Exposing your skin to the sun builds vitamin D. Organize a brisk walk around the block in the sun.

➤ **Learn a routine.** Follow an aerobics DVD or class with friends. Or find a local *tai chi* instructor, then make time for regular group practice.

➤ **Ease off.** Chip in to hire a massage therapist who will make a house call for an hour or two so that everyone gets a massage.

➤ **Put your feet up and watch a movie.** Laugh, share stories, have a glass of wine and some soy nuts (they're good for your bones).

---

increased by some antidepressant drugs. Eating good carbs throughout the day can help your brain maintain levels of feel-good serotonin to keep your mood sunny. The fiber in complex carbohydrates is what makes them beneficial. Their fiber slows the rate at which these foods enter your bloodstream, supporting a steady supply of tryptophan and more stable levels of serotonin.

Depression is a serious condition, yet many people aren't aware that it's tied to heart disease. Data from the Women's Health Initiative, which studied more than 93,000 postmenopausal women, found that those who were even mildly depressed were 50% more likely to die of heart disease than those without depression. Eating a diet rich in complex carbs can protect you in both areas. Simple carbohydrates, such as those found in white bread and most processed foods, don't produce the same effects; in fact, they make both conditions worse.

➤ **B better, feel better.** What if I told you that foods rich in B vitamins could help reverse menopause-related mood swings and depression? It's true. Of all the nutrients in our diets, the B vitamins seem to be most closely linked to mood. People deficient in any of the Bs, even if just borderline, are far more likely to suffer from depression than those who get adequate amounts. I'm so keen on the Bs that I recommend women take a daily B-complex 100 supplement. These vitamins are water soluble, meaning any excess leaves your body via urine (and brightly colored at that, if you're taking a supplement) so you can never OD on Bs.

The Mediterr-Asian Diet provides the range of the Bs found in a B complex tablet, including folate, which boosts serotonin and possibly also *melatonin*, a hormone that helps regulate your energy. Be sure to get at least 400 micrograms (mcg) of folate daily from leafy greens and sunflower seeds, among other sources. Research also shows that the majority of people with depression are low in vitamin B-6. If you're living on take-out and processed foods, you likely aren't getting enough. Leafy greens are loaded with B-6, as

are legumes, fish and chicken. Bananas and whole grains are good sources, too.

Getting enough vitamin B-12 can also be challenging for many menopausal women, because your body's ability to absorb it declines with age. Even borderline deficiency can cause depression, not to mention fatigue and memory problems. The good news is that B-12 is easily found in lean meats, low-fat yogurt and other dairy products. The recommended daily amount is 6 mcg. This doesn't sound like a lot, but it can take some work to get that amount from food alone—just another reason to take a B-complex 100 daily.

➤ **Bank on beans.** Don't overlook the humble bean, which is too often relegated to occasional use in chili or burritos. Beans are a superhealer hiding in an unassuming little package.

First, beans contain phytoestrogens—and by now you are familiar with the beneficial effects of these compounds on the symptoms of menopause. Beans also are a weight-loss dream food because they slow the rate at which glucose is absorbed into your bloodstream, quieting appetite for hours and driving down your risk for diabetes. Beans have a truckload of minerals and vitamins, including calcium, B-6 and folate.

Beans also surpass nearly every other plant food on earth in antioxidant power. Kidney, pinto and black beans all have more disease-fighting antioxidants than any other food, and science is still discovering others as I write this. Start sprinkling them on everything from eggs to salads and soups every day.

➤ **Mussel up on iron.** Many women going through menopause are astonished at the frequency and irregularity of their periods. You can lose impressive amounts of blood during this time, which can lead to iron-deficiency anemia and fatigue.

You can replace the iron you're losing with foods like mussels, oysters and clams. These are exceptional choices because they're extremely high in iron, while being much lower in calories than other iron-rich foods, such as liver and red meat. While you're putting iron in the bank, load up on fruits and veggies for their exceptional vitamin C content, which helps your body absorb iron more efficiently. Foods rich in vitamin C also strengthen capillaries to help shore up your blood loss. Aim for 1,000 mg of vitamin C daily. Supplement if you're not yet getting ten servings per day of nature's best vitamin C fruits and veggies.

➤ **Stop the sweats with sage.** Here's an easy experiment to try if hot flashes and night sweats are driving you a little crazy. Sage is an herbal remedy traditionally used to help the body to produce less perspiration. Add half a teaspoon of dried sage to a cup of boiling water, let it steep for about 10 minutes and sip the brew once or twice daily. Many menopausal women swear by it.

Foods That Make It Worse

Every calorie counts and that's especially true during menopause. Ever hear the term *nutrient dense*? It means that every bite of food you eat should be loaded with maximum health-giving nutrients. Since many women tend to gain weight where it's most risky—around the middle—you'll want to choose your calories carefully, minimizing sources of poor fats and bad carbs. If you focus on accentuating the positive, eliminating the negative is an easier task. Place your emphasis on foods that are health giving. *Meanwhile, cut way back on or eliminate these menopause-menacing foods…*

➤ **Go easier on meat products.** You don't need to follow a vegetarian diet to get relief from menopausal symptoms, but I do recommend that you consume red meat moderately. Putting vegetables at the center of your diet is one of the easiest ways to control your weight and to prevent diabetes. It also can reduce your risk for stroke by as much as 54%. Studies show that women who get the majority of their calories from plant foods have much higher levels of phytoestrogens and the natural menopause relief those estrogenlike foods deliver.

It's not that red meat is bad. Far from it. If it is pasture-raised and organically fed, red meat is a healthful food, providing valuable nutrients, such as iron and vitamin B-12. However, Americans tend to eat it in excess, and much of that red meat is poor quality. It also contains estrogenic growth hormones, antibiotics, pesticide residues and other contaminants. The ideal serving is about the size of a deck of cards, eaten perhaps once a week. Avoid all processed meats such as cold cuts, bacon and sausage, pepperoni and canned meat products. When buying poultry, choose only free-range and organic birds. These items may cost a bit more, but if you're eating less meat, the savings will balance out.

➤ **Back off sugar and refined carbs.** Sugar is the quintessential empty calorie. In other words, there's no nutrition there. That goes for any food that's been highly processed, such as white bread, cake, cookies, crackers and chips, too. They all dump a load of glucose into your blood, fast. This sugar rush is inevitably followed by a sugar crash, lower energy and renewed cravings for more bad carbs. The main source of sugar and calories in the United States diet is soft drinks, which account for an astonishing 21%. There are other culprits, including sweetened yogurt (choose plain, low fat instead) and most sweetened breakfast cereals. Read nutrition labels and walk away from anything with added sugar or high-fructose corn syrup.

Another downside of sugar: Women who eat a lot of it typically experience more mood swings and depression, in part because these foods trigger alternating spikes and dips in serotonin.

Low blood sugar means that cells throughout your body, including your brain, aren't getting the fuel that they need to function at their best. Studies show that the majority of people with low blood sugar, or *hypoglycemia*, usually suffer from depression, too. It's not worth it. An occasional sweet isn't the issue. It's okay to have a little and enjoy it every now and then, ideally after you've eaten a healthful meal to minimize the possibility of excess blood sugar. However, don't make a habit of it, particularly if you're filling up on so many snacks that you don't have the appetite to eat real food. If you

stick to the foods that will keep your blood and brain chemistry in balance, you'll enjoy better, more balanced moods!

➤ **Reduce your caffeine load.** Susan Lark, MD, author of *The Menopause Self-Help Book* and one of the country's leading experts in women's health, has noted that many women who drink coffee or other caffeinated beverages tend to have more hot flashes than those who consume less. If hot flashes are a problem for you, experiment with cutting back on the caffeine. If hot flashes don't seem to be causing you trouble, consume caffeine in moderation to ensure you're getting enough B vitamins. Too much caffeine depletes the body's stores of some Bs, which can lead to mood swings and depression.

➤ **Curb the cocktails.** If you're dealing with hot flashes, mood swings or other menopausal symptoms, try giving up alcohol for a week or two to see if it makes a difference. Then, if you feel like it, have a drink. If your symptoms reappear, they might be linked to alcohol. Some women report that their hot flashes worsen when they drink. Alcohol has its good and bad sides. People who drink some alcohol tend to have lower blood pressure, healthier hearts, better cholesterol readings and may be less likely to form clots in the arteries. However, even one alcoholic drink per day, the upper limit recommended for women, can sap some of the body's reserves of B vitamins and precious magnesium and calcium, thus increasing the risk for osteoporosis.

➤ **Don't overdo the oils.** With the exception of extra-virgin olive oil, most cooking oils, especially corn, safflower, sunflower and canola, are high in omega-6 fatty acids. Taking in too many omega-6s can reduce the enormous health benefits you get from the omega-3s in fish and flaxseed. One study reported that women who consumed a relatively large amount of omega-6s and not enough omega-3s had greater amounts of bone loss than those whose ratio of omega-3s to omega 6s was higher. Another reason that these polyunsaturated vegetable oils should be avoided is that they oxidize easily in the body, leading to heart disease and cancer.

Supplemental Help

Most of the herbs and supplements used for menopause either have estrogenic properties or stimulate hormones that help restore the body's natural balance. Read on, then experiment to see what feels right for your symptoms.

➤ **Consider black cohosh.** According to the American College of Obstetricians and Gynecologists, this is the one herb that's a proven alternative to hormone replacement therapy. Taken as a supplement, black cohosh helps reduce the severity of hot flashes. It's also used to ease depression, sharpen memory, improve sleep and increase the elasticity of vaginal tissues. Researchers believe it works by boosting the efficiency of the low levels of estrogen that remain during menopause, though new studies suggest that black cohosh attaches to opiate receptors involved in temperature regulation. Whatever the explanation, I recommend it and favor the product that's been successfully tested in

more than 90 different studies: Remifemin, available from Enzymatic Therapy.

➤ **St. John's for better mood.** If you've been feeling a little sadness, anxiety or depression, I'm happy to tell you that the herb St. John's wort is as effective for treating mild depression as some prescription antidepressant drugs. It increases brain levels of serotonin, important for improving outlook and stabilizing mood swings. You can take 300 mg, three times daily, or in combination with black cohosh in Remifemin. Researchers at the University of Illinois examined studies that tested a variety of herbs for menopausal mood problems and found this combo to be most effective. A word of caution: St. John's wort interacts with some prescription anti-anxiety medications, so consult with your physician first.

➤ **Get hip to hops.** Most of us hear hops and think beer, but you don't have to sip the suds to cool your hot flashes. Scientists in Belgium divided a group of post-menopausal women into two groups, one receiving a placebo and the other a hops extract supplement with high amounts of *8-prenylnaringenin*, a plant compound similar to estrogen. Twelve weeks later, those in the hops group displayed a significant reduction in hot flashes and other symptoms. Look for hops extract in supplement form.

➤ **Opt for omegas in fish oil.** Taking fish oil can help focus your mind and boost your moods, too. Falling levels of estrogen during menopause are tied to lower levels of serotonin, which, when in ample supply, helps brighten mood and keep the mind

257

sharp. Take two to three 1,000-mg fish oil capsules daily.

➤ **Pick Pycnogenol.** Pycnogenol, an antioxidant-rich extract from pine bark, may deliver real relief from menopause-related night sweats, hot flashes, sleep disturbances, poor memory and concentration, as well as problems with mood. Researchers in Germany and Taiwan studied more than 150 women in perimenopause, half of whom took Pycnogenol extract and half a placebo. Those taking the extract experienced real improvement. Women in the study took 200 mg daily.

Other Helpers and Healers

For all women, menopause is a perfect time to take your physical and emotional pulse. *If you aren't feeling as vibrant as you'd like, here are a few more suggestions for being better than ever during the second half of your life…*

➤ **Kick the habit.** If you're still smoking, this is a great time to stop. The menopause-induced reduction in heart-protective estrogen means that you've lost much of the cardio protection you had up until now. Ask your doctor for help and look for a stop-smoking group, so you will have support in the process.

➤ **Silence stress.** Getting rid of stress may be even more difficult if you're coping with symptoms of menopause. You're busy juggling a job, money, aging parents, children, grandchildren, a partner or lack thereof or a combo of all the above. That's a lot to deal with. It usually isn't the stress that's harmful, but how you deal with it. I

encourage you to start a stress-relieving program and practice it every day. Managing stress isn't a luxury—it's a necessity. Select something that appeals to you: yoga, *tai chi,* deep breathing, guided imagery, prayer or a hot bath. If you don't take care of yourself, who will?

➤ **Walk it off.** For brighter moods, weight control, stress relief and hot-flash reduction, walking really works. Get out most days and walk briskly for half an hour. Study after study shows that it helps relieve menopause-related symptoms, builds strong bones, improves circulation, gets your heart and circulation pumping and actually improves the way your body uses nutrients and oxygen.

➤ **Tighten up with kegels.** Urinary incontinence isn't a symptom of menopause per se, but plenty of women lose tone in the bladder and urethra with age. One in six women between the ages of 40 and 65 experience stress incontinence, that embarrassing scenario in which laughing, lifting or sneezing can cause you to leak some urine. Kegel exercises build up strength in your *pubococcygeus* (PC) muscle, the one you use to tighten to stop urinating. Australian scientists reviewed more than 20 studies and found that doing kegels regularly cured 73% of women of their stress incontinence.

Find your PC muscle by starting and stopping the flow of urine next time you're in the bathroom. Then, a few times daily, squeeze and hold for three beats. Don't tighten your abdomen by mistake. If you're doing them correctly, you'll feel a little pull in your rectum and lift in your vagina. The best part? Nobody knows you're doing

---

10 Ways to Manage Menopause

1. **Move your body every day.** Walk, dance, do an aerobic workout, lift weights or join a gym. These are all bone builders because they bear your full weight.
2. **Sleep for eight hours.** This will repair and restore your memory, mood, energy and your spirit.
3. **Stay connected to other women.** You need a reliable support network in both good times and bad.
4. **Have fun.** However that translates for you. Take long bike rides, travel, create a blog.
5. **Eat well.** Rely on the Mediterr-Asian Diet to support optimum nutrition and emphasize estrogenic foods. Visit *www.myhealingkitchen.com* for more foods and herbs that relieve menopausal discomfort.
6. **Learn to say no.** Don't be afraid to place yourself at the top of your to-do list if you're the kind of woman who places everyone's priorities ahead of your own.
7. **Keep your spirit nourished.** Good ways include prayer, meditation, arts or crafts, volunteering or walking in nature.
8. **Get some fresh air and sun.** Your mother was right. The vitamin D in sunshine is extremely good for you.
9. **Join a group.** Meet to talk about what you're interested in—smoking cessation, weight loss, grief support, divorce, great books.
10. **Treat yourself well.** To support happiness and relaxation, have a massage, buy a new book or CD, or take a class in something you've always wanted to learn.

---

them, so you can practice anywhere, anytime. Build up to 15 squeezes and do the set three times daily, perhaps while you're in the car, watching television or sitting on the porch. Incontinence improvement usually occurs quickly.

➤ **Stash the salt.** Even if salt didn't budge your blood pressure readings in the past, it might as you get older. About half of Americans with high blood pressure are sensitive to salt, and the hormonal changes of menopause can increase salt sensitivity, even in women who previously had normal blood pressure and weren't affected by salt. Check nutrition labels on canned foods such as beans, chopped tomatoes and tuna. Choose those labeled "low sodium." The upper limit for sodium intake is 1,500 mg daily, the amount in a half teaspoon of table salt. ∎

CHAPTER

17

Migraines

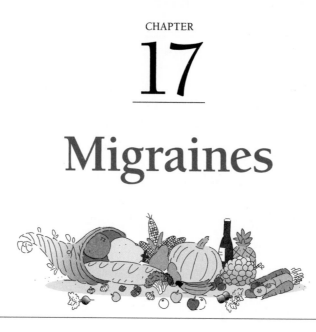

igraines aren't just very painful headaches. Yes, they can be excruciating, but pain is just a part of the larger migraine syndrome that can include dizziness, nausea and vomiting, and sensitivity to noise, light and sensory changes (known collectively as *migraine aura*). Migraines can last as little as four hours, but may persist for days. For many people they are recurring, causing long-term disability and depression. Studies reveal that people who suffer frequent migraines are four times more likely to suffer from major depression than those who have them only occasionally.

It's estimated that up to 17% of American women and 6% of men have migraines, yet fewer than half receive an accurate diagnosis. This is a real problem because treatments that work for other headaches (such as tension, cluster or sinus headaches) don't usually make a dent in a migraine. Doctors are working to sharpen their diagnoses to help differentiate migraines from other headaches.

If you're wondering whether your attacks are genuine migraines, ask yourself these questions: Has a headache limited your activities for one or more days over the past three months? Do you become nauseated during the headaches? Are you unusually sensitive to light during attacks? Researchers asked 400 patients these questions and found that more than 90% of those answering "yes" to two out of three had migraines. It's not a perfect quiz, but it can help you decide quickly if you need to see your doctor to discuss medications. It can also signal whether making changes in your diet, a cornerstone of migraine prevention and treatment, is likely to help.

SYMPTOMS

Migraine pain tends to be severe, with most people reporting a throbbing, pulsing pain on one or both sides of the head. Pain can appear suddenly, or may be preceded by an aura for 15 to 30 minutes. In this case, it's called a *classic migraine*. Auras are usually characterized by bright or flashing spots, zigzagging lines in the field of vision and tingling or numbness, usually in one arm or leg. Less often, you might have difficulty speaking or feel unusually weak during an aura. Even if you don't experience a classic migraine aura, you might have a vague premonition that a migraine is approaching. This premonition, called a *prodrome*, can occur hours or even a day or two before pain begins. Some people experiencing a migraine prodrome can feel highly energetic, while others may feel unusually fatigued or irritated. Some people crave sugar or have intense thirst before a migraine begins.

CAUSES

It's not entirely clear how migraines get started. Newer research leads scientists to believe that a nervous system disorder may be involved, with pain being relayed via the brain's *trigeminal nerve network* to a spot in the brain stem called the *trigeminal nucleus*. Pain signals might travel from there to the brain's sensory cortex, which plays a role in pain awareness. Still under investigation is what triggers the trigeminal nerves in the first place. It could be a wave of brain chemicals, called *neurotransmitters*, that stimulates the trigeminal nerves, or it could be a trigger in the brain stem that controls your light perception, smell and noise sensitivity, alertness and sensitivity to pain—all migraine-related factors. Another theory holds that some people have disturbances in the pain pathways of the brain or imbalances of the neurotransmitter *serotonin* and other brain chemicals that trigger the release of *neuropeptides*, inflammatory substances that cause blood vessels in your brain to dilate.

Neuroscientists also suspect that there's an area in the brain called a *migraine generator* that's activated during times of stress. It's possible that a single stressful event might be enough to trigger the release of chemicals that irritate nerves, dilate blood vessels and transmit pain signals. It's more likely, however, that the migraine generator becomes stimulated when you cross a certain stress threshold due to a combination of triggers, such as poor sleep, low blood sugar, eating certain foods and high stress. In other words, even though there are individual migraine triggers, they may not actually cause a migraine unless you're already close to the threshold and your level of stressors reaches critical mass.

Because women are about three times more likely than men to have migraines, fluctuations in estrogen related to the menstrual cycle are probably also a factor. Many women have migraines in the days preceding their periods, when estrogen levels are low. Menstrual-related migraines sometimes stop during the major hormonal shifts of pregnancy and after menopause.

TREATMENT

If you suffer from occasional migraines, you may be able to treat the pain yourself with a nonsteroidal anti-inflammatory drug (NSAID), such as ibuprofen or aspirin. However, there's a curious risk involved with this approach, apart from the potential stomach upset or gastrointestinal bleeding that frequent NSAID use can cause. Aspirin and ibuprofen can actually trigger *more* migraines. People who take them more than twice a week, or take them in large quantities, can develop rebound headaches, generating yet more headaches in the process of trying to stop a migraine.

Prescription drugs that treat migraines are divided into two groups: those that stop a migraine in progress and those taken regularly for prevention. A class of drugs called *triptans*, including *sumatriptan* (Imitrex) and *rizatriptan* (Maxalt), usually work very quickly to interrupt a migraine in progress, especially if they are taken at the first sign of symptoms. To prevent migraines, doctors often prescribe beta-blockers or calcium-channel blockers. Commonly used to treat hypertension and other cardiovascular diseases, these drugs are very effective. A class of antidepressants called *tricyclic antidepressants* also works well, but these have more side effects than SSRI antidepressants, such as Prozac. Many people can't tolerate the dizziness, blurred vision and persistent fatigue the tricyclics can cause.

For most people, keeping migraines at bay takes more than drugs. Other important prevention steps include eating well and regularly, avoiding trigger foods, limiting stress, exercising and taking nutritional supplements.

262

Foods That Make It Better

What and how you eat is a critical part of migraine management. About half of sufferers tend to have migraines when they've gone without eating for too long and their blood sugar is low. About 40% of patients have one or more food triggers. In addition to avoiding trigger foods, there are a number of antimigraine foods that can reduce both the frequency and severity of attacks. Don't expect instant results, however. It can take up to two months before dietary changes start to make a difference. Some of the best choices follow.

➤ **Fishing for migraine relief.** In the 1960s, scientists noticed that Greenland's population had surprisingly low rates of heart disease and migraines and wondered if their fish-based diet was a factor. Subsequent research showed that the omega-3 fatty acids in cold-water fish suppress the body's production of inflammatory chemicals, including *prostaglandins*, *leukotrienes* and *thromboxane*. People with elevated levels of these chemicals can experience abnormal vascular constriction, which restricts blood flow, elevates blood pressure and stimulates nerves, all of which may be involved in migraine attacks.

In one study, migraine patients were given either fish oil supplements or a placebo for six weeks. In the fish oil group, 60% reported significantly fewer migraines. Even when they had a migraine, they reported that their pain was 40% to 50% less severe.

You'll get the most omega-3s from cold-water fish, such as wild-caught salmon, trout, herring, sardines and mackerel. For migraine relief, eat about 16 ounces of fish per week, which will provide roughly the same amount of omega-3s as the supplements used in this and other studies. For extra protection, supplement a fresh-fish diet with 1 to 3 grams (g) of fish oil daily.

➤ **Up your magnesium.** Researchers have found that magnesium levels affect several brain chemicals thought to play key roles in migraines, and that people who have migraines tend to have lower than normal amounts of magnesium in their brain. Your best approach is to increase the amount and frequency of magnesium-rich foods you eat, including whole grains, such as brown rice, wheat berries, and oatmeal; kidney beans and other legumes, including chickpeas, lentils and split peas; pumpkin seeds and other seeds. At the same time, keep your plate green with magnesium-rich Swiss chard, spinach, broccoli and mustard greens. Try for a minimum of 400 milligrams (mg) daily.

Clinical studies confirm the power of magnesium to help reduce the frequency of migraine attacks. In one, a group of migraine sufferers took magnesium supplements for 12 weeks and experienced a 41% reduction in migraines compared with 15% for those taking a placebo. These are excellent results. If you have had kidney stones or currently have kidney disease, please talk to your doctor before taking magnesium or calcium.

➤ **Trust complex carbohydrates.** You can boost your brain's level of serotonin by eating complex carbohydrates, including whole unrefined foods such as beans, nuts, seeds, fruits, vegetables and unrefined grains like oatmeal and brown rice. These foods elevate brain levels of the amino acid *tryptophan*, which your body converts to serotonin.

In a study at Loma Linda University, migraine sufferers were given a diet high in complex carbohydrates and low in fat. Participants started out with an average of nine headaches per month. By the end of the study, the frequency had dropped to about two per month, an improvement of nearly 71%. The intensity of the headaches decreased by about 66% and duration and the need for painkillers also decreased.

➤ **Rev up with riboflavin.** Migraine sufferers appear to have impaired energy production in some of their brain cells. Riboflavin, or vitamin B-2, seems to help these cells generate more energy, which can reduce the number of migraines. If you're taking a B-complex supplement daily, you'll be getting 10 mg of riboflavin, which is a good start. However, some studies show that doses of 40 mg can cut the number of migraines. B-2 is a water-soluble vitamin, so overdose is not a concern. Any unneeded B-2 leaves your body in bright yellow urine.

Your best bet is to supplement your supplement with riboflavin-rich foods like calf's liver (a four-ounce serving provides 2.2 mg), cremini mushrooms (0.69 mg in five ounces) and spinach (0.42 mg per cup). Other good sources are romaine lettuce, chicken eggs, yogurt and broccoli.

➤ **Sip ginger tea.** Ginger is used in many parts of Asia to help prevent migraine, and some research suggests it might work nearly as well as prescription drugs. Ginger blocks the effects of *prostaglandins*, chemicals that cause painful inflammation in blood vessels in the brain. Ginger probably won't come to your rescue once a migraine is under way, but it can make a difference if you use it at the first hint of a coming migraine. Use a teaspoon or two of minced fresh gingerroot, steeping it in a cup of hot water. Or add it to a tall glass of cool lemonade. For more foods and recipes that help prevent and relieve migraines, visit *www.myhealingkitchen.com*.

Foods That Make It Worse

Foods that trigger migraines can vary with the sufferer. If you have migraine attacks, keep a food diary for a few weeks, writing down everything you eat and drink, including how much you ate and when you ate it. Make notes about other lifestyle factors, such as how frequently you're exercising, the stress in your life, how you've been sleeping and so on. You also should make notes about any headaches you experience. You should begin to see a connecting pattern between the migraines and your life.

Your headaches are most likely to be caused by a combination of foods and other factors. A food diary will help you keep all the variables straight. There are, however, a few foods that are commonly linked with migraines. *The main ones follow...*

➤ **Kick the caffeine.** Coffee is among the main migraine triggers. It's an interesting paradox. For some people, coffee works as well as prescription drugs at stopping a headache by constricting blood vessels in the brain that are temporarily dilated. If you read the labels on over-the-counter painkillers, you'll find that quite a few contain caffeine. In these products, caffeine acts as a *potentiator*, an ingredient that makes the medication more effective. However, if you consume a lot of caffeine, the blood vessels in your brain become more sensitive to its effects and are more likely to contract, then expand, which can cause blinding pain. This is similar to what happens when coffee drinkers don't get their usual morning cup and suffer a headache due to caffeine withdrawal.

If you're a coffee drinker who also gets migraines, you should definitely start reducing your consumption. Don't give up your java abruptly, however. Taper off gradually to one cup per day. Then start diluting your coffee with decaf until you've quit completely.

➤ **Oy, soy!** Foods like miso, tempeh and tofu are among the healthiest choices on the planet and are among the main reasons that so many people in Asian countries live healthier and longer lives than North Americans. However, if you have migraines, soy could be part of the problem, because it contains *tyramine*, an amino acid that stimulates the release of hormones that cause blood vessels to constrict.

Soy foods that have undergone the most processing, such as soy cheese, miso and soy burgers, seem to be stronger migraine triggers than products such as tofu, tempeh and soy milk, but there are no absolutes. Some people drink soy milk every day and only have migraines every few weeks. Does this mean that the milk is not a trigger? No. Remember, migraines are more likely to be caused by a confluence of *multiple* triggers than by any single one. When you drink soy milk, you're adding one more factor to your trigger load. Maybe you didn't sleep well the night before or you're more stressed than usual. Throwing soy into the mix can tip you into a migraine.

Since soy-based foods are generally healthful and healing, I don't recommend giving them up unless they trigger migraines for you. First, eliminate all other potential triggers. If soy still seems to be a problem, go without it for a few weeks to see if there's a change in your migraine pattern. If you have fewer migraines or none at all, then soy belongs on your no-no list. If your migraines stay the same (or you aren't sure if there's a connection), try eating less soy for awhile.

► **Not-so-golden oldies.** Tyramine, a very common migraine trigger, is formed when protein in foods breaks down as it ages, which is why aged cheeses and red wine are common triggers. Generally, the longer a cheese ages, the more tyramine it contains. Beware of blue cheese, gorgonzola, Parmesan, cheddar—they're all high in tyramine. Fresh cheeses contain a lot less tyramine than their aged counterparts. Cottage cheese, fresh mozzarella, ricotta, farmer cheese and cream cheese are virtually free of it.

► **Ditch the dogs.** Hot dogs and other cured meats, such as ham, salami, pepperoni and bacon, should be off-limits if you suffer from migraines. Most are high in preservatives called *nitrites*, powerful vasodilators that cause blood vessels to expand quickly, which can set off a migraine. As little as 1 mg of *sodium nitrate*, barely a speck, can trigger a migraine in some people.

► **Sack the sulfites.** Many commercially available dried fruits, such as apricots and dates, contain chemical compounds called *sulfites* that act as preservatives. These compounds are as bad for migraines as processed meats. Sulfites are used to keep dried fruits from turning brown and sometimes to maintain the fresh look of vegetables, fruits and salads on salad bars. They also occur naturally in all wines, although many wines have added sulfites to prevent spoilage. If you don't want to give up these foods, look for organic dried fruit advertising "no preservatives" on the label and organic wines that are free of added sulfites. Whole fresh fruits are also a good choice.

► **Watch for MSG.** Doctors formerly used the phrase "Chinese restaurant syndrome" to describe migraines caused by *monosodium glutamate* (MSG), a flavor enhancer once commonly used in Asian restaurants. The term is a bit outdated now that many restaurants have stopped using MSG in any form due to customer complaints/requests. Many even print "No MSG" on their menus. The packaged food industry, however, apparently can't live without MSG, which is added to literally thousands of processed foods, and isn't always labeled clearly. MSG masquerades under such aliases as *hydrolyzed vegetable protein* and *maltodextrin*, among others. Read food labels and menus carefully, and if you see MSG in any form, don't eat it. Better yet, don't eat processed, packaged foods of any kind.

► **Give up the red.** Red wine is one of the top sources of tyramine and one of the most common migraine triggers. All wines contain some naturally occurring sulfites, but many wines have more added. In truth, all alcoholic beverages dilate the blood vessels in your brain, increasing blood flow that leads to increased pressure, and this in turn can trigger migraines. White wine is generally safer than red because it lacks tyramine, and any clear liquor like vodka or gin is less likely than aged spirits (such as scotch, rum or whiskey) to cause headaches because clear alcohol contains fewer impurities. Moderation obviously matters. Know when to say when.

➤ **Beware of brain freeze.** Take your time with icy cold foods. What many people call *brain freeze*—the miserable, stabbing pain that occurs when you eat or drink something that's too cold too fast—can trigger a migraine attack. Brain freeze occurs when cold stimulates the nerves that transmit pain signals through the *trigeminal nerve*, one of the largest in our heads and one that's in charge of sending temperature impulses to the brain. The resulting headache doesn't last very long, but it can be ferociously painful. According to researchers at the Cleveland Clinic, more than 90% of people who suffer from migraines have learned to be very cautious with cold foods and drinks. Eat ice cream slowly, taking a small bite and letting your mouth warm up before you have more. Sip cold drinks slowly, even when you want to gulp.

Supplemental Help

It's not unusual for people with migraines to spend days in bed every month and hun-

Common Migraine Triggers

A survey of more than 400 migraine sufferers found that roughly 16% had problems with cheese or chocolate, about 28% were sensitive to alcohol and nearly 12% reacted to red wine. Most foods that cause migraines contain one or more of the amines: tyramine, *histamine* or *phenylethylamine*.

Foods Containing Tyramine
- Aged cheeses and cheese spreads
- Cured or pickled fish
- Aged, dried, fermented or pickled meats
- Processed meats such as bacon, hot dogs and cold cuts
- Soy foods, including soy sauce
- Meat tenderizer
- Yeast extracts

Foods Containing Histamine
- Overripe bananas
- Beer
- Chicken liver
- Processed meats, such as bacon, hot dogs and cold cuts
- Sauerkraut
- Soy foods
- Citrus fruits
- Pineapple

Foods Containing Phenylethylamine
- Citrus fruits
- Chocolate
- Yellow cheeses
- Red wine
- Canned berries

dreds of dollars a year on high-tech pharmaceuticals, but they may not need them. Scientists have identified a handful of supplements that can make a real difference in preventing migraines. It's well worth the effort to start experimenting with them and find the right ones for you.

➤ **Fight with feverfew.** Clinical studies have demonstrated that taking this herb regularly is among the best natural remedies for preventing migraines. In one of the studies, researchers examined 270 migraine patients who treated their headaches by chewing on fresh feverfew leaves. More than 70% reported that the herb reduced both the frequency and severity of attacks.

A few years later, scientists did a double-blind, placebo-controlled study, published in *The Lancet*. Patients in the active group, who took feverfew capsules containing the equivalent of two medium leaves, had a 24% reduction in attacks and also experienced less nausea and vomiting. Scientists believe feverfew works by making the brain chemical serotonin more effective.

If you live near an herb store, try the fresh leaves, eating one to four daily to prevent migraines. If you find the leaves too bitter, feverfew supplements are widely available. I recommend a dose of 125 mg of the freeze-dried leaf, taken twice daily with food.

➤ **Try CoQ10.** A few years ago, a study looked at coenzyme Q10 (CoQ10) for migraine prevention. People with a history of migraines took 150 mg of CoQ10 daily for three months. Prior to the study, the participants averaged seven migraines during a three-month period. During the course of the study, the attacks dwindled to less than three over three months, a 60% decrease.

CoQ10 is a powerful antioxidant that's necessary for cellular energy production. In fact, findings in a Swiss study supported earlier research showing that CoQ10 prevented migraines by allowing the so-called "power plant" in cells—the *mitochondria*—to function optimally. After agreeing they would not use any other migraine prevention during the research period, the migraine sufferers were told they would be taking either a placebo or 300 mg of CoQ10 daily. For the first 30 days, study directors gave every participant a placebo. They then started half the group on the daily CoQ10 300-mg dose, while the others continued on the placebo. The CoQ10-takers experienced significant results, with migraine incidence slashed by 50%. When they did have a migraine, symptoms were milder and shorter in duration. CoQ10 is safe, so you can take the 300 mg daily dose used in the study with confidence, dividing it into three 100 mg doses.

➤ **Fish oil works.** Compelling research shows that consuming more fish can help prevent migraines, and that fish oil supplements may be equally effective. One study, conducted at the University of Cincinnati, found that patients who took fish oil supplements for six weeks had a 60% decrease in migraines. Even when those studied had migraines, the attacks were significantly less severe. Most studies looking at the effects of omega-3s on migraines have used between 1,000 mg and 1,500 mg daily. Use a product that mainly contains DHA and EPA, the most beneficial types of omega-3.

Make sure the product's label says that it has undergone "molecular distillation," which eliminates mercury and other toxins.

➤ **Beat 'em with butterbur.** The butterbur plant increases brain circulation, and clinical trials have shown that it prevents migraines. Using a purified form of the herb in a product called *Petadolex*, researchers found that those who took it twice daily had a 50% reduction in migraine frequency. According to Dr. Alexander Mauskop of the New York Headache Center, patients who did have migraines while taking the butterbur extract reported that the duration and severity of the attacks tended to be less severe. The recommended dose is 50 mg three times daily for one month and twice daily thereafter. Expect to take butterbur for up to two months before experiencing any significant results.

Other Helpers and Healers

Give your digestion a boost. The body's digestive acids naturally decline with age, and there's some evidence that people with low levels of these acids might have a higher risk for developing migraines. You can buy digestive-acid supplements such as *betaine hydrochloride* at health food stores. Take one tablet with every meal.

➤ **Ask about allergies.** People with food allergies or food sensitivities are often susceptible to migraines (and tension headaches), probably because trigger foods can cause an increase in histamine and other body chemicals. If you suspect that food allergies are causing your migraines, see a doctor who specializes in nutritional therapy or allergies. You'll probably be advised to keep a food diary, writing down everything you eat for a few weeks, along with notes about any headaches, when they occur, how often, their severity and so on. Review your diary periodically to see if you notice links between certain foods and migraines.

➤ **Destress.** Stress can play a significant role in initiating chemical changes in the brain. If you frequently experience migraines, make stress prevention a cornerstone of your daily life. Unwind with exercise, yoga, meditation, biofeedback or guided imagery. It may be worth consulting an expert in relaxation training. Dozens of clinical studies have confirmed that people who practice relaxation techniques can reduce the severity and frequency of migraines.

➤ **Sleep and eat on schedule.** Try to go to bed at about the same time and sleep roughly the same number of hours. Don't short yourself on sleep and then try to make it up. Being underrested is a common migraine stressor. So is having low blood sugar. Munch healthy snacks like raw vegetables, walnuts and fruit periodically throughout the day, favoring six smaller meals to three larger ones. ■

18

Osteoporosis

O steoporosis is a decades-long process in which bones become more and more fragile. Once a woman reaches menopause and her estrogen levels start to decline, she's likely to lose from 1% to 3% of her total bone mass every year. Thin women face an even greater risk, because those with low body fat don't produce as much *estrogen*, the hormone that contributes to bone strength. Small-boned women also have less bone mass in reserve and therefore develop osteoporosis more rapidly. The numbers are grim for most women affected by osteoporosis. Five years after menopause, many will lose 25% of their bone density. By the time a woman reaches her seventies, she may have lost between 35% and 50% of her total bone mass.

Men also lose bone as they age, but not as rapidly. After age 75, men are just as likely to develop osteoporosis as women, but because men have denser, stronger bones to begin with, osteoporosis develops more slowly.

SYMPTOMS

Women lose bone for decades without a sign that anything's wrong. It's been estimated that the average doctor sees about 100 patients per week who have undetected bone loss. In fact, up to 28 million American women currently have osteoporosis, yet only three to four million actually will be diagnosed. The first noticeable symptom is often a bone fracture or a stooped appearance and loss of height. Women with advanced osteoporosis may have bones that are nearly as fragile as eggshells. They don't have to trip and fall to break a bone. Sneezing or coughing can do it, as can bending over to tie shoelaces. Fragile bones can quite literally fall to pieces.

Every woman should have a bone-density test once she's 65, but most, especially

269

if they are in menopause, should be tested earlier. If you're past menopause and have any osteoporosis risk factors, including any history of tobacco use, eating disorders, long-term use of corticosteroids or other bone-damaging drugs, or if you have a close family member with osteoporosis, ask your doctor about getting a bone-density scan. The best test, known as DEXA (*dual energy X-ray absorptiometry*), measures the density of bone in your hip and lower spine. Men with risk factors should also be tested.

CAUSES

Bones are living tissue. Your skeleton is in a constant state of reconstructing itself. This is a process called *remodeling*, in which new bone is constantly being created by cells called *osteoblasts*. At the same time, old bone is broken down by cells called *osteoclasts*. A full remodeling cycle takes between two and three months and, until you reach your early thirties, the building-up process occurs more rapidly than the breaking down. You accumulate more bone than you lose, resulting in strong, dense bones, provided that your diet includes sufficient calcium, plus other vitamins and minerals that support this rebuilding process. Once you reach your mid-thirties, however, the balance shifts. From this point forward, you lose more bone than you make and your bone balance starts dipping into the red.

Your body needs estrogen to build bone. Once estrogen declines due to the onset of menopause, the density of your bones rapidly falls off. This can occur at any age

270

if a woman has her ovaries removed, which induces what's called *surgical menopause*.

TREATMENT

Until recently, hormone replacement therapy (HRT) was the primary treatment for osteoporosis. Women were advised by their doctors to take HRT after menopause to replace the hormones (primarily estrogen) in decline. Then, in 2002, an important study found that women taking supplemental hormones for long periods were more likely to contract heart disease and breast cancer than those who didn't take HRT or who used it for shorter periods. This was the first large-scale study to reveal these risks; it represented a very important advance in our knowledge. What happened next, however, was unexpected. Within a month after the study was reported, about a third of women who were on HRT, horrified by the increased risks, stopped taking it. About 20% of the women who stopped HRT didn't take any new steps to protect their bones. Suddenly, these patients found themselves with an increased risk for osteoporosis, the leading cause of bone fractures after menopause.

Many newer osteoporosis treatments appear to improve bone density, and seem less likely to cause dangerous side effects. These include *bisphosphonate* drugs such as *alendronate* (Fosamax) and *risedronate* (Actonel). Another drug, *raloxifene* (Evista), apparently mimics the bone-strengthening effects of estrogen. Drugs such as *parathyroid hormone* and *calcitonin* also seem to improve bone strength and reduce the risk for fractures. Some studies show that long-term use of some bisphosphonates may lead to weaker, more brittle bones, so plan to discuss the risks and benefits with your doctor. The advice in this chapter presents the current best strategies for protecting and strengthening your bones through sound nutrition and regular exercise.

Foods That Make It Better

Osteoporosis is a disease that is almost entirely preventable if you start making your skeleton as strong as possible during the bone-forming years. You'll still lose bone later, but you'll have more in reserve to keep the bones relatively strong. Catching up once you move into the negative side of the equation is more difficult. Still, numerous studies show that dietary methods are the best strategy for preventing osteoporosis. In addition, eating the right foods can greatly improve bone density no matter how fragile bones are.

Calcium is the primary component of bones, and one of the best substances for maintaining strong bones or replacing

10 Top Calcium Foods

1. Yogurt, 1 cup low-fat — 447 mg
2. Sesame seeds, ¼ cup — 351 mg
3. Cow's milk, 1 cup 2% — 297 mg
4. Collard greens, 1 cup boiled — 226 mg
5. Turnip greens, 1 cup cooked — 197 mg
6. Mozzarella, 1 ounce, part skim — 183 mg
7. Bok choy, 1 cup cooked — 158 mg
8. Blackstrap molasses, 2 teaspoons — 118 mg
9. Tofu, 4 ounces raw — 100 mg
10. Cinnamon, 2 teaspoons ground — 56 mg

bone that's already lost. Women under 50 and men in general need 750 to 1,000 milligrams (mg) of calcium every day. After age 50, women should get at least 1,000 to 1,500 mg daily. One study found that people who got at least 1,000 mg of calcium daily reduced bone loss by 43%. However, calcium isn't the only player in building bone density. A variety of factors make calcium available to your bones. *Here are the most important...*

MAXIMIZE DAIRY PRODUCTS

To acquire calcium easily, drink organic milk and eat a cup of plain organic yogurt from pasture-raised cows every day. Calcium-fortified juices are another option. Each of these delivers about 300 mg of calcium per serving. Other dairy products, such as cottage cheese and other cheeses, added to your daily diet can get you partway to your total intake.

➤ **Keep it low-fat.** Low-fat dairy contains as much calcium as full-fat versions. In fact, skim milk can be a better choice than whole milk. A glass of fortified skim contains 352 mg of calcium, compared with 290 mg in whole milk. The bonus is that low-fat dairy products contain fewer calories.

➤ **Use the powdered kind.** When baking or making oatmeal, it's okay to use nonfat milk powder mixed with water if you want to save money and calories. A half-cup of powder has close to 420 mg of calcium. You can even make homemade yogurt with nonfat powdered milk.

➤ **Say yes to yogurt.** Choose plain yogurt with a label that says it contains active or live cultures. Sweeten with fresh fruit, chopped prunes or a little honey.

➤ **Eat more cheese.** Low-fat cheeses in particular are very high in calcium. Just one tablespoon of low-fat Parmesan, for example, has nearly 70 mg of calcium. Full-fat artisanal cheeses are an option, too. They contain more calories but a little goes a long way. Cheese and a fermented soy food called *natto* also contain vitamin K-2, another potent bone builder.

➤ **Sip a little juice.** Calcium-fortified juice is a good option, but it has more sugar and calories than skim milk. On the plus side, we seem to absorb between 36% and 42% of the calcium in juices, compared with 25% to 30% of the calcium in dairy.

➤ **Soy good for bones.** No one knows for sure why Asian women suffer fewer hip fractures than women in the US, but some experts attribute it to their consumption of soy foods. Tofu, tempeh, natto and other soybean-based foods are a staple in Asian countries. Studies show that Japanese women who consume the most natto and other soy foods have the lowest incidence of osteoporosis in the world. Soy foods are high in *phytoestrogens*, plant compounds that act like a weak form of estrogen and stimulate bone growth. Even better, recent research has shown that women who've been treated for breast cancer and who consume soy foods have lower risk for cancer recurrence—the opposite of what was originally thought. Discuss with your doctor.

Studies clearly show that soy is good for your heart and arteries. For the millions of Americans who can't digest (or don't like)

dairy, soy milk is a healthy alternative, particularly if you buy a brand that's calcium-fortified. Most contain roughly 300 mg of calcium per cup, about the same as cow's milk.

➤ **More produce, more bone.** Fruits and vegetables contain healthy amounts of potassium, magnesium and vitamin K, all essential minerals for building strong bones. Research shows that people who eat the most produce, particularly fruits and vegetables high in potassium (such as Swiss chard, spinach, lima beans, avocado and sweet potatoes) have greater bone densities and a lower risk for fractures. Fruits and vegetables also contain substances that are used by the body to generate *bicarbonate ions*, which help neutralize the natural acids that can leach calcium from your bones. At the same time, fruits and vegetables reduce the amount of calcium that's excreted in urine. A study published in *American Journal of Clinical Nutrition* found that women who took in the most potassium had bone density scores 8% higher than those who got the least.

➤ **DASH your bone loss.** You may already have heard of the DASH (Dietary Approaches to Stop Hypertension) diet (see page 205). It is based on research that shows how diet, including fruits and vegetables, can lower blood pressure. Researchers involved in the various DASH studies were primarily interested in hypertension, but noticed that those who followed this diet also seemed to have healthier bones. Subjects eating the most fruits and vegetables, along with three daily servings of low-fat dairy, experienced the least amount of bone loss.

calcium in their urine. The more salt you eat, the more calcium disappears. Those trying to control their blood pressure are advised to get no more than 1,500 mg a day, which is a healthy amount for most people. The best evidence suggests that if you're not concerned about bone health, you can have a little more—about 2,000 mg daily.

➤ **New rules for alcohol.** Experts once believed that even small amounts of alcohol were bad for the bones. It's true that excessive drinking causes a loss of bone density, resulting in more fractures from osteoporosis. Heavy alcohol intake seems to inhibit the absorption of calcium, as well as escalate the excretion of calcium in the urine. However, recent research suggests that mild drinking—say, a drink a day for women—isn't likely to diminish bone strength significantly. In fact, some studies now indicate that light-to-moderate drinkers might have better bone density.

➤ **Axe the oxalates.** Some of the healthiest foods for bone strength, including spinach, beet greens, chard and almonds, are high in chemical compounds called *oxalates*. These bind to calcium and inhibit calcium absorption. Another super-healthful group of foods, legumes, contain substances called *phytates* that also block the absorption of calcium. Luckily, there's a trick for getting around the phytate problem. Cook dried beans for a couple of hours, pour out the water, rinse and finish cooking in fresh water. This will neutralize some of the calcium-blocking effects.

Supplemental Help

Nearly everyone *can* get enough bone-building calcium and other nutrients from their food and other dietary sources, but that doesn't mean everyone *does*. And some essential bone builders, like vitamin D, are virtually impossible to get in sufficient quantities from food sources and must be supplemented. Fortunately, the essential supplements for preventing osteoporosis are inexpensive and safe. The extra insurance is clearly worth it.

➤ **Extra calcium counts.** To reduce the risk of fractures, you need plenty of calcium from food, but you should also take a good calcium supplement. Premenopausal women should take 1,000 mg of calcium; take 1,500 mg after menopause. Men should take 750 to 1,000 mg daily. The two forms that work best, *calcium citrate* and *calcium carbonate*, are equally effective. The main difference is that you can take calcium citrate any time, but calcium carbonate must be taken with food to be absorbed efficiently. If you are prone to constipation, choose calcium citrate.

The body can absorb only so much calcium at a time, generally 500 to 600 mg. If you're taking a bigger dose, anything in excess of this amount is being flushed away in your urine. It's better to take two 500-mg tablets per day, one in the morning one in the evening, after meals. Calcium carbonate supplements must be taken with food. Calcium taken at night will help you sleep better because it's a natural muscle relaxant.

➤ **Your secret need for vitamin D.** Vitamin D is just as important as calcium for bone density and strength. Without it, calcium isn't able to get into your bones. Studies show that D also helps your kidneys hold on to calcium, so that less is excreted, and suppresses *parathyroid hormone,* which governs bone loss. In addition, vitamin D strengthens muscles, which in turn decreases vulnerability to falls that can lead to bone fractures. Doctors have known for a long time that severe deficiencies of vitamin D can seriously affect bones, but they've only recently learned that even marginal deficiencies can lead to osteoporosis.

Many Americans have surprisingly low levels of vitamin D. Your body makes its own when skin is exposed to sunlight. Lighter skin educes more from solar rays than darker skin.

These days people are avoiding sunshine. They worry that it may cause skin cancer, so they don't go out, they cover up or they use sunscreen, which diminishes the body's ability to synthesize vitamin D from the sun. Worse, the body's ability to produce vitamin D actually declines with age. A 70-year-old's skin makes just about a quarter of the vitamin D that it manufactured from the sun's rays 50 years earlier.

Advice that says avoid the sun is dead wrong. Research confirms that because solar rays are the most significant source of vitamin D for humans—and vitamin D increases protection against many cancers—people who get less sun actually have *higher* rates of skin cancer. This includes melanoma. The sunshine vitamin also appears to play an effective role in preventing heart disease and many other serious conditions such as prostate cancer, according to a meta-analysis of 63 studies published the *American Journal of Public Health.*

However, getting 100% of your vitamin D requirements from food sources can be difficult. Many people are told to avoid eating vitamin D–rich foods such as calf's liver and other organ meats, dairy foods and eggs because they are so dense in calories and cholesterol.

So the trick is learning how to manage all your sources of vitamin D to make sure you get the full amount. To do this, most will need to take supplements, especially those who live in northern latitudes. I urge you to take at minimum 1,000 to 2,000 international units (IU) of vitamin D-3—which helps metabolize vitamin D from any other source—during the colder months. In the late spring, summer and early fall, make some of your own vitamin D by exposing your body to 10 to 20 minutes of sunshine. African-Americans, who have higher cancer rates and lower blood levels of vitamin D, should double this dose.

Don't Be Caught "D" Deficient

True or False? A research team in a Minnesota hospital found that during one July, *all* of the older adults admitted for bone fractures were vitamin D–deficient, even though half of them were supplementing with the vitamin.

True. Of the 82 women admitted to the hospital for broken bones, those taking supplements had just slightly higher levels of vitamin D in their blood than those not taking supplements. All had dangerously low levels of vitamin D, nowhere near the 40 nanograms per milliliter (ng/ml) that is recommended.

➤ **Potassium peak.** In 2004, the Institute of Medicine advised Americans to increase their potassium intake to 4,700 mg daily. This higher level was recommended partly to protect bones from osteoporosis. If you don't eat a lot of fresh vegetables, you may need a potassium supplement. Plenty of studies show that people who eat the most potassium-rich fruits and vegetables have higher bone densities and a lower risk for fractures. A cup of steamed Swiss chard, for example, contains at least 950 mg of potassium. I urge you to eat widely from potassium-rich sources, including cremini mushrooms (about 600 mg per five ounces) and raw celery (344 mg per cup), but also eggplant, avocado and sweet potatoes. To cover any gaps, take a daily multivitamin, which supplies 80 to 100 mg.

➤ **More K is okay.** A long-running study of more than 70,000 women found that those who had the lowest intake of vitamin K were almost a third more likely to suffer a bone fracture than women who got more. You can get plenty of vitamin K if you fill up on leafy greens such as kale, but if you don't eat greens regularly or take a daily multi that includes vitamin K-2 you won't get enough for bone support. The recommended dose is 150 to 300 mcg daily. Don't take doses in pill form if you're taking blood-thinning medication such as *warfarin* (Coumadin) because the supplemental form can interfere with blood clotting.

➤ **B is for better bones.** Chronic, low-level inflammation is linked to everything from cancer to heart disease. Research now suggests that it also contributes to osteoporosis. One of the main signs of inflammation is elevated *homocysteine* in the blood, which is readily lowered with B vitamins, particularly folic acid plus B-6 and B-12. To keep your bones healthy, take 100 mg of a B-complex daily.

➤ **Oh, omegas!** Research shows that omega-3 fatty acids, those highly beneficial fats in cold-water fish and flaxseed, boost the level of calcium in your bones and also improve their strength. A study of women over 65 found that those taking omega-3 supplements had significantly less bone loss over a three-year period than women taking a placebo. The omega-3 takers even improved their bone density.

Fish oil is a supplement I heartily endorse. So many people aren't eating enough fish to prevent osteoporosis, heart disease and other inflammation-driven medical conditions. Purchase fish oil that's labeled as having undergone "molecular distillation," a process that eliminates toxins.

Krill oil is another rich source of omega-3s. Krill, tiny oceanic crustaceans that feed on algae, are responsible for the high omega-3 content of salmon and other cold-water fish. Take one to three 1,000-mg fish oil or krill oil capsules daily, increasing to twice daily if you have any inflammation-driven condition.

Either of these oils can thin the blood, so if you're taking a blood-thinning drug such as Coumadin, check with your doctor before starting supplements. If you have a shellfish allergy, don't take krill oil—krill, after all, are shellfish. Take fish oil instead.

➤ **Say "strontium."** Strontium is a trace mineral that has huge potential for increasing bone density. *Strontium ranelate* is a patented type of strontium that has been closely observed. One study, published in *The New England Journal of Medicine* and involving 1,600 postmenopausal women with osteoporosis, found that those who were given strontium in addition to calcium and vitamin D had a 49% reduced risk of fractures during the first year of treatment and a 41% reduced risk over a three-year period, compared with women who received calcium and vitamin D alone.

In another study, 5,000 postmenopausal women with osteoporosis who took strontium ranelate saw their fracture risk drop by 16% over three years. The women with the lowest bone density saw the greatest benefit, experiencing a 39% reduced fracture risk compared with the placebo takers. That's twice as effective at building bone mass as hormone replacement or the leading osteoporosis drugs.

No adverse reactions have been identified in studies on strontium ranelate, sold as Protelos in Europe where it's used widely. It hasn't yet been approved for use in the US, but the mineral strontium is available in supplement form as *strontium citrate*, most commonly in 300 to 350 mg tablets. Take two daily to achieve the dose used in the successful studies. If you're taking any pharmaceutical drugs or have impaired kidney function, talk to your doctor first.

278

Other Helpers and Healers

➤ **Exercise builds bone.** Most of us exercise because we want to lose weight, strengthen our muscles, prevent illness or simply to age more gracefully. Bones need a good workout every day, too. Weight-bearing exercise (or any activity that puts stress on your bones) stimulates osteoblasts to produce stronger bone. Walking, tennis, dancing, aerobics and resistance training are ideal for bone strength. Swimming and cycling are good for your heart, but they don't stimulate bone to grow.

Exercise builds the most bone when you do it before about age 40, but if you're older don't give up. Young people who exercise regularly and get enough calcium and vitamin D have much stronger bones than adults—and greater bone reserves will offset the inevitable losses that come later in life. However, exercise also strengthens muscles and improves balance, essential in preventing falls that can stress bones to the breaking point. Try for 30 to 45 minutes of weight-bearing exercise two to three days a week.

➤ **Walk on.** Can merely walking protect your bones? The answer is yes. Researchers found that postmenopausal women who walked at either a low- or high-intensity pace three miles per day for four days per week actually prevented bone loss. In fact, walking may be the perfect physical activity for menopausal and postmenopausal women because it is so easy to do, it can be done at your convenience and it's free.

➤ **Shake it up, baby.** The first truly effective medical device for treating osteoporosis is here. It's called Juvent 1000 and it's so effective that National Aeronautics and Space Administration (NASA) is installing it on the International Space Station to help counter the bone loss that astronauts experience in zero gravity. This gently shaking platform delivers low-magnitude vibration up through the feet, stimulating muscle fibers and bone, improving balance and thus helping to prevent falls. Standing on the Juvent platform, which resembles a bathroom scale, stimulates circulation and bone building. The Juvent is currently sold in Europe, Canada, Australia and online. The company expects FDA approval by 2010 as a bona fide osteoporosis treatment.

➤ **Give up the smokes.** Studies show that people who smoke are far more likely to develop osteoporosis than nonsmokers. Researchers believe there might be something in tobacco smoke that changes the body's hormones, which adversely affect bone. Regardless of the mechanism, the advice is the same: Do everything you can to stop smoking. If you can't manage it cold-turkey—and many people can't—talk to your doctor about smoking-cessation aids like nicotine patches, gum or other strategies, including support-group meetings. Also, steer clear of secondhand smoke.

➤ **Heartburn drugs are bad to the bone.** If you're one of the millions of Americans who take drugs to put out the raging fire of heartburn, your bones might need a rescue team. A study in the *Journal of the American Medical Association* found that patients taking proton pump inhibitors (PPIs), drugs such as Prilosec, to control heartburn had a 44% higher risk of hip fractures than nonusers. These drugs reduce stomach acid, which might make it harder for the body to break down bone-building minerals like calcium for absorption into the system. Another class of heartburn drugs, H2 blockers, also increases bone risk, although not as much as the PPIs.

Studies like the one mentioned above are a solid reminder to use drugs only when you absolutely need them. Pharmaceuticals can be highly effective in limited circumstances, but they're riskier when used regularly to manage chronic conditions. In general, I hesitate to recommend pharmaceuticals unless the long-term benefits clearly outweigh the risks. For something like heartburn, it makes more sense to start out with lifestyle changes and natural approaches. Begin by giving up nicotine, caffeine and aspirin; each one is a heartburn trigger. So is going to bed on a full stomach. Wait until several hours after eating to lie down or go to sleep. While you're working on these changes, try a few supplemental remedies. Licorice extract tincture (one dropperful three times per day) is very effective, as is deglycyrrhizinated licorice, a compound developed to relieve pain from heartburn and ulcers. The amino acid *glutamine* is also effective (take 1 to 3 g daily). ◼

19

Overweight and Obesity

Most of us don't need a doctor or fitness coach to tell us we could benefit from losing a little weight. Even though perceptions aren't necessarily reality, what you see in the mirror and how you feel in your clothes should act as a gentle hint. The question is—How much weight do you need to lose? Obesity is defined as being more than 30 pounds heavier than your healthy weight, which is calculated by the body mass index (BMI). To calculate your BMI, see the directions at right. The accompanying chart will show you where you stand.

The Centers for Disease Control (CDC) reports that 30% of the US population is obese. More than 60% of us are overweight, or 20 pounds over our normal BMI range. Until very recently, BMI was the universal measure for healthy and unhealthy weight

How to Calculate Your Body Mass Index (BMI)

Divide your weight in pounds by your height in inches squared, then multiply the total by 703.

Formula: Weight in lbs/(height in inches)^2 x 703 = BMI

Example: [140 lbs/(63")^2] x 703 = 24.79

Check your status with this chart:

BMI	Weight Status
Below 18.5	Underweight
18.5–24.9	Normal
25–29.9	Overweight
30 & above	Obese

For everyone, a BMI of 19 to 24.9 is ideal. A BMI of 25 to 29.9 means you're overweight. And a score of 30 to 39.9 indicates obesity. Higher numbers reflect extreme obesity.

but, lately, scientists have revealed serious flaws in this system. Because muscle is heavier than fat, a person with more muscle mass may register as being overweight on the BMI scale, even though she is actually healthy and fit. For example, because of his height, actor Tom Cruise has a BMI that characterizes him as obese, which is ridiculous. On the other hand, elderly individuals who have less muscle mass can be underestimated by the BMI system when they may, in fact, be obese.

Doctors now believe that a more accurate way of determining your weight status, especially for health purposes, is by waist circumference. New research shows that, while how much you weigh still matters, it's more important where you are carrying the weight. Studies reveal that the larger your waist size, the greater your risk for cancer, diabetes, heart attack and dementia. One of the most compelling findings comes from Harvard research in which 44,000 female nurses had their waists measured. Kathryn Rexrode of the Harvard Medical School and Brigham and Women's Hospital in Boston found that even normal BMI women whose waist measurements were larger than ideal had twice the risk of early death from cancer or heart disease. For both women and men, waist size is a good way to determine if you're at increased risk for heart attack, high blood pressure and diabetes. One reason for this is that belly fat is metabolically active, which means that it secretes hormone-like substances that increase inflammation throughout the body. A large midsection also indicates that your body is storing fat around your heart and liver, which poses serious health risks. The connection between waistline and dementia is equally intriguing. Scientists at the Kaiser Permanente Division of Research in California evaluated data collected from 6,500 people for more than 30 years, and discovered that men and women with the largest waistlines in their forties had almost *triple* the risk of dementia in their seventies as those with normal

Proper Waist Management

Use a tape measure or a piece of string to measure the circumference of your waist at the level of your navel. The ideal waist measurement should be half your height or less. For a woman who is 5 foot 6 inches, or 66 inches, that's a 33-inch waist.

If you're running a bit on the wide side, Dr. Arya M. Sharma, chairman of obesity research and management at the University of Alberta, says your primary objective should be to stop adding pounds. Even if you don't lose waist inches or pounds, improving the quality of food you eat (easy to do on the Mediterr-Asian Diet) and adding some physical activity can reduce your risk for cardiovascular disease and other serious medical conditions. Many people ask me which is more effective for weight loss: diet or exercise? According to the newest research, diet is far more effective. It's also the easiest. For example, it takes 77 minutes of moderately paced bicycling to burn off the average 360-calorie blueberry muffin. Exercise is not effective as a single strategy for weight loss. It simply takes too long. The quicker solution is not to eat the muffin at all.

How Much Should I Weigh?

Here's a quick way to figure your ideal weight from the National Institutes of Health...

Women. Add 100 pounds for your first five feet in height then add five pounds for each extra inch. A 5-foot 6-inch woman would thus ideally weigh 130 pounds.

Men. Add 106 pounds for your first five feet in height and then add six pounds for each extra inch. A 5-foot 11-inch man would have an ideal weight of 172 pounds.

If your frame is small, subtract 10% from your total. If your frame is large, add 10%.

waistlines and weight. Researchers are still looking to pinpoint the precise link between the brain and abdomen.

Data from multiple studies indicate that a man's health risk increases when his waist reaches 37 inches and is boosted further when he jumps to 40 inches or more. A woman's health risks rise when her waist measurement reaches 31.5 inches and increase significantly with a waist measurement of 35 inches or more. See the box on page 281 to discover your healthy waist circumference.

CAUSES

Regardless of which standard of measurement is used, two-thirds of Americans are officially overweight; of that amount, one-third is clinically obese and that number is steadily increasing. The vast majority of people who gain weight do so because they consume more calories than they burn through activity. The excess calories are converted into fat

282

and stored in fat cells. The consumption of soft drinks has increased by more than 15 gallons per person annually from 1987 to 2000. Of course, genetic factors may also be involved in weight gain. Some people have an unnaturally low rate of *thermogenesis*, the amount of calories burned (as measured by the amount of heat produced) during resting metabolism. In other words, your friend sitting on the couch next to you watching television may be burning more calories than you are, even though you're both active people. A person who is lean might exhibit a 40% increase in thermogenesis after eating, compared with a 10% increase in someone who's overweight. This is also largely because muscle burns two times as many calories as fat, even when you're asleep—which is just another reason to preserve or build as much muscle mass as you reasonably can.

➤ **The myth of exercise.** According to new calculations published in *Obesity Research*, a pound of muscle burns about six calories a day while at rest, while a pound of fat burns two calories. So, if you work out vigorously enough to convert ten pounds of body fat to lean muscle—a Herculean achievement—you'd only be able to eat an extra 40 calories per day (about a teaspoon of butter) before you begin to gain weight again. Not too encouraging, is it?

Actually, it is. Because it emphasizes the importance diet has on weight gain and loss. The truth is that you'll lose more weight—and faster—by eating the high-volume, low-calorie foods in the Mediterr-Asian Diet (see page 19) than by exercising yourself into a sweaty heap.

➤ **The stress connection.** Stress is definitely involved in abdominal weight gain, too, with researchers linking *cortisol*, one of your body's main stress hormones, to the accumulation of belly fat. We know people with chronic stress produce very high levels of cortisol, which actually increases the ability to store fat. One study confirmed this when it discovered that women who felt the most stressed doing math or public speaking assignments had larger waists than the unstressed women.

➤ **Disability and immobility.** Finally, some people have physical limitations, such as degenerative arthritis and chronic joint pain, that prevent them from being as physically active as they'd like to be. For these people, calorie consumption must be monitored very carefully, or weight gain will rapidly accumulate.

TREATMENT

The weight-loss industry is one of the largest and most profitable industries in the US, primarily due to repeat business. A large percentage of overweight Americans hop from one fad diet to another, hoping to find the silver bullet that puts an end to their weight problems. Fad dieting, while immensely seductive, is a poor way to lose weight. Research from as far back as the 1950s found that about 95% of all diets fail to achieve lasting results. Losing weight in the short term is much easier than keeping the weight off for life, which should be the real goal of any weight-reduction strategy.

However, when it comes to improving your health, losing even a little weight goes a long way. Studies show that a mere 10% reduction in body weight produces significant reductions in the risk for heart disease, cancer, diabetes and other chronic conditions. The most important weight you lose may not be visible to the naked eye. In one study, very obese people lost about 20% of their total body weight, but while this showed up on the tape measure as a 23% smaller waist size, the big story was *internal*. They actually had shed 32% of their dangerous heart-padding fat.

➤ **Why dieting fails.** Virtually all quick-loss fad diets are about calorie restriction. Most maintain that there are certain foods you must abstain from, be they carbohydrates, fats, meat or sugars. Study after study confirms that deprivation never succeeds in the long run because most people wind up craving the foods they can't have. The only weight-loss strategies that truly succeed are the ones that focus on more healthful eating patterns and a more active lifestyle. That's another important reason why I favor the Mediterr-Asian Diet. Research shows that a Mediterranean style of eating is one of the best ways to lose weight and maintain that loss. Research conducted by Dr. Frank Sacks of Brigham and Women's Hospital and the Harvard School of Public Health found that "three times as many people were able to stick to a Mediterranean-style diet for 12 months versus the standard low-fat diet." Adding an Asian component to the Mediterranean plan makes it even more effective, because this increases the number of delicious foods and interesting dishes you can add to your repertoire.

283

➤ **Burn, baby, burn.** One of the easiest ways to lose weight is to trim or burn an extra 500 calories from your daily routine. Since one pound of body weight is the equivalent of 3,500 calories, cutting and/or burning this many calories in a week's time will result in a four-pound loss in a month. This is not a difficult goal to achieve. For example, if an average-sized woman gives up one soft drink per day, she will eliminate approximately 150 calories. If she walks briskly for a mile, she'll burn another 100 calories, equaling a 250-calorie deficit for the day. These two simple achievements put her halfway to her daily calorie-reduction goal.

Let's assume you need about 1,500 calories for basic metabolism and another 500 calories to sustain all other activities. If you eat exactly 2,000 calories a day, you'll maintain a consistent weight, without gaining an ounce. To *lose* weight requires that you create a calorie deficit. Continuing with our example, to lose one pound you'd have to eliminate 3,500 calories a week via diet and/or exercise, ideally both. I assure you that people who walk regularly and eat healthy foods can easily lose one to two pounds per week. That's an optimal rate of weight loss, too, because it means your body is shedding fat, not the lean muscle mass.

➤ **How many calories should I eat?** The number of calories you need every day is based on how much energy you use and how much lean muscle mass your body has. To calculate how many calories you need, just apply the Rule of 10. Multiply your body weight times ten to get the total number of daily calo-

284

ries to approximate your basal metabolic rate (BMR), which is the amount of energy your body requires to maintain itself in a resting state, like sitting or sleeping. If you weigh 150 pounds, you need about 1,500 calories for your BMR. This number accounts for 70% of the total calories your body needs to fuel its normal functions. If you are active, obviously you'll need more. How many more depends on factors such as your body composition, your activity level and your age. By the time we reach adulthood, we need fewer calories than we did when we were younger, because our metabolism slows by about 2% per decade. This explains why so many of us start gaining weight as we age, even though we may be eating and exercising as we always did.

➤ **More about your BMR.** Your body is always burning calories, even when you're resting on the couch or napping. People who go on deprivation diets usually experience a sharp drop in lean muscle, with a consequential drop in their BMR, and this is not good. A low BMR means your body is adapting to burning fewer calories at rest than it normally would. Even if you drastically cut your calorie intake and initially manage to lose a lot of weight, if you're losing muscle mass this will lead to a low BMR and will essentially stop your weight loss. This is what happens when dieters hit a discouraging plateau and give up. The Mediterr-Asian Diet has a built-in fail-safe protection against this, because the meal selection is vast and interesting, so it doesn't seem like a diet at all. The idea is simply to burn more calories than you take in by boosting your metabolism with more physical activity, and by filling you up on fewer calorie-rich foods. Some people might cut a mere 100 calories a day from their diet and burn another 100 with exercise. Others may be more aggressive and cut out 250 to 500 calories a day, increasing their exercise at the same time. If you maintain muscle mass, your body's engine and BMR will keep humming, so the weight will continue to come off easily. At the same time, the Mediterr-Asian Diet includes the kinds of foods, especially plenty of healthful fats, which actually *raise* your BMR.

Foods That Make It Better

The Mediterr-Asian plan gives you plenty of healthy choices to please your palate while you take off the pounds. As long as you're eating whole, unprocessed foods, easing up on calorie-rich (yet nutrient-poor) treats and getting some daily physical activity, you *will* lose weight. This is why there are no "overweight" recipes in *The Healing Kitchen*. Nearly everyone who follows the Mediterr-Asian guidelines (see page 22) can lose at least 10 to 15 pounds within the first few months, with the added bonus that your health will greatly improve. You can also find delicious recipes that will help you lose weight without "dieting" at the free Web site *www.my healingkitchen.com*.

What makes the Mediterr-Asian Diet so effective is that it's loaded with bulky, beneficial, high-fiber complex carbohydrates, making up 50% of your total food intake. Research suggests that these smart-carb foods, such as vegetables, fruits and whole grains, are the foundation of successful lifelong weight management.

During the most recent low-carb craze, mainstream health advice was so confusing that people actually stopped eating complex carbohydrate foods in the mistaken belief that they were fattening. The carbohydrate culprits in the typical American diet are highly processed carbs, such as white bread, white pasta, cookies, crackers and processed snack foods. With their fiber removed, these foods are nothing more than a concentrated source of calories that acts just like pure sugar in the bloodstream, spiking glucose and insulin levels, resulting in the constant craving for more unhealthy carbohydrates. The excess blood sugar, instead of going to cells for energy, is transformed into blood fats (*triglycerides*) and escorted to fat cells where it's stored as body fat. To lose weight without dieting or deprivation, eat less of those refined, processed foods and more of those that follow.

➤ **Eat more fat.** Read this section very carefully, as it runs counter to the standard medical advice you may have heard. *You need to eat fat in order to lose fat.* It's a scientific fact. You see, your body needs fat for its metabolism to operate efficiently. Your BMR, remember, is the engine that burns calories 24/7, even while you're sleeping. One reason that low-fat diets fail is that they slow down this critical calorie-burning process. In an important study conducted decades ago, researchers put people on an impossibly high-fat diet, with fully 90% of their calories coming from fat. That's not something I recommend you try, but in this instance it made an important point. The study participants were running on almost pure fat, yet they lost weight. When researchers switched them to a diet that was only 10% fat, they didn't lose a pound.

While it's never wise to go overboard on fat because it contains more calories than protein or carbohydrates, making sure you're consuming the healthful kind can indeed help you lose weight. Good fats improve your body's ability to burn off your reserves of body fat. In fact, all the fats in the Mediterr-Asian plan—olive and sesame oils, the fats in fish and nuts, and so on—are beneficial, healthy fats. These are the ones that don't cause silent inflammation, the primary cause of heart disease and so many other medical conditions.

If you follow the Mediterr-Asian Diet, you'll get at least 30% of your total calories from fat, possibly even a little more. In Spain, Italy and other Mediterranean countries, it's not unusual for people to get up to 40% of their total calories from fat, yet they're healthier and slimmer than most Americans. Olive oil is a treasured source of fat in these countries, and studies have shown that it's a big help in whittling the waistline. Researchers at Cornell University discovered that restaurant diners who dipped their bread in olive oil actually ate 23% less bread over the course of their meal compared with diners who did not use olive oil. When Harvard researchers placed a group of overweight people on either a low-fat diet or a moderate-fat Mediterranean diet for 18 months, the people in the Mediterranean group lost an average of nine pounds and three inches from their waistlines. Those in the low-fat group actually gained an inch and weighed

286

six pounds more than when they started. Only 20% of the low-fat group was able to stay on this meal plan until the end of the study, while more than 50% of the Mediterranean eaters were still on their plan.

➤ **Avocados, olive oil, hummus, fatty fish and nuts.** The staple foods of the Mediterr-Asian Diet certainly aren't typical diet foods. They're fatty, filling, satisfying and hearty. Clinical research confirms that eating such foods is the key to lifelong weight-loss success. In fact, a team of researchers followed 28,000 Spaniards for three years, and found that the Mediterranean way of eating actually does make the waistline lean. The adults in the study eating the Mediterranean way were 31% less likely to become obese.

➤ **Learn to love veggies.** Studies show that people who eat a vegetable-based diet typically weigh up to 20% less than those who consume the typical American diet. This makes sense when you consider that vegetables are so high in complex carbohydrates and fiber. Research at George Washington University School of Medicine found that even when overweight participants ate mostly vegetables, they tended to lose weight despite being allowed to eat as much food as they liked without restriction. Another study found that when a group of women followed a vegetable-based diet for just three months, each lost an average of 12 pounds.

➤ **Less gain with more grain.** Research shows that we'd all weigh less and be much healthier by having a few daily servings of whole grains, such as oatmeal, brown rice and whole-grain bread. One study found that people who regularly ate whole grains and consumed the most fiber were half as likely to gain weight as those who mainly ate refined grains, such as white rice and bread.

Whole grains are digested slowly, so you stay full longer after eating them. In addition, whole grains don't turn to sugar in your bloodstream as rapidly as refined carbs, so you'll avoid the insulin spikes that promote fat storage. One small study found that people who did nothing more than eat unprocessed oatmeal for breakfast were able to cut their daily snacking by 35%, compared with those who ate instant oatmeal. Think about that. This one small, seemingly insignificant change cut their snack intake by more than a third.

Whole grains are easy to cook in advance. My wife and I often cook a big pot of brown rice, quinoa or wheat berries at one time, then freeze them in serving-size containers. Frozen grains keep their original texture well and taste as good as fresh. Even if you forget to pull out a bag or two in the morning for that night's dinner, a frozen block of cooked grains can be heated quickly. I encourage you to experiment with a variety of whole grains, including quick-cooking quinoa and millet. Choose brown rice as a bed for a veggie stir-fry or as a hearty addition to a spinach salad. Cook whole barley, dress it with extra-virgin olive oil vinaigrette while it cools, then toss in some cold cucumber slices and chopped mint for a flavor-rich salad that will keep you satisfied all afternoon.

➤ **Snack well.** Losing weight doesn't mean you have to give up snacking. Quite the contrary. Snacking is *essential* for weight loss, because it helps to control your appetite between meals. People who go without food longer than two or three hours experience a sharp drop in metabolism. This makes it very difficult to lose weight because they invariably eat like horses the next time they have a meal. The key is to snack smart. It's the *quality* of the snacks that makes all the difference.

The ideal snack combines a complex carbohydrate food with a little protein. A good example is a small handful of walnuts with a piece of fresh fruit as a midmorning snack. The fruit releases glucose slowly and evenly because of its fiber content, so you won't get a sugar rush followed by a letdown. The protein in the walnuts digests even more slowly, so its effect on your appetite lasts longer. Because calories still count, a snack should contain no more than 150 calories, and you should limit yourself to two per day, equally spaced between meals.

Whatever you do, stay one step ahead of your hunger because, once your stomach starts growling, you're going to eat whatever's handy. Plan ahead and always carry some healthy snacks with you when you're away from home, like cut-up raw veggies. Dried fruit and nut mixes are good too, but they require a little discipline because they pack a lot of calories and are easy to overeat. Fruit is the original snack food. Eat it often throughout the day. Take a cup of plain organic yogurt with you to work, or a tin of omega 3–rich sardines and whole-grain crackers. Use the list of "My 10 Top 100-Calorie Snacks" on page 288 as a starting point and add your own smart snacks to it.

Stay away from sodas, fruit drinks and anything with sugar in it because they will just make you crave more sugary foods a short time later. Likewise, steer clear of granola bars and energy bars, which are just candy masquerading under a pseudo-healthful label. Other diet busters include yogurt-covered nuts or raisins, banana chips and so-called natural potato chips. Even innocent-looking pretzels act like sugar when they hit your bloodstream, because they're usually made with refined white flour. Did you know that just 18 Fat-Free Rold Gold Tiny Twists have 100 calories?

➤ **Always eat breakfast.** Too many overweight adults skip breakfast, and quite a few don't bother with lunch. People who don't eat breakfast think they'll lose weight, but the opposite often happens. They become so ravenous that when they finally do eat, they lose all control. Studies show that breakfast skippers eat more total calories by the end of the day than people who eat breakfast and snack wisely. Your metabolism is like an engine, and needs fuel in the morning to get it started. Not eating when you awaken is like starving your body and brain of fuel and nutrition it needs to operate. That first cup of coffee might feel like fuel, and the caffeine in it certainly provides a kick, but it won't last nearly as long as a nutritious breakfast with slow-burning calories. Besides, excess caffeine has a tendency to overwork your adrenal glands, resulting in long-term fatigue.

A 2008 study conducted at Virginia Commonwealth University shows that eating a big breakfast is one of the best ways

288

My 10 Top 100-Calorie Snacks

1. Two California sushi rolls
2. Two cups of fat-free popcorn
3. ½ whole-wheat pita with one tablespoon peanut butter (or two tablespoons hummus)
4. One tablespoon peanut butter with celery sticks
5. Organic yogurt, plain or flavored (6 ounces)
6. One hard-boiled egg
7. Ten almonds or walnuts
8. ¼ cup sunflower seeds
9. One small skim cafe latte or cappuccino
10. ½ cup of 1% reduced-fat cottage cheese (with cinnamon for extra control of blood sugar)

to lose weight and keep the pounds off over the long haul. Researchers took two groups of obese, physically inactive women in their thirties and fed one group a small, low-carb, 290-calorie breakfast consisting of a cup of milk, one egg, three slices of bacon and two teaspoons of butter. The other group ate a breakfast twice that size, including milk, turkey, cheese, two slices of bread, mayonnaise, an ounce of chocolate candy and a protein shake. Both groups stayed on the diet for four months to lose weight, then switched to maintenance mode for an equal amount of time.

At the end of the eight months, the researchers were stunned by the results. Even though the big-breakfast group initially ate more than 200 calories extra per day, they lost more weight than the group eating the smaller breakfast. After four months, the small-breakfast group had lost 28 pounds, while the big-breakfast women lost 23. By the end of the experiment, however, the small-breakfast group regained an average of 18 pounds, while the big-breakfast eaters continued to lose weight. In fact, they lost another 16.5 pounds on average. The women who ate the bigger breakfast lost more than 21% of their body weight, while the small-breakfast eaters lost only 4.5%.

"Those on the big-breakfast diet felt less hungry before lunch and all day," says Daniela Jakubowicz, MD, an endocrinologist and clinical professor at Virginia Commonwealth University in Richmond, who led the study.

These results should motivate you to eat a better breakfast every day. Sure, you're pressed for time in the morning, especially if you have a family to care for. Planning is your secret weapon. Make sure you get to bed early enough to allow for eight hours of sleep so you can wake up a little earlier to get things done. Waking up one hour earlier will allow you to enjoy a leisurely cup of green tea or coffee with breakfast as you reflect on the day ahead (see also page 299).

➤ **Egg yourself on.** The traditional American breakfast is making a comeback. For years people avoided eggs because of medical advice concerning cholesterol content. However, no study has ever proven the link between egg consumption and heart disease. Research shows that eggs are no more likely to raise cholesterol than any other food. In fact, eggs seem to be the perfect food, an ideal way to lose weight, because they are high in protein, nature's own appetite suppressant. One study found that overweight and obese women who started the day with an egg breakfast consumed 163 fewer calories at lunch than people who got the same number of breakfast calories from yogurt and a bagel with cream cheese. The hunger-satisfying effect of eggs didn't stop at lunch. By the end of the day, the egg eaters had consumed 418 fewer calories overall. They also consumed fewer calories at breakfast and lunch on the following day.

➤ **Fight fat with fish.** Seafood is an important source of protein in many parts of Asia and throughout the Mediterranean region. This is a major reason that people in these countries are healthier and longer-lived than Americans. It also explains why they're leaner. People who eat more fish naturally eat less calorie-rich red meat. An ounce of seafood has only about half as many calories as an ounce of beef, and only a third the calories of chicken. High-protein fish also fills you up and helps satisfy your appetite on fewer calories. Most of us would benefit from consuming more fish. Two to three weekly servings are ideal.

I don't recommend farm-raised fish, however, because it lacks many of the healthful compounds found in wild fish. For instance, farm-raised salmon lacks the amount of beneficial omega-3 fatty acids of wild salmon, and has many more omega-6 fatty acids and environmental toxins, all of which cause inflammation in the body. Small salt-water fish, including anchovies and sardines, are more reliable sources of omega-3s,

My Top 10 In-a-Hurry Breakfasts

1. **Oatmeal topped with nuts and fruit.** Prepare steel-cut or Irish oats in quantity over the weekend, so that daily portions are ready to be heated gently on weekday mornings. Add yogurt, skim or soy milk and top with your favorite fruit, chopped walnuts and a sprinkle of cinnamon. For a pumpkin-pie flavor, plus a big dose of antioxidants and fiber, mix a can of organic pumpkin into your weekly oatmeal preparation.

2. **Quickie burrito.** Scrambled egg with sliced onions and peppers, mashed black beans, a bit of your favorite cheese, spicy salsa all rolled up in a non-fat, whole-wheat tortilla. Grab it and go.

3. **Cottage cheese with fresh fruit.** Sprinkle one cup of 1% cottage cheese with cinnamon and top with chopped almonds, fresh fruit and ground flaxseed.

4. **Lox and bagel.** Toast half a whole-wheat, onion or garlic bagel, spread lightly with low-fat cream cheese or soft goat cheese, sprinkle on a few capers for a salty note and top with smoked wild salmon and tomato and onion slices. Squeeze a few drops of lemon juice on the fish if you like. Heavenly!

5. **Fresh berries and yogurt.** This is my all-time favorite. Fill a bowl with fresh, organic strawberries, blueberries and blackberries. Gently mix in ½ cup organic plain yogurt or vanilla soy yogurt, and top with 3 or 4 teaspoons ground flaxseed. Yum! This keeps me sated until lunch.

6. **Power smoothie.** Toss ½ cup fresh berries and any other fruit into a blender with 2 cups organic yogurt, soy milk, soft tofu and/or pomegranate juice. Add 1 tablespoon protein powder or spirulina, plus a few teaspoons of ground flaxseed.

7. **Hard-boiled eggs and cheese.** A European tradition. Keep a few peeled hard-boiled eggs in the fridge for mornings when you're really squeezed for time. Grab an egg, a chunk of hard artisanal cheese about the size of your thumb and an apple or banana and enjoy them on your way to work. The protein should keep you going until your midmorning snack.

8. **Whole-grain cereal.** If you rely on a packaged breakfast cereal, make sure it's truly made from whole grains, including bran, with no added sugars. Splash on some low-fat milk or soy milk and top with fruit. Sprinkle on a tablespoon of ground flaxseed to boost its fiber content.

9. **Muesli.** This is a terrific breakfast that you can prep the night before. Soak a bowl of dry muesli (available at your supermarket) in skim or soy milk in the fridge the night before. The grains and dried fruit in the muesli will soften and be ready to eat the next morning. All you'll need is a spoon.

10. **Turkey on whole grain.** Breakfast sandwiches can take many healthful shapes. Don't discount lean protein like turkey breast, layered onto whole-grain bread and topped with sliced tomato and avocado and a few leaves of romaine. Cut and enjoy the first half before you leave the house, and the rest on your way to work or for a midmorning snack.

especially if you broil them with a little olive oil, which also contains beneficial fats.

Studies show that overweight people who eat fish and other omega 3–rich foods reduce the level of inflammatory chemicals in their bloodstream. Don't cook fish (or anything) in oils made from corn, safflower, sunflower or canola. They're all high in omega-6 fatty acids, which counteract the good omega-3 fats in fish. These oils also oxidize quickly and become toxic. (To read more about "The Most Healthful Oils", see pages 190–94.)

Avoid shark, tuna, swordfish and tilefish because of probable mercury contamination.

➤ **Go green.** In much of Asia, people drink green tea with every meal, as well as in between meals. This may not be the main reason that most Asians are significantly slimmer than Americans, but it certainly helps. Recent studies show that green tea has *thermogenic* properties that rev up the body's metabolism and increase the number of calories it burns. In one study, researchers compared the effects of green tea extract, caffeine and a placebo. Only the people in the green-tea group had an increase in calorie expenditure. Two or more cups of green tea daily seem enough to achieve this measurable calorie-burn increase.

➤ **Don't nix the nuts.** For a long time, people trying to lose weight were advised to avoid nuts because they are high in fat and calories. This fear later turned out to be misdirected, because the fats in nuts are extremely healthful. Studies show that people who eat nuts tend to weigh less than people who don't. A study at City of Hope National

Medical Center, for example, compared two groups of people who were given a 1,000-calorie liquid diet. One group also ate three ounces of almonds while the other group ate a variety of complex carbohydrates. Even though the nut group consumed more fat, they lost 18% of their body weight over the six-month period, compared with the non-nut group, who lost only 11%.

➤ **Do dairy.** Low-fat dairy products are among the best sources of calcium, and calcium, it appears, can help you lose more weight. Multiple studies show that people who consume dairy foods and take in the most calcium—usually in the range of 1,300 mg to 1,400 mg daily—tend to weigh less than those who get less. The reasons for this aren't quite clear, although researchers have noted that fat cells containing a lot of calcium tend to burn more fat.

Other mechanisms may also be in play, according to Brazilian scientists studying calcium's role in weight loss. One explanation is the effect of calcium on hormones involved in fat accumulation. Another is that calcium binds with fats in the intestine, thus reducing reabsorption into the bloodstream. In one study, obese volunteers were assigned to one of two groups. The first group ate one daily serving of dairy, providing between 400 and 500 mg of calcium. The second group got about 1,100 mg of calcium daily from dairy products. People in both groups also trimmed their total calorie consumption by 500 calories per day. At the end of the study, the people in the higher-calcium group had lost an average of 14 pounds, compared with 11 pounds in the lower-calcium group.

To get this much calcium, treat yourself to three to four daily servings of low-fat milk, yogurt and cheese. Be sure to augment your diet with calcium from nondairy sources, such as leafy greens including kale and Swiss chard. If you don't enjoy dairy foods, focus on the greens and have a daily cup of calcium-fortified orange juice, in addition to taking a calcium and vitamin D supplement. For a list of the "Top 10 Calcium Foods," see page 271.

➤ **Stock up on ready-to-go protein.** You need protein to lose weight, so don't skimp. To make life easier, prepare a half-dozen hard-boiled eggs at a time and refrigerate, enjoying one each day for breakfast or lunch, alone or sliced onto whole-grain bread or into a salad. Cook a large package of skinless chicken breasts or thighs and separate into serving sizes. Later, you can use them cold or reheated in salads, bean dishes or on whole-grain bread with tomato and romaine.

Don't forget that tofu, low-fat milk and yogurt, as well as cheeses, are great protein sources, too, as are beans of all types. Canned beans are fine to use as long as the sodium content is minimal. Blend cooked, partially mashed beans with tomatoes, onions, fresh cilantro and garlic, wrapping the beans in a low-calorie corn or whole-wheat tortilla for a fast veggie burrito.

Use beans as a base for limitless salad variations. Toss beans in a bowl with raw chopped veggies of any kind, including green pepper, onion and celery, then dress with extra-virgin olive oil and aged balsamic vinegar. Add some sliced green olives or canned anchovies for a salty accent and/or

a can of whole or chunk tuna or salmon for extra protein.

➤ **Save time with frozen.** People in Asia and the Mediterranean eat far more vegetables than Americans, and they make time to enjoy shopping for and preparing fresh produce. If you're pressed for time, you can easily use frozen vegetables. The nutritional content can be very close to fresh. Just make sure you're not buying frozen vegetables with a lot of additives, such as fat, flavorings and salt.

➤ **Buy organic.** Studies show that organically grown produce contains more vitamins, minerals and phytonutrients than vegetables and fruits that were conventionally raised, which means organic food contains more healing power. In 2007, the largest study ever conducted of organic food was funded by the European Union. It discovered that organic vegetables and fruits possess up to 40% more disease-fighting antioxidants than their conventional equivalents. Earlier, a 1998 review of 34 studies confirmed that organic foods possess protein with fewer toxins, higher levels of vitamin C and greater mineral content.

Mineral levels are also dramatically higher. Organic food contained twice as much iron, for example. Another review of 41 studies found that organically grown produce contained 27% more vitamin C, 21% more iron, 29% more magnesium and 14% more phosphorus. The same meta-analysis also found that while five servings of organically grown vegetables provided the daily recommended intake of vitamin C, a major antioxidant, conventionally grown veggies did not.

What about the higher prices of organic food? When you take its nutritional superiority into consideration, organic food is actually a bargain compared with conventionally grown produce and animal products. You actually receive more nutrition per calorie and, thus, per serving. "By buying and consuming organic foods fairly consistently, consumers can easily double their daily intake of vitamins, minerals and antioxidants," explains Dr. Charles Benbrook, chief scientist at the Organic Center for Education and Promotion in Greenfield, Massachusetts. Some nutritionists report that you'd have to eat two to three times the amount of conventionally raised food to get the same nutrient value that organic food provides. That's certainly no way to lose weight.

Organic food is also healthier because it's free from pesticide and chemical residues, which have been shown to cause health problems such as abdominal pain, dizziness, headaches, nausea, vomiting, and eye disorders. Peer-reviewed research links pesticide exposure to severe medical conditions such as respiratory problems, memory disorders, dermatologic conditions, depression, neurological deficits, miscarriage and birth defects. It doesn't make sense to eat more of the healing fruits and vegetables discussed in this book if they contain toxins that can ultimately harm you.

➤ **Eat real food only.** If you read food labels, you'll notice a lot of ingredients not made by Mother Nature, such as hydrogenated oils, polysorbate and hydrolyzed vege-

table protein. The vast majority of processed foods, including soft drinks, snacks and frozen dinners, are jammed with sweeteners, excessive salt, artificial preservatives and other chemicals. In general, processed foods are the number-one source of ill health and overweight in our world today.

➤ **Bag it.** Another way to get both convenience and great taste is to stock up on cut vegetables and salad mixes offered today. Some of the salad mixes are fabulous, offering blends of arugula, romaine and butterhead lettuces. Washed and bagged organic baby spinach is a dream convenience food. (To assure food safety, be sure to wash again.) You can add the leaves to a bean salad, steam the entire contents to accompany chicken, stir-fry with garlic and sun-dried tomatoes for a tasty side dish, or just make a salad. While these packages are more expensive than bulk produce, the convenience is worth it for people on busy schedules.

➤ **More celery, less weight.** Celery is a curious vegetable. Even though it's mostly water, it's surprisingly high in essential nutrients. It's also an ideal snack food because it's very low in calories, high in fill-you-up fiber and quick to prepare. People who snack on celery generally report that they immediately feel less hungry. Other crunchy, watery foods, such as cucumber and watermelon, produce similar satiety effects.

➤ **Grapefruit is back.** Nutritionists once chuckled at proponents of the Grapefruit Diet who were convinced that this juicy citrus fruit contained the secret to long-lasting weight loss. As it turns out, the grapefruit lovers were right. In a 2006 study of obese adults conducted by researchers at Scripps Clinic, participants who ate half a grapefruit before each meal lost more weight than those in any of the other groups.

➤ **Slim down with cayenne.** Many of the spicy foods that are popular throughout Asia and the countries of the Mediterranean have thermogenic properties, meaning they can increase the rate your body burns calories. In a study at Quebec's Laval University, men who spiced up their daily diets with about a tablespoon of red pepper or other hot chilies had a significant increase in BMR, so their metabolism burned more calories while they were at rest. At the same time, the hot peppers acted as an appetite suppressant. In a 24-hour period, the pepper eaters consumed 883 fewer calories than men in a nonpepper group and the pepper eaters also burned an additional 77 calories without performing any additional physical activity.

Many spicy foods contain *capsaicin*, a fiery chemical compound that increases thermogenesis, even when you're doing nothing more strenuous than raising your fork. A study reported in *British Journal of Nutrition* found that men given food seasoned with a teaspoon of red pepper consumed about 18% fewer carbohydrates than men who ate unseasoned food.

➤ **Grab more garlic.** Like other spicy foods, garlic seems to increase the body's metabolic rate and make losing weight easier. When laboratory animals are given garlic or a garlic-based extract, they lose weight, or at least don't gain weight, compared with animals given their usual food. Scien-

294

tists aren't sure how garlic contributes to a healthy weight, but its active ingredients, including *allicin*, clearly increase metabolism. In addition, garlic's rich flavor makes it easy to eliminate higher-calorie ingredients, such as butter, without sacrificing flavor.

Foods That Make It Worse

Gaining or losing weight is mostly about calories. The reason it's so easy to overeat sugary carbs, fats and processed foods is because they pack a lot of calories into a small portion. By the time your stomach is filled and your brain receives the "I'm full" signal, you might easily have consumed a bag of chips, a large soda and perhaps a hot dog, which is the equivalent of 1,000 calories. That's half the calories the average person needs for the day. In addition, because there's almost no fiber in a meal like that, you're guaranteed of being hungry in a short time. You can't lose weight, or stay healthy, eating like that. It's a sure formula for weight gain, and perhaps diabetes or heart disease, as well.

The easiest way to lose weight is to base your diet on foods that are low in calories and high in volume. These foods take up more space in your stomach, so you can eat your fill and satisfy your hunger without calorie overload. Vegetables are at the top of this list, followed by whole grains, fruits, nuts, fish and poultry. Cut out as many processed foods and refined carbohydrates as possible (the more you refrain from eating them, the faster you'll lose weight).

Finally, regular physical activity will accelerate your weight loss Yes, it's really that easy. Shoot for losing two pounds per week and you can easily weigh 20 to 30 pounds less in six months. Stay away for the weight-loss saboteurs listed below and your progress will be steady and strong.

➤ **Trans fats.** Even though these synthetic, hydrogenated fats don't contain any more calories than olive oil, they cause your body to churn out inflammatory substances called *eicosanoids* that make it harder to burn stored fat. Trans fats should never be eaten. Aside from their harmful cardiovascular effects, they add to your calorie load. A surprising number of processed foods still contain them, as do most fast foods. When shopping, read food labels carefully. Any time you spot the word *hydrogenated*, you should put that food back on the shelf. It's just another way of saying trans fat. Most of the margarine sold in the US contains trans fat.

Don't be fooled by labels that say trans-fat free, because manufacturers are allowed to make this claim when their products contain .5 g or less of trans fat per serving. No amount of trans fat is safe. Any amount is a health danger because trans fats accumulate in the body, particularly in the arteries, and are not broken down the way normal fats are.

➤ **Added sugar.** Sugar is bad news for anyone who values good health and wants to control their weight. Unfortunately, our taste buds love sweetness because that's where the calories are. Our bodies are programmed to zero in on calories—we evolved that way to avoid starvation. Today, food manufacturers add sugar to just about everything, even to foods that are naturally sweet. Believe it or not, the average American eats 175 pounds of sugar annually, the equivalent of one cup per day. That doesn't include the amount of hidden sugar added to processed foods. This is beyond excessive.

So much sugar wreaks havoc on our metabolism, triggering massive insulin spikes that contribute to type 2 diabetes, heart disease, cancer and other inflammation-driven medical conditions. There is no way that the human body can deal with this amount of glucose. The sudden spike in insulin, the hormone whose job it is to remove all this glucose from the bloodstream, triggers a roller-coaster effect on your energy levels and hunger. Studies show that consuming sugary foods and refined carbohydrates on a regular basis leads to carbohydrate cravings and constant hunger. Overeating is the natural result, leading to weight gain and eventual obesity, both of which are linked directly to a number of serious degenerative diseases. It is a downward spiral that leads to an early grave. I urge you to break this vicious cycle while you still can.

Sugar, once the favored sweetener of food manufacturers, has now largely been replaced by high-fructose corn syrup (HFCS), a substance that makes gaining weight even easier. Research shows that your body metabolizes HFCS differently than sugar. It is actually converted into fat more quickly. Furthermore, studies show that HFCS doesn't satisfy hunger, so these calories don't count against satiety (the feeling that you are getting full). Thus, your body doesn't recognize the calories represented by HFCS, so you naturally eat more. HFCS has been banned in Europe.

Because it is so much cheaper than sugar, HFCS is now present in practically all processed foods, including breakfast cereals, pastries and puddings, and fruit juices. It's also added to many low-fat and fat-free foods, to compensate for the lack of flavor that results when the fat is removed. Start reading food labels carefully and you'll be surprised by the number of foods listing it as a major ingredient. Soft drinks are, by far, the worst offender. They are the number-one source of calories in the American diet. The statistics are shocking. Drinking soda increases your risk of obesity by 60%. Joseph Mercola, D.O.—osteopathic physician, health activist and Internet advocate for alternative health solutions—and other researchers have discovered that people who drink multiple soft drinks daily gain several additional pounds a year, even if the rest of their diet stays the same. Studies show that giving up one soft drink per day results in the loss of one pound of body weight per week, even if you do nothing else. Reporting in the British medical journal *The Lancet*, a team of Harvard researchers irrefutably linked soft drink consumption to childhood obesity, so please don't provide this stuff to your kids or grandchildren.

Although research shows that sweetened processed foods make people fat, manufacturers would rather we didn't know this. So, even though laws require that ingredients be listed in order of their greatest concentration to lesser concentration on all food labels, manufacturers have developed

code names for sweeteners such as *maltose* and others. This way, consumers don't realize that one of the main ingredients is actually a sweetener. Your best defense is to be suspicious of any processed food and trust your instincts. If a processed food comes in a brightly colored box or bag, chances are it contains added sweeteners and other empty calories, even if its label claims it is a healthy food. Stick to foods in their natural form to be safe and slim.

➤ **Sugar substitutes.** Artificial sweeteners are no better. They also confuse your body's innate ability to know when it's full. So, consuming fake sugar in any form can increase the amount of calories you take in. The consumption of artificially sweetened drinks and foods has increased dramatically in the last 25 years, and obesity has increased right along with it. In addition to weight gain, some clinical research has linked artificial sweeteners with migraines, seizures, depression, fatigue, hearing loss, tinnitus and memory loss, not to mention anxiety and panic attacks.

One of the most widely used artificial sweeteners, *aspartame,* is found in more than 5,000 diet foods, soft drinks, tabletop sweeteners, chewing gum, breakfast cereals, jams and jellies and even vitamins and over-the-counter medications. Sold commercially under brands such as NutraSweet and Canderel, more than two-thirds of the adult population and 40% of children regularly consume aspartame in one form or another. Since it contains no calories, aspartame is considered a boon to weight-conscious people, and believed to be safe because it has been FDA approved. However, independent research done by Dr. Mercola shows that aspartame can produce a range of adverse effects in humans, including headaches, memory loss, mood swings, seizures, multiple sclerosis and Parkinson's-like symptoms, tumors and even death.

Splenda (*sucralose*) may not be any better. As of 2006, only six human trials have been conducted on this artificial sweetener. Of these, only two studies, involving a total of 36 human subjects, were completed and published before sucralose was approved by the FDA for human consumption, according to Dr. Mercola. It's clear who the real guinea pig is here.

If you must have a sweetener and you want to avoid the extra calories, I recommend you try *stevia*, a supersweet herb from South America that has been used as a natural sweetener for more than 1,500 years. While it is 600 times sweeter than cane sugar, stevia contains zero calories and is completely safe. If you have diabetes or other blood sugar issues, you should limit your use of all sweeteners, including stevia, because it can decrease your blood sensitivity to insulin, says Dr. Mercola.

➤ **Large portions.** True or false—The original bottle of Coke contained 6.5 ounces and today's plastic version contains 20 ounces. The answer is *true*, but the real question is whether you think the larger bottle is a single serving or the two-and-a-half servings it actually is. I recommend you never consume soft drinks, which are mainly HFCS, food coloring and tap water. Any form of excess sugar is devastating to your health, not to mention your waistline. Consider that, in the last 30 years, purveyors of snack foods and restaurant meals figured out they could boost revenues and draw in extra customers by offering far larger portions of food for just a little extra money. Don't be fooled by giant bags of chips, super bottles of sugar-water or huge restaurant meals. Avoid the first two, and if you have trouble putting down your fork when eating out, ask for half your meal to be placed in a take-home box before you take your first bite.

➤ **Fast food.** Researchers at Harvard discovered that eating fast food more than a couple times per week pushes up the risk of obesity by 50% in young adults. It's no surprise that a University of Minnesota study of nearly 900 women found that frequent fast-food eaters consumed more calories and gained more weight than those who didn't eat fast food as often. When researchers at Children's Hospital in Boston tracked more than 500 schoolchildren for two years, they discovered that this incidence of obesity spiked an astonishing 60% for every serving of sugary drinks consumed per day. The Mediterr-Asian way of eating contains no fast food, but the recipes are fast and easy to prepare. In addition to helping you heal a specific medical condition, each recipe fits neatly into any weight-loss program.

Supplemental Help

Until recently, most health experts believed that weight-loss supplements were akin to snake oil, but that thinking is beginning to change. Some supplements actually *can* make a difference.

➤ **Fiber in a pill.** The dietary fiber that's present in all plant foods is one of nature's most powerful weight-control helpers. It's ideal to get your fiber from natural sources because it's accompanied by a host of healing nutrients and protective phytochemicals. However, fiber supplements can provide extra insurance during times when your diet falls short. For weight loss, choose water-soluble fiber products such as *glucomannan*, seaweed fibers such as *alginate* and *carrageenan* and/or *psyllium seed*. Studies show that people who use fiber supplements tend to have lower glucose and insulin. In addition, water-soluble fiber dissolves and forms a gel in your stomach and intestines, reducing appetite and also inhibiting the absorption of extra calories. Using a fiber supplement can help you cut 180 calories from your daily diet without increasing your hunger. This alone can result in significant weight loss over the course of a year.

➤ **Increase your energy with CoQ10.** A clinical study of obese people found that they lost more weight when they took coenzyme Q10 (CoQ10). I routinely recommend this supplement for heart health because it increases cellular energy, which is also ideal for burning more calories. Take 100 mg, twice daily.

➤ **Combine it with L-carnitine.** This amino acid helps CoQ10 work more efficiently. *L-carnitine* causes the *mitochondria* (the tiny "engines" inside your cells) to convert the food you eat into energy more efficiently and helps to shuttle out the toxic by-products of metabolism as well. Take 500 mg two or three times per day.

➤ **More magnesium.** Many obese people are deficient in magnesium. Research has found that this mineral works synergistically both with CoQ10 and L-carnitine for more energy. Take 200 mg twice a day for weight loss.

➤ **Crank up the calcium.** Studies show that calcium in dairy products and other food sources helps promote weight loss. Food is the best way to get calcium, but supplements can also make a difference. Data collected from the National Health and Nutrition Examination Surveys consistently show that calcium and body weight are closely linked. Researchers have learned, for example, that people who get the least amount of calcium are up to six times more likely to be overweight than those who get the most. High doses of calcium aren't necessary to induce this fat-burning effect. For most people, between 1,000 mg and 1,500 mg per day is sufficient. Your body can't absorb a lot of calcium at once, so take a 500-mg supplement once in the morning and again in the afternoon. Men should limit their total calcium to 1,000 mg a day because higher amounts can increase the risk of prostate problems. Women past menopause should get 1,500 mg daily.

Other Helpers and Healers

When you start on a food regimen to lose weight, you'll need to do more than eat the right foods. You'll need to change certain ingrained patterns of behavior, too. Here's

298

Habits of Overweight Kids

A fascinating survey published by *Consumer Reports* showed that children who are overweight have eating habits different from their normal-weight friends. *Overweight children, on average…*

➤ **Drink three or more sugar-containing drinks daily and have fast food,** carry-out food and frozen or packaged dinners several times weekly.

➤ **Are more likely to eat breakfast and lunch at school** and have dinner somewhere other than home.

➤ **Eat fewer than four servings of vegetables daily.**

➤ **Spend less time being active in sports,** play or other exercise-related activities and more time in front of video games.

➤ **Are more likely than their normal-weight counterparts** to ask their parents to go to restaurants seen on television and to purchase foods advertised there.

➤ **Are more likely to have parents who have weight problems themselves.**

If any of this sounds familiar, consider a gradual shift to the Mediterr-Asian way of eating described in this book. It represents an enormous first step in offsetting poor eating habits. Then, just add exercise.

some food for thought on how to support the hard work you're doing to eat right and lose weight.

REVISE LIFESTYLE AND EATING HABITS

➤ **Regain control of your life.** Very few of us gain weight consciously; mostly, it occurs when we lose control of our hunger, our time, our impulses and our schedule. So, the first step in losing weight is to regain control of all these things. If you are deprived of "me" time, try to wake an hour earlier every day. You can use this time to meditate, stretch or do a little yoga. It's up to you.

People often complain that losing weight is too hard, requires too much willpower and demands too many sacrifices. This is only true if you relinquish control over the fattening factors that a little wise planning can easily conquer. As I tell my patients, brainpower beats willpower every time.

➤ **Shop smart.** "If you don't buy it, you can't eat it." One of the smartest strategies for losing weight is to stop buying foods that pack on extra pounds. If you don't have it on hand, you won't have to fight temptation or sabotage your weight-loss goals. Never go to the supermarket hungry—that's when you're at your weakest. Eat a good meal first and have a shopping list to refer to. That way you'll avoid impulse purchases, which are usually fattening foods.

➤ **Don't eat late.** Your metabolism slows when you sleep, burning 10% to 15% fewer calories at night, making the calories in any late-night meal or snack likely to be stored as fat rather than burned as energy. A small after-dinner snack is fine. Choose plain air-popped popcorn, a handful of nuts or a small square or two of dark chocolate. Fresh fruit with yogurt is also good because the calcium in it will help you sleep better. Just remember that the earlier in the evening you eat, the more of those calories will be burned before bedtime.

➤ **Eat more meals to lose more weight.** Sounds crazy, doesn't it? But studies show that people who eat more frequently lose more weight and keep the weight off longer. The traditional three squares a day is almost a sure-fire guarantee of weight gain. Keep in mind that your metabolism can only process about 600 calories at a time, unless you are an extremely active athlete. Any calories in excess of 600 will be stored as fat for later use. However, when you eat three major meals a day, later never comes and the body fat keeps accumulating. Eating smaller, more frequent meals is known as *grazing*—and studies have shown that grazers tend to gain less weight, and lose more, than three-meal-a-day eaters. These people also tend to have healthier blood sugar levels and are less likely to experience food cravings. Give it a try and see if it works for you.

➤ **Graze only when you're hungry.** We all eat for reasons that have nothing to do with appetite, often when we're depressed or bored or busy working or watching television. Emotional or mindless eating can add up to a lot of extra calories every day. On the other hand, if you can harness the urge by snacking on raw vegetables and fruits, by all means do so. Just make sure you're actually hungry. If you're not, redirect your energies by taking a brisk walk around the block or stretching your body.

➤ **When you eat, just eat.** Don't watch television, drive, sit at your computer or do a crossword puzzle while you eat. Much of our eating today is mindless and unconscious, so we take in calories that we're hardly aware we 300

are eating. And never eat standing up. If you discipline yourself to always eat sitting down, you'll cut out the bulk of unconscious snacking that gets us into trouble. Try it.

➤ **Fill your plate halfway.** Nearly everyone overestimates their appetite. People tend to load their plates with what they think they want, even if it's too much food. Try serving yourself half of what you think you'll eat from now on. You can always help yourself to seconds if you're really hungry. Don't hurry eating. Give your stomach and brain time to decide if you really want more. Taking small servings initially is also helpful because, over time, it produces neurochemical brain changes that actually reduce appetite. Studies prove it!

➤ **Use smaller plates.** It might sound silly, but it works. Researchers at Cornell University threw an ice-cream party for members of the nutrition department, with guests randomly receiving a large bowl or a small one, and a large spoon or a small one. Those who used larger bowls ate 30% more than the small-bowl folks, though in a survey they reported being unaware of eating more. Spoon size mattered, too. Those with larger spoons took in 15% more ice cream than the small-spoon guests, even the large-spoon, small-bowl guests! People using a large spoon and a large bowl ate a staggering 57% more than the small-bowl, small-spoon group. This goes to show that sizing down your eating utensils can help prevent you from sabotaging your weight-loss efforts.

➤ **Chew.** If you're going to pay a premium for nutritionally superior organic food, here's a tip for extracting even more healing power from it—*chew.* A 2009 study from Purdue University demonstrated that giving each mouthful a few extra chews releases more healing nutrients into your bloodstream for your body's repair and regeneration. It's like driving more slowly to make a gallon of gasoline take you farther. Why speed through mealtime? Eating quickly is like throwing a portion of your food down the garbage disposal. Research shows that chewing your food thoroughly brings you greater satiety from less food. Since it takes about 10 to 15 minutes for your brain to receive the "I'm full" signal from your stomach, speedy eating is a major factor in weight gain. A few extra chews with each mouthful means you'll feel satisfied by a smaller portion. You'll lose weight without dieting or feeling deprived, and the extra time will allow you to enjoy yourself and those you're dining with.

Better-quality food naturally tastes better, especially when it's artfully prepared. Why not take a little extra time to really savor the flavor? Chewing slowly allows you to do this but, even before the food reaches your mouth, engage your other senses. Appreciate the colors of the food. Enjoy the aromas. Notice the textures as you bite and chew. Pause often and put your fork down occasionally, not out of discipline, but because you want the flavors to linger.

Research shows that diners eat less food when meals provide more pleasure. That's the secret behind the best-selling book *French Women Don't Get Fat* by Mireille Guiliano. Even though the French eat bread, cheese and pate, drink wine and regularly enjoy three-course meals, they manage to stay slim, live longer and suffer less often from heart disease than people in many other countries. The key to this French paradox is that they eat for pleasure. This way, a little food, even if it has a high-calorie price tag, can go a long way. Gastronomical pleasure is high on their *joie de vivre* list. I urge you to upgrade its place on your list, too.

LEARN TO LOVE TO MOVE

➤ **Burn off stress calories.** In Asian, Mediterranean and other European countries, daily exercise is part of life. People may not do as much formal exercise as do Americans, but they're often walking, riding bikes or working in gardens. This is good for calorie control, and it's just as good for stress relief. Physical activity—whether it's walking, doing *tai chi* or yoga or raking leaves—burns off excess cortisol, the stress hormone. Less stress means less emotional eating and a lot more enjoyment of the world around you. Remember the stressed nurses with larger waists whom we discussed earlier? Their bodies were churning out lots of stress hormones, which led to weight gain, especially around the middle. Taking control of your stress, just like taking control of your time, will make losing weight much easier.

➤ **Lace up your walking shoes.** Fitness fanatics of the 1980s considered walking an activity for older people. Doctors were the only ones who recommended it, and then usually only to people with bum knees or creaky hips. Walking wasn't generally considered real exercise until scientists started looking at it more closely. That research showed that walking may be the single most effective form of exercise of them all. Hold on to your hat here. Did you realize that walking burns an average of 100 calories per mile, and if you walk for an hour most days of the week, you'll lose about four pounds a month even if you never change your diet? All true. Walking also promotes steady weight loss, builds bone, improves cardiovascular conditioning and reduces the risk of diabetes. In addition, a daily hour of walking will add about five years to your life. Because it doesn't stress your joints or heart, it's something you can do for a lifetime.

➤ **The easiest calorie burner ever.** You don't need lessons or specialized gear to walk and you certainly don't need to be in great shape to start. The very simplicity of walking may have worked against its reputation as a fitness and weight-loss method, making it seem too easy to be effective. A study at Texas Woman's University found that people who walked at a moderate pace three miles per day (about 6,000 steps) for five days per week received the same cardiovascular benefits as joggers did. Even though it sounds counterintuitive, brisk walking actually burns *more* calories than jogging. Start walking today, and you'll start losing weight almost immediately. In addition, like compound interest at the bank, the results will multiply the longer you do it. That's because physical activity not only burns calories from the moment you start, it also builds muscle and keeps your metabolism revved up, so your body continues to burn calories while you're sleeping or reading a book.

➤ **Walking also builds muscle.** And you want that, because muscle burns 200 times more calories than body fat. I'm not suggesting you go for the muscle-bound bodybuilder look. Far from it. I don't believe in hard-core workouts for nonathletes because I've seen too many people hurt themselves. The truth is people in average shape who exercise too hard are at risk for joint damage, stroke and heart attack. Mild exercise, on the other hand, has none of these risks. Going for a walk, even if you start slowly, promotes lower blood pressure, better circulation and healthier blood lipid profiles. Walking also makes your body's cells more responsive to insulin and improves their ability to remove glucose from the blood. It also lowers blood sugar by burning more glucose for fuel. Best of all, it promotes weight loss, especially belly fat, which drives down your risk for diabetes and its complications even further. The landmark Diabetes Prevention Program study found that walking daily for 30 minutes at a moderate pace, along with the simple diet changes I've outlined here, reduces your risk for contracting diabetes by 58%. If you already have diabetes, walking will slow the progression of the disease and lower your chances of complications such as blindness or amputation.

➤ **You don't have to eat less.** Walking combined with the Mediterr-Asian Diet makes losing weight very easy, even if you have a lot of weight to drop. To lose one pound per week, you need a deficit of 500 daily calories (double that if you want to lose two pounds per week). The most painless way to achieve this deficit is to consume fewer calories every day and burn off a little extra. That doesn't mean you don't have to eat less, just smarter. Hold off on full-fat cheeses. Go easy on salad dressings and high-fat condiments. Substitute seltzer plus a little 100% juice for soft drinks. Eating just a little smarter can easily shave 500 calories a day. If you go for a walk at lunchtime or after dinner, you'll achieve your 1,000 calorie savings for the day. Once you see how easy this is, you'll find yourself making these smart shifts throughout your day. You'll cut calories from your daily diet and never miss them. Here's the best part—once you start seeing the results on the scale, in your mirror and in how your clothes fit, you'll be encouraged to lose even more. There's no better motivation than success. Once you actually experience how this strategy delivers results, there will be no stopping you!

➤ **10,000 steps to no-sweat weight loss.** Most of us will never be world-class athletes, or desire to be. We just want to slim down a bit, get our hearts pumping, feel stronger and give our energy level a boost. Walking accomplishes all of that and more, without a huge time commitment. In fact, studies show that all you need to do is take at least 10,000 steps a day to achieve a level of physical activity that will shed pounds and improve your health. That's it. No heart monitors, gym memberships or trendy outfits required (though I do recommend a good pair of shoes). Taking 10,000 steps every day can burn 250 to 500 calories each day. This means that you'll easily lose 10% of your body weight, and that's enough to

take most folks out of the danger zone when it comes to their health. A recent study by Johns Hopkins Medical School confirms that being overweight is a bigger risk factor for cardiovascular disease than being unfit. And losing weight, the doctors concluded, is more important than getting fit when it comes to avoiding a heart attack.

Now, 10,000 steps may sound like a lot, but it's not. Couch potatoes take about 3,000 steps a day. With a little effort, you can easily walk circles around them. Based on a two-and-a-half-foot stride, 10,000 steps will carry you approximately 4.5 miles. So, if you already take 3,000 steps, that leaves a mere 3.5 miles to go. A brisk one-hour walk will take you all the way there, but you don't have to meet this total in a single outing. By adding a few extra steps here and there during the day, you can easily meet your goal. When you walk and change your diet at the same time, not only will you stop gaining weight, you can easily drop two pounds or more a week. That means you'll be eight pounds lighter in a month and shed 24 pounds in three months.

➤ **Count steps, lose pounds.** The 10,000-step approach is equivalent to the amount of daily activity recommended by the surgeon general to reduce the size of your waistline and your risk of serious disease. How can you tell if you're taking 10,000 steps a day? The easiest way is to purchase a pedometer and clip it onto your belt or shoe. This device counts each step you take during the day and gives you the total whenever you want to know. You can launch into a calorie-burning walking program without any gadgetry at all, but pedometers are a great way to know where you're starting and how much farther you need to go. Once your pedometer is up and running (the instructions tell you how to adjust it to your usual walking stride), you can start counting steps and deciding how far and how fast you want to go. Remember, you don't have to take all your steps at one time. You're already walking through much of your day, and those steps count toward the total.

Most people clip on their pedometer first thing in the morning so that it records every step of the day. You'll start adding steps as you go about your usual business, whether it's ambling out to the mailbox, going up and down stairs, shopping at the mall or walking the dog. Research shows it's your total amount of daily activity that makes the difference. The pounds will drop away whether you take your steps all at once or incrementally throughout the day.

If you've been relatively sedentary, you already take about 3,000 steps a day, and you might not want to jump to 10,000 immediately. Take it gradually. When you begin, allow time for your muscles and cardiovascular system to get into shape, though this transition happens more quickly than you might expect. Increase your daily step count gradually by leapfrogging your goals. For example, shoot for 5,000 daily steps and when this total becomes easy, increase it. Keep it up until you hit 10,000 steps. At that point, you can continue to add more steps or shift your strategy, walking faster to get your heart and lungs pumping. That's when the pounds really start melting away. *Here are some other helpful tips...*

- **Establish your baseline.** Put on your pedometer first thing in the morning, wear it all day, then record how many steps you're currently taking before bedtime. Do this for about a week, going about your normal routine and recording each day's total. Add the numbers and divide by the number of days to get your baseline.
- **Power up by 10%.** Once you've established your baseline, boost your average daily steps by 10%. If your baseline was 4,000 steps per day, increase it consistently by 400 steps daily. Remember, you don't have to do it all at once. Take one extra turn around the block or find an excuse to go up and down the stairs once or twice. Park farther away from the mall. Walk to lunch. Remember, every step literally counts, and steps, like calories, add up quickly. Stay at your baseline plus 10% for a few days or a few weeks, whichever you're more comfortable with. When you're ready, kick it up another 10%. You might find walking to a store for the newspaper adds 800 steps and walking to the bus 500. Walking your dog might add another 1,000.
- **Log it in.** At the end of each day, jot down how many steps you took in your walking diary. You don't have to keep this log forever, but it's a good way to get a sense of what activities add significant steps to your daily total. Another idea is to record the number of steps it takes to reach specific destinations. If it takes 1,200 steps to walk to the park and circle it once, for example, that's a big chunk of steps you can always count on to help fill out your daily total. At the end of the week,

calculate an average for the number of steps you took each day.

- **Check it out.** Get in the habit of checking your pedometer a few times a day to see how you're progressing. If the day's half done and you haven't come close to your halfway step point, you'll need to get your feet moving. Try not to fall short of your daily goal. Find extra reasons to walk more, even if that means spending more time standing up and moving your feet instead of sitting. For instance, when you're talking on the phone, stand up and walk around. You'll be amazed how the steps add up during a brief conversation. You might find yourself thinking, "I just had a 220-step chat."

- **Kick it up a notch.** Every kind of walk, even a slow stroll, will burn calories and boost cardiovascular fitness. However, you'll burn more calories if you go a little faster. Let's say you start walking at a brisk clip of five miles an hour. Your diet stays the same, and you do all your serious walking in a single 45-minute stretch. Just walking like this four days a week for a year (with no diet changes at all) will knock 18 pounds off your frame. I'd say that qualifies as serious success.

- **Make sure it feels good.** As you move forward with the walking program, you'll actually notice that your heart and lungs are in much better shape. You'll definitely be leaner and your clothes will fit better. Plus, your muscles will be primed for more and faster walking. Congratulations! You're gaining more personal power and control over your schedule, your weight, your health, and your life. If you're logging a lot of daily steps and it feels

better than sitting on your rump, it means that physical activity is becoming a habit.

By staying with the walking plan, you're guaranteed to be stronger and fitter. Some people find sticking with any exercise tedious. The secret to long-term success is to build variation into your routine so that it doesn't become boring or a chore.

- **Up the challenge.** Turn your walks into workouts by adding variety. Try walking with lightweight dumbbells, pumping your arms so you get an upper-body workout in the process. You can buy a vest at sporting goods stores that has pockets for inserting small weights. This will help you burn even more calories because you're increasing the resistance. Perhaps you'll simply walk to the grocery and tote your food home. Take two bags so you're well balanced, and don't try to carry too much at once.

- **Stretch it out.** Incorporate a few minutes of stretching in your routine. About five minutes into a walk, for example, slowly lean down and grip your ankle, keeping your knees together. Or take a big step forward with one leg, bend the knee, and stretch until your thigh is parallel to the ground. Stretching after you've warmed up with a short walk is a great way to stay limber and prevent injuries. Besides, the extra exertion burns extra calories.

- **Hit the hills. To keep your interest,** look for more challenging places to walk. Set your sights on steep streets, mountain trails or multiple flights of stairs.

- **Grab your iPod.** Listen to your favorite music while walking, be it golden oldies or Vivaldi. Or maybe you'll want to download a book. Some walkers love to listen to inspirational lectures, while others prefer guided moving meditations, poetry or prayers.

• **Raise the bar.** If you walk 10,000 steps most days of the week, you may want to set aside an extreme day when you go for 12,000 or 14,000 steps. Your metabolism will buzz like a hummingbird's. Weight falls off more quickly when exercise intensity increases.

• **Push your speed.** Pretend you're late for an appointment and walk at that pace for a few minutes, then slow that down to your normal pace. Athletes call this *interval training* and it really builds stamina quickly. Doing this will cause your heart to beat at between 65% and 85% of its maximum rate. This target zone is the point at which your body is burning calories at its most efficient rate.

• **Join the crowd.** It can get lonely out there by yourself, and sometimes it's more fun to walk with a buddy or a group. Look for 5K or 10K walk/run events or charity walks. You'll meet other people who share your weight loss and fitness goals. You might even connect with a regular walking partner.

• **Pull in your abs.** As you walk, contract your abdominal muscles for four to 10 seconds, or until the muscles get fatigued. Relax and walk normally for a few minutes before repeating the contractions. This will build core strength and tone your midsection muscles. You're on your way to six-pack abs.

➤ **Weigh yourself daily.** Step on the scale every day and lose more weight? Studies show it really works to help you lose weight and keep it off. Scientists at Brown University tracked a group of people for 18 months and discovered that those who weighed themselves regularly made better food choices. The scale steppers were also less likely to gain back weight already lost and were less likely to binge. A University of Minnesota study confirms this effect. Researchers followed a group trying to prevent weight gain and another trying to lose weight. People in each group who weighed themselves regularly had the greatest weight loss and the smallest weight gain.

➤ **Focus on your progress.** During the first few months, the pounds may seem to drop off by magic, but one day you may find that the scale hardly budges and you could swear it's broken. Don't be discouraged. This is called a *plateau*, a time to remind yourself of how far you've come. Congratulate yourself for each small victory you've achieved, even if you only lost a quarter or a half pound that week. Those small amounts add up, and if you keep walking, it's unlikely the weight you've lost will ever come back. ∎

20

Prostate Problems

ost men don't think much about their prostate gland until they start to feel symptoms of an enlarged prostate, which can make the bathroom the most frequently visited room in the house. Enlarged prostate, also called *benign prostatic hyperplasia* (BPH), is the most common health problem affecting men over 50. In fact, half of men in their sixties are pestered by symptoms.

The prostate is the gland that produces the fluid that delivers sperm during ejaculation. Normally about the size of a walnut, the prostate wraps around the urethra, the tube that drains urine from the bladder. It's easy to quickly see why urinary changes are a hallmark of BPH. An enlarged prostate can squeeze the urethra and compromise the muscles that control urine flow.

There's no known link between BPH and prostate cancer, but nearly every man who lives long enough will have some prostate cancer cells in his lifetime. Generally, prostate cancer takes decades to reach the point where it causes discernible symptoms, and while up to 50% of all US males over 70 have prostate cancer to some degree, most die *with* it, not from it. Prostate cancer generally grows very slowly—so slowly, in fact, that older men who have it are often advised to leave it alone, since it's unlikely to progress quickly enough to affect health in any meaningful way. However, prostate cancer is still one of the most common male cancers and kills 29,000 men every year.

SYMPTOMS

Symptoms of BPH occur when the enlarged gland squeezes your urethra, leading to multiple bathroom visits day and night. Like a stepped-on garden hose, BPH can also significantly weaken urine flow, make it difficult to start urinating, cause an interrupted stream or incomplete emptying of the bladder, create an urgent need to urinate and result in dribbling at the end of urination. In a few men who have serious urine retention, complications can cause urinary tract infection, kidney problems, bladder damage and bladder stones.

BPH isn't life threatening, but it can slow you down and damage health by interrupting the REM sleep cycle during which the body repairs and regenerates itself. Symptoms usually get worse with age, but not all men with an enlarged prostate have symptoms that bother them enough to see their doctors. Even though about 90% of men in their seventies and eighties have an enlarged prostate, each man's symptoms are more closely related to how the enlargement is affecting his urethra and thus his urine flow. Some with enlarged prostates have few symptoms, while others with just a little enlargement in the right location have many.

Unlike BPH, prostate cancer doesn't announce itself with early symptoms. It's not until a cancerous tumor triggers swelling of the prostate or the malignancy spreads outside the prostate that symptoms become noticeable. When they do, they can include some of the same symptoms as BPH. In addition, blood in your semen or urine, or experiencing pain during ejaculation or urination may be a signal of cancer and should send you to your doctor.

308

CAUSES

Scientists aren't certain what causes BPH, but hormones are high on the list of suspects, and there are two schools of thought. Some doctors believe that aging prostate glands become more sensitive to circulating levels of free testosterone, prompting the gland to enlarge. Others think that the age-related change in the ratio of testosterone to the hormone estrogen encourages the prostate to enlarge, just as it does in breast cancer and other estrogen-driven cancers. I favor this theory, since testosterone levels tend to fall as a man ages.

The specific causes of prostate cancer are also unknown. In addition to hormone levels, risk factors include ethnicity, DNA/family history of prostate cancer and diet. Obesity also increases your risk, possibly because fat pumps up the production of estrogen, which can spur development of cancer cells in the prostate gland.

TREATMENT

If you're having symptoms of BPH, talk to your doctor. Current medical treatments try to reestablish normal urinary function. How you approach that goal is closely related to the extent of your symptoms. Certain drugs can relieve symptoms for about two-thirds of men, either by shrinking the prostate itself or by causing the muscles that ring the neck of the bladder to relax and thus improve urinary flow. All drugs come with side effects, however.

Medical procedures include using radio waves, microwaves, lasers to reduce prostate size or surgery called TURP (transurethral resection of the prostate) to remove part of the prostate and open the urinary channel. Nonsurgical approaches aim to reduce the size of the prostate gland or eliminate the part that's pressing on the urethra. A very new treatment, not yet FDA-approved, injects Botox into the prostate, shrinking a portion of the gland in order to alleviate symptoms.

All men 50 and over should be screened for prostate cancer annually. African-American men and those with a family history of cancer should ask their doctor for advice on being checked earlier and more frequently.

Screening consists of two tests. One check is a blood test that looks for levels of prostate-specific antigen (PSA), a marker for prostate abnormalities. However, an elevated PSA reading can also signal BPH or an infection called *prostatitis*, so PSA results are not definitive for prostate cancer. Doctors look for a sudden rise in PSA to tip them off to the possibility of cancer. In this case, a biopsy is usually proposed.

The digital rectal exam is another test for prostate cancer. Your doctor feels your prostate by inserting a gloved finger into the rectum to check for enlargement or swelling. This quick, low-tech exam can save your life. Ultrasound is often used to visually examine the prostate.

Depending on the extent of the cancer, treatments include radiation, chemotherapy, cryotherapy (cold), prostate removal or hormone therapy to halt the body's production of cancer-encouraging hormones. Many men with early and low-grade prostate cancers are advised to avoid side-effect-laden radical treatment in favor of watchful waiting, in which no immediate action is taken other than careful monitoring of the cancer. Whatever your diagnosis, take your time evaluating all the options available. Usually, there's no need to rush.

Foods That Make It Better

New evidence shows that men can reduce their risk for prostate cancer and even slow the growth of existing cancers simply by changing their diet. The US death rate for prostate cancer is nearly triple that of Japan and a whopping 16 times that of China. Asian men who eat diets high in vegetables, fish and soy foods, with limited amounts of dairy products and red meat, have a rate of prostate cancer ten times lower than that of US men. This underscores the Asian in the Mediterr-Asian Diet. If you're looking for a meal plan that's tailor-made for prostate health, this diet is ideal.

Fresh, high-fiber foods provide an essential dietary element that drives down the risk of hormone-driven prostate cancer. Fiber locks onto estrogen molecules and blocks them from being absorbed into the bloodstream. This lowers the total amount of estrogen circulating in the body and lessens the danger of it encouraging cancer in the prostate or elsewhere. Fiber may also put the brakes on existing prostate cancers by shifting insulin and testosterone levels, both thought to spur the development of tumors.

Eating a vegetable-rich diet, while limiting fat and limiting alcohol, can also reduce your symptoms of BPH, according to research published in the *American Journal of Epidemiology,* which evaluated the eating habits of more than 4,700 men, average age 63, over seven years. During the course of the study, BPH developed in 876 of the men. Using diet-tracking data, researchers found that men who ate four or more servings of vegetables daily lowered their risk of BPH by 32%, and those who drank fewer than two drinks per day trimmed their risk by 38%. BPH risk increased by 38% in those who ate red meat daily and by 31% in men who got a lot of their daily calories from fat. Reviewing this data and the suggestions that follow, you see how nutritional choices can dramatically influence the health of your prostate.

HEAD FOR SELENIUM CITY

Fish, shellfish, and whole grains such as barley and oats are good sources of selenium, a trace mineral that's a powerful antioxidant, an immune booster and a proven cancer fighter. Selenium improves your body's ability to recognize and knock out early cancer cells, yet it's estimated that as many as 30% of American men don't get enough of it, partly because modern farming methods have depleted it from the food supply. Harvard researchers studying 33,000 men found that those who took in the most selenium from food had one-third the risk of contracting advanced prostate cancer as men with the lowest intake. In another study, scientists at the University of Arizona discovered that prostate cancer was 63% less likely to develop in men whose selenium levels were highest. Follow the Mediterr-Asian diet to get at least 70 micrograms (mcg) of selenium daily. Higher amounts, up to 200 mcg, may be even more protective. Start your day with oatmeal and you'll get 19

310

12 Top Selenium-Rich Foods

For prostate health, enjoy a variety of foods with robust selenium content, getting between 70 and 200 mcg daily.

1. Calf's liver, 4 ounces — 58 mcg
2. Snapper, 4 ounces — 56 mcg
3. Salmon, Chinook, 4 ounces — 53 mcg
4. Cod, 4 ounces — 53 mcg
5. Shrimp, 4 ounces — 45 mcg
6. Cremini mushrooms, 5 ounces — 37 mcg
7. Barley, 1 cup — 36 mcg
8. Turkey breast, 4 ounces — 33 mcg
9. Sunflower seeds, ¼ cup, raw — 21 mcg
10. Oats, 1 cup — 19 mcg
11. Egg — 14 mcg
12. Brazil nuts (one shelled nut) — 12–25 mcg

mcg right off the bat. Check the box above for more selenium-rich foods.

TOMATOES ARE TERRIFIC

Tomatoes are your prostate's best friends. They get their red color from lycopene, a pigment that accumulates in the prostate gland and has demonstrated an amazing ability to ward off cancer. Lycopene is a type of *carotenoid,* an antioxidant that neutralizes cell-damaging free radicals, so you should eat tomatoes in as many ways as you can, from pizza to spaghetti sauce. A five-year study involving 48,000 men found that those who ate 10 or more weekly servings of tomatoes, including ketchup and tomato sauce, were two-thirds less likely to get prostate cancer than those who ate just two servings per week. A review of more than 20 studies confirms that this protection is decidedly dose related. Men who ate six ounces of raw tomatoes daily saw a 3% reduction in prostate cancer risk, but those eating the most cooked tomato preparations had a 19% lower risk.

➤ **Cooked is better than raw.** Lycopene becomes concentrated when tomatoes are cooked; it doesn't lose its potency when exposed to heat. Concentrated sources, such as tomato juice, tomato sauce, and tomato paste, provide about five times the protection of fresh tomatoes. Adding a little fat, such as olive oil, also makes the lycopene in tomatoes more absorbable, another healthful serendipity of Mediterranean-style eating.

Enjoy tomato sauce, paste and low-sodium juice as often as you can. Studies show that a single daily serving may be enough to stall the growth of prostate tumors. You'll also be helping your heart. A European study found that men who ate the most lycopene-containing foods had *half* the risk of heart attack as those who ate the least!

➤ **Get pasted regularly.** Tomato paste is one of the most concentrated sources of lycopene. Add it generously to soups, chili and stews for prostate protection, and to guard against skin cancer. Lycopene actually elevates your skin's levels of natural sun protection to defend itself against UV damage.

➤ **Ketchup with organics.** Organic ketchups contain as much as three times the lycopene of nonorganic brands, so choose it whenever you can. Happily, ketchup producers have noticed our interest and have made organic versions widely available.

➤ **Soak up the sauce.** Even my Italian grandmother would agree that the quality of a few of today's prepared tomato sauces rival that of homemade. Check labels carefully and avoid any that contain high-fructose corn syrup. Look at sugar and salt content, too, choosing the lowest you can find.

➤ **Get juiced, too.** Keep low-sodium tomato juice in the pantry and enjoy a small glass daily as an afternoon pick-me-up or morning eye-opener. Squeeze a big slice of fresh lemon into it for an extra vitamin C blast. If you're going to have a cocktail, which studies confirm is healthy for you as long as you don't overdo it, make it a Bloody Mary.

➤ **Bake, broil, sauté or stew.** I can't think of anything more succulent than a late-summer tomato. Keep your eye peeled for heirloom varieties at your farmers' market and serve them as slices, drizzling with a few drops of extra-virgin olive oil and a scattering of torn basil leaves. Fresh mozzarella is optional but makes this a perfect appetizer or snack. Or toss raw tomatoes with hot pasta for a delicious fresh tomato sauce. I especially enjoy broiled halved tomatoes that have been sprinkled with Parmesan cheese, herbs and cracked pepper. Be creative!

➤ **Make minipizzas.** Start with high-quality whole-grain prepared pizza crust or pocketless pita bread slathered with pizza sauce or other thick tomato sauce, sprinkle on some chopped onion and shredded part-skim mozzarella and broil until bubbly. Top with shredded fresh basil.

➤ **Combine the red and green.** Tomatoes pack an ever bigger punch against prostate cancer when teamed with broccoli, another proven cancer fighter. Researchers at the University of Illinois described it as the "additive effect," when they discovered that eating the two together increased the cancer-fighting potency of each other. The various anticancer compounds in each food act on different anticancer pathways. Combine the two whenever possible: in pasta sauce, soups, on pizza and in salads.

SAVOR SOME SOY

Men in Asian countries have far lower rates of prostate cancer than American men, and some studies indicate it's because of the soy foods in the Asian diet. Soy foods contain estrogenlike plant compounds called *isoflavones* that lower levels of *dihydrotestosterone* (DHT), a nasty form of testosterone that fuels the growth of cancer cells. Some research suggests that isoflavones may actually cause cancer cells to die. For instance, a study at Loma Linda University discovered that prostate cancer was 70% less likely to develop in men who drank more than one serving of soy milk daily. I recommend that you enjoy a serving of soy food daily, selecting products that have undergone the least amount of processing. For example, tofu burgers and soy dogs don't have nearly the isoflavone content of soy nuts, soy yogurt, soy milk, miso or tofu. Consider a half cup of tofu, an ounce of soy nuts or a cup of soy milk one serving. If you don't know much about soy, read on for tips.

➤ **Tofu.** Men in China eating the most tofu have a 42% reduced risk of prostate cancer compared with men eating the least,

312

according to a study done there. Firm tofu is a denser variety and easy to cut up for a stir-fry or soup. Silken tofu has a custardlike consistency and is better for smoothies and sauces.

➤ **Miso.** Traditional Japanese soup uses this fermented soy paste to create a broth rich in isoflavones. If you've never tried it, order it at a Japanese restaurant, then shop for miso packets to make your own. You can use the miso to make a quick and restorative soup or add it to vegetables, rice or chili to enrich a variety of foods.

➤ **Soy milk.** If you buy take-out java, try a soy latte or *chai,* a spiced black tea favored in India. If you make your own coffee, keep a carton of unsweetened soy milk in the fridge so you can top off your brew. Remember to read labels. The vast majority of soy milk contains cane sugar, so be sure to look for unsweetened and save the calories.

➤ **Soy nuts.** These aren't nuts at all but roasted soybeans. Munch them for a snack or toss them into a salad, but limit your intake to a quarter cup (about one ounce) at a sitting, which contains approximately 120 calories.

➤ **Edamame.** These tender green pealike vegetables are boiled green soybeans, served hot or cold in their pods at Japanese restaurants. You also can buy them frozen at many groceries, boiled in their pods or shelled. Toss the shelled soybeans into soups or stews and onto salads for an isoflavone boost.

TAKE TIME FOR TEA

A fascinating study in the *Asia Pacific Journal of Clinical Nutrition* found that drinking green tea regularly in conjunction with a diet rich in lycopene-containing foods generates a more powerful effect against prostate cancer than either did alone. The biggest green-tea drinkers had a whopping 86% lower risk.

In another study, three groups of men with prostate cancer who were scheduled to have their prostates removed drank five cups of experimental beverages for five days before their surgeries. One group drank green tea, another black tea and the third group soda. After surgery, scientists looked at cells from each prostate gland. The tea drinkers had fewer new cancer cells than those drinking soda, whose new cancer cells were proliferating.

PEPPERS AND POMEGRANATE

Meet a healthful odd couple. Both pomegranate juice and hot peppers seem to protect your prostate. Researchers at UCLA found that men who drank eight ounces of pomegranate juice daily had significantly lower levels of PSA. All the men in the study had undergone treatment for prostate cancer, yet none of the juice drinkers experienced *metastasis,* the spread of cancer cells throughout the body. That's reason enough to keep a bottle of pomegranate juice in your refrigerator.

We know the juice has potent anti-inflammatory and antioxidant properties, which some researchers believe alters the way prostate cancer grows. Be sure to choose juice with no added sugar.

Pomegranate juice can be a little strong, which is why I dilute it with soda water to create a sparkling "proprostate" cocktail.

Shoot for two to four ounces daily, blending some into your morning smoothie.

Now, about those hot peppers. The journal *Cancer Research* published a study showing that *capsaicin,* the compound that puts the heat in hot pepper, can cause prostate cancer cells to commit suicide, medically called *apoptosis.* That may be a good reason to make your favorite cocktail a *spicy* Bloody Mary.

LOAD UP ON LEGUMES

There are loads of other legumes besides soybeans that protect the prostate. Several studies give you every reason to eat them regularly. In the Netherlands, scientists studying more than 58,000 men discovered that those who ate the most legumes, such as kidney beans, split peas, lentils and chickpeas, had a 29% lower risk of prostate cancer than men with the lowest intake. A Seventh-day Adventist study looked at 14,000 US men and saw a similar trend. Those eating the most legumes had a significantly lower risk of prostate cancer than those who didn't. Legumes are magnificent for overall health. They help control blood sugar, lower the risk of colon cancer and strengthen the immune system, not to mention lowering cholesterol. Beans also contain at least five known anticancer compounds, and there are likely many more. Enjoy a half cup daily, any way you'd like. *Here are some suggestions…*

➤ **Drain and add.** Open a can of kidney or garbanzo beans, drain and toss into salads and soups. Or start with kidney beans and add chopped apple, tiny cubes of Swiss cheese, a few crushed walnuts and a light vinaigrette for a quick and easy lunch or dinner.

➤ **Make chili.** A favorite snack for football fans and weight watchers alike. Make your favorite recipe, but bump up the bean content, adding a range of different types to the standard red kidney beans, such as black beans and chickpeas. Be generous with the tomato paste. While you're at it, add a couple extra cans of chopped tomatoes, too, for their prostate-healthy lycopene.

➤ **Do the mash.** All manner of canned refried beans are available. Choose organic vegetarian types, some of which have jalapeño or other flavors added. Warm a corn tortilla and slather on a layer of refried beans, adding cilantro and salsa for a prostate-perfect snack. Add scrambled eggs for a hearty breakfast burrito on the run.

➤ **Blend your beans.** Puree white beans with a little rosemary, garlic and olive oil for a classic white bean dip (you can add a can of anchovies for an extra blast of omega-3). Or pour an almost-drained can of garbanzo beans into the blender with a squeeze of fresh lemon juice, minced garlic, salt, and sesame seed paste (called *tahini*) for a fast and easy hummus, adding liquid by the tablespoonful until you reach the desired consistency. Now you're ready to dip something into it, such as raw veggies or whole-wheat pita triangles.

➤ **Gassy?** Some beans produce less gas, black beans and Anasazi (also called Aztec beans) among them. To reduce their gassiness, soak beans overnight before cooking to release some of their indigestible compounds, called *oligosaccharides,* which can cause gas. Don't soak if gas isn't a problem, though. The

oligosaccharides that leach out into the water are healthful *prebiotics* that nourish helpful bacteria in your digestive tract, and they're a healing force once you ingest them. There's also a natural enzyme product called Beano that makes beans more sociable. Look for it in your supermarket or drugstore.

OPEN UP TO OMEGAS

Everywhere you look, you see more and more healthful reasons to eat cold-water fish. Treasured for their omega-3 fatty acids, they've been shown to halt inflammation in the body and are especially healing for heart problems, arthritis, hypertension and a long list of other medical conditions. Now, you can add prostate cancer.

New research shows that fish, such as wild salmon, herring, anchovies, sardines and mackerel stop prostate cancer cells from growing, according to *The Lancet*. Men who eat omega-3s regularly tend to have a stronger flow of urine, less urine retention in the bladder and smaller prostate glands. Swedish scientists discovered that prostate cancer was up to three times more likely to develop in men who rarely eat seafood. On the flip side, research on 48,000 men determined that eating fish several times a week led to half the risk of prostate cancer. There's even more reason to watch your ratio between pro-inflammatory omega-6 fats (found in sunflower, soybean, corn and safflower oil, refined carbohydrates and most fast foods) and anti-inflammatory omega-3 fats. Research in England found that excess consumption of omega-6 fats speeds up the spread of prostate cancer cells. Scientists now believe omega-6s may be used by cancer cells for energy. However, the presence of omega-3 fats actually blocked this spread. Enjoy wild-caught cold-water fish two to three times a week.

FEEL FREE TO VEG OUT

By now you've heard that eating ten servings of vegetables and fruit each day is a major way to stay healing and reverse a variety of health problems. If you're concerned about prostate health, there's even more reason to love your vegetables because new research shows they're highly prostate protective.

Studies evaluating the eating patterns of 32,000 men over a 14-year period found that those eating the most vegetables had an 11% reduced risk for BPH, or enlarged prostate, compared with those eating the least. Researchers say the antioxidants in vegetables reduce the harmful effects of free radicals on prostate cells. This protection has been proved in numerous studies. One, published in the *Journal of the National Cancer Institute,* found that men eating cruciferous (cabbage family) vegetables three or more times per week had a 40% reduced risk of prostate cancer compared with those who ate just one serving or less per week. This level of risk reduction should send you running to your farmers' market. If you don't think you can consume that many vegetables in a day, here are a few smart strategies that will make it significantly easier...

➤ **Snack on raw.** One of the simplest ways to get all your vegetable servings in a day is to cut up a variety of raw veggies. To get an easy six servings, slice up a large

organic carrot, green pepper, a few radishes and a small summer squash to equal about three cups. Getting veggies ready ahead of time is the key to success, and it requires a good sharp knife. Wash and slice a day's worth of veggies and stash in the fridge or take a bag of them to work with you. Munch a few whenever you have a snack attack. You'll be astonished at how quickly you'll go through three cups of vegetables without adding to your weight—in fact, they'll help you actually shed pounds. Add two pieces of fruit (or ½ cup of 100% fruit juice) and two steamed vegetables or a salad at dinner to reach 10 daily servings.

➤ **Make a slaw.** You can make slaw out of just about anything. Use a sharp grater and start with cabbage, beets, and turnips. Grate a bowlful and toss with mustardy vinaigrette, made from a teaspoon of Dijon mustard blended with a teaspoon of red wine vinegar, with extra-virgin olive oil whisked in until it tastes good. Don't forget the onion, fresh herbs and chopped pimento olives.

➤ **Stir the fry.** Stir-fries are a quick and easy way to enjoy veggies, especially when they're heaped over brown rice. It doesn't matter which veggies you use—every one of them has something healing to offer. Go for a different variety every day.

➤ **Crucify cancer cells.** Remember the study showing that cruciferous vegetables lowered prostate cancer risk by 40%? Let's review this potent group of cancer fighters, which includes kale, collards, cabbage, Brussels sprouts, broccoli, cauliflower, bok choy, turnips, rutabaga, radish, spicy arugula and watercress. Cruciferous vegetables are loaded with sulfur compounds called *glucosinolates,* the healing compound that smells during cooking. Chopping and chewing these crucifers also releases their healing phytochemicals, which increase healing hormones, while lowering levels of compounds that feed prostate cancers.

For an ultraquick lunch or dinner, cut any crucifer (such as broccoli) into bite-sized pieces and steam *al dente* just until a fork goes in easily. Drain and transfer to a glass bowl. In a small dish, combine a capful of sherry vinegar and a teaspoon of Dijon mustard, followed by a couple of teaspoons or so of extra-virgin olive oil. Whisk until blended and thickened, pour over broccoli and toss. Add a few capers, canned anchovies or water-packed sardines for a salty zip and serve warm. Use this dish as a basic recipe with endless variations, such as adding roasted red peppers, tomatoes or red onion. You'll discover more foods and easy recipes to heal your prostate at *www.myhealingkitchen.com.*

➤ **Be fond of broccoli.** Yes, it's one of the cruciferous vegetables, but it's *extra* powerful against prostate cancer. Broccoli abounds in a family of phytochemicals called *indoles,* including *indole-3-carbinol* (I3C), which boosts beneficial hormones in your body, while depressing other hormones that fuel prostate cancers. These healing substances in broccoli seem to activate genes that keep cancer from developing, and turn off genes that encourage its spread. Just a few servings each week can protect men from prostate cancer, according to research

published in the Public Library of Science journal *PloS One.* Scientists evaluated men who had precancerous areas on their prostates that increased their risk of cancer. The men were divided into two groups, one eating four additional servings of broccoli each week for a year and, the other eating four extra servings of peas. Tissue samples were taken periodically and researchers found the broccoli eaters showed hundreds of positive changes in the genes involved in fighting cancer. They credited broccoli's *sulforaphane* for the protection.

➤ **Start a sprout farm.** Broccoli sprouts have one of the highest concentrations of sulforaphane, which fuels your body's natural anticancer mechanisms. Sulforaphane enhances the action of the body's own enzymes that are in charge of fighting cancer-causing substances, making broccoli and broccoli sprouts a full-body detoxifier in a single vegetable. In fact, the sprouts have up to 50 times the amount of sulforaphane than full-grown broccoli. You can find broccoli sprouts at some groceries, or you can order the seeds online and start your own broccoli sprout farm on your kitchen countertop.

➤ **All hail allium.** Onions, scallions, shallots, leeks, chives and garlic, all members of the allium family, are big favorites, either raw or sautéed, on sandwiches or in chili. New research shows they can ward off prostate tumors by squashing the compounds that cause it. At the National Cancer Institute (NCI), scientists studied the consumption patterns of allium vegetables of men living in Shanghai. Those who ate five cloves of fresh garlic every week had half the risk of cancer. Those who ate just a tablespoon to a tablespoon and a half of scallions or onions daily drove down their prostate cancer risk by 49%.

➤ **Best produce bang.** If I could write a single vegetable prescription for my cancer patients, it would be to eat more leafy greens. They're nutritionally superb, with spinach topping the list. It contains more than 13 unique flavonoids, compounds that work against cancer in general, and prostate cancer specifically. These flavonoids appear to hasten the death of cancer cells and boost the creation of molecules that inhibit the development of new cancer cells. Research published in the *Journal of Nutrition* highlighted the spinach compound *neoxanthin,* which prevents replication of cancer cells and also causes them to self-destruct. Buy a bag of washed baby spinach and lay the leaves on sandwiches. Or rinse and steam them for a couple minutes before topping with some extra-virgin olive oil and a little grated Parmesan cheese. This certainly is an easy food prescription to fill.

POP A FEW PUMPKIN SEEDS

Pumpkin seeds are taking center stage in preventing prostate enlargement, or BPH. The star ingredients are the plant *sterol beta-sisterol* and plant compounds called *cucurbitacins.* They work to block testosterone from converting to dihydrotestosterone, a powerful metabolite that leads to prostate enlargement by encouraging the body's production of extra prostate cells. A study in *The Lancet* reported significant easing of urinary problems in men who took 20 mg of beta-sisterol three times daily. Beta-sisterol also works to lower cholesterol. Pumpkin seeds also contain zinc, another lead player in prostate health. A half cup has about 8 mg of zinc.

Foods That Make It Worse

With the incidence of prostate cancer so high in the US, something we're eating must be upping our risk. That something is found in two procancer food categories: too much sugar and too much fat.

➤ **Flee the sugar shack.** In 1931, German scientist Dr. Otto Warburg was awarded the Nobel Prize for discovering that cancer cells use sugar for fuel. Incredibly, even though this breakthrough finding is nearly 80 years old, only a minority of cancer specialists today acknowledge the role of glucose in cancer development. Fortunately, this is now beginning to change as more researchers recognize that a high intake of sugar, and the insulin production it triggers, is a major factor in cancer development.

Limit sugar (or quit it) and you'll be depriving any cancer cells in your body of the additional calories they need to reproduce and spread. Of course it's not just sugar in the form of table sugar, candy, and other sweets. Refined carbohydrates—white bread, chips, crackers, cookies, cake and many breakfast cereals—act just like sugar when they hit your bloodstream, kicking up insulin levels and raising the amount of *growth factor-I,* which encourages the development of tumors. Eating the Mediterr-Asian way will

317

help you replace refined white foods with fiber-rich whole grains, vegetables and fruits that keep your blood sugar stable. The food is so hearty and delicious that you'll never miss the junk.

➤ **Keep yourself lean.** Scientists found that obese men were more than three times as likely to have BPH as their leaner counterparts. Losing even a little weight can improve your condition. Scientists at the University of California San Diego discovered that men who were obese had three and a half times the risk of enlarged prostate as their leaner buddies. The same study revealed that a quartet of factors placed men at risk: high cholesterol, high blood pressure and high blood sugar as well as overweight. The message: Lose some weight and stay lean, fill your plate with more vegetables and less meat and enjoy the Mediterr-Asian menu.

➤ **Cut the fat.** A diet that's lower in all fats can put prostate cancer in the slow lane, according to a study published in the *American Journal of Epidemiology*. Researchers who studied 4,770 men over seven years discovered that the risk of BPH increased by a troubling 31% in men eating a high-fat diet. It doesn't matter what kind of fat was eaten, according to the study's author, Dr. Alan Kristal of the Fred Hutchinson Cancer Research Center in Seattle. Eating red meat every day boosted risk by 38%. On the flip side, researchers found that BPH risk was reduced 32% by eating four or more servings of vegetables every day.

An overview of all clinical studies conducted on diet and prostate health confirms that fruits, veggies and high-fiber foods put the kibosh on cancer and other prostate problems. Limiting animal products such as dairy and meat actually slows the development of prostate cancers. Trans fats, found in nearly all processed foods and junk foods, are definitely off-limits. Stay safe by eating the Mediterr-Asian way, which provides high-quality meat in moderate amounts.

➤ **To drink or not to drink.** How do you spell m-o-d-e-r-a-t-i-o-n? If it's two drinks a day or fewer, go to the head of the class. Moderate alcohol consumption is good for you and actually reduces your risk of BPH by 38%. However, excessive drinking drains your body of important nutrients such as zinc, which helps keep your prostate healthy.

Supplemental Help

Always inform your doctor about any supplements you're taking. Some can influence the outcome of tests while others can interfere with pharmaceutical drugs. A number of nutritional supplements have been shown to protect the prostate and ease symptoms. *Here are some of the best…*

DON'T BE "D" DEFICIENT

For years, doctors and other health experts have warned us about sun exposure. By now, most Americans are so afraid of sunshine that they won't go outdoors without being slathered in sunscreen. Meanwhile, cancer rates continue to rise, including skin cancer. What gives? We now know this has been bad advice because solar rays are the main source of vitamin D, the sunshine vitamin, and tons of studies show that vitamin D protects against all cancers, including those of the skin and prostate. Research shows that men living in low-sun areas of the country have higher rates of prostate cancer.

While your body makes its own vitamin D when skin is exposed to sun, those living in northern latitudes can't sunbathe during the winter months. Also, the skin's ability to convert vitamin D from sunlight declines with age, resulting in deficiencies among the elderly. Furthermore, dark skin doesn't turn UV rays into vitamin D efficiently, which helps explain why African-Americans have higher rates of many cancers, including that of the prostate. In these cases, a vitamin D supplement is essential.

➤ **The first step.** The majority of Americans are deficient in vitamin D, so the odds are good that you are among them. One way to be sure is to be tested. Request a 25-OH vitamin D blood test (25-hydroxy vitamin D). If your results show that you're in the normal range, take it with a grain of salt, because current recommendations are greatly underestimated. Your optimal range should be 45 to 65 ng/ml (or 115 to 128 nmol/l). If you're not, get more sun, eat more vitamin D-rich foods (such as soy foods, fortified milk and orange juice) or purchase a high-quality supplement.

➤ **Shopping tips.** The only supplement to buy is a high-quality brand of vitamin D-3 (*cholecalciferol*), the same form that your skin manufactures from UV rays. Cod liver oil is also acceptable. Don't purchase vitamin D-2 (*ergocalciferol*), because it isn't as good.

➤ **Doses.** The current typical recommended dose for adults between the ages of 51 and 70 is 400 international units (IU), while those 71 and older are advised to take 600 IU daily. The average multivitamin contains 400 to 600 IU. However, new research shows that these levels are far too low. Thankfully, scientists are starting to recognize this. Recent studies show that most people who are deficient in vitamin D, especially the elderly and African-Americans, should get 3,000 to 4,000 IU daily to maintain healthy 25 (OH) blood levels of vitamin D. If you are generally healthy, a daily dose of 1,000 IU should be enough, but in the winter months, I suggest you increase that to 2,000 IU. Please disregard any warnings of vitamin D toxicity at these levels. This advice is obsolete and even dangerous. The most recent studies conclusively show that daily doses up to 10,000 IU are not harmful, although I don't recommend taking this much, unless you are battling a chronic illness. Don't forget to include foods that are rich in vitamin D in your diet.

THE PROSTATE VITAMIN FOR SMOKERS

Smokers and former smokers have a higher risk of prostate cancer, so taking vitamin E is essential. Here's why: Research from the National Cancer Institute discovered that male smokers who had quit cigarettes within the previous ten years were able to reduce their risk of prostate cancer by 71% just by taking a minimum of 400 IU of vitamin E. Check with your doctor if you're on a blood thinner, as vitamin E also produces this effect.

SUCCEED WITH SELENIUM

One of the largest clinical trials tracked men for 13 years and found that advanced prostate cancer was nearly half as likely to develop in men who had the highest blood levels of selenium, compared with those with the lowest levels. Researchers believe that the superb antioxidant power of selenium might actually control the cell damage that leads to cancer. If you're eating the Mediterr-Asian way, you should be getting enough selenium (see the list of selenium-rich prostate protector foods on page 310). If your diet is low in selenium, however, you may want to take a supplement of up to 200 mcg daily.

DRUG-FREE RELIEF FOR BPH

▶ **Ease symptoms with saw palmetto.** Derived from palmetto shrub berries, saw palmetto has been used by many men with BPH to reduce urgency and increase urinary flow. One review of more than eight studies involving several thousand men revealed that saw palmetto boosted weak urine flow by 50%. It can take weeks to months for saw palmetto to work, so give it a chance. Take 160 mg twice daily.

▶ **Bet on beta-sitosterol.** While this plant extract doesn't shrink the prostate, it does boost the rate of urine flow and limit the amount of urine that stays in your bladder once you're done. *The Lancet* reported that men taking 20 milligrams (mg) daily found it offered significant help with BPH-related urinary problems.

▶ **Fee-Fi-Fo-*Pygeum*.** This extract of the bark of the African plum tree proved itself in clinical trials for BPH. It boosts urinary flow, limits frequency and lessens the amount of urine left in the bladder. Traditional healers in Africa have used the bark for thousands of years to treat urinary problems. Clinical trials used 100 mg to 200 mg of a product called Tadenan. It's widely used in Europe and is available online.

Other Helpers and Healers

▶ **Talk it out.** Women figured out long ago that sharing difficult experiences provides a load of healing that most medical procedures can't touch. Men who are going through difficult BPH symptoms or prostate cancer need to talk, and many find it easiest to talk to other men. You'll learn a lot and maybe even laugh a little, too. Ask your doctor about support groups for men with prostate cancer and BPH. Many hospitals sponsor them.

▶ **Make a little whoopee.** Sex is particularly good for your prostate: Studies show that men who have the most orgasms reduce their prostate cancer risk by a third, compared with men who have the fewest. This news comes from a prestigious National Cancer Institute study, published in the *Journal of the American Medical Association*. Researchers collected data from 30,000 middle-aged men to evaluate the connection between ejaculation and prostate cancer risk. The study found that it didn't matter how climax was reached. If you're a man whose sex life has changed because of prostate cancer or surgery, keep in mind that intimacy can take many forms. Stay closely connected to your partner, who is often your greatest support.

Exercise is essential to prostate health. Even a little workout can reduce the symptoms of BPH. In fact, a lack of activity can worsen urine retention. For men who have had difficulty accepting a prostate diagnosis, exercise is a great antidote to depression and sadness. Check out the walking recommendations in the previous chapter or visit Internet sites, such as *www.thewalkingsite. com*, for guidelines. Studies show that walking as little as 30 minutes a day four days a week can reap huge health benefits. How easy is that!

➤ **Mind your meds.** If you're having difficulty controlling urination because of BPH, clear the antihistamines and decongestants out of your medicine cabinet. Both types of drugs constrict the ring of muscles around your urethra, making it more difficult to urinate. Men with BPH who are taking diuretics should talk to their doctor about changing the dose or timing if these medications are making symptoms more troublesome.

➤ **Whittle your waistline.** Here are two more compelling reasons to cut back on calories and start exercising: Extra body fat generates inflammatory hormones linked to the growth of prostate cancer tumors. Research shows that obesity may even lead to aggressive prostate cancers that are more likely to recur and more likely to be fatal. In addition, men who weigh more often have larger prostate glands along with lower PSA numbers, making accurate screening challenging and increasing the chance that a prostate tumor will be overlooked.

➤ **Go when you gotta go.** If you wait to urinate and let your bladder overfill, you can damage it or stretch the bladder muscle itself so that it's less functional. The moment you sense the need to urinate, head for the bathroom.

➤ **Let the sun shine in.** Avoiding the sun can double your risk of prostate cancer, according to a study from the Northern California Cancer Center. Exposing your bare skin to the sun triggers your body's production of vitamin D, the sunshine vitamin that bestows all kinds of anticancer and good health properties. Expose as much of your skin as you're comfortable with for 15-minute periods on most days, if possible. Don't wear sunscreen, but do avoid burning.

➤ **Put a time limit on fluids.** Stop drinking most of your fluids about three hours before bedtime to trim the number of nighttime bathroom trips. ∎

Recipes

Cooking in a Healing Kitchen

My passion for fresh and delicious food began in my childhood. I had the great fortune to have two grandmothers—one Sicilian, one German—who taught me to prepare and love good food. I learned their special recipes as well as their secrets for choosing the best products from the butcher, the garden, or in my Grandmother Edna's case, from the Chesapeake Bay. We didn't call the place where we prepared our meals "a healing kitchen," but I now understand that's exactly what it was.

My kitchen is a healing one now, but I must confess that it has not always been this way. Even though I was raised by women who showed me how to make great-tasting, wholesome food, my adult life had become complicated. Pressured by work and my family's schedules, I was choosing convenience over quality and my family's eating habits had become pretty unhealthy.

As I began to develop the healing recipes here, my family and I adopted the Healing Kitchen way of life. We started eating Dr. Sinatra's Mediterr-Asian Diet and we experienced the positive results almost immediately. I felt stronger and healthier, my skin looked better, and my hair started to get thicker. Most important, I became happier... *much* happier. My energy level has increased dramatically and my mood swings are gone. My children are less hyperactive and more focused, friendly and interested in helping me in the kitchen. To a mother of three, that's a miracle.

In addition to creating the recipes and testing the foods in *The Healing Kitchen*, I re-introduced some of my grandmothers' techniques and I enjoy cooking as much as I did as a child. Making the time to rediscover the power of food has been worth the effort. My healing kitchen has changed our lives and my family's good health is the only reward I'll ever need.

* * *

All of the recipes included in *The Healing Kitchen* are grouped according to condition. Note that there are no recipes included here for "Obesity and Overweight." If you adopt Mediterr-Asian eating habits, your weight should stabilize at a healthy level.

Most of the following recipes are main entrées that include plenty of vegetables. I've started each section with easy healing soups and salads, most of which could be used as the basis for a light lunch or supper. There are also a few vegetable side dishes. Desserts (yes, you can have dessert when you're eating healthy foods!) are also included at the end of every section.

It's my hope that the recipes I developed with Dr. Sinatra for this book encourage you to embrace a healing kitchen philosophy of your own. You'll feel better and have more energy because you're eating real and delicious food. It's a life-changing adventure worth trying.

—*Rebecca Bent*

THE HEALING KITCHEN PANTRY

Once you start preparing and enjoying fresh food, I promise that you'll never turn back. As you start on your way to more healthful eating, here are some suggestions about choosing ingredients and stocking your kitchen.

➤ **Olive oil.** This is a key ingredient in the Mediterr-Asian Diet. As Dr. Sinatra

326

has mentioned in previous sections, cold-pressed, extra-virgin olive oil is the best oil for your health. Unfortunately, most of its healing properties are destroyed in cooking. It has what is known as a "low smoke point," which means you easily burn your food or scorch pans if you use a small amount on a high flame. So never use extra-virgin olive oil in high-heat frying. Extra-virgin olive oil has the richest olive flavor, which makes it an essential element in salad dressings or as a finishing touch to dishes, but can clash with other contrasting flavors (such as Asian). It's also expensive, so you'll want to use it with discretion.

➤ **High-heat cooking.** Light or extra-light olive oils, both widely available, are better choices for high-heat cooking. "Light" does not refer to the calorie or fat content—it has the same as the darker versions—but rather to the strength of the flavor. It does not possess the same healing qualities as extra-virgin, but it is a better choice over processed polyunsaturated fats such as vegetable or corn oil. Light olive oil is also neutral enough in flavor to use in baking. In Asian stir-fries, you may want to use a small amount of peanut or sesame oil (toasted or not). Most of my recipes call for light olive oil when frying, but feel free to experiment with other healthful oils such as grapeseed or coconut (see page 328).

Oils labeled "100% pure olive oil" are actually the cheapest grade of edible olive oil. It has the least flavor while having a higher smoke point, so it's a good frying oil. Like "light," it is of lesser nutritional quality than extra-virgin olive oil.

➤ **Salt.** These recipes do not have much added salt. Most people get far too much—most of it coming from processed foods. Try to eat only 1,500 to 2,300 milligrams (mg) of sodium a day if you're a healthy adult. I prefer sea salt in all my cooking because it has more flavor and beneficial minerals. Kosher salt (often used in home pickling) and sea salt have larger crystals that are easier to see when cooking. Fine sea salt has a bright flavor that you can feel on the front of your tongue and can be used in all cooking. Coarse sea salt is delicious on salad, veggies or meat, and it leaves a distinct and lasting flavor.

Sea salt and table salt have the same basic nutritional value—both consist mostly of two minerals: sodium and chloride. Table salt is highly processed to prohibit clumping, so it's best to use sea salt or herbs. Sea salt is produced through evaporation of seawater, usually with little processing, which leaves behind some trace minerals. These minerals add flavor and color to sea salt. Most table salt also has added iodine, an essential nutrient that appears naturally in sea salt.

➤ **Grass-fed and free-range meats and poultry.** Grass-fed and/or free-range meat and poultry products now can be found in regular grocery stores as well as health food stores. If not, ask your grocer to begin supplying them. Free-range implies these animals are not caged and therefore live healthier lives. Many studies show grass-fed animals are higher in omega-3 fatty acids, beta-carotene and important minerals like calcium and potassium.

"Grass-fed" implies that the animals are grazing in the field. This is not necessarily true. They can be fed grass in troughs, so it is worth looking up the vendor to see if the animals are truly free to graze. Overall, grass-fed and free-range usually indicate more humane treatment than feedlots where hundreds of cattle are confined in huge pens and fed highly processed grain products.

Ask your retail grocer about the source of meat and poultry you are purchasing. Make it clear that you care about more than price. The surest way to get the best is to buy your meat and poultry directly from the grower who can vouch for its purity.

➤ **Wild salmon.** Fresh omega-3 seafood is an important part of Mediterr-Asian eating. I prefer wild sockeye salmon. It has a bright orange color and distinctive flavor that's fresh and slightly salty. It can be purchased online frozen or from stores like Whole Foods. Make sure the label reads "wild-caught." You can also purchase canned wild salmon, which is surprisingly tasty and as inexpensive as tuna.

➤ **Sugar substitutes.** I use xylitol, a naturally occurring sweetener found in the fibers of many fruits and vegetables. Xylitol is sometimes referred to as birch sugar because it was first derived from birch trees in Finland in the 19th century and was popularized in Europe as a safe sweetener for people with diabetes. It has a low glycemic index and a sweet taste that's tarter than sugar.

Xylitol contains 40% fewer calories than sugar and can be purchased at Whole Foods. It is becoming increasingly popular, so it may soon be available in large grocery store chains. (See page 328 for more healthful sweeteners.)

Flours:

- **Gluten-free** (such as almond, brown rice, hazelnut, quinoa, sesame or walnut)
- **Ground flaxseed** (this is exceptionally healing but too dense to use alone; store in the fridge)
- **Whole-grain pastry flour** (whole-wheat pastry flour is the easiest to find; contains less protein than regular whole-wheat flour, which results in a lighter texture that is close to that of white flour)
- **Whole-wheat flour**

Sweeteners:

- **Birch sugar (xylitol)**
- **Honey,** especially dark, local honey
- **Maple syrup**
- **Raw agave nectar**
- **Stevia**

Organic low-fat milk:

- **Cow's milk**
- **Goat's milk** (available canned)
- **Nut milks** (such as almond)
- **Rice milk**
- **Soy milk** (look for unsweetened)

Butter and oils:

- **Almond oil**
- **Buttery spreads made from expeller-pressed oils** (vegan and trans fat free)
- **Coconut oil**
- **Flaxseed oil** (store in the fridge)
- **Grapeseed oil**
- **Olive oil,** both light and extra-virgin
- **Organic butter from grass-fed cattle**
- **Peanut oil**
- **Sesame oil**
- **Walnut oil**

Pasta:

- **Gluten-free pasta** (such as brown rice or quinoa)
- **Whole-grain pasta** (such as whole wheat)

Cheeses:

- **Artisanal hard cheeses** like Parmesan, Romano and Asiago
- **Grass-fed cow's, goat's and sheep's milk cheeses**

Frozen fruits and vegetables:

- **Blueberries,** broccoli, cherries, mixed berries, mixed stir-fry veggies and spinach

CONVENIENCE FOODS IN THE HEALING KITCHEN PANTRY

I always have certain staples in my pantry so I can make a great meal even when I haven't been shopping. Many of the products listed here are personal favorites—some varieties may sound unfamiliar, but all should be available at quality grocery store chains.

- **Garlic paste.** Look for it in the Italian section of almost any grocery store. One teaspoon equals approximately one garlic clove. It's very smooth, so it can flavor a dish easier than minced garlic. You can make your own by mashing a garlic clove together with a pinch of kosher salt into pulp with the flat of your knife.
- **Low-sodium stock (chicken, beef and vegetable).** This is always in my cupboard for quick soups.
- **"Lite" coconut milk.** This contains significantly fewer calories and less fat that regular coconut milk. It's an inexpensive flavorful ingredient that turns simple chicken and frozen veggies into a succulent curry. Do

not confuse with sweetened cream of coconut (used for mixed drinks) or coconut water.

- **Low-sodium canned tomatoes.** I prefer Muir Glen Organic No Salt Added or Del Monte No Salt Added Tomato Sauce.

- **Low-sodium soy sauce.** I use this for soup seasoning and stir-fries. My favorite brands include Yamasa Less-Salt Soy Sauce and Kikkoman Lite Soy Sauce.

- **Low-sodium teriyaki sauce.** This makes a delicious stir-fry or flavors poultry or lean meat as a marinade. My favorite is Kikkoman Low Sodium Teriyaki Marinade & Sauce.

OTHER ITEMS TO INSPIRE YOUR CULINARY CREATIVITY

- **Raw, unsalted nuts,** including Brazil nuts, walnuts, pecans and almonds
- **Seeds such as flaxseed,** sunflower seeds and sesame seeds
- **Unsweetened dried fruit,** especially cherries, raisins and figs
- **Organic low-sodium canned beans of all kinds** (rinse well before using)
- **Spices,** especially curry, cumin, cloves, nutmeg, allspice, cayenne and coriander
- **Dried herbs,** including thyme, oregano, sage, rosemary, parsley and mint

Recipes by Condition

Arthritis 331
Cancer 341
Depression 353
Diabetes 363
Digestive Disorders 373
Erectile Dysfunction 382
Eye Disease 392
Fatigue 402
Heart Disease 413
Hypertension 426
Insomnia 435
Memory Loss 443
Menopause 452
Migraines 462
Osteoporosis 470
Prostate Problems 480

Note: If you eat the Mediterr-Asian way, your weight will come under control naturally. So we have not included specific recipes for "Overweight and Obesity." If weight loss is a concern for you, please review the chapter starting on page 280. You'll find more Mediterr-Asian recipes at the free Web site *www.myhealingkitchen.com*.

🍽 *Arthritis-Fighting Thai Salmon Salad*

Makes 4 servings

This dish blends ten arthritis-healing ingredients into a delectable Thai dish. Crunchy greens and flaked salmon are lightly tossed with a savory homemade dressing. The cherries add a touch of sweetness. Perfect for lunch, dinner, a summer picnic or as a quick bite, tucked into a whole-wheat pita pocket.

Crunchy Greens Salad

1 pound **fresh salmon fillet**
2 teaspoons **light olive oil**
1 cup finely shredded **purple cabbage**
4 heaping cups fresh **spinach**
4 **basil leaves**, finely chopped
2 tablespoons **crushed walnuts**, for garnish

Miso-Pineapple Dressing

1 tablespoon **miso paste***
¼ cup **pineapple juice**
1 tablespoon **sesame oil**
1 tablespoon finely chopped **dried cherries**
¼ cup finely chopped **shallots**
1 tablespoon **brown-rice vinegar**, white-wine vinegar or other vinegar of your choice

1. Preheat oven to 400°F.

2. Lightly coat the salmon fillet with oil. Roast in oven for 8 to 10 minutes until slightly opaque in the center.

3. Cool salmon at room temperature, then chill for an hour or overnight. Break up into chunks, removing any fatty ends or dark spots.

4. In a large bowl, combine the miso, pineapple juice, sesame oil, dried cherries, shallots and vinegar, and whisk until well combined.

5. Add the cabbage, spinach, basil and broken-up salmon, and toss until the salad is evenly coated.

6. Divide among four plates, sprinkle with walnuts and serve.

Vegetarian Version

Add canned black beans instead of salmon for excellent protein, fiber and antioxidant content.

Frugal Options

Reduce the amount of salmon to 8 ounces and double the amount of cabbage and spinach.

*Miso substitute: ½ tablespoon low-sodium soy sauce and ½ tablespoon low-sodium chicken stock or bone broth (see page 55).

Per serving: calories 297.7, total fat 15.5 g, saturated fat 2.2 g, cholesterol 80.5 mg, sodium 313.9 mg, potassium 981.1 mg, total carbohydrate 7.9 g, dietary fiber 1.5 g, sugars 5.1 g, protein 31.2 g

🍽️ *Joint-Mending Mediterranean Stew*

Makes 8 servings

Bouillabaisse is a popular French soup in which all ingredients simmer together in a mouth-watering, nutritious broth. In this healing twist on the Mediterranean classic, garlic and onions form the soup base while halibut, cabbage and cauliflower build up layers of flavor. Fragrant saffron and fennel seed provide the finish. Make sure to use the freshest seafood.

1 teaspoon light olive oil
2 tablespoons minced garlic
1 large yellow onion, peeled and finely chopped
1 tablespoon finely chopped fresh thyme
¼ cup finely chopped fresh parsley
4 basil leaves
1 bay leaf
¼ head cabbage, finely chopped
1 pound cauliflower, finely chopped
2 quarts low-sodium fish stock
3 pounds halibut, cod, snapper or salmon fillets
2 cups kale, cut into 2-inch pieces
6 saffron threads, crumbled
1½ teaspoons salt
Pinch fennel seeds

1. Heat the olive oil in a large stockpot over medium-low heat. Add the garlic, onions, thyme, parsley, basil and bay leaf. Stir gently until aromatic, and the onions start to soften, about 3 minutes.

2. Add the cabbage, cauliflower, fish stock and seafood and bring the liquid to a slow boil. Simmer for 10 minutes, or until the fish starts to turn opaque.

3. Add the kale, saffron, salt and fennel seeds and cook for another 5 minutes.

4. Spoon the soup into deep bowls and serve.

Vegetarian Version

Substitute 2 pounds ½-inch cubed, firm tofu for the seafood.
Use vegetable broth instead of fish stock.

Frugal Options

Use water and a fish bouillon cube instead of fish stock.
Use frozen fish fillets. Thaw in refrigerator before adding.
Omit the saffron threads and use a prepackaged seasoning blend (often referred to as paella seasoning).

Per serving: calories 226.4, total fat 2.3 g, saturated fat 0.4 g, cholesterol 93.5 mg, sodium 657.4 mg, potassium 599.0 mg, total carbohydrate 6.9 g, dietary fiber 2.3 g, sugars 0.4 g, protein 16.8 g

🍽 *Pain-Buster Tuna Wraps with Zesty Asian Dipping Sauce*

Makes 4 servings

Bite into this wrap for the satisfying crunch of fresh green beans and walnuts alongside succulent spinach and omega-3 tuna. Drizzle the tangy dipping sauce into the salad before wrapping.

Tuna Salad Wraps

1 ounce whole-wheat angel hair pasta
16 ounces canned albacore tuna*
1 cup finely chopped fresh baby spinach
1½ cups finely chopped steamed green beans
1 tablespoon crushed walnuts
1 tablespoon finely chopped fresh pineapple
1 teaspoon curry powder, optional
4 whole-wheat wraps

Asian Dipping Sauce

4 tablespoons unsweetened pineapple juice
1 tablespoon miso paste
1 teaspoon minced roasted garlic
½ cup water or chicken or bone broth (see page 55)
2 tablespoons sesame oil

1. Prepare the pasta according to package directions.
2. In a large bowl, combine the tuna, spinach, green beans, walnuts, pasta, pineapple and curry powder, if using. Mix until well combined and set aside.
3. To prepare the dipping sauce, whisk together the juice, miso paste, garlic, broth and sesame oil in a small saucepan. Cook over medium heat, stirring occasionally, for 10 minutes.
4. To assemble, divide the tuna salad among the four wraps. Place a line of the salad mixture in the center of the wrap, leaving a ½-inch edge at each end. Very carefully roll up by bringing up the bottom of the wrap and tucking it around the filling. Once the wrap is firmly rolled, slice it in half with a sharp knife. Serve with dipping sauce.

Wheat-Free Version

Use brown-rice pasta and wrap the tuna salad in romaine or butter lettuce leaves.

Frugal Options

Reduce the amount of tuna to 8 ounces and double the amount of green beans and spinach.

*While many prefer the taste of albacore tuna, chunk-light tuna is known to have lower mercury levels.

Per serving: calories 228.4, total fat 8.1 g, saturated fat 0.6 g, cholesterol 6.3 mg, sodium 470.6 mg, potassium 172.3 mg, total carbohydrate 31.5 g, dietary fiber 6.1 g, sugars 3.2 g, protein 9.4 g

🍽 *Ease-Inflammation Curried Scallop Salad*

Makes 4 servings

This curried salad is a great way to serve scallops. They make the perfect foil for the spicy curry, savory basil and sweet coconut. Serve on a bed of stir-fried soybeans sprinkled with lemon zest. This salad is simple enough to make in a jiffy, elegant enough to serve to guests and powerfully healing.

Curried Scallops

1 teaspoon red curry paste*
½ teaspoon minced ginger
¼ cup fresh basil, julienned
2 tablespoons "lite" coconut milk
1 pound bay scallops (about 30–40 scallops)

Edamame Salad

1 teaspoon light olive oil
½ cup finely chopped red onion
2 cups cooked edamame**
1 teaspoon grated lemon zest

1. Place an oven rack on the middle shelf of the oven and preheat to 400°F.

2. In a small oven-safe dish, combine the curry paste, ginger, basil and coconut milk and mix. Add the scallops and toss until they are thoroughly coated. Bake for 12 minutes, or until the scallops are piping hot and opaque.

3. While the scallops are cooking, prepare the salad. Heat the olive oil in a wok or large deep skillet over medium-low heat. Sauté the onions for 10 minutes, or until they are translucent and soft.

4. Reduce the heat to low and add the edamame. Toss and remove from the heat. Edamame tastes best at room temperature.

5. To assemble, divide the salad among four plates and top with the scallops, about 8 scallops per plate. Spoon out any juices from the casserole dish and drizzle over the salad. Sprinkle with lemon zest and serve.

Vegetarian Version

Use sautéed tofu instead of scallops.

Frugal Options

Cut the amount of scallops to ½ pound and add 2 cups fresh spinach or shredded cabbage.

*Red curry paste is found in the Asian or international section of most grocery stores.

**Edamame is the green vegetable version of soybeans, harvested before the beans "harden." You can find edamame in the frozen foods section of most grocery stores.

Per serving: calories 209.9, total fat 7.8 g, saturated fat 1.4 g, cholesterol 21.3 mg, sodium 330.7 mg, potassium 723.2 mg, total carbohydrate 14.4 g, dietary fiber 4.3 g, sugars 1.1 g, protein 22.1 g

---

⦿ *Joint-Soothing Vegetarian Cellophane Noodles*

Makes 4 servings

Cellophane noodles are a very thin, translucent Asian bean thread, a mainstay in Thai diets. Because they easily absorb the flavor and color of sauces, they bring extra savor to the meal. A quick stir-fry of this tasty combo will keep the vegetables crunchy and succulent.

Miso-Garlic Sauce

> **2 teaspoons miso paste***
> **2 tablespoons peanut oil**
> **1 tablespoon oyster sauce**
> **2 teaspoons minced garlic**
> **1 teaspoon minced ginger**
> **2 tablespoons low-sodium soy sauce**
> **2 tablespoons finely chopped dried cherries**

Vegetable-Noodle Sauté

> **1 teaspoon sesame oil**
> **1 cup fresh green beans,** ends removed
> **1½–2 pounds fresh broccoli,** cut into florets with 2-inch stems
> **½ teaspoon salt**
> **½ cup water**
> **2 ounces cellophane noodles** (about one bunch, dried) or any thin whole-grain noodle
> **3 large kale leaves,** cut into 1-inch slices
> **2 cups fresh baby spinach**
> **Shredded basil leaves,** for garnish

1. In a small bowl, combine the miso, peanut oil, oyster sauce, garlic, ginger, soy sauce and dried cherries. Whisk until well combined.

2. Heat the sesame oil in a wok or large saucepan over medium heat. Add the green beans, broccoli, salt, water and cellophane noodles and cook, constantly stirring, until the broccoli and noodles are tender, about 4 minutes.

3. Reduce the heat to medium-low. Add the kale, spinach and sauce. Toss until greens are wilted.

4. To serve, divide among four plates, top with basil and serve.

Nonvegetarian Version

Add 6 ounces of chicken tenders or 1 pound fresh salmon cut into 1-inch pieces. Simmer 4 minutes with vegetables or until tender.

Frugal Options

Use frozen green beans, broccoli, cherries and/or spinach.

*Miso substitute: ½ tablespoon low-sodium soy sauce and ½ tablespoon low-sodium chicken stock or bone broth (see page 55).

Per serving: calories 153.6, total fat 8.4 g, saturated fat 1.1 g, cholesterol 0.0 mg, sodium 458.5 mg, potassium 255.7 mg, total carbohydrate 18.2 g, dietary fiber 3.4 g, sugars 3.0 g, protein 3.6 g

🍽 *Omega-Mighty Toasted Shrimp Pasta*

Makes 4 servings

The Mediterranean region is the source of many arthritis-friendly foods, and this recipe features a number of them. Here's an old Sicilian secret: Use toasted breadcrumbs—*mollica* in Italian or *muddica* in Sicilian—in pasta dishes to add volume, flavor and texture. Garlic, olive oil and basil are the basis of the topping.

Pasta with Wilted Spinach
> ¾ **pound whole-wheat penne**
> 1 **teaspoon salt**
> 3 **cups baby spinach**

Toasted Shrimp:
> 2 **tablespoons light olive oil,** divided
> ½ **cup whole-wheat breadcrumbs**
> ¼ **head cauliflower,** thinly sliced and cut into 1-inch-long pieces
> 1 **heaping teaspoon minced garlic**
> 8 **leaves fresh basil,** julienned
> ¼ **teaspoon sea salt**
> 12 **ounces medium shrimp,** peeled and deveined
> 4 **tablespoons freshly grated Parmesan cheese**

1. Cook the pasta according to package directions for al dente. Add salt to water just before pasta.
2. While the pasta is cooking, prepare the toasted shrimp topping. Heat 1 tablespoon of the olive oil in a large skillet over medium heat. Add the breadcrumbs, cauliflower, garlic, basil and salt and stir to combine. Sauté until breadcrumbs are lightly toasted (about 5 minutes) and cauliflower is tender. Stir constantly, so the crumbs don't burn. Set aside.
3. When the pasta is done, drain and return to the pot. Toss the spinach with the hot pasta until it begins to wilt. Add the breadcrumb mixture to the pasta pot and toss.
4. Wipe out the skillet. Add the remaining tablespoon of olive oil to the skillet and heat over medium heat. When it is hot, add the shrimp and sauté, 3 to 5 minutes.
5. Divide the pasta mixture among four plates and top with shrimp, sprinkle with Parmesan and serve.

Vegetarian Version
> Add extra vegetables or sautéed tofu instead of shrimp.

Frugal Options
> See "vegetarian version" above. Use frozen spinach or cauliflower. Use frozen shrimp.

Per serving: calories 457.2, total fat 6.2 g, saturated fat 1.4 g, cholesterol 169.0 mg, sodium 428.5 mg, potassium 176.2 mg, total carbohydrate 70.9 g, dietary fiber 9.4 g, sugars 1.1 g, protein 31.5 g

🍽 *Anti-Arthritis Grilled Tuna on Chopped Berry-Bean Salad*

Makes 2 servings

Fresh pineapple and strawberries are teamed with Serrano chilies for a sweet-spicy contrast typical of the flavorful foods of Asia.

Berry-Bean Salad
- ¼ cup finely chopped fresh pineapple
- 5 fresh strawberries, finely diced
- ¼ teaspoon finely chopped Serrano chilies
- 1 cup 1-inch fresh green bean pieces
- 1 teaspoon crushed walnuts
- Salt and pepper, to taste
- Pinch cayenne pepper
- 1 tablespoon finely chopped fresh cilantro
- 5 cups fresh spinach or shredded purple cabbage

Grilled Tuna
- Two 4-ounce tuna steaks
- 1 teaspoon light olive oil
- ¼ teaspoon salt

1. Heat a well-seasoned gas grill to medium heat for at least 4 minutes with the lid closed until it reaches 350°F. Or heat a seasoned grill pan on medium heat for 3 minutes.
2. While the grill is heating, prepare the salad. In a large bowl, combine the pineapple, strawberries, Serrano chilies, green beans, walnuts, salt, cayenne and cilantro. Mix until well combined and set aside.
3. Prepare the grilled tuna. Rub the tuna steaks with the olive oil and salt. Place the tuna on the grill and cook 2 minutes per side for medium-rare, 3 minutes for medium and 4 for well done.
4. To assemble, divide the spinach or cabbage between two plates, top with the salad and grilled tuna and serve.

Vegetarian Version

Substitute 1 tablespoon lightly toasted almonds plus two 4-ounce sautéed tofu slices for tuna.

Frugal Options

See "vegetarian version" above.
Use one-half the amount of pineapple and substitute frozen strawberries for the fresh.

Per serving: calories 216.9, total fat 4.2 g, saturated fat 0.4 g, cholesterol 0.0 mg, sodium 140.3 mg, potassium 556.4 mg, total carbohydrate 9.1 g, dietary fiber 3.8 g, sugars 0.3 g, protein 37.0 g

🍴 *Joint-Cooling Seafood Scampi Salad and Roasted Vegetables*

Makes 4 servings

Sauté a combination of shrimp and diced fish fillets in aromatic garlic and serve over delectable roasted vegetables. Let your favorite vegetables be the colorful centerpiece to balance the seafood.

Roasted Vegetables

1 pound vegetables, roughly chopped, such as cauliflower, cabbage, broccoli florets or fresh green beans
1 teaspoon olive oil
2 teaspoons finely chopped fresh basil, oregano or rosemary

Seafood Scampi Salad

1 tablespoon light olive oil
1 shallot, peeled and finely chopped
4 cloves garlic, sliced thin
1 pound fresh roughly chopped seafood, such as tuna, salmon, scallops, shrimp, halibut or trout
2 teaspoons commercial Italian seasoning blend
½ cup dry white wine
6 cups fresh baby spinach

1. Place the oven rack on the lowest shelf of the oven and preheat to 400°F.

2. Lay vegetables on a baking sheet and sprinkle with 1 teaspoon olive oil and the herbs. Toss until the vegetables are thoroughly coated. Roast for about 20 minutes. Vegetables are done when they are tender.

3. Heat the olive oil in a wok or large saucepan over medium heat. When the oil starts to ripple, carefully add the shallot to the wok and sauté 2 minutes. It is best to use a splatter screen as the shallots may pop and spray oil.

4. Reduce the heat to medium-low and add the garlic, seafood and Italian seasoning. Cook for 2 minutes until the seafood is opaque and cooked through.

5. Carefully add the wine. Do not pour directly from the bottle; pour the wine into a glass before pouring into the wok. Cook for another minute.

6. Remove from the heat and begin to fold the spinach into the sauce. As it wilts, continue adding spinach by the handful until all 6 cups are used.

7. Divide the vegetables among four plates and cover with a heaping mound of seafood and serve.

Vegetarian Version

Substitute sautéed tofu or black beans for seafood.

Per serving: calories 285.2, total fat 7.0 g, saturated fat 0.9 g, cholesterol 86.1 mg, sodium 176.3 mg, potassium 1,124.1 mg, total carbohydrate 20.2 g, dietary fiber 7.8 g, sugars 0.2 g, protein 34.5 g

---

🍽 *Arthritis-Soothing Cherry-Roasted Cauliflower*

Makes 2 servings

Roasting peppered cauliflower livens up this simple, nutritious vegetable. Cherries and lemon juice offer a subtle sweet-and-sour complement to the succulent cauliflower.

1 head cauliflower (intact), cut into ½-inch-thick slices from top to stem, so that the pieces lie flat
1 tablespoon light olive oil
3 tablespoons lemon juice
4 tablespoons roughly chopped dried cherries
1 teaspoon salt
Pinch freshly ground black pepper

1. Place an oven rack on the middle shelf of the oven and preheat to 350°F. On a sheet pan, spread the cauliflower in a single layer.
2. In a small bowl, combine the olive oil, lemon juice, cherries, salt and pepper and mix until well blended. Drizzle the cauliflower with the mixture and bake for 25 minutes, until the cauliflower is tender. Halfway through the cooking process, turn the cauliflower. Some of the smaller pieces may cook more quickly; watch them carefully to avoid burning.
3. Remove the cauliflower from the oven, making sure to scrape up all the bits, transfer to a dish and serve.

Nonvegetarian Version

Once the cauliflower is cooked, add 6 ounces lean, thinly sliced sautéed buffalo steak. Toss and serve.

Per serving: calories 248.9, total fat 10.1 g, saturated fat 1.3 g, cholesterol 0.0 mg, sodium 207.6 mg, potassium 1,407.2 mg, total carbohydrate 37.4 g, dietary fiber 11.6 g, sugars 9.8 g, protein 9.4 g

Arthritis-Busting Upside-Down Cherry and Strawberry Cobbler

Makes 4 cobblers, 2 servings each

I love to make upside-down cobblers because they are easy to assemble. You may substitute other arthritis-healing fruits for the cherries and strawberries. The cobbler dough-to-fruit filling ratio is about two to one. If you prefer less dough and more fruit, reduce the dough recipe by half.

Fruit Filling

1 teaspoon light olive oil
20 frozen cherries
10 **strawberries**, hulled and sliced
1 teaspoon xylitol or birch sugar

Cobbler Dough

1 cup whole-wheat pastry flour
2 tablespoons almond flour
2 tablespoons ground flaxseed
1 tablespoon baking powder
Pinch salt
1 tablespoon xylitol or birch sugar
3 tablespoons unsalted butter from grass-fed cows, melted
1 cup almond milk or vanilla soy milk

1. Preheat the oven to 350°F. Place the oven rack in the middle.
2. Heat the olive oil in a medium pan over medium heat. Add the cherries, strawberries and sugar. Sauté for 5 minutes or until the fruit starts to release its juices. Remove from the heat.
3. In a medium bowl, mix the flours, flaxseed, baking powder, salt, sugar, butter and milk until a dough forms.
4. Divide the dough among four 3-inch pie pans. Pour the cherries and strawberries, with their juices, on top and bake for about 20 minutes. The cobblers are done when the crust is a light golden brown and the fruit is bubbling.
5. Let the cobblers cool slightly before serving.

Per serving: calories 139.1, total fat 6.9 g, saturated fat 2.9 g, cholesterol 11.7 mg, sodium 221.7 mg, potassium 97.8 mg, total carbohydrate 19.0 g, dietary fiber 3.3 g, sugars 5.1 g, protein 3.1 g

---

🍽️ *Cancer-Clobbering Carrot Bisque*

Makes 2 servings

This Mediterr-Asian carrot soup has a gingery bite, but the goat cheese cools it off. If you want less bite, use only one tablespoon of ginger. For an eye-catching presentation, serve the bright orange soup next to a green garden salad.

6 large carrots, peeled and diced
2 heaping tablespoons plus 1 teaspoon fresh minced ginger
1 quart low-sodium vegetable broth
1 teaspoon ground coriander
1 tablespoon extra-virgin olive oil
1 ounce goat's milk cheese
Pinch nutmeg
Pinch cinnamon

1. In a medium saucepan over medium-high heat, combine the carrots, ginger, broth and coriander, and bring to a boil. Cook at a high boil, stirring constantly, for 35 minutes, or until the carrots are tender.

2. Remove from the heat, add the olive oil and blend the soup—either in a food processor or using an immersion blender—until it is smooth.

3. Ladle soup into two bowls. Garnish with a dab of goat cheese and a sprinkle of nutmeg and cinnamon and serve.

Nonvegetarian Version

Sauté chicken tenders in garlic, dice and add to the soup.

Per serving: calories 227.7, total fat 10.5 g, saturated fat 3.2 g, cholesterol 6.6 mg, sodium 487.4 mg, potassium 732.7 mg, total carbohydrate 28.7 g, dietary fiber 8.4 g, sugars 14.4 g, protein 4.9 g

---

🍴 *Cancer-Blocking Summer Fruity Soups*

Each recipe makes 2 servings

Chilled fruit soups are one of the most inexpensive, nourishing and easy dishes you can make, and they're full of cancer-healing vitamins and antioxidants. A garnish of fresh fruit slices, ground nuts, cilantro or mint adds a simple but artistic touch.

Mango-Peach Soup

Flesh of 1 freshly peeled mango
1 cup peach juice
½ peach, peeled and cut into thin slices

1. In a blender, combine the mango and peach juice and pulse until you reach the desired consistency, from chunky to smooth.
2. Transfer to a bowl and chill for 1 hour. Serve with peach slices floating on top.

> ***Per serving:*** calories 144.0, total fat 0.3 g, saturated fat 0.1 g, cholesterol 0.0 mg, sodium 10.8 mg, potassium 211.3 mg, total carbohydrate 37.2 g, dietary fiber 2.9 g, sugars 33.9 g, protein 1.1 g

Spicy Peach-Apple Soup

10 ounces frozen peaches
1 cup apple juice
¼ teaspoon red curry paste*
¼ apple, cored and cut into thin slices
1 tablespoon finely chopped fresh cilantro

*Red curry paste is found in the Asian or international section of most grocery stores.

1. In a blender, combine the peaches, apple juice and curry paste and pulse until you reach the desired consistency, from chunky to smooth.
2. Pour into two bowls, top with apple slices and cilantro, and serve.

> ***Per serving:*** calories 118.5, total fat 0.6 g, saturated fat 0.0 g, cholesterol 0.0 mg, sodium 15.1 mg, potassium 238.5 mg, total carbohydrate 27.3 g, dietary fiber 2.3 g, sugars 17.0 g, protein 1.1 g

Strawberry-Kiwi Soup

1 large or 2 medium fresh or frozen strawberries, chopped
2 kiwi, peeled
1 cup pomegranate juice
Leaves from 1 rosemary sprig, finely chopped
2 fresh basil leaves

In a blender, combine the strawberries, kiwi, pomegranate juice, rosemary and basil and pulse until you reach the desired consistency, from chunky to smooth. Serve immediately.

Per serving: calories 118.5, total fat 0.6 g, saturated fat 0.0 g, cholesterol 0.0 mg, sodium 15.1 mg, potassium 238.5 mg, total carbohydrate 27.3 g, dietary fiber 2.3 g, sugars 17.0 g, protein 1.1 g

Frozen Blueberry-Yogurt Soup

2 cups frozen blueberries
1 cup 2% Greek yogurt
1 cup orange juice
8 dried blueberries

1. In a blender, combine the blueberries, Greek yogurt and orange juice and pulse until you reach the desired consistency, from chunky to smooth.
2. Serve with a few dried blueberries floating on top.

Per serving: calories 256.9, total fat 3.0 g, saturated fat 1.1 g, cholesterol 10.0 mg, sodium 53.2 mg, potassium 481.3 mg, total carbohydrate 49.4 g, dietary fiber 5.4 g, sugars 37.1 g, protein 13.4 g

🍽 *Extra-Antioxidant Roasted Veggie-Spinach Salad*

Makes 2 large servings

If you're looking for a salad that's as satisfying as a whole meal, this is the one. Roasting Brussels sprouts gives this earthy vegetable a deeper and richer flavor. It is a filling lunch salad as is; add roasted wild salmon for a fine dinner.

Roasted Brussels Sprouts

10 Brussels sprouts, trimmed and cut into ¼-inch slices
1 tablespoon light olive oil
3 tablespoons lemon juice
1 teaspoon dried oregano
4 tablespoons roughly chopped unsweetened dried mango
1 teaspoon salt
⅛ teaspoon freshly ground black pepper

Spinach Salad and Dressing

1 tablespoon extra-virgin olive oil
1 teaspoon balsamic vinegar
1 tablespoon raw or roasted pumpkin seeds
4 cups fresh baby spinach
1 tablespoon broccoli sprouts

1. Place an oven rack on the middle shelf of the oven and preheat to 400°F.
2. Place the Brussels sprouts on a baking sheet in a single layer. In a small bowl, combine the light olive oil, lemon juice, oregano, mango, salt and pepper and whisk until well blended. Toss the Brussels sprouts with the olive-oil mixture. Roast for 15 minutes, or until the sprouts are tender. Halfway through the cooking process, toss the Brussels sprouts. Some of the smaller pieces may cook more quickly and begin to darken.
3. While the sprouts are roasting, prepare the salad dressing. In a large bowl, combine the light olive oil and vinegar and whisk until well blended. Stir in the pumpkin seeds.
4. Remove the Brussels sprouts from the oven and add them to the bowl with the salad dressing, along with the spinach and broccoli sprouts. Toss thoroughly and serve.

Nonvegetarian Version

While the sprouts are roasting, place two 4-ounce salmon fillets in a separate baking dish and roast in the hot oven for 7 minutes, or until opaque.

Per serving: calories 216.0, total fat 14.7 g, saturated fat 2.1 g, cholesterol 0.0 mg, sodium 194.0 mg, potassium 746.5 mg, total carbohydrate 20.0 g, dietary fiber 5.8 g, sugars 7.8 g, protein 5.4 g

🍽 *Estrogen-Balancing Spicy Tofu-Pineapple Salad*

Makes 4 servings

Tofu is seen as an alternative protein in the West, but it is a very popular ingredient in Asia. To serve this salad cold, simply place the tofu directly on a mound of chilled spicy pineapple. For a splash of extra flavor, spoon some juice from the pineapple salad on top. You can serve it hot by adding the spicy pineapple salad to the wok at the last minute.

Spicy Pineapple

4 canned pineapple rings, diced
4 plum tomatoes, cored, seeded and diced
2 tablespoons chopped unsweetened dried mango
1 apricot, seeded, peeled and chopped
½ teaspoon finely chopped Serrano pepper
Pinch salt
1 teaspoon ground flaxseed, optional

Fried Tofu Slices

2 teaspoons olive oil
4 ounces extra-firm tofu, cut into 8 slices

1. In a medium bowl, combine the pineapple, tomatoes, mango, apricot, Serrano pepper, salt and ground flaxseed (if using). Mix until well blended. Cover, then chill.
2. Heat the olive oil in a pan large enough to hold the tofu slices in a single layer (if your pan isn't big enough, cook the tofu in batches). Add the tofu, and fry until golden, about 4 minutes per side.
3. Place the pineapple salad on each plate, top with two tofu slices and serve.

Nonvegetarian Version

Top salad with bits of sautéed, all-natural turkey.

Per serving: calories 94.1, total fat 3.5 g, saturated fat 0.4 g, cholesterol 0.0 mg, sodium 54.8 mg, potassium 81.9 mg, total carbohydrate 13.9 g, dietary fiber 2.8 g, sugars 10.8 g, protein 3.0 g

---

🍽 *Cancer-Protective Spicy Tofu Kebabs with Pear Relish*

Makes 4 servings

Sweet pears and spicy chili sauce flavor this tasty Asian tofu kebab. When grilling, it's important not to burn your food—then it will be rendered unhealthy. This dish can also be prepared in a large skillet instead.

Pear Relish

> 1 teaspoon light olive oil
> ⅓ cup peeled and finely chopped shallots
> 1 whole pear, cored and finely chopped
> ½ cup pomegranate juice

Spicy Tofu and Onions

> 1 heaping teaspoon chili sauce
> 1 tablespoon sesame oil
> 1 tablespoon finely chopped parsley
> 1 tablespoon water
> 15 ounces extra-firm tofu, cut into 1-inch cubes
> 2 large red onions, peeled, root end intact and sliced into 8 wedges (make sure each wedge has a piece of the root end so that it will hold together)

1. To prepare the relish, heat the olive oil in a small pan over medium heat. Sauté the shallots and pear until they are tender, about 7 minutes. Reduce the heat to low and stir in the pomegranate juice. When the relish is well blended, remove from the heat, transfer to a bowl and place in the freezer to chill quickly.

2. In a large resealable plastic bag, combine the chili sauce, sesame oil, parsley and water. Mix gently, making sure the chili sauce is well distributed. Add the tofu and onions and seal the bag.

3. Heat a gas grill to medium. As the grill heats, scrape the grates clean, then wipe with a towel dipped (but not dripping) in olive oil.

4. When the grill is hot, remove the onions from the bag and grill them for 5 minutes.

5. Thread the tofu cubes onto 8 metal skewers, place them on the grates and grill for about 2 minutes per side. The onions are done when they are tender. The tofu is done when it has grill marks on both sides.

6. Remove the relish from the freezer. Mound the onions onto a platter, slide the kebabs off the skewers and place atop the onions. Top with the cool relish and serve.

Nonvegetarian Version

Substitute cubed chicken breast or buffalo sirloin for tofu.

Frugal Options

Use unsweetened canned pears instead of fresh. Use 100% pure apple juice instead of pomegranate juice.

Per serving: calories 228.2, total fat 11.5 g, saturated fat 1.6 g, cholesterol 0.4 mg, sodium 29.3 mg, potassium 302.2 mg, total carbohydrate 22.5 g, dietary fiber 2.3 g, sugars 7.9 g, protein 12.3 g

Beta-Carotene Roasted Winter Squash with Fruity Asian Vinaigrette
Makes 4 servings

Roasted winter squash has a rich, nutty flavor. It is especially tasty coated with this sweet and salty vinaigrette. The soybeans provide protein and gentle estrogen, as well as a garden-fresh flavor.

Roasted Squash
> **One 2-pound winter squash** (such as butternut), peeled, seeded and cut into 1-inch pieces
> **1 cup cooked shelled soybeans (edamame)**

Asian Vinaigrette
> **1 tablespoon chopped dried unsulphured apricots**
> **1 tablespoon chopped dried cherries**
> **1 tablespoon miso paste**
> **1 tablespoon soy sauce**
> **Freshly ground black pepper,** to taste
> **1 tablespoon light olive oil**
> **1 teaspoon balsamic vinegar**
> **1 tablespoon minced chives**
> **¼ cup water**

1. Place an oven rack on the middle shelf of the oven and preheat to 350°F.
2. Place the squash on a baking sheet sprayed with nonfat cooking spray, cover it with foil and bake in the oven for 50 minutes or until tender. A knife should easily pass through it. Let cool slightly.
3. While the squash is baking, prepare the vinaigrette. Combine the apricot, cherries, miso paste, soy sauce, pepper, olive oil, vinegar, chives and water in a standing blender. Pulse until well combined.
4. Divide the squash between four plates, top with edamame, drizzle with vinaigrette and serve.

Nonvegetarian Version
Bake four 4-ounce salmon fillets on a separate baking sheet for 7 minutes, or until opaque.

Frugal Options
Use frozen fruit instead of dried.

Per serving: calories 197.5, total fat 6.7 g, saturated fat 0.8 g, cholesterol 0.0 mg, sodium 492.6 mg, potassium 869.6 mg, total carbohydrate 30.9 g, dietary fiber 8.2 g, sugars 3.0 g, protein 8.2 g

🍽 *Cancer-Curbing Broccoli alla Cacciatore*

Makes 6 servings

Alla cacciatore indicates an Italian dish prepared hunter-style—that is, with mushrooms—and this vegetarian version pairs two very powerful cancer-healing ingredients: broccoli and tomatoes. My Sicilian grandmother always told me, "Everything you want to know about a sauce is in the tomatoes," and taught me to break them up in my hands for the best texture. Add the earthy flavors of Asian maitake or shiitake mushrooms and this old classic becomes a Mediterr-Asian gem.

1 teaspoon light olive oil
1 large white onion, peeled and sliced
2 cups sliced maitake or shiitake mushrooms
1 cup dry red wine
1 tablespoon minced roasted garlic
1 teaspoon commercial Italian seasoning blend
1 quart low-sodium vegetable broth
3 pounds Roma tomatoes, roughly chopped or broken up into pieces
2–3 heads broccoli, cut into florets with 1-inch stems
1 pound whole-wheat linguine

1. Heat the olive oil in a Dutch oven over medium heat. Add the onion and mushrooms and sauté until the mushrooms release their juices, about 3 minutes. Add a couple of tablespoons of water to the pan if the mushrooms seem to be drying out.

2. Raise the heat to high and add the wine, garlic and Italian seasoning while stirring constantly until the mushrooms absorb the liquid. Lower the heat to medium and add the broth, tomatoes and broccoli. Make sure the broccoli is completely submerged and cook at a medium simmer for 15 minutes. Stir the sauce occasionally to ensure it doesn't stick.

3. Prepare the pasta according to the package directions. When the pasta is done, drain and toss it with the vegetables and sauce.

4. Divide among six warmed deep bowls and serve.

Nonvegetarian Version

Add sautéed chicken tenders or shrimp to the simmering vegetables.

Frugal Options

Use white mushrooms instead of maitake and shiitake.

Per serving: calories 378.7, total fat 1.8 g, saturated fat 0.1 g, cholesterol 0.0 mg, sodium 144.6 mg, potassium 746.9 mg, total carbohydrate 77.2 g, dietary fiber 11.6 g, sugars 8.3 g, protein 13.1 g

---

🍽️ *Anti-Cancer Greek Spinach Pie*

Makes 2 servings

This is an easy, crustless version of the Greek spinach pie called spanokopita. It can be made with either regular or baby spinach. Whichever you choose, top with oregano for traditional Greek flavor. The extra vegetables add a nourishing bonus of texture. For the adventurous, instructions for a version with a phyllo-dough crust are included.

1 teaspoon light olive oil
2 scallions, ends removed, finely chopped
5 Brussels sprouts, trimmed and finely sliced
4 cups fresh spinach
½ cup low-fat feta cheese crumbles, rinsed
1 teaspoon finely chopped garlic
1 tablespoon finely chopped parsley
1 omega-3 egg, whisked
½ teaspoon salt
1 teaspoon fresh lemon juice
Few sprigs fresh oregano

1. Place an oven rack on the middle shelf of the oven. Preheat to 350°F. Brush a 9-inch loaf pan or 8-inch casserole dish with olive oil and set aside.

2. Heat the olive oil in a wok or large saucepan over medium heat. Sauté the scallions and Brussels sprouts until tender, about 7 minutes.

3. Reduce the heat to medium-low. Add the spinach, feta cheese, garlic, parsley, egg and salt and stir until well blended. Add the lemon juice. Remove from heat.

4. Scoop the spinach mixture into a prepared loaf pan or casserole dish, top with oregano sprigs and bake for 15 minutes. The top should turn golden brown. If the top starts to burn before cooking time is up, place a piece of foil over it.

5. Let the spinach pie cool slightly before slicing and serving.

Spanokopita with Phyllo-Dough Crust

Purchase a frozen or fresh package of phyllo-dough sheets. Brush six sheets of phyllo dough on both sides with olive oil. Place three pieces at the bottom of the oiled casserole. Add the filling. Place three remaining sheets of phyllo dough on top. Bake, uncovered, until golden brown, about 30 minutes.

Nonvegetarian Version

Cook sautéed chicken tenders or shrimp with the vegetables in the wok.

Frugal Options

Purchase feta cheese in a block instead of crumbled. Replace fresh oregano sprigs with a sprinkle of dried oregano.

Per serving: calories 182.4, total fat 9.2 g, saturated fat 3.6 g, cholesterol 110.0 mg, sodium 508.6 mg, potassium 538.1 mg, total carbohydrate 8.2 g, dietary fiber 3.7 g, sugars 1.3 g, protein 13.5 g

🍽 *Cancer-Conquering Warm Vegetable Salad with Asian Flavors*

Makes 4 servings

When vegetables are in season, they are best prepared simply so that their natural flavors shine through. You can use a wok for this recipe, but a large sauce pot works just as well.

Garlic Dressing

1 tablespoon minced garlic
1 teaspoon minced ginger
1 tablespoon sesame oil
1 tablespoon all-natural, low-sodium teriyaki sauce
1 teaspoon sesame seeds
1 tablespoon water
Dash lime juice

Vegetable Salad

2 teaspoons light olive oil
1 medium white onion, peeled and finely chopped
1 cup finely chopped carrot
1 bunch broccoli rabe, cut into small pieces
1 cup quartered canned artichoke hearts
1 cup finely sliced shiitake mushrooms
6 cups fresh baby spinach

1. To prepare the dressing, combine the garlic, ginger, sesame oil, teriyaki sauce, sesame seeds and water in a blender. Pulse until well blended. Add a dash of lime juice and set aside.
2. Heat the olive oil in a wok or large saucepan over medium heat. Make sure that the entire surface of the pan is coated. Add the onion and carrot, and sauté until they are golden, about 4 minutes. Stir constantly, so that the vegetables cook evenly.
3. Reduce the heat to medium-low and add the broccoli rabe, artichoke hearts and mushrooms. Cook until the broccoli is tender, about 2 minutes.
4. Remove from the heat and fold in the spinach. As the spinach hits the hot pan, it will wilt.
5. Divide the salad among four plates, drizzle with dressing and serve.

Nonvegetarian Version

Serve the salad on a lean piece of sautéed chicken or buffalo.

Frugal Option

Use frozen vegetables, thawed, instead of fresh.

Per serving: calories 111.9, total fat 6.5 g, saturated fat 0.9 g, cholesterol 0.0 mg, sodium 149.4 mg, potassium 327.8 mg, total carbohydrate 10.6 g, dietary fiber 3.8 g, sugars 3.6 g, protein 4.2 g

Lignan-Rich Bean Croquettes with Pomegranate Dipping Sauce

Makes 5 servings (2 croquettes each)

Bean croquettes are a fun dish to prepare. They're a delicious fusion of Asian and Mediterranean tastes, and they're a conversation piece because the name comes from the French *croquant* (which means crunchy or crisp). Popular in Europe, they are often eaten while on the go. Once you learn the technique, apply it to other minced ingredients, such as seafood or healing vegetables. Complete the meal with a side of steamed broccoli and a spicy tomato soup.

Bean Croquettes

½ cup minced white onions
12 ounces canned beans, such as white, lima or black beans, drained and rinsed
½ cup whole-wheat breadcrumbs
¼ cup finely grated Parmesan cheese
2 tablespoons fresh parsley
½ teaspoon curry powder
1 omega-3 egg

Pomegranate Dipping Sauce

½ cup pomegranate juice
½ cup canned mandarin orange segments
1 teaspoon minced garlic
1 tablespoon sesame oil

1. Place an oven rack on the middle shelf of the oven and preheat to 350°F.

2. In a blender, combine the onions, beans, breadcrumbs, cheese, parsley, curry and egg. Pulse until a paste has formed. Form into 10 balls, 2 tablespoons of the mixture for each. Set them on a baking sheet. Bake for 15 minutes. The croquettes are done when they are slightly firm and golden. Remove from the oven. Egg might have seeped out from some of the croquettes, because there is very little binder.

3. To prepare the dipping sauce, combine the pomegranate juice, mandarin oranges, garlic and sesame oil in a small bowl. Mix gently so as not to break up the orange segments. Set aside.

4. Place two croquettes on each of five plates, drizzle with the dipping sauce and serve.

Nonvegetarian Version

Substitute minced chicken or minced seafood for the beans.

Frugal Option

Use 100% pure apple juice instead of pomegranate juice.

Per serving: calories 202.0, total fat 6.0 g, saturated fat 1.7 g, cholesterol 41.9 mg, sodium 188.8 mg, potassium 320.9 mg, total carbohydrate 29.1 g, dietary fiber 4.5 g, sugars 7.8 g, protein 8.7 g

---

🍴 *Cancer-Healing Baked Apple-Berry Crisp*

Makes 6 servings

This dish can be made with any healing fruit. Bran flakes may be sprinkled on the oatmeal during the last five minutes of baking.

1½ **cups oats,** divided
2 **tablespoons unsalted butter from grass-fed cows,** melted and divided
2 **tablespoons ground flaxseed**
¼ **teaspoon baking powder**
¼ **teaspoon ground cinnamon**
¼ **cup xylitol or birch sugar**
1 **tablespoon raw agave nectar**
½ **cup applesauce**
1 **omega-3 egg,** whisked
1 **apple,** peeled, cored, and diced
½ **cup blueberries**
Vanilla soy ice cream, optional

1. With the oven rack placed in the middle, preheat the oven to 350°F.
2. In a medium bowl, mix 1 cup of the oats, 1 tablespoon of the butter, flaxseed, baking powder, cinnamon, sugar, agave and applesauce until well combined.
3. Mix in the egg, apple and blueberries. Transfer to a casserole dish. Bake for 20 minutes.
4. Place the remaining oats on a small baking sheet and drizzle with the remaining melted butter. Bake alongside the oatmeal-fruit mixture, stirring occasionally.
5. After the oatmeal-fruit mixture has baked for 15 minutes, top it with the toasted oats. Serve with soy ice cream, if using.

Per serving: calories 188.1, total fat 6.7 g, saturated fat 2.8 g, cholesterol 42.0 mg, sodium 232.8 mg, potassium 124.3 mg, total carbohydrate 23.6 g, dietary fiber 4.0 g, sugars 5.8 g, protein 4.8 g

⦿ *Mood-Lifting Tossed Shrimp Bean Rice Salad*

Makes 4 servings

Once the rice is cooked, this dish takes about 2 minutes to prepare. The texture of white beans complements shrimp, but navy, lima, black-eyed peas or chickpeas work, too. This recipe uses chicken stock instead of water for preparing the rice, which gives it a bit more flavor and healing properties.

Rice

- **1 cup jasmine or brown rice**
- **2 cups free-range, low-sodium chicken broth**
- **1 tablespoon finely chopped fresh cilantro**
- **1 tablespoon sesame seeds**
- **1 cup canned beans, drained and rinsed** (white, navy, lima, black eye or chickpeas)

Shrimp

- **1 teaspoon light olive oil**
- **½ teaspoon fresh ginger,** minced
- **1 teaspoon finely chopped fresh parsley**
- **1 teaspoon soy sauce**
- **1 pound medium shrimp,** peeled, deveined and tails removed
- **1 large bunch kale**
- **1 teaspoon toasted sesame oil**

1. In a medium saucepot with a lid, prepare the rice according to the package directions, using chicken broth instead of water. One cup of jasmine rice usually requires 2 cups of stock and takes 20 minutes to cook. (Brown rice will require 20 additional minutes cooking time.) When the rice is done, fluff with a fork and set aside. When it cools slightly, sprinkle it with the cilantro and sesame seeds, add the beans and toss.
2. Heat olive oil in a wok over medium heat. Add the ginger, parsley, soy sauce, shrimp and kale. Cook until the shrimp is cooked through, about 2 minutes per side, and the kale has wilted. Remove from the heat and add the rice and sesame oil. Toss and serve directly from the wok.

Vegetarian Version

Omit the shrimp. Use vegetable broth instead of chicken broth.

Frugal Option

Omit the shrimp.

Per serving: calories 317.0, total fat 6.6 g, saturated fat 1.0 g, cholesterol 173.0 mg, sodium 280.9 mg, potassium 722.9 mg, total carbohydrate 32.8 g, dietary fiber 8.6 g, sugars 1.8 g, protein 32.1 g

Brain-Building Hoisin Beef Tapas with Spicy Pear Skewers

Makes 2 servings

When you have little time to prepare a meal, this dish is an excellent choice. It takes just a few minutes and cleanup is easy. I like to combine the contrasting flavors and textures of soft fruit and hearty meat in one bite. If you prefer fish to meat, substitute fresh tuna for the steak. The fruit can also be varied. Instead of pear, try apple, mango, pineapple, plum or peach.

Spicy Sauce for Pear Skewers
   1 teaspoon chili sauce
   1 tablespoon toasted sesame oil
   ¼ teaspoon salt

Skewers
   1 **pear,** cored and cut into 1-inch pieces
   ½ **pound (8 ounces) grass-fed sirloin,** sliced very thin
   ¼ **cup hoisin sauce**

Seed-and-Nut Salad
   2 heaping cups baby spinach
   1 teaspoon sunflower seeds

1. To make the spicy sauce, in a small bowl, combine the chili sauce, sesame oil and salt. Add the pear pieces and toss until well coated. Set aside.
2. In a separate bowl, combine the sirloin strips and hoisin sauce and mix until well combined. Set aside.
3. Clean a gas grill by wiping the grates with water, dry, then coat with olive oil. Set the heat on medium to reach a temperature of 375°F to 400°F.
4. Prepare the skewers by alternating the pear and the beef. Add two pieces of thin beef at a time. Push together so that the beef is well sandwiched between the pear. You should be able to make 3 or 4 skewers.
5. Grill the skewers for 2 to 3 minutes per side or until the beef is medium-rare. Feel free to baste the skewered pear slices with leftover spicy sauce and the skewered beef with more hoisin. To assemble, divide the spinach and sunflower seeds between two plates, top them with the skewers and serve.

Vegetarian Version
   Substitute tofu for beef.

Frugal Option
   Use free-range chicken tenders for the beef.

Per serving: calories 401.4, total fat 17.3 g, saturated fat 4.7 g, cholesterol 101.3 mg, sodium 466.6 mg, potassium 655.9 mg, total carbohydrate 16.7 g, dietary fiber 2.3 g, sugars 1.7 g, protein 36.1 g

🍴 *Blues-Busting Hunan Lamb Chop Salad*

Makes 4 servings

Lamb is delicate and requires very little cooking time. It is low in fat, with a distinctive hearty flavor. Marinating the iron-rich meat overnight is an excellent way to tenderize it and infuse it with flavor. This recipe is worthy of the most chic dinner party, with the preparation time of a simple home-cooked meal.

Marinade
- 1 tablespoon sherry vinegar
- 1 teaspoon minced ginger
- 1 teaspoon garlic paste, (store-bought)
- 1 tablespoon hoisin sauce
- 1 cup dry red wine
- ½ fresh plum, thinly sliced

Sauce
- ½ cup low-sodium beef stock, (store-bought or homemade)
- 1 tablespoon hoisin sauce
- ¼ cup finely chopped dried cherries
- 2 tablespoons finely chopped fresh parsley
- 1 tablespoon finely chopped dried mango
- ½ cup crushed pecans or almonds, optional

Lamb Chop Salad
- 4 lamb chops (about 1 pound)
- 4 heaping cups fresh baby spinach
- 1 chopped Russet baked potato, leave skin on

1. To make the marinade, combine the sherry vinegar, ginger, garlic paste, hoisin sauce, wine, plums and lamb chops in a large glass bowl. Cover the bowl with plastic wrap and marinate overnight.
2. Place an oven rack 6 inches from the broiler and preheat the broiler.
3. To make the sauce, combine the beef stock, hoisin sauce, cherries, parsley and mango in a small saucepan. Cook over low heat for 6 minutes.
4. Remove the lamb chops from the marinade and shake off any excess liquid. Place on a sheet pan or broiler pan and under the broiler. Broil the lamb chops for 4 minutes on the first side and 3 minutes on the second for medium-rare. Remove from the oven and let rest briefly.
5. To assemble, divide the spinach and potato among four plates and place the lamb chops on top. Spoon the sauce over the lamb and salad, sprinkle with nuts, if using, and serve.

Vegetarian Version

Substitute tofu slices for lamb chops.

Frugal Option

See "vegetarian version" above.

*Salad: **per serving:** calories 337.7, total fat 11.9 g, saturated fat 2.7 g, cholesterol 72.7 mg, sodium 216.5 mg, potassium 1,084.0 mg, total carbohydrate 29.1 g, dietary fiber 4.7 g, sugars 6.9 g, protein 28.8 g*

*Marinade: **per serving:** calories 29.4, total fat 0.4 g, saturated fat 0.0 g, cholesterol 0.1 mg, sodium 60.1 mg, potassium 28.2 mg, total carbohydrate 2.9 g, dietary fiber 0.2 g, sugars 0.8 g, protein 0.1 g*

🍽 **Mood-Elevating Mackerel and Vegetables en Papillote**

Makes 2 servings

En papillote means "cooked in paper," which is a simple yet elegant way to retain flavor. In cooking, *papillote* most often refers to parchment paper, which can be found in most supermarkets. The *en papillote* method is the perfect choice for romantic dinners, when you have little time to slave over the stove. You toss (gently!) everything together and cook in the oven. The parchment paper makes cleanup a breeze.

Vegetables

1 heaping cup fresh baby spinach
12 young yellow beans, ends removed
12 young green beans, ends removed
10 pearl onions, peeled and ends removed
6 baby asparagus

Fish

Two 6-ounce mackerel fillets, boned and trimmed
1 tablespoon fresh dill, torn into 1-inch pieces
2 tablespoons lemon juice (about 1 lemon)
1 teaspoon garlic paste, store-bought
½ teaspoon salt
1 tablespoon crushed walnuts
4 lemon wedges

1. Place an oven rack on the middle shelf of the oven and preheat to 350°F.

2. Fold a 12-inch by 12-inch piece of parchment paper in half and place it on a baking sheet. Unfold. Decoratively arrange the vegetables in the center of the parchment by the fold, trying to keep ingredients as close together as possible. Place the fish on top of the vegetables and cover with the dill, lemon juice and garlic. Sprinkle with salt.

3. Fold the parchment paper over so that the ingredients are covered and crimp the edges to create a seal.

4. Bake for 15 minutes. The fish is done when the parchment paper puffs up slightly. Remove the baking sheet from the oven, place the packet on a serving plate and bring to the table. Open the parchment paper. Sprinkle with walnuts and serve with lemon wedges on the side.

Vegetarian Version

Substitute slices of eggplant for the mackerel.

Per serving: calories 561.8, total fat 4.4 g, saturated fat 0.4 g, cholesterol 0.0 mg, sodium 306.8 mg, potassium 416.8 mg, total carbohydrate 17.3 g, dietary fiber 6.9 g, sugars 0.2 g, protein 6.4 g

🍽️ *Iron-Rich Asian Steak Salad*

Makes 4 servings

This salad is for anyone who loves steak and lots of flavor. Leftovers are perfect tucked into an omelet or sandwich, and hold their own stuffed into a potato smothered in shredded cheese and broiled.

Steak Salad
- **2 teaspoons light olive oil or peanut oil,** divided
- **½–¾ pound broccoli,** sliced from stem to flower (¼- to ½-inch-wide slices), so that florets will lie flat
- **2 cups fresh spinach or beet greens**
- **Buffalo or grass-fed beef sirloin steak,** cut into ¼-inch strips
- **Pinch salt,** or to taste
- **1 cup bean sprouts**
- **2 tablespoons unsalted crushed almonds or peanuts**

Sauce
- **1 tablespoon hoisin sauce**
- **1 teaspoon minced ginger**
- **1 teaspoon garlic paste,** store-bought
- **1 tablespoon soy sauce**
- **1 tablespoon finely chopped fresh cilantro**
- **1 teaspoon toasted sesame oil**

1. Heat 1 teaspoon of the olive oil or peanut oil in a wok over medium heat. Add the broccoli and spinach and sauté for 4 minutes, or until the broccoli starts to become tender and the spinach wilts.
2. To make the sauce, in a large bowl, combine the hoisin, ginger, garlic, soy sauce, cilantro and sesame oil and whisk until well combined. Set aside.
3. When the broccoli is tender, push the vegetables along the sides of the wok so that there is a place in the middle for the steak. If the vegetables slip back down, remove and toss them into the bowl with the sauce.
4. Add the remaining olive or peanut oil to the wok. Add the steak and the salt. Sauté the steak for 2 to 3 minutes, turning so that both sides brown. Test one of the pieces for doneness. The timing will vary, depending on the heat of the wok and the thickness of the strips. Remove from the heat and transfer the steak (and vegetables, if not already transferred to the bowl) to the bowl and toss. Divide the steak salad among four plates, sprinkle with sprouts and almonds or peanuts and serve.

Vegetarian Version
Substitute tofu slices for steak.

Frugal Option
Replace sirloin with free-range turkey or chicken tenderloins, cut into ¼-inch strips.

Per serving: calories 151.8, total fat 7.1 g, saturated fat 0.9 g, cholesterol 30.3 mg, sodium 358.4 mg, potassium 129.8 mg, total carbohydrate 7.1 g, dietary fiber 2.3 g, sugars 1.6 g, protein 16.3 g

🍽 *Pasta Comfort Ragu di Carne ala Florentine*

Makes 4 servings

This dish hails its flavor from Florence, Italy, where it is served in many restaurants. If you are looking for a hearty pasta and meat dish, this is it. If you cannot find ground buffalo meat, try a lean grass-fed ground beef, such as sirloin.

1 teaspoon light olive oil
1 heaping cup finely chopped white onion
1 large carrot, peeled and finely chopped
½ ground free-range chicken breast
½ cup ground buffalo meat
¾ cup dry red wine
5 fresh plum tomatoes, cored, seeded if desired and roughly chopped
½ teaspoon salt
¼ teaspoon garlic paste, store-bought
¾ pound whole-wheat penne
4 cups fresh spinach
3 tablespoons pitted and thinly sliced black olives
½ cup freshly grated Parmesan cheese

1. Heat the olive oil in a wok over medium heat. Sauté the onions and carrot until tender, about 7 minutes. Stir occasionally so that the vegetables cook evenly.
2. Reduce the heat to medium-low. Add the chicken and buffalo and cook for another 2 minutes, stirring. Add the red wine, tomatoes, salt, and garlic. Cook for 20 minutes.
3. When the sauce has 10 minutes left to cook, prepare the pasta according to package directions. Penne usually takes approximately 9 minutes.
4. After the pasta is done, drain and toss into the wok with the spinach. Stir and remove from the heat. Serve the pasta and sauce directly from the wok, topping each plate with sliced olives and cheese.

Vegetarian Version

Substitute tofu or a very meaty mushroom, such as a portobello, for the meat.

Frugal Option

Use free-range ground turkey meat in place of the buffalo.

Per serving: calories 536.0, total fat 9.5 g, saturated fat 4.1 g, cholesterol 27.5 mg, sodium 474.1 mg, potassium 424.3 mg, total carbohydrate 77.5 g, dietary fiber 10.9 g, sugars 4.7 g, protein 28.5 g

🍽 *Brain-Boosting Calf's Liver in Fig-and-Port Sauce*

Makes 2 servings

Calf's liver is very popular throughout the Mediterranean and can be found everywhere, from the finest restaurants to the local bistro. It requires very little cooking and can easily be overdone. Make sure the liver is completely covered in the liquid during the cooking process to meld the flavors together. If port is not handy, use red wine or medium-dry sherry.

Fig-and-Port Sauce

1 tablespoon finely chopped shallot
4 dried figs, stems removed, quartered
¼ cup inexpensive port
½ cup low-sodium free-range chicken or vegetable broth, plus additional ¼ cup, if needed
Pinch freshly ground black pepper

Calf's Liver and Asparagus

1 teaspoon light olive oil
1 pound calf's liver, cut into ½-inch slices
1 teaspoon salt
¼ teaspoon ground nutmeg
1 bunch green asparagus (¾ pound), woody bottom of stems removed and cut into 2-inch pieces
½ cup whole-wheat couscous
2 tablespoons lemon zest

1. To make the fig sauce, in a small saucepan over medium-low heat, combine the shallots, figs (cut side down), port, vegetable broth and pepper. Cook 10 minutes, until the figs soften.
2. Heat the olive oil in a wok over medium heat. When the wok is hot, add the calf's liver, salt, nutmeg and asparagus. Pour in the fig-and-port sauce and stir so the sauce is well distributed. Cook for another 5 to 7 minutes or until the liver is cooked through and no longer pink. If there is very little liquid in the wok, add ¼ cup of broth, let warm slightly, then remove from the heat and add the couscous. Cover the wok with a piece of foil, let it stand for 5 minutes or until the couscous has absorbed all the liquid and serve.

Vegetarian Version

Substitute portobello mushrooms for the liver.

Per serving: calories 617.2, total fat 19.1 g, saturated fat 6.8 g, cholesterol 1,280.0 mg, sodium 228.4 mg , potassium 1,122.7 mg, total carbohydrate 46.7 g, dietary fiber 7.7 g, sugars 18.6 g, protein 56.4 g

---

🍽 *Calming Croquettes with Spicy Hummus Dipping Sauce*

Makes 4 servings

Croquettes can be created from your favorite ingredients and, once you learn the technique, it's easy. I like to use a food processor to mix my croquette fillings, which saves a lot of chopping time.

Croquette Coating
½ cup whole-wheat panko or breadcrumbs
½ cup finely chopped cilantro
2 omega-3 rich eggs

Croquettes
½ teaspoon tomato paste
2 tablespoons finely grated Parmesan cheese
2 tablespoons whole-wheat panko or breadcrumbs
1½ tablespoons hoisin sauce
1 teaspoon garlic paste (store-bought)
1 teaspoon chopped parsley
½ pound of healing B-12-rich ingredients, such as shrimp, butterflied and peeled, or turkey tenderloins, flank steak or chicken breast, roughly chopped

Sauce and Salad
¾ cup hummus (store-bought is fine)
1 tablespoon Sriracha chili sauce* or any chili sauce
4 heaping cups fresh baby spinach

1. Place an oven rack on the middle shelf of the oven and preheat the oven to 350°F.
2. In a small shallow bowl, combine the breadcrumbs and cilantro and toss until well combined. Crack the eggs into a separate small bowl and whisk until frothy.
3. In a food processor, combine the tomato paste, cheese, breadcrumbs, hoisin sauce, garlic, parsley and B-12-rich protein. Pulse until a paste is formed. Scoop out the mixture and make 8 equal balls, about 1½ tablespoons each.
4. Dip the croquettes into the egg and shake slightly to remove any excess. Transfer to the breadcrumbs and roll around until well coated. Place the croquettes on a sheet pan. Bake the croquettes for 12 minutes or until just cooked through. Croquettes should be firm to the touch.
5. Meanwhile, prepare the hummus dipping sauce by combing the hummus and the chili sauce and mixing until blended.
6. Serve the croquettes warm on a bed of spinach with a dollop of dipping sauce.

*Sriracha chili sauce can be found at most specialty grocery stores, such as Whole Foods, in the Asian section.

Per serving: calories 358.9, total fat 12.6 g, saturated fat 2.6 g, cholesterol 130.0 mg, sodium 625.8 mg, potassium 475.3 mg, total carbohydrate 34.9 g, dietary fiber 6.7 g, sugars 1.4 g, protein 25.1 g

🍽 *Mood-Lifting Peach and Cherry Ricotta Tarts*

Makes 4 tarts, up to 8 servings

I like to prepare mini tarts so that my guests can make requests. Other great healing fruits to use are apricots, strawberries, apples, raspberries, mango and blueberries.

Crust

    ½ cup whole-wheat pastry flour
    ¼ cup almond flour
    4 tablespoons grass-fed unsalted butter
    1 tablespoon 70% real cacao powder
    1 tablespoon birch sugar or xylitol

Topping

    ¾ cup low-fat ricotta
    2 tablespoons birch sugar or xylitol
    2 cups frozen peaches, thawed and chopped
    10 frozen cherries

1. Preheat the oven to 350°F and place the rack in the middle.
2. In a food processor, pulse the flours, butter, cacao and sugar until thoroughly blended.
3. Slowly add ¼ cup ice-cold water a little at a time and pulse until the dough comes together. You may not need the entire ¼ cup. When the dough is formed, remove it from the processor and form it into four balls. Press the dough into the bottom of four 3-inch spring pans. Bake for 10 minutes. Remove from the oven.
4. Combine the ricotta and the sugar and spread on the bottom of the tart crust. Top with the peaches and cherries. Bake for 15 minutes. Remove them from the oven to cool slightly and then serve.

Per serving: calories 331.3, total fat 17.2 g, saturated fat 9.0 g, cholesterol 46.1 mg, sodium 121.6 mg, potassium 252.7 mg, total carbohydrate 29.6 g, dietary fiber 4.6 g, sugars 7.1 g, protein 9.4 g

¶◉¶ *Feel-Good Flourless Chocolate Cakes with Raspberry Sauce*

Makes 8 individual cakes

These cakes are divine. However, if you aren't accustomed to 70% cacao dark chocolate, I suggest adding an additional ¼ cup of sugar.

Chocolate Cake

6 ounces 70% or more cacao dark chocolate, roughly chopped
1 tablespoon vanilla extract
½ cup maple or xylitol or birch sugar
Light olive oil, or coconut oil, for greasing
½ cup vanilla whole-milk yogurt
⅓ cup roasted sweet potato, peeled and mashed
⅓ cup honey
1 omega-3 egg
3 egg whites

Raspberry Sauce

8 ounces raspberries
1 tablespoon honey

1. Place a rack on the center shelf of the oven and preheat to 375°F.
2. Bring water in the bottom of a double boiler to a simmer. Add the chocolate to the top of the double boiler and melt over medium heat. Remove from the heat. Stir in the vanilla and sugar. Grease eight 4-ounce ramekins with light olive oil. Using a mixer, blend the yogurt, sweet potato, honey and egg until smooth. Fold into the chocolate.
3. Beat the egg whites until stiff peaks are formed. Fold about 1 cup of egg whites into the chocolate mixture. Once incorporated into the chocolate, gently fold in the remaining egg whites until thoroughly blended.
4. Carefully divide the mixture among the ramekins and place on a baking sheet. Bake for 12 minutes. The cakes are done when they are soft and have risen slightly, become puffy, and the inside is moist.
5. While the cakes are baking, place the raspberries in a small pot over medium heat. As the raspberries begin to soften, stir in the honey. Mix with a fork until the raspberries reduce to a pulp. Remove from the heat. Drizzle the sauce over the cakes and serve immediately. If you don't like raspberry seeds, press the sauce through a sieve.

Per serving: calories 224.3, total fat 8.7 g, saturated fat 5.0 g, cholesterol 24.4 mg, sodium 19.1 mg, potassium 89.6 mg, total carbohydrate 31.1 g, dietary fiber 4.3 g, sugars 22.6 g, protein 3.3 g

🍽 *Diabetes-Fighting Mediterranean Broccoli-Red Pepper Soup*

Makes 4 servings

This soup has a little kick to it, so be sure to serve it with a generous amount of Greek yogurt to soften its edge. The soup is delicious served cold, accompanied by artisanal whole-wheat bread. It is also great drizzled over rice, pasta and chicken as a sauce.

1 tablespoon light olive oil
4 medium shallots, finely chopped, about ½ cup
2 roasted red bell peppers, finely chopped
2–3 pounds fresh broccoli, finely chopped
1 quart low-sodium vegetable stock
¼ teaspoon finely chopped fresh oregano leaves
¼ teaspoon finely chopped fresh marjoram leaves
Pinch of cayenne pepper
¼ teaspoon salt, plus more to taste
Freshly ground black pepper, to taste
1 teaspoon minced garlic
¼ cup Greek yogurt (store-bought or homemade, see page 406)

1. Heat the olive oil in a large stockpot over medium-high heat. Add the shallots and bell peppers, and sauté until the shallots are translucent, about 7 minutes. Reduce the heat to medium-low and add the broccoli, vegetable stock, oregano, marjoram, cayenne, salt, pepper and garlic. Cook for about 30 minutes, stirring occasionally.

2. Taste and correct seasoning. Serve in a deep bowl with a 1-tablespoon dollop of Greek yogurt.

Nonvegetarian Version

Sauté chicken tenders in the pot before adding vegetables.

Frugal Option

Use regular plain yogurt instead of Greek yogurt.

Per serving: calories 139.5, total fat 4.8 g, saturated fat 1.0 g, cholesterol 0.0 mg, sodium 223.6 mg, potassium 672.7 mg, total carbohydrate 20.6 g, dietary fiber 6.8 g, sugars 4.1 g, protein 7.1 g

🍽️ *Glucose-Balancing Asian Scallop-Bean Salad*

Makes 4 servings

This salad takes just minutes to prepare. Beans are a low-glycemic, high-fiber superfood for diabetics. The dressing blends traditional Asian flavors of toasted sesame oil, ginger and garlic. Lemon zest wakes up the sautéed beans and scallops. You can use any healing seafood such as tuna, salmon or trout. Cut them into bite-sized pieces so that they will cook quickly.

Dressing

1 tablespoon honey
1 tablespoon brown-rice vinegar
1 tablespoon toasted sesame oil
½ cup orange juice
1 tablespoon soy sauce
2 teaspoons fresh grated ginger
2 teaspoons roasted minced garlic

Scallop-Bean Salad

1 teaspoon light olive oil
1 pound fresh sea scallops, quartered
1 cup canned pinto beans, drained and rinsed
1 cup canned navy beans, drained and rinsed
¼ red bell pepper, cored, seeded and diced
½ teaspoon sea salt, to taste
1 tablespoon lemon zest, for garnish

1. To make the dressing, combine the honey, vinegar, sesame oil, orange juice, soy sauce, ginger and garlic in a small bowl and whisk until well combined.
2. To make the salad, heat the olive oil in a large skillet over medium heat. Sauté the scallops for about 3 minutes, stirring frequently so that they cook evenly. When the scallops are done (they should be opaque throughout), reduce the heat to low and add the beans, red bell pepper and salt. Toss until well combined. Add the dressing and stir again until well coated. Remove from the heat.
3. Divide the bean salad among four plates, sprinkle with lemon zest and serve.

Vegetarian Options

Omit the scallops and add some steamed broccoli to the bean salad.

Frugal Options

Use less-expensive seafood, such as frozen shrimp (thaw before cooking) or tilapia.

Per serving: calories 301.1, total fat 6.0 g, saturated fat 0.8 g, cholesterol 37.4 mg, sodium 474.2 mg, potassium 851.6 mg, total carbohydrate 35.0 g, dietary fiber 8.9 g, sugars 7.3 g, protein 27.0 g

¶◎¶ *Diabetes-Busting Orange Broccoli Salad*

Makes 4 servings

Broccoli is best cooked *al dente*, so that it has a bit of crunch and retains its nutrients. Orange *supremes*—sections from which the skin, pith and membrane have been removed—give a sweet citrus flavor to the dressing. Red peppers and broccoli add crunch and color.

Orange Dressing

> 2 tablespoons unsweetened pomegranate juice
> ½ teaspoon minced ginger
> 1 teaspoon minced garlic
> 1 tablespoon finely chopped shallots
> 1 tablespoon finely chopped fresh cilantro
> 1 teaspoon soy sauce
> 1 teaspoon toasted sesame oil
> 1 orange, supremed

Broccoli Salad

> 1 teaspoon olive oil (extra-virgin or light)
> 1 red bell pepper, cored, seeded and finely diced
> 3–3½ pounds (about 4 small heads) fresh broccoli, cut into florets with 1-inch stems
> ¼ teaspoon salt
> Freshly ground black pepper, to taste

1. In a medium saucepan over medium-low heat, combine the pomegranate juice, ginger, garlic, shallots, cilantro, soy sauce and sesame oil, and simmer for 10 minutes. Remove from the heat and add the orange supremes. Set aside.
2. While the dressing simmers, prepare the vegetable salad. Heat the olive oil in a wok over medium heat. Add the red bell pepper and sauté for 4 minutes or until softened. Add the broccoli, salt and pepper and cook the broccoli about 2 minutes until it is al dente, or 1 minute longer to render it softer. Stir the broccoli so that it cooks evenly.
3. Divide the vegetables among four plates, drizzle it with the dressing and serve.

Nonvegetarian Version

Before cooking the broccoli, stir-fry thin slices of range-fed beef in olive oil. Remove when medium-rare. Add to the vegetables after the broccoli is done, toss a few times to heat through and serve.

Frugal Option

Use unsweetened apple juice instead of pomegranate juice.

Per serving: calories 135.8, total fat 3.4 g, saturated fat 0.5 g, cholesterol 0.0 mg, sodium 166.9 mg, potassium 1,130.3 mg, total carbohydrate 22.8 g, dietary fiber 10.2 g, sugars 1.1 g, protein 9.8 g

---

🍽 *Sugar-Busting Spicy Shrimp 'n' Rice*

Makes 6 servings

Shrimp will take on almost any seasoning you cook it with, so it is perfect for this mildly spicy broth. This South Asian–style meal is lightly aromatic and surprisingly filling, because shrimp are full of sugar-balancing protein. Add vegetables to the broth for variety and extra healing power.

Rice

> 1 cup brown rice
> 2¼ cups low-sodium chicken broth

Spicy Shrimp

> 2¼ cups low-sodium vegetable broth
> 1 teaspoon minced garlic
> 1 teaspoon minced ginger
> ½ teaspoon red curry paste
> 1 teaspoon lime juice
> 1 teaspoon salt, or to taste
> Pinch chili powder, to taste
> ½ cup dry white wine
> 2 pounds medium shrimp, peeled and deveined

1. In a medium saucepan with a lid, prepare the rice according to the package directions, using chicken broth instead of water. One cup of brown rice usually requires 2¼ cups of stock and takes 45 minutes to cook. When the rice is done, fluff with a fork and set aside.
2. While the rice is cooking, prepare the broth. Heat the vegetable broth, garlic, ginger, curry, lime juice, salt, chili powder, and wine in a large saucepan over medium-high heat for 5 minutes.
3. Reduce the heat to medium-low, add the shrimp and cover the pot. Cook the shrimp until they are opaque, about 2 minutes. Remove the lid and remove from the heat.
4. To serve, divide the rice among four shallow bowls, spoon the spicy shrimp and broth into each bowl and serve.

Vegetarian Version

Cook the rice in low-sodium vegetable broth and substitute sliced zucchini for shrimp.

Frugal Option

Use frozen shrimp. Thaw before cooking.

Per serving: calories 221.9, total fat 2.9 g, saturated fat 0.6 g, cholesterol 229.7 mg, sodium 332.8 mg, potassium 327.3 mg, total carbohydrate 10.9 g, dietary fiber 1.0 g, sugars 0.7 g, protein 32.2 g

⦿ *Diabetes Delight Vegetarian Paella*

Makes 8 servings

Paella is a traditional Spanish rice and seafood dish seasoned with saffron, a spice cherished by many cultures as a unique flavor component. This simple vegetarian version is prepared in a 12-inch wok or a 12-inch-wide deep skillet. Two kinds of high-fiber beans create a black-and-white contrast as well as rich flavor, texture and protein.

1 tablespoon light olive oil
1 large white onion, chopped
1 red bell pepper, cored, seeded and cut into ¼-inch pieces
2 large tomatoes, cored and chopped
2 large garlic cloves, minced
1 teaspoon kosher salt
Pinch black pepper
1 quart low-sodium vegetable broth, plus additional ¼ cup, if needed
2 cups brown rice
8 saffron threads
1 cup canned black beans
1 cup canned navy beans

1. Pour the olive oil into a large wok or stockpot over medium heat. Add the onion, bell pepper, tomatoes, garlic, salt and pepper. Lightly sauté the ingredients, stirring often, for 10 minutes. Lower the heat if the ingredients are sticking to the pan.
2. Turn the heat to medium-low and add the vegetable broth, rice and saffron. Stir the ingredients and shake the pan to distribute the ingredients. Carefully add the black and navy beans, gently pressing them into the liquid. All the solid ingredients should be submerged. Do not stir the rice; rotate the pan on the burner. A thin crust will form on the bottom of the wok. Do not disturb it, as it may break up and become mixed into the paella.
3. Cook until the rice has absorbed the liquid, about 55 minutes.
4. Depending on the level of heat, you may need to cook the rice another 5 minutes, until it is tender. Remember to move the pan around on the heat. If the water is absorbed but the rice isn't finished cooking, slowly add ¼ cup of water. Let the rice absorb the water before testing again.
5. Once the rice is tender, reduce the heat to low. Cook the paella another 5 minutes. Remove from the heat and let stand for 5 minutes before serving in eight bowls.

Nonvegetarian Version

Sauté small shrimp, peeled and deveined, or chicken tenders, with the vegetables.

Per serving: calories 155.1, total fat 2.4 g, saturated fat 0.4 g, cholesterol 0.0 mg, sodium 92.2 mg, potassium 309.9 mg, total carbohydrate 27.9 g, dietary fiber 6.2 g, sugars 1.9 g, protein 5.6 g

---

🍽 *Diabetes-Defeating Tuna Cakes*

Makes 4 servings

These tuna cakes are very delicate. They are baked, not pan-fried, so they will hold together and have a crispy crust. If fresh tuna is hard to come by, canned Sicilian tuna will also work.

Tuna Cakes

> ½ cup whole-wheat breadcrumbs
> 1 teaspoon chili sauce
> 2 tablespoons finely chopped fresh cilantro
> 1 omega 3–rich egg, beaten
> ⅛ teaspoon freshly squeezed lemon juice
> Pinch salt
> 2 tablespoons low-fat Greek yogurt (store-bought or homemade, see page 406)
> 1 pound fresh tuna
> Olive oil spray

Broccoli with Dressing

> 2–3 pounds fresh broccoli, cut into florets with 1-inch stems
> ¼ cup extra-virgin olive oil
> 1 tablespoon balsamic vinegar
> ¼ teaspoon sea salt, or to taste
> Pinch freshly ground black pepper
> 1 teaspoon freshly squeezed lemon juice
> 1 tablespoon chopped parsley leaves

1. Place an oven rack on the middle shelf of the oven and preheat to 350°F.

2. Prepare the tuna cakes. In a food processor or blender, combine the breadcrumbs, chili sauce, cilantro, egg, lemon juice, salt, yogurt and tuna. Pulse until a paste is formed. Form into four cakes. Lightly spray a baking sheet. Place the tuna cakes on the baking sheet and bake for 15 minutes, or until golden brown. Remove from the oven and cool slightly.

3. In a medium saucepan, bring 1 inch of water to a boil. Add the broccoli and cook for 2 minutes, or until *al dente*. Drain the broccoli and place it in a large bowl. In a small bowl, whisk together the olive oil, vinegar, salt, pepper, lemon juice and parsley and then add it to the broccoli and stir until everything is well combined.

4. Divide the broccoli among four plates, and top each with a tuna cake and serve.

Vegetarian Version

> Substitute canned navy beans, drained and mashed, for the tuna.

Frugal Option

> Use canned Italian tuna instead of fresh.

Per serving: calories 418.5, total fat 19.1 g, saturated fat 3.3 g, cholesterol 99.5 mg, sodium 410.5 mg, potassium 610.3 mg, total carbohydrate 29.4 g, dietary fiber 6.7 g, sugars 2.4 g, protein 35.8 g

🍽 *Insulin-Leveling Mediterranean Stuffed Peppers*

Makes 4 servings

Stuffed peppers are easy to prepare and very decorative. Just about any meat or vegetable can be included in this recipe, such as ground lamb, shredded chicken, corn or spinach. Stuffed peppers can be served hot or cold, so take some of these on a picnic or to work.

½ cup quinoa, rinsed
1 cup water
4 red bell peppers
6 fresh basil leaves, finely chopped
1 teaspoon minced garlic
1 ripe tomato, cored, seeded and minced
½ cup canned navy beans
½ pound sea scallops, diced, or other protein of your choice
4 tablespoons finely grated Parmesan cheese, divided

1. In a medium saucepan over medium heat, combine the quinoa and water; bring to a boil, stir, lower heat, cover and simmer for 20 minutes. Separate the grains with a fork.
2. While the quinoa is cooking, prepare the peppers: Cut the tops off, then remove the seeds and ribs.
3. When the quinoa is almost done, place an oven rack on the middle shelf of the oven and preheat to 350°F.
4. In a medium bowl, combine the quinoa, basil, garlic, tomato, beans, scallops (if using) and 2 tablespoons of the cheese. Mix until well blended. Stuff the peppers with the mixture. Place the peppers in a loaf pan, so that they don't tip over. Bake for 10 to 15 minutes, until piping hot. Transfer to a serving dish. Cut each pepper into quarters or serve them whole. Serve with the remaining cheese on the side for sprinkling.

Vegetarian Version

Use diced tofu instead of seafood.

Per serving: calories 229.4, total fat 3.8 g, saturated fat 1.0 g, cholesterol 22.7 mg, sodium 188.9 mg, potassium 493.2 mg, total carbohydrate 32.1 g, dietary fiber 6.6 g, sugars 2.4 g, protein 17.9 g

---

〔◎〕 *Glucose-Lowering Balsamic Salmon with Figgy Brown Rice*

Makes 4 servings

If you like figs, this dish may soon become a favorite. The figs are caramelized in the balsamic vinegar, then combined with the rice, which soaks up the vinegar reduction. This sauce can also be used to dress salads and vegetables. It's also great for marinating meats before cooking.

1 cup brown rice
2 tablespoons balsamic vinegar
2 tablespoons light olive oil
6 dried figs (black mission preferred), stems removed and cut in half
4 wild salmon fillets, 4 ounces each
Salt and pepper, to taste
1 teaspoon finely chopped fresh savory leaves or fresh thyme, mint or sage

1. Place an oven rack on the middle shelf of the oven and preheat to 350°F.
2. In a medium saucepan, prepare the rice according to the package directions, using chicken broth instead of water. When the rice is done, fluff it with a fork and set aside.
3. In a large skillet over medium-low heat, combine the vinegar, olive oil and figs. Lightly sauté the figs (cut side down) for 10 minutes, or until they soften and caramelize. When the figs are caramelized, add the cooked rice to the skillet and stir gently to incorporate the balsamic reduction. It should transfer to the rice and start to darken it. Add salt to taste.
4. Place the salmon on a lightly greased sheet pan and season with salt and pepper. Bake for 7 minutes, or until opaque.
5. Divide the rice among four plates and sprinkle with fresh savory. Place the salmon fillets alongside the rice and serve.

Vegetarian Version

Omit salmon and serve rice mixture on a bed of cress or arugula, adding a dollop of goat cheese and a sprinkling of ground walnuts.

Frugal Option

Substitute a baked, skinless, boneless, free-range chicken breast sprinkled with fresh thyme leaves for salmon.

Per serving: calories 332.4, total fat 12.0 g, saturated fat 2.0 g, cholesterol 85.5 mg, sodium 100.2 mg, potassium 234.8 mg, total carbohydrate 30.9 g, dietary fiber 3.7 g, sugars 14.8 g, protein 25.2 g

¡◎¡ *Diabetes-Defying Deep Dark Chocolate Brownies*

Makes 24 brownies

These brownies are healing and wonderfully sweet. However, if you aren't used to 70% cacao dark chocolate, you may want to add an additional ¼ cup of xylitol or birch sugar to sweeten them further. Enjoy, but watch your portion size.

3 ounces 70% or more cacao dark chocolate, roughly chopped
1 teaspoon vanilla
5 tablespoons grass-fed unsalted butter, melted
Light olive oil, for greasing
¾ cup xylitol or birch sugar
¼ cup raw agave nectar
2 omega-3 eggs
¼ cup whole-wheat pastry flour
¼ cup almond flour

1. Place a rack on the center shelf of the oven and preheat to 375°F.

2. Bring water in the bottom of a double boiler to a simmer. Add the chocolate to the top of the double boiler and melt over medium heat. Remove from the heat. Stir in the vanilla and butter.

3. Let cool slightly. Lightly grease an 8-inch square baking pan with olive oil.

4. Using a mixer, blend the sugar, agave and eggs and mix until smooth. Add the chocolate and mix until well combined. Sift in the flours and mix well.

5. Pour the batter into the pan and bake for 40 minutes. The brownies are done when they are somewhat firm and moist. Cool slightly and serve.

Per brownie: calories 77.8, total fat 4.7 g, saturated fat 2.5 g, cholesterol 21.1 mg, sodium 4.9 mg, potassium 1.0 mg, total carbohydrate 5.0 g, dietary fiber 0.6 g, sugars 3.2 g, protein 1.2 g

🍽 *Sugar-Steady Peach Quinoa Cobblers*

Makes 4 individual cobblers, up to 8 servings

I like cobblers with a nut crunch topping and prepared upside down. The topping can be omitted, if you prefer. If you do, assemble the cobbler with the crust on top.

Crust

    1 cup cooked quinoa
    ½ cup almond flour
    1 teaspoon baking powder
    Pinch salt
    1 cup almond milk or vanilla rice milk
    1 teaspoon ground cinnamon
    1 tablespoon grass-fed unsalted butter, melted

Fruit Filling

    4 cups canned sliced peaches (in natural juices)
    1 tablespoon vanilla
    1 tablespoon xylitol or birch sugar

Nut Crunch Topping

    2 tablespoons raw agave nectar
    1 teaspoon lemon zest
    3 tablespoons crushed almonds
    ¼ cup almond flour
    Pinch of cinnamon, optional

1. Preheat the oven to 350°F with the rack placed in the middle.
2. In a food processor, pulse the quinoa, flour, baking powder, salt, milk, cinnamon and butter until thoroughly blended. Divide into four even portions and press each section into a 3-inch pie pan.
3. In a medium bowl, toss the peaches, vanilla and sugar until well combined. Arrange the peaches on top of the crust.
4. In a small bowl, mix the agave, zest, almonds, flour and cinnamon until well combined. Distribute evenly over the peaches.
5. Bake for 30 minutes or until the peaches are bubbling. Cool briefly and serve.

Per serving: calories 249.1, total fat 8.0 g, saturated fat 1.2 g, cholesterol 3.9 mg, sodium 111.2 mg, potassium 208.3 mg, total carbohydrate 36.3 g, dietary fiber 4.9 g, sugars 5.2 g, protein 6.4 g

🍽 *Tummy-Taming Vegetable Bean Salad*

Makes 4 servings

Beans are a staple throughout the Mediterranean. The delicate flavors of fiber-filled cannellini and chickpeas (garbanzo beans) allow the vegetables in this dish to shine through. Sage gives it a smoky depth, while lemon gives it zing. As a bonus, you'll get the complex carbs you need for added energy without any gluten or refined flours.

1 bunch asparagus, woody ends broken off, cut into 1-inch pieces; or
2–3 pounds broccoli, cut into florets; or **1 container Brussels sprouts**, trimmed and
    quartered; or **10 ounces green beans,** trimmed, cut into 1-inch pieces
1 clove garlic, peeled and minced
1 teaspoon dried, rubbed sage
One 15-ounce can cannellini beans, drained and rinsed
One 15-ounce can chickpeas, drained and rinsed
1 teaspoon salt
Pinch freshly ground black pepper
2 tablespoons extra-virgin olive oil
2 tablespoons fresh lemon juice
2 tablespoons grated Parmesan cheese

1. Steam the vegetables for 2 minutes, or until tender.
2. Transfer to a large bowl and add the garlic, sage, beans, chickpeas, salt, pepper, oil and lemon juice and toss until well combined.
3. Cover the salad with plastic wrap and let marinate in the refrigerator for 30 minutes.
4. Toss again, then sprinkle with cheese before serving.

Nonvegetarian Version

Add 1 pound large shrimp, steamed in their shells 3–5 minutes, then peeled, deveined and roughly chopped.

Per serving: calories 402.3, total fat 10.0 g, saturated fat 1.8 g, cholesterol 2.0 mg, sodium 455.7 mg, potassium 1,462.6 mg, total carbohydrate 63.0 g, dietary fiber 17.6 g, sugars 0.0 g, protein 21.1 g

🍽 *Gently Digesting Teriyaki Vegetables and Spinach Salad*

Makes 4 servings

Teriyaki is more than just a sauce. It's one of the world's best-loved cooking techniques, in which food is cooked in a sweet sauce comprised of soy, sake, sugar and ginger. The sauce melds perfectly with juicy stir-fried veggies, meats and seafood. The healing ingredients make this meal complete. Omega-3- and magnesium-rich spinach is added to the fiber and vitamin C-packed veggies.

Teriyaki Vegetables

1 teaspoon light olive oil
1 bunch asparagus, woody ends broken off, cut into 1-inch pieces; or 2–3 pounds broccoli, cut into florets; or 1 container Brussels sprouts, trimmed and cut into eighths; or 10 ounces green beans, ends trimmed, cut into 1-inch pieces
½ cup all-natural, low-sodium teriyaki sauce

Spinach Salad

6 heaping cups fresh baby spinach
2 teaspoons lemon juice
1 tablespoon sesame seeds

1. Heat the olive oil in a wok or large saucepot over medium heat.
2. Add the vegetables and sauté for 1 minute, or until al dente (note that the Brussel sprouts will require more time). Reduce the heat to low, add the teriyaki sauce and toss until the vegetables are thoroughly coated.
3. Remove from the heat and add the spinach, lemon juice and sesame seeds.
4. Toss until well blended and the spinach starts to wilt. Serve directly from the wok.

Nonvegetarian Version

Add canned tuna or salmon to the salad.

Frugal Option

Use frozen vegetables.

Per serving: calories 78.5, total fat 2.6 g, saturated fat 0.4 g, cholesterol 0.0 mg, sodium 677.7 mg, potassium 439.3 mg, total carbohydrate 5.3 g, dietary fiber 2.6 g, sugars 6.2 g, protein 4.2 g

🍽 *Seared Omega-3 Tuna Steaks with Lemon-Fig Sauce*

Makes 4 servings

When ingredients are truly fresh, they hardly need much fussing over. The best way to dress up omega-3–rich tuna is to combine it with an interesting sauce such as this. You can also try an orange- or lime-based sauce, or even use chopped fresh cherries instead of figs.

Tuna Steaks

Four 4-ounce tuna steaks, ¾-inch thick
1 teaspoon salt
3 tablespoons light olive oil

Lemon-Fig Sauce

2 fresh figs, stem removed and finely diced
2 tablespoons fresh lemon juice
1 tablespoon balsamic vinegar
½ teaspoon freshly ground white pepper
4 tablespoons extra-virgin olive oil

1. In a large resealable plastic bag, combine the tuna steaks, salt, and light olive oil. Seal the bag and turn until the tuna is thoroughly coated. Marinate for 15 minutes.
2. Combine the figs, lemon juice, vinegar, pepper and olive oil in a small bowl. Mix well.
3. Heat a well-seasoned cast-iron pan large enough to hold the tuna steaks over medium-high heat. Remove the tuna from the marinade and carefully lay the steaks on the pan to cook for about 3 minutes per side or until the outside is seared, but the inside is still rare.
4. Place each tuna steak on a plate, top with a tablespoon of the lemon-fig sauce and serve.

Vegetarian Version

Substitute fresh broccoli, sliced lengthwise, coated in olive oil and grilled, for the tuna.

Frugal Option

Use a cheaper cold-water omega-3 fish.

Per serving: calories 317.4, total fat 20.4 g, saturated fat 3.1 g, cholesterol 52.0 mg, sodium 85.9 mg, potassium 82.2 mg, total carbohydrate 7.3 g, dietary fiber 1.0 g, sugars 5.7 g, protein 26.7 g

🍴 *Colon-Calming Salmon Burgers with Asian Sauerkraut*

Makes 4 servings

This recipe is great fun to prepare during grilling season. Simply cover the grates with a little foil before cooking. Sauerkraut is filled with omega-3s, and fermented foods are known all over the world for aiding digestion. I love to add extra spices to my salmon. I find that the Asian flavors of this sauerkraut make it an excellent companion for the fish.

Asian Sauerkraut

1 tablespoon teriyaki sauce
1 tablespoon soy sauce
½ teaspoon minced ginger
½ teaspoon minced garlic
1 tablespoon honey
1 cup sauerkraut, store-bought, rinsed and drained
¼ cup water

Salmon Burgers

16 ounces canned wild salmon
1 teaspoon kosher salt
1 teaspoon minced garlic
Pinch freshly ground black pepper
½ cup whole-grain breadcrumbs
1 teaspoon toasted sesame oil
1 teaspoon olive oil
Gluten-free minibuns, optional

1. In a 1-quart saucepan, bring the teriyaki, soy sauce, ginger, garlic, honey, sauerkraut and water to a boil. Lower the heat and simmer until the liquid lightly coats the back of a spoon, about 10 minutes. Set aside, but keep warm.

2. Put the salmon, salt, garlic, pepper and breadcrumbs in a blender and pulse until it comes together. Shape into 16 balls, then flatten them into small patties.

3. Heat the sesame and olive oils in a large pan over medium heat. Fry the patties for 2 minutes per side, or until golden brown.

4. Place four patties on each plate, cover with a generous helping of the sauerkraut and serve. You might also want to serve the burgers on gluten-free buns.

Vegetarian Option

Use mashed beans instead of canned salmon.

Per serving: calories 236.6, total fat 10.9 g, saturated fat 0.4 g, cholesterol 0.0 mg, sodium 505.1 mg, potassium 113.0 mg, total carbohydrate 12.6 g, dietary fiber 1.7 g, sugars 5.7 g, protein 19.9 g

🍽 *Bella (Pretty) Pizza*

Makes 4 servings

Nothing quite equals eating pizza—no wonder it is one of the world's most popular foods. The origins of pizza date back 3,000 years and versions of this dish can be found in Egyptian, Roman and Greek history. However, it didn't become what we eat today until it was perfected in Naples. Healing ingredients turn this favorite meal into a sumptuous treat for your digestion, too. You'll be helping yourself by using mild cheeses and omega-3–packed spinach, as well as the complex carbs and fiber of gluten-free whole grains.

Olive oil spray
Store-bought gluten-free pizza shells, thawed if frozen
4 ounces low-fat farmer's cheese or other soft cheese, crumbled
4 ounces low-fat mozzarella cheese, shredded
1 teaspoon light olive oil
10 cherry tomatoes, halved
4 cups fresh spinach
2 finely chopped canned artichoke hearts
2 tablespoons pesto (store-bought or homemade), divided

1. Place an oven rack on the lowest shelf of the oven and preheat to 500°F.
2. Lightly spray a rimmed baking sheet with the olive oil spray. Position the pizza shells on the sheet and sprinkle evenly with the cheeses.
3. Bake the pizzas for 8 minutes, or until the cheese has melted and the crust is golden brown.
4. While the pizza is cooking, prepare the toppings. Heat the olive oil in a wok over medium heat. Add the cherry tomatoes, spinach and artichoke bottoms and toss. The spinach should start to wilt after a few minutes. When it does, remove from the heat. Stir in 1 tablespoon of the pesto.
5. When the pizzas are done, evenly divide the remaining pesto among the pizzas, and spread over the cheese. Top with the vegetable mixture, and fold in half and serve.

Nonvegetarian Version

Add in 2 ounces of cooked ground bison meat to the toppings.

Per serving: calories 341.8, total fat 13.5 g, saturated fat 0.9 g, cholesterol 12.5 mg, sodium 463.7 mg, potassium 267.4 mg, total carbohydrate 37.9 g, dietary fiber 5.4 g, sugars 1.8 g, protein 20.1 g

🍽 *Easy-Eating Mushroom Pasta*

Makes 4 servings

You're sure to love this gluten-free pasta dish, which is a sweet marriage of Greek and Italian cuisines. This pasta gets its rustic flavor from mushrooms, feta cheese and herbs. Portobello mushrooms are a hearty highlight, with their thick and meaty texture. The mild ricotta provides a rich, creamy feel, while salty feta provides tangy contrast. Your digestive system will love it, too.

¾ pound gluten-free pasta
1 teaspoon light olive oil
1 cup chopped white onions
2 portobello mushrooms, stemmed and cut into strips
6 cups fresh spinach
½ cup low-fat ricotta cheese
½ cup rinsed and crumbled feta cheese
1 tablespoon roasted garlic, minced
¼ teaspoon ground nutmeg
½ teaspoon salt
1 tablespoon finely chopped fresh parsley

1. Fill a large pot about ¾ full with cold water and place over high heat. Cook pasta according to package directions. Drain it well, reserving ½ cup of pasta water (see note below).

2. While the pasta is cooking, prepare the mushroom sauce. Heat the olive oil in a wok or large saucepan over medium-low heat, add in the onions and mushrooms, and sauté for 4 minutes or until they start to sweat.

3. Add the spinach and the reserved pasta water. Reduce the heat to low and cook for 3 minutes, or until the spinach wilts. Stir occasionally to make sure that the sauce does not stick.

4. After the spinach wilts, turn the heat to medium and add the cheeses, garlic, nutmeg and salt. Cook, stirring, until well combined (about 2 minutes).

5. Add the cooked pasta to the pot and stir until all the liquid is absorbed. If the water does not disappear after a few minutes, raise the heat for 2 minutes, then remove the pot from the heat.

6. Serve the pasta directly from the pot onto four plates. Drizzle each plate with liquid from the bottom of the pot (if there is any), sprinkle the pasta with parsley and serve.

Note about pasta water: The use of pasta water in this dish is optional. I find it helps pull the dish together by thickening the sauce. In Italy, pasta water is commonly used when making a sauce for pasta.

Nonvegetarian Version

Place 6 shelled, deveined steamed shrimp on top of the pasta.

Frugal Version

Use canned mushrooms instead of fresh.

Per serving: calories 578.9, total fat 17.4 g, saturated fat 1.2 g, cholesterol 10.0 mg, sodium 273.1 mg potassium 534.7 mg, total carbohydrate 71.1 g, dietary fiber 5.2 g, sugars 2.7 g, protein 38.3 g

Stomach-Soothing Tarts with Spinach, Fig and Sweet Potato

Makes 4 servings

Tarts are easy to make and perfect for parties because the presentation is so elegant. This distinctly Mediterranean recipe will heal your belly with digestible goat cheese and the distinctive rich flavor of figs. Sweet potatoes offer a bit of smokiness, along with complex carbs and fiber. If you would like to prepare the tarts in advance, assemble in the springform pans and place them in the freezer. Remove from freezer and bake in the oven until golden brown, adding an additional 10 minutes to the baking time.

Approximately 6½ cups baby spinach (about 10 ounces)
4 ounces goat cheese, or low-fat ricotta
4 tablespoons finely chopped leeks
Pinch curry powder
1 tablespoon golden raisins
2 fresh figs, stems removed and finely chopped
1 sweet potato, peeled and cut into ⅛-inch-thick slices

1. Preheat the oven to 350°F.
2. In a medium pot over low heat, wilt the fresh spinach. Add the goat cheese, leeks, curry, raisins and figs, and mix until a paste is formed. Remove from the heat and set aside.
3. Divide the ingredients into four to six batches, depending on the number of tarts you are preparing. In small springform tart pans, alternate layers of sweet potato with 1 tablespoon of the spinach-goat cheese mixture. Start and end with a layer of potato and use a few potato slices per layer. Fill up each pan entirely (there should be about 6 layers in total), cover with foil and bake in the oven for 40 minutes, or until the sweet potatoes are soft.
4. Remove the tarts from the pans and serve.

Nonvegetarian Version
Add finely chopped free-range chicken to the spinach-goat cheese layers.

Frugal Option
Use thawed and drained frozen spinach instead of fresh.

Per serving: calories 161.7, total fat 6.4 g, saturated fat 4.2 g, cholesterol 13.0 mg, sodium 150.6 mg, potassium 466.3 mg, total carbohydrate 20.2 g, dietary fiber 3.4 g, sugars 6.2 g, protein 7.7 g

🍴 *Refreshing Greek Yogurt Vegetable Towers*

Makes 2 servings

Greek yogurt salads are easy to prepare and offer a new twist on something familiar. In this recipe, the asparagus is cut into ¼-inch rounds and cooked quickly to caramelize slightly before mixing them with a savory yogurt blend. I suggest packing the yogurt mixture into a food mold, then carefully unmolding to make a striking salad tower.

Vegetable Salads
1 teaspoon light olive oil
½ pound asparagus, bottom inch of spears removed, sliced into rounds ¼ inch thick
2 heaping cups fresh baby spinach
1 cup finely chopped fresh broccoli or halved fresh green beans
2 teaspoons finely chopped cilantro, divided
¼ teaspoon salt, or to taste
1 tablespoon pumpkin seeds

Yogurt Dressing
½ teaspoon lime juice
½ teaspoon curry powder
½ teaspoon minced fresh ginger
1 teaspoon garlic paste
4 leaves fresh basil, finely chopped
½ cup Greek yogurt (store-bought or homemade, see page 406)

1. Heat the olive oil in a wok or skillet over medium heat. Add the asparagus, spinach and broccoli, and stir until the asparagus is tender, about 3 minutes.

2. While the vegetables are cooking, prepare the yogurt. In a small bowl, mix the lime juice, curry, ginger, garlic, basil and yogurt until well combined. Set aside.

3. When the asparagus is done, remove from the heat, add 1 teaspoon of the cilantro and salt and toss. Combine with the yogurt. Stir until it is well combined and taste for salt, adding more if needed.

4. To assemble the dish, place a 3-inch ring mold in the center of a plate and press half the yogurt mixture into the mold. Carefully remove the mold. Repeat for the second plate. When both plates are prepared, sprinkle them with the remaining 1 teaspoon of chopped cilantro and the pumpkin seeds and serve.

Nonvegetarian Version
Top the salad with 6 ounces thinly sliced sautéed lean grass-fed beef.

Per serving: calories 137.1, total fat 6.0 g, saturated fat 1.4 g, cholesterol 0.0 mg, sodium 154.7 mg, potassium 650.5 mg, total carbohydrate 15.2 g, dietary fiber 4.5 g, sugars 1.1 g, protein 8.4 g

ᴵᴼᴵ *Celiac-Disease-Fighting Banana and Prune Pudding*

Makes 2 servings

There's nothing more comforting than a creamy pudding. This one combines traditional tastes of childhood for the ultimate comfort food.

2 cups prepared tapioca pudding
½ cup roughly chopped canned stewed prunes
1 medium banana, sliced thin
¼ cup raisins, optional
Shaved dark chocolate, optional

1. Divide the pudding between two bowls and top with the prunes and bananas.
2. Serve warm or chill as desired. Sprinkle the dessert with raisins and dark chocolate shavings, if using, and serve.

Per serving: calories 311.4, total fat 0.5 g, saturated fat 0.2 g, cholesterol 0.0 mg, sodium 7.2 mg, potassium 390.9 mg, total carbohydrate 80.4 g, dietary fiber 2.5 g, sugars 7.3 g, protein 1.5 g

ᴵᴼᴵ *Celiac-Perfect Frozen Vanilla Fig Yogurt Pops*

Makes 2 servings

This yogurt pop recipe can easily be adapted to include other healing ingredients, such as prunes and raisins.

2 cups low-fat vanilla yogurt (store-bought)
½ cup low-fat ricotta cheese or prepared tapioca pudding
4 fresh figs, stems removed and chopped
1 banana, cut into slices

1. In a blender, pulse the yogurt, ricotta, figs and banana until well combined.
2. Transfer the mixture to ice-pop molds. Freeze until firm.

Per serving: calories 389.0, total fat 5.7 g, saturated fat 3.7 g, cholesterol 30.0 mg, sodium 301.9 mg, potassium 530.6 mg, total carbohydrate 71.4 g, dietary fiber 5.1 g, sugars 59.1 g, protein 17.5 g

🍽 *Lovers' Oysters Rockefeller Dip*

Makes 4 main-dish servings or 8 appetizer servings

First prepared in 1899 at Antoine's Restaurant in New Orleans, the original Oysters Rockefeller tasted so rich that it was named for the richest man in the country, industrialist John D. Rockefeller. Our version has that same depth of flavor, but with far fewer calories. Don't forget that oysters have a long-standing, well-deserved reputation as an aphrodisiac!

1 teaspoon light olive oil
2 medium shallots, finely chopped
2 cups fresh baby spinach
12 oysters, shucked and coarsely chopped
1 red bell pepper, finely chopped
1 cup canned crushed tomatoes
¼ cup 2% milk
2 ounces Pernod
2 tablespoons all-purpose whole-grain pastry flour
8 ounces low-fat feta cheese, at room temperature, rinsed and cubed
1 tablespoon chopped parsley
Whole-wheat crackers or fresh whole-wheat bread slices

1. Place an oven rack on the middle shelf of the oven and preheat to 350°F.
2. Heat the olive oil in a wok or large pan over medium-low heat. Add the shallots and sauté for 5 minutes.
3. Add the spinach, oysters, red pepper, tomatoes and milk. Stir until well combined. Add the Pernod.
4. Remove a small portion of liquid from the skillet; with a fork, mix the flour into the liquid until well combined. Add the flour mixture to the pan.
5. Transfer the seafood mixture into an attractive baking dish or individual ramekins. Top with the feta cubes. Bake for about 20 minutes, or until the feta is melted and creamy.
6. Remove from the oven. Let cool about 5 minutes. Sprinkle with the parsley and serve with the crackers or bread.

Frugal Option

Use canned or frozen oysters.

Per serving: calories 393.0, total fat 19.6 g, saturated fat 0.2 g, cholesterol 38.1 mg, sodium 160.3 mg, potassium 69.4 mg, total carbohydrate 14.3 g, dietary fiber 1.2 g, sugars 2.0 g, protein 36.0 g

¡©¡ *Libido-Lighting Salmon Fillets with Pecan Rice*

Makes 4 servings

Light, delicate, omega-3-rich salmon is often used in Japanese cuisine. In this libido-lighting dish, it takes on the rich sweetness of cooked plums and peppercorns—flavors that go well with nutty brown or wild rice. Be careful not to overcook salmon, as it takes only seven minutes or so.

Plum Marinade

> **2 tablespoons minced garlic**
> **2 cups dry white wine**
> **1 tablespoon salt**
> **1 plum,** seeded and coarsely chopped
> **1 tablespoon black peppercorns**
> **Four 6-ounce wild Pacific salmon fillets**

Pecan Rice

> **2 cups cooked brown jasmine or wild rice**
> **1 tablespoon finely chopped fresh parsley leaves**
> **2 tablespoons very finely crushed pecans**
> **1 cup kidney beans**
> **2 heaping cups of vegetables,** such as shredded carrots, cucumbers cut into matchsticks, baby spinach, sautéed asparagus rounds, steamed broccoli florets or steamed cauliflower florets

1. In a large bowl, combine the garlic, wine, salt, plums, peppercorns and salmon. Make sure the salmon fillets are covered in liquid as much as possible. Cover and refrigerate overnight.
2. Place an oven rack on the middle shelf of the oven and preheat to 350°F.
3. Remove the salmon fillets from the marinade, gently shaking off any excess liquid. Place the salmon on a large rimmed baking sheet. Bake for 7 minutes, or until the salmon's flesh is opaque and flakes easily. Remove from the oven.
4. In a large bowl, combine the rice, parsley, pecans, beans and vegetables and toss until well combined.
5. Divide the rice among four plates, top each with a salmon fillet and serve.

Frugal Option

Use frozen wild salmon. Thaw for a couple hours in the refrigerator before placing in marinade.

Per serving: calories 409.9, total fat 10.7 g, saturated fat 2.0 g, cholesterol 127.5 mg, sodium 318.2 mg, potassium 303.8 mg, total carbohydrate 35.3 g, dietary fiber 6.9 g, sugars 1.7 g, protein 40.9 g

Marinade per serving: calories 48.0, total fat 0.0 g, saturated fat 0.0 g, cholesterol 0.0 mg, sodium 875.5 mg, potassium 73.8 mg, total carbohydrate 2.4 g, dietary fiber 0.3 g, sugars 0.8 g, protein 0.2 g

---

¡©¡ *Romantic Baked Clam Lasagna*

Makes 8 servings

Inspired by the flavors of Venice—one of the most romantic cities in the world—this delicious seafood lasagna is perfect for dinner for two (with plenty of delicious leftovers!) or a crowd. It's especially easy for entertaining because you can prepare it in advance, refrigerate and bake just before serving.

1 teaspoon salt
½ pound whole-wheat lasagna noodles
1 teaspoon light olive oil
1 small shallot, finely chopped
16 ounces canned clams, diced, liquid discarded
1 tablespoon minced garlic
1 tablespoon finely chopped pimentos
1 tablespoon dry white wine
1 cup low-fat ricotta cheese
2 cups fresh spinach, wilted in the microwave for 30 seconds
32 ounces low-sodium marinara sauce (store-bought)
¼ cup freshly grated Parmesan cheese

1. Place an oven rack on the middle shelf of the oven and preheat to 350°F.
2. Fill a pot with water and add the salt. Bring to a boil and cook the pasta according to package directions. Drain.
3. Heat the olive oil in a medium pan over medium heat. Add the shallots and clams. Sauté for 5 minutes.
4. Reduce the heat to low. Add the garlic, pimentos, and wine. Stir until well combined. Remove from the heat and set aside to cool.
5. Transfer the clam mixture to a medium bowl. Add the ricotta and spinach. Mix until well blended and smooth.
6. Assemble the lasagna layers in a 9-inch casserole dish in the following order: sauce, pasta, ricotta, repeat. Reserve enough sauce, so that when the casserole is almost full, you can cover the top layer, which should be pasta, with sauce and Parmesan cheese.
7. Bake for 45 minutes. Halfway through the cooking time, cover the lasagna with foil to prevent burning. Remove from the oven and let it sit for 10 minutes before serving.

Frugal Option

Use frozen spinach instead of fresh.

Per serving: calories 214.6, total fat 3.9 g, saturated fat 1.7 g, cholesterol 39.2 mg, sodium 499.8 mg, potassium 398.1 mg, total carbohydrate 26.3 g, dietary fiber 3.0 g, sugars 1.1 g, protein 18.8 g

¶◎¶ *Love Shack Spicy Shellfish with Asparagus*

Makes 4 servings

This creamy, zingy shellfish dinner was inspired by a similar dish at the legendary Nobu restaurant in Manhattan's Tribeca. Quite simply, it's one of the most addictive shellfish dishes you'll ever taste.

Spicy Shellfish

1 cup fat-free mayonnaise
½ teaspoon salt
⅛ teaspoon freshly ground white pepper (can substitute black pepper)
1 tablespoon plus 1 teaspoon chili-garlic sauce, such as Sriracha*, optional
1 pound fresh shellfish, such as snow crab, king crab or blue crab, freshly shucked oysters, quartered sea scallops or canned clams
¼ cup thinly sliced scallions

Asparagus

15 asparagus spears, woody ends removed
1 tablespoon light olive oil

1. Set an oven rack on the middle shelf and preheat oven to 400°F.
2. In a large bowl, stir together the mayonnaise, salt, pepper and chili-garlic sauce (if using) until well blended.
3. Add the shellfish and scallions. Mix thoroughly.
4. Spoon into a 9-inch ovenproof casserole and pat down gently.
5. Place the asparagus on a large rimmed baking sheet and drizzle with olive oil.
6. Roast the shellfish and the asparagus in the same oven for 15 minutes. Remove the asparagus and the shellfish, then reposition the rack at least 6 inches from the broiler.
7. Turn the oven setting to broil and return the shellfish to the oven. Broil for about 1 minute, or until golden brown. Watch closely to avoid burning.
8. Divide the asparagus among four plates. Using a spatula to keep the casserole's crispy topping intact, place a serving of shellfish on top of the asparagus and serve.

Frugal Option

Use frozen shellfish.

*Sriracha is available in the Asian section of specialty grocery stores.

Per serving using scallops: calories 159.8, total fat 3.9 g, saturated fat 0.5 g, cholesterol 18.7 mg, sodium 632.4 mg, potassium 346.6 mg, total carbohydrate 18.3 g, dietary fiber 3.5 g, sugars 7.0 g protein 12.4 g

---

🍽️ *In the Mood Thai Mackerel with Avocado Salsa*

Makes 4 servings

With its spicy, chili-infused fish sauce, this simple and healthy meal packs a true Thai punch. Leave out the chili or chili sauce if you prefer a bit milder flavor.

Spicy Sauce

1 red chili, seeded and chopped (or 1 tablespoon chili sauce)
1 tablespoon freshly squeezed lime juice
¼ cup oyster sauce diluted with ¼ cup low-sodium chicken broth
½ cup low-sodium soy sauce
2 tablespoons freshly minced garlic cloves
¼ teaspoon freshly ground black pepper
1 tablespoon fish sauce

Fish

Two 1-pound whole mackerel, with 5 diagonal cuts slashed on the body of each (salmon fillets may be substituted)
½ cup fresh basil leaves
½ cup fresh cilantro leaves

Avocado Salsa

1 ripe avocado, peeled, pit removed and diced
Juice of ½ fresh lime
2 very large beefsteak tomatoes, cored and diced, or 14 ounces canned organic diced tomatoes, drained
1 cup canned black beans, rinsed
Pinch salt
2 tablespoons finely chopped fresh cilantro

1. Place an oven rack on the middle shelf of the oven and preheat to 350°F.
2. In a medium bowl, combine the chili or chili sauce, lime juice, oyster sauce, soy sauce, garlic, pepper and fish sauce. Whisk until well combined.
3. Lay a piece of foil large enough to wrap up both fish on a rimmed baking sheet. Place the two whole fish on top of the foil. Sprinkle the fish with the basil and cilantro and pour the sauce over them. Fold up the foil packet, keeping the seam at the top so the sauce won't leak during baking.
4. Bake for 30 minutes. The fish is done when it is opaque and flakes easily.
5. Make the salsa while the fish bakes. In a medium bowl, combine the avocado, lime juice, tomato, beans, salt and cilantro. Toss gently until well combined. Chill.
6. Remove the fish from the oven and open the foil packet. Reserving the sauce that remains, transfer the fish to a plate and let cool slightly. Separate the fish into four fillets, carefully removing all the bones.
7. Place a fillet on each of four plates, top with the sauce, mound some salsa alongside and serve.

Per serving: calories 288.4, total fat 9.3 g, saturated fat 1.4 g, cholesterol 57.8 mg, sodium 444.6 mg, potassium 937.8 mg, total carbohydrate 19.3 g, dietary fiber 7.8 g, sugars 0.4 g, protein 28.2 g

Sexy Baked Stuffed Fish

Makes 4 servings

Savory stuffed fish is popular throughout the Mediterranean. There, fresh fish are plentiful and the stuffing changes according to what's in season at the local market. Combining spinach, kale, pecans and a touch of red wine, this simple stuffing is also delicious with buffalo, lamb and turkey.

1 teaspoon light olive oil
2 cloves garlic, sliced thin
Pinch salt, plus extra to taste
Pinch freshly ground black pepper
½ cup finely chopped sun-dried tomatoes, packed in oil and drained
½ cup whole-wheat breadcrumbs
2 tablespoons finely chopped pecans
1 tablespoon chopped parsley
1 teaspoon Italian Seasoning blend (store-bought or follow recipe on page 482)
2 tablespoons red wine or water
6 cups fresh baby spinach
2 cups fresh kale leaves, finely chopped
Eight 2- to 3-ounce skinless wild Pacific salmon fillets

1. Place an oven rack on the middle shelf of the oven and preheat to 350°F.
2. Heat the olive oil in a wok or large saucepan over medium heat. Add the garlic, salt, pepper, sun-dried tomatoes, breadcrumbs, pecans, parsley, Italian Seasoning and red wine and sauté for about 10 minutes until the breadcrumbs lightly brown.
3. Put the spinach and kale in a large pot with a tablespoon or so of water, cover and heat on high for about 30 seconds. Add to the breadcrumb mixture. Stir until well combined.
4. Lay four of the fish fillets on a rimmed baking sheet. Cover each with a mound of loosely packed stuffing. Place the remaining fillets over the stuffing-topped fillets. Bake for 20 minutes or until the flesh is opaque and flakes easily.
5. Divide among four plates and serve.

Frugal Option

Use any fillet of wild fish that is on sale.

Per serving: calories 332.0, total fat 10.9 g, saturated fat 1.8 g, cholesterol 85.0 mg, sodium 515.9 mg, potassium 783.0 mg, total carbohydrate 28.2 g, dietary fiber 5.7 g, sugars 3.7 g, protein 29.9 g

---

Asian Beef Kebabs Testosteroni

Makes 4 servings

Hearty grilled kebabs are easy to prepare and fun to eat. Bathing the beef in the hot-and-spicy Japanese-inspired marinade is the key to the kebabs' deep, rich flavor. If you're in a hurry, skip the overnight marination and brush the marinade on the kebabs as they cook.

Spicy Marinade

1 **shallot,** finely chopped
1 **teaspoon minced ginger**
2 **tablespoons oyster sauce**
1 **cup red wine**
1 **dried apricot,** finely chopped

Beef Kebabs

1½ **pounds pasture-fed beef or buffalo sirloin,** cut into 1-inch cubes
25 **cherry tomatoes**
Zest from 1 large lime

Rice

½ **cup brown jasmine rice**
2 **tablespoons finely chopped fresh parsley**

1. In a large resealable bag, combine the shallots, ginger, oyster sauce, wine and apricots. Add the beef kebabs to the marinade. Seal the bag and refrigerate overnight.
2. Cook the rice according to package directions. Fluff with a fork and stir in the parsley.
3. Heat a gas grill to medium, or set a grill pan on medium heat. Remove the beef from the marinade, shaking the pieces to remove excess marinade. Discard remaining marinade. Thread the beef and the tomatoes on skewers, alternating the meat with the vegetables.
4. Grill for about 1 minute per side for medium-rare beef, a total of 4 minutes per skewer.
5. Remove the kebabs from the grill, divide among four plates and sprinkle the beef with the lime zest. Serve with cooked rice.

Vegetarian Version

Use healing vegetables instead of beef.

Per serving: calories 289.8, total fat 3.8 g, saturated fat 0.8 g, cholesterol 90.1 mg, sodium 172.8 mg, potassium 380.4 mg, total carbohydrate 12.9 g, dietary fiber 2.0 g, sugars 3.9 g, protein 40.9 g

Lamb Love Burgers with Greek Yogurt Dressing

Makes 4 servings

Greek herbs and creamy yogurt bring a mellow flavor to the grass-fed lamb in these delightfully different burgers, which are a healthy, tasty departure from familiar beef patties. Make the patties small enough so that you can stuff them into pita pockets or serve them on top of another flatbread.

Lamb Burgers

1–2 tablespoons light olive oil
1½ pounds organic grass-fed ground lamb
3 tablespoons Greek Seasoning (store-bought or prepared following recipe below)
2 teaspoons salt
⅛ teaspoon plus 1 pinch freshly ground black pepper
1 cup low-fat Greek yogurt (store-bought or prepared following recipe on page 406)
3 tablespoons chopped parsley
4 whole-wheat pita pockets
Grated zest of 1 lemon

Grilled Vegetables

½ pound yellow squash, ends removed, sliced
½ pound zucchini, ends removed, sliced
1 tablespoon light olive oil

1. Heat gas grill to medium-high or set a grill pan on medium-high heat. Lightly grease with olive oil.
2. In a large bowl, combine the lamb, Greek Seasoning, salt and black pepper. Mix well and divide into 4 patties about ¾ inch thick.
3. Place the squash and zucchini on a rimmed baking sheet and drizzle with olive oil.
4. Grill the burgers until medium-rare, 4 to 4½ minutes per side.
5. Grill the vegetables alongside the burgers, and turn when you turn the burgers.
6. In a small bowl, combine the yogurt and parsley.
7. Slice open one end of each pita pocket, tuck the burgers inside and sprinkle with lemon zest. Spoon some yogurt into each pita and serve.

Per serving: calories 672.8, total fat 48.0 g, saturated fat 18.2 g, cholesterol 123.7 mg, sodium 291.6 mg, potassium 593.8 mg, total carbohydrate 21.8 g, dietary fiber 4.9 g, sugars 2.1 g, protein 37.5 g

Greek Seasoning

1 teaspoon dried oregano
1 teaspoon dried thyme
1 teaspoon sweet paprika
1 tablespoon ground fennel seed
1 tablespoon ground coriander seed

Combine the oregano, thyme, paprika, fennel and coriander. Store in a jar.

🍽 *Sublime Pumpkin Pie*

Makes one 10-inch pie, 10 servings

If you have any pumpkin filling left over, pour it into a ramekin and bake alongside the pie, or freeze it for another time.

Pie Crust

> 1 cup whole-wheat pastry flour
> ½ cup almond flour
> 1 tablespoon ground flaxseed
> ½ teaspoon salt
> 1 teaspoon xylitol or birch sugar
> ¼ teaspoon ground cinnamon
> 4 tablespoons unsalted butter from grass-fed cows

Pumpkin Custard

> 15 ounces all-natural pumpkin puree
> ½ cup low-fat milk
> 2 omega-3 eggs
> 2 teaspoons vanilla extract
> 1 cup low-fat vanilla yogurt
> 1 tablespoon pumpkin pie spice
> ½ cup xylitol or birch sugar

1. In a food processor, combine the flours, flaxseed, salt, sugar, cinnamon and butter. Pulse until thoroughly blended.
2. Pour ½ cup ice-cold water through the feed tube and pulse until the dough comes together. Remove from the processor and shape into a ball. Refrigerate for 15 minutes.
3. Place an oven rack on the middle shelf and preheat the oven to 350°F.
4. Place the pie crust on a well-floured piece of wax paper. Flour a rolling pin and carefully roll out the dough into a 12-inch circle no thicker than ½ inch. Transfer to a 10-inch pie pan and tuck any extra dough under the edges. Pinch the dough between your fingers and one knuckle to create a scalloped crust.
5. Cover the crust with aluminum foil and fill the foil with dried beans or pie weights. Place the plate into the oven to bake for 15 minutes. Remove the foil and beans and bake for another 10 minutes or until the crust starts to turn golden. Remove from the oven.
6. Using a mixer, mix the pumpkin, milk, eggs, vanilla, yogurt, spice and sugar until well combined. Pour into the baked pie crust and place in the oven for 30 minutes. If the pie crust starts to darken, cover the pie loosely with foil.
7. Remove from the oven and cool before serving.

Per serving: calories 193.7, total fat 8.9 g, saturated fat 3.7 g, cholesterol 57.0 mg, sodium 51.0 mg, potassium 147.6 mg, total carbohydrate 17.6 g, dietary fiber 3.6 g, sugars 5.3 g, protein 5.8 g

🍽️ *Sweets for Men Pumpkin Cheesecakes*

Makes 4 individual cheesecakes, 8 servings

A food processor and a stand mixer make quick work of these sumptuous individual cheese-cakes. But it does require some advance planning, since the cakes must be refrigerated overnight.

Fruit-Nut Crust

1 tablespoon vanilla extract
4 tablespoons unsalted butter from grass-fed cows
¼ cup finely chopped walnuts
6 dried roughly chopped figs
¼ cup xylitol or birch sugar
1½ cups quick-cooking oats
¼ cup almond flour

Cheesecake Filling

½ cup pumpkin puree
16 ounces low-fat cream cheese
¾ cup xylitol or birch sugar
1 tablespoon almond flour
1 tablespoon orange zest
4 omega-3 eggs
1 teaspoon vanilla extract
1 teaspoon cornstarch

1. Place a rack on the middle shelf of the oven and preheat to 350°F.
2. In a food processor fitted with the steel blade, pulse the vanilla, butter, walnuts, figs, sugar, oats and almond flour until a dough forms.
3. Divide the dough into 4 pieces and press each into the bottom of individual springform pans. Cover the dough with aluminum foil and bake for 6 minutes. Allow to cool, then cover the bottom edges of the pans with aluminum foil.
4. Place the pumpkin puree, cream cheese, sugar, flour, zest, eggs, vanilla and cornstarch in the bowl of a stand mixer. Mix on medium speed until well combined.
5. Pour the filling over the baked crusts. Place them in a large roasting pan and on the oven rack. Using a kettle, carefully pour boiling water into the roasting pan until it reaches halfway up the sides of the springform pans.
6. Reduce the heat to 200°F and bake the cheesecakes for 60 minutes, until they no longer wobble in the center. Turn off the oven, leaving the door ajar, for 60 minutes.
7. Remove the cheesecakes and let cool slightly before covering them with plastic wrap and refrigerating overnight. This process of baking and cooling the cheesecakes prevents splitting, which can happen when cheesecake is overcooked.

Per serving (½ cheesecake): calories 407.6, total fat 23.2 g, saturated fat 11.2 g, cholesterol 154.8 mg, sodium 304.2 mg, potassium 308.6 mg, total carbohydrate 23.1 g, dietary fiber 3.7 g, sugars 8.0 g, protein 12.6 g

---

🍽 *Visionary Lentil Carrot Soup*

Makes 4 servings

Lentils are used in inexpensive and nutritious soups from India to Europe to South America. This robust soup requires only few steps to prepare, and can also be spooned over vegetables, pasta, rice, even seafood. Thick, flavorful and earthy, this soup is loaded with carrot's sight-healing beta-carotene.

1 teaspoon light olive oil
½ cup chopped white onions
1 tablespoon tomato paste
1 tablespoon minced garlic
1 large carrot, peeled and thinly sliced
1 cup dried red or green lentils
1 quart low-sodium vegetable stock
½ teaspoon salt

1. Heat the olive oil in a stockpot over medium-high heat. Add the onions and sauté until they are translucent, about 7 minutes.

2. Add the tomato paste, garlic, carrot, lentils, vegetable stock and salt. Cook for 30 minutes, or until the lentils and carrots are tender.

3. Adjust seasonings and serve from the pot.

Nonvegetarian Version

Sauté strips of chicken with the onion or add shrimp along with the tomato paste and garlic.

Per serving: calories 104.5, total fat 1.4 g, saturated fat 0.2 g, cholesterol 0.0 mg, sodium 224.2 mg, potassium 317.3 mg, total carbohydrate 18.2 g, dietary fiber 5.9 g, sugars 3.3 g, protein 5.1 g

⦿ *Anti-Cataract Tuna Tapas with Spicy Marinated Red Peppers*

Makes 4 servings

Tapas, which are Spanish in origin, are small plates that, in this country, are often eaten as appetizers, but in Spain comprise an entire meal. Tapas bars are now found all over the world. Make a double batch of the vitamin-rich, spicy marinated peppers, and keep them in the fridge. They are delicious with chicken, fish, meat, soups, sandwiches and salads.

Spicy Marinated Red Peppers

2 red bell peppers, cored, seeded and sliced into 1½-inch strips
1 cup red wine vinegar
1 Serrano pepper, seeded and thinly sliced
1 tablespoon lime juice
6 parsley stems
6 whole black peppercorns

1. In a large glass jar, combine the red bell peppers, vinegar, Serrano pepper, lime juice, parsley and black peppercorns.
2. Add enough water to cover. Close the jar and marinate in the refrigerator overnight. If you would prefer them spicier, add another Serrano pepper.

Herb Vinaigrette

½ cup olive oil
2 tablespoons white wine vinegar
½ tablespoon finely chopped fresh cilantro
1 teaspoon raw sunflower seeds
⅛ teaspoon freshly ground black pepper

Tuna Skewers

1 pound fresh tuna, cut into 1-inch cubes
8 broccoli florets
8 Brussels sprouts, trimmed and sliced in half
12 Spicy Marinated Red Bell Pepper strips, with 1 tablespoon of marinade

1. Heat a well-seasoned outdoor grill to medium heat.
2. Combine the olive oil, vinegar, cilantro, sunflower seeds and ground pepper in a small bowl. Whisk until well combined.
3. Thread the tuna, broccoli, sprouts and marinated peppers onto four metal skewers.
4. Grill, turning and brushing occasionally with the herb vinaigrette, for a total of 10 minutes.
5. To serve, remove the fish and vegetables from the skewers and offer the vinaigrette on the side.

Per serving: calories 163.2, total fat 1.3 g, saturated fat 0.1 g, cholesterol 50.0 mg, sodium 58.3 mg, potassium 351.6 mg, total carbohydrate 13.6 g, dietary fiber 3.5 g, sugars 1.0 g, protein 28.6 g

🍴 C Better Greek Shrimp Salad

Makes 4 servings

Greek salads have become a staple in American restaurants, but you can't beat one prepared at home with the freshest, healthiest ingredients. The simple goodness of olive oil, vinegar, feta cheese and lemon never disappoints. This fruity dressing, loaded with vitamin C, is a delightfully bright twist on the classic. Add the dressing just before serving.

Greek Salad

1 large head romaine lettuce, torn into bite-sized pieces
2 heaping cups fresh baby spinach
¼ cup pitted kalamata olives
4 Brussels sprouts, trimmed and thinly sliced
1 carrot, peeled, and thinly sliced
1 red bell pepper, cored, seeded and cut into ¼-inch pieces
1 small red onion, sliced and separated into rings
1 tomato, cored and diced
1 teaspoon light olive oil
1 pound medium shrimp, peeled and deveined

Dressing

1 plum, or 1 cup fresh papaya, peeled, pitted and cut up
4 tablespoons extra-virgin olive oil
1 tablespoon red wine vinegar
Leaves from 8 sprigs Italian (flat-leaf) parsley, chopped
1 teaspoon minced garlic
1 teaspoon dried oregano

¼ cup feta cheese, rinsed, then crumbled

1. In a large bowl, combine the lettuce, spinach, olives, Brussels sprouts, carrot, red bell pepper, onion and tomato and toss until well combined.
2. In the bowl of a food processor, combine the plum or papaya, olive oil, red wine vinegar, parsley, garlic and oregano. Pulse until well blended. Set aside.
3. Heat the light olive oil in a small skillet over medium heat. Add the shrimp and sauté until pink, 2–3 minutes.
4. Add to the salad. Add the dressing and toss until the salad is well coated.
5. Divide among four shallow bowls, sprinkle with the feta cheese and serve.

Vegetarian Version

Omit shrimp. Add sautéed green beans.

Per serving: calories 350.8, total fat 20.7 g, saturated fat 4.0 g, cholesterol 177.3 mg, sodium 451.4 mg, potassium 752.5 mg, total carbohydrate 13.1 g, dietary fiber 4.2 g, sugars 2.8 g, protein 29.2 g

---

¡◎¡ *Eye-Saving Caesar Salad*

Makes 4 servings

Salty, crunchy Caesar salad is a universal favorite. To add more vision-healing power, we've added cauliflower croutons in the place of the traditional bread cubes. In the last few minutes of baking, finely grated Parmesan cheese is added to make an Italian *frico*, a crispy cheese wafer, sometimes called "lacy Parmesan."

Cauliflower Croutons

1–1½ pounds cauliflower, broken into florets and cut into slices ½ inch thick
1 tablespoon light olive oil
¼ cup freshly grated Parmesan cheese
¼ cup finely chopped parsley

Caesar Dressing

1 tablespoon anchovy paste
1 tablespoon garlic paste
1 teaspoon Dijon mustard
Freshly squeezed lemon juice, or to taste
⅛ teaspoon freshly ground black pepper
1 teaspoon salt
1 tablespoon freshly grated Parmesan cheese
¼ cup extra-virgin olive oil

2 heads romaine lettuce, torn into bite-sized pieces
¼ cup raw sunflower seeds

1. Place an oven rack on the middle shelf of the oven and preheat to 400°F.
2. Prepare the croutons. Toss the cauliflower with the light olive oil on a rimmed baking sheet that holds the vegetables in a single layer. Bake for 15 minutes.
3. Meanwhile, combine the anchovy paste, garlic paste, mustard, lemon juice, pepper, salt, Parmesan and olive oil in a medium bowl and whisk until well combined.
4. When the cauliflower is tender enough to pierce with a fork, sprinkle it with ¼ cup Parmesan. The cheese will turn golden and lacy in about 4 minutes. Check it once or twice to prevent burning. Remove from the oven and sprinkle with the parsley. The cheese should harden slightly.
5. Place the romaine lettuce in a large bowl, add the dressing and toss.
6. Divide the lettuce among four plates and top with the cauliflower croutons. Sprinkle with sunflower seeds and serve.

Nonvegetarian Versions

Top with sautéed halibut fillets or shrimp.

Per serving: calories 310.9, total fat 26.4 g, saturated fat 4.3 g, cholesterol 6.2 mg, sodium 442.2 mg, potassium 870.7 mg, total carbohydrate 14.3 g, dietary fiber 6.6 g, sugars 0.5 g, protein 9.7 g

🍽 **Warm Italian See-Food Salad with Asian Dressing**

Makes 2 servings

The best salads make you feel as though you've just visited the farmers' market and brought home the healthiest local ingredients. Sauté the broccoli and cauliflower very quickly, so that the vegetables retain their color and crunch.

1 teaspoon light olive oil
2 pounds cauliflower, broken into florets and cut into slices ½-inch thick
1–2 pounds broccoli, cut into florets
6 large shelled and butterflied shrimp
¼ cup finely chopped dried pineapple
1 teaspoon garlic paste (store-bought)
1 teaspoon minced ginger
½ teaspoon salt
½ cup pomegranate juice, or unsweetened apple or pear juice
2 heaping cups fresh baby spinach
4 lime wedges

1. Heat the olive oil in a wok or large sauté pan over medium heat. Add the cauliflower and broccoli and sauté, stirring, for 4 minutes.
2. Add the shrimp and reduce the heat to medium low. Add the pineapple, garlic paste, ginger, salt and pomegranate juice. Stir together quickly, and cook until the shrimp turns pink. Remove from heat.
3. Divide the spinach and lime wedges between 2 plates, and top them with the cooked vegetable-shrimp mixture and serve.

Vegetarian Version

Instead of shrimp, use ½-inch tofu slices sautéed in olive oil. When golden on both sides, add to broccoli and cauliflower with the dressing.

Frugal Options

Use frozen shrimp instead of fresh.

Per serving: calories 337.6, total fat 5.8 g, saturated fat 0.7 g, cholesterol 36.5 mg, sodium 423.4 mg, potassium 2,216.8 mg, total carbohydrate 62.1 g, dietary fiber 17.9 g, sugars 9.2 g, protein 21.0 g

Sight-Saving Italian Green Spaghetti with Buffalo

Makes 4 servings

In this pasta dish, parsley is more than a garnish. It joins salty anchovies and crunchy sunflower seeds in a vision-healing green version sauce that is served all over Italy. There will be plenty of extra green sauce for another day, so keep it in the refrigerator and try it on baked potatoes, other vegetables and poultry.

¾ pound whole-wheat spaghetti

Italian Green Sauce

1 bunch fresh Italian (flat-leaf) parsley
1–1½ pounds broccoli, cut into florets
1 cup fresh spinach
1 tablespoon white vinegar
1 teaspoon capers, drained
1 tablespoon minced garlic
1 teaspoon anchovy paste
1 teaspoon raw sunflower seeds
2 tablespoons light olive oil, plus additional for sautéing
1 pound buffalo sirloin, sliced into ½-inch-thick strips
Freshly ground black paper, to taste

1. Cook the pasta according to package directions. Drain.
2. Fill a large saucepan halfway full with water. Bring to a boil. Blanch the parsley (saving 4 sprigs for use as a garnish), broccoli and spinach by dropping them into the boiling water for 30 seconds. Remove from the water.
3. Transfer the parsley, broccoli and spinach to a blender. Add the vinegar, capers, garlic, anchovy paste, sunflower seeds, 2 tablespoons olive oil and ½ cup water. Pulse until well combined. If the ingredients are not thoroughly blended, add another tablespoon of water and pulse again.
4. Heat olive oil in a medium pan, over medium-high heat. Sauté the buffalo strips until pink, about 2 minutes per side. Season with black pepper.
5. Toss the pasta with the green sauce. Divide the pasta among four plates, top with buffalo strips and a sprig of parsley and serve.

Vegetarian Version

Omit buffalo strips and anchovy paste. Top the spaghetti with some sautéed cauliflower, red bell peppers and red onion.

Frugal Options

Use frozen broccoli and spinach instead of fresh.

Per serving: calories 513.6, total fat 10.3 g, saturated fat 1.6 g, cholesterol 60.4 mg, sodium 166.8 mg, potassium 386.3 mg, total carbohydrate 69.1 g, dietary fiber 10.6 g, sugars 0.1 g, protein 38.5 g

---

🍽 *Cataract-Conquering Thai Halibut-Carrot Stew*

Makes 10 appetizer servings

The best soups are made in a few simple steps. This is a slightly spicy, hearty Thai fish stew. Cilantro gives it a bright finish in both color and flavor, and everyone knows carrots are great for better vision.

> 2 quarts low-sodium vegetable or fish stock
> 1 teaspoon red curry paste*
> 1 teaspoon minced ginger
> 1 teaspoon minced garlic cloves
> 3 leaves fresh basil
> ¼ cup finely chopped fresh cilantro
> 2 tablespoons fish sauce
> ¼ cup finely chopped lemongrass, optional
> 1 tablespoon low-sodium soy sauce
> 3 large carrots, peeled and cut into ¼-inch slices
> 4 fresh halibut fillets

1. Heat the stock in a large stockpot over medium heat. Add the red curry paste, ginger, garlic, basil, cilantro, fish sauce, lemongrass (if using), soy sauce and carrots to the stock. Cook for 20 minutes or until the carrots are tender.
2. Add the fish fillets and lower the heat to medium-low. Cook for another 10 minutes or until the fish is opaque and flakes easily. Stir gently, so as not to break up the fish.
3. Divide the soup among four bowls, place a fillet in each and serve.

Vegetarian Version

Instead of halibut, add 2 cups bite-sized pieces of broccoli florets with the carrots and a few cups of spinach a few minutes before serving. You may also serve the soup over ½ cup cooked brown rice.

Frugal Option

Use frozen fish and vegetables, thawed, instead of fresh.

*Red curry paste is found in the Asian or international section of most grocery stores.

Per serving: calories 75.6, total fat 1.2 g, saturated fat 0.2 g, cholesterol 14.4 mg, sodium 504.2 mg, potassium 304.0 mg, total carbohydrate 5.4 g, dietary fiber 1.4 g, sugars 2.6 g, protein 10.0 g

◉ *Mighty Omega-3 Mandarin Salmon Burgers*

Makes 4 servings

Here's an Asian twist on the traditional burger. Wild salmon is an excellent match for the fruity and bold ketchup. There are two universal rules when cooking burgers: Never press on the burger and only flip once.

Salmon Burger

1 teaspoon light olive oil, plus 1 tablespoon
2 tablespoons finely chopped shallots
1 teaspoon minced ginger
1 teaspoon minced garlic
12 ounces canned salmon
¼ cup whole-wheat breadcrumbs
1 omega-3 egg
2 kale leaves, finely chopped
Two 9-inch (large) whole-wheat wraps, cut in half
¼ cup feta cheese, rinsed and crumbled, optional

Mandarin Sesame Ketchup

1 cup canned mandarin orange segments
½ red bell pepper, cored and seeded
1 tablespoon toasted sesame oil
1 teaspoon toasted sesame seeds
1 tablespoon hoisin sauce
1 teaspoon garlic paste

1. Heat 1 teaspoon of olive oil in a small pan over medium heat. Add the shallots and sauté until they soften, about 7 minutes.

2. To make the ketchup, in a blender, combine the mandarin oranges, red bell pepper, sesame oil, sesame seeds, hoisin sauce and garlic paste with 1 tablespoon water and pulse until well combined. Set aside.

3. Scrape the shallots into a food processor and wipe out the pan. Add the ginger, garlic, salmon, breadcrumbs and egg to the food processor bowl and pulse until well blended and a paste is formed.

4. Shape the paste into four burgers, and fry them in 1 tablespoon of olive oil in the pan used for the shallots, over medium-low heat. Cook uncovered for 2 minutes per side. They are done when they have a golden crust.

5. To serve, place a handful of chopped kale on each of the four wrap halves and top with a salmon burger. Add a generous spoonful of the ketchup, a sprinkle of feta cheese and serve.

Per serving: calories 346.5, total fat 16.3 g, saturated fat 2.7 g, cholesterol 52.5 mg, sodium 483.3 mg, potassium 131.1 mg, total carbohydrate 26.9 g, dietary fiber 2.8 g, sugars 1.7 g, protein 22.5 g

---

🍽 *Sight-Sharpening Asian Salmon with Salad*

Makes 4 servings

Sesame seeds and almonds add crunch to the tender wild salmon. The Asian citrus dressing adds hints of citrus plus heat from the cayenne. This dish is mildly spicy but can be adjusted for your particular tastes.

Sesame Coating

½–1 teaspoon curry powder, to taste
2 tablespoons white sesame seeds
2 tablespoons crushed almonds

Salmon and Salad

1 large piece wild salmon, about 1½ pounds, cut into 1-inch pieces
1 teaspoon light olive oil
6 cups fresh baby spinach
1 teaspoon orange zest

Asian Citrus Dressing

1 tablespoon roughly chopped cilantro
½ teaspoon garlic paste
1 tablespoon orange juice
1 teaspoon grapefruit juice
Pinch cayenne
¼ cup sesame oil

1. Combine the curry, sesame seeds and almonds in a shallow pie plate.
2. Place the salmon pieces into the coating mixture and press to make sure as much of the coating sticks as possible.
3. Heat the olive oil in a wok or large skillet over medium heat. Carefully add the salmon pieces and cook about 1 minute on each side.
4. For the dressing, combine the cilantro, garlic paste, orange juice, grapefruit juice, cayenne and sesame oil in a small bowl and whisk.
5. Pour the dressing into the wok, reserving about 1 tablespoon. Remove from the heat.
6. Divide the spinach among four plates and top with the sesame-encrusted salmon. Sprinkle with the orange zest, drizzle with the reserved dressing and serve.

Vegetarian Version

Use eggplant or zucchini instead of salmon.

Frugal Options

Use cubed chicken breast instead of salmon.

Per serving: calories 344.4, total fat 22.9 g, saturated fat 4.1 g, cholesterol 60.0 mg, sodium 175.2 mg, potassium 313.3 mg, total carbohydrate 4.4 g, dietary fiber 2.1 g, sugars 0.8 g, protein 32.9 g

🍽 *Vision Perfect Carrot Cake*

Makes one 9-inch loaf, 9 servings

This carrot cake is a snap to prepare. You might want to add a pinch of pumpkin pie spice or ground nutmeg.

½ cup xylitol or birch sugar
2 omega-3 eggs
2 heaping cups shredded carrots
¼ cup light olive oil, plus additional for greasing
¼ cup raw agave nectar
1 teaspoon vanilla extract
Pinch salt
1 teaspoon ground cinnamon
1 teaspoon baking soda
1 tablespoon slivered almonds
¾ cup whole-wheat pastry flour
½ cup almond flour

1. Place the oven rack in the middle and preheat the oven to 350°F. Lightly grease a 9-inch loaf pan with olive oil.
2. Using a mixer, combine the sugar and eggs well on medium. Add the carrots, olive oil, agave, vanilla, salt, cinnamon, baking soda and almonds and continue to mix. Lower the speed and add the flours. Mix to blend thoroughly.
3. Scrape the batter into the prepared loaf pan. Bake for 45 minutes, turning about halfway through the cooking time. The cake is done when a toothpick comes out clean.
4. Remove from the pan by running a sharp knife around the edge of the pan. Turn over to remove, then place right-side up on a wire rack to cool for 10 minutes. Slice and serve while still warm.

Per 1-inch-thick slice: calories 198.6, total fat 10.3 g, saturated fat 1.3 g, cholesterol 42.2 mg, sodium 186.3 mg, potassium 124.3 mg, total carbohydrate 16.5 g, dietary fiber 2.8 g, sugars 7.0 g, protein 4.2 g

🍴 *Smart-Carb Pumpkin and Potato Soup with Asian Salad*

Makes 2 servings

Soup and salad make a wonderful lunch or light dinner. Pumpkin soup has a smooth, comforting flavor and is loaded with fatigue-busting B vitamins. Cinnamon and cardamom are the scents of autumn and the Asian-inspired salad is a lovely balance of smooth and crunchy, sweet and salty. Store extra batches in the freezer for quick, easy meals.

Asian Salad

1 whole spaghetti squash, cut in half, seeds removed
3 tablespoons store-bought plum sauce*
2 leaves Napa cabbage, rib removed, finely chopped
1 heaping tablespoon finely chopped fresh cilantro

Soup

1 can organic pumpkin purée
1 pound new potatoes, boiled
Pinch ground cinnamon
¼ teaspoon ground cardamom
2 cups low-sodium vegetable broth
¼ cup light coconut milk
½ teaspoon red curry paste*
Pinch salt
1½ ounces herbed goat cheese
Whole-grain crackers, for serving

*Plum sauce and red curry paste are available in the Asian foods section of most supermarkets.

1. Preheat the oven to 375°F.

2. Slice the spaghetti squash in half (lengthwise) or quarters, and gently scrape out the seeds and the pulp. Place the squash on a large sheet pan, cut side down, and bake it in the oven for 30 to 40 minutes until tender. Set it aside to cool slightly. With a fork, scrape the inside of the squash to release the spaghetti-like strands, and transfer to a large bowl. Add the plum sauce, cabbage, and cilantro and toss until well combined.

3. In a medium saucepot over medium heat, combine the pumpkin, potatoes, cinnamon, cardamom, broth, coconut milk, curry paste, salt and goat cheese. Mix until well combined. If the soup starts to boil, reduce the heat to medium-low. If you prefer your soup smooth, pulse with an immersion blender until your desired texture.

4. Divide the soup between two bowls, the salad between two plates and serve with crackers.

Per serving: calories 435.1, total fat 8.6 g, saturated fat 3.5 g, cholesterol 7.5 mg, sodium 514.3 mg, potassium 901.5 mg, total carbohydrate 82.7 g, dietary fiber 17.7 g, sugars 16.5 g, protein 14.0 g

---

🍽 *High-Protein Niçoise Salad*

Makes 6 servings

This salad comes from the French city of Nice, on the Mediterranean Sea. Originally, the salad had no tuna at all, just anchovies. The traditional dressing has a touch of mustard and shallot; we've loaded it up with fresh herbs and some walnuts for crunch.

Niçoise Dressing

¼ cup minced shallots
1 tablespoon finely chopped parsley
1 teaspoon finely chopped fresh chives
1 tablespoon crushed walnuts
1 tablespoon Dijon mustard
1 teaspoon minced garlic
¼ cup extra-virgin olive oil
¼ cup white or red wine vinegar

Salad

8 heaping cups baby spinach
½ pound green beans, ends trimmed and cut in half
2 English cucumbers, ends trimmed and cut into ¼-inch slices
½ cup thinly sliced shallots
2 hard-boiled omega-3 eggs, quartered lengthwise
8 new potatoes, boiled or steamed, and quartered
6 large Niçoise olives, pitted and finely chopped
2 tomatoes, cut into wedges
1 large very ripe avocado, peeled and sliced into thin wedges
4 ounces Sicilian tuna, packed in oil and drained
6 anchovy fillets

To make the dressing, mix the shallots, parsley, chives, walnuts, mustard, garlic, olive oil and vinegar and stir until well blended.

To serve in composed individual portions: Divide the spinach among six wide salad bowls. Top each bowl with equal portions of green beans, cucumbers, shallots, eggs, potatoes, olives, tomatoes and avocados, in a decorative pattern. Top each salad with a heaping tablespoon of tuna and an anchovy fillet, drizzle dressing evenly over each and serve.

To serve tossed, family style: In a very large bowl, combine the spinach, green beans, cucumbers, shallots, eggs, potatoes, olives, tomatoes, avocados, tuna and dressing. Toss the salad gently until well coated. Divide the salad among six wide salad bowls, top each with an anchovy and serve.

Per serving: calories 479.7, total fat 22.1 g, saturated fat 2.5 g, cholesterol 71.9 mg, sodium 423.3 mg, potassium 1,418.1 mg, total carbohydrate 52.4 g, dietary fiber 9.4 g, sugars 2.0 g, protein 19.5 g

Hot 'n' Lively Thai Oyster Soup and Garden Salad

Makes 2 servings

Oyster soups and stews are rich, hearty and truly healing. We've added Thai red curry paste to fuse this dish into a Mediterr-Asian delight, and give it some extra heat. As the soup cooks, the flavor will deepen. Its subtle sweetness will pair nicely with a fresh garden salad and fruity vinaigrette.

Oyster Soup
- 1 teaspoon light olive oil
- ½ cup finely chopped shallot
- 1 pound raw oysters, roughly chopped
- 2 cups low-sodium vegetable stock
- Pinch mace
- 1 teaspoon red curry paste*
- Whole-grain crackers

Salad
- 3 cups washed baby greens
- 2 large carrots, peeled and julienned
- 3 radishes, washed, trimmed and sliced thin
- 2 medium tomatoes, washed, cored and quartered

Vinaigrette
- ¼ cup extra-virgin olive oil
- 1 tablespoon balsamic vinegar
- ¼ teaspoon salt
- Pinch freshly ground black pepper
- 1 teaspoon freshly squeezed lemon juice
- 2 tablespoons finely chopped fresh parsley
- 1 teaspoon crushed walnuts
- 1 tablespoon unsweetened dried cherries

1. To make the soup, heat 1 teaspoon olive oil in a medium saucepan over medium heat. Add the shallots and sauté until they begin to soften, about 5 minutes. Add the oysters and cook for 2 minutes, stirring. Add the vegetable stock, mace and curry paste, and cook for 5 minutes. If the soup approaches a boil, reduce the heat to medium low.

2. To make the vinaigrette, combine ¼ cup olive oil, vinegar, salt, pepper, lemon juice, parsley, walnuts and cherries in a large bowl. Whisk until the vinaigrette emulsifies.

3. Add the greens, carrots, radishes and tomatoes to the bowl with the vinaigrette. Gently toss just before serving.

4. Divide the soup between two bowls, the salad between two plates and serve with whole-grain crackers.

Vegetarian Version

Use canned navy beans, rinsed, instead of oysters.

Frugal Options

Use canned oysters instead of fresh.

*Available in the Asian foods section of most supermarkets.

Oyster Soup 1¼ cup per serving: calories 230.7, total fat 6.3 g, saturated fat 0.3 g, cholesterol 100.0 mg, sodium 431.8 mg, potassium 133.6 mg, total carbohydrate 18.2 g, dietary fiber 1.0 g, sugars 2.3 g, protein 21.0 g

Garden Salad per serving: calories 163.7, total fat 14.6 g, saturated fat 2.1 g, cholesterol 0.0 mg, sodium 70.5 mg, potassium 148.6 mg, total carbohydrate 6.9 g, dietary fiber 1.9 g, sugars 3.1 g, protein 1.3 g

---

⦿ *Fatigue-Fighting "Skinny" Quiche with Caramelized Vegetables*

Makes 2 servings

Traditional quiches are French custard tarts that use butter in the crust and eggs in the filling. In this much lighter crustless quiche, Greek yogurt replaces eggs and firms up the filling just as well. Hard to believe? Try it! Skinny quiche has a savory, slightly sweet flavor, and the yogurt offers plenty of protein for steady energy. You'll never miss the crust.

1 teaspoon light olive oil
1 shallot, trimmed, peeled and sliced into thin rings
2 asparagus spears, tough ends removed and cut into ⅛-inch rounds
1 ounce boneless, skinless chicken breast, chopped into ¼-inch bits
1 teaspoon finely chopped fresh thyme leaves
¼ teaspoon salt
½ cup finely grated Parmesan cheese
1 cup 2% Greek yogurt (store-bought, or follow recipe, page 406)
3 heaping cups fresh baby spinach

1. Place an oven rack on the middle shelf of the oven and preheat to 350°F.
2. Heat the olive oil in a wok over medium heat. Add the shallots and sauté until tender, about 7 minutes. Reduce the heat to medium-low and add the asparagus and chicken. Cook until the asparagus is tender and the chicken opaque, about 5 minutes.
3. Remove from the heat. Transfer the mixture to a medium bowl and let cool slightly. Add the thyme, salt, cheese and Greek yogurt. Mix until well blended.
4. Divide the mixture between two 4-inch springform pans and bake for 20 minutes, or until the cheese starts to bubble and the Greek yogurt has set. Remove from the oven and release each quiche from the springform pans (you may need to run a knife around the edge of each quiche). Let them sit on the pans' bottom discs until slightly cooled, 2 to 3 minutes.
5. Divide the spinach between two plates, top each with a quiche and serve.

Vegetarian Version
Substitute broccoli florets for the chicken.

Per serving: calories 253.1, total fat 9.9 g, saturated fat 4.5 g, cholesterol 20.0 mg, sodium 481.7 mg, potassium 618.5 mg, total carbohydrate 22.4 g, dietary fiber 1.5 g, sugars 7.8 g, protein 16.0 g

 ## *Greek Yogurt*

Makes 12 ounces

1 quart 2% milk, organic, from pasture-fed cows
¼ cup plain yogurt (container should read "contains active cultures")

1. In a saucepan over medium heat, scald the milk (bring almost to a boil, about 170°F). Transfer it to a nonreactive bowl, and let cool to 110° to 120°F. Gently stir in the plain yogurt.

2. Set the bowl in a warm place, such as next to a heater or warm oven and surround it with kitchen towels to create a nest to keep the bowl warm. You may also use an electric yogurt tray. Drape a towel over the bowl. Let the milk sit out overnight or for 8 to 12 hours. The yogurt should be left completely alone until it is thick. If, at the end of 12 hours, the yogurt isn't thick, set it atop a stove set to 200°F for 2 hours (alternatives are to place it on top of a heater or a warm place in the house). If the yogurt is still very runny after letting it sit on the stove, the yogurt simply needs more time to set.

3. To make thick Greek yogurt, transfer the yogurt to a cheesecloth-lined colander and drain for at least 2 hours. I like to suspend the cheesecloth from a wooden spoon laid over a medium bowl, as quite a bit of liquid will drain off. Scrape the Greek yogurt from the cloth into a bowl and refrigerate up to one week.

Per serving (3 ounces): calories 130.6, total fat 4.8 g, saturated fat 3.1 g, cholesterol 19.8 mg, sodium 111.8 mg, potassium 39.0 mg, total carbohydrate 12.6 g, dietary fiber 0.0 g, sugars 13.5 g, protein 8.9 g

---

🍽 *Kick-Up-Your-Heels Chicken Paella*

Makes 4 servings

Great energy is all about balancing complex carbs with protein, and this Spanish paella delivers just the right mix of brown rice, poultry, seafood and veggies to replenish the nutrients that fight fatigue. The delicate and smoky sweetness of saffron is this dish's signature flavor.

1 tablespoon light olive oil (Spanish olive oil preferred)
1 large white onion, chopped
1 red bell pepper, cored, seeded and cut into ¼-inch dice
2 large tomatoes, cored and chopped
2 large garlic cloves, minced
1 teaspoon sea salt
Pinch black pepper
2 skinless, boneless chicken breasts, cut into ½-inch pieces
½ cup dry sherry
1 quart low-sodium vegetable or chicken broth, plus additional ¼ cup, if needed
2 cups brown rice
½ teaspoon curry powder, optional, if you like a little spicy kick
8 saffron threads (or paella spice mix—located in most grocery stores in the international spice section)
1 pound live baby clams or cockles, scrubbed and rinsed well
4 cups fresh baby spinach

1. Heat the olive oil in a large heavy stockpot over medium heat. Add the onions, peppers, tomatoes, garlic, salt, pepper and chicken breast. Sauté for 10 minutes, stirring frequently to prevent sticking.

2. Add the sherry, vegetable broth, rice, curry (if using) and saffron. Stir, then gently shake the pan to combine ingredients, all of which should be beneath the liquid. Cover.

3. Reduce the heat to medium-low and cook until the rice starts to appear above the water (it's okay to uncover the pot to check occasionally), about 55 minutes. If the water is totally absorbed but the rice isn't tender, slowly add ¼ cup of water and let it cook off before testing the rice again.

4. Add the clams or cockles to the rice, hinge side down, and reduce the heat to low. Cook for another 5 minutes, after which all the clams or cockles should have opened. Unopened clams or cockles should be discarded. Remove from the heat and let the paella sit for 5 minutes before serving. Serve the paella on plates lined with fresh spinach, which will wilt when covered with the rice.

Vegetarian Version

Omit seafood and poultry and add extra vegetables, black beans or cubed sautéed tofu.

Frugal Option

Use frozen vegetables instead of fresh. Use frozen shrimp instead of fresh clams.

Per serving: calories 444.5, total fat 4.6 g, saturated fat 0.7 g, cholesterol 0.0 mg, sodium 208.9 mg, potassium 461.1 mg, total carbohydrate 39.6 g, dietary fiber 4.5 g, sugars 5.6 g, protein 40.6 g

---

🍽 *Zingy Chicken and Okra Curry*

Makes 4 servings

Curry powder has a rich and spicy flavor that goes well with almost anything, especially chicken and okra. Okra is full of potassium and other immune-building nutrients. If you've never cooked okra before, this is an excellent recipe to start with. When okra is cooked for just 30 minutes, it retains its shape and has a nice crunch.

Rice

1 cup brown jasmine rice
2 tablespoons finely chopped fresh cilantro

Chicken and Okra Curry

1 teaspoon light olive oil
1 pound okra, trimmed and rinsed just before cooking
1 teaspoon minced roasted garlic
2 teaspoons curry powder
1 cup light coconut milk
2 cups canned crushed tomatoes
2 tablespoons golden raisins
1 pound boneless, skinless chicken breasts, pounded thin, cut into 4 pieces
1 teaspoon salt
Pinch cayenne pepper

1. Cook the rice according to package directions. Remove from the heat, and fluff lightly with a fork. Toss with the cilantro.

2. To make the curry, heat the olive oil in a wok or large pot over medium heat. Add the okra and sauté for 2 minutes. Add the garlic, curry powder, coconut milk, tomatoes and 1 cup of water. Stir until well combined. Cook for 20 minutes or until the okra starts to become tender. Stir occasionally to ensure that the okra does not stick.

3. Reduce the heat to medium-low and add the raisins, chicken and salt. Mix gently. The chicken should be covered with liquid. Cook for 12 minutes, or until the chicken is opaque and tender. Season with cayenne.

4. Divide the rice among four plates, add a generous amount of okra and ¼ cup of the sauce, top with a piece of chicken and serve.

Vegetarian Version

Omit chicken and add slices of zucchini and/or sautéed tofu.

Per serving: calories 297.1, total fat 6.0 g, saturated fat 3.5 g, cholesterol 0.0 mg, sodium 213.8 mg, potassium 501.9 mg, total carbohydrate 28.4 g, dietary fiber 5.7 g, sugars 6.0 g, protein 32.7 g

---

○ *Blah-Busting Mediterr-Asian Grilled Tuna*

Makes 2 servings

This combination of very ripe, sweet pineapple coupled with flavorful green tomatoes and hearty tuna is a Mediterr-Asian winner. A bit of Serrano pepper ignites the sauce. You can use any seafood instead of tuna, but most notable are grilled wild salmon or mackerel.

Green Tomato Sauce

2 green tomatoes, cored and seeded, cut into ¼-inch-thick slices
1 tablespoon toasted pumpkin seeds
¼ teaspoon salt
Pinch freshly ground black pepper
2 heaping teaspoons finely chopped fresh cilantro, or other herb of your choice

Grilled Tuna

Two 4-ounce tuna steaks
1 teaspoon light olive oil
¼ teaspoon salt

Chopped Pineapple Salad

¼ cup finely chopped fresh pineapple
¼ cup fresh finely diced mango
¼ cup canned white corn
¼ teaspoon finely chopped Serrano pepper

1. Place the oven rack 6 to 8 inches from the broiler. Preheat the broiler. Place green tomatoes on a sheet pan 6 inches from the broiler and cook for 5 minutes. Move the rack 3 inches from the broiler, and cook for an additional minute. Remove and let cool.
2. Heat a well-seasoned gas grill to medium-high heat for at least 4 minutes with the lid closed.
3. To make the green tomato sauce, mix the pumpkin seeds, salt, pepper and cilantro in a small bowl until well combined. Peel tomatoes (skins should remove easily after broiling) and add pulp to the pumpkin-seed blend, stirring until the tomatoes break down into a sauce.
4. Place the tuna steaks on a plate and rub with the olive oil and salt. Place the tuna on the grill and cook 2 minutes per side for medium-rare, 3 minutes for medium and 4 minutes for well done.
5. To make the chopped pineapple salad, combine the pineapple, mango, corn and Serrano pepper in a small bowl. Toss until well blended.
6. Divide the chopped pineapple salad between two plates and top with a tuna steak, drizzle with half of the green tomato sauce and serve.

Vegetarian Version

Instead of tuna, use ½-inch slices of eggplant drizzled with sesame oil. Grill 10 minutes each side, turning once.

Frugal Option

Use whatever fresh tomato is available.

Per serving: calories 243.7, total fat 4.5 g, saturated fat 0.4 g, cholesterol 50.0 mg, sodium 223.4 mg, potassium 291.1 mg, total carbohydrate 22.2 g, dietary fiber 2.1 g, sugars 14.2 g, protein 28.7 g

---

⭐ *High-Protein Spicy Mediterranean Buffalo Burgers*

Makes 4 servings

Buffalo burgers are all the rage these days. Buffalo are pasture fed, and the burgers have a clean and hearty taste, as well as being extremely low in fat and high in iron. They should be served medium-rare or they will become dry. We've spiced things up with the Tabasco and Worcestershire sauce, and the cilantro adds freshness and color. To add a little variation to this recipe, try making sliders.

1–2 tablespoons light olive oil, for greasing
½–1 teaspoon Tabasco sauce, to taste
1 teaspoon Worcestershire sauce
2 tablespoons chopped cilantro
¼ teaspoon salt
⅛ teaspoon freshly ground black pepper
¼ cup pinto beans, mashed
2 tablespoons finely chopped white onion
2 pounds ground buffalo
4 slices Cheddar cheese, optional
4 whole-wheat wraps

1. Lightly grease a grill or cast-iron skillet with olive oil and heat over medium-high heat. In a large bowl, combine the Tabasco and Worcestershire sauces, cilantro, salt, pepper, beans and onion. Taste to test the level of spiciness. Keep in mind that once it's added to the meat and cooked, it will seem much less spicy.

2. Fold the buffalo into the spices, beans and onion until it is evenly mixed. Divide the buffalo into 4 burgers about ½ inch thick. Cook over medium-high heat until medium-rare: 3½ minutes per side on the grill, 4 minutes per side in a skillet. Do not overcook! About 2 minutes before removing the burgers from the heat, place 1 cheese slice on each burger and cover the skillet or grill to melt the cheese. Serve whole-wheat wraps on the side.

Vegetarian Version

Omit the buffalo and create a bean burger with 1½ cups extra mashed pinto beans.

Frugal Option

Use ground turkey instead of buffalo. Cook patties 7 minutes per side.

Per serving: calories 371.5, total fat 22.6 g, saturated fat 9.0 g, cholesterol 100.0 mg, sodium 304.6 mg, potassium 456.7 mg, total carbohydrate 4.0 g, dietary fiber 1.0 g, sugars 0.2 g, protein 34.8 g

---

🍽️ *Energy-Rich Apricot Crumble*

Makes 8 servings

This apricot crumble is versatile and easy. Prepare it with other healing fruits, such as strawberries or bananas.

Crust

> 1 cup whole-wheat pastry flour
> ½ cup almond flour
> 1 teaspoon baking powder
> Pinch salt
> 1 cup low-fat milk, vanilla soy milk or almond milk
> 2 tablespoons xylitol or birch sugar
> 4 tablespoons grass-fed unsalted butter, melted

Crumble Topping

> 1½ cups rolled oats
> 3 tablespoons grass-fed unsalted butter or olive oil
> 1 tablespoon crushed walnuts
> ¼ cup almond flour
> ¼ teaspoon ground nutmeg
> ¼ teaspoon ground cinnamon
> ¼ cup xylitol or birch sugar

Filling

> 4 fresh apricots, peeled, pitted and sliced into wedges

1. Preheat the oven to 350°F with the rack placed in the middle.
2. In a large bowl, mix the flours, baking powder, salt, milk, sugar and butter until well combined.
3. In a medium bowl, combine the oats, butter, walnuts, almond flour, nutmeg, cinnamon and sugar. Mix until thoroughly blended.
4. To assemble the apricot crumble, spoon the crust into a 2-inch-high, 8-inch round pan. Top with the apricot slices and cover with the topping. Bake for 30 minutes. The apricots should be bubbling. Let cool and serve.

Per serving: calories 400.7, total fat 22.4 g, saturated fat 9.5 g, cholesterol 38.3 mg, sodium 302.9 mg, potassium 289.6 mg, total carbohydrate 34.6 g, dietary fiber 6.7 g, sugars 4.8 g, protein 10.3 g

---

🍽 *Powerful Apricot Almond Biscotti*

Makes 15 to 20 biscotti

Biscotti dough is very delicate after its first baking, so be careful when slicing it. These are delightful served with a scoop of low-fat ice cream.

3 tablespoons grass-fed unsalted butter
½ cup xylitol or birch sugar
2 omega-3 eggs
1 teaspoon vanilla extract
½ cup blanched coarsely chopped almonds
½ cup finely chopped dried or fresh figs
½ cup finely chopped dried apricots
1 tablespoon ground flaxseed
1 teaspoon baking powder
½ teaspoon baking soda
Pinch salt
1¼ cups whole-wheat pastry flour, plus more for dusting
¼ cup almond flour or whole-wheat flour
¼ cup rolled oats

1. Preheat the oven to 350°F with the rack placed in the middle.
2. Using a mixer set on medium speed, mix the butter and sugar until well combined. Add the eggs, vanilla, almonds and figs and mix until well combined. In a medium bowl, mix with a fork the apricots, flaxseed, baking powder, baking soda, salt, flours and oats until well blended. Slowly add to the egg mixture until a well-blended dough is formed.
3. Turn the dough out onto a floured surface and divide it into two 6 x 3 x 1-inch logs. Transfer to a baking sheet. Bake for 25 minutes, or until golden brown.
4. Carefully transfer the log to a work area and, using a serrated knife, cut the log on a sharp diagonal into ¼-inch-thick slices. Transfer them to the baking sheet pan. Bake them flat for 5 to 7 minutes. Remove from the oven. Let cool and serve.

Per biscotti: calories 105.7, total fat 4.4 g, saturated fat 1.4 g, cholesterol 26.2 mg, sodium 80.9 mg, potassium 105.3 mg, total carbohydrate 12.2 g, dietary fiber 2.3 g, sugars 4.5 g, protein 2.8 g

---

🍽 *Guacamole with Diced Tomatoes*

Makes 6 servings

Grab a few avocados and have this tasty, timeless appetizer/accompaniment ready in minutes. Your heart will love you for it.

3 ripe avocados, sliced in half, pitted, and avocado scooped out and mashed
2 plum tomatoes, seeded and diced
1 tablespoon jalapeno chili (for less heat, remove seeds and ribs)
3 tablespoons minced onions, optional
3 tablespoons fresh lime juice
Pinch lime zest
5 tablespoons finely chopped fresh cilantro leaves
Pinch cumin, optional (for extra zest)
Coarse salt, to taste

Combine the mashed avocado, tomatoes, jalapeno, onions, lime juice, lime zest, cilantro and cumin if desired. Mix until well blended. Taste and correct with salt.

Per serving: calories 153.7, total fat 13.4 g, saturated fat 1.9 g, cholesterol 0.0 mg, sodium 9.6 mg, potassium 510.5 mg, total carbohydrate 9.7 g, dietary fiber 6.3 g, sugars 0.9 g, protein 2.0 g

¦◎¦ *Mighty Omega-3 Bean Soup with Sardines*

Makes 2 servings

Local variations on bean soup are found throughout the small fishing villages that dot the Mediterranean coastline. The sardines may be added to the soup, but I prefer them on the side with a nice piece of artisanal whole-grain bread. If sage isn't your favorite herb, you can substitute parsley, cilantro, basil or thyme.

15 ounces canned navy beans, drained
4 new potatoes, small dice
1 teaspoon minced garlic
2 cups low-sodium vegetable stock
1 leek, cleaned and thinly sliced
2 leaves fresh sage, finely chopped
1 teaspoon sea salt, or to taste
1 can sardines in olive oil, drained
1 small loaf whole-grain bread, sliced

1. In a large pot over medium heat, combine the beans, potatoes, garlic, vegetable stock, leeks, sage and salt and cook for 20 minutes, stirring occasionally. When the potatoes and leeks are tender, remove from the heat. Carefully place an immersion blender into the pot and pulse until the soup becomes thick and smooth, or serve chunky. Taste and add more salt, if needed.

2. Serve the soup in 2 deep bowls with sardines and bread on the side.

Vegetarian Version

Omit sardines and serve with herbed goat cheese.

Per serving: calories 603.4 total fat 5.7 g, saturated fat 1.2 g, cholesterol 17.5 mg, sodium 580.5 mg, potassium 938.1 mg, total carbohydrate 109.0 g, dietary fiber 31.7 g, sugars 5.5 g, protein 33.2 g

---

¶⊙¶ *Heart-Healing Sweet 'n' Spicy Thai Halibut Salad*

Makes 4 servings

This salad is a stunning combination of sweet apricots, nutty sesame and spicy radish. Salads are full of fiber and vitamins, and easy to prepare in advance. Store the greens before rinsing, so that they stay crisp. Add dressing when you're ready to eat.

Dressing

1 tablespoon miso or miso substitute*
1 tablespoon toasted sesame oil
1–2 cloves garlic, minced
1 tablespoon crushed pecans
2 dried apricots, finely chopped
1 cup finely chopped shallots
1 tablespoon rice vinegar

Salad

1 cup grated daikon radish
2 fresh figs, stems removed and thinly sliced
1 cup canned chickpeas, drained and rinsed
4 heaping cups fresh spinach
Four 6-ounce halibut fillets
Olive oil, for drizzling
2 tablespoons toasted sesame seeds

1. In a medium bowl, combine the miso, sesame oil, garlic, pecans, apricots, shallots, rice vinegar and 1 tablespoon of water. Mix with a fork until well blended.
2. Toss the radish, figs, chickpeas and spinach in a large bowl. Add the dressing, reserving a little for the halibut, and toss.
3. Place an oven rack on the middle shelf of the oven and preheat to 350°F. Place the fish fillets on a baking sheet. Drizzle with olive oil and bake for 10 minutes, or until the flesh is opaque and flakes easily. Remove from the oven and set aside.
4. Divide the salad among four plates, top with the halibut, drizzle with the dressing, sprinkle with sesame seeds and serve.

Vegetarian Version

Use 4–6 pounds fresh broccoli, cut into florets with 2-inch stems, covered with foil and roasted for 10 minutes, instead of halibut.

*Miso substitute: ½ tablespoon low-sodium soy sauce and ½ tablespoon chicken stock.

Per serving: calories 364.8, total fat 9.3 g, saturated fat 1.1 g, cholesterol 60.0 mg, sodium 337.3 mg, potassium 618.2 mg, total carbohydrate 33.1 g, dietary fiber 5.7 g, sugars 8.1 g, protein 40.9 g

---

Antioxidant Asian Chicken Rice

Makes 4 servings

Rice is a staple in the heart-healthy Asian diet. It is also popular in Italy, which is the largest rice grower in Europe. For our Mediterr-Asian fusion, we added sweet mango and robust fig to seasoned brown jasmine rice. Lovely as a side dish, it is a balanced main dish when served with free-range chicken tenders.

½ cup finely chopped unsweetened, unsulphured dried mango
3 large fresh figs, stems removed and finely chopped
1 cup cooked brown jasmine rice
2 teaspoons lime juice
2 tablespoons finely chopped fresh cilantro
Four 4-ounce free-range chicken tenders
Pinch black pepper, to taste
1 teaspoon light olive oil
1 tablespoon raw pumpkin seeds
Pinch salt, to taste

1. In a large bowl, combine the mango, figs, rice, lime juice and cilantro, and toss until well coated. Set aside.
2. Sprinkle the chicken tenders with black pepper. Heat the olive oil in a skillet over medium heat. Add the chicken and sauté until tender, turning once.
3. Divide the chicken among four plates and place the rice either next to or over the chicken. Sprinkle with pumpkin seeds, season to taste and serve.

Vegetarian Version

Omit chicken. Add some navy beans or grilled tofu to the rice for extra protein.

Per serving: calories 317.4, total fat 3.2 g, saturated fat 0.5 g, cholesterol 70.0 mg, sodium 90.3 mg, potassium 161.9 mg, total carbohydrate 42.0 g, dietary fiber 3.5 g, sugars 18.0 g, protein 29.0 g

Heart-Healing Buffalo Salad with Peanut-Sesame Dressing

Makes 4 servings

Chopped salads are fabulous because each bite has a bit of everything, and this one has three vitamin- and mineral-rich greens dressed in an Asian-inspired peanut-sesame dressing. Orange juice and vinegar add zip. It's topped with grilled low-fat buffalo. This recipe prepares enough peanut-sesame dressing for a week.

Buffalo Salad

1 teaspoon light olive oil
16 ounces buffalo sirloin,
    cut into ½-inch strips
1½ cups finely sliced white onion
1 head escarole, cut into 1-inch pieces
4 cups spinach
2 heads romaine lettuce,
    cut into ¼-inch pieces

Peanut-Sesame Dressing

⅔ cup sugar-free crunchy peanut butter
1–2 cloves garlic, minced
4 tablespoons low-sodium soy sauce
1 tablespoon grated ginger
¼ cup rice vinegar
½ cup orange juice
2 tablespoons sesame oil
½ cup light olive oil
1 teaspoon salt

1. For the salad, heat the olive oil in a wok or large saucepan over medium heat. Add the buffalo and sauté for 2 minutes. Remove the strips to a plate and set aside.
2. Return the wok to the stove, add the onions and sauté for 7 minutes, or until softened. Add the escarole and spinach and reduce the heat to low. Stir the greens occasionally until they wilt, about 5 minutes. Remove from the heat.
3. To make the dressing, in a small pan over low heat, add the peanut butter, garlic, soy sauce and ginger and whisk until the peanut butter is soft and easily stirred. Turn off the heat. In a small bowl, stir the vinegar, orange juice, sesame oil, olive oil and salt together. Add to the warm peanut butter mixture and whisk until smooth.
4. To assemble, add the romaine lettuce, buffalo strips, and ¼ cup of dressing to the wok containing the escarole-spinach mixture and toss until well combined. Divide among four plates and serve. Store the remaining dressing in the refrigerator in a well-sealed container for up to 10 days.

Vegetarian Version

Substitute grilled smoked tempeh for the buffalo.

Frugal Option

Replace buffalo with a less expensive cut of lean pasture-fed beef or free-range chicken breast.

Heart-Healing Buffalo Salad per serving: calories 205.0, total fat 4.2 g, saturated fat 0.7 g, cholesterol 60.0 mg, sodium 142.5 mg, potassium 243.6 mg, total carbohydrate 13.5 g, dietary fiber 7.9 g, sugars 1.0 g, protein 30.4 g

Peanut-Sesame Dressing per serving (scant 2 tablespoons): calories 71.2, total fat 4.5 g, saturated fat 0.9 g, cholesterol 0.0 mg, sodium 236.3 mg, potassium 20.8 mg, total carbohydrate 5.5 g, dietary fiber 0.8 g, sugars 2.6 g, protein 2.1 g

🍽 *Super-Fiber Mediterranean Ratatouille*

Makes 8 servings

Ratatouille is a traditional French vegetable stew. It's a dish that you can serve time and again, knowing that it has an alphabet of Mediterranean healing foods that range from basil to zucchini. It does require a little bit of preparation, but you'll have enough for a week. It's great by itself, as well as folded into omelets or spooned over chicken, lamb or pasta.

4 large eggplants, trimmed and cut into ½-inch cubes
½ teaspoon salt, or to taste
1 teaspoon light olive oil
1 large white onion, chopped into ¼-inch pieces
2 zucchini, sliced ½ inch thick and halved
2 red bell peppers, cored, seeded and cut into ¼-inch slices
4 cloves garlic, smashed
2 cans (28 ounces each) whole tomatoes, drained
Leaves from 1 large bunch of basil, torn in half
1 cup finely chopped parsley
1 tablespoon finely chopped fresh thyme

1. Place the eggplant in a large colander in a clean sink or over a plate and sprinkle with the salt and set aside.
2. Heat the olive oil in a stockpot over medium heat. Add the onions, zucchini and peppers, and toss until they are lightly browned, about 8 minutes. Add the garlic.
3. Rinse and dry the eggplant.
4. Reduce the heat to medium-low and add the eggplant and tomatoes. Break up the tomatoes with a wooden spoon. Cook for 20 minutes. Add the basil, parsley and thyme and cook for 15 minutes. Remove from the heat and allow to cool slightly. Serve from the pot.

Nonvegetarian Version

Serve over baked chicken or lamb.

Per serving: calories 138.4, total fat 1.4 g, saturated fat 0.2 g, cholesterol 0.0 mg, sodium 57.0 mg, potassium 1,251.0 mg, total carbohydrate 31.0 g, dietary fiber 9.8 g, sugars 2.9 g, protein 5.6 g

Heart's Delight Pasta Puttanesca

Makes 4 servings

This classic Italian dish *puttanesca* is named for urban "ladies of the night" who needed to prepare satisfying meals in a hurry and could not shop at the market every day for fresh produce—pantry items are the key ingredients here. It is loaded with tomatoes, the best heart-healing vegetable. After the pasta has finished cooking, toss it into the sauce with a little of its cooking water. The noodles will be infused with flavor.

¾ **pounds whole-wheat spaghetti or brown rice spaghetti**
1½ **tablespoon minced roasted garlic**
1 **teaspoon capers,** drained
1 **teaspoon black olive paste**
1 **teaspoon anchovy paste**
28 **ounces canned whole tomatoes with their liquid,** broken into bite-sized pieces.
½ **pound Italian chicken sausage**
2 **chopped kalamata olives**
2 **tablespoons chopped fresh parsley leaves,** plus a few whole leaves for garnish

1. Cook pasta according to package directions. Reserve ½ cup cooking water before draining.
2. Add the garlic, capers and olive and anchovy pastes to a wok or large pot over medium-low heat. Sauté about 1 minute, until aromatic. Add the tomatoes and sausage. Reduce the heat to medium low and cook for 10 minutes, stirring occasionally.
3. Add the spaghetti, pepper and reserved pasta water to the pot and reduce the heat to low. Gently toss until well combined and pasta water is absorbed.
4. Transfer the pasta directly from the pot onto 4 plates, add additional sauce from the pot, sprinkle with chopped olives and parsley and serve.

Vegetarian Version

Omit the sausage. The sauce will still have a fabulous flavor.

Per serving: Calories 425.8, total fat 4.4 g, saturated fat 1.7 g, cholesterol 32.4 mg, sodium 405.0 mg, potassium 568.9 mg, total carbohydrate 75.7 g, dietary fiber 10.2 g, sugars 0.0 g, protein 18.2 g

🍴 *Artery-Healing Whole-Grain Farro Shrimp*

Makes 4 servings

Farro, from the Near East and Mediterranean, has a long history and has been called "grain of the legions," because it is said to have fed Roman soldiers. A different, less common variety of wheat, it can easily be cooked whole. The trick in this recipe is to start with farro that is already cooked, so that the grains become creamy, like risotto. Figs, garlic and red wine are the rich base for this heart-warming feast. If you can't find farro, barley will do very well.

Olive oil, for greasing pan
6 fresh figs, stems removed and finely chopped
1 teaspoon minced garlic
1 teaspoon miso paste*
½ cup red wine
1 pound medium shrimp, peeled, deveined and butterflied
2 cups cooked farro
1 teaspoon sea salt, or to taste
1 teaspoon finely chopped fresh marjoram
1 teaspoon turmeric
3 cups fresh baby spinach
1 lime, quartered

1. Lightly grease a wok or large pot with olive oil, and heat over medium-low heat. Sauté the figs until they begin to give up their juices, about 3 minutes. Reduce the heat to low and add the garlic, miso paste and wine. Stir until well combined. Remove from the heat.

2. Transfer the fig mixture to a large plate, using a spatula.

3. Return the pot to the heat and add a bit more olive oil. Raise the heat to medium-high and add the shrimp, farro, salt, marjoram and turmeric. Sauté the shrimp until the flesh turns pink and opaque, about 2 minutes per side. Remove from the heat and add the spinach to the pot. Add salt, if needed.

4. Gently toss, divide among four deep bowls and serve with lime wedges.

Vegetarian Version

Omit shrimp and add Italian white beans or sautéed tofu.

Miso substitute: ½ tablespoon low-sodium soy sauce and ½ tablespoon chicken stock for the miso

---

Per serving: calories 226.7, total fat 2.4 g, saturated fat 0.5 g, cholesterol 172.3 mg, sodium 227.5 mg, potassium 628.1 mg, total carbohydrate 23.4 g, dietary fiber 3.9 g, sugars 16.0 g, protein 24.7 g

---

Heart-Healthy Spanish Gazpacho with Tuna

Makes 8 servings

Gazpacho is a very popular chilled Spanish soup. Most restaurants have their own twist on the traditional dish, and ours is served as a side soup or a sauce over succulent broiled tuna. Traditionally, the ingredients are chopped by hand, which gives the gazpacho a delectable chunky texture. However, it is a lot of chopping, so if time is an issue, a carefully guided food processor will do the trick.

1 red bell pepper, cored, seeded and finely chopped
1 small purple onion, finely chopped
8 tomatoes, cored, seeded and finely chopped
1 cucumber, trimmed, peeled, seeded and chopped
1 teaspoon grated lemon zest
1 tablespoon sherry
2 teaspoons garlic paste
3 cups tomato juice
Pinch cayenne
Four 4-ounce tuna steaks
Pinch salt
2 teaspoons sesame oil
1 tablespoon pumpkin seeds, for garnish

1. In a large bowl, combine the peppers, onions, tomatoes, cucumbers, lemon zest, sherry, garlic, tomato juice and cayenne. Mix until well blended. Cover the bowl with plastic wrap and place it in the refrigerator to chill.

2. Set an oven rack 6 inches from the heat. Preheat the broiler. Season both sides of the tuna with salt and drizzle it with sesame oil. Broil the tuna 2–3 minutes on each side for medium-rare.

3. To serve gazpacho, spoon out into deep bowls and sprinkle with pumpkin seeds. Serve tuna on the side.

Vegetarian Version
Omit tuna and serve gazpacho over brown rice.

Per serving: calories 125.5, total fat 1.6 g, saturated fat 0.0 g, cholesterol 25.0 mg, sodium 85.9 mg, potassium 293.5 mg, total carbohydrate 8.2 g, dietary fiber 1.9 g, sugars 3.6 g, protein 15.1 g

▌◍▐ *Heart-Loving Whole-Grain Tabbouleh*

Makes 6 servings

Tabbouleh originated in Lebanon but is popular throughout the Middle East and the Mediterranean. It's not difficult to prepare but requires a fair amount of chopping and dicing. Make extra, because it keeps well for a healing meal on the go. Tabbouleh is delicious spooned on soups or salads, tucked in wraps or omelets.

1 cup bulgur
2 bunches flat-leaf parsley, finely chopped
½ bunch fresh mint, finely chopped
4 vine-ripened tomatoes, cored, seeded and finely chopped
½ cup finely chopped white onion
1 large cucumber, trimmed, peeled and finely chopped
¼ cup extra-virgin olive oil
¾ cup lemon juice
¼ teaspoon ground cinnamon
¼ teaspoon ground allspice
¼ teaspoon ground cumin
1 teaspoon salt, or to taste
Pinch black pepper
1 teaspoon finely chopped unsweetened dried cranberries
1 lemon, cut into wedges

1. Cook the bulgur according to package directions. Drain and set aside to cool slightly.
2. In a large bowl, combine the parsley, mint, tomatoes, onions, cucumbers, olive oil, lemon juice, cinnamon, allspice, cumin, salt and pepper. Toss until well coated. Add the bulgur and toss. Cover and refrigerate for at least 1 hour.
3. Mix in cranberries just before serving and serve with lemon wedges on the side.

Nonvegetarian Version

Add 1 pound small shrimp, grilled or sautéed.

Per serving: calories 205.7, total fat 9.7 g, saturated fat 1.4 g, cholesterol 0.0 mg, sodium 37.6 mg, potassium 187.5 mg, total carbohydrate 26.5 g, dietary fiber 6.7 g, sugars 1.4 g, protein 4.4 g

---

🍽 *Artery-Strengthening Asian Portobello Salad with Buffalo*

Makes 2 servings

You'll love this earthy mushroom salad seasoned with sesame and pomegranate. It's extremely easy to make. The cellophane noodles are also called glass noodles because of their translucent appearance. They have plenty of heart-healing selenium, but if you can't find them, use whole-grain vermicelli.

Asian Sauce

½ cup pomegranate juice
½ cup mandarin orange, supremed (sectioned with white pith removed)
1 clove garlic, minced
1 tablespoon sesame oil

Salad

½ teaspoon light olive oil
Two 4-ounce sirloin buffalo strips
1 portobello mushroom cap, cut into ⅛-inch slices
¼ head white cabbage, cut into ⅛-inch slices
1 teaspoon low-sodium soy sauce
1 cup beet greens or fresh spinach, rinsed and pat dry, hard stems removed
1 ounce cellophane noodles, soaked in hot water for 2 minutes

1. In a small bowl, combine the pomegranate juice, mandarin oranges, garlic and sesame oil. Gently mix, being careful not to break up the oranges. Set aside.

2. Heat olive oil in a small skillet over medium heat. Sauté the buffalo strips, mushroom and cabbage with the soy sauce for 4 minutes, or until the cabbage begins to wilt and the buffalo is pink in the middle. Remove from the heat. Add the beet greens and cellophane noodles. Toss gently until well combined.

3. Divide the mushroom salad between 2 plates, drizzle each generously with the sauce and serve.

Vegetarian Version

Substitute your favorite healing vegetables for the buffalo. Good options are beans and broccoli.

Per serving: calories 331.5, total fat 10.8 g, saturated fat 1.7 g, cholesterol 60.0 mg, sodium 241.0 mg, potassium 880.8 mg, total carbohydrate 30.7 g, dietary fiber 4.8 g, sugars 13.5 g, protein 30.3 g

---

⑩ *Heart-Happy Chocolate-Covered Strawberries*

Makes about 20 pieces

This recipe is a classic. Save any leftover chocolate for another dessert.

½ pound 70% cacao or other dark chocolate, chopped
¼ cup finely chopped pistachios
1 ounce 70% real cacao powder
1 pound organic strawberries with stems, rinsed and patted dry

1. Bring water in the bottom of a double boiler to a simmer. Add the chocolate to the top of the double boiler and melt over medium heat.
2. Line a sheet pan or other flat surface with waxed paper. In a small shallow bowl, combine the pistachios and cacao powder.
3. Dip the strawberries, one at a time, into the melted chocolate. Turn the strawberry in the chocolate to make sure it is well coated. Lift the strawberry and let any excess chocolate drip off. Roll the strawberry in the pistachio mixture. Repeat the process with the remaining berries. Refrigerate for 10 to 15 minutes to allow the chocolate to set before serving.

Per strawberry: calories 72.2, total fat 5.0 g, saturated fat 2.6 g, cholesterol 0.0 mg, sodium 9.7 mg, potassium 37.6 mg, total carbohydrate 7.7 g, dietary fiber 1.8 g, sugars 3.5 g, protein 1.3 g

🍽 *Don't Miss a Beat Chocolate and Apple Tarte Tatin*

Makes approximately 8 servings

Make the crust moments before you place it on the apples because the crust tends to thicken and then becomes a little cumbersome to spoon into the pan. I enjoy this recipe with many kinds of fruit, such as apricots, berries, pears, and peaches.

Topping

> 1 tablespooon light olive oil
> 2 tablespoons xylitol birch sugar
> 2 apples, peeled, cored and sliced into wedges
> 1 ounce shaved 70% or more cacao dark chocolate
> 2 finely chopped dried figs, optional

Crust

> 1 cup whole-wheat pastry flour
> ½ cup almond flour
> 1 teaspoon baking powder
> Pinch salt
> 1 cup almond milk
> 2 tablespoons xylitol or birch sugar
> ¼ cup light olive oil or grass-fed unsalted butter, melted

1. Preheat the oven to 425°F with the rack placed in the middle.
2. Coat the bottom of a 10-inch iron pan with the olive oil. Sprinkle with the sugar. Arrange the apple slices closely together in two concentric circles, round side down. Place the pan over medium heat and cook for 15 minutes. Do not stir the apples, but let their juices fill the pan and bubble. Remove from the heat. Carefully place the skillet in the oven and bake for 15 minutes. Place the pan on a baking sheet, as the apples may bubble over.
3. To make the crust, in a large bowl, mix the pastry and almond flour, baking powder, salt, milk, sugar and olive oil until well combined.
4. Carefully remove the pan from the oven and pour the crust over the apples. Bake for 20 minutes, or until golden brown.
5. Remove from the oven. Let cool for 10 minutes. Place a plate on top of the pan. Carefully turn over. The tart should release onto the plate. If any apples remain on the skillet, remove with a spatula and place on the tart. Top with chocolate shavings and dried figs if using, and serve.

Per serving: calories 234.3, total fat 13.6 g, saturated fat 2.3 g, cholesterol 0.0 mg, sodium 99.6 mg, potassium 138.3 mg, total carbohydrate 23.3 g, dietary fiber 4.5 g, sugars 4.5 g, protein 3.9 g

🍽 *Diastolic-Calming Udon-Miso Soup*

Makes 8 servings

Udon-miso soup combines two traditional Japanese staples—miso (soy) paste and thick udon noodles. This soup takes about 15 minutes to prepare and is an excellent main course. Miso has a sweet and subtle flavor, which allows the flavor of the vegetables to shine through. This soup can also be made with beef broth.

3 tablespoons red miso paste
1 cup cremini mushrooms
1 teaspoon low-sodium soy sauce
1 large celery stalk, trimmed and sliced thinly
1 cup green beans, trimmed and cut into ¼-inch pieces
2 large Swiss chard leaves, cut into bite-sized pieces
1 cup finely chopped broccoli florets
1 cup fresh spinach
1 scallion, white and light green parts only, chopped
3 tablespoons finely chopped fresh cilantro
1 teaspoon sea salt
¼ pound udon noodles
1 omega-3 egg, beaten

1. In a large stockpot over medium heat, combine 2 quarts of water, the miso paste, mushrooms, soy sauce, celery, green beans, Swiss chard, broccoli, spinach, scallion, cilantro and salt and stir until well combined. Cook the soup for 12 minutes, or until the broccoli is al dente.

2. Cook the udon according to package directions. Drain.

3. Reduce the heat to medium-low. Add the egg and stir. The egg should set immediately.

4. Remove from the heat. Add the noodles and stir. Taste and adjust seasonings, if needed.

5. Ladle into four bowls and serve.

Beef Broth Variation

Substitute 2 quarts low-sodium beef broth for the miso and water; prepare as above.

Frugal Option

Consider using frozen broccoli and spinach.
Substitute 1½ tablespoons low-sodium soy sauce and 1½ tablespoons chicken stock for the miso.

Per serving: calories 100.5, total fat 1.0 g, saturated fat 0.2 g, cholesterol 23.8 mg, sodium 430.1 mg, potassium 267.9 mg, total carbohydrate 17.9 g, dietary fiber 1.6 g, sugars 1.6 g, protein 4.6 g

🍽 *Heart-Pumping Beet Greens Salad with Greek Yogurt*

Makes 2 servings

Beet greens are extremely easy to cook with and have a hearty taste. They make a lovely base for a warm green salad. If fresh beet greens are hard to come by, substitute artery-opening spinach, chard or any green that becomes tender when cooked for a few minutes. If you would like to add some cheese to round out this salad, try feta or some shaved Parmesan.

Yogurt Dressing

½ teaspoon orange juice
1 teaspoon finely chopped fresh parsley
1 teaspoon freshly minced garlic
½ cup low-fat Greek yogurt, store-bought or homemade (see recipe on page 406)

Beet Green Salad

½ pound beet greens, stems removed
10 pearl onions
1 teaspoon finely chopped fresh dill
1 teaspoon balsamic vinegar
2 tablespoons feta cheese, rinsed and crumbled, optional

1. In a small bowl, combine the orange juice, parsley, garlic and yogurt and mix until well combined. Set aside.
2. Fill a medium pot halfway with water. Bring to a boil over high heat. Add the beet greens and pearl onions. Boil for 3 minutes.
3. Drain the greens and onions in a colander. Remove the hot greens very carefully, transfer them to the bowl with the yogurt and stir until well combined. Set aside.
4. Run the onions under cool water. When they are cool to the touch, peel them by slicing off the stem end, then carefully pushing them out of their skins.
5. Slice the onions in half and place them in a small skillet over medium heat. Stir in the dill and balsamic vinegar and cook for 2 minutes. Remove from the heat.
6. Mound half of the beet green mixture in the center of a plate and top with the onion mixture, then the cheese, if using, and serve with the dressing.

Nonvegetarian Version

Add 6 ounces of sautéed chicken to the beet green mixture.

Per serving: calories 341.5, total fat 1.1 g, saturated fat 0.6 g, cholesterol 2.5 mg, sodium 383.8 mg, potassium 861.7 mg, total carbohydrate 85.2 g, dietary fiber 14.2 g, sugars 40.9 g, protein 14.0 g

---

🍽 **Lower Blood Pressure Broiled Salmon with Asian Pear Salad**

Makes 4 servings

This salad is a combination of omega-3-rich salmon, potassium-rich asparagus and Asian pear. It's a blend that has great healing power plus wonderful flavor and texture. The dish can also be prepared with canned salmon—add it to the salad while you are broiling the asparagus. If Asian pears are not in season, use canned pears.

Broiled Salmon

Four 4-ounce wild salmon fillets
15 fresh asparagus, tough ends removed, sliced into 1-inch pieces
1 teaspoon light olive oil

Asian Pear Salad

2 fresh Asian pears, cored, peeled and julienned
15 ounces canned white beans, drained and rinsed
Pinch salt
1 tablespoon sesame oil
1 tablespoon low-sodium teriyaki sauce
1 tablespoon orange juice
1 tablespoon honey
1 tablespoon red wine vinegar
¼ cup finely chopped fresh parsley leaves

1. Place an oven rack 6 inches from the broiler and preheat.
2. Place the salmon and asparagus on a rimmed baking sheet and drizzle with the olive oil. Broil the salmon for 7 minutes. Turn asparagus to keep from burning. Do not turn the salmon.
3. In a medium bowl, combine the pears, beans, salt, sesame oil, teriyaki sauce, orange juice, honey, vinegar and parsley and toss until well combined. Set aside.
4. Divide the salad among four plates, top with the salmon and asparagus and serve.

Vegetarian Option

Omit the salmon.

Frugal Option

Use canned pears in their own juice.

Per serving: calories 386.4, total fat 13.1 g, saturated fat 0.8 g, cholesterol 60.0 mg, sodium 175.6 mg, potassium 1,298.6 mg, total carbohydrate 38.5 g, dietary fiber 8.7 g, sugars 9.7 g, protein 33.6 g

---

🍽️ *Hypertension-Be-Gone Salmon-Squash Stack with Asian Fruit Sauce*

Makes 4 servings

Citrus, ginger and cilantro make this a vibrant and flavorful meal. It's also simple to make and beautiful to present. A food processor or blender makes the preparation of the fruit sauce easy.

1 tablespoon light olive oil
2 tablespoons orange juice
1 pear, peeled, cored and roughly chopped
½ teaspoon minced ginger
½ teaspoon freshly minced garlic
1 tablespoon finely chopped onion
1 teaspoon low-sodium soy sauce
1 heaping tablespoon fresh cilantro leaves
2 tablespoons fresh parsley leaves
¼ teaspoon sea salt
Freshly ground black pepper, to taste
3 pounds winter squash, ends removed, peeled, seeded and grated
Four 4-ounce salmon steaks

1. Place an oven rack on the middle shelf of the oven and preheat to 400°F.
2. In a food processor, combine the olive oil, orange juice, pear, ginger, garlic, onion, soy sauce, cilantro, parsley, salt and pepper and pulse until smooth.
3. Spread the grated squash on a baking sheet. Place the salmon on top of the squash. Drizzle with the pear sauce and bake for 15 minutes. The seafood is done when it is opaque and flakes easily.
4. Divide the squash and salmon among four plates and serve.

Vegetarian Option

Instead of baking seafood on top of the squash, consider turning this dish into a baked vegetarian delight. Great healing vegetables to bake include chopped white onions, sliced cremini mushrooms, broccoli florets, whole green beans and trimmed asparagus. Prepare the dish as described, drizzling sauce over the vegetables and squash.

Per serving: calories 413.9, total fat 12.1 g, saturated fat 0.6 g, cholesterol 60.0 mg, sodium 145.9 mg, potassium 2,120.8 mg, total carbohydrate 57.3 g, dietary fiber 16.1 g, sugars 0.7 g, protein 28.2 g

---

🍽️ *Doctor's-Orders Grilled Mackerel Over Asian Rice Salad*

Makes 4 servings

Mackerel is a rich fish, which is why it's the perfect match for this slightly sweet rice salad. Try to make the salad a couple hours in advance. The flavors will become more vibrant over time. If you don't have a grill, bake the fish in a 375°F oven until the flesh becomes tender, about 15 minutes.

Grilled Mackerel

> 1 teaspoon light olive oil
> 1 teaspoon sesame oil
> 1 teaspoon fresh minced garlic
> 1 tablespoon low-sodium soy sauce
> ½ teaspoon salt
> 1 teaspoon finely chopped fresh oregano
> 2 whole cleaned Atlantic mackerel (about 1 pound each), with 4 or 5 small diagonal slashes on each side

Asian Rice Salad

> 1 cup brown rice
> 2¼ cups low-sodium chicken broth, plus another ½ cup if needed
> 1 tablespoon finely chopped fresh parsley
> 1 cup canned low-sodium white, navy or lima beans, black-eyed peas or chickpeas, rinsed
> 4 heaping cups fresh baby spinach
> 4 finely chopped dried apricots

1. In a shallow bowl, whisk the olive oil, sesame oil, garlic, soy sauce, salt and oregano.
2. Place the mackerel in the bowl, turn to coat with dressing and set aside.
3. Cook the rice according to package directions, using chicken broth instead of water. Remove from the heat. Fluff, then stir in the parsley, beans, spinach and apricots, until the spinach starts to wilt.
4. Light a well-seasoned gas grill to medium heat.
5. Remove the fish from the dressing and set them on the center grate. Grill for 5 minutes per side or until the flesh becomes opaque and is cooked through. Baste the mackerel occasionally with dressing as it cooks.
6. Remove them from the grill and carefully fillet each fish, creating a total of four fillets.
7. Divide the mackerel and rice salad among four plates and serve.

Vegetarian Option

Marinate and grill portobello mushrooms instead of mackerel.

Frugal Option

Consider using frozen fish instead of fresh or omit altogether.

> ***Per serving:*** calories 663.1, total fat 4.6 g, saturated fat 0.8 g, cholesterol 0.0 mg, sodium 208.0 mg, potassium 1,709.3 mg, total carbohydrate 114.2 g, dietary fiber 19.2 g, sugars 3.7 g, protein 28.0 g

Healing Vegetables Fried Brown Rice

Makes 4 servings

Fried rice is a very easy dish to prepare and variations on it are a staple in most Asian countries. This rice dish is a great accompaniment for healing omega 3–rich seafood.

1 teaspoon peanut oil
½ cup finely chopped white onions
1 cup finely chopped broccoli florets
½ stalk celery, sliced paper thin
1 teaspoon minced garlic
1 tablespoon chopped dried cherries
1 teaspoon chopped fresh parsley
1 tablespoon hoisin sauce
6 cups fresh baby spinach
3 large leaves Swiss chard, finely chopped
2 cups cooked brown jasmine rice, broken up to remove clumps
1 tablespoon low-sodium soy sauce

1. Heat the peanut oil in a wok or large pot over medium heat. Add the onions, broccoli and celery. Sauté until the onions have begun to soften and are transparent, about 5 minutes.
2. Reduce the heat to low and add the garlic, cherries, parsley, hoisin sauce, spinach and Swiss chard. Toss until the greens are wilted.
3. Return the heat to medium. Add the cooked rice and mix well. Stir in the soy sauce. Remove from the heat.
4. Divide the rice among four plates and serve.

Frugal Options

Use frozen vegetables instead of fresh.

Per serving: calories 223, total fat 1.6 g, saturated fat 0.2 g, cholesterol 0 mg, sodium 322 mg, total carbohydrate 46.0 g, dietary fiber 4.5 g, potassium 713.3 mg, sugars 2.7 g, protein 6.0 g

🍽 *Anti-Hypertensive Roasted Beet Lasagna*

Makes 10 servings

Lasagna is versatile and easy to make. This version is hearty as well as healing. If you want to prepare this dish in advance, simply assemble the lasagna, cover it in an airtight container and place it in the freezer. Bake an additional 20 minutes until piping hot.

½ pound whole-wheat lasagna noodles
1 cup low-fat ricotta cheese
1 tablespoon finely chopped fresh parsley
2 tablespoons finely chopped dried cherries, optional
¼ teaspoon sea salt
2 cups fresh spinach, covered and wilted in a microwave for 30 seconds
3 large beets, ends removed, peeled and finely chopped
4 ounces herbed goat cheese
32 ounces low-sodium marinara sauce, (store-bought or homemade, see recipe on page 482)
2 yellow squash, 12 ounces each, ends removed, peeled and grated
¼ cup finely grated Parmesan cheese

1. Place an oven rack on the middle shelf of the oven and preheat to 350°F.
2. Cook the pasta according to package directions. Drain and set aside.
3. Combine the ricotta, parsley, dried cherries, salt and spinach in a medium bowl, and stir until well blended and smooth.
4. In a medium bowl, combine the beets and goat cheese.
5. Assemble the lasagna in a deep 9-inch casserole dish in the following order: sauce, lasagna noodles, shredded squash, beets and ricotta; repeat. The final layer should be pasta covered with sauce and a sprinkling of the Parmesan cheese, so be sure to reserve a little sauce for this.
6. Bake the lasagna for 45 minutes. Halfway through the cooking process, cover the lasagna with foil to prevent burning. Cool for 10 minutes before serving.
7. To serve, evenly divide the lasagna into 10 servings and use a flat spatula to remove each piece from the casserole dish.

Nonvegetarian Version

Add sautéed free-range ground chicken to each layer.

Per serving: calories 179.6, total fat 3.3 g, saturated fat 2.0 g, cholesterol 14.6 mg, sodium 339.5 mg, potassium 431.9 mg, total carbohydrate 28.3 g, dietary fiber 4.7 g, sugars 7.1 g, protein 10.0 g

🍴 *Low-Pressure Stuffed Tomatoes with Asian Celery Dressing*

Makes 8 appetizer servings

Stuffed tomatoes are a wonderful way to combine the super heart-healing ingredients of celery and tomatoes in a smart and compact package. These fresh and firm tomato cups are very popular in Mediterranean countries. If both sides of the halved tomato are in good shape, put them back together after the tomatoes are stuffed and bake them whole for a nice presentation.

Tomato Cups
1 bunch fresh asparagus spears, tough ends removed, cut into ¼-inch pieces
4 cups finely chopped fresh baby spinach
½ cup cooked and finely chopped fava beans or kidney beans
¼ teaspoon sea salt
2 ounces low-fat feta cheese, rinsed and crumbled
1 teaspoon fresh thyme leaves, optional
1 tablespoon finely chopped fresh parsley
¼ cup rolled oats
4 large, firm beefsteak tomatoes, sliced in half, insides scooped out to create 8 cups

Celery Dressing
2 celery stalks, trimmed and roughly chopped
3 dried apricots, chopped
3 tablespoons orange juice
1 teaspoon fresh garlic, minced
1 tablespoon low-sodium soy sauce
¼ teaspoon salt
1 tablespoon fresh cilantro leaves
2 teaspoons extra-virgin olive oil

1. Place an oven rack on the middle shelf of the oven and preheat to 350°F.

2. In a medium bowl, combine the asparagus, spinach, beans, salt, cheese, thyme (if using), parsley and oats. Mix thoroughly.

3. Place the 8 tomato cups on a baking sheet. Divide the stuffing among the tomatoes and pack firmly. Bake for 25 minutes.

4. In a blender or food processor, combine the celery, apricots, orange juice, garlic, soy sauce, salt, cilantro, olive oil and 4 tablespoons of water. Pulse until the ingredients come together. If the mixture is too thick, add another tablespoon of water. Process until quite smooth.

5. Divide the stuffed tomatoes among eight plates, drizzle with dressing and serve.

Nonvegetarian Version
Substitute ¼ pound ground, grass-fed beef, lightly sautéed, for the beans.

Per serving: calories 80.8, total fat 2.7 g, saturated fat 0.9 g, cholesterol 2.5 mg, sodium 221.5 mg, potassium 279.5 mg, total carbohydrate 8.5 g, dietary fiber 2.2 g, sugars 2.0 g, protein 4.6 g

---

🍽 *Yummy Antioxidant Dessert Fruit Salad with Custard*

Makes 2 servings

Custard spooned over your favorite ripe fruit is divine. This is a perfect dessert for guests, because it is very easy to prepare. The secret of thickening the custard is to temper the eggs properly. When eggs are added to something hot, they must be tempered first; otherwise they will scramble. Adding a little of the hot mixture to the eggs helps them adjust to the temperature slowly.

Custard

> 1 cup 2% milk
> 1 omega-3 egg at room temperature, beaten
> 2 tablespoons maple syrup
> ½ vanilla bean, split lengthwise
> 2 teaspoons cornstarch

Fruit Salad

> ½ ripe mango, peeled, pitted and diced
> 1 cup diced ripe pineapple
> 1 cup diced ripe melon
> 1 ripe banana, sliced
> ½ cup store-bought oat bran flakes cereal
> 2 tablespoons dried cherries or cranberries

1. In a small saucepan over medium-high heat, heat the milk almost to a boil, about 3 minutes.
2. In a small bowl, combine the eggs and maple syrup.
3. Reduce heat to medium-low and scrape some of the vanilla seeds from the split pod into the milk. Scrape the remainder into the egg mixture and stir.
4. Pour 2 tablespoons of hot milk into the egg mixture, stirring constantly until well combined. Slowly pour the egg mixture into the saucepan, stirring constantly.
5. Carefully whisk the cornstarch into the milk and continue to cook it on medium-low until the mixture begins to thicken, about 5 minutes.
6. Remove from the heat. Transfer the custard to a clean bowl and refrigerate for 1 hour.
7. To serve, arrange the mango, pineapple, melon, banana and oat bran flakes on two plates. Pour the slightly chilled custard over the fruit and sprinkle with dried cherries.

Per serving: calories 377.8, total fat 6.4 g, saturated fat 2.6 g, cholesterol 104.8 mg, sodium 193.4 mg, potassium 715.7 mg, total carbohydrate 74.4 g, dietary fiber 5.4 g, sugars 44.9 g, protein 10.3 g

---

These recipes are restful bedtime snacks or light meals full of soothing ingredients.

Rest-Easy Mango Lassi

Makes 2 servings

This is supereasy, and any healing fruit will work. Make small batches because once the ice melts, it doesn't taste quite the same.

1 cup low-fat plain yogurt
1 heaping cup chopped fresh mango
½ cup ice
1 tablespoon raw agave nectar

In a blender, combine the yogurt, mango, ice, agave and ½ cup water. Blend until smooth. Pour into a tall glass and serve.

Per serving: calories 160.8, total fat 2.1 g, saturated fat 1.3 g, cholesterol 7.4 mg, sodium 87.4 mg, potassium 415.4 mg, total carbohydrate 30.1 g, dietary fiber 1.5 g, sugars 28.3 g, protein 6.9 g

Dreamy Whole-Grain Egg Sandwich

Makes 2 servings

This sandwich is easy to prepare and lends itself to great toppings, like fresh spinach, kale or sliced avocado.

2 slices whole-grain bread
1 teaspoon olive oil (extra-virgin or light)
2 omega-3 eggs, beaten
Pinch salt
1 teaspoon Italian Seasoning blend, store-bought or following the recipe on page 482
Pinch shredded Parmesan cheese

1. Toast the whole-grain bread. In a medium nonstick pan, heat the olive oil over medium heat. Add the eggs. Gently swirl the pan to keep the eggs moving. Lower the heat to medium-low. Season with salt and Italian Seasoning. With a large spatula, scramble the eggs for a few seconds, cook for a few seconds longer, then scramble them again. Repeat this process for about 2 minutes or until you see the eggs begin to cook and change to pale yellow. They should still be wet. Sprinkle with the cheese. Remove from the heat.

2. To serve, make a sandwich with the eggs and toast. Slice the sandwich in half and divide it between two plates.

Per serving: calories 179.9, total fat 8.8 g, saturated fat 2.3 g, cholesterol 190.0 mg, sodium 245.0 mg, potassium 0.0 mg, total carbohydrate 19.0 g, dietary fiber 3.0 g, sugars 0.0 g, protein 11.0 g

Sleepy-Time Warm Broccoli Soup

Makes 2 servings

This soup is very thick. If you prefer yours thinner, add a little more water.

2–3 pounds of broccoli, woody bottom part of stalk removed, remaining stalk peeled; chop
    remaining stem and florets
1 low-sodium organic vegetable bouillon cube, or 3 cups low-sodium vegetable stock
Pinch Asian seasoning such as lemongrass powder, ground ginger or five-spice powder
2 heaping teaspoons Greek yogurt (see page 406)

1. Place the broccoli in a medium pot with 3 cups water (or stock, if using instead of bouillon cube)
and bring to a boil. Reduce the heat to medium and cook for 6 minutes, or until the broccoli is
tender. Add in the bouillon cube and Asian seasoning. Using an immersion blender, puree the
soup. This may also be transferred to a standing blender and pureed.
2. Pour into two bowls and top with Greek yogurt. Serve warm.

Per serving: calories 109.8, total fat 2.2 g, saturated fat 0.7 g, cholesterol 0.0 mg, sodium 171.2 mg,
potassium 996.6 mg, total carbohydrate 19.6 g, dietary fiber 9.2 g, sugars 0.3 g, protein 10.3 g

Soothing Cauliflower Soup

Makes 4 servings

This recipe is perfect for just about any vegetable, and may be seasoned with your favorite herbs.
Fresh herbs are best, but dried may be used.

1 cauliflower head, core removed and chopped
1 low-sodium organic vegetable bouillon cube, or 6 cups low-sodium vegetable stock
½ teaspoon finely chopped herbs, such as parsley, thyme, oregano and basil
4 heaping tablespoons shredded part-skim mozzarella cheese

Place the cauliflower in a large pot with 6 cups water (or 6 cups vegetable stock, if using instead
of bouillon) and bring to a boil. Reduce the heat to medium and cook for 6 minutes, or until the
cauliflower is tender. Add the bouillon cube and herbs. Using an immersion blender, puree the soup.
This may also be transferred to a standing blender and pureed. Remove from the heat. Stir in the
mozzarella cheese and serve warm.

Per serving: calories 110.1, total fat 2.4 g, saturated fat 0.1 g, cholesterol 5.0 mg, sodium 363.1 mg,
potassium 637.1 mg, total carbohydrate 15.4 g, dietary fiber 6.8 g, sugars 3.0 g, protein 8.2 g

Lazy Lentil Bean Soup

Makes 4 servings

Use canned beans to make quick work of this soothing recipe.

1 teaspoon olive oil
½ cup chopped white onion
½ cup canned pinto beans, drained and rinsed
1 cup canned lentils, drained and rinsed
1 quart no-sodium vegetable stock
½ teaspoon salt

1. Heat the olive oil in a stockpot over medium heat. Sauté the onions until they are translucent, about 7 minutes. Add the pinto beans, lentils, vegetable stock and salt and cook for 30 minutes, or until the lentils are tender. Taste, and add more salt, if needed.
2. Divide the soup among four bowls and serve.

Per serving: calories 119.2, total fat 1.5 g, saturated fat 0.2 g, cholesterol 0.0 mg, sodium 231.2 mg, potassium 314.1 mg, total carbohydrate 20.2 g, dietary fiber 7.1 g, sugars 2.0 g, protein 6.5 g

Sleep-Ease Halibut Stew

Makes 8 nighttime servings

This stew is great prepared earlier in the day because the flavors will meld over time. To save time, purchase organic cole slaw mix, found in the produce section of most grocery stores.

1 teaspoon fresh thyme leaves
1 teaspoon garlic paste
¼ cup finely chopped fresh parsley
¼ cup low-sodium fish stock
2 quarts low-sodium vegetable stock
1½ cups shredded cabbage
Four 4-ounce halibut fillets

1. Place the thyme, garlic, parsley, fish stock, vegetable stock and cabbage in a wide pot over medium heat and cook for 20 minutes, or until the cabbage is tender.
2. Carefully add the fish fillets, making sure they are covered with liquid. Lower the heat to medium-low. Stir gently and cook for another 10 minutes, or until the fish is opaque and flakes easily.
3. Divide the soup among eight small bowls, placing a fillet in each and serve.

Per serving: calories 73.5, total fat 0.9 g, saturated fat 0.0 g, cholesterol 20.0 mg, sodium 212.2 mg, potassium 52.0 mg, total carbohydrate 4.3 g, dietary fiber 1.5 g, sugars 2.1 g, protein 11.8 g

🍽️ *Soothing Wild Salmon Frittata*

Makes one 6-inch frittata, about 8 appetizer servings

This is also delightful with smoked salmon as well as your favorite healing vegetables.

Light olive oil, for greasing
2 cups fresh spinach, washed, stems trimmed
12-ounce can boneless wild salmon
6 omega-3 eggs, beaten
8 ounces nonfat cottage cheese
1 cup shredded low-fat Swiss cheese
½ cup shredded low-fat Cheddar
1 teaspoon Italian Seasoning blend, store-bought or prepared following the recipe on page 482

1. Preheat the oven to 375°F.
2. Lightly grease a 6-inch nonstick ovenproof skillet with olive oil.
3. Place fresh spinach in a glass container, cover with microwave-safe plastic and microwave for 20 seconds to wilt. You can also drop the spinach into boiling water for 10 seconds (do not cover). Remove, and shock the spinach leaves in ice water to stop cooking. Drain briefly on paper towels.
4. In a medium bowl, flake the canned salmon and mix with the eggs, cottage cheese, Swiss cheese, Cheddar cheese, wilted spinach and Italian Seasoning until well blended. Pour into the skillet and bake for 30 minutes, or until the frittata is set and the eggs are cooked through. The frittata is done when a toothpick comes out clean. Slice and serve.

Per serving: calories 224.6, total fat 12.8 g, saturated fat 5.1 g, cholesterol 163.6 mg, sodium 250.3 mg, potassium 41.9 mg, total carbohydrate 3.5 g, dietary fiber 0.8 g, sugars 1.2 g, protein 22.7 g

🍽 *Peaceful Pecan Banana Bread*

Makes one 9-inch loaf to serve 12, or 12 muffins

This recipe can be used to make either banana bread or muffins, both of which are delicious warm with a smear of nonfat or tofu cream cheese. Birch sugar is a naturally occurring sweetener found in fruits and vegetables. It's very low on the glycemic index and has no aftertaste. You should be able to find it in most health food stores.

3 tablespoons unsalted grass-fed butter
½ cup birch sugar or xylitol
2 bananas, mashed
1 omega-3 egg
1 tablespoon light olive oil or coconut oil, plus additional for greasing
Pinch salt
3 tablespoons raw agave syrup
¾ cup brown rice flour
½ cup coconut flour
¼ cup oats
1 teaspoon baking soda
1 teaspoon baking powder
¼ cup almond milk
¼ cup chopped pecans

1. Preheat the oven to 350°F.
2. In a standing mixer, blend the butter and sugar and mix until well combined. Add the bananas, egg, olive oil, salt and agave. In a separate bowl, combine the flours, oats, baking soda and baking powder. Alternate adding the dry ingredients with the almond milk and pecans until well blended.
3. Lightly grease a 9-inch loaf pan. Scrape the batter into the loaf pan. Bake for 1 hour 10 minutes, turning it around halfway through the baking time. The bread is done when a toothpick comes out clean. *To make muffins:* Lightly grease a muffin tin and fill the cups halfway with batter. Bake for 20 minutes, until a toothpick comes out clean.
4. Remove the banana bread from the pan by running a sharp knife around the edge. Turn it over to remove, then place right-side up on a wire rack to cool.

Per serving: calories 171.6, total fat 7.2 g, saturated fat 2.7 g, cholesterol 23.6 mg, sodium 184.3 mg, potassium 127.2 mg, total carbohydrate 26.4 g, dietary fiber 2.4 g, sugars 5.6 g, protein 2.3 g

🍽 *Warming Whole-Grain Almond Flatbread with Honey*

Makes 8 flatbreads

> **1 cup warm water (100°F to 110°F)**
> **1 package active dry yeast**
> **1 tablespoon raw agave nectar**
> **2–3 cups whole-wheat pastry flour,** plus more for dusting
> **½ cup semolina flour**
> **2 heaping tablespoons almond flour**
> **¼ cup slivered almonds**
> **1 teaspoon salt**
> **2 tablespoons light olive oil,** plus additional for greasing
> **½ cup honey**

1. Pour the warm water into a small bowl and add the yeast and agave. Stir the mixture with a fork until the yeast dissolves and the water begins to foam slightly and turn tan. Let stand as it continues to foam, about 7 minutes. In the bowl of an electric stand mixer or food processor fitted with a dough blade, combine 2 cups of the whole-wheat pastry flour, semolina flour, almond flour, almond slivers and the salt and mix until well combined. Add the yeast mixture and olive oil. Mix or pulse until the dough comes together, adding flour as needed. The dough should be smooth and supple. Cut the dough into 8 equal pieces. Roll the dough pieces into balls and let rest for about 5 minutes.

2. With a rolling pin, roll out the balls one at a time until they are about ¼ inch thick and resemble pancakes.

3. Grease a large skillet with a little olive oil and set over medium heat for 2 minutes. Transfer one dough pancake at a time to the skillet and cook it for 1 minute per side. The flatbread is done when it is cooked through and dotted with tan spots and bubbly.

4. Place the flatbread on a plate and cover with a dish towel to keep it warm. Cook the remaining in the same fashion. Serve drizzled with honey.

Per serving: calories 296.9, total fat 6.6 g, saturated fat 0.8 g, cholesterol 0.0 mg, sodium 21.0 mg, potassium 78.7 mg, total carbohydrate 55.7 g, dietary fiber 5.8 g, sugars 19.5 g, protein 7.6 g

🍽 *Sleep-Tight Oatmeal Apricot Cookies with Walnuts*

Makes 12 large cookies

These cookies are delicious and perfect for a light snack before bed. Since there is no gluten in these flours, you will need to be careful when forming the balls, as the dough tends to fall apart.

Light olive oil, for greasing
1¼ cups rolled oats
¼ cup almond flour
¼ cup brown rice flour
⅓ cup coconut flour
½ teaspoon salt
¼ cup almond butter
4 tablespoons unsalted grass-fed butter
½ cup raw agave nectar
1 teaspoon vanilla extract
2 tablespoons molasses
2 tablespoons brown rice syrup
1 omega-3 egg
½ heaping cup finely chopped dried apricots
½ cup walnut pieces

1. Preheat the oven to 350°F.
2. Lightly grease a cookie sheet with light olive oil or cooking spray.
3. In a medium bowl, combine the oats, almond flour, brown rice flour, coconut flour and salt. In a standing mixer with the paddle attached, set on medium speed, mix the almond butter, butter, agave, vanilla, molasses and brown rice syrup until smooth. Add the egg, apricots and walnuts and mix until well blended. Reduce the mixer to low and slowly add the flour mixture. When well blended, remove from the mixer and divide the dough into 12 pieces. Form into balls.
4. Place the balls on the cookie sheet about 4 inches apart and flatten to about ¾ inch thick. Bake for 20 minutes or until lightly golden. Remove from the oven and cool for a few minutes. Remove the cookies from the pan and place on a wire rack to cool further before serving.

Per cookie: calories 243.1, total fat 12.6 g, saturated fat 3.5 g, cholesterol 26.2 mg, sodium 110.6 mg, potassium 236.8 mg, total carbohydrate 28.3 g, dietary fiber 2.9 g, sugars 15.1 g, protein 4.5 g

Nerve-Calming Banana Cake

Makes one 9-inch loaf, up to 8 servings

This moist banana cake is delightful served warm with a scoop of low-fat vanilla ice cream. If you plan to use the chocolate chips, make sure to look for ones with the highest percentage of cacao.

3 tablespoons grass-fed unsalted butter or light olive oil
½ cup birch sugar or xylitol
2 bananas, mashed
1 omega-3 egg
1 tablespoon light olive oil, plus additional for greasing pan
Pinch salt
3 tablespoons raw agave nectar
2 heaping tablespoons dark chocolate chips, optional
1 cup whole-wheat pastry flour
¼ cup almond flour
1 teaspoon baking soda
1 teaspoon baking powder
¼ cup low-fat milk
Low-fat vanilla ice cream, optional

1. Preheat the oven to 350°F with the oven rack placed in the middle.
2. Using a mixer, combine the butter and sugar until well mixed. Add the bananas, egg, olive oil, salt, agave and chocolate chips, if using. In a separate bowl, combine the flours, baking soda and baking powder. Alternate pouring in the dry ingredients with the milk until just blended (don't over-mix). Lightly grease a 9-inch loaf pan with olive oil. Add the batter. Bake for 45 minutes, turning it about halfway through the cooking time. The cake is done when a toothpick comes out clean.
3. Remove the banana loaf from the pan by running a sharp knife around the edge of the pan. Turn over to remove, then place right-side up on a wire rack to cool slightly. Serve warm slices with a scoop of low-fat vanilla ice cream, if you'd like.

Per serving: calories 225.7, total fat 9.7 g, saturated fat 4.1 g, cholesterol 35.6 mg, sodium 250.6 mg, potassium 140.2 mg, total carbohydrate 37.6 g, dietary fiber 3.1 g, sugars 22.3 g, protein 4.0 g

Memory-Boosting Minestrone Soup

Makes 8 servings

Minestrone is very popular in Italy and often served as a first course. However, this soup is hearty enough to be considered a complete meal. This dish can also be served as a salad by omitting the broth. If fresh plum tomatoes are not in season or are hard to come by, use low-sodium canned plum tomatoes instead. In fact, canned tomatoes are full of healing ingredients and aren't quite as tart as fresh.

1 teaspoon light olive oil
1 medium white onion, finely chopped
1 stalk celery, strings removed, finely chopped
1 large carrot, peeled and finely chopped
2 quarts low-sodium vegetable stock
1 teaspoon sea salt
1 ear of corn, kernels removed, or ½ cup frozen, thawed
6 plum tomatoes, cored, seeded and diced
1 teaspoon minced garlic
1 cup finely chopped fresh parsley
1 teaspoon dried marjoram
⅛ teaspoon freshly ground black pepper, or to taste
4 cups arugula, spinach, Swiss chard, cabbage or kale, leaves torn if large
1 cup cooked whole-wheat tubettini pasta
Salt, to taste
½ cup finely shredded Parmesan cheese

1. Heat the olive oil in a saucepan over medium heat. Add the onions, celery, and carrots. Sauté about 4 minutes.
2. Raise the heat to medium-high and add the vegetable broth, salt, corn, tomatoes and garlic and cook for 10 minutes, stirring frequently.
3. Remove from the heat. Add the parsley, marjoram, pepper, arugula and pasta. Gently stir until well blended. Add salt, if needed.
4. Serve in eight bowls, each topped with 2 tablespoons of cheese.

Nonvegetarian Version
Add omega-3 seafood of choice.

Per serving: calories 115.7, total fat 3.0 g, saturated fat 1.3 g, cholesterol 4.9 mg, sodium 298.5 mg, potassium 204.7 mg, total carbohydrate 14.3 g, dietary fiber 3.8 g, sugars 2.9 g, protein 5.4 g

Vitalizing Vietnamese Pho Bo Soup

Makes 6 servings

Pho Bo soup, or Vietnamese beef soup, is prepared by placing razor-thin slices of raw beef in the soup bowl, then pouring piping hot soup on top to cook it. This method ensures that the beef is very tender. It is important to use the highest-quality lean beef you can find. Make sure it is grass-fed for extra omega-3s. The secret, regardless of what cut you use, is to slice the beef paper thin—easily done if the beef is partially frozen. Other protein choices that work in this soup are buffalo, venison, scallops and shrimp. If you want to try this with chicken, cook the thin slices in the pot with the rest of the soup until opaque.

Beef Broth

1 quart low-sodium beef stock
½ cup finely chopped onion
1 teaspoon minced fresh ginger
1 teaspoon minced fresh garlic
4 fresh basil leaves
1 tablespoon finely chopped scallions
Pinch cinnamon
Pinch cloves
1 star anise
½ teaspoon Sichuan pepper or chili sauce, optional
½ fresh fennel bulb, finely chopped
½ teaspoon sea salt, or to taste

Pho Bo

½ pound flat rice noodles
½ pound grass-fed sirloin beef steak, very lean, sliced paper thin
1 cup bean sprouts
2 large Swiss chard leaves, thinly sliced

1. In a large pot over medium heat, combine the beef stock, 1 quart of water, onions, ginger, garlic, basil, scallions, cinnamon, cloves, star anise, Sichuan pepper or chili sauce, if using, fennel and salt. Cook at a medium boil for 20 minutes, or until the fennel and onions are tender.

2. Prepare the flat rice noodles according to package directions. Drain and set aside.

3. To serve, divide the noodles, beef, sprouts and Swiss chard among six large bowls and pour the boiling soup over the ingredients to cook them. The beef should cook within a few minutes. Once it does, serve immediately.

Per serving: calories 152.3, total fat 3.2 g, saturated fat 1.2 g, cholesterol 33.6 mg, sodium 427.1 mg, potassium 424.5 mg, total carbohydrate 14.8 g, dietary fiber 2.3 g, sugars 1.2 g, protein 15.4 g

🍽 *Memorable Veal Chops and Spinach Salad*

Makes 4 servings

Mediterranean veal chops are a nearly effortless meal, requiring hardly any cooking time. Veal is naturally delicate, so be careful not to overcook it. The veal really livens up a nourishing spinach salad.

Veal Chops

1 tablespoon plus 1 teaspoon **light olive oil,** divided
Four 4-ounce grass-fed boneless veal chops, pounded to a thickness of ¼ inch
1 teaspoon salt
¼ teaspoon freshly ground black pepper
2 smashed garlic cloves
1 teaspoon finely chopped fresh rosemary needles
6 heaping cups fresh baby spinach
1 tablespoon crushed walnuts

Salad Dressing

¼ cup extra-virgin olive oil
1 tablespoon balsamic vinegar
¼ teaspoon salt, or to taste
Pinch ground black pepper
1 teaspoon freshly squeezed lemon juice
Pinch turmeric

1. In a large resealable plastic bag, combine 1 tablespoon olive oil, the veal chops, salt, pepper, garlic and rosemary. Turn until the veal chops are thoroughly coated. Set aside to marinate for 20 minutes.

2. Heat 1 teaspoon olive oil in a cast-iron skillet over medium-high heat. Remove the veal chops from the marinade and place in the hot skillet. Cook until they are medium-rare, slightly under 2 minutes per side. Remove from the heat and set aside for 4 minutes.

3. Prepare the salad. In a small bowl, combine the olive oil, vinegar, salt, pepper, lemon juice, turmeric, and 1 tablespoon of water. Whisk until well combined.

4. In a large bowl, combine the spinach and salad dressing. When the veal chops are done, add them to the bowl and gently mix until the chops are coated with the dressing.

5. Divide the salad among four plates, place a veal chop atop each, sprinkle with walnuts and serve.

Vegetarian Version

Substitute marinated and sautéed sliced tofu for the veal.

Frugal Option

See "vegetarian version" above.

Per serving: calories 336.4, total fat 21.7 g, saturated fat 3.3 g, cholesterol 0.0 mg, sodium 244.6 mg, potassium 732.3 mg, total carbohydrate 3.1 g, dietary fiber 1.2 g, sugars 0.8 g, protein 34.8 g

🍽 *Thoughtful Asian Salmon Salad*

Makes 4 servings

I love to marinate my fish before cooking. It imparts extra layers of flavor. Salmon is a hearty fish that can be served warm, cold or at room temperature. This is a quick, easy recipe that's perfect for picnics, bag lunches or as a quick bite tucked into a whole-wheat pita pocket.

Marinade

1 tablespoon light olive oil
¼ cup dry white wine
4 basil leaves

Salmon

Four 4-ounce wild Pacific salmon fillets
1 tablespoon sesame seeds

Salad and Dressing

2 tablespoons sesame oil
½ cup finely chopped dried cranberries
1 cup finely chopped shallots
1 tablespoon white wine vinegar
6 heaping cups fresh spinach

1. In a large bowl, combine the olive oil, wine, basil and 1 cup of water. Add the salmon fillets and make sure they are completely covered with liquid. Cover the bowl with plastic wrap and refrigerate overnight.

2. Place an oven rack on the middle shelf of the oven and preheat to 350°F.

3. Remove salmon from the marinade, shake off any excess liquid and place on a baking sheet. Bake the fish for 10 minutes, or until the flesh is opaque and flakes easily. Set aside to cool briefly. Discard any remaining marinade.

4. In a medium bowl, combine the sesame oil, cranberries, shallots, vinegar and 1 tablespoon of water, and whisk until well combined.

5. Add the spinach and toss to coat.

6. To serve, divide the salad among four dishes, top with the salmon and sprinkle with sesame seeds.

Vegetarian Version

Substitute cubed, baked winter squash for the salmon.

Frugal Option

Use canned wild Alaskan salmon instead of fresh.

Per serving: calories 362.2, total fat 19.5 g, saturated fat 1.6 g, cholesterol 60.0 mg, sodium 89.4 mg, potassium 957.3 mg, total carbohydrate 21.8 g, dietary fiber 2.3 g, sugars 11.2 g, protein 26.7 g

Clear-the-Fog Kale-Rice Salad with Chicken

Makes 4 servings

In the Mediterranean, rice is often cooked in broth or a pat of butter for added flavor. Cooked al dente, brown rice adds wonderful texture as well as whole-grain nutrients. The best thing about it is that you can serve it with just about any vegetable, sauce, meat or seafood. Here, memory-boosting kale mixed with the rice makes a tasty bed for the curried chicken strips. Rice salads can be served warm or cold.

Kale-Rice Salad

1 cup brown jasmine rice
1½ cups low-sodium chicken or beef stock
1 teaspoon light olive oil
2 bunches escarole, chopped into ¼-inch slivers
4 leaves kale, chopped into ¼-inch slivers
2 teaspoons garlic paste
¼ teaspoon salt

Chicken Strips

1 teaspoon light olive oil
4 chicken breasts, pounded to ¼ inch thick and cut into 1-inch-wide strips
1 teaspoon curry powder, or to taste

1. Prepare the rice according to package directions, using chicken stock instead of water. Fluff with a fork, and set aside.
2. Heat the olive oil in a wok or large pan over medium heat. Add the escarole, kale, garlic paste and salt. Sauté until the escarole starts to wilt.
3. Scrape the ingredients onto a large plate. Add the rice to the escarole mixture and gently toss until evenly dispersed.
4. Wipe out the wok or pan, and set over medium heat. Add 1 teaspoon of olive oil. Add the chicken strips and sauté until the chicken is opaque throughout, about 7 minutes. Remove from the heat. Sprinkle the chicken with the curry powder. Toss until thoroughly coated.
5. To serve, place a mound of rice in the center of each of four plates and top it with the chicken strips.

Vegetarian Version

Substitute a crunchy vegetable like sautéed broccoli or cauliflower for the chicken strips.

Frugal Option

Use frozen spinach instead of escarole and kale.

Per serving: calories 268.9, total fat 6.1 g, saturated fat 0.9 g, cholesterol 66.0 mg, sodium 333.2 mg, potassium 410.0 mg, total carbohydrate 23.0 g, dietary fiber 8.9 g, sugars 1.7 g, protein 31.9 g

🍽 *Thought-Provoking Wild Salmon with Spinach and Fruit Tapenade*

Makes 4 servings

A tapenade is usually a combination of ground olives, capers and balsamic vinegar, but ours is a vitamin-rich fruit blend that is wildly delicious with wild salmon.

Salmon

Four 4-ounce wild Pacific salmon fillets
½ teaspoon salt
⅛ teaspoon ground white pepper
1 teaspoon light olive oil

Fruit Tapenade

1 teaspoon light olive oil
½ cup finely chopped shallots
1 tablespoon balsamic vinegar
1 Gala apple, peeled, cored and diced
½ cup hulled, diced fresh strawberries
1 teaspoon garlic paste
1 tablespoon pumpkin seeds

Salad

6 heaping cups fresh baby spinach

1. Set an oven rack on the middle shelf and preheat the oven to 350°F.
2. Place the salmon fillets skin side down on a baking sheet, sprinkle with salt and white pepper, and drizzle with olive oil. Bake about 12 minutes, or until the salmon's flesh is opaque and flakes easily.
3. For the fruit tapenade, heat the olive oil in a small sauté pan over medium heat. Add the shallots and balsamic vinegar, and sauté until the shallots are tender, about 4 minutes.
4. Remove from the heat and scrape into a food processor. Add the apples, strawberries, garlic paste and pumpkin seeds and pulse until a paste is formed.
5. Divide the spinach among four plates and top each with a salmon fillet. Add a generous spoonful of tapenade and serve.

Vegetarian Version

Omit the salmon and use the tapenade on a wild rice blend.

Frugal Option

Use frozen fish instead of fresh.

Per serving: calories 244.3, total fat 11.3 g, saturated fat 0.4 g, cholesterol 60.0 mg, sodium 184.4 mg, potassium 952.1 mg, total carbohydrate 13.3 g, dietary fiber 2.7 g, sugars 4.7 g, protein 26.1 g

Brainy Balsamic-Berry Chicken and Couscous

Makes 2 servings

Balsamic glazes are delightful and pair wonderfully with berries for a perfect savory-sweet taste sensation. This dish has lots of Mediterranean influences, and the technique can be applied to a variety of healing ingredients. Add more vegetables, if you'd like.

Fruit Sauce

2 tablespoons balsamic vinegar
2 tablespoons olive oil
1 cup blueberries, stems removed
½ teaspoon salt
1 Gala apple, peeled, cored and diced

Chicken

1 tablespoon light olive oil
2 boneless, skinless chicken breast halves, pounded ¼ inch thick

Couscous

½ cup couscous
½ cup frozen green peas, thawed

1. Place a small saucepot over medium-low heat and add the vinegar, olive oil, blueberries, salt, apples and 2 tablespoons of water. Cook for 12 minutes or until the apples have softened and the sauce is thick.
2. Set a skillet large enough to hold both chicken breasts over medium heat and add the olive oil. Sauté the chicken 4 minutes per side, or until opaque throughout. Set aside.
3. Prepare the couscous according to package directions. Fluff with a fork, then stir in the peas. Cover to allow the legumes to warm.
4. Divide the couscous between two plates, place a piece of chicken on top, drizzle with the fruit sauce and serve.

Vegetarian Version

Substitute sautéed tofu for chicken.

Per serving: calories 569.8, total fat 22.0 g, saturated fat 3.2 g, cholesterol 66.0 mg, sodium 207.8 mg, potassium 569.4 mg, total carbohydrate 58.8 g, dietary fiber 7.8 g, sugars 19.4 g, protein 33.6 g

🍽 *Remember-More Moo Shu Vegetable Stir-Fry*

Makes 4 servings

Homemade moo shu, besides being delicious, is also versatile—it can include almost any ingredient to suit any taste. My rule of thumb is that if an ingredient can cook quickly to tenderness, it can be included. Use store-bought whole-wheat wraps, sliced in half if they are large.

Moo Shu

1 teaspoon light olive oil
2 tablespoons finely chopped shallots
2 cups finely slivered purple cabbage
2 cups finely slivered white cabbage
½ carrot, shredded
1–1½ pounds broccoli, cut into 1-inch florets
8 asparagus spears, tough ends removed, cut into 1-inch pieces
1 small yellow squash, grated
½ fresh plum, pitted and thinly sliced
4 whole-wheat wraps

Sauce

1 tablespoon low-sodium soy sauce
1 teaspoon minced ginger
1 teaspoon minced garlic
1 teaspoon honey

1. Heat the olive oil in a wok or large pot over medium heat. Add the shallots and sauté until soft, about 3 minutes. Add the cabbages, carrot, broccoli, asparagus, and squash and toss until well blended.

2. At this point, you can prepare the sauce in a separate bowl or add the ingredients to the pot. Keep tossing the mixture as the sauce ingredients are added, to make sure everything is well coated. Cabbage should be crisp-tender and not soft.

3. Remove from the heat and stir in the plum slices.

4. To assemble, divide the moo shu among four plates, topping with any juices remaining in the pot. Serve with the wraps on the side.

5. To wrap the moo shu, lay the wrap on a plate and place a mound of moo shu in the middle. Fold in the ends, then roll up from the bottom. Eat with your hands.

Nonvegetarian Version

Add sautéed free-range chicken tenders.

Per serving: calories 128.1, total fat 3.4 g, saturated fat 0.7 g, cholesterol 0.0 mg, sodium 412.3 mg, potassium 619.9 mg, total carbohydrate 22.0 g, dietary fiber 8.6 g, sugars 5.1 g, protein 9.0 g

---

🍽️ *Bright-Eyed Fruit Custards*

Makes 4 servings

It's hard to believe that some scrumptious desserts are so easy to prepare and yet full of healing nutrients. These fruit-studded custards can be prepared ahead of time, or baked while you are eating the main course. They are quite versatile, so use whatever fruits are in season.

2 omega-3 eggs, whisked
2 tablespoons maple syrup
1 tablespoon finely chopped dried mango slices
1 tablespoon finely chopped dried papaya slices
2 cups thinly sliced strawberries
2 plums, cored and sliced thin
2 tablespoons raw almond slivers
½ cantaloupe, sliced into four wedges

1. Preheat the oven to 350°F.
2. In a medium bowl, mix the eggs with the maple syrup, mango, papaya, strawberries, and plums until well combined.
3. Divide the mixture among four small ramekins and place in a large casserole dish. Use a kettle to fill the casserole dish with water halfway up the sides of the ramekins. Bake in the oven for 35 minutes, or until the eggs have cooked.
4. Remove from the oven, sprinkle with almond slivers, place a cantaloupe wedge alongside each dessert and serve.

Frugal Option

Use frozen strawberries, thawed, instead of fresh.

Per serving: calories 149.7, total fat 4.7 g, saturated fat 0.9 g, cholesterol 95.0 mg, sodium 42.6 mg, potassium 314.2 mg, total carbohydrate 23.8 g, dietary fiber 3.3 g, sugars 13.6 g, protein 4.8 g

---

🍽️ *Iron-Rich Mushroom Caps Stuffed with Italian Garlic Spinach*

Makes 8 appetizer servings, about 4 mushroom caps per serving

Mushroom caps are probably the most user-friendly finger food you could find. Just about any mushroom with a medium to large cap will work here, such as white, portobello or cremini mushrooms. Before stuffing the mineral-rich mushroom caps, they must be steamed. Otherwise when you bake them, they will wilt and release their juices, causing the filling to spread.

2 pounds large white mushrooms (about 32), wiped clean, stems removed and reserved
1 teaspoon light olive oil
1 large white onion, finely chopped
2 teaspoons Italian Seasoning blend, store-bought or prepared following recipe on page 482
6 heaping cups fresh baby spinach
½ teaspoon salt
1 cup whole-wheat breadcrumbs, soaked in 2 tablespoons of water
¼ cup freshly grated Parmesan cheese
6 ounces part-skim milk mozzarella cheese, shredded

1. Place an oven rack on the middle shelf of the oven and preheat to 400°F.

2. In a food processor, pulse the mushroom stems until finely chopped.

3. Heat the olive oil in a wok or large pan over medium heat. Add the onions, chopped mushrooms stems, Italian Seasoning, spinach and salt. Sauté until the onions are translucent and the mushroom stems have released their juices, about 10 minutes.

4. Remove from the heat. Stir in the soaked breadcrumbs and cheeses, until well blended.

5. In a pot that will hold a steamer basket, bring 1 inch of water to a boil. Place the mushrooms in the steamer basket, place over water and cover. Steam for 2 minutes. Transfer the mushrooms to several layers of paper towels to drain.

6. When the mushrooms are slightly cooled, place them on a baking sheet and stuff them. Don't pack the too tightly. Bake the stuffed mushrooms for about 15 minutes, or until the filling turns golden brown. Remove from the oven and serve.

Nonvegetarian Version

Salmon Stuffed Mushrooms: salmon, pumpkin seeds, mashed beans.

Per serving (4 mushroom caps): calories 193.1, total fat 7.8 g, saturated fat 3.8 g, cholesterol 17.9 mg, sodium 353.4 mg, potassium 610.8 mg, total carbohydrate 18.9 g, dietary fiber 3.6 g, sugars 2.2 g, protein 14.4 g

🍽 *Feel-Better Broccoli-Brown Rice Al Diavolo*

Makes 4 servings

Al diavolo means "to the devil" in Italian, and in the style of the devil means spicy. You can adjust the heat to suit your taste by adding more or less red pepper flakes. This recipe can be served two ways: with tomatoes or without.

1 teaspoon light olive oil
½ cup finely chopped white onions
2 pounds fresh broccoli, cut into 2-inch florets
2 teaspoons finely chopped roasted garlic
¼–½ teaspoon red pepper flakes, adjusted to taste
1 tablespoon roughly chopped fresh basil
¼ teaspoon salt
1 can (28 ounces) diced low-sodium tomatoes with their liquid, optional
1 cup cooked brown rice
Lemon wedges
¼ teaspoon finely chopped rosemary leaves
½ cup freshly grated Parmesan cheese

1. Heat the olive oil in a wok or large saucepan over medium-low heat. Add the onions and broccoli and sauté for 7 minutes, stirring occasionally. Add the garlic, red pepper flakes, basil, salt and tomatoes, if using. Reduce the heat to medium-low and cook the sauce for 10 minutes, stirring occasionally. Add the brown rice and reduce the heat to low. Gently stir until well combined.

2. Divide the sauce and rice mixture among four plates, along with a lemon wedge. Sprinkle with rosemary and Parmesan cheese (pass more at the table), if desired.

Nonvegetarian Version

Add sautéed grass-fed ground beef.

Per serving: calories 274.4, total fat 6.6 g, saturated fat 2.8 g, cholesterol 9.9 mg, sodium 430.8 mg, potassium 1,119.4 mg, total carbohydrate 46.3 g, dietary fiber 14.7 g, sugars 10.5 g, protein 17.5 g

🍽 **Estrogen-Boosting Shrimp Scampi with Sweet Potatoes**

Makes 4 servings

What better way to highlight the clean and sweet flavor of shrimp than with wine and garlic in a dish often known as *scampi*? Combined with baby spinach and sweet potatoes, you have a chorus of healing.

Sweet Potato

4 large sweet potatoes
1 tablespoon light olive oil

Shrimp Scampi Salad

1 tablespoon light olive oil
2 pounds large shrimp, peeled and deveined
1 small onion, finely chopped
½ cup white wine
2 cloves garlic, thinly sliced
2 teaspoons Italian Seasoning blend, store-bought or prepared following the recipe on page 482
½ cup canned white beans, rinsed
6 cups fresh baby spinach
2 teaspoons lemon zest, optional

1. Place the oven rack on the lowest shelf of the oven and preheat to 400°F.
2. Place the potatoes on a baking sheet and coat with olive oil. Pierce each potato with a fork. Roast for 40 minutes, or until tender.
3. For the scampi, heat the olive oil in a wok or large pan over medium heat. Add the shrimp and onions and sauté for 2 minutes per side or until the shrimp is pink.
4. Carefully add the wine. *Do not pour directly from the bottle*; pour the wine into a glass before adding to the shrimp. Stir in the garlic and Italian Seasoning. Cook 1 minute.
5. Remove from the heat. Add the white beans and spinach by the handful, stirring as the spinach begins to wilt. Continue folding in the spinach, until all 6 cups are used.
6. To assemble, place a potato on each plate, slice it open lengthwise, cover with a portion of shrimp scampi, sprinkle with lemon zest and serve.

Vegetarian Version

Use sautéed tofu cubes instead of shrimp.

Frugal Option

Use frozen shrimp instead of fresh.

Per serving: calories 482.0, total fat 11.0 g, saturated fat 1.8 g, cholesterol 344.5 mg, sodium 375.0 mg, potassium 1,423.7 mg, total carbohydrate 37.1 g, dietary fiber 6.9 g, sugars 7.6 g, protein 52.4 g

❚●❙ *High-Fiber Baked Eggplant, Sweet Potatoes and Mushrooms*

Makes 4 servings

Baked eggplant, sweet potatoes and mushrooms are a delicious and hearty combination of flavors. This casserole is easy to assemble and lends itself to lots of tasty variations.

Eggplant and Mushrooms

    1 large eggplant, peeled and cubed, or shredded using a food processor
    1 tablespoon salt
    16 ounces marinara sauce, store-bought or prepared following the recipe on page 482
    2 large portobello mushrooms, cut into ¼-inch-thick slices
    1 sweet potato, cut into thin rounds

Cheese Mixture

    2 cups fresh escarole or baby spinach, wilted in a microwave for 30 seconds
    1 ounce goat cheese, softened in the microwave for 15 seconds
    1 ounce Greek yogurt, store-bought or prepared following the recipe on page 406
    ½ cup finely chopped onions
    ½ cup rinsed and mashed white beans

1. In a large bowl, combine the eggplant with the salt and let sit for 30 minutes. Rinse thoroughly and wring it out to dry. Place an oven rack on the middle shelf of the oven and preheat to 350°F.

2. In a small bowl, combine the escarole, goat cheese, yogurt, onions and white beans and mix until well blended.

3. In a 9- to 10-inch casserole, layer the ingredients in the following order: sauce, eggplant, cheese, mushrooms and sweet potatoes. Make as many layers as possible, finishing with the marinara.

4. Bake for 40 minutes or until the eggplant is tender. Cool slightly and serve.

Nonvegetarian Version

Add sautéed ground buffalo to the casserole.

Per serving: calories 182.1, total fat 3.2 g, saturated fat 1.3 g, cholesterol 3.3 mg, sodium 149.8 mg, potassium 864.9 mg, total carbohydrate 32.2 g, dietary fiber 7.7 g, sugars 8.3 g, protein 8.6 g

---

🍽 *Symptom-Busting Halibut and Balsamic Glazed Date-Fruit Rice*

Makes 4 servings

The combination of mango with omega-3–rich halibut is outstanding, as the fish is very hearty and the mango salad is slightly sweet and tender. This recipe calls for the fish to be cooked in the oven, but if you are a grilling aficionado, by all means, prepare the fish on the grill. You can also use other fruits, such as apricots, pineapple or orange sections.

Seafood

Four 6-ounce halibut steaks
1 teaspoon salt

Chopped Date-Fruit Rice

1 teaspoon light olive oil
10 pearl onions, trimmed and sliced in half
6 dates, quartered
1 teaspoon balsamic vinegar
1 cup cooked brown rice
1 teaspoon freshly squeezed lemon juice
1 tablespoon finely chopped fresh cilantro
1 teaspoon garlic paste (store-bought)
1 ripe mango, cut in to ¼-inch dice
1 tablespoon golden raisins
1 tablespoon raw pumpkin seeds

1. Place an oven rack in the middle shelf of the oven and preheat to 350°F.
2. Place the fish on a sheet pan and season with salt. Bake for 10 minutes or until fish is opaque and flakes easily.
3. Heat the olive oil in a wok or large pan over medium heat. Add the pearl onions, dates and balsamic vinegar. Sauté for 3 to 4 minutes, or until the onions start to soften. Remove from the heat. Gently stir in the brown rice.
4. In a large bowl, combine the lemon juice, cilantro, garlic paste, mango, raisins and pumpkin seeds. Stir in the pearl onions, dates and rice. Toss until well combined.
5. Divide the rice among four plates, top with fish and serve.

Vegetarian Version

Substitute baked thinly sliced sweet potatoes for the halibut.

Frugal Option

Use four 4-ounce pieces of chicken breast tenderloins instead of the fish.

Per serving: calories 454.8, total fat 4.1 g, saturated fat 0.4 g, cholesterol 60.0 mg, sodium 226.7 mg, potassium 230.0 mg, total carbohydrate 72.4 g, dietary fiber 7.9 g, sugars 35.7 g, protein 41.5 g

Mediterr-Asian Miso Soy Scallops with Tossed Brussels Sprouts

Makes 4 servings

The scallops will soak up the rich and slightly sweet flavors of soy sauce and miso. This dish takes less than 10 minutes cooking time. Serve on its own or atop a bed of brown rice or other whole grain.

Marinade

1 tablespoon miso paste
1 tablespoon low-sodium soy sauce
½ cup dry white wine
1 teaspoon freshly minced garlic cloves
4 sprigs parsley

Scallops

¾ pound scallops
1 tablespoon light olive oil

Brussels Sprouts

1 pounds Brussels sprouts, trimmed and cut in half
1 tablespoon light olive oil
¼ teaspoon salt
1 tablespoon minced roasted garlic
½ tablespoon low-sodium soy sauce
1 tablespoon sesame oil

1. In a large resealable plastic bag, combine the miso paste, soy sauce, wine, garlic, parsley and scallops. Seal the bag and turn to combine ingredients. Make sure that the miso paste dissolves. Marinate in the refrigerator overnight.
2. In a pot that will hold a steamer basket, bring 1 inch of water to a boil. Place the Brussels sprouts in the steamer basket, place over water and cover. Steam 2 minutes for al dente. Remove from the heat. Add the Brussels sprouts to a large bowl. Add the olive oil, salt, garlic, soy sauce and sesame oil. Toss until well combined.
3. Remove the scallops from the marinade, shaking off excess. Heat olive oil in a large pan over medium-high heat. Sauté the scallops for 2 minutes per side until opaque. Divide the scallops among four plates, and serve with Brussels sprouts on the side.

Vegetarian Version

Substitute cubed extra-firm tofu for the scallops.

Frugal Option

Substitute free-range chicken tenderloins for the scallops.

Per serving: calories 222.6, total fat 11.2 g, saturated fat 1.5 g, cholesterol 23.4 mg, sodium 492.8 mg, potassium 708.8 mg, total carbohydrate 13.9 g, dietary fiber 4.6 g, sugars 2.8 g, protein 16.5 g

¶◉| *Mid-Life Salmon Over Asian Date Rice*

Makes 4 servings

Dates are one of the oldest recorded fruits and are very popular in Mediterranean cooking. Omega-3 salmon will soothe those hot flashes, too.

Asian Date Rice

1 teaspoon red curry paste
3 cups low-sodium vegetable stock, plus additional cup, if needed
2 cups jasmine rice
2–3 pounds broccoli, cut into 2-inch florets
6 pineapple rings, cut into ¼-inch bits
3 dried dates, diced

Salmon

5 tablespoons finely chopped fresh cilantro
1 teaspoon chili powder
1 tablespoon freshly squeezed lemon juice
Pinch salt
1½ pounds wild salmon fillet, cut into four serving pieces

1. Place the broiler rack 6 inches from the broiler. Preheat.
2. Stir the curry paste into the vegetable stock until well blended. Prepare the rice according to package directions, using the curry-stock blend in place of water. About 2 minutes before the rice is finished cooking, stir in the broccoli. When the rice is done, stir in the pineapple and dates.
3. In a large bowl, mix the cilantro, chili, lemon juice and salt and until well blended. Add the salmon and turn in the sauce until coated. Broil the salmon, skin side down, for 7 minutes, until its flesh is opaque and flakes easily. Remove from the heat.
4. Divide the rice among four plates, top each with a salmon fillet and serve.

Vegetarian Version

Omit the salmon and serve the rice as a main dish.

Frugal Options

Use free-range chicken breast instead of salmon.

Per serving: calories 457.0, total fat 13.7 g, saturated fat 0.3 g, cholesterol 90.0 mg, sodium 307.1 mg, potassium 1,462.4 mg, total carbohydrate 43.3 g, dietary fiber 8.3 g, sugars 5.6 g, protein 43.5 g

---

🍽 *Omega-Rich Grilled Salmon and Warm Kale Salad*

Makes 4 servings

Salmon always shines when it's grilled. It becomes juicy, smoky and melt-in-your-mouth good. Paired with a beautiful Asian-inspired kale salad, this meal is a perfect pick-me-up for that sluggish menopausal moment.

Salmon
- ½ **cup sugar-free BBQ sauce** (store-bought, such as Walden Farms)
- ½ **tablespoon hoisin sauce**
- **Four 4-ounce wild salmon fillets,** skin on

Kale Salad
- 1 **teaspoon light olive oil**
- 1 **large head kale,** trimmed and finely sliced
- ¼ **teaspoon salt**
- 1 **tablespoon rice wine vinegar**
- 1 **tablespoon crushed walnuts**
- 2 **tablespoons golden raisins**
- 2 **tablespoons dried apricots,** chopped
- 1 **tablespoon finely chopped fresh cilantro**
- **Pinch pepper**

1. In a resealable bag, combine the BBQ sauce, hoisin sauce and salmon. Set aside to marinate.
2. Heat the olive oil in a wok or large pan over medium heat. Add the kale, salt and vinegar and sauté until softened, about 3 minutes.
3. Reduce the heat to medium-low and stir in the walnuts, raisins, apricots, cilantro and pepper until well blended. Remove from the heat.
4. Heat a gas grill to medium heat or 375°F.
5. Remove the salmon from the BBQ sauce and place it on a well-seasoned grill skin side down. Cook for 4 minutes per side. The salmon is done when it turns opaque. If you have a special grill rack for fish, use this instead.
6. Divide the salad among four plates, place the fish on top and serve.

Vegetarian Version
Marinate, skewer and grill cubes of tofu or eggplant.

Per serving: calories 281.3, total fat 12.1 g, saturated fat 0.5 g, cholesterol 60.1 mg, sodium 372.1 mg, potassium 943.8 mg, total carbohydrate 16.4 g, dietary fiber 3.3 g, sugars 5.1 g, protein 27.1 g

---

🍽 *High-Fiber Chocolate Date Biscotti*

Makes 15 to 20 biscotti

Biscotti dough is very delicate after its first baking, so be careful when slicing it. Biscotti are wonderful dipped in chilled soy milk and great as dessert and served for breakfast.

3 tablespoons grass-fed unsalted butter
½ cup xylitol or birch sugar
2 omega-3 eggs
1 teaspoon vanilla extract
½ cup blanched coarsely chopped almonds
½ cup finely chopped dates
½ cup semisweet chocolate chips
1 tablespoon ground flaxseed
1 teaspoon baking powder
½ teaspoon baking soda
Pinch salt
1¼ cups whole-wheat pastry flour, plus more for dusting
¼ cup almond flour or whole-wheat flour
¼ cup rolled oats

1. Preheat the oven to 350°F with the rack placed in the middle.
2. Using a mixer, mix the butter and sugar until light and smooth. Add the eggs, vanilla, almonds and dates. Mix until well combined. In a medium bowl, mix the chocolate chips, flaxseed, baking powder, baking soda, salt, flours and oats until well blended. Slowly add to the egg mixture and combine until a dough forms.
3. Turn the dough out onto a floured surface and divide it into two 6 x 3 x 1-inch logs. Transfer to a baking sheet. Bake for 25 minutes, or until golden brown.
4. Carefully transfer the log to a work area and, using a serrated knife, cut the log on a sharp diagonal into ¼-inch-thick slices. Transfer them back to the sheet pan. Bake them flat for 5 to 7 minutes. Remove from the oven. Let cool and serve.

Per biscotti: calories 118.7, total fat 5.6 g, saturated fat 2.2 g, cholesterol 26.2 mg, sodium 37.4 mg, potassium 75.0 mg, total carbohydrate 13.1 g, dietary fiber 2.2 g, sugars 5.3 g, protein 2.9 g

🍽 *Menopause Date Cheesecake*

Makes 4 individual pies, about 8 servings

This delectable cheesecake recipe is a no-bake alternative to the baked version. It is so creamy and delicious that it may become your standard cheesecake recipe.

Crust
½ cup whole-wheat pastry flour
¼ cup almond flour
½ tablespoon ground flaxseed
¼ teaspoon salt
1 teaspoon xylitol or birch sugar
¼ teaspoon ground cinnamon
3 tablespoons grass-fed unsalted butter

Filling
14 ounces silken tofu or low-fat ricotta
8 ounces low-fat cream cheese
½ cup xylitol or birch sugar
1 teaspoon vanilla extract
1 teaspoon cornstarch
1 teaspoon shaved 70% or more cacao dark chocolate
4 dates, finely chopped

1. Preheat the oven to 350°F with the rack placed in the middle.
2. In a food processor, combine the flours, flaxseed, salt, sugar, cinnamon and butter. Pulse until it looks like coarse crumbs. Slowly add ¼ cup ice-cold water a little at a time and pulse until the dough comes together. You may not need the entire ¼ cup.
3. Divide the dough into 4 parts, and press into 4-inch pie pans. Bake in the oven for 12 minutes.
4. In a medium bowl, mix the tofu or ricotta, cream cheese, sugar, vanilla and cornstarch until the ingredients are well combined. Pour into the baked pie shells. Refrigerate for 2 hours. Sprinkle the cheesecake with shaved chocolate and dates and serve.

Per serving (½ pie): calories 184.8, total fat 8.3 g, saturated fat 3.6 g, cholesterol 15.8 mg, sodium 105.7 mg, potassium 186.5 mg, total carbohydrate 13.3 g, dietary fiber 1.9 g, sugars 3.7 g, protein 7.2 g

🍽 *Migraine-Chasing Bean and Artichoke Soup*

Makes 4 servings

Vegetable soup is a Healing Kitchen staple. It's quick, cheap, delicious and nutritious. It's also particularly soothing for migraine sufferers when it's made with anti-inflammatory ginger and headache-calming beans.

1 tablespoon light olive oil
½ cup finely chopped shallots
1 can (19 ounces) white beans, drained and rinsed
1 quart low-sodium vegetable stock (store-bought or homemade)
4 canned artichoke hearts, finely chopped
1 tablespoon finely chopped fresh parsley
¼ teaspoon salt, or to taste
⅛ teaspoon freshly ground black pepper
1 teaspoon minced fresh garlic
1 teaspoon powdered ground ginger
4 tablespoons low-fat Greek yogurt (store-bought or homemade, see page 406)

1. Heat the olive oil in a large stockpot over medium-high heat. Add the shallots. Sauté the shallots until they are translucent, about 7 minutes. Reduce the heat to medium-low and add the beans, vegetable stock, artichokes, parsley, salt, pepper, garlic and ginger. Simmer for about 30 minutes, stirring occasionally. Taste and add more salt, if needed.

2. Distribute among four deep bowls, top with yogurt and serve.

Per serving: calories 307, total fat 4.2 g, saturated fat 0.8 g, cholesterol 0.0 mg, sodium 279.3 mg, potassium 981.0 mg, total carbohydrate 52.6 g, dietary fiber 11.1 g, sugars 3.2 g, protein 15.7 g

🍽 *Migraine-Healing Greek Yogurt Asparagus Salad*

Makes 2 servings

Caramelizing brings out the essence of vitamin-rich asparagus and makes it extra flavorful when combined with a savory yogurt sauce. For a lovely presentation, shape the salad using a food mold with an open top and bottom. It's equally good piled on a plate topped with a bit of cilantro.

Asparagus Salad

1 teaspoon light olive oil
½ **pound asparagus,** bottom inch of spears removed, and sliced into ¼-inch pieces
2 heaping cups fresh baby spinach
1 cup finely chopped fresh broccoli or halved fresh green beans
1 heaping tablespoon finely chopped dried cherries
2 teaspoons finely chopped fresh cilantro, divided
¼ teaspoon salt
1 tablespoon raw pumpkin seeds

Yogurt Dressing

½ teaspoon freshly squeezed lime juice
½ teaspoon curry powder
½ teaspoon freshly minced ginger
1 teaspoon minced fresh garlic
4 leaves fresh basil, finely chopped
½ **cup low-fat Greek yogurt** (store-bought or homemade, see page 406)

1. Heat the olive oil in a wok or large saucepan over medium-low heat. Add the asparagus, spinach, broccoli and cherries. Sauté until the asparagus is tender, about 3 minutes.

2. To make the dressing, in a small bowl, mix the lime juice, curry, ginger, garlic, basil and yogurt until well combined.

3. Add 1 teaspoon of the cilantro and the salt to the vegetables and toss. Add the vegetables to the bowl with the yogurt dressing. Stir until well blended.

4. To assemble the dish, place a round 3-inch mold in the center of a plate. Fill the mold with half the yogurt-vegetable mixture and press down lightly. Carefully remove the mold. Repeat this procedure on the second plate. Sprinkle each plate with the remaining teaspoon of cilantro and the pumpkin seeds and serve.

Per serving: calories 151.2, total fat 4.9 g, saturated fat 1.6 g, cholesterol 0.0 mg, sodium 179.9 mg, potassium 816.0 mg, total carbohydrate 18.4 g, dietary fiber 4.8 g, sugars 6.2 g, protein 8.6 g

🍴 *Head-Clearing Baked Vegetable Pie*

Makes 4 servings

Sweet fresh figs add an element of surprise to this crustless vegetable pie, which is held together by omega-3–rich eggs and the moisture from the migraine-fighting vegetables spinach and broccoli. It's excellent on its own, but try adding the optional toppings suggested. To prepare in advance, follow the recipe for the basic pie but bake only 10 minutes, then freeze. To serve, thaw the pie in the refrigerator, then bake for 20 minutes. Add toppings, if desired.

> **2 large omega-3 eggs**
> **1 tablespoon finely chopped fresh parsley**
> **¼ teaspoon salt**
> **1 cup shredded carrots**
> **1 cup fresh corn**
> **1 cup fresh spinach,** blanched and shocked (or microwaved for 20 seconds)
> **4 fresh figs,** stems removed and chopped
> **1 cup finely chopped broccoli florets**

1. Preheat the oven to 350°F.
2. In a medium bowl, whisk the eggs with the parsley and salt. Assemble successive layers of carrots, corn, spinach, figs and broccoli in two 4-ounce springform tart pans. Fill the pans almost to the top. Pour one-half of the egg mixture into each pan, distributing evenly over the vegetables. Cover each pan with foil to create a seal. Bake for 20 minutes, or until the egg has cooked through and is no longer runny.
3. Remove from the oven and let the tarts sit for a minute. Remove the pies from the springform pans. Serve, or add one of these optional toppings, which you can prepare while the pie is baking.

Vegetable Pie Toppings

> **1 teaspoon light olive oil**
> **Pinch salt**

One of the following:

> **5 large scallops,** quartered
> **6 ounces fresh salmon,** cut into 1-inch chunks
> **4 artichoke hearts** (frozen or canned), quartered
> **1 baked sweet potato,** peeled and diced
> **6 ounces free-range chicken tenders,** cut into 1-inch chunks
> **6 ounces buffalo fillet,** cut into 1-inch chunks

Heat the olive oil in a small pan over medium heat. Sauté the topping of your choice for 3 minutes or until golden brown. Season with salt and spoon on top of the vegetable pie.

Per serving: calories 302.9, total fat 6.9 g, saturated fat 1.8 g, cholesterol 202.4 mg, sodium 268.5 mg, potassium 1,038.7 mg, total carbohydrate 48.3 g, dietary fiber 9.0 g, sugars 25.9 g, protein 18.0 g

Migraine-Conquering Moroccan Chicken and Couscous

Makes 4 servings

This easy, one-pot meal gets its flavor from the most popular (and healthy!) seasonings of Morocco: cardamom, ginger, turmeric and cinnamon. If you don't finish it at dinner, tuck the leftovers into whole-grain pita pockets for a flavorful lunch.

2 large free-range boneless, skinless chicken breasts, cut into 1-inch cubes
1 tablespoon Moroccan Seasoning (recipe follows)
1 teaspoon light olive oil
1 large white onion, cut into ¼-inch slices
2½ cups low-sodium chicken broth, plus ¼ cup, if needed
1 cup couscous
4 fresh figs, stemmed and roughly chopped
4 heaping cups fresh baby spinach
1 tablespoon finely chopped fresh mint

1. Coat the chicken breasts with 1 tablespoon of Moroccan Seasoning.
2. Heat the olive oil in a Dutch oven over medium heat. Add the onions and sauté for 3 minutes. Add the chicken and cook until all sides are golden brown, about 3 minutes. Don't worry if the chicken sticks initially; it will release as it browns.
3. Add the broth to the pan, making sure the chicken is completely covered. Lower the heat to a moderate simmer and cook for 25 minutes, stirring occasionally. After 20 minutes, stir in the couscous, figs and spinach. The couscous will cook quickly, about 5 minutes, and the figs and spinach will soften.
4. Divide among four deep bowls, sprinkle with mint and serve.

Moroccan Seasoning

1 tablespoon ground turmeric
1 tablespoon ground ginger
1 teaspoon ground cinnamon
1 teaspoon ground cardamom
Pinch cayenne pepper

In a small bowl, thoroughly mix the turmeric, ginger, cinnamon, cardamom and cayenne. Store any leftover seasoning in a jar.

Vegetarian Version

In place of chicken, use 6 whole artichoke hearts (frozen or canned), quartered, or 2 potatoes, baked and diced.

Per serving: calories 333.6, total fat 3.0 g, saturated fat 0.6 g, cholesterol 48.4 mg, sodium 129.5 mg, potassium 710.5 mg, total carbohydrate 48.9 g, dietary fiber 5.8 g, sugars 10.4 g, protein 27.3 g

¶◉¶ *Headache-Calming Clams with Vinaigrette*

Makes 4 servings

Try serving these easy-to-prepare Mediterranean-inspired clams as an appetizer. The clams are loaded with migraine-friendly riboflavin and delicious spooned over brown rice, which is also soothing.

1 tablespoon light olive oil
1½ cups yellow bell pepper, cored, seeded and finely chopped
2 tablespoons minced roasted garlic
2 cups low-sodium vegetable broth
1 teaspoon salt
½ cup white wine
Approximately 50 littleneck clams, cleaned (see below)
5 large spinach leaves, stems removed and finely chopped
2 whole canned artichoke hearts, quartered
2 tablespoons finely chopped fresh parsley
Pinch cayenne

1. Heat the olive oil in a large pot over medium heat. Add the bell peppers and garlic. Sauté for about 2 minutes or until the peppers have softened. Add the vegetable broth, salt, wine and clams. Cover and cook until the clams are opened, about 3 minutes. Discard all clams that have not opened.

2. Add the spinach and artichokes. Stir gently. The spinach should wilt immediately. Add the parsley and cayenne.

3. Divide among four shallow bowls and serve.

To clean clams: Soak in cold water with a pinch of cornmeal or flour for 10 minutes, scrub the outside shells, then rinse with fresh water. Repeat this process until the water runs clean, or about 4 times. The clams will open to digest the cornmeal and therefore release any sand. The clams are clean when the soaking water is free of sand.

Per serving: calories 213.6, total fat 4.8 g, saturated fat 0.5 g, cholesterol 62.5 mg, sodium 215.8 mg, potassium 156.9 mg, total carbohydrate 10.7 g, dietary fiber 1.1 g, sugars 1.1 g, protein 24.6 g

---

Migraine-Fighting Spinach and Goat Cheese Tarts

Makes 4 servings

Savory tarts made with goat cheese and spinach, which has lots of migraine-fighting omega-3 fatty acids, are perfect for parties and open to improvisation. Once you've perfected this recipe, try adding other healthy ingredients (like tuna, halibut or wild Pacific salmon) to the mix. To prepare the tarts ahead of time, assemble in the springform pan, seal it well with plastic wrap and freeze. To serve, just thaw in the refrigerator and bake.

6½ cups fresh baby spinach, washed
4 ounces goat or ricotta cheese
4 tablespoons mashed white beans (canned is fine, rinse before using)
Fresh herbs, such as parsley, basil, chives, rosemary or dill
1 sweet potato, peeled and cut into ⅛-inch-thick slices
1 tablespoon crushed pecans
1 teaspoon raw pumpkin seeds

1. Preheat the oven to 350°F.
2. In a medium pot, wilt the fresh spinach over low heat using the water left on the leaves after washing. Add the goat cheese, white beans and herbs and mix until smooth. Remove from the heat.
3. In four individual 4-ounce springform pans, assemble the tarts by alternating layers of sweet potato slices and 1 tablespoon of the spinach-goat cheese mixture. Use a few potato slices per layer. Fill up each springform pan, loosely cover with foil and bake for 40 minutes, or until the sweet potatoes are soft.
4. Remove the tarts from the oven and let them sit for a minute or so to firm up. Remove the tarts from the springform pans. Sprinkle with pecans and pumpkin seeds and serve.

Per serving: calories 120.2, total fat 3.6 g, saturated fat 1.2 g, cholesterol 15.0 mg, sodium 111.7 mg, potassium 497.1 mg, total carbohydrate 15.7 g, dietary fiber 4.0 g, sugars 6.1 g, protein 9.4 g

🍽 *No More Migraines Salmon Croquette Pita Pockets*

Makes 2 servings

These Healing Kitchen croquettes, which are packed with omega-3 fatty acids from the salmon and egg, are lightly sautéed…but just as tasty as the traditional versions.

Croquettes

1 teaspoon light olive oil, plus 1 tablespoon for sautéing croquettes
½ cup minced white onions
6 ounces fresh salmon, cut into 1-inch pieces
¼ cup whole-wheat breadcrumbs
2 tablespoons feta cheese, rinsed and crumbled
1 omega-3 egg
3 tablespoons finely chopped fresh mint
½ teaspoon finely chopped fresh oregano

Yogurt Sauce

½ cup no-fat Greek yogurt (store-bought or homemade, see page 406)
1 tablespoon finely chopped fresh cilantro
Pinch freshly ground black pepper

Pita Pockets

1 fresh whole-wheat pita pocket
1 cup fresh spinach
¼ avocado, peeled, pit removed and sliced
2 plum tomatoes, cored and sliced
1 lemon, cut into wedges

1. Heat 1 teaspoon olive oil in a medium pan over medium-low heat. Add the onions. Sauté until they soften, about 5 minutes. Remove from heat. Transfer the onions to a food processor. Add the salmon, breadcrumbs, feta cheese, egg, mint and oregano to the food processor and pulse until well blended. Divide the mixture into four parts and roll each into a firm ball.

2. Heat 1 tablespoon olive oil in a large sauté pan over medium heat. Place the croquettes in the pan and sauté until golden brown, about 2 minutes per side. These croquettes are delicate and fall apart easily, so turn them gently. Cook each croquette thoroughly. The salmon will become firm and opaque when it's done.

3. In a small bowl, mix the yogurt, cilantro and pepper until well blended.

4. Cut the pita in half to form two smaller pockets. Stuff each with spinach, avocado and tomatoes and carefully add two croquettes to each pocket. Generously cover each pocket's stuffing with half of the yogurt sauce and serve with lemon wedges.

Vegetarian Version

Substitute one 14.5-ounce can navy beans, rinsed, for the salmon.

Per serving: calories 376, total fat 17.9 g, saturated fat 3.3 g, cholesterol 145.0 mg, sodium 374.8 mg, potassium 716.0 mg, total carbohydrate 20.6 g, dietary fiber 4.8 g, sugars 2.2 g, protein 29.7 g

---

🍽 *Headache-Be-Gone Banana Cream Pie*

Makes one 10-inch pie, about 10 servings

I like to freeze my banana cream pie before serving to help it set. This recipe can also be prepared as individual pies; simply divide as appropriate.

Crust

> 1 cup whole-wheat pastry flour
> ¼ cup almond flour
> ¼ cup quick-cooking oats
> 1 tablespoon ground flaxseed
> 2 tablespoons chopped pumpkin seeds
> 4 tablespoons unsalted butter from grass-fed cows

Filling

> 8 ounces low-fat cream cheese, softened
> 14 ounces low-fat vanilla yogurt
> 2 very ripe bananas, mashed
> ¾ cup xylitol or birch sugar
> 1 teaspoon vanilla extract

1. Preheat the oven to 350°F with the rack placed in the middle.
2. In a blender, pulse the flours, oats, flaxseed and pumpkin seeds until well blended. Add the butter and pulse until it starts to come together. Add 1 tablespoon ice water, if necessary, and pulse again. Press into a 10-inch pie pan. Prick the bottom of the crust with a fork.
3. Line the crust with aluminum foil and fill with dried beans. Bake for 10 minutes, remove the foil and beans and bake for another 2 minutes. Remove from the oven.
4. In a large bowl, mix the cream cheese, yogurt, banana, sugar and vanilla until well combined. Pour into the pie shell and freeze for 1½ hours before serving.

Per serving: calories 255, total fat 10.6 g, saturated fat 5.6 g, cholesterol 25.1 mg, sodium 122.8 mg, potassium 263.5 mg, total carbohydrate 25.1 g, dietary fiber 2.7 g, sugars 9.5 g, protein 7.2 g

🍽 *Bone-Strengthening Greek Tzatziki Dip with Vegetables*

Makes 4 servings

Greek tzatziki dip is a creamy combo of yogurt, garlic and cucumbers that's great as a bone-strengthening dip with fresh vegetables. Don't hesitate to slather it on roasted vegetables—or roasted meats or fish, for that matter. Refrigerate the dip before serving—it's extra refreshing when cold, especially if you're serving it with something spicy. The fresher the yogurt, the better the dip, so consider taking the time to make Greek yogurt from scratch (recipe on page 406).

Raw Vegetables

   2 cups baby carrots
   2 cups zucchini spears
   2 cups broccoli florets
   2 cups cucumber spears
   2 cups baby green beans

Tzatziki Dip

   2 cups low-fat Greek yogurt (store-bought or homemade, see page 406)
   1 large fresh garlic clove, mashed with a pinch of salt
   1 tablespoon lemon juice
   2 tablespoons fresh dill, chopped
   1 teaspoon freshly ground black pepper
   1 teaspoon salt
   1/3 cup peeled, finely diced cucumbers (Kirby or English seedless)

1. Arrange the vegetables on a decorative platter with a ramekin in the center for the dip.
2. In a medium bowl, mix the yogurt, garlic, lemon juice, dill, pepper, salt and cucumbers until well combined.
3. Transfer to the ramekin and serve.

Per serving: calories 188.2, total fat 3.9 g, saturated fat 2.2 g, cholesterol 0.0 mg, sodium 207.5 mg, potassium 831.1 mg, total carbohydrate 26.1 g, dietary fiber 6.2 g, sugars 11.6 g, protein 10.4

Super-Calcium Shrimp and Vegetable Egg-Drop Soup

Makes 6 servings

You'll be tempted to stir the omega-3 egg once you pour it into the hot broth, but resist the urge. You'll be rewarded with a soup that looks and tastes like the kind served at your favorite Chinese restaurant. Calcium- and vitamin-dense greens and broccoli make every spoonful of this egg-drop soup as nutritious as it is delicious.

½ **teaspoon miso paste***
1 **teaspoon minced fresh garlic**
½ **teaspoon minced fresh ginger**
2 **quarts low-sodium vegetable broth**
1 **large carrot,** peeled and shredded
1–1½ **pounds fresh broccoli,** cut into 2-inch florets (about 4 cups)
4 **cups finely chopped greens,** such as escarole or kale
½ **teaspoon salt**
1 **pound small shrimp,** deveined and shelled
2 **omega-3 eggs,** beaten

1. In a stockpot, combine the miso paste, garlic, ginger, vegetable broth, carrot, broccoli, greens and salt. Cook on medium-high heat for 10 minutes or until the vegetables are somewhat tender.
2. Reduce the heat to medium. Add the shrimp and the eggs. Do not stir the soup; instead, allow it to rest until the shrimp and eggs are cooked through, about 2 minutes.
3. Divide among six soup bowls and serve.

Frugal Options

Consider omitting the shrimp.

Miso substitute: ½ tablespoon of low-sodium soy sauce mixed with ½ tablespoon of chicken stock for the miso.

Per serving: calories 182.5, total fat 3.6 g, saturated fat 0.7 g, cholesterol 178.2 mg, sodium 387.2 mg, potassium 707.7 mg, total carbohydrate 16.3 g, dietary fiber 6.5 g, sugars 4.3 g, protein 22.2 g

---

Osteoporosis-Conquering Athena Salad

Makes 4 servings

This salad is bursting with distinctive flavors, thanks to classic Mediterranean ingredients such as garlic, anchovies, olives and feta cheese. Try doubling the dressing recipe. You can store it in the refrigerator for up to seven days, and it's so good that you'll find all kinds of ways to use it.

Athena Salad

2 large heads romaine lettuce, rinsed, dried and torn into bite-sized pieces
5 radishes, ends removed and thinly sliced
1 cucumber, peeled, seeded and thinly sliced
½ scallion, ends removed and thinly sliced
1 cup canned beans (your choice)
4 canned artichoke hearts, quartered
1 heaping tablespoon raw sunflower seeds

Mediterranean Flavors Dressing

1 tablespoon finely chopped fresh dill
1 tablespoon thinly sliced garlic or 1 large garlic clove, mashed with a pinch of salt
1 tablespoon red wine vinegar
3 tablespoons extra-virgin olive oil
8 black California olives, finely chopped, or 1 teaspoon olive paste
2 tablespoons feta cheese, rinsed and crumbled
½ teaspoon capers
½ teaspoon anchovy paste
1 teaspoon freshly squeezed lemon juice

1. In a large bowl, toss the lettuce, radishes, cucumbers, scallions, beans, artichoke hearts and sunflower seeds until well combined.
2. In a medium bowl, mix the dill, garlic, vinegar, olive oil, olives, feta cheese, capers, anchovy paste, and lemon juice until well blended.
3. Pour the dressing over the salad and toss until the leaves are well coated. Divide among four plates and serve.

Frugal Option

Omit the feta cheese.

Per serving: calories 243.4, total fat 14.2 g, saturated fat 2.5 g, cholesterol 2.7 mg, sodium 384.9 mg, potassium 737.7 mg, total carbohydrate 22.2 g, dietary fiber 7.2 g, sugars 1.2 g, protein 9.7 g

🍽 *Strong Bones Salmon with Kale Salad*

Makes 4 servings

This dish is served with a kale salad that's loaded with calcium, among other healing nutrients. Experiment until you find just the right balance of flour and oil, so that the fish is neither too heavy nor too oily.

Salmon Fillet

1 cup whole-wheat pastry flour
½ cup finely chopped fresh parsley
2 egg yolks, beaten, or ½ cup skim milk
1 pound fresh wild salmon fillet, skin removed, cut widthwise into 1-inch pieces
1 tablespoon light olive oil
1 teaspoon salt

Kale Salad

¼ cup finely chopped shallots
¼ cup finely chopped fresh cilantro
½ cup low-fat Greek yogurt, store-bought or prepared following the recipe on page 406
1 avocado, peeled, pit removed and finely diced
7 cups fresh kale, finely chopped
1 tablespoon raw pumpkin seeds

1. In a shallow bowl, combine the flour and parsley. Mix until well blended. Pour the egg or milk into another shallow bowl and place it next to the flour mixture.
2. Dip each salmon piece into the egg or milk, shake off excess liquid, then dredge in the flour mixture. Let the dredged pieces dry on a rack for a few minutes.
3. Heat the olive oil in a large sauté pan over medium heat. Carefully place the fish in the hot oil, sprinkle it with the salt and fry until golden brown, about 2 minutes per side. Remove from the heat and transfer to a plate.
4. In a large bowl, mix the shallots, cilantro, yogurt and avocado until well combined. Add the kale and stir until well coated.
5. Divide the salad among four plates and sprinkle each with pumpkin seeds. Top with the salmon and serve.

Vegetarian Option

In place of salmon in this recipe, use broccoli or cauliflower florets or tofu, cut into 1-inch pieces. Coat the cut-up vegetables in the flour mixture, as described above, and fry following recipe instructions.

Frugal Option

Use frozen fish in place of fresh.

Per serving: calories 410.3, total fat 19.4 g, saturated fat 2.1 g, cholesterol 73.6 mg, sodium 198.1 mg, potassium 1,568.3 mg, total carbohydrate 27.8 g, dietary fiber 8.7 g, sugars 4.9 g, protein 31.4 g

---

🍴 *Mighty Calcium Citrus Salmon Burgers Over Salad Greens*

Makes 4 servings

The all-American burger goes Mediterr-Asian and in the process becomes a more healing taste treat. Salmon, which is rich in calcium and vitamin D, makes a light and zesty burger when spiced with garlic and black pepper. The citrus glaze adds fruity zing. Serve atop a pile of leafy greens, with zinc-rich pumpkin seeds for extra crunch.

Citrus Glaze

> 1 teaspoon light olive oil
> ¼ cup finely chopped shallots
> ½ cup canned mandarin orange segments

Salmon Burger

> 1 egg
> 1 pound fresh wild salmon, bones removed and roughly chopped
> 1 teaspoon salt
> 1 teaspoon minced garlic
> Pinch freshly ground black pepper
> ½ cup whole-grain breadcrumbs* or cooked brown rice
> 2 tablespoons light olive oil

Salad Greens

> 4 heaping cups leafy greens
> 1 tablespoon raw pumpkin seeds

*To make your own breadcrumbs, tear two slices of lightly toasted whole-grain bread into pieces and chop up finely with a food processor.

1. For the glaze, heat the olive oil in a small saucepan over medium heat. Sauté the shallots for 7 minutes, or until they have softened.
2. Reduce the heat to low and add the mandarin segments and cook for another 2 minutes.
3. Make the patties next. In a food processor, combine the egg, salmon, salt, garlic, pepper and breadcrumbs. Pulse for a few seconds, until the mixture begins to hold together. Form the mixture into four patties. They will be fairly moist.
4. Heat the olive oil, in a skillet large enough to hold the burgers, over medium heat. The pan is ready when the oil ripples across the pan, or about 1 minute. Fry the burgers until golden brown, about 3 minutes per side, gently turning once with a thin metal spatula.
5. Mound some of the greens on each of four plates. Top each with a burger, drizzle glaze over the top, sprinkle with pumpkin seeds and serve.

Frugal Option

> Canned salmon makes a burger almost as delicious as fresh (and it's higher in healing calcium).

Per serving: calories 304.2, total fat 16.8 g, saturated fat 1.4 g, cholesterol 120.8 mg, sodium 143.2 mg, potassium 917.5 mg, total carbohydrate 11.4 g, dietary fiber 1.4 g, sugars 2.1 g, protein 26.1 g

---

Bone-Building Asian Broccoli and Chicken

Makes 4 servings

Sweet, calcium-rich mango gives this quick and easy stir-fry a delightful zing. The secret is in the sauce, which is added to the wok at the very last minute. As the sauce heats, the mango juices meld with the sesame oil and pungent cilantro to infuse the dish with flavor.

Stir-Fry

1 teaspoon light olive oil
1½ pounds free-range boneless, skinless chicken breast, cut into 1-inch cubes
1–1½ pounds fresh broccoli, cut into florets with 1-inch stems, about 4 cups
4 cups greens, such as kale or escarole
½ teaspoon salt, or to taste

Mango Sauce

2 tablespoons finely chopped dried mango
2 tablespoons finely chopped fresh cilantro leaves
8 fresh basil leaves, finely chopped
1 teaspoon fresh minced garlic
1 tablespoon sesame oil

1. Heat the olive oil in a wok or large skillet over medium heat. Add the chicken and sauté for 5 minutes, stirring occasionally.
2. To make the mango sauce, in a small bowl, combine the mango, cilantro, basil, garlic and sesame oil.
3. Add the broccoli to the pan and sauté for another 2 minutes. The chicken should now be cooked through and its flesh opaque. Remove from the heat.
4. Stir in the sauce and greens. Toss until well combined. The greens should wilt.
5. Divide among four plates and serve with a sprinkle of salt.

Vegetarian Option

Use quartered frozen or canned artichoke hearts or cubes of cooked winter squash instead of chicken.

Per serving: calories 286.8, total fat 7.3 g, saturated fat 1.3 g, cholesterol 99.0 mg, sodium 214.8 mg, potassium 1,113.0 mg, total carbohydrate 10.4 g, dietary fiber 5.4 g, sugars 1.1 g, protein 44.8 g

Fracture-Fighting Winter Squash Teriyaki

Makes 4 servings

Although teriyaki sauce is often paired with chicken or fish, it's also surprisingly tasty when served with antioxidant-rich winter squash. Teriyaki sauce's flavor mellows as it cooks, so you may want to add more before serving.

1 teaspoon light olive oil
1 large butternut or other winter squash, peeled, seeded and shredded, about 3 pounds
1 cup pineapple juice
1 teaspoon minced ginger
1 teaspoon minced garlic
2 teaspoons low-sodium soy sauce
3 tablespoons low-sodium teriyaki sauce
½ teaspoon salt
½ head cabbage, or 4 cups kale, sliced into thin ribbons
¼ cup crushed pecans, optional

1. Heat the olive oil in a wok or large sauté pan over medium heat. Add the squash, pineapple juice, ginger, garlic, soy sauce, teriyaki sauce and salt. Make sure the squash is completely covered by the liquid.

2. Cook until the squash is tender, about 15 minutes.

3. Bring ½ cup of water to a boil in a large, deep skillet. Add the cabbage and reduce the heat to a simmer. Cook until the cabbage has softened and the water has evaporated, about 8 minutes.

4. Remove from the heat. Stir into the squash mixture.

5. Divide evenly among four plates, sprinkle with pecans if desired and serve.

Per serving: calories 271.6, total fat 7.1 g, saturated fat 0.7 g, cholesterol 0.0 mg, sodium 355.0 mg, potassium 1,432.5 mg, total carbohydrate 53.5 g, dietary fiber 13.9 g, sugars 11.0 g, protein 5.3 g

Calcium-Rich Sautéed Spaghetti

Makes 4 servings

Spaghetti is one of the most popular and versatile pastas and can be served with just about anything. To add a healing dimension, serve spaghetti dishes with more vegetables and sauce than pasta and protein. This veggie-based sauce is rich in bone-building calcium and antioxidants. Feel free to experiment by adding or substituting your favorite healing ingredients.

¾ pound whole-wheat spaghetti
1 teaspoon light olive oil
2 tablespoons finely chopped shallots
1 red bell pepper, cored, seeded and finely chopped
1 tablespoon fresh chopped parsley leaves
12 ounces of healthy protein: choose from sea scallops (quartered), tofu (½-inch cubes) or
   free-range chicken breast (½-inch cubes)
1 teaspoon freshly squeezed lemon juice
1 teaspoon garlic paste
4 cups torn greens, such as escarole or kale
Pinch of salt

1. Cook the pasta according to package directions (it should be a little firm, because it will cook more in the pan). Drain.
2. Heat the olive oil in a wok or large sauté pan over medium heat. Add the shallots and red bell peppers. Sauté until soft, about 5 minutes.
3. Add the parsley, your choice of protein, lemon juice and garlic. Sauté for 2 minutes, or until the scallops or chicken pieces (if using) are cooked through.
4. Reduce the heat to low. Add the greens, spaghetti and salt. Toss until the greens begin to wilt.
5. Divide the spaghetti among four plates and serve.

Vegetarian Option
   Substitute 12 ounces cauliflower for the chicken or seafood.

Frugal Option
   Consider using frozen peppers instead of fresh.

Per serving: calories 409.5, total fat 4.5 g, saturated fat 0.3 g, cholesterol 28.1 mg, sodium 221.0 mg, potassium 645.2 mg, total carbohydrate 73.9 g, dietary fiber 12.2 g, sugars 4.6 g, protein 27.7 g

---

🍴 *Osteoporosis-Banishing Braised Chicken and Vegetable Ragout*

Makes 4 servings

Rich, savory and perfect for building healthy bones due to its osteoporosis-fighting beans and winter squash, this thick ragout is perfect on a chilly fall or winter evening. The sauce will thicken as it cools, resulting in a dish that's heartier than it might at first appear. Make sure to use a whole chicken or bone-in parts, not boneless breasts, because the bones add much to the dish's flavor and calcium content. If you're feeling creative, substitute turkey parts or a whole rabbit for the chicken.

One 2-pound free-range chicken
½ cup whole-grain pastry flour
1 tablespoon light olive oil
1 white onion, finely diced
1 butternut or other winter squash, about 3 pounds, peeled, seeded and shredded
1½ quarts low-sodium chicken stock
2 teaspoons finely chopped fresh thyme leaves
1 tablespoon finely chopped fresh parsley leaves
¼ teaspoon black pepper
¼ cup red or white wine, optional
1 cup canned white beans

1. Place the chicken on a flat surface. Cut it up into pieces or leave it whole. Dredge the chicken in the flour, pressing the flour into the meat with your fingers, if necessary, to make the flour adhere.
2. Heat the olive oil in a large Dutch oven over medium heat. Carefully add the chicken and brown on both sides, about 3 to 4 minutes per side. The chicken may stick, but it will release as it browns.
3. Add the onions and sauté for about 5 minutes, until they have softened.
4. Add the squash, chicken stock, thyme, parsley, pepper and wine, if using. Bring to a boil, then reduce the heat to a simmer.
5. Add the beans, cover and cook for 40 minutes. Turn the chicken after 20 minutes.
6. Remove from the heat and partially uncover. Let rest for about 10 minutes. Spoon the vegetables, chicken and sauce onto each of four plates and serve.

Vegetarian Option

Substitute kale for the chicken.

Note: To reduce the fat content, remove the skin and skip the browning process.

Per serving: calories 635.2, total fat 21.0 g, saturated fat 5.4 g, cholesterol 100.8 mg, sodium 124.4 mg, potassium 1,869.9 mg, total carbohydrate 80.3 g, dietary fiber 20.7 g, sugars 0.0 g, protein 34.6 g

---

🍽 *Better Bones Chocolate Ricotta Tart*

Makes 4 individual tarts, for 8 servings

I like to prepare individual tarts for easier storage and serving.

Fruit-Nut Crust

1 tablespoon vanilla extract
4 tablespoons unsalted butter from grass-fed cows
¼ cup finely chopped walnuts
6 roughly chopped dried figs
¼ cup xylitol or birch sugar
1½ cups quick-cooking oats
¼ cup almond flour

Ricotta Filling

1 pound low-fat ricotta
1 cup low-fat vanilla yogurt
1 cup xylitol or birch sugar
4 omega-3 eggs
1 teaspoon orange zest
3 fresh figs, stems removed and sliced
1 tablespoon 70% cacao powder, optional

1. Place an oven rack on the middle shelf of the oven and preheat to 350°F.
2. In a food processor fitted with the steel blade, pulse the vanilla, butter, walnuts, figs, sugar, oats and almond flour until a smooth dough is formed.
3. Divide the dough into four pieces and press into four 4-inch springform pans.
4. In a medium bowl, mix the ricotta, yogurt, sugar, eggs and zest until well blended. Pour into the springform pans. Bake for 1 hour.
5. Remove from the oven to cool slightly.
6. Serve topped with the figs and chocolate, if using.

Per ½ tart: calories 386.0, total fat 16.1 g, saturated fat 7.0 g, cholesterol 144.3 mg, sodium 313.5 mg, potassium 230.8 mg, total carbohydrate 28.6 g, dietary fiber 3.8 g, sugars 16.8 g, protein 14.6 g

🍽 *Prostate-Healing Vegetable Teriyaki*

Makes 4 servings

No more excuses for not eating right when time is tight: You can prepare this delectable Japanese-inspired dish in 15 minutes or so, including prep time. Teriyaki sauce and tangy pomegranate juice add a complex flavor to nutrient-dense vegetables like broccoli and cauliflower. For more protein power, try adding shrimp or grass-fed beef or buffalo.

1 teaspoon light olive oil
3 large heads broccoli, trimmed into 2-inch florets
1½ cups finely chopped cauliflower
1 cup pomegranate juice
1 teaspoon minced ginger
3 tablespoons low-sodium teriyaki sauce
½ teaspoon salt
1 cup cooked brown rice
4 cups finely chopped kale
2 tablespoons raw pumpkin seeds

1. Heat the olive oil in a wok or large saucepan over medium heat. Add the broccoli, cauliflower, pomegranate juice, ginger, teriyaki sauce and salt. Cook until the broccoli is tender, about 5 minutes. Stir the mixture occasionally, to be sure that the vegetables cook evenly.

2. Lower the heat to medium-low and add the brown rice and kale. Toss until well coated.

3. Divide the vegetable teriyaki among four plates, spoon any additional sauce from the pot over the vegetables, sprinkle with pumpkin seeds and serve.

Frugal Option

Use 100% unsweetened apple juice for pomegranate juice.

Per serving: calories 230.0, total fat 3.4 g, saturated fat 0.6 g, cholesterol 0.0 mg, sodium 362.7 mg, potassium 1,318.2 mg, total carbohydrate 44.7 g, dietary fiber 11.3 g, sugars 12.4 g, protein 12.0 g

---

Virility Veggies with Edamame-Miso Rice

Makes 4 servings

Edamame—or fresh soybeans—are very popular in Japan, where they're often eaten steamed and sprinkled with coarse salt or spices. You can find these green, high-protein beans in the frozen food section of almost any grocery store.

Edamame-Miso Rice

> 2 teaspoons miso paste*
> 1 cup brown jasmine rice
> 2 cups frozen shelled edamame beans
> Pinch salt
> 1 tablespoon pumpkin seeds
> Pinch red pepper flakes, optional

Vegetables

> 1 teaspoon light olive oil
> 1 pound healing vegetables in any combination, such as the following:
> Asparagus, woody ends removed
> Broccoli, stems removed and cut into 2-inch florets
> Fresh green beans, ends trimmed
> Carrot, peeled and minced
> Fresh baby spinach

1. Add 2 cups water to a medium saucepan. Whisk the miso paste into the water until it dissolves. Cook the rice, using the miso-infused water, according to package directions.
2. When the rice is almost done, stir in the frozen edamame. Replace the lid and finish cooking.
3. Heat olive oil in a wok or large saucepan over medium heat. Add the vegetables and sauté until tender, about 4 minutes. Remove from the heat. Add the spinach, if using, which will wilt when it hits the pan.
4. Divide the rice among four plates, top with vegetables, sprinkle with salt, pumpkin seeds and red pepper flakes, if using, and serve.

Frugal Option

Substitute canned black beans for edamame.

Miso substitute: ½ tablespoon low-sodium soy sauce mixed with ½ tablespoon low-sodium chicken stock.

Per serving: calories 224.1, total fat 7.9 g, saturated fat 1.0 g, cholesterol 0.0 mg, sodium 419.1 mg, potassium 780.1 mg, total carbohydrate 27.2 g, dietary fiber 7.0 g, sugars 1.0 g, protein 14.6 g

---

Super-Lycopene Italian Marinara Sauce with Eggplant

Makes 4 servings

Eggplant adds a twist to this well-seasoned, lycopene-packed marinara. Try it over omega-3 baked wild snapper for mega prostate-healing power.

Eggplant

1 large eggplant, peeled, ends removed and cut into 1-inch cubes
1 tablespoon salt
1 tablespoon olive oil

Marinara Sauce

1 tablespoon light olive oil
1 large white onion, finely chopped
2 anchovy fillets, rinsed, dried and finely chopped
1 can (28 ounces) organic crushed tomatoes
1 teaspoon Italian Seasoning blend (store-bought or prepared following the recipe below)
4 fresh basil leaves, whole
1 teaspoon salt
¼ teaspoon freshly ground black pepper

1. Place the eggplant cubes in a colander in the sink and sprinkle with salt. Set aside for 1 hour. Rinse the eggplant to remove excess salt. Pat dry.

2. To make the sauce, heat the olive oil in a large, heavy pot over medium-high heat. Add the onions and sauté until translucent, about 8 minutes. Reduce the heat to medium-low and add the anchovies, crushed tomatoes, Italian Seasoning, basil leaves, salt and pepper. Stir until well combined. Reduce the heat to low, and simmer for 20 minutes.

3. Heat the olive oil in a wok or pan over medium heat. Sauté the eggplant until tender, about 8 minutes. Remove from the heat. Add the eggplant to the sauce. Divide the eggplant among four bowls and serve.

Italian Seasoning

Makes ½ cup

2 tablespoons dried basil
2 tablespoons dried marjoram
2 tablespoons dried oregano
2 tablespoons dried ground rosemary

Combine and mix well. Store in a jar.

Per serving: calories 159.4, total fat 7.1 g, saturated fat 1.0 g, cholesterol 0.9 mg, sodium 155.1 mg, potassium 319.3 mg, total carbohydrate 23.9 g, dietary fiber 6.6 g, sugars 10.5 g, protein 3.4 g

---

Prostate-Soothing Mighty Omega Baked Cod with Parmesan Rice

Makes 4 servings

Cod—rich in vitamins and omega-3 fatty acids—is as healing as it is versatile. Serve it on a bed of baked Parmesan rice for a simple but rich meal. Try adding a bit of minced hot peppers to the rice to give it extra bite and extra prostate-healing power.

Cod

Four 4-ounce cod fillets
½ teaspoon salt
Pinch freshly ground white pepper
1 tablespoon light olive oil

Baked Parmesan Rice

1 cup cooked brown jasmine rice
Pinch salt
2 plum tomatoes, cored, seeded and chopped
1–1½ pounds broccoli, trimmed and cut into 2-inch florets
1 cup frozen peas
¼ cup freshly grated Parmesan cheese
2 tablespoons raw pumpkin seeds

1. Position racks on the bottom and middle shelves of the oven and preheat to 400°F. Place the cod fillets on a baking sheet, skin side down. Season with salt and white pepper and drizzle with olive oil. Bake for 20 minutes or until the cod is opaque and flakes easily.

2. Spread the rice out in a casserole dish and season with salt. Top the rice with the chopped tomatoes, broccoli and peas. Bake for 12 minutes. Sprinkle the rice with Parmesan cheese and pumpkin seeds and bake for 5 more minutes, or until the cheese is crispy.

3. To serve, place one scoop of rice in the center of each of four plates, place a cod fillet on top of the rice and serve immediately.

Frugal Option

Use organic canned tomatoes instead of fresh.

Per serving: calories 277.0, total fat 7.4 g, saturated fat 2.0 g, cholesterol 46.9 mg, sodium 308.9 mg, potassium 821.8 mg, total carbohydrate 22.1 g, dietary fiber 5.1 g, sugars 1.9 g, protein 29.0 g

🍽 *Asian Pomegranate Shrimp-Noodle Salad*

Makes 4 servings

Tart pomegranate juice, spicy garlic and salty peanut butter combine to infuse this luscious noodle salad with light, bright flavor. (The sauce is so good you'll want to use it on other dishes.) Large shrimp may be used: Leave them in the wok for a minute or two longer, until they are opaque.

Asian Sauce

> 1 tablespoon pomegranate juice
> 1 tablespoon miso paste*
> 2 teaspoons tahini paste, optional
> 1 teaspoon lemon juice
> ½ teaspoon garlic paste
> 1 heaping tablespoon peanut butter
> 1 teaspoon sesame oil

Noodles and Shrimp

> ¾ pound rice noodles or whole-wheat linguini
> 1 teaspoon light olive oil
> 1 bunch kale, rinsed and cut into bite-sized pieces
> ½ pound medium shrimp, deveined, shelled and butterflied
> ¼ cucumber, peeled and slivered
> 1 tablespoon sesame seeds or raw pumpkin seeds

1. In a mini food processor, combine the pomegranate juice, miso paste, tahini paste, if using, lemon juice, garlic paste, peanut butter, sesame oil and 2 tablespoons of water. Pulse until a smooth paste is formed. If it is very thick, add up to 1 more tablespoon of water.
2. Cook the noodles according to package directions. Drain and return to the pot. Add the sauce and toss to blend well.
3. Heat the olive oil in a wok or pan over medium heat. Add the kale and sauté until it begins to wilt, or about 1 minute. Add the shrimp and sauté until opaque. Remove from the heat.
4. Divide the noodles among four plates, top with the shrimp and kale, sprinkle with the cucumbers and pumpkin seeds and serve.

Vegetarian Option

Instead of shrimp, use 1 cup of cauliflower florets, broccoli florets, asparagus and/or green beans.

Frugal Option

Use 100% unsweetened apple juice instead of pomegranate juice.

Miso substitute: ½ tablespoon low-sodium soy sauce and ½ tablespoon chicken stock.

Per serving: calories 274.9, total fat 8.9 g, saturated fat 1.3 g, cholesterol 86.1 mg, sodium 311.9 mg, potassium 451.0 mg, total carbohydrate 32.5 g, dietary fiber 4.5 g, sugars 3.1 g, protein 17.2 g

Spicy Asian Shrimp with Beans

Makes 4 servings

Shrimp will reflect any flavor it is cooked with, and this recipe is a perfect example. The base recipe can also be used for broccoli or thinly sliced free-range chicken breast or grass-fed beef.

1 teaspoon light olive oil
½ head Napa or white cabbage, shredded
¼ teaspoon salt
1 cup low- or no-sodium vegetable broth
1–2 teaspoons minced hot peppers, optional
½ pound fresh shrimp, peeled, deveined and finely chopped
1 cup cooked white beans (canned is fine, drain before using)
2 tablespoons finely chopped fresh chervil or parsley
1 cup cooked brown rice
Pinch salt
2 tablespoons pumpkin seeds

1. Heat the oil in a wok or saucepan over medium heat. Add the cabbage and salt. Sauté until the cabbage releases its juices, about 8 minutes. Raise the heat to medium-high and add the broth and peppers, if using. Cook until the broth reduces, about 10 minutes, stirring occasionally.
2. When the broth has disappeared and the cabbage is soft, add the shrimp and cook for 2 minutes. Once the shrimp is opaque, remove from the heat. Add the white beans, chervil or parsley and brown rice and toss. Sprinkle with pumpkin seeds. Divide among four bowls and serve.

Vegetarian Option

Omit the shrimp.

Per serving: calories 243.4, total fat 3.5 g, saturated fat 0.6 g, cholesterol 86.1 mg, sodium 194.9 mg, potassium 751.1 mg, total carbohydrate 34.3 g, dietary fiber 6.9 g, sugars 0.5 g, protein 19.5 g

🍽 **Pro-Prostate Snapper with Thai Bean Salad**

Makes 2 servings

Light, healing Thai Bean Salad is particularly refreshing when paired with Asian-inspired garlic-and-ginger snapper. This recipe can also be made with vegetables or meat. My vegetable suggestions would include prostate-healing spinach or tomatoes, but cauliflower, eggplant, squash, escarole or cabbage would be delicious too. My meat preferences would be free-range chicken breast or grass-fed buffalo.

Snapper

½ teaspoon **miso paste***
½ teaspoon **minced fresh ginger**
½ teaspoon **minced fresh garlic**
¼ cup **fresh basil**, cut chiffonade (into thin strips)
One 8-ounce **wild snapper fillet**

Thai Bean Salad

1 teaspoon **light olive oil**
1 cup **finely chopped white onions**
1–1½ pounds **broccoli**, trimmed into 2-inch florets, cut in half lengthwise
1 teaspoon **finely chopped fresh thyme leaves**
1 cup **frozen edamame**, thawed
2 tablespoons **raw pumpkin seeds**

1. Position the oven rack on the middle shelf and preheat to 400°F.
2. In a small casserole dish, combine the miso paste, ginger, garlic and basil with 1 tablespoon of water. Place the snapper fillet in the casserole dish and coat with the miso mixture. Bake for 15 minutes, until opaque.
3. Heat the olive oil in a wok or large pan over medium-low heat. Add the onions and sauté for at least 8 minutes. Add the broccoli and sauté for another 2 minutes, or until the onions are translucent and soft. The broccoli should be al dente.
4. Reduce the heat to low and add the thyme and edamame. Toss well for a few minutes and remove from the heat. The edamame won't be very hot, which is fine, as they taste best when served at room temperature.
5. Divide the snapper between two plates, top with the soybean salad, add any sauce remaining in the casserole dish, sprinkle with pumpkin seeds and serve.

Frugal Option

Use great northern beans instead of edamame.

Miso substitute: ½ tablespoon low-sodium soy sauce and ½ tablespoon chicken stock.

Per serving: calories 339.2, total fat 11.7 g, saturated fat 1.2 g, cholesterol 0.0 mg, sodium 333.5 mg, potassium 1,342.1 mg, total carbohydrate 28.9 g, dietary fiber 10.8 g, sugars 0.2 g, protein 41.5 g

---

🍽 *Prostate Power Baked Stuffed Tomatoes*

Makes 6 servings

Stuffed tomatoes are popular throughout the Mediterranean region. This prostate power version combines antioxidant-rich vegetables with a little cheese. Try adding wild snapper, ground grass-fed beef or ground free-range chicken breast for meaty flavor and extra protein.

Stuffing

1 large carrot, peeled and diced
1 large zucchini, peeled, cored and diced
1 large yellow squash, peeled, cored and diced
1–1½ pounds broccoli, florets only, minced
2 tablespoons raw pumpkin seeds
1 cup cooked legumes, such as black or navy beans
8 ounces extra-firm tofu, cut into ½-inch cubes
¼ cup coarsely chopped fresh cilantro
1 tablespoon minced garlic
1 tablespoon minced hot peppers
Pinch salt

Tomatoes

6 large beefsteak tomatoes, tops removed and insides scooped out
1 teaspoon light olive oil
½ cup low-fat cheese, such as crumbled feta, crumbled goat cheese or grated Parmesan
cheese, optional

1. Position the rack in the center of the oven and preheat to 350°F.

2. In a large bowl, combine the carrot, zucchini, squash, broccoli, pumpkin seeds, legumes, tofu, cilantro, garlic, hot peppers and salt. Toss until well combined.

3. Place the tomatoes on a baking sheet pan and fill each with stuffing. Do not overload them. Drizzle with olive oil. Bake for 20 minutes.

4. If using cheese, sprinkle over the tomatoes after 15 minutes of cooking time. Remove from the oven and serve.

Frugal Option

Use bell peppers instead of tomatoes.

Per serving: calories 198.6, total fat 6.7 g, saturated fat 2.2 g, cholesterol 6.7 mg, sodium 323.0 mg, potassium 559.9 mg, total carbohydrate 16.1 g, dietary fiber 6.5 g, sugars 2.0 g, protein 14.5 g

---

¶◉¶ *Prostate-Healing Poached Wild Snapper and Broccoli Salad*

Makes 2 servings

Poaching—defined as gently cooking in liquid—is a great way to prepare mild, delicate fish, such as red snapper. Poached fish is moist and flaky, and can take on flavors from simple to sophisticated. Leftovers are delicious when tucked into a whole-wheat pita or served over brown rice.

Wild Snapper

Two 4-ounce fillets wild snapper
1 cup dry white wine
5 whole black peppercorns
1 sprig fresh dill
1 teaspoon lemon juice
1 tablespoon finely chopped fresh parsley

Broccoli Salad

1 teaspoon light olive oil
1–1½ pounds broccoli, cut into 2-inch florets
2 tablespoons finely chopped sun-dried tomatoes packed in oil
½ cup cooked brown rice
¼ cup pomegranate juice
¼ teaspoon salt
½ cup chopped tomatoes
1 heaping cup baby spinach leaves
2 tablespoons raw pumpkin seeds

1. Place the snapper fillets side by side in a deep sauté pan. Pour wine over the snapper, then add water into the pan until the fillets are just covered. Add the peppercorns and dill. Cook over medium-low heat for 20 minutes until the fillets are cooked through, or until they are opaque and flake easily.

2. Heat the olive oil in a wok or pan over medium heat. Add the broccoli, sun-dried tomatoes and brown rice. Sauté until the broccoli is tender, about 5 minutes. Reduce the heat to medium-low. Add the pomegranate juice, salt, tomatoes, spinach and pumpkin seeds. Cook for an additional 5 minutes.

3. Divide the broccoli salad between two plates, top with a snapper fillet, drizzle with lemon juice, sprinkle with parsley and serve.

Frugal Option

Substitute 100% unsweetened apple juice for pomegranate juice.

Per serving: calories 346.9, total fat 6.4 g, saturated fat 0.7 g, cholesterol 0.0 mg, sodium 243.4 mg, potassium 1,040.0 mg, total carbohydrate 31.8 g, dietary fiber 6.8 g, sugars 5.7 g, protein 31.1 g

---

🍽️ *Feisty Fruit Pies*

Makes 4 individual pies

Here's a delicious way to up your daily fruit intake. Almost any type of fruit works here, such as apricots, blueberries, raspberries, apples, mango, papaya and pineapple. I suggest you try them all.

Topping

 1 teaspoon light olive oil
 2 tablespoons sugar
 1 **peach,** pitted and diced, peeled, if desired
 20 **strawberries,** hulled and sliced

Crust

 ½ cup whole-wheat pastry flour
 ¼ cup almond flour
 1 teaspoon baking powder
 Pinch salt
 ½ cup low-fat milk
 1 tablespoon xylitol or birch sugar
 2 tablespoons melted grass-fed unsalted butter

 Low-fat ice cream, optional

1. Preheat the oven to 350°F with the rack placed in the middle.
2. Heat the olive oil a medium saucepan over medium heat. Add the sugar and peaches and sauté for 4 minutes, or until the peaches are soft. Remove from the heat and stir in the strawberries.
3. In a medium bowl, mix the flours, baking powder, salt, milk, sugar and butter until well combined. Divide into four pieces, and press into four pie pans. Pour the peaches and strawberries with their juices into the pans. Place on a baking sheet and bake for 20 minutes. Let cool slightly and serve topped with low-fat ice cream, if desired.

Per serving: calories 219.0, total fat 10.5 g, saturated fat 4.1 g, cholesterol 16.2 mg, sodium 178.0 mg, potassium 244.7 mg, total carbohydrate 27.0 g, dietary fiber 4.4 g, sugars 6.5 g, protein 4.9 g

Select Bibliography

Introduction

Cordain, L., S. Eaton, J. Miller, N. Mann, and K. Hill. "The Paradoxical Nature of Hunter-Gatherer Diets: Meat-Based, Yet Non-atherogenic." *European Journal of Clinical Nutrition* 2002;56:S42–S52.

Kaput, J., and R. Rodriguez. *Nutritional Genomics: Discovering the Path to Personalized Nutrition.* Hoboken, NJ: John Wiley & Sons, 2006.

_____. "The Therapeutic and Preventative Potential of the Hunter-Gatherer Lifestyle: Insights from Australian Aborigines." In: N.J. Temple and D.P. Burkitt, eds. *Western Disease.* Clifton, NJ: Humana Press, 1994.

Milburn, Michael P. "Indigenous Nutrition." *American Indian Quarterly* 2004;28(3):411–434.

Pollan, Michael. *In Defense of Food: An Eater's Manual.* New York: The Penguin Press, 2008.

Urbina, Ian. "In the Treatment of Diabetes, Success Often Does Not Pay." *The New York Times,* January 11, 2006.

The Two Healthiest Diets on Earth

Ahsan, S.K. "Magnesium in Health and Disease." *Journal of the Pakistan Medical Association* 1998;48(8):246–250.

Albert, C.M., et al. "Nut Consumption and Decreased Risk of Sudden Cardiac Death in the Physicians' Health Study." *Archives of Internal Medicine* 2002;162(12):1382–1387.

Ali, M., M. Thomson, and M. Aful. "Garlic and Onions: Their Effect on Eicosanoid Metabolism and Its Clinical Relevance." *Prostaglandins, Leukotrienes, and Essential Fatty Acids* 2000;62(2):55–73.

_____, T. Bordia, and T. Mustafa. "Effect of Raw Versus Boiled Aqueous Extract of Garlic and Onion on Platelet Aggregation." *Prostaglandins, Leukotrienes, and Essential Fatty Acids* 1999;60(1):43–47.

Apitz-Castro, R., et al. "Ajoene, the Antiplatelet Principle of Garlic, Synergistically Potentiates the Antiaggregatory Action of Prostacyclin, Forskolin, Indomethacin and Dypiridamole on Human Platelets." *Thrombosis Research* 1986;42(3):303–311.

Ascherio, A., E.B. Rimm, M.A. Hernan, et al. "Intake of Potassium, Magnesium, Calcium and Fiber and Risk of Stroke Among US Men." *Circulation* 1998; 98:1198–1204.

Augusti, K.T. "Therapeutic Values of Onion (Allium Cepa 1.) and Garlic (Allium Sativum 1.)." *Indian Journal of Experimental Biology* 1996;34(7):634–640.

_____. "Hypercholesterolemic Effect of Garlic (Allium Sativum Uno.)." *Indian Journal of Experimental Biology* 1977;15:489.

Awad, A.B., and C.S. Fink. "Phytosterols as Anticancer Dietary Components: Evidence and Mechanism of Action. *Journal of Nutrition* 2000;130:2127–2130.

Bauer, Joy. *Joy Bauer's Food Cures: Easy 4-Step Nutrition Programs for Improving Your Body.* New York: Rodale Press, 2007.

Block, E. "The Chemistry of Garlic and Onions." *Scientific American* 1985;252:114–119.

Bordia, A.K., et al. "Essential Oil of Garlic on Blood Lipids and Fibrinolytic Activity in Patients with Coronary Artery Disease." *Atherosclerosis* 1977;28:55.

_____. "The Effective of Active Principle of Garlic and Onion on Blood Lipids and Experimental Atherosclerosis in Rabbits and Their Comparison with Clofibrate." *Journal of the Association of Physicians of India* 1977; 25:509.

_____. "Effect of the Essential Oil (Active Principle) of Garlic on Serum Cholesterol, Plasma Fibrinogen Whole Blood Coagulation Tune and Fibrinolytic Activity in Alimentary Lipaemia." *Journal of the Association of Physicians of India* 1974;22:267.

_____. "Effect of the Essential Oils of Garlic and Onion on Alimentary Hyperlipemia." *Atherosclerosis* 1975; 21:15–19.

_____. "Effect of Garlic on Blood Lipids in Patients with Coronary Heart Disease." *American Journal of Clinical Nutrition* 1981;34:2100.

Borek, C. "Garlic Reduces Dementia and Heart-Disease Risk." *Journal of Nutrition* 2006;136(3):810S–812S.

Bowden, Jonny. *The 150 Healthiest Foods on Earth: The Surprising, Unbiased Truth about What You Should Eat and Why.* Minneapolis: Quayside, 2007.

Carper, Jean. *The Food Pharmacy: Dramatic New Evidence That Food Is Your Best Medicine.* New York: Pocket Books, 1998.

Challier, B., J.M. Perarnau, and J.F. Viel. "Garlic, Onion and Cereal Fibre as Protective Factors for Breast Cancer: A French Case-Control Study." *European Journal of Epidemiology* 1998;14(8):737–747.

Chutani, S.K., et al. "The Effect of Fried vs. Raw Garlic on Fibrinolytic Activity in Man." *Atherosclerosis* 1981; 38:417.

Daley, Rosie, and Andrew Weil. *The Healthy Kitchen.* New York: Knopf, 2003.

Delaha, E.C., et al. "Inhibition of Mycobacteria by Garlic Extract (Allium sativum)." *Antimicrobial Agents and Chemotherapy* 1985;27(4):485–486.

Dixon, L.B., et al. "Choose a Diet That Is Low in Saturated Fat and Cholesterol and Moderate in Total Fat: Subtle Changes to a Familiar Message. *Journal of Nutrition* 2001;13:510S–526S.

Dorant, E., P.A. van den Brandt, and R.A. Goldbohm. "Allium Vegetable Consumption, Garlic Supplement Intake, and Female Breast Carcinoma Incidence." *Breast Cancer Research and Treatment* 1995; 33(2):163–170.

———. "A Prospective Cohort Study on the Relationship Between Onion and Leek Consumption, Garlic Supplement Use and the Risk of Colorectal Carcinoma in the Netherlands." *Carcinogenesis* 1996; 17(3):477–484.

Dorsch, W., M. Ettl, G. Hein, et al. "Antiasthmatic Effects of Onions. Inhibition of Platelet-Activating Factor-Induced Bronchial Obstruction by Onion Oils." *International Archives of Allergy and Applied Immunology* 1987;82(3–4):535–536.

Feldman, Elaine B. "The Scientific Evidence for a Beneficial Health Relationship Between Walnuts and Coronary Heart Disease." *Journal of Nutrition* 2002; 132:1062S–1101S.

Fenwick, G.R. "The Genus Allium-Part 3." *CRC Critical Reviews in Food Science & Nutrition* 1985;23(1):1–73.

Fukushima, S., N. Takada, T. Hori, and H. Wanibuchi. "Cancer Prevention by Organosulfur Compounds from Garlic and Onion." *Journal of Cellular Biochemistry* 1997;27:100–105.

Garg, Manohar L., Robert J. Blake, and Ron B.H. Wills. "Macadamia Nut Consumption Lowers Plasma Total and LDL Cholesterol Levels in Hypercholesterolemic Men." *Journal of Nutrition* 2003;133:1060–1063.

Gupta, N.N., et al. "Effect of Onion on Serum Cholesterol, Blood Coagulation Factors and Fibrinolytic Activity in Alimentary Lipaemia." *Indian Journal of Medical Research* 1966;54(1):43–53.

Harris, Lloyd J. *The Book of Garlic.* Berkeley, CA: Aris Books, 1980.

Hu, Frank B., Meir J. Stampfer, JoAnn E. Manson, et al. "Dietary Fat Intake and the Risk of Coronary Heart Disease in Women." *New England Journal of Medicine* 1997;337(12):1491–1499.

Jain, R.C., et al. "Onion and Blood Fibrinolytic Activity." *British Medical Journal* 1969;258:514.

Jiang, Rui, JoAnn E. Manson, Meir J. Stampfer, et al. "Nut and Peanut Butter Consumption and Risk of Type 2 Diabetes in Women." *Journal of the American Medical Association* 2002;288(20):2554–2560.

Knekt, P., J. Kumpulainen, R. Jarvinen, H. Rissanen, M. Heliovaara, A. Reunanen, T. Hakulinen, and A. Aromaa. "Flavonoid Intake and Risk of Chronic Diseases." *The American Journal of Clinical Nutrition* 2002;76(3):560–568.

Kris-Etherton, Penny M., et al. "High-Monounsaturated Fatty Acid Diets Lower Both Plasma Cholesterol and Triacylglycerol Concentrations." *The American Journal of Clinical Nutrition* 1999;70:1009–1015.

———. "Nuts and Their Bioactive Constituents: Effects on Serum Lipids and Other Factors That Affect Disease Risk." *The American Journal of Clinical Nutrition* 1999;70(Suppl.):504S.

———. "Recent Discoveries in Inclusive Food-Based Approaches and Dietary Patterns for Reduction in Risk for Cardiovascular Disease." *Current Opinion in Lipidology* 2002;13(4):397–407.

Lau, B.H.S., et al. "Allium Sativum (Garlic) and Atherosclerosis: A Review." *Nutrition Research* 1983;3:119–128.

Liu, M., et al. "Mixed Tocopherols Inhibit Platelet Aggregation in Humans: Potential Mechanisms." *The American Journal of Clinical Nutrition* 2003;77(3):700–750.

Lovejoy, J.C., et al. "Effect of Diets Enriched in Almonds on Insulin Action and Serum Lipids in Adults with Normal Glucose Tolerance or Type 2 Diabetes." *The American Journal of Clinical Nutrition* 2002;76(Suppl.):1000–1006.

Mateljan, George. *The World's Healthiest Foods: Essential Guide for the Healthiest Way of Eating.* Grand Rapids, MI: GMF, 2007.

Menon, Sudhakaran I. "Onions and Blood Fibrinogenolysis." *British Medical Journal* 1970;2:421.

Mitrou, Panagiota N., Victor Kipnis, et al. "Mediterranean Dietary Pattern and Prediction of All-Cause Mortality in a US Population." *Archives of Internal Medicine* 2007;167(22):2461–2468.

Moon, J.H., R. Akata, S. Oshima, et al. "Accumulation of Quercetin Conjugates in Blood Plasma after the Short-Term Ingestion of Onion by Women." *American Journal of Physiology—Regulatory, Integrative and Comparative Physiology* 2000;279(2):R461–R467.

Morgan, W.A., et al. "Pecans Lower Low-Density Lipoprotein Cholesterol in People with Normal Lipid Levels." *Journal of the American Dietetic Association* 2000;100:312–318.

Morris, M.C., et al. "Dietary Intake of Antioxidant Nutrients and the Risk of Incident Alzheimer Disease in a Bi-racial Community Study." *Journal of the American Medical Association* 2002;287(24):3223–3229.

Murray, Michael T., Joseph Pizzorno, and Lara Pizzorno. *The Encyclopedia of Healing Foods.* New York: Atria, 2005.

Ostlund, R.E., et al. "Effects of Trace Components of Dietary Fat on Cholesterol Metabolism: Phytosterols, Oxysterols, and Squalene." *Nutrition Reviews* 2002; 60(11):349–359.

Papas, A.M. (ed.). *Antioxidant Status, Diet, Nutrition, and Health.* Boca Raton, FL: CRC Press, 1999.

Pratt, Steven G., and Kathy Matthews. *SuperFoods Rx: Fourteen Foods That Will Change Your Life.* New York: HarperCollins, 2005.

Riley, D.M., F. Bianchini, and H. Vainio. "Allium Vegetables and Organosulfur Compounds: Do They Help Prevent Cancer?" *Environmental Health Perspectives* 2001;109(9):893–902.

Sabate, J. "Nut Consumption, Vegetarian Diets, Ischemic Heart Disease Risk, and All-Cause Mortality: Evidence from Epidemiologic Studies." *The American Journal of Clinical Nutrition* 1999;70(Suppl.):500S–503S.

Sainani, G.S., D.B. Desai, N.H. Gohre, et al. "Effect of Dietary Garlic and Onion on Serum Lipid Profile in Jain Community." *Indian Journal of Medical Research* 1979;69:776–780.

Sharma, K.K., et al. "Antihyperglycemic Effect of Onion: Effect on Fasting Blood Sugar and Induced Hyperglycemia in Man." *Indian Journal of Medical Research* 1977;65(3):422–429.

Sheela, C.G., K. Kumud, and K.T. Augusti. "Antidiabetic Effects of Onion and Garlic Sulfoxide Amino Acids in Rats." *Planta Medica* 1995;61(4):356–357.

Silagy, C.A., and A.W. Neil. "A Meta-Analysis of the Effect of Garlic on Blood Pressure." *Journal of Hypertension* 1994;12:463–468.

Song, K., and J.A. Milner. "The Influence of Heating on the Anticancer Properties of Garlic." *American Society for Nutritional Sciences* 2001;131(Suppl.):1054S–1057S.

Spigelski, D., and P.J. Jones. "Efficacy of Garlic Supplementation in Lowering Serum Cholesterol Levels." *Nutrition Reviews* 2001;59(7):236–241.

Spiller, G.A., et al. "Nuts and Plasma Lipids: An Almond-Based Diet Lowers LDL-C While Preserving HDL-C. *Journal of the American College of Nutrition* 1998:17:285–290.

Srivastava, K.C. "Evidence for the Mechanism by Which Garlic Inhibits Platelet Aggregation." *Prostaglandins, Leukotrienes, and Medicine* 1986;22(3):313–321.

Stewart, J.R., et al. "Resveratrol: A Candidate Nutritional Substance for Prostate Cancer Prevention." *Journal of Nutrition* 2003;133(7 Suppl.):2440S–2443S.

Sueur, M. "Effect of Garlic on Serum Lipids and Lipoproteins in Patients Suffering from Hyperlipoproteinemia." *Diabetologia Croatica* 1980;9:323.

Thomson, M., K.K. Al-Qattan, T. Bordia, and Ali M. "Including Garlic in the Diet May Help Lower Blood Glucose, Cholesterol, and Triglycerides." *Journal of Nutrition* 2006;13(3 Suppl.):800S–802S.

Mediterr-Asian Diet

Adlercreutz, H., and W. Mazur. "Phyto-oestrogens and Western diseases." *Annals of Medicine* 1997;29(2):95-120.

_____, H. Markkanen, and S. Watanabe. "Plasma Concentrations of Phyto-estrogens in Japanese Men." *The Lancet* 1993:342:1209–1210.

Alarcon de la Lastra, C., V. Motilva Barranco, and J.M. Herrerias. "Mediterranean Diet and Health: Biological Importance of Olive Oil." *Current Pharmaceutical Design* 2001;7(10):933–950.

Anderson, J.W. "Meta-Analysis of the Effects of Soy Protein Intake on Serum Lipids." *New England Journal of Medicine* 1995;333(5):276–282.

Bhathena, Sam J., and Manuel T. Velasquez. "Beneficial Role of Dietary Phyto-estrogens in Obesity and Diabetes." *The American Journal of Clinical Nutrition* 2002; 76(6):1191–1201.

Carper, Jean. *The Food Pharmacy: Dramatic New Evidence That Food Is Your Best Medicine.* New York: Pocket Books, 1998.

Chang, S.K.C. "Isoflavones Form Soybeans and Soy Foods." In: Shi, J., G. Mazza, and M. Le Maguer (eds.). *Functional Foods: Biochemical and Processing Aspects, vol. 2.* Boca Raton, FL: CRC Press, 2002. pp. 39–70.

Chen, Y.M., S.C. Ho, S.S. Lam, et al. "Soy Isoflavones Have a Favorable Effect on Bone Loss in Chinese Postmenopausal Women with Lower Bone Mass: A Double-Blind, Randomized, Controlled Trial." *Journal of Clinical Endocrinology & Metabolism* 2003; 88(10):4740–4747.

Da Silva Queiroz, K., A.C. de Oliveira, E. Helbig, et al. "Soaking the Common Bean in a Domestic Preparation Reduced the Contents of Raffinose-Type Oligosaccharides but Did Not Interfere with Nutritive Value." *Journal of Nutritional Science and Vitaminology* (Tokyo) 2002;48(4):283–289.

De Lorgeril, M., P. Salen, J.-L. Martin, et al. "Mediterranean Diet, Traditional Risk Factors, and the Rate of Cardiovascular Complications After Myocardial Infarction. Final Report of the Lyon Diet Heart Study." *Circulation* 1999;99(6):779–785.

Desroches, S., I.F. Mauger, L.M. Ausman, et al. "Soy Protein Favorably Affects LDL Size Independently of Isoflavone in Hypercholesterolemic Men and Women." *Journal of Nutrition* 2004;134(3):574–579.

Dwyer, J.T., et al. "Tofu and Soy Drinks Contain Phytoestrogens." *Journal of the American Dietetic Association* 1994;94(7):739–743.

Erdman, J.W. Jr. "AHA Science Advisory: Soy Protein and Cardiovascular Disease: A Statement for Healthcare Professionals from the Nutrition Committee of the AHA." *Circulation* 2000;102(20):2555–2559.

Funayama, S., et al. "Hypotensive Principle of Laminaria and Allied Seaweeds." *Journal of Medicinal Plants Research* 1981;41(1):29–33.

Furusawa, E., et al. "Anticancer Activity of a Natural Product, VivaNatural, Extracted from Undaria Pinnantifida on Intraperitoneally Implanted Lewis Lung Carcinoma." *Oncology* 1985;42(6):364–369.

Grundy, S.M., et al. "Comparison of Actions of Soy Protein and Casein on Metabolism of Plasma Lipoproteins and Cholesterol in Humans." *The American Journal of Clinical Nutrition* 1983;38:245–252.

Haub, M.D., A.M. Wells, M.A. Tarnopolsky, and W.W. Campbell. "Effect of Protein Source on Resistive-Training-Induced Changes in Body Composition and Muscle Size in Older Men." *The American Journal of Clinical Nutrition* 2002;76(3):511–517.

Hopps, H.A., et al. (eds.). *Marine Algae in Pharmaceutical Science.* New York: DeGruyter, 1982.

Jenkins, David J.A., Cyril W.C. Kendall, and Chung-Ja C. Jackson. "Effects of High- and Low-Isoflavone Soyfoods on Blood Lipids, Oxidized LDL, Homocysteine, and Blood Pressure in Hyperlipidemic Men and Women." *The American Journal of Clinical Nutrition* 2002;76(1):365–372.

Keys, A. "Mediterranean Diet and Public Health: Personal Reflections." *The American Journal of Clinical Nutrition* 1995;61:1321S–1323S.

Kreijkamp-Kaspers, S., et al. "Phyto-oestrogens and Cognitive Function." In: Watson, D.H. (ed.). *Performance Functional Foods.* Boca Raton, FL: CRC Press, 2003. pp. 61–77.

Kritz-Silverstein, D., and D.L. Goodman-Gruen. "Usual Dietary Isoflavone Intake, Bone Mineral Density, and Bone Metabolism in Postmenopausal Women." *Journal of Women's Health and Gender-Based Medicine* 2002;11(1):69–78.

Lee, M.M., S.L. Gomez, J.S. Chang, et al. "Soy and Isoflavone Consumption in Relation to Prostate Cancer Risk in China." *Cancer Epidemiology Biomarkers & Prevention* 2003;12:665–668.

Lo, G.S., et al. "Soy Fiber Improves Lipid and Carbohydrate Metabolism in Primary Hyperlipidemic Subjects." *Atherosclerosis* 1986;62:239–248.

Mateljan, George. *The World's Healthiest Foods: Essential Guide for the Healthiest Way of Eating.* Grand Rapids, MI: GMF, 2007.

Matvienko, Oksana A., Douglas S. Lewis, and Mike Swanson. "A Single Daily Dose of Soybean Phytosterols in Ground Beef Decreases Serum Total Cholesterol and LDL Cholesterol in Young, Mildly Hypercholesterolemic Men." *The American Journal of Clinical Nutrition* 2002;76(1):57–64.

Menotti, A., D. Kromhout, H. Blackburn, et al. "Food Intake Patterns and 25-Year Mortality from Coronary Heart Disease: Cross-cultural Correlations in the Seven Countries Study. The Seven Countries Study Research Group." *European Journal of Epidemiology* 1999;15(6):507–515.

Messadi, D.V., et al. "Inhibition of Oral Carcinogenesis by a Protease Inhibitor." *Journal of the National Cancer Institute* 1986;76(3):447–452.

Messina, Mark J. "Emerging Evidence on the Role of Soy in Reducing Prostate Cancer Risk." *Nutrition Reviews* 2003;61(4):117–131.

———. "Legumes and Soybeans: Overview of Their Nutritional Profiles and Health Effects. *The American Journal of Clinical Nutrition* 1999;70(3 Suppl.):439S–450S.

———, and Virginia Messin. "Provisional Recommended Soy Protein and Isoflavones Intake for Healthy Adults." *Nutrition Today* 2003;38(3):100–109.

Munro, I.C., M. Harwood, J.J. Hlywka, et al. "Soy Isoflavones: A Safety Review." *Nutrition Reviews* 2003;61(1):1–33.

Nagata, Chisato, Hiroyuki Shimizu, Rieko Takami, et al. "Soy Product Intake Is Inversely Associated with Serum Homocysteine Level in Premenopausal Japanese Women." *Journal of Nutrition* 2003;133: 797–800.

Ogura, Chikara, Haruo Nakamoto, et al. "Prevalence of Senile Dementia in Okinawa." *International Journal of Epidemiology* 1995;24:373–380.

Pratt, Steven G., and Kathy Matthews. *SuperFoods Rx: Fourteen Foods That Will Change Your Life.* New York: HarperCollins, 2005.

Rabin, Roni Caryn. "For Sharp Brain, Stimulation." *The New York Times,* May 13, 2008.

Renaud, S., M. de Lorgeril, J. Delaye, et al. "Cretan Mediterranean Diet for Prevention of Coronary Heart Disease." *The American Journal of Clinical Nutrition* 1995;61:1360S–1367S.

Sass, Lorna J., and Jonelle Weaver. *The New Soy Cookbook.* San Francisco: Chronicle Books, 1998.

Setchell, K.D.R., et al. "Bioavailability, Disposition, and Dose-Response Effects of Soy Isoflavones When Consumed by Healthy Women at Physiologically

Typical Dietary Intake." *Journal of Nutrition* 2003;133(4):1027–1035.

Shimada, A. "Regional Differences in Gastric Cancer Mortality and Eating Habits of People." [Article in Japanese] *Gan No Rinsho* (*Japan Journal of Cancer Clinics*) 1986;32(6):692–698.

Shurtleff, W., et al. *The Book of Tofu.* Berkeley, CA: Ten Speed Press, 1998.

Sirtori, C.R., et al. "Studies on 1M Use of a Soybean Protein Diet for the Management of Hyperlipoproteinemias." In: *Animal and Vegetable Proteins in Lipid Metabolism and Atherosclerosis.* New York: Alan R. Liss, 1983. pp. 135–148.

Steinberg, F.M., et al. "Soy Protein with Isoflavones Has Favorable Effects on Endothelial Function That Are Independent of Lipid and Antioxidant Effects in Healthy Postmenopausal Women." *The American Journal of Clinical Nutrition* 2003;78(1):123–130.

Takeshi, H. "Epidemiology of Human Carcinogenesis: A Review of Food-Related Diseases." In: Stich, H.F. (ed.). *Carcinogens and Mutagens in the Environment.* Boca Raton, FL: CRC Press, 1982. pp. 13–30.

Teas, J. "The Consumption of Seaweed as a Protective Factor in the Etiology of Breast Cancer." *Medical Hypotheses* 1981;7(5):601–613.

_____. "The Dietary Intake of Laminaria, a Brown Seaweed, and Breast Cancer Prevention." *Nutrition and Cancer* 1983;4(3):217–222.

Wagner, J.D., D.C. Schwenke, K.A. Greaves, et al. "Soy Protein with Isoflavones, but Not an Isoflavone-Rich Supplement, Improves Arterial Low-Density Lipoprotein Metabolism and Atherogenesis." *Arteriosclerosis, Thrombosis, and Vascular Biology* 2003;23(12):2241–2246.

Watson, R.R. *Vegetables, Fruits, and Herbs in Health Promotion.* Boca Raton, FL: CRC Press, 2001. pp. 117–134.

Yamamoto, I., et al. "Antitumor Activity of Edible Marine Algae: Effect of Crude Fucoidan Fractions Prepared from Edible Brown Seaweeds against L-1210 Leukemia." *Hydrobiologia* 1984;116–117(1):145–148.

Why Organic Matters

Burros, Marian. "You Are What You Eat: 2006 and the Politics of Food." *The New York Times,* December 27, 2006.

Hansen, Nanette. "Organic Food Sales See Healthy Growth." CNBC, December 3, 2004, *www.msnbc.msn.com/id/6638417.*

Konrad, Walecia. "Organic Growth." *Fast Company* 2007 March;113, *http://www.fastcompany.com/magazine/113.*

Kuban, Adam. "How to Decode PLU Stickers on Produce." April 19, 2008, *http://www.seriouseats.com/2008/04/how-to-decode-plu-stickers-on-produce.html.*

Long, Cheryl and Lynn Keiley. "Is Agribusiness Making Food Less Nutritious?" *Mother Earth News,* June/July 2004, *http://www.motherearthnews.com.*

"Why Go Organic?" *Natural Solutions* (formerly *Alternative Medicine Magazine*), October 1, 2005, *http://www.naturalsolutionsmag.com.*

Worthington, V. "Effect of Agricultural Methods on Nutritional Quality: A Comparison of Organic with Conventional Crops." *Alternative Therapies in Health and Medicine* 1998 Jan;4 (1):58–69.

Arthritis

Altman, R.D., and K.C. Marcussen. "Effects of a Ginger Extract on Knee Pain in Patients with Osteoarthritis." *Arthritis and Rheumatism* 2001;44(11):2531–2538.

American Diabetes Association. "Evidence Builds: Diet High in Magnesium Lowers Diabetes Risk." *http://www.diabetes.org.*

American Institute for Cancer Research. "A Closer Look at Antioxidants." *http://www.aicr.org.*

_____. "In the News: Antioxidant Supplements and Cancer." *http://www.aicr.org.*

Arthritis Research Campaign. "Food for Thought." *http://www.arc.org.uk.*

Australasian College of Nutritional and Environmental Medicine. "Insulin Resistance, Obesity and Diabetes: The Connection." *http://www.acnem.org.*

Bastyr Center for Natural Health. "Vitamin C May Aid People with Diabetes." *http://www.bastyrcenter.org.*

Bauer, Joy. *Joy Bauer's Food Cures: Easy 4-Step Nutrition Programs for Improving Your Body.* New York: Rodale, 2007.

Belch, J., and A. Hill. "Evening Primrose Oil and Borage Oil in Rheumatologic Conditions." *American Journal of Clinical Nutrition* 2000;71(Suppl. 1):352S–356S.

Carper, Jean. *The Food Pharmacy: Dramatic New Evidence That Food Is Your Best Medicine.* New York: Pocket Books, 1998.

Carroll, K. "Biological Effects of Fish Oils in Relation to Chronic Diseases." *Lipids* 1986;21:731–732.

Childers, Norman F., ed. *Childers' Diet to Stop Arthritis: Nightshades, Aging and Ill Health.* Minneapolis: Dr. Norman F. Childers Publications, 1995.

_____, and M.S. Margoles. "An Apparent Relation of Nightshades (Solanaceae) to Arthritis." *Journal of Neurological and Orthopaedic Medicine and Surgery* 1993;14:227–231.

Clegg, D.O., D.J. Reda, C.L. Harris, et al. "Glucosamine, Chondroitin Sulfate, and the Two in Combination for Painful Knee Osteoarthritis." *New England Journal of Medicine* 2000;354(8):795–808.

Cleland, L.G., M.J. James, and S.M. Proudman. "The Role of Fish Oils in the Treatment of Rheumatoid Arthritis." *Drugs* 2003;63:845–853.

Diabetes Mall. "Glycemic Index: How Quickly Do Foods Raise Your Blood Sugar?" *http://www.diabetesnet.com*.

Dunkin, Mary A. "Elimination Diets." Arthritis Foundation. *http://ww2.arthritis.org*.

EurekAlert. "First Link Found Between Obesity, Inflammation and Vascular Disease." *http://www.eurekalert.org*.

Felson, D.T., Y. Zhang, and J.M. Anthony. "Weight Loss Reduces the Risk for Symptomatic Knee Osteoarthritis in Women. The Framingham Study." *Annals of Internal Medicine* 1992;116:353–539.

Hafstrom, I., B. Ringertz, and A. Spangberg. "A Vegan Diet Free of Gluten Improves the Signs and Symptoms of Rheumatoid Arthritis: The Effects on Arthritis Correlate with a Reduction in Antibodies to Food Antigens." *Rheumatology* 2001;40:1175–1179.

Harris, W.S. "Health Effects of Omega-3 Fatty Acids." *Contemporary Nutrition* 1985;10:8.

Healthcastle.com. "Alcohol and Cancer." *http://www.healthcastle.com*.

Heliovaara, M., K. Aho, and P. Knekt. "Coffee Consumption, Rheumatoid Factor, and the Risk of Rheumatoid Arthritis." *Annals of the Rheumatic Diseases* 2000;59:631–635.

Johns Hopkins Arthritis Center. "Role of Diet in the Incidence of Gout." *http://www.hopkins-arthritis.org*.

Kjeldsen-Kragh, J. "Rheumatoid Arthritis Treated with Vegetarian Diets." *The American Journal of Clinical Nutrition* 1999;70:594S–600S.

Linos, A., V.G. Kaklamani, and Y. Koukmantaki. "Dietary Factors in Relation to Rheumatoid Arthritis: A Role for Olive Oil and Cooked Vegetables." *The American Journal of Clinical Nutrition* 1999;70:1077–1082.

Linus Pauling Institute. "Legumes." *http://lpi.oregonstate.edu*.

Mangge, H., J. Hermann, and K. Schauenstein. "Diet and Rheumatoid Arthritis—A Review." *Scandinavian Journal of Rheumatology* 1999;28:201–209.

Manners, Deborah B. "The Elimination Diet and the Detection Diet." *http://www.foodintol.com*.

Mateljan, George. *The World's Healthiest Foods: Essential Guide for the Healthiest Way of Eating*. Grand Rapids, MI: GMF, 2007.

MayoClinic.com. "Rheumatoid Arthritis." *http://www.mayoclinic.com*.

——. "Type 2 Diabetes." *http://www.mayoclinic.com*.

——. "Carbohydrate Counting and Diabetes." *http://www.mayoclinic.com*.

——. "Diabetes Diet: New Guidelines for Healthy Eating with Diabetes." *http://www.mayoclinic.com*.

——. "Diabetes Diet: Create Your Healthy Eating Plan." *http://www.mayoclinic.com*.

McDougall Newsletter. "How to Prevent and Treat Degenerative (Osteo) Arthritis." *http://www.drmcdougall.com*.

McIlwain, Harris H. *Diet for a Pain-Free Life: A Revolutionary Plan to Lose Weight, Stop Pain, Sleep Better and Feel Great in 21 Days*. New York: Da Capo Press, 2007.

Mendosa.com. "Revised International Table of Glycemic Index and Glycemic Load Values." *http://www.mendosa.com*.

Messier, S.P., D.J. Gutekunst, C. Davis, and P. DeVita. "Weight Loss Reduces Knee-Joint Loads in Overweight and Obese Older Adults with Knee Osteoarthritis." *Arthritis and Rheumatism* 2005;52(7):2026–2032.

Michaud, Ellen, and Anita Hirsch. *The Healing Kitchen: From Tea Tin to Fruit Basket, Breadbox to Veggie Bin—How to Unlock the Power of Foods That Heal*. New York: BenBella Books, 2006.

Muller, H., F.W. De Toledo, and K.L. Resch. "Fasting Followed by Vegetarian Diet in Patients with Rheumatoid Arthritis: A Systematic Review." *Scandinavian Journal of Rheumatology* 2001;30:1–10.

Murray, Michael, J. Pizzorno, and L. Pizzorno. *The Encyclopedia of Healing Foods*. New York: Atria, 2005.

National Center for Complementary and Alternative Medicine. "Questions and Answers: NIGH Glucosamine/Chondroitin Arthritis Intervention Trial." *http://nccam.nih.gov*.

National Diabetes Information Clearinghouse. "Complementary and Alternative Medical Therapies for Diabetes." *http://diabetes.niddk.nih.gov*.

Pratt, Steven G., and Kathy Matthews. *SuperFoods Rx: Fourteen Foods That Will Change Your Life*. New York: HarperCollins, 2005.

Reginster, J.Y., R. Deroisy, and L. Rovati. "Long-Term Effects of Glucosamine Sulphate on Osteoarthritis Progression: A Randomized, Placebo-Controlled Clinical Trial." *The Lancet* 2001;357:251–256.

Soy Stats Information. *http://www.soystats.com*.

Venn, B.J., and J.I. Mann. "Cereal Grains, Legumes, and Diabetes." *European Journal of Clinical Nutrition* 2004;58:1443–1461.

Williams, David G. *Alternatives for the Health-Conscious Individual* 2004, April.

Yeager, Selene, and *Prevention* Magazine Health Books (eds.). *New Foods for Healing*. New York: Bantam Books, 1998.

Cancer

American Association for Cancer Research. "Intake of Carrots, Spinach, and Supplements Containing Vitamin A in Relation to Risk of Breast Cancer." *Cancer Epidemiology, Biomarkers & Prevention* 1997;6:887–892.

American Institute for Cancer Research. "Apples: Neglected Power Food." *www.aicr.org*.

_____. "A Closer Look at Antioxidants." *www.aicr.org*.

_____. "Does Juice Fight Cancer as Well as Whole Vegetables and Fruit?" *www.aicr.org*.

_____. "Get Punchy without Alcohol." *www.aicr.org*.

_____. "Just Two Servings of Broccoli Provide Protection." *www.aicr.org*.

_____. "Nutrition Wise." *www.aicr.org*.

_____. "Onions and Garlic for Your Health." *www.aicr.org*.

_____. "Stronger Than Iron, Curcumin May Prevent Tumors." *www.aicr.org*.

_____. "Too Much Red Meat May Raise Breast Cancer Risk." *www.aicr.org*.

_____. "What's the Link?" *www.aicr.org*.

Augustin, L.S., L. Dal Maso, C. La Vecchia, M. Parpinel, E. Negri, S. Vaccarella, C.W. Kendall, D.J. Jenkins, and S. Francesch. "Dietary Glycemic Index and Glycemic Load, and Breast Cancer Risk: A Case-Control Study." *Annals of Oncology* 2001;12:1533–1538.

_____, S. Gallus, C. Bosetti, F. Levi, E. Negri, S. Franceschi, L. Dal Maso, D.J. Jenkins, C.W. Kendall, and C. La Vecchia. "Glycemic Index and Glycemic Load in Endometrial Cancer." *International Journal of Cancer* 2003;105:404–407.

Barber, M.D., D.C. McMillan, T. Preston, J.A. Ross, and K.C. Fearon. "Metabolic Response to Feeding in Weight-Losing Pancreatic Cancer Patients and Its Modulation by a Fish-Oil-Enriched Nutritional Supplement." *Clinical Science* 2000;98:389–399.

_____, J.A. Ross, A.C. Voss, M.J. Tisdale, and K.C. Fearon. "The Effect of an Oral Nutritional Supplement Enriched with Fish Oil on Weight Loss in Patients with Pancreatic Cancer." *British Journal of Cancer* 1999;81:80–86.

Bauer, Joy. *Joy Bauer's Food Cures: Easy 4-Step Nutrition Programs for Improving Your Body*. New York: Rodale, 2007.

Bennett, Connie, Stephen T. Sinatra, and Nicholas Perricone. *Sugar Shock!: How Sweets and Simple Carbs Can Derail Your Life—and How You Can Get Back on Track*. New York: Berkley Trade, 2007.

Beresford, S.A., et al. "Low-Fat Dietary Pattern and Risk of Colorectal Cancer: The Women's Health Initiative Randomized Controlled Dietary Modification Trial." *Journal of the American Medical Association* 2006;295:643–654.

Bernstein, Richard. *Diabetes Solution: The Complete Guide to Achieving Normal Blood Sugars*. Boston: Little Brown and Company, 2003.

Boehm, S., et al. "Estrogen Suppression as a Pharmacotherapeutic Strategy in BPH." *British Journal of Cancer* 1998;110:817–823.

Borugian, M.J., S.B. Sheps, A.S. Whittemore, A.H. Wu, J.D. Porter, and R.P. Gallagher. "Carbohydrates and Colorectal Cancer Risk among Chinese in North America." *Cancer Epidemiology, Biomarkers & Prevention* 2002;11:187–193.

Bounous, G. "Whey Protein Concentrate (WPC) and Glutathione Modulation in Cancer Treatment." *Anticancer Research* 2000;20:4785–4792.

Bowden, Jonny. *The 150 Healthiest Foods on Earth: The Surprising, Unbiased Truth about What You Should Eat and Why*. Minneapolis: Quayside, 2007.

Calder, P.C., and P. Yaqoob. "Glutamine and the Immune System." *Amino Acids* 1999;17:227–241.

Campbell, Colin T. *The China Study*. Dallas: BenBella, 2005.

Carper, Jean. *The Food Pharmacy: Dramatic New Evidence That Food Is Your Best Medicine*. New York: Pocket Books, 1998.

Cover, C.M., S.J. Hsieh, E.J. Cram, et al. "Indole-3-Carbinol and Tamoxifen Cooperate to Arrest the Cell Cycle of MCF-7 Human Breast Cancer Cells." *Cancer Research* 1999;59:1244–1251.

Edenharder, R., G. Keller, K.L. Platt, and K.K. Unger. "Isolation and Characterization of Structurally Novel Antimutagenic Flavonoids from Spinach (Spinacia oleracea)." *Journal of Agricultural and Food Chemistry* 2001;49:2767–2773.

Edwards, A.J., et al. "Consumption of Watermelon Juice Increases Plasma Concentrations of Lycopene and Beta-Carotene in Humans." *Nutrition* 2003;133(4):1043–1050.

Etminan, M., B. Takkouche, and F. Caamano-Isorna. "The Role of Tomato Products and Lycopene in the Prevention of Prostate Cancer: A Meta-Analysis of Observational Studies." *Cancer Epidemiology, Biomarkers & Prevention* 2004;13:340.

Fahey, J.W., Y. Zhang, and P. Talalay. "Broccoli Sprouts: An Exceptionally Rich Source of Inducers of Enzymes That Protect Against Chemical Carginogens." *Proceedings of the National Academy of Sciences of the United States of America* 1997;94:10367–10372.

Favero, A., M. Parpinel, and M. Monrella. "Energy Sources and Risk of Cancer of the Breast and Colon-Rectum in Italy." *Advances in Experimental Medicine and Biology* 1999;472:51–55.

Fernandez, E., L. Chatenoud, C. La Vecchia, et al. "Fish Consumption and Cancer Risk." *American Journal of Clinical Nutrition* 1999;70(1):85–90.

Franceschi, S., L. Dal Maso, L. Augustin, E. Negri, M. Parpinel, P. Boyle, D.J. Jenkins, and C. La Vecchiao. "Dietary Glycemic Load and Colorectal Cancer Risk." *Annals of Oncology* 2001;12(2):173–178.

Giovannucci, E. "Tomatoes, Tomato-Based Products, Lycopene, and Cancer: Review of the Epidemiologic Literature." *Journal of the National Cancer Institute* 1999;91(4):317–331.

Goodwin, Pamela J., Marguerite Ennis, Kathleen I. Pritchard, Maureen E. Trudeau, Jarley Koo, Yolanda Madarnas, Warren Hartwick, Barry Hoffman, and Nicky Hood. "Fasting Insulin and Outcome in Early-Stage Breast Cancer: Results of a Prospective Cohort Study." *Journal of Clinical Oncology* 2002;20(1):42–51.

Grogan, M., L. Tabar, B. Chua, H.H. Chen, and J. Boyages. "Estimating the Benefits of Adjuvant Systemic Therapy for Women with Early Breast Cancer." *British Journal of Surgery* 2001;88:1513–1518.

Gupta, S., N. Ahmad, and H. Mukhtar. "Prostate Cancer Chemoprevention by Green Tea." *Seminars in Urologic Oncology* 1999;17:70–76.

Higginbotham, Susan, Zuo-Feng Zhang, I-Min Lee, Nancy R. Cook, Edward Giovannucci, Julie E. Buring, and Simin Liu. "Dietary Glycemic Load and Risk of Colorectal Cancer in the Women's Health Study." *Journal of the National Cancer Institute* 2004;96:229–233.

Hitti, Miranda. "High-Carb Diet Linked to Breast Cancer: Associations Seen in Study of Mexican Women." WebMD.com, August 6, 2004.

Inoue, M., K. Mizutani, and M. Tajima. "Regular Consumption of Green Tea and the Risk of Breast Cancer Recurrence." *Cancer Letters* 2001;167:175–182.

Kennedy, R.S., G.P. Konok, G. Bounous, S. Baruchel, and T.D. Lee. "The Use of a Whey Protein Concentrate in the Treatment of Patients with Metastatic Carcinoma: A Phase I-II Clinical Study." *Anticancer Research* 1995;15:2643–2649.

Key, Timothy J. "Diet, Nutrition and the Prevention of Cancer." *Public Health Nutrition* 2004;7:187–200.

Khachik, F., et al. "Lutein, Lycopene, and Their Oxidative Metabolites in Chemoprevention of Cancer." *Cell Biochemistry* 1996:22(Suppl.):236–246.

Kimmick, G.G., and H.B. Muss. "Systemic Therapy for Older Women with Breast Cancer." *Oncology* 2001;15:280–291.

Lee, M.M., S.L. Gomez, J.S. Chang, et al. "Soy and Isoflavone Consumption in Relation to Prostate Cancer Risk in China." *Cancer Epidemiology, Biomarkers & Prevention* 2003;12(7):665–668.

Life Extension. "Coenzyme Q10 New Applications for Cancer Therapy." *http://www.lef.org.*

_____. "Melatonin and Cancer Treatment." *http://www.lef. org.*

Lipschitz, David A. *Breaking the Rules of Aging.* Washington, D.C.: LifeLine Press, 2002.

Longnecker, M.P., P.A. Newcomb, R. Mittendorf, et al. "Intake of Carrots, Spinach, and Supplements Containing Vitamin A in Relation to Risk of Breast Cancer." *Cancer Epidemiology, Biomarkers & Prevention* 1997;6:887–892.

Mateljan, George. *The World's Healthiest Foods: Essential Guide for the Healthiest Way of Eating.* Grand Rapids, MI: GMF, 2007.

Medina, M.A. "Glutamine and Cancer." *The Journal of Nutrition* 2001;131(Suppl. 9):S2539–S2542.

Mercola.com. "Sugar and Cancer." *http://www.mercola.com.*

Michaud, Dominique S., Simin Liu, Edward Giovannucci, Walter C. Willett, Graham A. Colditz, and Charles S. Fuchs. "Dietary Sugar, Glycemic Load, and Pancreatic Cancer Risk in a Prospective Study." *Journal of the National Cancer Institute* 2002;94(17):1293–1300.

Michaud, Ellen, and Anita Hirsch. *The Healing Kitchen: From Tea Tin to Fruit Basket, Breadbox to Veggie Bin—How to Unlock the Power of Foods That Heal.* New York: BenBella Books, 2006.

Moerman, C., H.B. Bueno de Mesquita, and S. Rurua. "Dietary Sugar Intake in the Aetiology of Biliary Tract Cancer." *International Journal of Epidemiology* 1993;22(2):207–214.

Moss, Ralph. "The Moss Report" *http://www.cancerdecisions. com.*

Murray, Michael, Joseph Pizzorno, and Lara Pizzorno. *The Encyclopedia of Healing Foods.* New York: Atria, 2005.

Pratt, Steven G., and Kathy Matthews. *SuperFoods Rx: Fourteen Foods That Will Change Your Life.* New York: HarperCollins, 2005.

Prentice, R.L., et al. "Low-Fat Dietary Pattern and Risk of Invasive Breast Cancer: The Women's Health Initiative Randomized Controlled Dietary Modification Trial." *Journal of the American Medical Association* 2006;295(6):629–642.

Rose, D.P., and J.M. Connolly. "Omega-3 Fatty Acids as Cancer Chemopreventive Agents." *Pharmacology and Therapeutics* 1999;83(3):217–244.

Sanjoaquin, M.A., P.N. Appleby, M. Thorogood, J.I. Mann, and T.J. Key. "Nutrition, Lifestyle and Colorectal Cancer Incidence: A Prospective Investigation of 10,998 Vegetarians and Nonvegetarians in the United Kingdom." *British Journal of Cancer* 2004;90(1):118–121.

Saydah, S.H., Catherine M. Loria, Mark S. Eberhardt, and Frederick L. Brancati. "Abnormal Glucose Tolerance and the Risk of Cancer Death in the United States." *American Journal of Epidemiology* 2003;157(12):1092–1100.

Setiawan, V.W., Z.-F. Zhang, G.-P. Yu, et al. "Protective Effect of Green Tea on the Risks of Chronic Gastritis and Stomach Cancer." *International Journal of Cancer* 2001;92:600–604.

Silvera, S.A., M. Jain, G.R. Howe, A.B. Miller, and T.E. Rohan. "Dietary Carbohydrates and Breast Cancer Risk: A Prospective Study of the Roles of Overall Glycemic Index and Glycemic Load." *International Journal of Cancer* 2005;114(4):653–658.

Sirtori, C.R. "Risks and Benefits of Soy Phytoestrogens in Cardiovascular Diseases, Cancer, Climacteric Symptoms and Osteoporosis." *Drug Safety* 2001; 24:665–682.

Stefansson, Vilhjamur. *Cancer: A Disease of Civilization?* New York: Hill and Wang, 1960.

van Poppel, G., D.T. Verhoeven, H. Verhagen, and R.A. Goldbohm. "Brassica Vegetables and Cancer Prevention. Epidemiology and Mechanisms." *Advances in Experimental Medicine and Biology* 1999;472:159–168.

Warburg, Otto. "On the Origin of Cancer Cells." *Science* 1956;123(3191):309–314.

Willett, Walter C. "Diet and Cancer: One View at the Start of the Millennium." *Cancer Epidemiology, Biomarkers & Prevention* 2001;10:3–8.

Yeager, Selene, and *Prevention* Magazine Health Books (eds.). *New Foods for Healing.* New York: Bantam Books, 1998.

Zhang, S., et al. "Measurement of Retinoids and Carotenoids in Breast Adipose Tissue and a Comparison of Concentrations in Breast Cancer Cases and Control Subjects." *American Journal of Clinical Nutrition* 1997;66:626–632.

Depression

Alpert, J.E., and M. Fava. "Nutrition and Depression: The Role of Folate." *Nutrition Reviews* 1997;55:145–149.

Bauer, Joy. *Joy Bauer's Food Cures: Easy 4-Step Nutrition Programs for Improving Your Body.* New York: Rodale, 2007.

Bennett, Connie, Stephen T. Sinatra, and Nicholas Perricone. *Sugar Shock!: How Sweets and Simple Carbs Can Derail Your Life—and How You Can Get Back on Track.* New York: Berkley, 2007.

Bottiglieri, T. "Homocysteine and Folate Metabolism in Depression." *Progress in Neuropsychopharmacology & Biological Psychiatry* 2005;29(7):1103–1112.

Christensen, L. "Psychological Distress and Diet Effects of Sucrose and Caffeine." *Journal of Applied Nutrition* 1988;40:44–50.

Coppen, A., and C. Bolander-Gouaille. "Treatment of Depression: Time to Consider Folic Acid and Vitamin B12." *Journal of Psychopharmacology* 2005;19(1):59–65.

Diehl, D.J., and S. Gershon. "The Role of Dopamine in Mood Disorders." *Comprehensive Psychiatry* 1992;33(2):115–120.

Fife, Bruce. "Do You Eat Enough Fat?" *http://www.jctonic.com/include/healingcrisis/14enough_fat.htm.*

Gettis, A. "Food Sensitivities and Psychological Disturbance: A Review." *Journal of Nutrition, Health & Aging* 1989;6:135–146.

Gloth, F.M. III, W. Alam, and B. Hollis. "Vitamin D vs. Broad Spectrum Phototherapy in the Treatment of Seasonal Affective Disorder." *Journal of Nutrition, Health & Aging* 1999;3(1):5–7.

Haskell, C.F., D.O. Kennedy, K.A. Wesnes, and A.B. Scholey. "Cognitive and Mood Improvements of Caffeine in Habitual Consumers and Habitual Non-consumers of Caffeine." *Psychopharmacology* (Bed.) 2005; 179(4):813–825.

Hypericum Depression Trial Study Group. "Effect of Hypericum Perforatum (St. John's Wort) in Major Depressive Disorder: A Randomized Controlled Trial. *Journal of the American Medical Association* 2002;287(14):1807–1814.

James, J.E., and P.J. Rogers. "Effects of Caffeine on Performance and Mood: Withdrawal Reversal Is the Most Plausible Explanation." *Psychopharmacology* (Berl.) 2005;182(1):1–8.

Lansdowne, A.T., and S.C. Provost. "Vitamin D3 Enhances Mood in Healthy Subjects During Winter." *Psychopharmacology* (Bed.) 1998;135(4):319–323.

Lee, S., K.M. Gura, S. Kim, et al. "Current Clinical Applications of Omega-6 and Omega-3 Fatty Acids." *Nutrition in Clinical Practice* 2006;21(4):323–341.

Maes, M., A. Christophe, J. Delanghe J., et al. "Lowered Omega-3 Polyunsaturated Fatty Acids in Serum Phospholipids and Cholesterol Esters of Depressed Patients." *Psychiatry Research* 1999;85:275–291.

Mart, Krista. "A Depression-Free Diet." *http://www.dukehealth.org.*

Murray, Michael, Joseph Pizzorno, and Lara Pizzorno. *The Encyclopedia of Healing Foods.* New York: Atria, 2005.

Noaghiul, S., and J.R. Hibbeln. Cross-national Comparisons of Seafood Consumption and Rates of Bipolar Disorders. *American Journal of Psychiatry* 2003;160(12):2222–2227.

Parker, G., N.A. Gibson, H. Brotchie, et al. Omega-3 Fatty Acids and Mood Disorders. *American Journal of Psychiatry* 2006;163(6):969–978.

Penninx, B., J.M. Guralnik, and L. Ferrucci. "Vitamin B (12) Deficiency and Depression in Physically Disabled Older Women: Epidemiologic Evidence from the Women's Health and Aging Study." *American Journal of Psychiatry* 2000;157:715–721.

Police Psychology. "Caffeine and Health: The Latte Letdown." *http://www.policepsych.com.*

Prevention Magazine Health Books. *Healing with Vitamins.* Emmaus, PA: Rodale Press, 1996.

Schrader, D. "Equivalence of St. John's Wort Extract (ZE 117) and Fluoxetine: A Randomized, Controlled Study in Mild-Moderate Depression." *International Clinical Psychopharmacology* 2000;15:61–68.

Schwarcz, Joe, and Frances Berkoff. *Foods That Harm, Foods That Heal: An A–Z Guide to Safe and Healthy Eating.* Pleasantville, NY: Reader's Digest Association, 2004.

Shelton, R.C., M.B. Keller, A. Gelenberg, et al. "Effectiveness of St. John's Wort in Major Depression: A Randomized Controlled Trial." *Journal of the American Medical Association* 2001;285(15):1978–1986.

Smith, A., D. Sutherland, and G. Christopher. "Effects of Repeated Doses of Caffeine on Mood and Performance of Alert and Fatigued Volunteers." *Journal of Psychopharmacology* 2005;19(6):620–626.

Somer, Elizabeth. *Food and Mood: The Complete Guide to Eating Well and Feeling Your Best.* New York: Henry Holt, 1999.

Sontrop, J., and M.K. Campbell. "Omega-3 Polyunsaturated Fatty Acids and Depression: A Review of the Evidence and a Methodological Critique." *Preventive Medicine* 2006;42(1):4–13.

Stoll, A.L., W.E. Severus, M.P. Freeman, et al. "Omega 3 Fatty Acids in Bipolar Disorder. A Preliminary Double-Blind, Placebo-Controlled Trial." *Archives of General Psychiatry* 1999;56:407–412.

Szegedi, A., R. Kohnen, A. Dienel, M. Kieser. "Acute Treatment of Moderate to Severe Depression with Hypericum Extract WS 5570 (St. John's Wort): Randomized Controlled Double Blind Non-inferiority Trial versus Paroxetine." *British Medical Journal* [serial online] 2005;330(7490):503.

Trivedi, M.H., T.L. Greer, B.D. Grannemann, et al. "Exercise as an Augmentation Strategy for Treatment of Major Depression." *Journal of Psychiatric Practice* 2006;12(4):205–213.

Volz, H.P., and P. Laux. "Potential Treatment for Subthreshold and Mild Depression: A Comparison of St. John's Wort Extracts and Fluoxetine." *Comprehensive Psychiatry* 2000;41(2 Suppl. 1):133–137.

Weber, B., U. Schweiger, M. Deuschle, and I. Heuser. "Major Depression and Impaired Glucose Tolerance." *Experimental and Clinical Endocrinology & Diabetes* 2000;108:187–190.

Woelk, H. "Comparison of St. John's Wort and Imipramine for Treating Depression: Randomized Controlled Trial." *British Medical Journal* 2000;321:536–539.

Vieth, R., S. Kimball, A. Hu, and P.G. Walfish. "Randomized Comparison of the Effects of the Vitamin D3 Adequate Intake versus 100 mcg (4000 IU) per Day on Biochemical Responses and the Well-Being of Patients." *Nutrition Journal* [serial online] 2004;3:8.

Yeager, Selene, and *Prevention* Magazine Health Books (eds.). *New Foods for Healing.* New York: Bantam Books, 1998.

Diabetes

American Diabetes Association. "Complications Associated to Type 2 Diabetes." *http://www.diabetes.org.*

———. "The Diabetes Food Pyramid: Fat." *http://www.diabetes.org.*

———. "Diabetes Statistics." *http://www.diabetes.org.*

———. "Direct and Indirect Costs of Diabetes in the United States." *http://www.diabetes.org.*

———. "A Guide to Beans, Lentils, Legumes and Pulses." *http://www.diabetes.org.*

———. "Identifying Symptoms for Diabetes." *http://www.diabetes.org.*

———. "National Diabetes Fact Sheet." *http://www.diabetes.org.*

———. "The Scoop on Sugar." *http://www.diabetes.org.*

———. "Standards of Medical Care in Diabetes—2006." *http://care.diabetesjournals.org.*

———. "Statement Regarding Sugar." *http://www.diabetes.org.*

———. "Sugar and Sugar Substitutes." *http://www.diabetes.org.*

Boyle, James P., Michael P. Milburn, et al. "Projection of Diabetes Burden Through 2050: Impact of Changing Demography and Disease Prevalence in the U.S." *Diabetes Care* 2001;24:1936–1940.

Brynes, A.E., J.L. Lee, R.E. Brighton, et al. "A Low Glycemic Diet Significantly Improves the 24-Hour Blood Glucose Profile in People with Type 2 Diabetes, as Assessed Using the Continuous Glucose MiniMed Monitor." *Diabetes Care* 2003;26:548–549.

Center for Science in the Public Interest. "Calcium, D, & Diabetes." *Nutrition Action Healthletter* 2006;May.

Chandalia, M., A. Garg, D. Lutjohann, et al. "Beneficial Effects of High Dietary Fiber Intake in Patients with Type 2 Diabetes Mellitus." *The New England Journal of Medicine* 2000;342:1392–1398.

Gannon, Mary C., and Frank Q. Nuttall. "Control of Blood Glucose in Type 2 Diabetes Without Weight Loss by Modification of Diet Composition." *Nutrition and Metabolism* 2006;3:16.

_____. "Effect of a High-Protein, Low-Carbohydrate Diet on Blood Glucose Control in People with Type 2 Diabetes." *Diabetes* 2004;53(9):2375–2382.

Gray, Liz. "Does the Food Pyramid Diet Lead to Additional Diseases in Diabetics? Research Says...Yes." *Native American Times*, April 22, 2004.

Gross, Lee S., Li Li, Earl S. Ford, and Simln Liu. "Increased Consumption of Refined Carbohydrates and the Epidemic of Type 2 Diabetes in the United States: An Ecologic Assessment." *American Journal of Clinical Nutrition* 2004;79:774–779.

Diabetes in Control. "Low-Carb Diet Controls Diabetes Without Weight Loss or Insulin Use." *http://www.diabetesincontrol.com.*

Giacco, R., M. Parillo, A.A. Rivellese, et al. "Long-Term Dietary Treatment with Increased Amounts of Fiber-Rich Low-Glycemic Index Natural Foods Improves Blood Glucose Control and Reduces the Number of Hypoglycemic Events in Type 1 Diabetic Patients." *Diabetes Care* 2000;23:1461–1466.

Hodge, A.M., D.R. English, K. O'Dea, and G.G. Giles. "Glycemic Index and Fiber as Risk Factors for Type 2 Diabetes in the MCCS." *Diabetes Care* 2004;27(11):2701–2706.

_____. "Increased Diabetes Incidence in Greek and Italian Migrants to Australia: How Much Can Be Explained by Known Risk Factors." *Diabetes Care* 2004;27(10):2330–2334.

Howarth, N.C., T.T. Huang, S.B. Roberts, and M.A. McCrory. "Dietary Fiber and Fat Are Associated with Excess Weight in Young and Middle-Aged US Adults." *Journal of the American Dietetic Association* 2005;105:1365–1372.

Hu, F.B., J.E. Manson, M.J. Stampfer, et al. "Diet, Lifestyle and the Risk of Type 2 Diabetes Mellitus in Women." *New England Journal of Medicine* 2001;345:790–797.

Hung, T., J.L. Sievenpiper, A. Marchie, C.W. Kendall, and D.J. Jenkins. "Fat Versus Carbohydrate in Insulin Resistance, Obesity, Diabetes and Cardiovascular Disease." *Current Opinion in Clinical Nutrition & Metabolic Care* 2003;6:165–176.

Jarvi, A.E., B.E. Karlstrom, Y.E. Granfeldt, et al. "Improved Glycemic Control and Lipid Profile and Normalized Fibrinolytic Activity on a Low Glycemic Index Diet in Type 2 Diabetic Patients." *Diabetes Care* 1999;22:10–18.

Khan, A., M. Safdar, M.M. Ali Khan, K.N. Khattak, and R.A. Anderson. "Cinnamon Improves Glucose and Lipids of People with Type 2 Diabetes." *Diabetes Care* 2003;26(12):3215–3218.

Kleinfield, N.R. "Diabetes and Its Awful Toll Quietly Emerge as a Crisis." *The New York Times,* January 9, 2006.

_____. "Living at an Epicenter of Diabetes, Defiance and Despair." *The New York Times*, January 10, 2006.

Littman, A.J., A.R. Kristal, and E. White. "Effects of Physical Activity Intensity, Frequency, and Activity Type on 10-Y Weight Change in Middle-Aged Men and Women." *International Journal of Obesity* 2005;29:524–533.

Liu, Simin, JoAnn E. Manson, Meir J. Stampfer, Michelle D. Holmes, Frank B. Hu, Susan E. Hankinson, and Walter C. Willett. "Carbohydrate Metabolism and Diabetes: Dietary Glycemic Load Assessed by Food-Frequency Questionnaire in Relation to Plasma High-Density-Lipoprotein Cholesterol and Fasting Plasma Triacylglycerols in Postmenopausal Women." *American Journal of Clinical Nutrition* 2001;73:560–566.

MacKenzie, Debora. "Cinnamon Spice Produces Healthier Blood." *New Scientist* 2003;17:52.

MayoClinic.com. "Diabetes Foods: Is Honey a Good Substitute for Sugar." *http://www.mayoclinic.com.*

_____. "Diabetes Nutrition: Including Sweets in Your Meal Plan." *http://www.mayoclinic.com.*

Meyer, Katie A., Lawrence H. Kush, David R. Jacobs, Jr., Joanne Slaving, Thomas A. Sellers, and Aaron R. Folsom. "Carbohydrate Metabolism and Diabetes: Carbohydrates, Dietary Fiber, and Incident Type 2 Diabetes in Older Women." *American Journal of Clinical Nutrition* 2000;71:921–930.

Narayan, K., M. Venkat, et al. "Lifetime Risk for Diabetes Mellitus in the United States." *Journal of the American Medical Association* 2003;290(14):1884–1890.

National Diabetes Information Clearinghouse. "Diabetes Prevention Program (DPP)." *http://diabetes.niddk.nih.gov.*

_____. "The Pima Indians, Pathfinders for Health." *http://diabetes.niddk.nih.gov.*

O'Connor, Andrew S., and Jeffrey R. Schelling. "Diabetes and the Kidney." *American Journal of Kidney Diseases* 2005;46(4):766–773.

O'Dea, Kerin. "Diabetes in Australian Aboriginal and Torres Strait Islander Peoples." *Papua and New Guinea Medical Journal* 2001;44:164–170.

_____. "Marked Improvement in Carbohydrate and Lipid Metabolism in Diabetic Australian Aborigines After Temporary Reversion to Traditional Lifestyle." *Diabetes* 1984;33:596–603.

Pittas, A.G., B. Dawson-Hughes, and T. Li. "Vitamin D and Calcium Intake in Relation to Type 2 Diabetes in Women." *Diabetes Care* 2006;29:650–656.

Popov, D., M. Simionescu, and P.R. Shepherd. "Saturated-Fat Diet Induces Moderate Diabetes and Severe Glomerulosclerosis in Hamsters." *Diabetologia* 2003;46:1408–1418.

Prevention Magazine Health Books (eds.). *The Healthy Cook*. Emmaus, PA: Rodale, 1997.

Tuomilehto, J., J. Lindstrom, and J.G. Eriksson. "Prevention of Type 2 Diabetes Mellitus by Changes in Lifestyle Among Subjects with Impaired Glucose Tolerance." *New England Journal of Medicine* 2001;344:1343–1350.

Upritchard, J.E., et al. "Effect of Supplementation with Tomato Juice, Vitamin E, and Vitamin C on LDL Oxidation and Products of Inflammatory Activity in Type 2 Diabetes." *Diabetes Care* 2000;23(6):733–738.

Weigley, E.S. "Average? Ideal? Desirable? A Brief Overview of Height-Weight Tables in the United States." *Journal of the American Dietetic Association* 1984;84:417–423.

Wild, Sarah, G. Roglic, A. Green, et al. "Global Prevalence of Diabetes: Estimates for the Year 2000 and Projections for 2030." *Diabetes Care* 2004;27(5):1047–1053.

Willett, Walter, JoAnn Manson, and Simin Liu. "Glycemic Index, Glycemic Load, and Risk of Type 2 Diabetes." *American Journal of Clinical Nutrition* 2002;76(1):274S–280S. Presented at a symposium held at Experimental Biology 2001, Orlando, Florida, April 1, 2001.

Wolever, T.M., D. Jenkins, V. Vuksan, A.L. Jenkins, G.S. Wong, and R.G. Josse. "Beneficial Effect of Low-Glycemic Index Diet in Overweight NIDDM Subjects." *Diabetes Care* 1992;15:562–564.

World Health Organization. "Diabetes: The Cost of Diabetes." *http://www.who.org*.

Yeh, G.Y., D.M. Eisenberg, T.J. Kaptchuk, and R.S. Phillips. "Systematic Review of Herbs and Dietary Supplements for Glycemic Control in Diabetes." *Diabetes Care* 2003;26:1277–1294.

Digestive Disorders

Boutin, Chad. "Vitamin E in Plant Seeds Could Halt Prostate, Lung Cancer." Purdue News Service, December 14, 2004, *www.purdue.edu/newsroom*.

Celiac Disease Foundation. "Cause of Celiac Disease." *http://www.celiac.org*.

Ellis, H.J., and Ciclitira, P. J. "Should Celiac Sufferers Be Allowed Their Oats?" *European Journal of Gastroenterology & Hepatology* 2008;20(6):492–493.

Edelberg, David, and Hough, Heidi. *The Triple Whammy Cure*. New York: Free Press, 2007.

MayoClinic.com. "Celiac Disease: Lifestyle and Home Remedies." *http://www.mayoclinic.com*.

Naruszewicz, Marek, et al. "Effect of *Lactobacillus plantarum* 299v on Cardiovascular Disease Risk Factors in Smokers." *American Journal of Clinical Nutrition* 2002;76(6):1249–1255.

National Digestive Diseases Information Clearinghouse (NDDIC). "Constipation." *http://digestive.niddk.nih.gov/ddiseases/pubs/constipation/*.

University of Maryland School of Medicine. "What Is Celiac Disease?" *http://www.celiaccenter.org/faq.asp*.

WebMD. "11 Meal Planning Tips to Prevent Heartburn." *http://www.webmd.com*.

Erectile Dysfunction

Advanced Health and Life Extension. "Zinc in Health and Nutrition." *http://www.advance-health.com*.

Altmedicine.about. "Natural Remedies for Erectile Dysfunction." *http://altmedicine.about.com*.

American Academy of Anti-Aging Medicine. "Chocolate: A Boon for the Libido and the Heart." *http://www.worldhealth.net*.

Health.MSN.com. "Oysters May Be an Aphrodisiac After All." *http://health.msn.com*.

Lewis, Benjamin, Marianne Legato, and Harry Fisch. "Medical Implications of the Male Biological Clock." *Journal of the American Medical Association* 2006;296:2369–2371.

Men's Health Magazine (eds.). "Factors that Affect Spermatogenesis." In: *The Complete Book of Men's Health*. Emmaus, PA: Rodale Press, 2000.

Raloff, Janet. "Smoking Away Vitamin C—Cigarette Smoking Depletes Vitamin C Levels." *Science News*, June 8, 1991.

U.S. News & World Report. "Erectile Dysfunction." *http://health.usnews.com*.

Yeager, Selene, and *Prevention* Magazine Health Books (eds.). *New Foods for Healing*. New York: Bantam Books, 1998.

Eye Disease

Abel, Robert. *The Eye Care Revolution*. Grand Rapids, MI: Kensington Corporation, 1999.

American Optometric Association. "Antioxidants and Age-Related Eye Disease." *http://www.aoa.org*.

_____. "Lutein and Zeaxanthin—Eye-Friendly Nutrients." *http://www.aoa.org*.

Aviation Flight Medicine. "Optimum Vision and Eye Protection." *http://www.aviationmedicine.com*.

Chiro.org. "Quercetin: A Review of Clinical Applications." *http://www.chiro.org*.

Ferrigno, L., R. Aldigeri, F. Rosmini, et al. "Associations Between Plasma Levels of Vitamins and Cataract in the Italian-American Clinical Trial of Nutritional

Supplements and Age-Related Cataract (CTNS): CTNS Report #2." *Ophthalmic Epidemiology* 2005; 12(2): 71–80.

Gale, C.R., N.F. Hall, D.I.W. Phillips, and C.N. Martyn. "Lutein and Zeaxanthin Status and Risk of Age-Related Macular Degeneration." *Investigative Ophthalmology & Visual Science* 2003;44(6):2461–2465.

Illinois Eye & Ear Infirmary. "The Eye Digest." *http://www.agingeye.net*.

Jacques, P. "The Potential Preventive Effects of Vitamins for Cataract and Age-Related Macular Degeneration." *International Journal for Vitamin and Nutrition Research* 1999;69:198–205.

Jacques, P.F., A. Taylor, S. Moeller, et al. "Long-Term Nutrient Intake and 5-Year Change in Nuclear Lens Opacities." *Archives of Ophthalmology* 2005;123(4):517–526.

Kuzniarz, M., P. Mitchell, R.G. Cumming, and V.M. Flood. "Use of Vitamin Supplements and Cataract: The Blue Mountains Eye Study." *American Journal of Ophthalmology* 2001;132(1):19–26.

Leske, M.C., L.T. Chylack Jr., and Sy Wu. "The Lens Opacities Case-Control Study. Risk Factors for Cataract." *Archives of Ophthalmology* 1991;109(2):244–25l.

Lipschitz, David A. *Breaking the Rules of Aging*. Washington, D.C.: LifeLine Press, 2002.

McGuire, R. "Fish Oil Cuts Lower Ocular Pressure." *Medical Tribune* 1991;September 19:25.

Medical News Today. "Nutrition Scientists Take a Look at Cataract Prevention." *http://www.sciencedaily.com*.

Moeller, S.M., A. Taylor, K.L. Tucker, et al. "Overall Adherence to the Dietary Guidelines for Americans Is Associated with Reduced Prevalence of Early Age-Related Nuclear Lens Opacities in Women." *Journal of Nutrition* 2004;134(7):1812–1819.

Murray, Michael, Joseph Pizzorno, and Lara Pizzorno. *The Encyclopedia of Healing Foods*. New York: Atria, 2005.

Newsome, D.A., and R.J. Rothman. "Zinc Uptake in Vitro by Human Retinal Pigment Epithelium. *Investigative Ophthalmology & Visual Science* 1987;28(11):1795–1799.

Pratt, Steven G., and Kathy Matthews. *SuperFoods Rx: Fourteen Foods That Will Change Your Life*. New York: HarperCollins, 2005.

Prevention Magazine Health Books. *Healing with Vitamins*. Emmaus, PA: Rodale Press, 1996.

Richer, S. "Nutritional Influences on Eye Health." *Optometry* 2000;71(l0):657–666.

_____, W. Stiles, L. Statkute, et al. "Double-Masked, Placebo-Controlled, Randomized Trial of Lutein and Antioxidant Supplementation in the Intervention of Atrophic Age-Related Macular Degeneration: The Veterans LAST Study (Lutein Antioxidant Supplementation Trial). *Optometry* 2004;76(4):216–230.

Robertson, J.M., A.P. Donner, and J.R. Trevithick. "A Possible Role for Vitamins C and E in Cataract Prevention." *American Journal of Clinical Nutrition* 1991;53(1 Suppl.):346S–351S.

Fatigue

Arieli, Amichai, Yoram Epstein, Shay Brill, Michael Winer, and Yair Shapiro. "Effect of Food Intake on Exercise Fatigue in Trained and Untrained Subjects." *European Journal of Applied Physiology and Occupational Physiology* 1985;54:297–300.

Bastyr Center for Natural Health. "Iron Deficiency and Exercise Fatigue." *http://www.bastyrcenter.org*.

Doctor Yourself.com. "Chronic Fatigue and Immune Dysfunction Syndrome: Alternative Approaches." *http://www.doctoryourself.com*.

Knowles, David "Facts on Fatigue." *http://www.bodybuilding.com/fun/david32.htm*.

Linus Pauling Institute. "Vitamin C." *http://lpi.oregonstate.edu*.

MayoClinic.com. "Vitamin Deficiency Anemia." *http://www.mayoclinic.com*.

Medline Plus. "Potassium in Diet." *http://www.nlm.nih.gov/medlineplus*.

Prevention Magazine Health Books. *Healing with Vitamins*. Emmaus, PA: Rodale Press, 1996. pp. 182–184, 247.

Somer, Elizabeth. *Food and Mood: The Complete Guide to Eating Well and Feeling Your Best*. New York: Henry Holt, 1999.

Strand, Erik. "Fighting Fatigue with Diet." *Psychology Today*, October 1, 2003.

The Triple Whammy Cure. "Health Tip from David Edelberg, M.D." *http://mail.dredelberg.com*.

USDA. "Dietary Guidelines for Americans 2005." Appendix B, Food Sources of Selected Nutrients, *http://www.cnpp.usda.gov/DietaryGuidelines.htm*.

Yeager, Selene, and *Prevention* Magazine Health Books (eds.). *New Foods for Healing*. New York: Bantam Books, 1998.

Heart Disease

Abbassi, F., T. McLaughlin, C. Lamendola, H.S. Kim, A. Tanaka, T. Wang, K. Nakajima, and G.M. Reaven. "High Carbohydrate Diets, Triglycerides-Rich Lipoproteins, and Coronary Heart Disease Risk." *American Journal of Cardiology* 2000;85:45–48.

Albert, C.M., H. Campos, M.J. Stampfer, et al. "Blood Levels of Long-Chain N-3 Fatty Acids and the Risk of

Sudden Death." *The New England Journal of Medicine* 2002;346:1113–1118.

American Heart Association. "AHA Scientific Statement, AHA Dietary Guidelines, Revision 2000: A Statement for Healthcare Professionals from the Nutrition Committee of the American Heart Association." *http://circ.ahajournals.org.*

———."Dietary Guidelines." *http://www.heart.org/HEARTORG/.*

———. "Diets Rich in Omega-3 Fatty Acids May Lower Blood Pressure." *http://www.heart.org/HEARTORG/.*

———. "Heart Disease Still No.1 Killer, 2006 Statistics Update Reports." *http://www.heart.org/HEARTORG/.*

———. "Metabolic Syndrome." *http://www.heart.org/HEART ORG/.*

———. "Metabolic Syndrome May Be an Important Link to Stroke." *http://www.heart.org/HEARTORG/.*

———. "Profiling High Blood Pressure as a Silent Killer." *http://www.heart.org/HEARTORG/.*

Archer, S.L., K. Liu, A.R. Dyer, K.J. Ruth, D.R. Jacobs, Jr., L. Van Horn, J.E. Hilner, and P.J. Savage. "Relationship Between Changes in Dietary Sucrose and High-Density Lipoprotein Cholesterol: The CARDIA Study. Coronary Artery Risk Development in Young Adults." *Annals of Epidemiology* 1998;8(7):433–438.

Bauer, Joy. *Joy Bauer's Food Cures: Easy 4-Step Nutrition Programs for Improving Your Body.* New York: Rodale Press, 2007.

BBC News. "Hibiscus May Reduce Cholesterol." *http://news.bbc.co.uk.*

Bougnoux, P. "N-3 Polyunsaturated Fatty Acids and Cancer." *Current Opinion in Clinical Nutrition & Metabolic Care* 1999;2:121–126.

Brody, Jane E. "Sorting Out Coffee's Contradictions." *The New York Times,* August 5, 2008.

Bucher, H.C., P. Hengstler, C. Schindler, and G. Meier. "N-3 Polyunsaturated Fatty Acids in Coronary Heart Disease: A Meta-Analysis of Randomized Controlled Trials." *American Journal of Medicine* 2002;112:298–304.

Carper, Jean. *The Food Pharmacy: Dramatic New Evidence That Food Is Your Best Medicine.* New York: Pocket Books, 1998.

Cater, N.B., and A. Garg. "Serum Low-Density Lipoprotein Cholesterol Response to Modification of Saturated Fat Inake: Recent Insights." *Current Opinion in Lipidology* 1997;8:332–336.

Cooper, Kenneth. *Controlling Cholesterol the Natural Way.* New York: Bantam, 1999.

DeNoon, Daniel J. "Dark Chocolate Is Healthy Chocolate: Dark Chocolate Has Health Benefits Not Seen in Other Varieties." *http://www.WebMD.com.*

Desroches, S., Mauger, I.F., Ausman, L.M., et al. "Soy Protein Favorably Affects LDL Size Independently of Isofla-

vones in Hypercholesterolemic Men and Women." *Journal of Nutrition* 2004;134(3):574–579.

El-Enein, A.M.A. "The Role of Nicotinic Acid and Inositol Hexaniacinate as Anticholesterolemic and Antilipemic Agents." *Nutrition Reports International* 1983;28:899–911.

Ellis, R.W. "Infection and Coronary Heart Disease." *Journal of Medical Microbiology* 1997;46:535–539.

FDA News. "FDA Allows Qualified Health Claim to Decrease Risk of Coronary Heart Disease." *http://www.fda.gov.*

Fernandez, M.L. "Soluble Fiber and Nondigestible Carbohydrate Effects on Plasma Lipids and Cardiovascular Risk." *Current Opinion in Lipidology* 2001;12(1):35–40.

Fleming, Richard M. *Stop Inflammation Now.* New York: Avery, 2004.

Ford, E.S., and S. Liu. "Glycemic Index and Serum High-Density Lipoprotein Cholesterol Concentration among U.S. Adults." *Archives of Internal Medicine* 2001;161(4):572–576.

Fried, S.K., and S.P. Rao. "Sugars, Hyperuiglyceridemia, and Cardiovascular Disease." *American Journal of Clinical Nutrition* 2003;78(4):873S–880S.

Gaziano, Michael J., Charles H. Hennekens, Christopher J. O'Donnell, Jan L. Breslow, and Julie E. Buring. "Fasting Triglycerides, High-Density Lipoprotein, and Risk of Myocardial Infarction." *Circulation* 1997;96:2520–2525.

Gotto, Antonio M., Jr. "Triglyceride: The Forbore Risk Factor." *Circulation* 1998;97:1027–1028.

Grady, Denise. "A Search for Answers in Russert's Death." *The New York Times,* June 17, 2008.

Harvard School of Public Health. "Fats & Cholesterol." *http://www.hsph.harvard.edu.*

Hayes, Sharonne. "Heart Disease in Women: A Mayo Clinic Specialist Answers Questions." *http://www.mayoclinic.com.*

Hayward, Rodney A., Timothy P. Hofer, and Sandeep Vijan. "Narrative Review: Lack of Evidence for Recommended Low-Density Lipoprotein Treatment Targets: A Solvable Problem." *Annals of Internal Medicine* 2006;145(7):520–530.

The Heart.org. *http://www.theheart.org.*

Howard, B.Y., et al. "Low-Fat Dietary Pattern and Risk of Cardiovascular Disease: The Women's Health Initiative Randomized Controlled Dietary Modification Trial." *Journal of the American Medical Association* 2006;295(6):655–666.

Howard, Barbara Y., and Judith Wylie Rosett. "Sugar and Cardiovascular Disease: A Statement for Healthcare Professionals from the Committee on Nutrition of the Council on Nutrition, Physical Activity, and

Metabolism of the American Heart Association." *Circulation* 2002;106:523–527.

Hu, F.B., L. Bronner, W.C. Willett, et al. "Fish and Omega-3 Fatty Acid Intake and Risk of Coronary Heart Disease in Women." *Journal of the American Medical Association* 2002;287:1815–1821.

Illingworth, D.R., et al. "Comparative Effects of Lovastatin and Niacin in Primary Hypercholesterolemia." *Archives of Internal Medicine* 1994;154:1586–1595.

Jeppesen, Jorgen, Hans Ole Hein, Poul Suadicani, and Finn Gyntelberg. "Triglyceride Concentration and Ischemic Heart Disease: An Eight-Year Follow-Up in the Copenhagen Male Study." *Circulation* 1998;97:1029–1036.

Johns Hopkins Health Alerts. "Heart Health." *http://www. johnshopkinshealthalerts.com.*

Knekt, P., J. Kumpulainen, R. Jarvinen, H. Rissanen, M. Heliovaara, A. Reunanen, T. Hakulinen, and A. Aromaa. "Flavonoid Intake and Risk of Chronic Diseases." *The American Journal of Clinical Nutrition* 2002;76(3):560–568.

Kromhout, D., A. Menotti, B. Bloemberg, et al. "Dietary Saturated and Trans Fatty Acids and Cholesterol and 25-Year Mortality from Coronary Heart Disease: The Seven Countries Study." *Preventive Medicine* 1995;24:308–315.

Lill, Simin, et al. "A Prospective Study of Dietary Glycemic Load, Carbohydrate Intake, and Risk of Coronary Heart Disease in U.S. Women." *American Journal of Clinical Nutrition* 2000;71:1455–1461.

Lipschitz, David A. *Breaking the Rules of Aging.* Washington, D.C.: LifeLine Press, 2002.

Liu, Simin, Walter C. Willett, Meir J. Stampfer, Frank B. Hu, Mary Franz, Laura Sampson, Charles H. Hennekens, and JoAnn E. Manson. "Lipids and Cardiovascular Risks: A Prospective Study of Dietary Glycemic Load, Carbohydrate Intake, and Risk of Coronary Heart Disease in U.S. Women." *American Journal of Clinical Nutrition* 2000;71(6):1455–1461.

Mateljan, George. *The World's Healthiest Foods: Essential Guide for the Healthiest Way of Eating.* Grand Rapids, MI: GMF, 2007.

Mayo Clinic.com. "Trans Fat: Avoid This Cholesterol Double Whammy." *http://www.mayoclinic.com.*

――――. "Soy: Does It Reduce Cholesterol?" *http://www.mayo clinic.com.*

McNamara, D.J. "Dietary Cholesterol and Atherosclerosis." *Bichimica et Biophysica Acta* 2000;1529:310–320.

Medical News Today. "Heart Attack Risk 30% Higher with Western Diet." *http://www.medicalnewstoday.com.*

――――. "Men with Cardiovascular Disease May Be at Considerably Increased Risk for Death Even When Their Blood Sugar Level Remains in the 'Normal' Range." *http://www.medicalnewstoday.com.*

Medicinal Food News. "Blueberries Should Be in Your Diet." *http://www.medicinalfoodnews.com.*

Meggs, William Joel. *The Inflammation Cure.* New York: McGraw-Hill, 2004.

Menotti, A., D. Krornhout, H. Blackburn, et al. "Food Intake Patterns and 25-Year Mortality from Coronary Heart Disease: Cross-cultural Correlations in the Seven Countries Study. The Seven Countries Study Research Group." *European Journal of Epidemiology* 1999;15(6):507–515.

Mercola, Joseph. "High Triglycerides Risk for Heart Attack." *http://www.mercola.com.*

――――. "Omega-3: How to Properly Increase Intake of Omega-3 with Krill Oil to Protect against Disease." *http:// www.mercola.com.*

――――. "Omega-3's Protect against Clogged Arteries." *http:// www.mercola.com.*

――――. "Triglycerides May Predict Heart Risk." *http://www. mercola.com.*

Michaud, Ellen, and Anita Hirsch. *The Healing Kitchen: From Tea Tin to Fruit Basket, Breadbox to Veggie Bin—How to Unlock the Power of Foods That Heal.* New York: BenBella Books, 2006.

Murray, Michael, J. Pizzorno, and L. Pizzorno. *The Encyclopedia of Healing Foods.* New York: Atria, 2005.

Natural News. Browning, Leslee D. "Artichoke Leaf Extract Lowers Cholesterol." *http://naturalnews.com.*

――――. Connealy, Leigh E. "Getting to the Heart of Women's Health." *http://naturalnews.com.*

――――. "Just One Meal High in Saturated Fat Alters Cholesterol Chemistry for the Worse." *http://naturalnews. com.*

Nelson, G.J. "Dietary Fat, Trans Fatty Acids, and Risk of Coronary Heart Disease." *Nutrition Reviews* 1998;56:250–252.

Pan, J., M. Lin, R.L. Kesala, J. Van, M.A. Charles. "Niacin Treatment of the Atherogenic Lipid Profile and Lp(a) in Diabetes." *Diabetes Obesity & Metabolism* 2002;4:255–261.

Piscatella, Joseph. *Take a Load Off Your Heart.* New York: Workman, 2003.

Port, Sidney C., Noel G. Boyle, Willa A. Hsueh, Manuel J. Quiñones, Robert I. Jennrich, and Mark O. Goodarzi. "The Predictive Role of Blood Glucose for Mortality in Subjects with Cardiovascular Disease." *American Journal of Epidemiology* 2006;163(4):342–351.

Pratt, Steven G., and Kathy Matthews. *SuperFoods Rx: Fourteen Foods That Will Change Your Life.* New York: HarperCollins, 2005.

Prevention.com. "Top 10 Cholesterol Fighting Foods." *http:// www.prevention.com.*

Rimm, E. "Commentary: Alcohol and Coronary Heart Disease—Laying the Foundation for Future Work." *International Journal of Epidemiology* 2001;30:738–739.

Science Daily. "Increased Consumption of Soy Protein May Help Lower Cholesterol." *http://www.sciencedaily.com*.

Science News Online. "Reevaluating Eggs' Cholesterol Risks." *http://www.sciencenews.org*.

Simopoulos, A.P. "The Importance of the Ratio of Omega-6/Omega-3 Essential Fatty Acids." *Biomedicine & Pharmacotherapy* 2002;56:365–379.

Stamler, J., P. Elliott, and B. Dennis. "INTERMAP: Background, Aims, Design, Methods, and Descriptive Statistics (Nondietary)." *Journal of Human Hypertension* 2003;17:591–608.

Swircenski, Mark. "Toxic Blood Syndrome." *Alaska Wellness*, July 2001. *http://www.alaskawellness.com*.

The Triple Whammy Cure. "Health Tip from David Edelberg, M.D.: Zzzzz: You're Getting Sleepy and Your Heart is Happy." *http://mail.dredelberg.com*.

USDA Nutrient Data Laboratory. "Search the USDA National Nutrient Database for Standard Reference." *http://www.nal.usda.gov*.

Wagner, J.D., D.C. Schwenke, K.A. Greaves, et al. "Soy Protein with Isoflavones, but Not an Isoflavone-Rich Supplement, Improves Arterial Low-Density Lipoprotein Metabolism and Atherogenesis." *Arteriosclerosis, Thrombosis, and Vascular Biology* 2003;23(12):2241–2246.

WebMD. "Pass the Olive Oil." *http://www.webmd.com*.

Whitaker, Julian. "Dr. Julian Whitaker's Health & Healing: Your Definitive Guide to Wellness Medicine." *http://www.drwhitaker.com*.

Yale-New Haven Hospital. "A Glass of Red Wine a Day Keeps the Doctor Away." *http://www.ynhh.org*.

Yeager, Selene, and *Prevention* Magazine Health Books (eds.). *New Foods for Healing*. New York: Bantam Books, 1998.

Hypertension

American Family Physician. "Health Effects of Garlic." *http://www.aafp.org*.

Appel, L.J., T.J. Moore, E. Obarzanek, et al. "A Clinical Trial of the Effects of Dietary Patterns on Blood Pressure. DASH Collaborative Research Group." *The New England Journal of Medicine* 1997;336:1117–1124.

Carper, Jean. *The Food Pharmacy: Dramatic New Evidence That Food Is Your Best Medicine*. New York: Pocket Books, 1998.

Castleman, Michael. *The Healing Herbs*. Emmaus, PA: Rodale Press, 1991.

Duke, James A. *The Green Pharmacy*. Emmaus, PA: Rodale Press, 1997.

Ecology Health Center. "Folic Acid Helps Hypertension in Women." *http://www.crohns.net*.

Fujita, H., T. Yamagami, K. Ohshima. "Effect of an ACE-Inhibitory Agent, Katuobishi Oligopeptide, in the Spontaneously Hypertensive Rat and in Borderline and Mildly Hypertensive Subjects." *Nutrition Research* 2001;21:1149–1158.

———. "Antihypertensive Activity of 'Katsuobushi Oligopeptide' in Hypertensive and Borderline Hypertensive Subjects." *Japanese Pharmacology & Therapeutics* 1997;25:147–151.

Garcia-Palmieri, M.R., R. Costas Jr., M. Cruz-Vidal, P.D. Sorlie, J. Tillotson, and R.J. Havlik. "Milk Consumption, Calcium Intake, and Decreased Hypertension in Puerto Rico. Puerto Rico Heart Health Program Study." *Hypertension* 1984;6:322–328.

Mateljan, George. *The World's Healthiest Foods: Essential Guide for the Healthiest Way of Eating*. Grand Rapids, MI: GMF, 2007.

MayoClinic.com. "Alcohol: Does It Affect Blood Pressure?" *http://www.mayoclinic.com*.

———. "Doing the DASH: Healthy Eating to Lower Your Blood Pressure." *http://www.mayoclinic.com*.

———. "High Blood Pressure." *http://www.mayoclinic.com*.

———. "Sodium: Are You Getting Too Much?" *http://www.mayoclinic.com*.

Michaud, Ellen, and Anita Hirsch. *The Healing Kitchen: From Tea Tin to Fruit Basket, Breadbox to Veggie Bin—How to Unlock the Power of Foods That Heal*. New York: BenBella Books, 2006.

Moore, T.J., P.R. Conlin, J. Ard, and L.P. Svetkey. "DASH (Dietary Approaches to Stop Hypertension) Diet Is Effective Treatment for Stage 1 Isolated Systolic Hypertension." *Hypertension* 2001;38:155–158.

Murray, Michael, J. Pizzorno, and L. Pizzorno. *The Encyclopedia of Healing Foods*. New York: Atria, 2005.

Pratt, Steven G., and Kathy Matthews. *SuperFoods Rx: Fourteen Foods That Will Change Your Life*. New York: HarperCollins, 2005.

Rivas, M., R.P. Garay, J.F. Escanero, P. Cia Jr., and J.O. Alda. "Soy Milk Lowers Blood Pressure in Men and Women with Mild to Moderate Essential Hypertension." *Journal of Nutrition* 2002;132:1900–1902.

Rossi, Gian Paolo. "Eating the Health of Your Endothelium: Is It Too Early to Say?" *Journal of Hypertension* 2006;24:259–261.

Sacks, F.M., L.P. Svetkey, V.M. Vollmer, et al. "Effects on Blood Pressure of Reduced Dietary Sodium and the Dietary Approaches to Stop Hypertension (DASH) Diet. DASH-Sodium Collaborative Research Group." *The New England Journal of Medicine* 2001;344:3–10.

Sahelian, Ray. "Hypertension Natural Options." *http://www.raysahelian.com*.

Schwarcz, Joe, and Frances Berkoff. *Foods That Harm, Foods That Heal: An A–Z Guide to Safe and Healthy Eating.* Pleasantville, NY: Reader's Digest Association, 2004.

ScienceDaily. "Skimmed Milk Reduces the Risk of Hypertension by 50 Percent." *http://www.sciencedaily.com*.

USDA. "Dietary Guidelines for Americans 2005." Appendix B, Food Sources of Selected Nutrients, *http://www.cnpp.usda.gov/DietaryGuidelines.htm*.

Wait, Marianne. *Food Cures: Breakthrough Nutritional Prescriptions for Everything from Colds to Cancer.* Pleasantville, NY: Reader's Digest Association, 2007.

Whelton, P.K., and J. He. "Potassium in Preventing and Treating High Blood Pressure." *Seminars in Nephrology* 1999;19:494–499.

Whitaker, Julian. "Dr. Julian Whitaker's Health & Healing: Your Definitive Guide to Wellness Medicine." *http://www.drwhitaker.com*.

Yeager, Selene, and *Prevention* Magazine Health Books (eds.). *New Foods for Healing.* New York: Bantam Books, 1998.

Your Health Base.com. "Treatment of Hypertension." *http://www.yourhealthbase.com*.

Insomnia

Bakalar, Nicholas. "Aging: Study Links Falls to Lack of Sleep." *The New York Times,* September 15, 2008.

Edelberg, David, and Hough, Heidi. *The Triple Whammy Cure.* New York: Free Press, 2007.

Imhof, Hugh. "Study Indicates Majority of Patients Complaining of Insomnia Are Diagnosed with a Mental Disorder," *ScienceDaily,* September 10, 1999.

Mercola, Joseph. "Overactive Adrenals Leads to Insomnia." Mercola.com, August 29, 2001. *http://articles.mercola.com/sites/articles/archive/2001/08/29/insomnia-part-one.aspx*.

Naska, Androniki, et al. "Siesta in Healthy Adults and Coronary Mortality in General Population." *Archives of Internal Medicine* 2007;167(3)296–301.

HealthTree.com. "Foods That Help You Sleep." *http://www.healthtree.com/articles/sleep-disorders/treatment/sleep-inducing-foods/*.

Memory Loss

Bauer, Joy. *Joy Bauer's Food Cures: Easy 4-Step Nutrition Programs for Improving Your Body.* New York: Rodale Press, 2007.

Bryan, J., E. Calvaresi, and D. Hughes. "Short-Term Folate, Vitamin B-12 or Vitamin B-6 Supplementation Slightly Affects Memory Performance but Not Mood in Women of Various Ages." *Journal of Nutrition* 2002;132(6):1345–1356.

Carper, Jean. *The Food Pharmacy: Dramatic New Evidence That Food Is Your Best Medicine.* New York: Pocket Books, 1998.

Clarke, R., D. Smith, and K.A. Jobst. "Folate, Vitamin B12, and Serum Total Homocysteine Levels in Confirmed Alzheimer Disease." *Archives of Neurology* 1998;55:1449–1455.

Daley, Rosie, and Andrew Weil. *The Healthy Kitchen.* New York: Knopf, 2003.

Dang-Vu, T.T., M. Desseilles, M.P. Peigneux, and P. Maquet. "A Role for Sleep in Brain Plasticity." *Pediatric Rehabilitation* 2006;9(2):98–118.

Ebly, Erika M., Jeffrey P. Schaefer, Norman R. Campbell, and David Hogan. "Folate Status, Vascular Disease and Cognition in Elderly Canadians." *Age and Ageing* 1998;27:485–491.

Grant, William B. "Dietary Links to Alzheimer's Disease." *Journal of Alzheimer's Disease* 1999;1:197-201.

Jennings, J.R., M.F. Muldoon, C. Ryan, J.C. Price, P. Greer, K. Sutton-Tyrrell, F.M. van der Veen, and C.C. Meltzer. "Reduced Cerebral Blood Flow Response and Compensation among Patients with Untreated Hypertension." *American Academy of Neurology* 2005;64(8):1358–1365.

Jones, Nicola, and Peter J. Rogers. "Preoccupation, Food, and Failure: An Investigation of Cognitive Performance Deficits in Dieters." *International Journal of Eating Disorders* 2003;33(2):185–192.

Kang, Jae H., Alberto Ascherio, and Francine Grodstein. "Fruit and Vegetable Consumption and Cognitive Decline in Aging Women." *Annals of Neurology* 2005;57(5):713–720.

Mahoney, Caroline R., Holly A. Taylor, Robin B. Kanarek, and Priscilla Samuel. "Effect of Breakfast Composition on Cognitive Processes in Elementary School Children." *Physiology and Behavior* 2005;85(5):635–645.

Maquet, P. "The Role of Sleep in Learning and Memory." *Science* 2001;294:1048–1052.

Mateljan, George. *The World's Healthiest Foods: Essential Guide for the Healthiest Way of Eating.* Grand Rapids, MI: GMF, 2007.

Michaud, Ellen, and Anita Hirsch. *The Healing Kitchen: From Tea Tin to Fruit Basket, Breadbox to Veggie Bin—How to Unlock the Power of Foods That Heal.* New York: BenBella Books, 2006.

Morris, Martha C., Denis A. Evans, Christine C. Tangney, Julia L. Bienias, Robert S. Wilson. "Fish Consumption and Cognitive Decline with Age in a

Large Community Study." *Archives of Neurology* 2005;62(12):1849–1853.

Mosavi Jazayeri, S.M., R. Amani, and N. Khajeh Mugahi. "Effects of Breakfast on Memory in Healthy Young Adults." *Asia Pacific Journal of Clinical Nutrition* 2004;13(Suppl.):S130.

Murray, Michael T., Joseph Pizzorno, and Lara Pizzorno. *The Encyclopedia of Healing Foods.* New York: Atria, 2005.

O'Brien, Laurie T., and Mary Lee Hummert. "Memory Performance of Late Middle-Aged Adults: Contrasting Self-Stereotyping and Stereotype Threat Accounts of Assimilation to Age Stereotypes." *Social Cognition* 2006;24(3):338–358.

Rovio, S., I. Karebolt, E. Helkala, M. Viitanen, B. Winblad, J. Tuomilehto, H. Soininen, A. Nissinen, and M. Kivipelto. "Leisure-Time Physical Activity at Midlife and the Risk of Dementia and Alzheimer's Disease." *Lancet Neurology* 2005;4(11):705–711.

Singh, Amanpreet, S. Pattipati, S. Naidu, and Shrinivas K. Kulkarni. "Reversal of Aging and Chronic Ethanol-Induced Cognitive Dysfunction by Quercetin, a Bioflavonoid." *Free Radical Research* 2003;37(11): 1245–1252.

Solfrizzi, V., F. Panza, and A. Capurso. "The Role of Diet in Cognitive Decline." *Journal of Neural Transmission* 2003;110(1):95–110.

Tucker, Katherine L., Ning Qiao, Tammy Scott, Irwin Rosenberg, and Avron Spiro III. "High Homocysteine and Low B Vitamins Predict Cognitive Decline in Aging Men: The Veterans Affairs Normative Aging Study." *American Journal of Clinical Nutrition* 2005;82(3): 627–635.

Pratt, Steven G., and Kathy Matthews. *SuperFoods Rx: Fourteen Foods That Will Change Your Life.* New York: HarperCollins, 2005.

Smith, M.A., G.J. Petot, and G. Perry. "Diet and Oxidative Stress: A Novel Synthesis of Epidemiological Data on Alzheimer's Disease." *Alzheimer's Disease Review* 1997;2:58–59.

Tully, A.M., H.M. Roche, R. Doyle, C. Fallon, I. Bruce, D. Coakley, and M.J. Gibney. "Low Serum Cholesteryl Ester-Docosahexaenoic Acid Levels in Alzheimer's Disease: A Case-Control Study." *British Journal of Nutrition* 2003;89(4):483–489.

Wait, Marianne. *Food Cures: Breakthrough Nutritional Prescriptions for Everything from Colds to Cancer.* Pleasantville, NY: Reader's Digest Association, 2007.

Wesnes, K.A., C. Pincock, D. Richardson, et al. "Breakfast Reduces Declines in Attention and Memory over the Morning in Schoolchildren." *Appetite* 2003;41(3):329–331.

Zimmerman, F.J., and D.A. Christakis. "Children's Television Viewing and Cognitive Outcomes: A Longitu-dinal Analysis of National Data." *Archives of Pediatric and Adolescent Medicine* 2005;159(7):619–625.

Menopause

Barton, D.L., C.L. Loprinzi, S.K. Quella, et al. "Prospective Evaluation of Vitamin E for Hot Flashes in Breast Cancer Survivors." *Journal of Clinical Oncology* 1998;16:495–500.

Erkkila, A., A. Lichtenstein, D. Mozaffarian, et al. "Fish Intake Is Associated with a Reduced Progression of Coronary Artery Atherosclerosis in Postmenopausal Women with Coronary Artery Disease." *American Journal of Clinical Nutrition* 2004;80(3):626–632.

Fitzpatrick, L.A. "Libido and Perimenopausal Women." *Menopause* 2004;11(2):136–137.

Kritz-Silverstein, D., and D.L. Goodman-Gruen. "Usual Dietary Isoflavone Intake, Bone Mineral Density, and Bone Metabolism in Postmenopausal Women." *Journal of Women's Health and Gender-Based Medicine* 2002;11(1):69–78.

Lieberman, S. "A Review of the Effectiveness of Cimicifuga Racemosa (Black Cohosh) for the Symptoms of Menopause." *Journal of Women's Health* 1998;7(5): 431–432.

MayoClinic.com. "Menopause." *http://www.mayoclinic.com.*

MedicineNet.com. "Managing Menopause Symptoms through Diet." *http://www.medicinenet.com.*

Murray, Michael T., Joseph Pizzorno, and Lara Pizzorno. *The Encyclopedia of Healing Foods.* New York: Atria, 2005.

News-Medical.Net. "Atherosclerosis at Menopause Slowed by Diet and Exercise." *http://www.news-medical.net.*

Pratt, Steven G., and Kathy Matthews. *SuperFoods Rx: Fourteen Foods That Will Change Your Life.* New York: HarperCollins, 2005.

Prevention Magazine Health Books. *Healing with Vitamins.* Emmaus, PA: Rodale Press, 1996. pp. 390–391.

Prevention.com. "Herbs for Menopause." *http://www.preven tion.com.*

U.S. Food and Drug Administration. "Soy: Health Claims for Soy Protein." *http://www.fda.gov.*

Wait, Marianne. *Food Cures: Breakthrough Nutritional Prescriptions for Everything from Colds to Cancer.* Pleasantville, NY: Reader's Digest Association, 2007.

Yeager, Selene, and *Prevention* Magazine Health Books (eds.). *New Foods for Healing.* New York: Bantam Books, 1998.

Migraines

Allais, G., G. Bussone, C. De Lorenzo, et al. "Advanced Strategies of Short-Term Prophylaxis in Menstrual

Migraine: State of the Art and Prospects." *Neurological Science* 2005;26(Suppl. 2):S125–S129.

Aubuchon, Vaughn. "High Magnesium Foods Summary." *Magnesium Nutrition*, November 13, 2008.

Bauer, Joy. *Joy Bauer's Food Cures: Easy 4-Step Nutrition Programs for Improving Your Body.* New York: Rodale Press, 2007.

Bic, Z., G.G. Blix, P.P. Hopp, F.M. Leslie, and N.J. Schell. "The Influence of a Low-Fat Diet on Incidence and Severity of Migraine Headaches." *Journal of Women's Health and Gender-Based Medicine* 1999;8(5):623–630.

Bigal, Marcelo E., Joshua N. Liberman, and Richard B. Lipton. "Obesity and Migraine: A Population Study." *Neurology* 2006;66:545-550.

Biondi, David M. "Physical Treatments for Headache: A Structured Review." *Headache* 2005;45(6):738–746.

Boardman, Helen F., Elaine Thomas, David S. Millson, and P.R. Croft. "Psychological, Sleep, Lifestyle and Comorbid Associations with Headache." *Headache* 2005;45(6):657–669.

Carper, Jean. *The Food Pharmacy: Dramatic New Evidence That Food Is Your Best Medicine.* New York: Pocket Books, 1998.

Crawford, Paul, and Michael Simmons. "What Dietary Modifications Are Indicated for Migraines?" *Journal of Family Practice* 2006;55(1):62–64.

Dexter, J.D., J. Roberts, and J.A. Byer. "The Five-Hour Glucose Tolerance Test and Effect of Low Sucrose Diet in Migraine." *Headache* 1978;18:91–94.

Diener, H.C., V. Pfaffenrath, L. Pageler, et al. "The Fixed Combination of Acetylsalicylic Acid, Paracetamol and Caffeine Is More Effective Than Single Substances and Dual Combination for the Treatment of Headache: A Multicentre, Randomized, Double-Blind, Single-Dose, Placebo-Controlled Parallel Group Study." *Cephalalgia* 2005;25(10):776–787.

Egger, J., C.M. Carter, J.E. Soothill, and J. Wilson. "Oligoantigenic Diet Treatment of Children with Epilepsy and Migraine." *Journal of Pediatrics* 1989;114:51–58.

Goldstein J., S.D. Silberstein, J.R. Saper, et al. "Acetaminophen, Aspirin, and Caffeine Versus Sumatriptan Succinate in the Early Treatment of Migraine: Results from the ASSET Trial." *Headache* 2005;45(8):973–982.

Harel, Z., G. Gascon, S. Riggs, et al. "Supplementation with Omega-3 Polyunsaturated Fatty Acids in the Management of Recurrent Migraines in Adolescents." *Journal of Adolescent Health* 2002;31(2):154–161.

Headaches.org. "Fish Oil for Migraine." *http://www.headaches.org.*

Jakubowski, M., P.J. McAllister, Z.H. Bajwa, et al. "Exploding vs. Imploding Headache in Migraine Prophylaxis

with Botulinum Toxin A." *Pain* 2006;125(3):286–295.

Koehler, S.M., and A. Glaros. "The Effect of Aspartame on Migraine Headache." *Headache* 1988;28:10–13.

MayoClinic.com. "Migraine." *http://mayoclinic.com.*

Modi, S., and D.M. Lowder. "Medications for Migraine Prophylaxis." *American Family Physician* 2006;73(1):72–78.

Murray, Michael T., Joseph Pizzorno, and Lara Pizzorno. *The Encyclopedia of Healing Foods.* New York: Atria, 2005.

Nadelson, C. "Sport and Exercise-Induced Migraines." *Current Sports Medicine Reports* 2006;5(1):29–33.

Office of Dietary Supplements. National Institutes of Health. "Dietary Supplement Fact Sheet: Vitamin B6." *http://ods.od.nih.gov/.*

Rasura, M., A. Spalloni, M. Ferrari, S. Castro, R. Patella, F. Lisi, and M. Beccia. "A Case Series of Young Stroke in Rome." *European Journal of Neurology* 2006;13(2):146–152.

Sandor, P.S., L. Di Clemente, G. Coppola, et al. "Efficacy of Coenzyme Q10 in Migraine Prophylaxis: A Randomized Controlled Trial." *Neurology* 2005;64(4):713–715.

University of California Irvine. Headache and Migraine Prevention. "Migraine Headache Study." *http://www.ics.uci.edu.*

Wagner, W., and U. Nootbaar-Wagner. "Prophylactic Treatment of Migraine with Gamma-Linolenic and Alpha-Linolenic acids." *Cephalalgia* 1997;17(2):127–130.

WebMd.com. "Migraines and Headaches Guide: Fighting Food-Related Headaches." *http://www.webmd.com.*

Wilkinson, C.F., Jr. "Recurrent Migrainoid Headaches Associated with Spontaneous Hypoglycemia." *American Journal of the Medical Sciences* 1949;218:209–212.

Yeager, Selene, and *Prevention* Magazine Health Books (eds.). *New Foods for Healing.* New York: Bantam Books, 1998.

Osteoporosis

Bacon, L., J.S. Stern, N.L. Keirn, and M.D. Van Loan. "Low Bone Mass in Premenopausal Chronic Dieting Women." *European Journal of Clinical Nutrition* 2004;58(6):966–971.

Bauer, Joy. *Joy Bauer's Food Cures: Easy 4-Step Nutrition Programs for Improving Your Body.* New York: Rodale Press, 2007.

Bone Health for Life. "Interpretation of DEXA Measures." *http://bonehealthforlife.org.au.*

Bonjour, J.P. "Dietary Protein: An Essential Nutrient for Bone Health." *Journal of the American College of Nutrition* 2005;24(6 Suppl.):526S–536S.

Booth, S.L., K.L. Tucker, H. Chen, et al. "Dietary Vitamin Kintakes Are Associated with Hip Fracture but Not with Bone Mineral Density in Elderly Men and Women." *American Journal of Clinical Nutrition* 2000;71(5):1201–1208.

Bowden, Jonny. *The 150 Healthiest Foods on Earth: The Surprising, Unbiased Truth about What You Should Eat and Why.* Minneapolis: Quayside, 2007.

Center for Science in the Public Interest. "Caffeine." *Nutrition Action Healthletter* 2008;March.

Chen, Y.M., S.C. Ho, S.S. Lam, et al. "Soy Isoflavones Have a Favorable Effect on Bone Loss in Chinese Postmenopausal Women with Lower Bone Mass: A Double-Blind, Randomized, Controlled Trial." *The Journal of Clinical Endocrinology & Metabolism* 2003;88(10):4740–4747.

Cohen, Suzy. *The 24-Hour Pharmacist: Advice, Options, and Amazing Cures from America's Most Trusted Pharmacist.* New York: HarperCollins, 2007.

Dawson-Hughes, B. "Interaction of Dietary Calcium and Protein in Bone Health in Humans." *The Journal of Nutrition* 2003;133(3):S852–S854.

Evans, C.E., A.Y. Chughtai, A. Blumsohn, et al. "The Effect of Dietary Sodium on Calcium Metabolism in Premenopausal and Postmenopausal Women." *European Journal of Clinical Nutrition* 1997;51:394–399.

Feskanich, D., W.C. Willett, M.J. Stampfer, and G.A. Colditz. "Protein Consumption and Bone Fractures in Women." *American Journal of Epidemiology* 1996; 143:472–479.

_____, P. Weber, W.C. Willett, et al. "Vitamin K Intake and Hip Fractures in Women: A Prospective Study." *American Journal of Clinical Nutrition* 1999;69(1):74–79.

Gjesdal, C.G., S.E. Vollset, P.M. Ueland, et al. "Plasma Total Homocysteine Level and Bone Mineral Density: The Hordaland Homocysteine Study." *Archives of Internal Medicine* 2006;166(1):88–94.

Help Guide.org. "Preventing and Healing Osteoporosis." *http://www.helpguide.org.*

Hernandez-Avila M., G.A. Colditz, M.J. Stampfer, et al. "Caffeine, Moderate Alcohol Intake, and Risk of Fractures of the Hip and Forearm in Middle-Aged Women." *The American Journal of Clinical Nutrition* 1991;54:157–163.

Hunt, I.F., N.J. Murphy, C. Henderson, et al. "Bone Mineral Content in Postmenopausal Women: Comparison of Omnivores and Vegetarians." *The American Journal of Clinical Nutrition* 1989;50:517–523.

Ikeda, Y., M. Iki, A. Morita, et al. "Intake of Fermented Soybeans, Natto, Is Associated with Reduced Bone Loss in Postmenopausal Women: Japanese Population-Based Osteoporosis Study OPOS." *Journal of Nutrition* 2006;136(5):1323–1328.

_____, J.E. Kerstetter. "Nutrition in Bone Health Revisited: A Story Beyond Calcium." *Journal of the American College of Nutrition* 2000;19(6):715–737.

Ilich, Jasminka Z., Rhonda A. Brownbill, Lisa Tamborini, and Zeljka Crncevic-Orlic. "To Drink or Not to Drink: How Are Alcohol, Caffeine and Past Smoking Related to Bone Mineral Density in Elderly Women?" *Journal of the American College of Nutrition* 2002;21(6):526–544.

Jacka, F.N., J.A. Pasco, M.J. Henry, et al. "Depression and Bone Mineral Density in a Community Sample of Perimenopausal Women: Geelong Osteoporosis Study." *Menopause* 2005;12(1):88–91.

Judge, J.O., A. Kleppinger, A. Kenny, et al. "Home-Based Resistance Training Improves Femoral Bone Mineral Density in Women on Hormone Therapy." *Osteoporosis International* 2005;16(9):1096–1108.

Juvent.com. "The Safe & Balanced Approach to Musculoskeletal Health." *http://juvent.com.*

Kamer, A.R., N. EI-Ghorab, N. Marzec, et al. "Nicotine Induced Proliferation and Cytokine Release in Osteoblastic Cells." *International Journal of Molecular Medicine* 2006;17(1):121–127.

Karadeniz, F., R.W. Durst, and R.E. Wrolstad. "Polyphenolic Composition of Raisins." *Journal of Agricultural and Food Chemistry* 2000;48(11):5343–5350.

Karakaya, S., S.N. El, and A.A. Tas. "Antioxidant Activity of Some Foods Containing Phenolic Compounds." *International Journal of Food Sciences and Nutrition* 2001;52(6):501–508.

Kerstetter, J.E., and I.H. Allen. "Dietary Protein Increases Urinary Calcium." *The Journal of Nutrition* 1990;12:134–136.

_____, A.C. Looker, and K.I. Insogna. "Low Dietary Protein and Low Bone Density." *Calcified Tissue International* 2000;66:313.

_____, K.O. O'Brien, D.M. Caseria, et al. "The Impact of Dietary Protein on Calcium Absorption and Kinetic Measures of Bone Turnover in Women." *Journal of Clinical Endocrinology & Metabolism* 2005;90(1):26–31.

_____, K.O. O'Brien, and K.L. Insogna. "Dietary Protein, Calcium Metabolism, and Skeletal Homeostasis Revisited." *American Journal of Clinical Nutrition* 2003;78(3 Suppl.):584S–592S.

_____. "Low Protein Intake: The Impact on Calcium and Bone Homeostasis in Humans." *Journal of Nutrition* 2003;133(3):855S–861S.

Kim, S.H., D.J. Morton, and E.I. Barrett-Connor. "Carbonated Beverage Consumption and Bone Mineral Density Among Older Women: The Rancho Bernardo Study." *American Journal of Public Health* 1997;87:276–279.

Linus Pauling Institute. "Preventing Osteoporosis Through Diet and Lifestyle." *http://lpi.oregonstate.edu.*

MacDonald, H.M., S.A. New, W.D. Fraser, M.K. Campbell, and D.M. Reid. "Low Dietary Potassium Intakes and High Dietary Estimates of Net Endogenous Acid Production Are Associated with Low Bone Mineral Density in Premenopausal Women and Increased Markers of Bone Resorption in Postmenopausal Women." *American Journal of Clinical Nutrition* 2005;81(4):923–933.

_____, M.H.N. Golden, et al. "Nutritional Associations with Bone Loss during the Menopausal Transition: Evidence of a Beneficial Effect of Calcium, Alcohol, and Fruit and Vegetable Nutrients and of a Detrimental Effect of Fatty Acids." *American Journal of Clinical Nutrition* 2004;79(1):155–165.

Mannan, M.T., K. Tucker, B. Dawson-Hughes, et al. "Effect of Dietary Protein on Bone Loss in Elderly Men and Women: The Framingham Osteoporosis Study." *Journal of Bone Mineral Research* 2000;15:2504–2512.

Mateljan, George. *The World's Healthiest Foods: Essential Guide for the Healthiest Way of Eating.* Grand Rapids, MI: GMF, 2007.

MayoClinic.com. "Osteoporosis." *http://www.mayoclinic.com.*

Mazariegos-Ramos, E., F. Guerrero-Romero, F. Rodriguez-Moran, et al. "Consumption of Soft Drinks with Phosphoric Acid as a Risk Factor for the Development of Hypocalcemia in Children: A Case-Control Study." *Journal of Pediatrics* 1995;126:940–942.

Moriguti, J.C., E. Ferriolli, and J.S. Marchini. "Urinary Calcium Loss in Elderly Men on a Vegetable: Animal (1:1) High-Protein Diet." *Gerontology* 1999;45:274–278.

Murray, Michael T., Joseph Pizzorno, and Lara Pizzorno. *The Encyclopedia of Healing Foods.* New York: Atria, 2005.

Mussolino, M.E. "Depression and Hip Fracture Risk: The NHANES I Epidemiologic Follow-up Study." *Public Health Reports* 2005;120(1):71–75.

New, S.A., S.P. Robins, M.K. Campbell, et al. "Dietary Influences on Bone Mass and Bone Metabolism: Further Evidence of a Positive Link between Fruit and Vegetable Consumption and Bone Health?" *American Journal of Clinical Nutrition* 2000;71(1):142–151.

Nieves, J.W. "Osteoporosis: The Role of Micronutrients." *American Journal of Clinical Nutrition* 2005;81(5):1232S–1239S.

Osteopenia-Osteopenia Treatment. "Osteopenia, Osteoporosis Alcohol Connection—Fact or Fiction?" *http://www.osteopenia3.com.*

Potter, S.M., J.A. Baum, H. Teng, et al. "Soy Protein and Isoflavones: Their Effects on Blood Lipids and Bone Density in Postmenopausal Women." *The American Journal of Clinical Nutrition* 1998;68(Suppl.):S1375–S1379.

Pratt, Steven G., and Kathy Matthews. *SuperFoods Rx: Fourteen Foods That Will Change Your Life.* New York: HarperCollins, 2005.

Prevention.com. "Fruits and Vegetables Can Bolster Your Bones." *http://www.prevention.com.*

Rainey, C.J., L.A. Nyquist, R.E. Christensen, et al. "Daily Boron Intake from the American Diet." *Journal of the American Dietetic Association* 1999;99(3):335–340.

Rapuri, P.B., J.C. Gallagher, K.E. Balhorn, and K.L. Ryschon. "Alcohol Intake and Bone Metabolism in Elderly Women." *American Journal of Clinical Nutrition* 2000;72(5):1206–1213.

Reinwald, S., and C.M. Weaver. "Soy Isoflavones and Bone Health: A Double-Edged Sword?" *Journal of Natural Products* 2006;69(3):450–459.

Ryder, K.M., R.I. Shorr, A.J. Bush, et al. "Magnesium Intake from Food and Supplements Is Associated with Bone Mineral Density in Healthy Older White Subjects." *Journal of the American Geriatric Society* 2005;53(11):1875–1880.

Shu, X.O., Zheng, Ying, Cai, Hui, et al. "Soy Food Intake and Breast Cancer Survival." *The Journal of the American Medical Association* 2009;302(22):2437–2443.

Suominen, H. "Muscle Training for Bone Strength." *Aging Clinical and Experimental Research* 2006;18(2):85–93.

Tesar, R., M. Notelovitz, E. Shim, et al. "Axial and Peripheral Bone Density and Nutrient Intakes of Postmenopausal Vegetarian and Omnivorous Women." *The American Journal of Clinical Nutrition* 1992;56:699–704.

Tucker, K.L, M.T. Hannan, H. Chen, et al. "Potassium, Magnesium, and Fruit and Vegetable Intakes Are Associated with Greater Bone Mineral Density in Elderly Men and Women." *American Journal of Clinical Nutrition* 1999;69(4):727–736.

van Meurs, J.B., R.A. Dhonukshe-Rutten, S.M. Pluijm, et al. "Homocysteine levels and the risk of osteoporotic fracture." *New England Journal of Medicine* 2004;350(20):2033–2041.

Weaver, C.M., and J.M. Cheong. "Soy Isoflavones and Bone Health: The Relationship Is Still Unclear." *Journal of Nutrition* 2005;135(5):1243–1247.

Weber, P. "Vitamin K and Bone Health." *Nutrition* 2001;17(10):880–887.

WebMD.com. "Osteoporosis Guide." *http://www.webmd.com.*

Wyshak, G., and R.E. Frisch. "Carbonated Beverages, Dietary Calcium, the Dietary Calcium/Phosphorus Ratio, and Bone Fractures in Girls and Boys." *Journal of Adolescent Health* 1994;15:210–215.

Yeager, Selene, and *Prevention* Magazine Health Books (eds.). *New Foods for Healing.* New York: Bantam Books, 1998.

Zhang, X., X.O. Shu, H. Li, et al. "Prospective Cohort Study of Soy Food Consumption and Risk of Bone Fracture

Among Postmenopausal Women." *Archives of Internal Medicine* 2005;165(16):1890–1895.

Overweight & Obesity

Andrade, A., T. Minaker, and K. Melanson. "Eating Rate and Satiation." Presentation at the 2006 Annual Scientific Meeting of NAASO: The Obesity Society. Boston: October 20–24, 2006.

Bauer, Joy. *Joy Bauer's Food Cures: Easy 4-Step Nutrition Programs for Improving Your Body.* New York: Rodale Press, 2007.

Bowden, Jonny. *The 150 Healthiest Foods on Earth: The Surprising, Unbiased Truth about What You Should Eat and Why.* Minneapolis: Quayside, 2007.

Brehm, B.J., R.J. Seeley, S.R. Daniels, et al. "A Randomized Trial Comparing a Very Low Carbohydrate Diet and a Calorie-Restricted Low-Fat Diet on Body Weight and Cardiovascular Risk Ractors in Healthy Women." *Journal of Clinical Endocrinology & Metabolism* 2003;88:1617–1623.

Cohen, Suzy. *The 24-Hour Pharmacist: Advice, Options, and Amazing Cures from America's Most Trusted Pharmacist.* New York: HarperCollins, 2007.

Crister, Greg. *Fat Land: How Americans Became the Fattest People in the World.* Boston: Houghton Mifflin, 2003.

Czernichow, S., S. Bertrais, P. Preziosi, et al. "Indicators of Abdominal Adiposity in Middle-Aged Participants of the SU.VI.MAX Study: Relationships with Educational Level, Smoking Status and Physical Inactivity." *Diabetes & Metabolism* 2004;30:153–159.

Davis, J.R., V.A. Hodges, and M.B. Gillham. "Normal-Weight Adults Consume More Fiber and Fruit Than Their Age-and-Height-Matched Overweight/Obese Counterparts." *Journal of the American Dietetic Association* 2006;106(6):833–840.

Dominguez, Alex. "Waistline Good Indicator of Diabetes Risk." *Associated Press News Wire*, March 22, 2005.

Duyff, Roberta Larson. *The American Dietetic Association's Complete Food and Nutrition Guide, 3rd ed.* Hoboken, NJ: John Wiley & Sons, 2006.

Ebbeling, Cara B., Michael M. Leidig, Kelly B. Sinclair, Linda G. Seger-Shippee, Henry A. Feldman, and David S. Ludwig. "Effects of an Ad Libitum Low-Glycemic Load Diet on Cardiovascular Disease Risk Factors in Obese Young Adults." *American Journal of Clinical Nutrition* 2005;81(5):976–982.

Engeland, Anders, Tone Bjorge, Anne Johanne Sogaard, and Aage Tverdal. "Body Mass Index in Adolescence in Relation to Total Mortality: 32-Year Follow-Up of 227,000 Norwegian Boys and Girls." *American Journal of Epidemiology* 2003;157:517–523.

Foster, Gary D., Holly R. Wyatt, James O. Hill, Brian G. McGuckin, Carrie Brill, B. Selma Mohammed, Philippe O. Szapary, Daniel J. Rader, Joel S. Edman, and Samuel Klein. "A Randomized Trial of a Low-Carbohydrate Diet for Obesity." *New England Journal of Medicine* 2003;348(21):2082–2090.

Gillum, R.F., and T. Sempos. "Ethnic Variation in Validity of Classification of Overweight and Obesity Using Self-Reported Weight and Height in American Women and Men: The Third National Health and Nutrition Examination Survey." *Nutrition Journal* [serial online] 2005;4:27.

Gray, D.S., and K. Fujioka. "Use of Relative Weight and Body Mass Index for the Determination of Adiposity." *Journal of Clinical Epidemiology* 1991;44(6):545–550.

Harrison, G.G. "Height-Weight Tables." *Annals of Internal Medicine* 1985;103(6):989–994.

Harvard School of Public Health. "Frequent Consumption of Sugar-Sweetened Beverages Linked to Greater Weight Gain and Type 2 Diabetes in Women." Press release, August 24, 2004.

Howard, B.V., J.E. Manson, M.L. Stefanick, S.A. Beresford, G. Frank, B. Jones, R.J. Rodabough, L. Snetselaar, C. Thomson, L. Tinker, M. Vitolins, and R. Prentice. "Low-Fat Dietary Pattern and Weight Change Over 7 Years: The Women's Health Initiative Dietary Modification Trial." *Journal of the American Medical Association* 2006;295(1):39–49.

Howarth, N.C., T.T. Huang, S.B. Roberts, and M.A. McCrory. "Dietary Fiber and Fat Are Associated with Excess Weight in Young and Middle-Aged US Adults." *Journal of the American Dietetic Association* 2005;105(9):1365–1372.

_____, E. Saltzman, and S.B. Roberts. "Dietary Fiber and Weight Regulation." *Nutrition Reviews* 2001;59(5): 129–139.

James, Janet, Peter Thomas, David Cavan, and David Kerr. "Preventing Childhood Obesity by Reducing Consumption of Carbonated Drinks: Cluster Randomized Controlled Trial." *British Medical Journal* 2004;328:1237–1241.

Littman, A., A.R. Kristal, and E. White. "Effects of Physical Activity Intensity, Frequency, and Activity Type on 10-Y Weight Change in Middle-Aged Men and Women." *International Journal of Obesity* 2005;29(5):524–533.

Mateljan, George. *The World's Healthiest Foods: Essential Guide for the Healthiest Way of Eating.* Grand Rapids, MI: GMF, 2007.

Miller-Kovach, Karen. *Weight Watchers, He Loses, She Loses.* Hoboken, NJ: John Wiley & Sons, 2007.

Monti, Veronica, Joseph J. Carlson, Steven C. Hunt, Ted D. Adams. "Relationship of Ghrelin and Leptin Hormones with Body Mass Index and Waist Circumference in a Random Sample of Adults." *Journal of the American Dietetic Association* 2006;106(6):822–828.

Moss, Ralph. "The Pima Indians, Obesity and Diabetes." *http://diabetes.niddk.nih.gov.*

Murray, Michael T., Joseph Pizzorno, and Lara Pizzorno. *The Encyclopedia of Healing Foods.* New York: Atria, 2005.

National Heart, Lung, and Blood Institute, National Institute of Diabetes and Digestive and Kidney Diseases. "Obesity Education Initiative." In: "Clinical Guidelines on the Identification, Education, and Treatment of Overweight and Obesity in Adults: The Evidence Report." Bethesda, MD: NIH, publication no. 98-4083, 1998.

Nelson, L.H., and L.A. Tucker. "Diet Composition Related to Body Fat in a Multivariate Study of 203 Men." *Journal of the American Dietetic Association* 1996;96(8):771–777.

New York Times.com. "The Overflowing American Dinner Plate." *http://www.nytimes.com.*

Pereira, Mark, Janis Swain, Allison B. Goldfine, Nader Rifai, and David S. Ludwig. "Effects of a Low Glycemic Load Diet on Resting Energy Expenditure and Heart Disease Risk Factors During Weight Loss." *Journal of the American Medical Association* 2004;292:2482–2490.

Price, G.M., R. Uauy, E. Breeze, et al. "Weight, Shape, and Mortality Risk in Older Persons: Elevated Waist-Hip Ratio, Not High Body Mass Index, Is Associated with a Greater Risk of Death." *American Journal of Clinical Nutrition* 2005;84(2):449–460.

Samaha, Frederick F., Nayyar Iqbal, Prakash Seshadri, et al. "A Low-Carbohydrate as Compared with a Low-Fat Diet in Severe Obesity." *New England Journal of Medicine* 2003;348(21):2074–2081.

Sanders, T.A. "High- Versus Low-Fat Diets in Human Diseases." *Current Opinion in Clinical Nutrition and Metabolic Care* 2003;6(2):151–155.

Schoeller, D.A., and A.C. Buchholz. "Energetics of Obesity and Weight Control: Does Diet Composition Matter?" *Journal of the American Dietetic Association* 2005; 105(5 Suppl. 1);S24–S28.

St. Jeor, S.T., B.V. Howard, T.E. Prewitt, et al. "Dietary Protein and Weight Reduction: A Statement for Healthcare Professionals from the Nutrition Committee of the Council on Nutrition, Physical Activity, and Metabolism of the American Heart Association." *Circulation* 2001;104(15):1869–1874.

U.S. Department of Health and Human Services, Centers for Disease Control and Prevention. "Physical Activity for Everyone." *http://www.cdc.gov.*

Wait, Marianne. *Food Cures: Breakthrough Nutritional Prescriptions for Everything from Colds to Cancer.* Pleasantville, NY: Reader's Digest Association, 2007.

WebMD.com. "'Big Breakfast' Diet Helps Shed Pounds." *http://www.webmd.com.*

Weigley, E.S. "Average? Ideal? Desirable? A Brief Overview of Height-Weight Tables in the United States." *Journal of the American Dietetic Association* 1984;84(4):417–423.

Willett, W.E. "The Mediterranean Diet: Science and Practice." *Public Health Nutrition* 2006;9(1A):105–110.

Williams, P.T., and R.R. Pate. "Cross-sectional Relationships of Exercise and Age to Adiposity in 60,617 Male Runners." *Medicine and Science in Sports and Exercise* 2005;37(8):1329–1337.

_____, and W.A. Satariano. "Relationships of Age and Weekly Running Distance to BMI and Circumferences in 41,582 Physically Active Women. *Obesity Research* 2005;13(8):1370–1380.

_____, and P.D. Wood. "The Effects of Changing Exercise Levels on Weight and Age-Related Weight Gain." *International Journal of Obesity* 2006;30(3):543–551.

Yao, M., and S.B. Roberts. "Dietary Energy Density and Weight Regulation." *Nutrition Reviews* 2001;59(8 Pt 1):247–258.

Zemel, M.B. "The Role of Dairy Foods in Weight Management." *Journal of the American College of Nutrition* 2005;24(6 Suppl.):537S–546S.

Prostate

Bennett, Connie, Stephen T. Sinatra, and Nicholas Perricone. *Sugar Shock!: How Sweets and Simple Carbs Can Derail Your Life—and How You Can Get Back on Track.* New York: Berkley Trade, 2007.

Berges, R.R., J. Windeler, H.J. Trampisch, et al. "Randomized, Placebo-Controlled, Double-Blind Clinical Trial of Beta-Sitosterol in Patients with Benign Prostatic Hyperplasia." *The Lancet* 1995;345:1529–1532.

Bombardelli, E., and P. Morazzoni. "Cucurbita Pepo L." *Fitoterapia* 1997;68:291–302.

Bowden, Jonny. *The 150 Healthiest Foods on Earth: The Surprising, Unbiased Truth about What You Should Eat and Why.* Minneapolis: Quayside, 2007.

Carbin, B.E., B. Larsson, and O. Lindahl. "Treatment of Benign Prostatic Hyperplasia with Phytosterols." *British Journal of Urology* 1990;66:639–641.

Cohen, Suzy. *The 24-Hour Pharmacist: Advice, Options, and Amazing Cures from America's Most Trusted Pharmacist.* New York: HarperCollins, 2007.

Daley, Rosie, and Andrew Weil. *The Healthy Kitchen.* New York: Knopf, 2003.

Edamame. "What Is Edamame?" *http://edamame.com.*

Edenharder, R., G. Keller, K.L. Platt, et al. "Isolation and Characterization of Structurally Novel Anti-Inutagenic Flavonoids from Spinach (Spinacia Oleracea)." *Journal of Agricultural and Food Chemistry* 2001;49(6):2767–2773.

Essortment. "Health Benefits of Tomatoes." *http://essortment. com.*

Farnsworth, W. "Estrogen in the Etiopathogenesis of BPH." *Journal of Basic and Clinical Physiology and Pharmacology* 2003;14(3):301–308.

Fayed, Lisa. "Hot Peppers and Prostate Cancer." *http://cancer. about.com.*

Giovannucci, E., E.B. Rimm, Y. Liu, M.J. Stampfer, and W.C. Willett. "A Prospective Study of Tomato Products, Lycopene, and Prostate Cancer Risk." *Journal of the National Cancer Institute* 2002;94(5):391–398.

Key, T.J., P.B. Silcocks, G.K. Davey, P.N. Appleby, and D.T. Bishop. "A Case-Control Study of Diet and Prostate Cancer." *British Journal of Cancer* 1997;76:678–687.

Khachik, F., L. Carvalho, P.S. Bernstein, et al. "Chemistry, Distribution, and Metabolism of Tomato Carotenoids and Their Impact on Human Health." *Experimental Biology and Medicine* 2002;227(10):845–851.

Kohlmeyer, L., J.D. Kark, E. Gomez-Gracia, et al. "Lycopene and Myocardial Infarction Risk in the EUROMIC Study." *American Journal of Epidemiology* 1997;146: 618–626.

Kono, S., K. Shinchi, K. Wakabayashi, S. Honjo, I. Todoroki, Y. Sakurai, K. Imanishi, H. Nishikawa, S. Ogawa, and M. Katsurada. "Relation of Green Tea Consumption to Serum Lipids and Lipoproteins in Japanese Men." *Journal of Epidemiology* 1996;6(3):128–133.

Krieg, M., et al. "Effect of Aging on Endogenous Level of 5 DHT, Estradiol, and Esnone in Human Prostate." *Journal of Clinical Endocrinology & Metabolism* 1993;77:375–38l.

Lee, J. "Prostate Disease and Hormones." *The John R. Lee, M.D. Medical Letter* 2002;Feb. *http://www.johnlee md.com.*

Ludikhuyze, L., L. Rodrigo, and M. Hendrickx. "The Activity of Myrosinase from Broccoli (Brassica Oleracea L. cv. Italica): Influence of Intrinsic and Extrinsic Factors." *Journal of Food Protection* 2000;63(3):400–403.

Mark Sisson's Daily Apple. "10 Things to Know about Tofu." *http://www.marksdailyapple.com.*

Mateljan, George. *The World's Healthiest Foods: Essential Guide for the Healthiest Way of Eating.* Grand Rapids, MI: GMF, 2007.

MayoClinic.com. "Enlarged Prostate." *http://www.mayoclinic. com.*

Mercola, J. "Progesterone Cream Can Help Prostate Cancer." *http://www.mercola.com.*

Michaud, Ellen, and Anita Hirsch. *The Healing Kitchen: From Tea Tin to Fruit Basket, Breadbox to Veggie Bin—How to Unlock the Power of Foods That Heal.* New York: BenBella Books, 2006.

Murray, Michael T., Joseph Pizzorno, and Lara Pizzorno. *The Encyclopedia of Healing Foods.* New York: Atria, 2005.

Nakhla, A., et al. "Estradiol Causes the Rapid Accumulation of cAMP in Human Prostate." *Proceedings of the National Academy of Sciences of the United States of America* 1994;91:5402–5405.

Peat, R. "Men with Normal PSA Are Also at Risk for Prostate Cancer." *Journal of Urology* 2005;174(6):2191–2196.

Petrow, V. "Endocrine Dependence of Prostatic Cancer upon Dihydrotestosterone and Not upon Testosterone." *Journal of Pharmacology* 1984;36:352–353.

Pratt, Steven G., and Kathy Matthews. *SuperFoods Rx: Fourteen Foods That Will Change Your Life.* New York: HarperCollins, 2005.

Schiebel-Schlosser, G., and M. Friederich. "Phytotherapy of BPH with Pumpkin Seeds—A Multicenter Clinical Trial." *Zeits Phytotherapy* 1998;19:71–76.

Sigounas, G., J. Hooker, A. Anagnostou, and M. Steiner. "S-allylmercaptocysteine Inhibits Cell Proliferation and Reduces the Viability of Erythroleukemia, Breast, and Prostate Cancer Cell Lines." *Nutrition and Cancer* 1997;27:189–191.

Thompson, Ian M., Donna K. Pauler, Phyllis J. Goodman, et al. "Prevalence of Prostate Cancer Among Men with a Prostate-Specific Antigen Level < or =4.0 ng per Milliliter." *New England Journal of Medicine* 2004;350(22):2239–2246.

Wait, Marianne. *Food Cures: Breakthrough Nutritional Prescriptions for Everything from Colds to Cancer.* Pleasantville, NY: Reader's Digest Association, 2007.

WebMd.com. "Prostate Cancer Health Center." *http://www. webmd.com.*

Weisburger, J.H. "Lycopene and Tomato Products in Health Promotion." *Experimental Biology and Medicine* 2002;227(10):924–927.

Wilt, T.J., A. Ishani, G. Stark, et al. "Saw Palmetto Extracts for Treatment of Benign Prostatic Hyperplasia. A Systematic Review." *Journal of the American Medical Association* 1998;280:1604–1609.

Recipe Index

A

Warming Whole-Grain **Almond** Flatbread with Honey, 440

Cancer-Healing Baked **Apple**-Berry Crisp, 352

Energy-Rich **Apricot** Crumble, 411

Powerful **Apricot** Almond Biscotti, 412

Sleep-Tight Oatmeal **Apricot** Cookies with Walnuts, 441

Migraine-Healing Greek Yogurt **Asparagus** Salad, 463

Osteoporosis-Conquering **Athena** Salad, 472

B

Celiac-Disease-Fighting **Banana** and Prune Pudding, 381

Headache-Be-Gone **Banana** Cream Pie, 469

Nerve-Calming **Banana** Cake, 442

Peaceful Pecan **Banana** Bread, 439

Lignan-Rich **Bean** Croquettes with Pomegranate Dipping Sauce, 351

Mighty Omega-3 **Bean** Soup with Sardines, 414

Migraine-Chasing **Bean** and Artichoke Soup, 462

Tummy-Taming Vegetable **Bean** Salad, 373

Asian **Beef** Kebabs Testosteroni, 388

Brain-Building Hoisin **Beef** Tapas with Spicy Pear Skewers, 354

Anti-Hypertensive Roasted **Beet** Lasagna, 432

Heart-Pumping **Beet** Greens Salad with Greek Yogurt, 427

Blueberry-Yogurt Soup, 343

Bone-Building Asian **Broccoli** and Chicken, 475

Cancer-Curbing **Broccoli** alla Cacciatore, 348

Diabetes-Busting Orange **Broccoli** Salad, 365

Diabetes-Fighting Mediterranean **Broccoli**-Red Pepper Soup, 363

Feel-Better **Broccoli**-Brown Rice Al Diavolo, 453

Sleepy-Time Warm **Broccoli** Soup, 436

Heart-Healing **Buffalo** Salad with Peanut-Sesame Dressing, 417

High-Protein Spicy Mediterranean **Buffalo** Burgers, 410

C

Eye-Saving **Caesar** Salad, 395

Brain-Boosting **Calf's Liver** in Fig-and-Port Sauce, 359

Cancer-Clobbering **Carrot** Bisque, 341

Vision Perfect **Carrot** Cake, 401

Arthritis-Soothing Cherry-Roasted **Cauliflower**, 339

Soothing **Cauliflower** Soup, 436

Menopause Date **Cheesecake**, 461

Arthritis-Busting Upside-Down **Cherry** and Strawberry Cobbler, 340

Antioxidant Asian **Chicken** Rice, 416

Brainy Balsamic-Berry **Chicken** and Couscous, 449

Clear-the-Fog Kale-Rice Salad with **Chicken**, 447

Kick-Up-Your-Heels **Chicken** Paella, 407

Migraine-Conquering Moroccan **Chicken** and Couscous, 465

Osteoporosis-Banishing Braised **Chicken** and Vegetable Ragout, 478

Zingy **Chicken** and Okra Curry, 408

Better Bones **Chocolate** Ricotta Tart, 479

Diabetes-Defying Deep Dark **Chocolate** Brownies, 371

Don't Miss a Beat **Chocolate** and Apple Tarte Tatin, 425

Feel-Good Flourless **Chocolate** Cakes with Raspberry Sauce, 362

Heart-Happy **Chocolate**-Covered Strawberries, 424

High-Fiber **Chocolate** Date Biscotti, 460

Headache-Calming **Clams** with Vinaigrette, 466

Romantic Baked **Clam** Lasagna, 384

Prostate-Soothing Mighty Omega Baked **Cod** with Parmesan Rice, 483

Calming **Croquettes** with Spicy Hummus Dipping Sauce, 360

E

Dreamy Whole-Grain **Egg** Sandwich, 435

High-Fiber Baked **Eggplant**, Sweet Potatoes and Mushrooms, 455

Super-Lycopene Italian Marinara Sauce with **Eggplant**, 482

F

Sexy Baked Stuffed **Fish**, 387

Bright-Eyed **Fruit** Custards, 451

Cancer-Blocking Summer **Fruity** Soups, 342–43

Feisty **Fruit** Pies, 489

Yummy Antioxidant Dessert **Fruit** Salad with Custard, 434

G

Guacamole with Diced Tomatoes, 413

H

Cataract-Conquering Thai **Halibut**-Carrot Stew, 398

Heart-Healing Sweet 'n' Spicy Thai **Halibut** Salad, 415

515

Sleep-Ease **Halibut** Stew, 437
Symptom-Busting **Halibut** and Balsamic Glazed Date-Fruit Rice, 456

L

Blues-Busting Hunan **Lamb** Chop Salad, 355
Lamb Love Burgers with Greek Yogurt Dressing, 389
Lazy **Lentil** Bean Soup, 437
Visionary **Lentil** Carrot Soup, 392

M

Doctor's-Orders Grilled **Mackerel** Over Asian Rice Salad, 430
In the Mood Thai **Mackerel** with Avocado Salsa, 386
Mood-Elevating **Mackerel** and Vegetables en Papillote, 356
Mango-Peach Soup, 342
Rest-Easy **Mango** Lassi, 435
Joint-Mending **Mediterranean** Stew, 332
Memory-Boosting **Minestrone** Soup, 443
Easy-Eating **Mushroom** Pasta, 378
Iron-Rich **Mushroom** Caps Stuffed with Italian Garlic Spinach, 452

N

High-Protein **Niçoise** Salad, 403
Joint-Soothing Vegetarian Cellophane **Noodles**, 335

O

Hot 'n' Lively Thai **Oyster** Soup and Garden Salad, 404
Lovers' **Oysters** Rockefeller Dip, 382

P

Diabetes Delight Vegetarian **Paella**, 367
Heart's Delight **Pasta** Puttanesca, 419
Pasta Comfort Ragu di Carne ala Florentine, 358
Mood-Lifting **Peach** and Cherry Ricotta Tarts, 361
Spicy **Peach**-Apple Soup, 342
Sugar-Steady **Peach** Quinoa Cobblers, 372
Insulin-Leveling Mediterranean Stuffed **Peppers**, 369
Vitalizing Vietnamese **Pho Bo** Soup, 444
Bella (Pretty) **Pizza**, 377

Artery-Strengthening Asian **Portobello** Salad with Buffalo, 423
Smart-Carb **Pumpkin** and Potato Soup with Asian Salad, 402
Sublime **Pumpkin** Pie, 390
Sweets for Men **Pumpkin** Cheesecakes, 391

Q

Fatigue-Fighting "Skinny" **Quiche** with Caramelized Vegetables, 405

R

Super-Fiber Mediterranean **Ratatouille**, 418

S

Arthritis-Fighting Thai **Salmon** Salad, 331
Colon-Calming **Salmon** Burgers with Asian Sauerkraut, 376
Glucose-Lowering Balsamic **Salmon** with Figgy Brown Rice, 370
Hypertension-Be-Gone **Salmon**-Squash Stack with Asian Fruit Sauce, 429
Libido-Lighting **Salmon** Fillets with Pecan Rice, 383
Lower Blood Pressure Broiled **Salmon** with Asian Pear Salad, 428
Mid-Life **Salmon** Over Asian Date Rice, 458
Mighty Calcium Citrus **Salmon** Burgers Over Salad Greens, 474
Mighty Omega-3 Mandarin **Salmon** Burgers, 399
No More Migraines **Salmon** Croquette Pita Pockets, 468
Omega-Rich Grilled **Salmon** and Warm Kale Salad, 459
Sight-Sharpening Asian **Salmon** with Salad, 400
Soothing Wild **Salmon** Frittata, 438
Strong Bones **Salmon** with Kale Salad, 473
Thoughtful Asian **Salmon** Salad, 446
Thought-Provoking Wild **Salmon** with Spinach and Fruit Tapenade, 448
Joint-Cooling **Seafood** Scampi Salad and Roasted Vegetables, 338
Warm Italian **See-Food** Salad with Asian Dressing, 396
Ease-Inflammation Curried **Scallop** Salad, 334

Glucose-Balancing Asian **Scallop**-Bean Salad, 364
Mediterr-Asian Miso Soy **Scallops** with Tossed Brussels Sprouts, 457
Love Shack Spicy **Shellfish** with Asparagus, 385
Artery-Healing Whole-Grain Farro **Shrimp**, 420
Asian Pomegranate **Shrimp**-Noodle Salad, 484
C Better Greek **Shrimp** Salad, 394
Estrogen-Boosting **Shrimp** Scampi with Sweet Potatoes, 454
Mood-Lifting Tossed **Shrimp** Bean Rice Salad, 353
Omega-Mighty Toasted **Shrimp** Pasta, 336
Spicy Asian **Shrimp** with Beans, 485
Sugar-Busting Spicy **Shrimp** 'n' Rice, 366
Super-Calcium **Shrimp** and Vegetable Egg-Drop Soup, 471
Pro-Prostate **Snapper** with Thai Bean Salad, 486
Prostate-Healing Poached Wild **Snapper** and Broccoli Salad, 488
Calcium-Rich Sautéed **Spaghetti**, 477
Sight-Saving Italian Green **Spaghetti** with Buffalo, 397
Anti-Cancer Greek **Spinach** Pie, 349
Gently Digesting Teriyaki Vegetables and **Spinach** Salad, 374
Migraine-Fighting **Spinach** and Goat Cheese Tarts, 467
Stomach-Soothing Tarts with **Spinach**, Fig and Sweet Potato, 379
Beta-Carotene Roasted Winter **Squash** with Fruity Asian Vinaigrette, 347
Fracture-Fighting Winter **Squash** Teriyaki, 476
Iron-Rich Asian **Steak** Salad, 357
Strawberry-Kiwi Soup, 343

T

Heart-Loving Whole-Grain **Tabbouleh**, 422
Cancer-Protective Spicy **Tofu** Kebabs with Pear Relish, 346
Estrogen-Balancing Spicy **Tofu**-Pineapple Salad, 345
Low-Pressure Stuffed **Tomatoes** with Asian Celery Dressing, 433

Prostate Power Baked Stuffed **Tomatoes**, 487

Anti-Arthritis Grilled **Tuna** on Chopped Berry-Bean Salad, 337

Anti-Cataract **Tuna** Tapas with Spicy Marinated Red Peppers, 393

Blah-Busting Mediterr-Asian Grilled **Tuna**, 409

Diabetes-Defeating **Tuna** Cakes, 368

Heart-Healthy Spanish Gazpacho with **Tuna**, 421

Pain-Buster **Tuna** Wraps with Zesty Asian Dipping Sauce, 333

Seared Omega-3 **Tuna** Steaks with Lemon-Fig Sauce, 375

Bone-Strengthening Greek **Tzatziki** Dip with Vegetables, 470

U

Diastolic-Calming **Udon**-Miso Soup, 426

V

Memorable **Veal** Chops and Spinach Salad, 445

Cancer-Conquering Warm **Vegetable** Salad with Asian Flavors, 350

Head-Clearing Baked **Vegetable** Pie, 464

Healing **Vegetables** Fried Brown Rice, 431

Prostate-Healing **Vegetable** Teriyaki, 480

Remember-More Moo Shu **Vegetable** Stir-Fry, 450

Extra-Oxidant Roasted **Veggie-Spinach** Salad, 344

Virility **Veggies** with Edamame-Miso Rice, 481

Y

Celiac-Perfect Frozen Vanilla Fig **Yogurt** Pops, 381

Greek **Yogurt**, 406

Refreshing Greek **Yogurt** Vegetable Towers, 380

Index

A

abdominal fat, 101, 204, 302
ACE (angio-tensin-converting enzyme), 209, 211
acerola berry, 146
acetylcholine, 229, 238, 241, 242, 243
acetyl-L-carnitine (ALC), 241
acidophilus, 123
acid reflux, 128
acupuncture, 55–56
adaptogen, 166
additive effect, 312
adenosine-5'-triphosphate (ATP), 165, 167
adrenal fatigue, 157, 166, 223
adrenal glands, 226
adrenal hormones, 160, 166
adrenaline, 164, 166
aerobics, 133, 253
age-related cognitive decline, 228, 230, 233; see also Alzheimer's disease; memory loss
agribusiness, 31–32
alcohol, 8–9
    benefits of, 93–94
    and blood pressure, 213
    and calcium, 275
    and cancer, 78
    and depression, 90, 94
    and diabetes, 110
    as diuretic, 81
    and erectile problems, 136, 139
    and eyes, 153–54
    and heartburn, 129
    and menopause, 256
    and prostate, 318
    and sleep, 167, 225
alfalfa sprouts, 248, 250
alginates, 11, 199, 298
alkaloids, 49

allergies
    exclusion phase, 50
    food diary, 50
    food sensitivities, 50, 268
    and migraines, 268
    reintroducing foods, 50
allicin, 16, 65
allium, 61, 64, 316–17
allyl sulfides, 64, 106
almonds, 27, 70, 104, 162, 190, 225, 251
alpha-linolenic acid (ALA), 42, 70, 122, 179, 183
alpha-lipoic acid (ALA), 114, 241
alprostadil, 137
Alzheimer's disease
    and brain plaques, 238
    early signs of, 229
    and exercise, 243–44
    foods that protect from, 233–39
    and Mediterranean diet, 4
    and memory, 228–31
    mental deterioration in, 229, 230
    risk factors for, 233
    supplemental help, 240–43
amino acids, 86, 145, 151, 159, 185
amyloid-beta, 235
anemia, 96, 162
    iron-deficiency, 241
    pernicious, 87
angina, 169
angioplasty, 171
angiotensin II, 206
anthocyanins, 26, 31, 45, 151, 180, 234, 235
antidepressants, 84–85, 87, 226
    tricyclic, 262
anti-endomysium, 120
anti-inflammation tea, 47
antioxidants
    and arthritis, 41

    and cancer, 59–60, 62, 65–67, 79, 80
    and celiac disease, 122
    and eyes, 149–50, 151, 152
    and heart disease, 176, 179, 180–81, 184, 187, 189
    and ORAC score, 191
    sources of, 8, 12, 26, 31, 41, 43–46, 47, 93, 96, 177, 188, 191, 213, 234–35, 239, 315
anti-tTg antibody, 120
anxiety, 219, 229–30
apigenin, 209, 224
apoptosis, 62, 313
appetite, changes in, 84
apple cider, 66
apples, 35, 65–66, 163
    antioxidants in, 66, 191, 234–35
    and D-glucarate, 72–73
    fiber in, 104
    flavonoids in, 66
    peels, 66, 150
    and pesticides, 66
    quercetin in, 150, 178
aqua aerobics, 54–55
arachidonic acid, 49
arame, 24
arginine, 8, 138–39, 178, 185
arteries, hardening of, 169
arthritis, 39–57
    causes, 39, 40–41, 101
    and exercise, 25
    and food sensitivities, 50
    foods that make it better, 41–47
    foods that make it worse, 47–49
    osteo-arthritis (OA), 39
    other helpers and healers, 54–57
    pain causes in, 39–40
    rheumatoid (RA), 39
    supplemental help, 50–54
    symptoms, 40

treatment, 41
wear-and-tear, 39
artichokes, 97, 106, 191, 200, 208
ashwagandha, 241
Asian Diet, 1–2, 9–18, 20, 68, 187, 206
asparagus, 35, 151, 179, 210
aspartame, 296–7
aspirin, 129, 200, 262
astaxanthin, 27
asthma, 4
atherosclerosis, 136, 168, 170, 171, 177, 180, 203
avocados, 26, 35, 151, 154, 190
    and brain performance, 240
    and lime, 139–40
    in Mediterranean diet, 7, 286
    and potassium, 207
    and weight, 286

B

bananas, 35, 88, 159, 207
bariatric (bypass) surgery, 56, 101
barley, 86, 123–24, 251, 311
basal metabolic rate (BMR), 284–86
basil, 46–47, 106
beans, 26–27, 97
    antioxidants in, 12, 179–80, 191, 254
    and blood sugar, 107–8, 147, 225
    and cancer, 27, 68
    carbs in, 159, 263
    chili, 314
    and digestion, 131
    fermented black, 24
    fiber in, 104, 108, 131
    folate in, 234
    and gas, 314
    green, 34, 43, 207
    and heart disease, 179–80
    in Mediterr-Asian Diet, 22
    and prostate, 313–14
    refried, 314
    in salads, 160, 292
    white, canned, 208
bean sprouts, 72–73
beef, 106, 240
bee propolis, 82
beer, 123
beet greens, 152
beets, 209–10
belly fat, 101, 204, 302
benign prostatic hyperplasia (BPH), 307–10, 320
beriberi, 159

berries, 34, 35
    antioxidants in, 26, 45, 66, 151, 191, 234, 235
    and arthritis, 43, 45
    for breakfast, 290
    and heart disease, 177–78
    phytoestrogen in, 250
beta-amyloid plaque, 230, 238
beta-carotene, 46, 65
    daily intake of, 155
    and eye diseases, 149, 151, 154, 155
    and heart disease, 176, 178, 179
    sources of, 152, 154
beta-glucan, 71, 105
betaine hydrochloride, 155
beta-sitosterol, 185, 321
bicarbonate ions, 272
bile acids, 74, 132
bison meat, 26
blackberries, 66
black cohosh, 257
blackstrap molasses, 271
blood, "thick," 170
blood clots, 168, 181
blood pressure
    diastolic, 203
    and produce, 177
    and salt, 144, 212–13, 259, 274–75
    systolic, 201
    see also hypertension
blood pressure monitor, 215–16
blood sugar (serum glucose), 98
    and brain function, 239–40
    and breakfast, 157, 158
    and energy, 163
    and Glycemic Index, 103, 223, 256
    and sexual performance, 147
    and sleep, 225
    see also diabetes
blueberries, 26, 66, 178, 235
blue-green algae, 80
body mass index (BMI), 216, 280–81
bok choy, 271
bone-building snacks, 253
bone density, 251–52, 269
bones
    remodeling, 270
    see also osteoporosis
boron, 250, 273
brain, intellectual engagement of, 245
brain fog, 239–40

brain freeze, 266
breakfast, 157–58, 243, 288–89
    top ten choices, 290
breakfast sandwich, 159
breast cancer, 61, 82
    and alcohol, 78
    and Asian diet, 9–10
    and estrogen, 247, 248
    and sugar, 76
breathing, 167, 217, 226
brewer's yeast, 106
broccoli, 26, 35, 43, 44, 273
    and cancer, 61, 62, 63, 73, 316
    and tomatoes, 63, 312–13
    vitamin C in, 107, 150, 161
broccoli sprouts, 73, 316
bromelain, 44, 53
Brussels sprouts, 62, 73, 161, 177
buckwheat, 105, 208
burrito, 290
butter, 190, 194
butterbur, 268
buttermilk, 252

C

cabbage, 35, 43, 44, 61, 73, 131, 177
cabbage juice, 131
cabbage slaw, 316
cachexia, 79
caffeic acids, 82
caffeine, 141, 164
    and blood pressure, 213–14
    and brain function, 237–38
    and decaf coffee, 187
    and depression, 93
    and diabetes, 109
    and digestion, 127, 129
    and menopause, 256
    and migraines, 264
    and sleep, 225
    in tea, 188
calcification, 171
calcium, 81, 161, 210, 223
    and bones, 120, 271–75, 277
    daily intake of, 114, 134, 211, 252, 275
    and diabetes, 114
    and digestion, 120, 122, 134
    excretion of, 274
    and menopause, 251–52
    sources of, 122, 252, 271, 273
    supplementation, 275
    and tofu, 249
    and weight control, 298–99

calcium carbonate, 275
calcium citrate, 275
calf's liver, 97, 106, 233, 234, 310
calories
    and body weight, 284, 294–95,
        301–3
    burning, 282, 284, 285–86, 303
    control of, 284–85, 303
    daily intake of, 284, 303
    from fat, 285–86
    and Rule of 10, 284
    in snacks, 287–88
cancer, 5, 58–82
    causes, 59–60
    and chemotherapy, 60, 72, 79–81
    foods that make it better, 60–75
    foods that make it worse, 75–78
    and HRT, 247–48, 270
    metastasis of, 59, 70, 71, 313
    as multifactorial disease, 59
    other helpers and healers, 81–82
    prevention, 60
    supplemental help, 78–81
    symptoms, 59
    treatments, 60
canola oil, 196, 197
cantaloupe, 207
capillaries, 110
capsaicin, 44, 54, 189, 294, 314
carbohydrates
    and cancer, 75–77
    and comfort food, 86–87
    complex, 86, 91, 97, 102, 158,
        253–54, 263
    controlling intake of, 103
    and heart disease, 174, 196–97
    and mood, 253–54
    and protein, 159
    refined, 12, 49, 91, 92, 100, 102,
        174, 196–97, 256, 318
    simple, 254
    sources of, 86, 263
cardiovascular disease, see heart
    disease
carminative herbs, 126
carnitine, 167
carnosic acid, 75
carnosol, 17
carotenoids, 27, 74, 151, 154, 310
carotid arteriosclerosis, 215
carrageenan, 199, 298
carrot juice, 154
carrots, 34, 65, 151, 152, 154, 178
cartilage, 39–47, 50–51
casein, 127

cataracts, 148; see also eye diseases
catechins, 70, 238
cauliflower, 34, 43, 61, 62, 161, 177
cayenne, 294
celery, 34, 209, 293
celiac disease, 49, 120–24
cells, apoptosis, 62, 313
cereals, 158, 290
    iron-enriched, 97
    whole-grain, 88, 140–41
chamomile tea, 126, 224
change, 244, 245
cheese, 24, 134, 158, 163, 265
    for breakfast, 290
    calcium in, 271, 272
    in DASH diet, 205
    and fats, 97, 190
    protein in, 292
    vitamin K in, 252
chemotherapy, 60, 72, 79–81
cherries, 35, 45, 191
chewing, 37–38, 300–1
chicken, 162, 233
chicken soup, 211
chickpeas, 97
chili, 314
chili peppers, 152, 189
chlorogenic acid, 109
chocolate, 75, 96, 129, 141, 163,
    185–86, 225
cholecalciferol, 320
cholesterol, 11
    and erectile dysfunction, 140–43,
        147
    HDL, 7, 16, 139, 143, 172, 186,
        187, 192, 196, 208, 213, 229,
        232, 251
    and heart disease, 170, 171–74,
        177, 178, 190
    LDL, 7, 10, 139, 143, 171, 172,
        177, 185, 186, 187, 196, 251
choline, 236
chromium, 105–6, 112–13
    sources of, 106
chromium picolinate, 113
chronic fatigue syndrome (CFS), see
    fatigue
cilantro, 110, 152
cinnamaldehyde, 189
cinnamon, 18, 96, 109, 141, 163,
    189, 191, 238, 271
citrulline, 140
clams, 97, 255
clothes, loose, 129
cloves, 18, 46, 53, 141

cobalamin, 87
cocoa beans, 185
coconut oil, 193, 194
cod liver oil, 319
coenzyme Q10 (CoQ10), 112, 199,
    214, 241, 267
    and cancer, 78–79
    and fatigue, 165, 167, 298
coffee
    antioxidants in, 93, 213
    and blood pressure, 213–14
    and brain function, 237–38
    and calcium loss, 274
    decaf, 187
    and depression, 93
    and diabetes, 108–9
    as diuretic, 81
    and fatigue, 163–64
    and heart disease, 187
    and menopause, 256
    and migraines, 264
cognitive decline, see Alzheimer's
    disease; memory loss
collagen, 211
collard greens, 15, 271
colon cancer, 61, 76
comfort foods, 86
community-supported agriculture
    (CSA), 34
condiments, 153
congestive heart failure (CHF), 167
constipation, 125–27
cookies, 163
copper, 155
corn, 35
coronary heart disease, see heart
    disease
cortisol, 166, 217, 219, 220, 229,
    243, 283, 301
COX-1 and COX-2, 39–40, 45, 46
cranberries, 192, 232
C-reactive protein, 170, 200, 201
crocin, 74
cucumbers, 34
cucurbitacins, 317
curcumin, 18, 46, 74, 192, 238–39
curry, 18, 46, 74, 188–89, 192
cysteine, 151
cytokines, 39, 42, 47

D
daffodil bulbs, 242
daidzein, 68, 249
dairy products
    calcium in, 271–72

and constipation, 127
in DASH diet, 205
in Mediterranean diet, 15
protein in, 87, 292
and weight control, 291–92
DASH (Dietary Approaches to Stop
Hypertension), 177, 205; diet,
205–6, 272–73
daylight, 222
dehydration, 126, 140
dementia, 228
risk factors for, 229
see also Alzheimer's disease;
memory loss
dental hygiene, 201–2
depression, 83–97
causes, 84
and diabetes, 116
foods that make it better, 85–90
foods that make it worse, 90–94
and mental performance, 229–30,
231
and mood swings, 92, 253–54
other helpers and healers, 96–97
supplemental help, 94–95, 254
symptoms, 83–84
treatment, 84–85
detox, 72–73, 165
D-glucarate, 72–73
diabesity, 101
diabetes, 98–118
and Alzheimer's, 230, 231, 240
causes, 100
complications with, 117
and depression, 116
and exercise, 25, 115–16
foods that make it better, 102–10
foods that make it worse, 110–12
and Mediterranean diet, 14
other helpers and healers, 115–18
paying serious attention to,
116–18
prediabetic stage, 100–101, 113
as preventable, 118
public awareness of, 117–18
risk factors, 99–100
and sexual performance, 147
supplemental help, 112–15
symptoms, 99–100
treatment, 100–102
type 1 (juvenile-onset), 100, 101
type 2 (adult-onset), 100, 101
as wasting disease, 99
and weight, 101, 102, 115–16
diabetic retinopathy, 114

diallyl disulfide, 16, 178
diallyl trisulfide, 16
digestive disorders, 119–34
celiac disease, 120–24
constipation, 125–27
diverticulitis, 121
diverticulosis, 121
heartburn, 127–29
irritable bowel syndrome, 130–33
lactose intolerance, 133–34
ulcers, 131
dihydrotestosterone (DHT), 313, 318
dihydroxy-phenyl isatin, 126
diindolylmethane (DIM), 62
dimethylaminoethanol (DMAE), 242
diosgenin, 250
diverticulitis, 121
diverticulosis, 121
DNA, 58
docosahexaenoic acid (DHA), 42,
181, 236
dopamine, 84, 157, 229, 237
D-ribose, 165, 167

E

E. coli, 35
edamame, 23, 313
eggplant, 35, 49
eggs, 49, 106, 151, 236, 311
for breakfast, 290
and cholesterol, 186
from free-range hens, 32
and iron, 97
omega-3 fortified, 237
and weight, 288, 289
eicosanoids, 48, 295
eicosapentaenoic acid (EPA), 42, 181
8-prenylnaringenin, 257
electrolytes, 81
endorphins, 97
endothelial cells, 203
endothelium, 169
energy, 157, 163
epigallocatechin-3-gallate (EGCG),
47, 70, 238
erectile dysfunction, 135–47
causes, 135–37
foods that make it better, 138–42
foods that make it worse, 142–44
other helpers and healers, 146–47
supplemental help, 144–46
symptoms, 135
treatment, 137–38
esophagus, 127–29
essential fatty acids (EFAs), 194

estrogen, 136
and menopause, 247–49, 251,
257, 258
and osteoporosis, 269–70
and soy products, 80–81, 249
ethanols, 82
eugenol, 46, 47
exercise
aerobic, 133, 253
benefits of, 24–25, 27, 301–6
and blood pressure, 216–17
and bones, 278–79
and brain function, 243–44, 245
and calories burned, 282
and cholesterol, 192
and depression, 96–97
and diabetes, 25, 115–16
and fatigue, 166
and heart disease, 200, 202
interval training, 306
movement, 54–55, 133
and prostate, 321
and sexual performance, 146–47
and sleep, 221, 227
walking, 301–6; *see also* walking
weight-bearing, 253
eye diseases, 148–55
causes, 149
foods that make it better, 149–53
foods that make it worse, 153–54
supplemental help, 154–55
symptoms, 148–49
treatment, 149
eyes, protection from the sun, 149

F

fast food, 297
fat, body
and heart disease, 201
and obesity, see obesity; weight
fatigue, 97, 156–67
adrenal, 157, 166, 223
causes, 156–57
chronic, 156, 165
and depression, 84, 93
foods that make it better, 157–63
foods that make it worse, 163–64
and heart failure, 167
other helpers and healers, 166–67
supplemental help, 164–66, 254
symptoms, 156
treatment, 157
fats, dietary
and beta-carotene, 154
and carbohydrates, 159

and diabetes, 111
and digestion, 127, 129, 132
and erectile dysfunction, 142–43
and heartburn, 225
and heart disease, 189–90, 197
hydrogenated, 49, 193, 195–96, 295
interesterified, 49
in Mediterranean diet, 6–8
and mental performance, 240
monounsaturated, 185, 189, 190
polyunsaturated, 12–14, 111, 174, 185, 189, 194–95, 240, 257
and prostate, 318
saturated, 13, 127, 132, 173–74, 189–90
shopping tips, 193
fennel seed, 126
fenugreek, 109–10
fermented foods, 11, 24, 126
feverfew, 267
fiber
    and blood pressure, 208
    and blood sugar, 103–4, 108
    and cancer, 67, 72, 73–74
    and cholesterol, 140, 147
    and digestion, 119, 125–27, 128, 131–32
    and diverticulitis, 121
    and heart disease, 180–81
    insoluble, 74, 103–4, 125
    lipophilic, 250
    and prostate, 309
    soluble, 74, 104, 125–26
    sources of, 104, 107, 126, 181
    supplements, 298
    and weight, 287
fibrinogen, 170–71
fight-or-flight response, 164, 166
figs, 207
fish
    and arthritis, 42
    and blood pressure, 208, 209
    and cancer, 69–70
    canned, 42
    and cholesterol, 192
    and digestion, 130–31
    and eyes, 152
    farm-raised, 182, 289
    in Mediterr-Asian Diet, 22, 286
    and menopause, 251
    and mental performance, 233, 237
    mercury contamination, 182, 291

and migraines, 262–63
omega-3s in, 13, 20, 22, 42, 43, 69, 89–90, 93, 95, 102, 122, 139, 152, 181–82, 224, 236–37, 240, 251, 262–63, 277, 314–15
and prostate, 310, 314–15
and weight, 289, 291
fish oil, 131
    and blood pressure, 209
    daily intake of, 90, 183, 226, 258, 263
    and heart disease, 182–83
    and mental performance, 237, 242
    and migraines, 267–68
    molecular distillation of, 183, 268
    omega-3s in, 42, 50, 51–52, 69, 90, 95, 182, 199, 257, 277
5-hydroxytryptophan (5-HTP), 95, 226
5-lipoxygenase (5-LO), 39
flammulin, 72
flatulence, 126
flavonoids, 8, 31, 63, 66, 82, 141, 176, 177, 185, 234, 273, 317
flaxseed oil, 192, 194
flaxseeds, 183, 236, 248
    as fiber source, 104, 126, 181
    omega-3s in, 42–43, 68, 90, 93, 126, 253, 277
    storage and uses of, 122, 126–27, 237
folate, folic acid
    and blood pressure, 210
    and cancer, 79
    daily intake of, 87, 165
    and dementia, 233
    and depression, 85, 87
    and fatigue, 160, 165
    and heart disease, 180, 181
    sources of, 87, 165, 210, 234
food diary, 50
food poisoning, 35
forgetfulness, 228
free radicals
    and arthritis, 41, 43
    and cancer, 59–60, 62, 79, 82, 315
    and eye diseases, 149
    and heart disease, 169–70, 172, 193
    and memory loss, 230, 235
    and ORAC score, 191
    and sugar, 92–93

French paradox, 78, 173–74, 186, 301
fried foods, 129, 153
friendship, 244–45
fructose, 107
fruit juice, 71, 81, 164
fruits
    antioxidants in, 43–46, 93, 149–50, 177
    and blood sugar, 225
    and bones, 272
    for breakfast, 158, 290
    carbs in, 86, 97, 253, 263
    and cholesterol, 192
    citrus, 67, 107, 150, 161
    in DASH diet, 205
    and diabetes, 107
    dried, 97
    fiber in, 142
    and heart disease, 175–80
    in Mediterranean diet, 5–6
    in Mediterr-Asian Diet, 22
    and menopause, 250
    and mental performance, 234
    organic, 292–93
    and pesticides, 34–35
    and prostate, 316
    washing and rinsing, 34–35, 36
    and weight, 287
fucans, 11
fullness, 301

G
galantamine, 242
gallbladder, 226
gamma-aminobutyric acid (GABA), 208, 226
gamma-tocopherol, 27, 123
garlic, 27, 294
    antioxidant powers of, 239
    and blood pressure, 206, 214
    and cancer, 61, 64–65, 316–17
    and heart disease, 178
    in Mediterranean diet, 16
    mincing and cutting, 65
gas, flatulence, 126, 315
genetically modified food, 33
genistein, 68–69, 211, 249
GERD (gastroesophageal reflux disease), 128
ginger, 18, 141, 189
    and inflammation, 46, 53
    for nausea, 80
    tea, 75, 126, 128, 263–64
gingerols, 46

ginkgo, 144, 155, 188, 241
ginkgolide, 188, 238
ginseng, 112, 145, 166
glaucoma, 155
glucomannan, 199, 298
glucosamine, 50–51
glucosamine/chondroitin, 51
    homemade, 55
glucose, 12, 17, 197
    and cancer, 317
    and depression, 86, 91–92, 97
    and diabetes, 98–99, 103–4, 109,
        117
    and fatigue, 157
    serum glucose, 98
    see also blood sugar
glucose tolerance factor (GTF), 112
glucose tolerance test, 100
glucosinolates, 316
glucuronic acid, 73
glutamine, 131, 279
glutathione, 26, 95, 151, 210
gluten, 49, 120–24
gluten-sensitive enteropathy, 120–24
glycation, 12, 73, 153, 197, 219
Glycemic Index (GI), 103, 147, 153,
    223, 256
glycemic load, 108
grains
    carbs in, 253, 263
    in DASH diet, 205
    and diabetes, 104–5, 147
    estrogenic effect of, 248
    fiber in, 74, 105
    gluten in, 120, 122
    iron-enriched, 97
    in Mediterr-Asian Diet, 23
    and menopause, 250–51
    and sleep, 223–24
    and weight, 286–87
    whole, 12, 14, 88, 140–41, 181,
        223–24, 225
grapefruit, 67, 72–73, 104, 107,
    178–79, 293–4
    pink, 180
grapefruit juice, 71, 161
grapefruit seed extract (GSE), 35, 36
grape juice, 9, 187
grapes, 35, 71, 180
grapeseed oil, 193, 194
grazing, 80, 97, 128, 133, 163, 268,
    287, 300
grilled foods, 77–78
groats, 251
growth factor-1, 317

guava, 161, 208

H
H2 blockers, 279
hawthorn, 214
headaches
    rebound, 262
    see also migraines
heartbeats, ectopic (skipped), 180
heartburn, 127–29, 225
    triggers, 129
heartburn drugs, 279
heart disease, 4, 168–202
    and Alzheimer's, 231
    causes, 169–71
    and exercise, 25
    foods that make it better, 104,
        175–94
    foods that make it worse, 194–97
    other helpers and healers,
        200–202
    risk factors, 202
    supplemental help, 197–200
    symptoms, 169
    treatment, 171–75
heart failure, congestive (CHF), 167
Helicobacter pylori, 131
hemoglobin, 160
herbs
    anti-inflammatory, 46–47
    cancer-fighting, 74–75, 80
    for flavor, 144
    in Mediterranean Diet, 15–18
    see also specific herbs
hesperidin, 71
heterocyclic amines (HCAs), 17, 77
hibiscus leaves, 140, 199–200, 215,
    216
high-fructose corn syrup (HFCS), 91,
    112, 295–6
hijiki, 24
histamine, 266, 268
homemade glucosamine/chondroitin,
    55
homocysteine, 171, 179, 180, 230,
    231, 233, 277
honey, 188, 223, 224
hops, 257
hormone replacement therapy
    (HRT), 247–48, 270–71
hormones, 248
hot flashes, 246, 248, 249, 251,
    256–58
human growth hormone (HGH),
    146, 218

hummus, 286
hydration, 81, 227
hydroxychloroquine, 41
hydroxytyrosol, 184
hyperarousal, 220
hyperresponders, 186
hypertension, 143, 203–17
    causes, 204
    foods that make it better, 205–12
    foods that make it worse, 212–14
    and heart disease, 169, 176
    other helpers and healers, 25,
        215–17
    prehypertension, 203–4
    primary, 204
    supplemental help, 214–15
    symptoms, 204
    treatment, 204–5
    white-coat, 215
hypertension punch, 216
hyperzine A, 241–42
hypoglycemia, 91, 256
hypothyroidism, 146, 229

I
ibuprofen, 41, 262
ice cream, and brain freeze, 266
imagery, 227
immune system
    and gluten intolerance, 120
    and inflammation, 101
impotence, see erectile dysfunction
indigestion, 225
indoles, 62, 317
inflammation
    anti-inflammation tea, 47
    anti-inflammatory herbs, 46–47
    chronic, 101
    and heart disease, 170, 174, 189,
        194–97, 201
    and immune system, 101
inositol hexanicotinate, 192, 199
insomnia, 218–27
    causes, 219–20
    foods that make it better, 221,
        223–25
    foods that make it worse, 225
    other helpers and healers, 226–27
    supplemental help, 225–26
    symptoms, 218–19
    treatment, 220–21
insulin, 12, 98, 100, 101, 153
insulin-receptor sites, 108
insulin resistance, 98, 113, 239–40
intellectual engagement, 245

interleukins, 39, 41
interval training, 306
inulin, 106
iron, 75, 160–61, 202, 255
 sources of, 97, 160
iron deficiency, 96, 241
iron pots and pans, 161
irritable bowel syndrome (IBS),
 130–33
isoflavones, 10, 20, 60, 68, 187, 249,
 313
isothiocyanates, 11, 62

J

Jim's Joint Juice, 57
joint replacement, 41
journal, 50, 132, 222, 264, 304–5
Juvent 1000, 279

K

kale, 43, 61, 152, 161, 177, 273
kegel exercises, 258–59
kelp, 24
Kempner Rice Diet, 211–12
ketchup, 63, 311
kimchi, 11
kiwi, 35, 44, 107, 161, 178
kombu, 24, 249
konjac, 199
krill oil, 242, 277

L

lactase, 123, 134
lacto-fermentation, 126
lactose intolerance, 124, 133–34,
 211
lamb, 233
L-arginine, 138–39, 145, 198, 215
lauric acid, 193
lavender, 226
L-carnitine, 165, 214–15, 241, 298
L-citrulline, 198
leafy green vegetables
 and arthritis, 44
 as calcium source, 122, 252, 271,
  273
 and cancer, 61, 63, 318
 as chromium source, 106
 cooking tip, 87
 and eyes, 151, 152
 as folate source, 210
 as iron source, 97
 see also spinach
legumes, 22, 26–27, 86, 122, 205,
 314–15
lentils, 97, 234

lentinan, 72
lettuce, 34, 106, 152
leukotrienes, 39, 42, 181, 262
licorice extract tincture, 279
life expectancy, 1
lignans, 20, 67–68, 122, 253
lime and avocado combo, 139–40
limonene, 67
lipid peroxidation, 188
lipoproteins, 171, 172, 199
liquids, warm, 127
liquors, triple-distilled, 123
local foods, 34
lovastatin, 175
lox and bagel, 290
L-theanine, 224
lutein, 150–51, 179
lycopene, 60, 63, 176, 177, 180,
 311–12

M

macadamia nuts, 185, 192
mackerel, 209, 224, 251
macula, 148
macular degeneration
 dry form vs. wet form, 155
 what it is, 148
 see also eye diseases
magnesium
 and blood pressure, 208
 and bones, 272, 273–74
 and brain function, 236
 chelated, 114
 and diabetes, 106, 108, 113–14
 and fatigue, 165, 167
 and migraines, 263
 and potassium, 162
 sources of, 106, 114, 125, 180,
  207–8, 223, 225, 263, 273–74
 and weight, 298
magnifying glasses, 149
maltose, 296
mango, 35
massage, 54, 202, 253
meat
 and arthritis, 49
 and cancer, 77–78
 in DASH diet, 205
 and eyes, 153
 free-range, 37
 of grass-fed animals, 237, 240
 grilled, 77–78
 iron in, 97, 160–61
 lean, 131, 143
 in Mediterr-Asian Diet, 23

and menopause, 255
 moderate intake of, 20
 nutrients, 143
 processed, 255, 265
 protein in, 87, 274
 quality vs. quantity, 77
 red, 14–15, 111, 143, 255
 serving size of, 255
 well-done, 78
medications
 drug interactions, 240, 243
 not discontinuing, 215
 and prostate, 322
 and sleep deprivation, 220
meditation, 133, 167, 202, 226
Mediterranean diet, 1–9, 12–18, 20
 and Alzheimer's, 231–32
 and blood pressure, 206
 and erectile problems, 145
 and heart disease, 175, 183–84,
  190
 and weight, 286
Mediterr-Asian Diet, 19–27
 animal products, 20
 and cancer, 61–62
 and exercise, 24–27
 how to start, 22–24
 as lifetime approach, 21
 phytoestrogens, 20, 248
 real-life plan, 21
 and weight, 286
melatonin, 79, 87, 95, 221, 224,
 226
memory, and exercise, 25, 27
memory loss, 228–45
 causes, 229–30
 foods that make it better, 231–39
 foods that make it worse, 92,
  239–40
 other helpers and healers, 243–45
 supplemental help, 240–43
 symptoms, 229
 treatment, 230–31
men
 ideal weight of, 282
 and prostate, 307–21
menopause, 84, 246–59
 and bone mass, 269
 causes, 247
 foods that make it better, 248–55
 foods that make it worse, 255–57
 and mood swings, 253–54
 other helpers and healers, 258–59
 perimenopause, 246, 247
 supplemental help, 257–58

symptoms, 246–47
tips for managing, 259
treatment, 247–48
metabolism, 158, 167, 282, 287, 300
BMR, 284–86
metabolites, 250
metastasis, 59, 70, 71, 314
methotrexate, 41
methylsulfonylmethane (MSM),
53–54
microvascular complications, 110
microvascular disease, 202
midday slump, 91
migraine aura, 260, 261
migraine generator, 261
migraines, 260–68
causes, 261
classic, 261
foods that make it better, 262–64
foods that make it worse, 264–66
other helpers and healers, 268
questions about, 260
supplemental help, 266–68
symptoms, 261
treatment, 261–62
triggers, 264–65, 266
milk
acidophilus, 123
calcium in, 123, 161, 252, 271
in DASH diet, 205
and digestion, 123, 124, 134,
186
and hypertension, 210–11
powdered, 271
protein in, 158
and tryptophan, 224–25
milk sugars, 134
mints, 129
miso, miso soup, 11, 23, 249, 312
mitochondria, 162, 165, 267, 298
mobility, 283
Monday, most stress on, 201
mood swings, 92, 253–54
motility, 127
MSG (monosodium glutamate), 265
mushrooms, 34
cremini, 233, 311
enoki, 72
maitake, 71–72
shiitake, 72
mussels, 255
mustard greens, 152
mutation, 58
myristic acid, 193

N

naringin, 71
natto, 24, 252
nausea
from chemo, 79–80
ginger for, 80
nectarines, 35
neurogenesis, 25, 243, 244–45
neurons, 85, 232
neuropathy, 110
neuropeptides, 261
neurotransmitters, 84, 85, 157, 261
niacin, 192, 199, 233
sources of, 233
nicotinamide adenine dinucleotide
(NADH), 165
nicotine, 227
nightshade family, 49
night vision, 151
nitric oxide (NO), 138, 145, 180–81,
198, 210
nitrites, 265
norepinephrine, 84, 145, 157, 237
nori, 11, 24
NSAIDS, 41
nutmeg, 141
nutraceuticals, 27
nutrient density, 255
nutrition, and mental activity, 230
nuts
and blood pressure, 208
and brain function, 236, 237, 240
and cancer, 69, 70
carbs in, 86, 263
and celiac disease, 122–23
in DASH diet, 205
and diabetes, 108
estrogenic effect of, 248
and heart disease, 175, 184–85,
190
in Mediterranean diet, 7–8
and menopause, 251
omega-3s in, 8, 70, 93
and prostate, 311
and sleep, 223
and weight control, 291

O

oat bran, 104
oats, oatmeal, 211, 223, 263, 290,
311
and carbs, 86, 158
and digestion, 123, 250
and fiber, 105, 140–41, 250
folate in, 181

and weight, 286–87
obesity, 151, 280–306
causes of, 282–83
foods that make it better, 285–94
foods that make it worse, 294–97
midsection (belly fat), 101, 204,
302
other helpers and healers,
298–306
supplemental help, 297–98
treatment, 283–85
oil
rancid, 194
smoking point, 194
see also fats, dietary; olive oil
oleic acid, 7, 139, 190
oleocanthal, 43
oleuropein, 184
oligosaccharides, 314
olive oil
and arthritis, 43
and brain function, 237, 240
and cholesterol, 141
cold-pressed extra-virgin, 43,
184, 190, 192, 194
for cooking, 184
and diabetes, 108, 111
dipping bread in, 184, 286
and heart disease, 183–84,
190–91, 194
in Mediterranean diet, 7, 183–84,
206
in Mediterr-Asian Diet, 22–23,
286
and menopause, 252–53, 256–57
in salad dressings, 184
storing, 184
and weight, 286
omega-3 fatty acids
and arthritis, 42–43, 48, 50
eggs fortified with, 237
in fish, see fish
in fish oil, 42, 50, 51–52, 69, 90,
95, 182, 199, 257, 277
in flaxseeds, 42–43, 68, 90, 93,
126, 253, 277
and heart disease, 195
in Mediterranean diet, 12–15
in nuts, 8, 70, 93
sources of, 43
storage of, 52
omega-6 fatty acids, 14, 15, 195
and cancer, 314–15
and inflammation, 174
sources of, 48, 111, 240, 257, 314

onions, 26, 35, 151, 178, 192
    and bones, 273
    and cancer, 61, 64, 316–17
    chromium in, 106
    cutting, 64
    in Mediterranean diet, 16–17,
      206
    vitamin C in, 150
ORAC score, 191
orange juice, 71, 87, 161
oranges, 35, 44, 45–46, 67, 107
organic food, 28–38, 292–93
    and connectivity, 38
    freshness of, 33–34
    nutrients in, 31
    and political action, 35–36
    Price Look-Up (PLU) codes, 33
    prices of, 32, 37, 38
    safety of, 32–33
    taste of, 33, 38
    what it is, 29–30
organization, 244
osteo-arthritis (OA), 39
osteoblasts, 270
osteocalcin, 252
osteoclasts, 270
osteoporosis, 251–52, 269–79
    causes, 270
    and celiac disease, 120
    foods that make it better, 271–74
    foods that make it worse, 274–75
    other helpers and healers, 278–79
    supplemental help, 275–78
    symptoms, 269–70
    treatment, 270–71
overweight, see obesity; weight
oxalates, 275
oxidization, 177
oysters, 43, 97, 106, 138, 152, 255

P

palm oil, 193
pantothenic acid, 223
papaya, 46, 180, 207
parathyroid hormone, 275–76
passionflower, 224
peaches, 35
peanut butter, 108, 159, 185, 225
peanut oil, 192–93
peanuts, 108, 185, 190, 225, 233
pears, 35
peas, 35, 233
pectin, 61, 108, 178–79
pedometer, 303–5
penile implant, 137

penis, erectile problems, 136–37,
    143
peppers
    alkaloids in, 49
    bell, 34
    beta-carotene in, 152
    hot, 34, 44, 54
    and prostate, 313
    vitamin C in, 107, 150, 161
peptides, 209
peripheral artery disease (PAD), 198
peristalsis, 125, 130
peroxidation, 194
peroxynitrite radical, 27
pesticides, 29, 30, 32, 34–35, 37, 66
pets, stress relief from, 217
phase II enzymes, 71
phenols, 45, 64, 179
phenylalanine, 236
phenylethylamine, 96, 266
phosphatidylserine (PS), 242
phosphodiesterase inhibitors, 137
phosphoric acid, 274
physical activity, see exercise
phytates, 275
phytic acid, 68
phytochemicals, 6, 232
phytoestrogens, 20, 23, 62, 67, 69,
    80, 248–49
    sources of, 250, 254, 255
phytonutrients, 67, 106
pineapples, 35, 44, 53
pine bark, 258
plaque, 153, 168, 169–71, 179, 190,
    203
plateau, in weight loss, 306
plums, 35, 191
polyphenols, 66, 70, 164, 183, 188
pomegranate juice, 26, 45, 70–71,
    140, 216, 313
portion size, 103, 297, 300–301
potassium, 81
    and adrenal function, 223
    and blood pressure, 15, 207,
      212–13
    and bones, 272, 273, 276
    and magnesium, 162
    sources of, 106, 206–7, 223, 276
potatoes, 34, 49, 106, 191, 206–7
potentiators, 264
poultry, 255
prebiotics, 314
pregnancy, and drug interactions, 240
premature ovarian failure, 247
probiotics, 123, 126, 131, 133, 134

procyanidins, 66
prodome, 261
produce, see fruits; vegetables
prostaglandins, 39–40, 42, 70, 177,
    181, 195, 262, 263–64
prostate problems, 307–21
    cancer, 61, 308, 310
    causes, 308
    foods that make it better, 309–17
    foods that make it worse, 317–18
    other helpers and healers, 320–21
    supplemental help, 318–20
    symptoms, 307–8
    treatment, 308–9
prostatitis, 309
protease inhibitors, 68
protein, 77, 80, 86, 87–88, 159, 274,
    287, 292
proteolytic enzyme, 44
proton pump inhibitors (PPIs), 279
prunes, 126, 191, 273
psyllium, 104, 199, 298
pulse monitor, 217
pumpkin, 141, 152
pumpkin seeds, 87, 104, 180, 208,
    236, 274, 318
pycnogenol, 114, 258
pygeum, 321

Q

quercetin, 8, 44, 110, 139, 150, 178,
    206, 234

R

radishes, 177
raisins, 86, 159
raspberries, 35, 45, 104
red yeast rice, 11, 197–98
relaxation, 202, 217, 259
resolvins, 42
restless leg syndrome, 220
resurfacing, 41
resveratrol, 8, 45, 71, 139, 178, 185,
    186, 235
retina, 114
rheumatoid arthritis (RA), 39
riboflavin, 263
rice
    and blood pressure, 211–12
    brown, 86, 208, 212, 223, 250,
      251, 263, 286
    wild, 86
romaine, 106
rosemarinic acid, 17
rosemary, 17–18, 75, 239
rye (grain), 105, 123–24

S

saffron, 74
sage, 243, 255
St. John's wort, 94, 257
salads, 293
salicylates, 176
salicylic acid, 31, 43–44
salmon
    and brain function, 233
    destruction of, 37
    farmed, 182, 289
    omega 3s in, 42, 152, 224, 236, 251
    and sexual performance, 139
    wild Alaskan, 27
Salmonella, 35
salt
    and blood pressure, 15, 143–44, 212–13, 259, 274–75
    and calcium, 274–75
    and eye problems, 154
    sea, 144, 213
    and sodium, 15, 212–13
    salt sensitivity, 212
SAM-e (S-adenosylmethionine), 53, 94–95
saponin glycosides, 8
sardines, 182, 224, 251
saw palmetto, 320
scallops, 97
seafood, iron in, 160–61
Seanol, 24
sea salt, 144, 213
seasonal affective disorder (SAD), 88–89
sea vegetables, 11, 23–24, 27, 199, 249, 298
secoisolariciresinol, 67
selective serotonin reuptake inhibitors (SSRIs), 86
selenium, 52–53, 95, 310, 320
    sources of, 53, 310
serotonin
    and brain function, 229–30, 236
    and depression, 84, 85, 86, 88–89, 91, 93, 95
    and fatigue, 159, 167
    and migraines, 261, 263
    and mood, 253, 257
    and sleep, 221, 223, 224, 226
serrapeptase, 54
sesame oil, 193, 194
sesame seeds, 236, 271
sex, and prostate, 320

shellfish, 51, 277
shrimp, 233
sinusitis, 101
skin cancer, 81–82, 276, 318–19
slaw, 315
sleep
    changing habits, 84
    cycles, 227
    and fatigue, 156–57
    and heartburn, 129
    and metabolism, 300
    and migraines, 268
    napping, 201, 226
    REM (rapid eye movement), 219, 225, 227
    and sexual performance, 146
    tips for, 222, 259
    see also insomnia
sleep apnea, 220, 221, 225
sleep deprivation, 218–19
sleeping pills, 220–21
sleep-wake cycle, 221, 222
smoking
    and blood pressure, 216
    and bones, 279
    and cancer, 319
    and free-radical damage, 79
    and heart disease, 169, 171, 201, 202, 258
    and mental function, 232, 244
    and sexual function, 137, 145
    and sleep, 167, 227
    and vitamin C, 145, 155
smoking-cessation aids, 279
smoothies, 80, 158, 290
snacks
    100-calorie, 288
    tryptophan, 224–25
snoring, 220, 225
social connections, 244–45, 259, 320
sodium, 81, 207, 209, 210
    and blood pressure, 15, 144, 212–13, 259
    daily intake of, 259
    "low sodium" on labels, 259
sodium nitrate, 265
soft drinks, 93, 111–12, 274, 296
sorbitol, 132
soups, 81
    glucosamine/chondroitin, 55
soy foods, 10–11, 43
    and calcium, 272
    and cancer, 68–69, 80–81, 248
    daily intake of, 249
    and heart disease, 187

    in Mediterr-Asian Diet, 23
    and menopause, 248–49, 252
    and migraines, 264–65
    and prostate, 312
sparkling water, 164
spices
    anti-inflammatory, 46
    cancer-fighting, 74–75, 80
    in Mediterranean diet, 15–18
    see also specific spices
spinach, 26, 34, 43
    and blood pressure, 207, 208, 210
    and the brain, 235–36
    and cancer, 63, 317
    and digestion, 125
    and eyes, 150–51, 152
    folate in, 87, 179, 210
    iron in, 161
spirituality, 259
spirulina, 57, 80
sprouts, 248, 250, 316
sprue, celiac, 120
spurs, 40
squamous cell carcinoma, 67
squash
    butternut, 152
    winter, 34, 65, 86, 152, 179, 207, 272
statin drugs, 170, 174–75
stearic acid, 186
stenosis, 40
sterols, 141–42, 317
stevia, 140, 297
stomach acid, 128–29, 155
strawberries, 34, 35, 43, 45, 66, 161, 177
stress
    and blood pressure, 217
    and digestion, 130, 132–33
    and fatigue, 159–60, 166–67
    and heart disease, 201
    and menopause, 258
    and mental performance, 229, 231, 243, 245
    and migraines, 261, 268
    and sexual performance, 146–47
    and sleep deprivation, 219–20, 221, 224, 226
    and weight, 283
strontium citrate, 278
subfraction, 171
subscription farming, 34
substance P, 54
sucralose, 297

sugar, 12, 132, 153
  blood, *see* blood sugar
  and calcium, 274
  and cancer, 75–77, 317–18
  and depression, 90–93, 256
  and diabetes, 102, 110
  and erectile performance,
    142–43
  and fatigue, 163
  and heart disease, 174, 196–97
  and menopause, 256
  in soft drinks, 111–12
  and weight, 295–96
sugar blues, 90, 91
sugar high, 91, 92
sugar substitutes, 296–97
sulfites, 265
sulforaphane, 62, 177, 316
sulfur, 44
sun
  and cancer, 81–82, 276, 318–19
  and eye diseases, 149
  vitamin D from, 52, 82, 88–89,
    115, 199, 253, 259, 276,
    318–19, 321
sunflower seeds, 87, 236, 273, 310
superoxide dismutase (SOD), 60
sweet potatoes, 65, 86, 104, 106–7
Swiss chard, 152, 208, 273

T
tai chi, 132–33, 167, 253
tamari, 23
tangerines, 35
tannin, 8
tarragon, 109
tea
  anti-inflammation, 47
  antioxidants in, 47, 188
  black, 70, 188
  and brain function, 238
  caffeine in, 188
  chai, 312
  chamomile, 126, 224
  cinnamon in, 109
  drinking, 57
  ginger, 75, 126, 128, 263–64
  ginkgo, 188, 238
  green, 47, 70, 140, 164, 188,
    216, 224, 238, 291, 312–13
  herbal, 127, 164, 224
  hibiscus, 215
  hypertension punch, 216
  passionflower, 224
  rooibos, 110

sage, 243, 255
tempeh, 23, 24, 249
tension, *see* stress
testosterone, 84, 136, 138, 143, 147,
  312, 317
theobromine, 141, 225
theophylline, 225
thermogenesis, 282, 291
thirst, 81, 125
3-n-butylphthalide, 209
thromboembolism, 189
thrombosis, 168
thromboxane, 181, 189, 262
thyroid, 146, 157, 229
tobacco, 49
tocopherols, 155
tocotrienols, 155
tofu, 23, 43, 187, 249, 252, 271,
  292, 312
tomatoes, 49, 106, 177, 310–12
  and blood pressure, 208
  and broccoli, 63, 311–12
  heirloom, 311
tomato juice, 311
tomato paste, 63, 311
tomato sauce, 63, 207, 311
trans fats, 48–49, 111, 143, 174,
  193, 195–96, 240, 295, 318
trigeminal nerve, 266
triglycerides, 188, 251, 285
tryptophan, 221
  and complex carbs, 86, 91, 253,
    263
  and depression, 86, 88, 93, 95
  snacks for sleep, 224–25
tumor necrosis factor (TNF), 46
tuna, 182
turkey, 88, 97, 162, 290, 310
turmeric, 53, 74–75, 188, 238–39
tyramine, 264, 265, 266
tyrosine, 162, 237

U
ubiquinone, 214
ulcers, 131
urinary incontinence, 258–59
urination
  and blood glucose, 99
  and prostate, 321

V
vaginal dryness, 248
valerian, 225–26
vascular dementia, 242
vasodilator, 144
vegetable juice, 57, 80, 81, 154

vegetables
  antioxidants in, 43–46, 93,
    149–50, 177, 315
  and blood sugar, 103, 225
  and bones, 272
  carbs in, 86, 97, 253, 263
  and cholesterol, 192
  colors of, 65
  cruciferous, 11, 44, 61, 62, 73,
    177, 315–16
  in DASH diet, 205
  frozen, 292
  and heart disease, 175–80
  iron in, 161
  Jim's Joint Juice, 57
  in Mediterranean diet, 5–6,
    14–15
  in Mediterr-Asian Diet, 22
  and menopause, 250
  organic, 292–93
  and pesticides, 34–35
  and prostate, 309–10, 315
  raw, 160, 315
  slaw, 315
  stir-fries, 315
  tossed with olive oil, 184
  washing and rinsing, 34–35, 36
  and weight, 286
vegetarianism, 233
villi, 120, 121
vinpocetine, 242
visual imagery, 227
vitamin A, 151
vitamin B complex
  and Alzheimer's, 233, 233–34,
    241
  and bones, 277
  and depression, 87–88, 95
  and digestion, 122
  and fatigue, 159–60, 166, 254
  and protein, 87–88
  and stress, 224
vitamin C
  and arthritis, 44, 45, 46
  and blood pressure, 208, 214
  and brain function, 242
  and cancer, 60, 67, 71, 79
  and circulation, 139–40
  daily intake of, 114, 255
  and diabetes, 106, 107
  and erectile performance,
    145–46
  and eyes, 149, 150, 154–55
  and fatigue, 162–63, 164
  and heart disease, 180

and iron, 161
sources of, 107, 150, 161
vitamin D
and blood sugar, 114–15
and bones, 275–76, 277
and brain function, 242
and calcium, 252
and cancer, 318–19
daily intake of, 114, 242, 252, 320
and heart disease, 198–99
and joint health, 52
and serotonin, 88–89
sun as source of, 52, 82, 88–89, 115, 199, 253, 259, 276, 318–19, 321
testing of, 115
vitamin E
and arthritis, 44, 46, 52
and brain function, 242
daily intake of, 114, 155
and eyes, 150, 152, 155
and free radicals, 92
and heart disease, 185
and menopause, 251
and prostate, 319
sources of, 8, 70, 114, 123, 152, 185
vitamin K, 252, 272, 273, 277
vitamins
fat-soluble, 90
multivitamins, 241

W

waist measurement, 281
wakame, 24
wake-up chemicals, 157
walking
and bones, 259, 278
with buddy or group, 306
and digestion, 127
and heart disease, 200, 202
and mental function, 232, 243, 245
and moods, 258
and pedometer, 303–5
and sleep, 221, 226
and stress, 167
10,000 steps, 303–4
and weight, 301–6
walnut oil, 194, 237
walnuts, 8, 43, 70, 90, 93, 158, 163, 236, 237, 251, 287
warfarin, 155, 178, 277
water
daily intake of, 162
drinking, 57, 81, 126, 127, 128, 129, 131, 162, 227, 321
and fiber, 125, 126
and sexual performance, 140
sparkling, 164
watercress, 152, 273
watermelon, 140, 180
weight
and arthritis, 56
body mass index, 216, 280–81
and calories, 284, 294–95, 301–3
and cancer, 318, 321
and chewing your food, 38
control of, 255, 306
and dementia, 239
and diabetes, 101, 102, 115–16
and diet, 282, 283
eating habits, 299–301
and erectile problems, 136
and exercise, 301–6
and glucose absorption, 254
and heartburn, 129
and heart disease, 201
ideal, 282
and Mediterranean diet, 286
obesity, *see* obesity
and portion size, 297, 300–301
and sexual performance, 137
and snacks, 287–88
and walking, 301–6
weighing yourself daily, 306
and willpower, 299–300
wheat, 123–24
whey, whey protein, 80
wine, 8–9, 24, 45, 123, 139, 186–87
and Alzheimer's, 235
and blood pressure, 206, 213
and migraines, 265–66
women
and breast cancer, 9–10, 61, 76, 78, 82, 247, 248
and heart disease, 202
ideal weight of, 282
and menopause, *see* menopause
and migraines, 261
and osteoporosis, 269–71
work, shifts, 220, 221

X

xanthines, 225

Y

yams, 250
yoga, 55, 132, 167, 202, 217, 226
yogurt, 24, 97, 123, 126, 131, 134, 158, 252, 271–72, 287, 290, 292
yohimbe, 144–45

Z

zeaxanthin, 44, 151, 179
zest, citrus, 35
zinc
and copper, 155
daily intake of, 155
and erectile dysfunction, 138
and eyes, 152–53, 155
and prostate, 317, 318